The Handbook of Conflict Resolution

The Handbook
of Conflict Resolution

Theory and Practice

Morton Deutsch
Peter T. Coleman, Editors

Jossey-Bass Publishers
San Francisco

Published by Jossey-Bass
A Wiley Imprint
989 Market Street, San Francisco, CA 94103-
1741   www.josseybass.com

Jossey-Bass books and products are available through most bookstores.
To contact Jossey-Bass directly call our Customer Care Department
within the U.S. at 800-956-7739, outside the U.S. at 317-572-3986 or
fax 317-572-4002.

Jossey-Bass also publishes its books in a variety of electronic formats.
Some content that appears in print may not be available in electronic
books.

Library of Congress Cataloging-in-Publication Data

The handbook of conflict resolution: theory and practice /
  Morton Deutsch and Peter T. Coleman, editors.—1st ed.
    p. cm.
  Includes bibliographical references and indexes.
  ISBN 0-7879-4822-5 (alk. paper)
  1. Conflict management. I. Deutsch, Morton, date.
II. Coleman, Peter T., date.
HM1126 .H35   2000   99-050875
303.6'9—dc21

FIRST EDITION
HC Printing   10 9 8 7 6

CONTENTS

Preface   xi

Introduction   1
Morton Deutsch

PART ONE: INTERPERSONAL AND INTERGROUP PROCESSES   19

1 Cooperation and Competition   21
Morton Deutsch

2 Justice and Conflict   41
Morton Deutsch

3 Constructive Controversy: The Value of Intellectual Opposition   65
David W. Johnson, Roger T. Johnson, Dean Tjosvold

4 Trust, Trust Development, and Trust Repair   86
Roy J. Lewicki, Carolyn Wiethoff

5 Power and Conflict   108
Peter T. Coleman

6 Communication and Conflict   131
Robert M. Krauss, Ezequiel Morsella

7 Persuasion in Negotiations and Conflict Situations 144
Shelly L. Chaiken, Deborah H. Gruenfeld, Charles M. Judd

8 Intergroup Conflict 166
Ronald J. Fisher

9 Problem Solving and Decision Making in Conflict Resolution 185
Eben A. Weitzman, Patricia Flynn Weitzman

PART TWO: INTRAPSYCHIC PROCESSES 211

10 Judgmental Biases in Conflict Resolution
and How to Overcome Them 213
Leigh Thompson, Janice Nadler

11 Anger and Retaliation in Conflict: The Role of Attribution 236
Keith G. Allred

12 Self-Regulation in the Service of Conflict Resolution 256
Walter Mischel, Aaron L. DeSmet

PART THREE: PERSONAL DIFFERENCES 277

13 Process and Outcome Goal Orientations in Conflict Situations:
The Importance of Framing 279
Tal Y. Katz, Caryn J. Block

14 Personality and Conflict 289
Sandra V. Sandy, Susan K. Boardman, Morton Deutsch

15 The Development of Conflict Resolution Skills in Children:
Preschool to Adolescence 316
Sandra V. Sandy, Kathleen M. Cochran

PART FOUR: CREATIVITY AND CHANGE 343

16 Creativity and Conflict Resolution: The Role of Point of View 345
Howard E. Gruber

17 Some Guidelines for Developing a Creative Approach to Conflict 355
Peter T. Coleman, Morton Deutsch

18 Change Processes and Conflict 366
Eric C. Marcus

19 Learning Through Reflection 382
Victoria J. Marsick, Alfonso Sauquet

PART FIVE: DIFFICULT CONFLICTS 401

20 Aggression and Violence 403
Susan Opotow

21 Intractable Conflict 428
Peter T. Coleman

PART SIX: CULTURE AND CONFLICT 451

22 Culture and Conflict 453
Paul R. Kimmel

23 Cooperative and Competitive Conflict in China 475
Dean Tjosvold, Kwok Leung, David W. Johnson

PART SEVEN: MODELS OF PRACTICE 497

24 Teaching Conflict Resolution Skills in a Workshop 499
Ellen Raider, Susan Coleman, Janet Gerson

25 Mediation 522
Kenneth Kressel

26 Managing Conflict Through Large-Group Methods 546
Barbara Benedict Bunker

PART EIGHT: LOOKING TO THE FUTURE 569

27 A Framework for Thinking About Research
on Conflict Resolution Training 571
Morton Deutsch

Concluding Overview 591
Peter T. Coleman

Recommended Reading 601

Contributors 611

Name Index 621

Subject Index 629

PREFACE

This book is meant for those who wish to deepen their understanding of the processes involved in conflicts and their knowledge of how to manage them constructively. It provides the theoretical underpinnings that throw light on the fundamental social psychological processes involved in understanding and managing conflicts at all levels: interpersonal, intergroup, organizational, and international.

As an area of scholarship and professional practice, conflict resolution is relatively young, having emerged as a discipline after World War II. Practice and theory have been only loosely linked. This book aims to foster closer connection between the two by demonstrating the relevance of theoretical ideas to practice. Though the link between theory and practice is inherently bidirectional, this handbook primarily emphasizes the path from theory to practice.

The theoretical ideas presented in this book were for the most part not developed specifically in relation to understanding conflict, nor to facilitate professional practice in this area. They have relevance to any area in which it is important to understand the basic processes involved in social interactions of all sorts, in various contexts—at work; in politics, schools, families, clinics, courts, and bedrooms; on highways; and elsewhere. For the purposes of this book, the authors have developed their chapters to bring out the relevance of the theories being discussed to understanding conflict specifically.

When appropriate, chapters contain three sections. The first deals with the theoretical ideas in the substantive area being discussed. The second draws out the implications of these ideas for understanding conflict, and the third is concerned with the implications of these ideas for educating or training people to manage their conflicts more constructively.

The *Handbook of Conflict Resolution* is divided into sections somewhat arbitrarily, and inevitably there is overlap among them. The introductory chapter gives examples of real conflicts and indicates the kinds of questions one might pose to understand what is going on in the conflicts—questions that are addressed in many of these chapters. The Introduction also has a brief discussion of the orientations of the practitioners on the one hand and the researcher-theorists on the other, to permit some insight into the misunderstandings that often occur between these two groups. It also contains an abbreviated history of the study of conflict, from a social psychological perspective, and indicates the sorts of questions that have been and are being addressed.

The major portion of the book, comprising Parts One through Five, presents the theoretical ideas that have been developed (mainly in areas of social psychology) that are useful in understanding conflict processes as well as in helping people to learn to manage their conflicts constructively. The authors of Chapters One through Twenty-One discuss the practical implications of their ideas for conflict as well as the theoretical foundations underlying the implications they draw.

Even apart from their usefulness for conflict, the theoretical ideas should be of value to anyone interested in understanding the nature of basic social psychological processes involved in social interactions of any kind. The table of contents for Parts One through Five indicates to the reader the broad range of theoretical ideas, and their implications for conflict, that are discussed in this section. They are grouped, arbitrarily, into interpersonal and intergroup processes, intrapsychic processes, personal difference, creativity and change, and difficult conflicts. Almost all of the chapters discuss matters that cross such arbitrary boundaries.

Part Six contains two chapters that consider the relation between culture and conflict, each from a somewhat different perspective. Chapter Twenty-Two examines some of the common sorts of misunderstanding that can arise when people from varying cultural backgrounds interact and what can be done to help people learn to understand one another's cultural background. Then Chapter Twenty-Three examines an influential theoretical approach to conflict resolution, developed in the United States, to see how it is (or is not) applicable to conflict in the entirely different context of China.

Part Seven is most directly concerned with practice. The first of its three chapters presents the Coleman-Raider model for training in constructive conflict resolution, which has been extensively used by our colleagues in the International Center for Cooperation and Conflict Resolution. Chapter Twenty-Five discusses mediation, as well as its values and limitations, from the perspective of someone who is both a highly respected mediator and an outstanding researcher in this area. Chapter Twenty-Six then discusses recently developed methods of managing conflict in large groups by someone who has coauthored the first book in this area and who is a distinguished scholar and practitioner of these methods.

Finally, in Part Eight, we look to the future. Chapter Twenty-Seven presents a framework for thinking about research on conflict resolution training. As of this writing, there has been little good and systematic research in this area. If the field is to develop and have a bright future, it needs more research. The concluding chapter is an overview and commentary on the current state of the field; it considers such issues as what substantive questions need to be addressed that have not received the attention they warrant—that is, the practice as well as theoretical issues.

The contributors to the *Handbook of Conflict Resolution* are an illustrious group of experts in the areas with which their chapters are concerned. We have asked them to write chapters that can be easily understood by readers who are not social scientists but that are also credible to other experts in their areas. Further, we asked them to suggest additional sources of information (listed by chapter at the back of the book in the section headed "Recommended Reading") and to limit considerably the number of technical references. Given the opaqueness of much writing in the social sciences, it is surprising how well the contributors have succeeded in writing clear, informative, interesting, useful, and authoritative chapters.

We believe the *Handbook of Conflict Resolution* is accessible and valuable to a wide variety of groups who have an interest in constructive conflict management: to undergraduate and graduate students, as well as their professors, in a number of academic fields such as psychology, education, sociology, political science, business, international relations, law, social work, and health care. It is also of value to such practitioners as conflict resolution trainers and consultants, negotiators, mediators, and those who manage or supervise others. In editing this handbook, we have learned a great deal, so we believe that even those considered "experts" can find much of value in it.

One final word about the *Handbook*'s orientation. This handbook is concerned with finding cooperative, win-win solutions to conflict, no matter how difficult. The "black arts" of conflict (such as violence, coercion, intimidation, deceit, blackmail, and seduction) are not discussed except, if at all, in the context of how to respond to or prevent the use of such tactics by oneself or others. In our view, such tactics are used too often, are commonly destructive and self-defeating, and are less productive in the long run than a constructive approach.

We wish to thank our faculty colleagues who participated in an informal seminar on conflict resolution at Teachers College; the inspiration for this book emerged from the lively discussions in the seminar. We also wish to thank Riva Kantowitz, Kathleen Vaughan, Joanne Lim, and Danny Mallonga, who typed, e-mailed, did editorial work, and provided the other invaluable services necessary to produce a completed manuscript.

January 2000   Morton Deutsch
New York, New York   Peter T. Coleman

The Handbook of Conflict Resolution

INTRODUCTION

Morton Deutsch

I n this chapter, I give some examples of conflicts and indicate the kinds of
   questions one might pose to understand what is going on in the conflicts—
   questions that are addressed in many of the following chapters. It also includes
a brief discussion of the orientations of both practitioners and researcher-theorists
to provide some insight into the misunderstandings that often occur between
these two groups. It concludes with an abbreviated history of the study of conflict from a social psychological perspective.

A CONFLICT BETWEEN HUSBAND AND WIFE

Some time ago, I had the opportunity to do therapeutic work with a professional
couple who were involved in bitter conflicts over issues they considered nonnegotiable. The destructiveness of their way of dealing with their conflicts was reflected in their tendency to escalate a dispute about almost any specific issue (for
example, a household chore, the child's bedtime) into a power struggle in which
each spouse felt that his or her self-esteem or core identity was at stake. The
destructive process resulted in (as well as from) justified mutual suspicion; correctly perceived mutual hostility; a win-lose orientation to their conflicts; a tendency to act so as to lead the other to respond in a way that would confirm one's
worst suspicion; inability to understand and empathize with the other's needs and
vulnerabilities; and reluctance—based on stubborn pride, nursed grudges, and fear

1

of humiliation—to initiate or respond to a positive, generous action so as to break out of the escalating vicious cycle in which they were entrapped.

Many couples involved in such conflicts do not seek help; they continue to abuse one another, sometimes violently, or they break up. The couple that I worked with sought help for several reasons. On the one hand, their conflicts were becoming physically violent. This frightened them, and it also ran counter to their strongly held intellectual values regarding violence. On the other hand, there were strong constraints making it difficult for them to separate. Their child would suffer; they felt they'd be considerably worse off economically; and they had mutually congenial intellectual, aesthetic, sexual, and recreational interests that would be difficult to continue engaging in together if they separated. As is often the case in such matters, it was the woman—being less ashamed to admit the need for help—who took the initiative to seek the assistance of a skilled third party.

The wife, who worked (and preferred to do so), wanted the husband to share equally in the household and child care responsibilities; she considered equality of the genders to be a core personal value. The husband wanted a "traditional marriage" with a conventional division of responsibilities in which he'd be the primary income-producing worker outside the home, while his wife would principally do the work related to the household and child care. The husband considered household work and child care inconsistent with his deeply rooted image of adult masculinity. The conflict seemed nonnegotiable to the couple. For the wife, it would mean betrayal of her feminist values to accept her husband's terms; for him, it would violate his sense of male adult identity to become deeply involved in housework and child care.

Yet this nonnegotiable conflict became negotiable when, with the help of the therapist, the husband and wife were able to listen to and really understand the other's feelings and how their respective life experiences had led them to the views they each held. Understanding the other's position fully, and the feelings and experiences behind them, made each person feel less hurt and humiliated by the other's position and readier to seek solutions that would accommodate the interests of both. They realized that with their joint incomes they could afford to pay for household and child care help that would enable the wife to be considerably less burdened by such responsibilities without increasing the husband's chores in these areas (though doing so, of course, lessened the amount of money they had available for other purposes).

This solution wasn't perfect for either partner. Each would have preferred that the other share his or her own view of what a marriage should be like. But their deeper understanding of the other's position made them feel less humiliated and threatened by it and less defensive toward the other. It also enabled them to negotiate a mutually acceptable agreement that lessened tensions, despite the continuing differences in basic perspective. (See Deutsch, 1988, for further discussion of negotiating the nonnegotiable.)

AN INTERGROUP CONFLICT AT A SCHOOL

A conflict has developed between two groups of teachers at a high school in New York City: the Black Teachers Caucus (BTC) and the newly formed Site-Based Management Committee (SBM). The SBM committee's eighteen members consist of the principal, the union chairperson, a representative from the parents' association, a student, and an elected teacher representative from each academic department. All of the SBM members are European American, with the exception of an African American teacher chosen from the math department.

At the last SBM meeting, the math teacher proposed that an official voting seat be designated for an African American teacher. After much heated discussion, the proposal was voted down. But the problems raised by the proposal didn't go away. Much personal bitterness has ensued.

The school has experienced a recent demographic shift from a predominantly white student body to one that's now mainly composed of students of color. This has occurred for two reasons. First, there's been a large influx of students of color from the city-owned housing projects constructed in the district during the past two years. Second, as a result the number of science-oriented students coming from other parts of the city has dropped.

The present student population is approximately 40 percent African American, 30 percent Latino American, 25 percent European American, and 5 percent Asian American. The faculty is 90 percent European American and 10 percent African American. The parents' association is 100 percent European American.

The Position of the BTC

The BTC believes that the SBM committee needs its input to make the changes needed—specifically, the curriculum is Eurocentric and many school policies are out of touch with the cultural perspective of the current student population. In addition, the caucus is very concerned about an increase in bias-related incidents in the community and wants to initiate antiracism classes at all grade levels.

The members of the BTC believe that even though the majority of the management committee members are sincerely interested in bringing about positive school change and are good, dedicated teachers, they lack personal understanding of the impact of racism on the African American experience. Some even seem to still value the old melting-pot approach to race relations, a position the caucus members believe is naïve and dysfunctional when it comes to positive educational change.

The BTC believes that having its representative present as a voting member on the committee will add a needed multicultural and antiracist perspective at this critical time of change. The caucus wants to be part of this change and won't take no for an answer.

The Position of the Euro-American SBM Committee Members

There are many reasons the European Americans voted against an African American seat on the SBM committee, and they deeply resent the implication that they're racists for so doing. First of all, they believe that if any particular black teacher wants a seat, he or she should go through regular democratic procedures and get elected by the respective department. New elections will be held in May.

Second, it wouldn't be fair to give a special seat to the black teachers without opening up other seats for the Latino, Asian, Jewish, Greek, or "you name it" teachers. SBM is about department representation, the members say, not about representation based on race or ethnicity.

Third, designating a seat for blacks or establishing quotas of any kind based on race would give the appearance of catering to pressure from a special-interest group and be difficult to explain to the rest of the faculty and the parents' association. They believe that the best direction for the school and society as a whole is a color-blind policy that would assimilate all races and ethnic groups into the great American melting pot. The site-management members sincerely believe that they don't discriminate because of race, and they resent the implication that they're incapable of teaching children of color.

The principal of the school, who is strongly committed to both site-based management and multiculturalism, very much wants this conflict to be resolved constructively. After several months of unproductive discussions between the two groups, during which they become progressively hardened in their respective positions, the principal calls in a mediator (Ellen Raider, the lead author of Chapter Twenty-Four) to help the groups resolve their conflict. By various means over a period of time, she—as well as the principal—encourages a civil problem-solving discussion of the issue. Together, the groups brainstorm and come up with twenty-seven ideas for handling the problem. Ultimately, they agree on one solution as being the best, namely, each year the principal will appoint seven faculty members to a multicultural task force that reflects the student composition. Two of the task-force members will also be members of the SBM committee, one to be elected by the task-force members and one selected from the ethnic group most heavily represented in the student population.

The solution, though not perfect, is acceptable to both sides and is implemented to the satisfaction of the teachers. It goes on contributing to the reduction of intergroup tensions as well as to the effectiveness of the SBM committee.

THE CONFLICT IN NORTHERN IRELAND

As Cairns and Darby (1998) point out, "The conflict in Northern Ireland is at its most basic a struggle between those who wish to see Northern Ireland remain part of the United Kingdom and those who wish to see the reunification of the island of Ireland" (p. 754). The roots of the conflict go back centuries to the period when the English colonized the island, occupied 95 percent of the land, and introduced a community of foreigners (mainly Scottish Protestants) in Northern Ireland. They became a majority in this area. in contrast to a Catholic majority in the south of the island.

Cairns and Darby (1998) also state that "years of oppression by the colonists and rebellion by the native Irish culminated in the Treaty of 1921, which partitioned the island into two sections: the 6 predominantly Protestant counties of the North, which remained an integral part of the United Kingdom, and the 26 mainly Catholic counties of the South, which separated from the United Kingdom" (p. 755) and ultimately became known as the Republic of Ireland. Despite the partition, significant violence has occurred periodically in Northern Ireland.

The use of the terms *Catholic* and *Protestant* to label the conflicting groups is not meant to indicate that the conflict is primarily a religious one, although that is an element. A small sector of the Protestant population is virulently anti-Catholic and fears for its religious freedom if union occurs with the Irish republic, whose population is 98 percent Catholic. The Irish Roman Catholic hierarchy has heavily influenced the laws of the Republic of Ireland in such matters as divorce and birth control.

Other elements come into play. The Catholics mainly consider themselves to be Irish, while the Protestants prefer to be viewed as British. Economic inequality has been an important factor in fueling the conflict: there has been considerably more unemployment, less education, and poorer housing among the Catholics as compared with the Protestants. The two communities are largely separated psychologically even though they are not always physically separated. Each has developed separate social identities that affect how the members in each community view themselves and the people of the community. The social identities of the two groups have, until recently, been negatively related: a perceived gain for one side is usually associated with a perceived loss for the other.

Although the costs of the intergroup conflict in Northern Ireland have been relatively small compared to ethnic conflicts in such areas as Rwanda, Lebanon, Bosnia, Sri Lanka, and Kosovo, they have not been insignificant. Taking into account population size, the deaths due to violence in Northern Ireland are equivalent to 500,000 deaths in the United States. There are not only the direct costs of violence in terms of death and injury (about 3,000 killed and 30,000 injured between 1969 and 1994) but also the indirect, harder-to-measure economic and mental health costs. Some of these costs were borne by England: the economic, psychological, and political toll from seeing some of its soldiers attacked and killed in an attempt to control the violence.

Over the years, various attempts have been made to reduce the explosiveness of the conflict, including efforts by the Northern Ireland government to improve the economic situation of the Catholics, stimulation of intergroup contact under favorable circumstances, conduct of intergroup workshops for influentials in both groups, organization of women's groups that conducted various demonstrations against violence, integration of some of the Catholic and Protestant schools, recognition and honoring of the cultural traditions of both groups, and so forth. Many of these efforts were sabotaged by extremist groups on both sides. However, cumulatively they began to create the recognition that peaceful relations might be possible and that continued violence would not lead to victory for either side. Most of the ordinary people on both sides became increasingly alienated from the perpetrators of violence.

The conditions for possible successful negotiation of a solution to the conflict were beginning to develop. The heads of three interested and concerned governments—U.S. President Clinton, Prime Minister Blair of Great Britain, and Prime Minister Ahern of Ireland—played key roles in getting the leaders of the various factions involved in the conflict to the negotiating table. Appointing former U.S. Sen. George Mitchell, a highly respected and influential political figure, as a mediator was an important, positive step. He was acceptable to both sides and was a well-practiced, skilled political mediator.

At this writing, there have been substantial popular votes in Northern Ireland as well as in Ireland in favor of an agreement negotiated among leaders of the main Protestant and Catholic factions in Northern Ireland that hopefully will end their protracted, sometimes violent conflict. The agreement was developed with the aid of a skillful mediator, and with strong pressures from the leaders of the three interested governments in constant telephone contact with the negotiators during the difficult phases of the process. In coming to an agreement, each of the conflicting parties had to modify long-held positions, reduce their aspirations, and act with greater civility toward one another as well as bring the extremists in their groups under control. This was difficult to do. The level of distrust among the conflicting groups is still very high despite the agreement. Its successful implementation over a period of time requires a high level of vigilance among those committed to its successful implementation, to prevent misunderstandings or the actions of extremists from unraveling it. The agreement itself was a creative attempt to respond to the apprehensions as well as interests of the various participants in the conflict. Its achievement was honored in 1998 by the Nobel Peace Prize, awarded to John Hume and David Trimble, the leading negotiators for the Catholics and Protestants respectively.

SOME QUESTIONS ABOUT CONFLICT

Conflicts such as these three suggest many questions pertinent to conflicts of all sorts—interpersonal, intergroup, and international. These questions relate to fundamental processes that have been studied extensively by social psychologists. The chapters in this book address many of the fundamental social psychological processes involved in conflict and develop the implications of these processes for understanding conflict and for managing conflicts more effectively. Here is an outline of some of the processes affecting conflict that are addressed in one or more chapters.

- *Cooperation-Competition.* Each of the conflicts I have described had a destructive phase characterized by a win-lose or competitive orientation to the conflict. What determines whether a conflict takes a destructive, win-lose course or a constructive, cooperative, problem-solving one?

- *Social Justice.* All of the parties in the three conflicts had initially differing conceptions of what would be a fair resolution. What are the important sources of perceived injustice?

- *Motivation.* What needs do the parties in conflict have? Are their needs the same as their positions? What motives foster conflict, and which are fostered *by* conflict and tend to perpetuate it? Which facilitate constructive conflict resolution?

- *Trust.* Distrust is common whenever a conflict takes a destructive course. What processes give rise to trust, and which give rise to distrust?

- *Communication.* Faulty communication engenders misunderstanding, which may lead to conflict, and conflict often leads to breakdown of communication. What are the characteristics of effective communication in terms of the communicator and the listener? What can be done to develop such communication?

- *Attribution Processes.* Our emotional responses toward the actions of another are very much influenced by what intentions we attribute to the other as well as how much responsibility for the actions we attribute to that person. What are the nature and consequences of common errors in attribution?

- *Persuasion.* In most negotiations and conflicts, much of each party's effort is channeled into attempting to persuade the other of the soundness of the former's position. What insights into the conditions resulting in effective persuasion have resulted from systematic research of the processes involved in persuasion?

- *Self-Control.* Effective goal-directed actions, particularly those that have to be sustained over a period of time, require effective self-control. During the course of conflict, various distractions, unexpected events, and emotions (such as rage, wounded pride, despair, anxiety) may, when uncontrolled, lead one to lose sight of one's important, enduring needs and goals. Knowing how to keep oneself on course during a conflict is obviously valuable; what help does theory provide?

- *Power.* The distribution of power among parties in conflict and how power is employed strongly influence conflict processes. How do the bases of each party's power (including economic resources, weapons, information, legitimate authority, effective social organization) determine the type of influence exerted during a conflict?

- *Violence.* When conflict takes a destructive course, it sometimes leads to violence. What factors contribute to violent behavior? What sorts of intervention reduce the likelihood of violence?

- *Judgmental Biases.* A host of misunderstandings, misperceptions, and potential biases interfere with the ability to resolve a conflict constructively. What gives rise to misunderstandings and biases, and how can their occurrence be reduced?

- *Personality.* How do unresolved self-conflict and individual personality characteristics affect how conflict is managed? How important is it to know the conflictual styles of various types of people (anxious, obsessive, analytical, and so on)?

- *Development.* What differences typically exist in managing conflict depending on whether it is between children, adolescents, or adults? How does psychological development (such as acquisition of language, increase in physical strength, and decreasing dependence on adults) affect response to conflict?

- *Group Problem Solving and Creativity.* Constructive management of conflict can be viewed as a creative, cooperative problem-solving process in which the conflict is defined as the mutual problem to be solved. What leads to effective group problem solving, and what enables individuals to be creative in their approach to nonroutine problems?

- *Intergroup Conflict.* Conflict between groups that differ in ethnicity, race, religion, gender, sexual orientation, and the like appear to have become prevalent and salient in recent years. How do the processes involved in intergroup conflicts differ from those in interpersonal conflicts?

- *Culture.* How does the culture in which an individual group is embedded affect how conflicts develop and are managed? What problems are faced by negotiators from diverse cultural backgrounds?

- *Intractable Conflicts.* Difficult, long-standing, intractable conflicts occur at all levels—interpersonal, intergroup, and international. When are such conflicts "ripe" for intervention? What methods of intervention are likely to be productive? How can reconciliation and forgiveness be encouraged between historically bitter enemies?

- *Mediation.* Third-party intervention, such as mediation, can sometimes help people resolve their conflicts when they are unable to do so by themselves. When is mediation likely to be effective? What are the processes involved in mediation?

- *Managing Conflict in Large Groups.* When the conflict occurs among factions within a large group, are there ways of bringing the total group, or its relevant components, together so that the group as a whole can contribute to resolving the conflict?

- *Constructive Controversy.* Conflict can take the form of lively, constructive controversy, which stimulates creativity and richer thought processes; yet differences in belief and opinion often produce quarrels that lead to hardening of positions and breakdown of relations. What leads to lively controversy rather than deadly quarrel?

- *Culture and Conflict.* Is conflict theory, largely developed in Western culture, applicable elsewhere? Can it be usefully applied in China, for example? What modifications, if any, are necessary?

These and other questions relevant to all sorts of conflict are addressed in one or more of the chapters of this handbook—sometimes directly and sometimes indirectly by articulating the fundamental social psychological processes that occur in all sorts of conflict.

SOME DIFFERENCES BETWEEN THE ORIENTATION OF THEORISTS AND PRACTITIONERS

Inevitable differences in the theory and practice orientations can lead to misunderstanding and alienation if these inherent differences are not understood. In many disciplines of the natural as well as social sciences, the "scientist" and the "practitioner" tend to stereotype each other: the scientist viewing the practitioner as "unscientific" and the practitioner considering the scientist to be "impractical." In the hope of fostering mutual respect and understanding of each other's orientation, we contrast several aspects of each orientation.

The Analytical Versus the Synthetic Approach

The practitioner must synthesize the knowledge from many theories and research studies; she must make a collage or mosaic of many theoretical ideas of the kind presented in this book rather than relying on any single one. In contrast, the theorist-researcher generates knowledge by analysis and isolation of the object of inquiry; the focus is often narrowly defined. Breadth of theoretical knowledge is more important for the practitioner than precision, consistency, or elegance, although the opposite is true for the theoretically oriented researcher. Moreover, since there are no well-established procedures for combining theories to fit them to a given practical problem, practitioners must often work intuitively without being able to specify precisely how they are weaving together the theoretical ideas employed. In contrast, the pressure on theorist-researchers is to be explicit and specific about their ideas and procedures.

The Skeptical Versus the Pragmatic

The practitioner is rewarded if what he does "works" even if his practice is not grounded in well-established knowledge. Moreover, he is usually more persuasive and effective if he has a positive, confident attitude about what he is doing and recommending. The scientist, on the other hand, knows very well that the path of progress in science is littered with discarded theories, and honor goes to those who help to determine the well-established ones. Thus, it is no wonder that the professional stance of the theorist-researcher is hesitant, self-critical, and skeptical toward the theory and research that social technologists often use with a confident attitude.

Enduring Versus Useful Truths

The theorist has the (rarely achieved) aim of developing knowledge that is universally true; enduringly valid for different times and places; and relevant for understanding cavepeople as well as spacepeople, aborigines in Kakadu as well as Park Avenue sophisticates. Such theoretical knowledge is usually general and abstract, and developing its implications for specific situations requires considerable additional thought and effort. The scientist is especially interested in developing the surprising and thus interesting implications of a theory because its validity and generality seem enhanced by the ability to predict the unexpected.

In contrast, the practitioner is necessarily concerned with the mundane and practical, namely, with those aspects of a specific situation that can be altered with minimum cost to produce the desired consequence. Her interest is more focused on the here and now, on the concrete aspects of the situation in which she has to work, rather than on the general and abstract. Of course, the practitioner also seeks to have general knowledge of the kind of situation and type of people with whom her model of intervention is effective, but the focus of attention is on what can be done to produce the desired effects. In practical work, it is more important to know that a child's ability to learn may be improved more easily and economically by changing motivation rather than by modifying genes, even though the child's genes may play an important role in determining the ability to learn.

A BRIEF HISTORY OF SOCIAL
PSYCHOLOGICAL THEORIZING ABOUT CONFLICT

This section of the Introduction is an overview of the progress made during the past one hundred years or so in the social psychological study of conflict. The writings of three intellectual giants—Darwin, Marx, and Freud—dominated the intellectual atmosphere during social psychology's infancy. These three theorists significantly influenced the writings of the early social psychologists on conflict as well as in many other areas. All three appeared, on a superficial reading, to emphasize the competitive, destructive aspects of conflict.

Darwin stressed "the competitive struggle for existence" and "the survival of the fittest." He wrote that "all nature is at war, one organism with another, or with external nature. Seeing the contented face of nature, this may at first be well doubted; but reflection will inevitably prove it is too true" (quoted in Hyman, 1966, p. 29).

Marx emphasized class struggle, and as the struggle proceeds, "the whole society breaks up more and more into two great hostile camps, two great, directly antagonistic classes: bourgeoisie and proletariat." He and Engels end their *Communist Manifesto* with a ringing call to class struggle: "The proletarians have nothing to lose but their chains. They have a world to win. Working men of all countries, unite."

Freud's view of psychosexual development was largely that of constant struggle between the biologically rooted infantile id and the socially determined, internalized parental surrogate, the superego. As Schachtel (1959) has noted, "The concepts and language used by Freud to describe the great metamorphosis from life in the womb to life in the world abound with images of war, coercion, reluctant compromise, unwelcome necessity, imposed sacrifices, uneasy truce under pressure, enforced detours and roundabout ways to return to the original peaceful state of absence of consciousness and stimulation" (p. 10).

Thus the intellectual atmosphere prevalent during the period when social psychology began to emerge contributed to viewing conflict from the perspective of "competitive struggle." Social conditions too—the intense competition among businesses and among nations, the devastation of World War I, the economic depression of the 1920s and 1930s, the rise of Nazism and other totalitarian systems—reinforced this perspective.

The vulgarization of Darwin's ideas in the form of "social Darwinism" provided an intellectual rationale for racism, sexism, class superiority, and war. Such ideas as "survival of the fittest," "hereditary determinism," and "stages of evolution" were eagerly misapplied to the relations between human social groups—classes and nations, as well as social races—to rationalize imperialist policies. The influence of pseudoevolutionary thinking was so strong that, as a critic suggested, it gave rise to a new imperialist beatitude: "Blessed are the strong, for they shall prey upon the weak" (Banton, 1967, p. 48). The rich and powerful were biologically superior; they had achieved their positions as a result of natural selection. It would be against nature to interfere with the inequality and suffering of the poor and weak.

Social Darwinism and the mode of explaining behavior in terms of innate, evolutionary, derived instincts were in retreat by the mid-1920s. The prestige of the empirical methods in the physical sciences, the point of view of social determinism advanced by Karl Marx and various sociological theorists, and the findings of cultural anthropologists all contributed to their decline. With the waning of the instinctual mode of explaining such conflict phenomena as war, intergroup hostility, and human exploitation, two others have become dominant: the psychological and the social-political-economic.

The psychological mode attempts to explain such phenomena in terms of "what goes on in the minds of men" (Klineberg, 1964) or "tensions that cause war" (Cantril, 1950). In other words, it explains such phenomena in terms of the perceptions, beliefs, values, ideology, motivations, and other psychological states and characteristics that individual men and women have acquired as a result of their experiences and as these characteristics are activated by the particular situation and role in which people are situated. The social-political-economic mode, by contrast, seeks an explanation in terms of such social, economic, and political factors as levels of armament, objective conflicts between economic and political interests, and the like.

Although the two modes of explanation are not mutually exclusive, there is a tendency for partisans of the psychological mode to consider that the causal arrow points from psychological conditions to social-political-economic conditions and for partisans of the latter to believe the reverse is true. In any case, much of the social psychological writing in the 1930s, 1940s, and early 1950s on the topics of war, intergroup conflict, and industrial strife was largely nonempirical, and in one vein or the other. The psychologically trained social psychologist tended to favor the psychological mode; the Marxist-oriented or sociologically trained social psychologist more often favored the other.

The decline of social Darwinism and the instinctivist doctrines was hastened by the development and employment of empirical methods in social psychology. This early empirical orientation to social psychology focused on the socialization of the individual; in part as a reaction to the instinctivist doctrine. It led to a great variety of studies, including a number investigating cooperation and competition. These latter studies are, in my view, the precursors to the empirical, social psychological study of conflict.

Field Theory, Conflict, and Cooperation-Competition

During the 1920s, 1930s, and 1940s, quite independently of the work being conducted in the United States on cooperation-competition, Kurt Lewin and his students were theorizing and conducting research that profoundly affected later work in many areas of social psychology. Lewin's field theory—with its dynamic concepts of tension systems, "driving" and "restraining" forces, "own" and "induced" forces, valences, level of aspiration, power fields, interdependence, overlapping situations, and so on—created a new vocabulary for thinking about conflict and cooperation-competition.

As early as 1931, employing his analysis of force fields, Lewin (1931, 1935) presented a penetrating theoretical discussion of three basic types of psychological conflict: approach-approach, in which the individual stands between two positive valences of approximately equal strength; avoidance-avoidance, where the individual stands between two negative valences of approximately equal strength; and approach-avoidance, meaning the individual is exposed to opposing forces deriving from positive and negative valences. Hull (1938) translated Lewin's analysis into the terminology of the goal gradient, and Miller (1937, 1944) elaborated and did research on it. Numerous experimental studies supported the theoretical analysis.

My own initial theorizing on cooperation-competition (Deutsch, 1949b) was influenced by Lewinian thinking on tension systems, which was reflected in a series of brilliant experiments on the recall of interrupted activities (Zeigarnik), the resumption of interrupted activities (Ovsiankina), substitutability (Mahler), and the role of ego in cooperative work (Lewis and Franklin). But even more of my thinking was indebted to the ideas that were in the air at the MIT Research Center for Group Dynamics. Ways of characterizing and explaining group processes and group functioning, employing the language of Lewinian theorizing, were under constant discussion there among the students and faculty. Thus, it was quite natural that when I settled on cooperation-competition as the topic of my doctoral dissertation, I employed the Lewinian dynamic emphasis on goals and how they are interrelated as my key theoretical wedge into this topic.

Even more important, the preoccupation at the MIT center with understanding group processes pressed me to formulate my ideas about cooperation and competition so that they would be relevant to the psychological and interpersonal processes occurring within and between groups. This pressure forced my theory and research (Deutsch, 1949a, 1949b) to go considerably beyond the prior social psychological work on cooperation-competition. My theorizing and research were concerned not only with the individual and group outcomes of cooperation and competition but also with the social psychological processes that would give rise to those outcomes. This work has central relevance to understanding the processes involved in conflict. It is summarized in Chapter One.

Game Theory and Games

In 1944, von Neumann and Morgenstern published their now-classic work, *Theory of Games and Economic Behavior*. Game theory has made a major contribution to the work of social scientists by formulating in mathematical terms the problem of conflict of interest. However, it is neither the mathematics nor the normative prescriptions for minimizing losses when facing an intelligent adversary that have made game theory of considerable value to social psychologists. Rather, it is the core emphasis on the parties in conflict having interdependent interests; their fates are woven together. Although the mathematical and normative development of game theory has been most successful in connection with pure competitive conflict (zero-sum games), game theory also recognizes that cooperative as well as competitive interests may be intertwined in conflict (as in coalition games or non-zero-sum games).

Game theory's recognition of the intertwining of cooperative and competitive interests in situations of conflict (or, in Schelling's useful term, the mixed-motive nature of conflict; Schelling, 1960) has had a productive impact on the social psychological study of conflict, theoretically as well as methodologically. Theoretically, at least for me, it helped buttress a viewpoint that I had developed prior to my acquaintance with game theory, namely, that conflicts were typically mixtures of cooperative and competitive processes and that the course of conflict would be determined by the nature of the mixture. This emphasis on the cooperative elements involved in conflict ran counter to what was then the dominant view of conflict as a competitive struggle.

Methodologically, game theory had an impact on an even larger group of psychologists. The mathematical formulations of game theory had the indirect but extremely valuable consequence of laying bare some fascinating paradoxical situations in such a way that they were highly suggestive of experimental work. Game matrices as an experimental device were popular because they facilitated precise definition of the reward structure encountered by the subjects, and hence of the way they are dependent on one another. Partly stimulated by and partly in reaction to the research using game matrices, other research games for the study of conflict were also developed. Well over one thousand studies based on experimental games had been published by 1985. Much of this research, as is true in other areas of science, was mindless—being done because a convenient experimental format was readily available. But some of it has, I believe, helped to develop systematic understanding of conflict processes and conflict resolution. Fortunately, in recent years, experimental gaming has been supplemented by other experimental procedures and by field studies that overcome some of the inherent limitations of experimental gaming.

Themes in Contemporary Social Psychological Research on Conflicts

Social psychological research and theorizing on conflict during the past forty years have primarily addressed eight major questions (see Deutsch, 1990, for more detail about the first five):

1. *What conditions give rise to a constructive or destructive process of conflict resolution?* In terms of bargaining and negotiation, the emphasis here is on determining the circumstances that allow the conflicting parties to arrive at a mutually satisfactory agreement that maximizes their joint outcomes. In a sense, this first question arises from focusing on the cooperative potential inherent in conflict. In social psychology, this question has been most directly addressed in the work of my students and myself and summarized in my 1973 book, *The Resolution of Conflict: Constructive and Destructive Processes.* All of the chapters in this handbook are relevant; the chapters focusing on constructive controversy and cooperation-competition are most relevant.

2. *What circumstances, strategies, and tactics lead one party to do better than another in a conflict situation?* The stress here is on how one can wage conflict, or bargain, so as to win or at least do better than one's adversary. This second question emerges from focusing on the competitive features of a conflict situation. It has been mainly addressed by economists and political scientists. In social psychology, research related to this question focuses on such bargaining tactics as "being ignorant," "being tough," "being belligerent," "the effects of threats," and how to increase one's bargaining power. This question is treated only indirectly in this handbook, by inference, because of the book's emphasis on constructive conflict resolution.

3. *What determines the nature of the agreement between conflicting parties, if they are able to reach an agreement?* Here the concern is with the cognitive and normative factors that lead people to conceive a possible agreement and to perceive it as a salient possibility for reaching a stable agreement—one that each of the conflicting parties sees as "just" under the circumstances. This third question is a recent one and has been addressed under the heading of research on the social psychology of equity and justice. Chapter Two, on social justice, is most directly relevant to this question, but other chapters bear on it as well.

4. *How can third parties be used to prevent conflicts from becoming destructive or to help deadlocked or embittered negotiators move toward constructive management of their conflicts?* This fourth question has been reflected in studies of mediation and in strategies for deescalating conflict. Chapter Twenty-Five, on mediation, pertains most directly, but all of the chapters have some relevance.

5. *How can people be educated to manage their conflicts constructively?* This has been a concern of consultants working with leaders in industry and government and also with those who have

responsibility for educating children in our schools. All the chapters bear on this question.

During the past fifteen years, three additional questions have emerged as foci of work in the field of conflict resolution:

6. *How and when to intervene in prolonged, intractable conflicts?* Much of the literature in conflict resolution has been preventive rather than remedial in its emphasis. It is concerned with understanding the conditions that foster productive rather than destructive conflict (as in question one) or developing knowledge about the circumstances that lead to intractable, destructive conflict, in the hope of preventing such conflict. More recently, the reality that many protracted, destructive conflicts exist in the world has induced some scholars to focus their attention on this problem. In this book, the discussions of intractable conflicts (Chapter Twenty-One), mediation (Chapter Twenty-Five), and intergroup conflict (Chapter Eight) are particularly relevant.

7. *How are we to understand why ethnic, religious, and identity conflicts frequently take an intractable, destructive course?* With the end of the Cold War, there appears to be a proliferation of such conflicts. In the past ten years, interest in such conflicts has been renewed. The chapters most directly pertaining to this question are those dealing with intergroup and cultural conflict, but almost all are relevant.

8. *How applicable in other cultural contexts are the theories related to conflict that have largely been developed in the United States and Western Europe?* In recent years, there has been much discussion in the literature of the differences that exist in how people from varying cultural backgrounds deal with negotiations and, more generally, manage conflict. We have not attempted to summarize the cultural differences that exist with regard to conflict management. However, in discussing culture and conflict (Chapter Twenty-Two) as well as in Chapter Twenty-Three, on applying conflict theory in China, there is discussion of the issue of cross-cultural generalizability.

Although various chapters of this book have direct relevance to the questions listed here, the aim of the *Handbook of Conflict Resolution* is not to summarize the work done, so far, in the field of conflict resolution. Rather, its aim is to enrich the field by presenting the theoretical underpinnings that throw light on the fundamental social psychological processes involved in all levels of conflict. None of the theories is adequate to deal by itself with the complexities involved in any specific conflict or any type of conflict. As indicated earlier in this chapter, each theory is a component of the particular mosaic that needs to be created to understand and manage a unique conflict constructively.

References

Banton, M. *Race Relations.* New York: Basic Books, 1967.

Cairns, E., and Darby, J. "The Conflict in Northern Ireland: Causes, Consequences, and Controls." *American Psychologist,* 1998, *53,* 754–760.

Cantril, H. (ed.). *Tensions That Cause Wars.* Urbana: University of Illinois Press, 1950.

Deutsch, M. "An Experimental Study of the Effects of Cooperation and Competition upon Group Processes." *Human Relations,* 1949a, *2,* 199–231.

Deutsch, M. "A Theory of Cooperation and Competition." *Human Relations,* 1949b, *2,* 129–152.

Deutsch, M. *The Resolution of Conflict: Constructive and Destructive Processes.* New Haven: Yale University Press, 1973.

Deutsch, M. "Commentary: on Negotiating the Nonnegotiable." In B. Kellerman and J. Rubin (eds.), *Leadership and Negotiation in the Middle East.* New York: Praeger, 1988.

Deutsch, M. "Sixty Years of Conflict." *International Journal of Conflict Management,* 1990, *1,* 237–263.

Hull, C. L. "The Goal-Gradient Hypothesis Applied to Some 'Field Force' Problems in the Behavior of Young Children." *Psychological Review,* 1938, *45,* 271–279.

Hyman, S. E. *The Tangled Bank.* New York: Grosset & Dunlap, 1966.

Klineberg, O. *The Human Dimensions in International Relations.* Austin, Tex.: Holt, Rinehart and Winston, 1964.

Lewin, K. "Environmental Forces in Child Behavior and Development." In C. Murchison (ed.), *A Handbook of Child Psychology.* Worcester, Mass.: Clark University Press, 1931.

Lewin, K. *A Dynamic Theory of Personality.* New York: McGraw-Hill, 1935.

Miller, N. E. "Analysis of the Form of Conflict Reactions." *Psychological Bulletin,* 1937, *34,* 720.

Miller, N. E. "Experimental Studies of Conflict." In J. M. Hunt (ed.), *Personality and the Behavior Disorders.* Vol. 1. New York: Ronald Press, 1944.

Schachtel, E. G. *Metamorphosis: On the Development of Affect, Perception, Attention, and Memory.* New York: Basic Books, 1959.

Schelling, T. C. *The Strategy of Conflict.* Cambridge, Mass.: Harvard University Press, 1960.

von Neumann, J., and Morgenstern, O. *Theory of Games and Economic Behavior.* New York: Wiley, 1944.

PART ONE

INTERPERSONAL AND INTERGROUP PROCESSES

CHAPTER ONE

Cooperation and Competition

Morton Deutsch

Some time ago, in the garden of a friend's house, my five-year-old son and his chum were struggling over possession of a water hose. (They were in conflict.) Each wanted to use it first to water the garden. (They had a competitive orientation.) Each was trying to tug it away from the other and both were crying. Each was very frustrated, and neither was able to use the hose to sprinkle the flowers as he'd desired. After reaching a deadlock in this tug-of-war, they began to punch one another and call each other names. (As a result of their competitive approach, the conflict took a destructive course for both of them—producing frustration, crying, and violence.)

Now imagine a different scenario. The garden consists mainly of two sections, flowers and vegetables. Each kid wants to use the hose first. Let's suppose they want to resolve their conflict amicably. (They have a cooperative orientation.) One says to the other, "Let's flip a coin to see who uses the hose first." (A fair procedure for resolving the conflict is suggested.) The other agrees and suggests that the loser be given the right to select which section of the garden he waters. They both agree to the suggestion. (A cooperative, win-win agreement is reached.) Their agreements are implemented and both kids feel happy and good about one another. (These are common effects of a cooperative or constructive approach to a conflict.)

As this example illustrates, whether the participants in a conflict have a cooperative orientation or a competitive one is decisive in determining its course and outcomes. This chapter is concerned with understanding the processes involved in cooperation and competition, their effects, and the factors that contribute to developing a cooperative or competitive relationship. It is important to understand the nature of cooperation and competition since almost all conflicts are mixed-motive, containing elements of both cooperation and competition.

A THEORY OF COOPERATION AND COMPETITION

The theory being presented here was initially developed by Morton Deutsch (1949a, 1949b, 1973, 1985) and much elaborated by David W. Johnson (Johnson and Johnson, 1989). The Johnsons have provided the most extensive summary of the theory and the research bearing on it; their 1989 book should be consulted for greater detail.

The theory has two basic ideas. One relates to the type of *interdependence among goals* of the people involved in a given situation. The other pertains to the *type of action* taken by the people involved.

I identify two basic types of goal interdependence: positive (where the goals are linked in such a way that the amount or probability of a person's goal attainment is positively correlated with the amount or probability of another obtaining his goal) and negative (where the goals are linked in such a way that the amount or probability of goal attainment is negatively correlated with the amount or probability of the other's goal attainment). To put it colloquially, if you're positively linked with another, then you sink or swim together; with negative linkage, if the other sinks, you swim, and if the other swims, you sink.

It is well to realize that few situations are "purely" positive or negative. In most situations, people have a mixture of goals so that it is common for some of their goals initially to be positive and some negatively interdependent. In this section, for analytical purposes, I discuss pure situations. In mixed situations, the relative strengths of the two types of goal interdependency, as well as their general orientation to one another, largely determine the nature of the conflict process.

I also characterize two basic types of action by an individual: "effective actions," which improve the actor's chances of obtaining a goal, and "bungling actions," which worsen the actor's chances of obtaining the goal. (For the purpose of simplicity, I use dichotomies for my basic concepts; the dichotomous types of interdependence and the dichotomous types of actions are, I assume, polar ends of continua.) I then combine types of interdependence and types of action to posit how they jointly affect three basic social psychological processes that are discussed later in this chapter: "substitutability," "attitudes," and "inducibility."

People's goals may be linked for various reasons. Thus, positive interdependence can result from people liking one another, being rewarded in terms of their joint achievement, needing to share a resource or overcome an obstacle together, holding common membership or identification with a group whose fate is important to them, being unable to achieve their task goals unless they divide up the work, being influenced by personality and cultural orientation, being bound together because they are treated this way by a common enemy or an authority, and so on. Similarly, with regard to negative interdependence, it can result from people disliking one another; or from their being rewarded in such a way that the more the other gets of the reward, the less one gets, and so on.

In addition to positive and negative interdependence, it is well to recognize that there can be lack of interdependence, or *independence,* such that the activities and fate of the people involved do not affect one another, directly or indirectly. If they are completely independent of one another, no conflict arises; the existence of a conflict implies some form of interdependence.

One further point. Asymmetries may exist with regard to the degree of interdependence in a relationship; suppose that what you do or what happens to you may have a considerable effect on me, but what I do or what happens to me may have little impact on you. I am more dependent on you than you are on me. In the extreme case, you may be completely independent of me and I may be highly dependent on you. As a consequence of this asymmetry, you have greater power and influence in the relationship than I. This power may be general if the asymmetry exists in many situations, or it may be situation-specific if the asymmetry occurs only in a particular situation. A master has general power over a slave, while an auto mechanic repairing my car's electrical system has situation-specific power.

The three concepts mentioned previously—substitutability, attitudes, and inducibility—are vital to understanding the social and psychological processes involved in creating the major effects of cooperation and competition. *Substitutability* (how a person's actions can satisfy another person's intentions) is central to the functioning of all social institutions (the family, industry, schools), to the division of labor, and to role specialization. Unless the activities of other people can substitute for yours, you are like a person stranded on a desert island alone: you have to build your own house, find or produce your own food, protect yourself from harmful animals, treat your ailments and illnesses, educate yourself about the nature of your new environment and about how to do all these tasks, and so on, without the help of others. Being alone, you can neither create children nor have a family. Substitutability permits you to accept the activities of others in fulfilling your needs. *Negative substitutability* involves active rejection and effort to counteract the effects of another's activities.

Attitudes refer to the predisposition to respond evaluatively, favorably or unfavorably, to aspects of one's environment or self. Through natural selection, evolution has ensured that all living creatures have the capacity to respond positively to stimuli that are beneficial to them and negatively to those that are harmful. They are attracted to, approach, receive, ingest, like, enhance, and otherwise act positively toward beneficial objects, events, or other creatures; in contrast, they are repelled by harmful objects and circumstances and avoid, eject, attack, dislike, negate, and otherwise act negatively toward them. This inborn tendency to act positively toward the beneficial and negatively toward the harmful is the foundation on which the human potentials for cooperation and love as well as for competition and hate develop. The basic psychological orientation of cooperation implies the positive attitude that "we are *for* each other," "we benefit one another"; competition, by contrast, implies the negative attitude that "we are *against* one another," and in its extreme form, "you are out to harm me."

Inducibility refers to the readiness to accept another's influence to do what he or she wants; *negative inducibility* refers to the readiness to reject or obstruct fulfillment of what the other wants. The complement of substitutability is inducibility. You are willing to be helpful to another whose actions are helpful to you, but not to someone whose actions are harmful. In fact, you reject any request to help the other engage in harmful actions and, if possible, obstruct or interfere with these actions if they occur.

THE EFFECTS OF COOPERATION AND COMPETITION

Thus, the theory predicts that if you are in a positively interdependent relationship with someone who bungles, his bungling is not a substitute for effective actions you intended; thus the bungling is viewed negatively. In fact, when your net-playing tennis partner in a doubles game allows an easy shot to get past him, you have to extend yourself to prevent being harmed by the error. On the other hand, if your relationship is one of negative interdependence, and the other person bungles (as when your tennis opponent double-faults), your opponent's bungle substitutes for an effective action on your part, and it is regarded positively or valued. The reverse is true for effective actions. An opponent's effective actions are not substitutable for yours and are negatively valued; a teammate can induce you to help him make an effective action, but you are likely to try to prevent or obstruct a bungling action by your teammate. In contrast, you are willing to help an opponent bungle, but your opponent is not likely to induce you to help him make an effective action (which, in effect, harms your chances of obtaining your goal).

The theory of cooperation and competition, then, goes on to make further predictions about different aspects of intrapersonal, interpersonal, intragroup, and intergroup processes from the predictions about substitutability, attitudes, and inducibility. Thus, assuming that the individual actions in a group are more frequently effective than bungling, among the predictions that follow from the theory are that *cooperative relations* (those in which the goals of the parties involved are predominantly positively interdependent), as compared with competitive ones, show more of these positive characteristics:

1. *Effective communication* is exhibited. Ideas are verbalized, and group members are attentive to one another, accepting of the ideas of other members, and influenced by them. They have fewer difficulties in communicating with or understanding others.

2. *Friendliness, helpfulness, and less obstructiveness* is expressed in the discussions. Members also are more satisfied with the group and its solutions and favorably impressed by the contributions of the other group members. In addition, members of the cooperative groups rate themselves high in desire to win the respect of their colleagues and in obligation to the other members.

3. *Coordination of effort, division of labor, orientation to task achievement, orderliness in discussion, and high productivity* are manifested in the cooperative groups (if the group task requires effective communication, coordination of effort, division of labor, or sharing of resources).

4. *Feeling of agreement with the ideas of others and a sense of basic similarity in beliefs and values, as well as confidence in one's own ideas and in the value that other members attach to those ideas,* are obtained in the cooperative groups.

5. *Willingness to enhance the other's power* (for example, the knowledge, skills, resources, and so on) to accomplish the other's goals increases. As the other's capabilities are strengthened, you are strengthened; they are of value to you as well as to the other. Similarly, the other is enhanced from your enhancement and benefits from your growing capabilities and power.

6. *Defining conflicting interests as a mutual problem to be solved by collaborative effort* facilitates recognizing the legitimacy of each other's interests and the necessity to search for a solution responsive to the needs of all. It tends to limit rather than expand the scope of conflicting interests. Attempts to influence the other tend to be confined to processes of persuasion.

In contrast, a *competitive process* has the opposite effects:

1. Communication is impaired as the conflicting parties seek to gain advantage by misleading the other through use of false promises, ingratiation tactics, and disinformation. It is reduced and seen as futile as they recognize that they cannot trust one another's communications to be honest or informative.

2. Obstructiveness and lack of helpfulness lead to mutual negative attitudes and suspicion of one another's intentions. One's perceptions of the other tend to focus on the person's negative qualities and ignore the positive.

3. The parties to the process are unable to divide their work, duplicating one another's efforts such that they become mirror images; if they do divide the work, they feel the need to check what the other is doing continuously.

4. The repeated experience of disagreement and critical rejection of ideas reduces confidence in oneself as well as the other.

5. The conflicting parties seek to enhance their own power and to reduce the power of the other. Any increase in the power of the other is seen as threatening to oneself.

6. The competitive process stimulates the view that the solution of a conflict can only be imposed by one side on the other, which in turn leads to using coercive tactics such as psychological as well as physical threats and violence. It tends to expand the scope of the issues in conflict as each side seeks superiority in power and legitimacy. The conflict becomes a power struggle or a matter of moral principle and is no longer confined to a specific issue at a given time and place. Escalating the conflict increases its motivational significance to the participants and may make a limited defeat less acceptable and more humiliating than a mutual disaster.

As the conflict escalates, it perpetuates itself by such processes as autistic hostility, self-fulfilling prophecies, and unwitting commitments. *Autistic hostility* involves breaking off contact and communication with the other; the result is that the hostility is perpetuated because one has no opportunity to learn that it may be based on misunderstandings or misjudgments, nor to learn if the other has changed for the better.

Self-fulfilling prophecies are those wherein you engage in hostile behavior toward another because of a false assumption that the other has done or is preparing to do something harmful to you; your false assumption comes true when it leads you to engage in hostile behavior that then provokes the other to react in a hostile manner to you. The dynamics of an escalating, destructive conflict have the inherent quality of a *folie à deux* in which the self-fulfilling prophecies of each side mutually reinforce one another. As a result, both sides are right to think that the other is provocative, untrustworthy, and malevolent. Each side, however, tends to be blind to how it as well as the other have contributed to this malignant process.

In the case of *unwitting commitments,* during the course of escalating conflict the parties not only overcommit to rigid positions but also may unwittingly commit to negative attitudes and perceptions, beliefs, defenses against the other's expected attacks, and investments involved in carrying out their conflictual activities. Thus, during an escalated conflict, a person (a group, a nation) may commit to the view that the other is an evil enemy, the belief that the other is out to take advantage of oneself (one's group, nation), the conviction that one has to be constantly vigilant and ready to defend against the danger the other poses to one's vital interests, and also invest in the means of defending oneself as well as attacking the other. After a protracted conflict, it is hard to give up a grudge, to disarm without feeling vulnerable, as well as to give up the emotional charge associated with being mobilized and vigilant in relation to the conflict. As Johnson and Johnson (1989) have detailed, these ideas have given rise to a large number of research studies indicating that a cooperative process (as compared to a competitive one) leads to greater group productivity, more favorable interpersonal relations, better psychological health, and higher self-esteem. Research has also shown that more constructive resolution of conflicts results from cooperative as opposed to competitive processes.

For understanding the nature of the processes involved in conflict, this last research finding is of central theoretical and practical significance. It suggests that constructive processes of conflict resolution are similar to cooperative processes of problem solving, and destructive processes of conflict resolution are similar to competitive processes. Since our prior theoretical and research work gave us considerable knowledge about the nature of the processes involved in cooperation and competition, it is evident that this knowledge provides detailed insight into the nature of the processes entailed in constructive and destructive conflict resolution. This kind of knowledge contributes to understanding what processes are involved in producing good or bad outcomes of conflict. There are many ways of characterizing the outcomes of a conflict: satisfaction-dissatisfaction of the parties, material benefits and costs, improvement or worsening of their relationship, effects on self-esteem and reputation, precedents set, kinds of lessons learned, effects on third-parties (such as children of divorcing parents), and so on. Thus, there is reason to believe that a cooperative-constructive process of conflict resolution leads to such good outcomes as mutual benefits and satisfaction, strengthening relationship, positive psychological effects, and so on, while a competitive-destructive process leads to material losses and dissatisfaction, worsening relationship, and negative psychological effects in at least one party (the loser if it is a win-lose outcome) or both parties (if it is a lose-lose outcome).

CONSTRUCTIVE AND DESTRUCTIVE COMPETITION

Competition can vary from destructive to constructive: unfair, unregulated competition being at the destructive end; fair, regulated competition being in between; and constructive competition being at the positive end. In constructive competition, the losers as well as the winners gain. Thus, in a tennis match that takes the form of constructive competition, the winner suggests how the loser can improve her game, offers an opportunity for the loser to learn and practice skills, and makes the match an enjoyable or worthwhile experience for the loser. In constructive competition, winners see to it that losers are better off, or at least not worse off than they were before the competition.

The major difference, for example, between constructive controversy and competitive debate is that in the former people discuss their differences with the objective of clarifying them and attempting to find a solution that integrates the best thoughts that emerge during the discussion, no matter who articulates them (see Chapter Three for a fuller discussion). There is no winner and no loser; both win if during the controversy each party comes to deeper insights and enriched views of the matter that is initially in controversy. Constructive controversy is a process for constructively coping with the inevitable differences that people bring to cooperative interaction because it uses differences in understanding, per-spective, knowledge, and world view as valued resources. By contrast, in com-petitive contests or debates there is usually a winner and a loser. The party judged to have "the best"—ideas, skills, knowledge, and so on—typically wins, while the other, who is judged to be less good, typically loses. Competition eval-uates and ranks people based on their capacity for a particular task, rather than integrating various contributions.

By my emphasis throughout this chapter, I do not mean to suggest that com-petition produces no benefits. Competition is part of everyday life. Acquiring the skills necessary to compete effectively can be of considerable value. More-over, competition in a cooperative, playful context can be fun. It enables one to enact and experience, in a nonserious setting, symbolic emotional dramas re-lating to victory and defeat, life and death, power and helplessness, dominance and submission; these dramas have deep personal and cultural roots. In addi-tion, competition is a useful social mechanism for selecting those who are more able to perform the activities involved in the competition. Further, when no ob-jective, criterion-referenced basis for measurement of performance exists, the relative performance of students affords a crude yardstick. Nevertheless, seri-ous problems are associated with competition when it does not occur in a co-operative context and if it is not effectively regulated by fair rules (see Deutsch, 1973, pp. 377–388, for a discussion of regulating competition).

INITIATING COOPERATION AND COMPETITION

If we know that cooperative and competitive processes have important effects on conflict resolution, a question follows: What initiates or gives rise to one or the other process? We did much research (see Deutsch, 1973) in an attempt to find the answer. The results of our many studies fell into a pattern I slowly began to grasp. They seemed explainable by an assumption I have immodestly labeled "Deutsch's Crude Law of Social Relations":

> The characteristic processes and effects elicited
> by a given type of social relationship also tend to
> elicit that type of social relationship.

Thus, cooperation induces and is induced by perceived similarity in beliefs and attitudes, readiness to be helpful, openness in communication, trusting and friendly attitudes, sensitivity to common interests and deemphasis of opposed interests, orientation toward enhancing mutual power rather than power differences, and so on. Similarly, competition induces and is induced by use of tactics of coercion, threat, or deception; attempts to enhance the power differences between oneself and the other; poor communication; minimization of the awareness of similarities in values and increased sensitivity to opposed interests; suspicious and hostile attitudes; the importance, rigidity, and size of issues in conflict; and so on.

In other words, if one has systematic knowledge of the effects of cooperative and competitive processes, one has systematic knowledge of the conditions that typically give rise to such processes, and by extension to the conditions that affect whether a conflict takes a constructive or destructive course. My early theory of cooperation and competition is a theory of the *effects* of cooperative and competitive processes. Hence, from the Crude Law of Social Relations, it follows that this theory brings insight into the conditions that give rise to cooperative and competitive processes.

This law is certainly crude. It expresses surface similarities between effects and causes; the basic relationships are genotypical rather than phenotypical. The surface effects of cooperation and competition are due to the underlying type of interdependence (positive or negative) and type of action (effective or bungling), the basic social psychological processes involved in the theory (substitutability, attitudes, and inducibility), and the social medium and social context in which these processes are expressed. Thus, how a positive attitude is expressed in an effective, positively interdependent relationship depends on what is appropriate to the social medium and social context; that is, presumably one would not seek to express it in a way that is humiliating or embarrassing or likely to be experienced negatively by one's partner.

Similarly, the effectiveness of any typical effect of cooperation or competition as an initiating or inducing condition of a cooperative or competitive process is not due to its phenotype but rather to the inferred genotype of type of interdependence and type of action. Thus, in most social media and social contexts, "perceived similarity in basic values" is highly suggestive of the possibility of a positive linkage between oneself and the other. However, we are likely to see ourselves as negatively linked in a context that leads each of us to recognize that similarities in values impel seeking something that is in scarce supply and available for only one of us. Also, it is evident that although threats are mostly perceived in a way that suggests a negative linkage, any threat perceived as intended to compel you to do something that is good for you or that you feel you should do is apt to be suggestive of a positive linkage.

Although the law is crude, my impression is that it is reasonably accurate; phenotypes are often indicative of the underlying genotypes. Moreover, it is a synthesizing principle, which integrates and summarizes a wide range of social psychological phenomena. The typical effects of a given relationship tend to induce that relationship, similarly, it seems that any of the typical effects of a given relationship tend to induce the other typical effects. For example, among the typical effects of a cooperative relationship are positive attitudes, perception of similarities, open communication, and orientation toward mutual enhancement. One can integrate much of the literature on the determinants of positive and negative attitudes in terms of the other associated effects of cooperation and competition. Thus, positive attitudes result from perceptions of similarity, open communication, and so on. Similarly, many of the determinants of effective communication can be linked to the other typical effects of cooperation or competition, such as positive attitudes and power sharing.

SUMMARY OF THE THEORY OF CONFLICT RESOLUTION

In brief, the theory equates a constructive process of conflict resolution with an effective cooperative problem-solving process in which the conflict is the mutual problem to be resolved cooperatively. It also equates a destructive process of conflict resolution with a competitive process in which the conflicting parties are involved in a competition or struggle to determine who wins and who loses; often, the outcome of the struggle is a loss for both parties. The theory further indicates that a cooperative-constructive process of conflict resolution is fostered by the typical effects of cooperation. The theory of cooperation and competition outlined in the beginning of this chapter is a well-verified theory of the *effects* of cooperation and competition and thus allows insight into what can give rise to a constructive or destructive process.

The theory cannot serve as a "cookbook" for a practitioner in the field of conflict resolution. It is a general intellectual framework for understanding what goes on in conflicts and how to intervene in them. Additionally, understanding and intervening in a specific conflict requires specific knowledge about the conflicting parties, their social contexts, their aspirations, their conflict orientations, the social norms, and so on.

Cooperation-competition, although of central importance, is only one factor influencing the course of conflict. The other chapters in this volume detail some of the other ingredients affecting conflict: power and influence, group problem solving, social perception and cognition, creativity, intrapsychic conflict, and personality. A practitioner must develop a mosaic of theories relevant to the specific situation of interest, rather than relying on any single one. The symptoms or difficulties in one situation may require emphasis on the theoretical theme related to power; in another, it may require focusing on problem-solving deficiencies.

IMPLICATIONS OF THE
THEORY FOR UNDERSTANDING CONFLICT

Kurt Lewin, a famous psychologist, used to tell his students, of whom I was one, that "there is nothing so practical as a good theory." To this point, I have presented the basic ideas of a good theory; in what follows, I indicate their usefulness in conflict situations.

The Importance of a Cooperative Orientation

The most important implication of cooperation-competition theory is that a cooperative or win-win orientation to resolving a conflict enormously facilitates constructive resolution, while a competitive or win-lose orientation hinders it. It is easier to develop and maintain a win-win attitude if you have social support for it. The social support can come from friends, coworkers, employers, the media, or your community.

To have a win-win attitude in a hostile environment, it is valuable to become part of a network of people or a member of groups with similar orientations that can extend social support to you. It is also helpful to develop the personal strengths and skills that are useful in bucking the tide.

If you are the manager in a system (for example, a principal in a school, a CEO in a company, a parent in a family), it is worthwhile to recognize that basic change in the system involves more than educating students, employees, or children to have a win-win orientation. It also involves educating yourself and other key people in the system such as supervisors, staff, teachers, and parents so that their actions reflect and support a win-win orientation. Additionally, it often requires fundamental change in the incentive structure so that the rewards, salaries, grades, perks, etc., in the system do not foster a win-lose relationship among the people in it.

Reframing

The second most important implication of the theory has to do with the cooperative process that is involved in constructive conflict resolution. At the heart of this process is reframing the conflict as a mutual problem to be resolved (or solved) through joint cooperative efforts. Reframing helps to develop a cooperative orientation to the conflict even if the goals of the conflicting parties are seen, initially, to be negatively interdependent. A cooperative orientation to what is initially a win-lose conflict leads the parties to search for just procedures to determine who is the winner as well as for helping the loser gain through compensation or other means. Reframing has inherent within it the assumption that whatever resolution is achieved, it is acceptable to each party and considered to be just by both. This assumption is made explicit when one or both parties to a conflict communicate to the other something like, "I won't be satisfied with any agreement unless you also feel satisfied with it and consider it to be just, and I assume that you feel the same way. Is my assumption correct?"

Thus, consider the school that is developing site-based management procedures but faces a conflict (the second opening vignette of the Introduction). One group of teachers, mainly white, insists on having teachers elected to the SBM executive committee from the various academic departments by majority vote. Another group of teachers, the Black Teachers Caucus, demand that several members of the committee be from minority groups to represent their interests. This conflict can be reformulated as a joint problem: "How to develop SBM procedures that empower and are responsive to the interests and needs of faculty, parents, and students from minority groups without abandoning the regular democratic procedures whereby teachers are elected to the SBM committee by their respective departments?"

This joint problem is not easy to solve, but similar problems have been faced and resolved in many organizations. There is reason to believe that if the conflicting groups—the SBM committee members elected by their departments and the BTC—define the conflict as a joint problem to be resolved cooperatively, they can come up with a solution that is mutually satisfactory. (See Chapter Two for a discussion of resolving conflicts about "what is just.")

The Norms of Cooperation

Of course, the parties are more apt to succeed in reframing their conflict into a mutual problem if the participants abide by the norms of cooperative behavior, even when in conflict, and have the skills that facilitate effective cooperation. The norms of cooperative behavior basically are similar to those for respectful, responsible, honest, and caring behavior toward friends or fellow group members. Some of these norms, particularly relevant to conflict, are the following:

- Place the disagreements in perspective by identifying common ground and common interests.

- When there is disagreement, address the issues and refrain from making personal attacks.

- When there is disagreement, seek to understand the other's views from his or her perspective; try to feel what it would be like if you were on the other's side.

- Build on the ideas of the other, fully acknowledging their value.

- Emphasize the positive in the other and the possibilities of constructive resolution of the conflict. Limit and control expression of your negative feelings so that they are primarily directed at the other's violation of cooperative norms (if that occurs), or at the other's defeatism.

- Take responsibility for the harmful consequences—unwitting as well as intended—of what you do and say; seek to undo the harm as well as openly accept responsibility and make sincere apology for it.

- If the other harms you, be willing to forgive if the other accepts responsibility for doing so, sincerely apologizes, and is willing to try to undo it; seek reconciliation rather than nurturing an injury or grudge.

- Be responsive to the other's legitimate needs.

- Empower the other to contribute effectively to the cooperative effort; solicit the other's views, listen responsively, share information, and otherwise help the other—when necessary—be an active, effective participant in the cooperative problem-solving process.

- Be appropriately honest. Being dishonest, attempting to mislead or deceive, is of course a violation of cooperative norms. However, one can be unnecessarily and inappropriately truthful. In most relationships, there is usually some ambivalence, a mixture of positive as well as negative thoughts and feelings about the other and about oneself. Unless the relationship has developed to a very high level of intimacy, communicating every suspicion, doubt, fear, and sense of weakness one has about oneself or the other is apt to be damaging to the relationship—particularly if the communication is blunt, unrationalized, and unmodulated. In effect, one should be open and honest in communication but appropriately so, realistically taking into account the consequences of what one says or does not say and the current state of the relationship.

- Throughout conflict, remain a moral person—therefore, a person who is caring and just—and consider the other as a member of one's moral community—therefore, as a person who is entitled to care and justice.

In the heat of conflict, there is often a tendency to violate the norms of cooperation. For example, you begin to attack the other as a person ("you're stubborn," "you're selfish," "you're unreasonable," "you're inconsiderate," "you're narcissistic," "you're paranoid"). Recognize when you start to do this, stop, apologize, and explain what made you angry enough to want to belittle and hurt the other. If the other starts to do this to you, then interrupt, explain why you are interrupting, and try to resume a mutually respectful dialogue ("You're calling me names; that's making me angry and makes me want to retaliate, so pretty soon we'll be in a name-calling contest and that will get us nowhere. Let's stick to the issues and be respectful of one another. If you're angry with me, tell me why. If I'm at fault, I'll remedy it.").

It is wise to recognize that you, as well as the other, have hot buttons that, if pressed, are likely to evoke strong emotions. The emotions evoked may be anxiety, anger, rage, fear, depression, withdrawal, and so on. It is important to know your own hot buttons and how you tend to react when they are pressed, so that you can control your reactions in that event. Sometimes you need to take time out to control your emotional reactions and to consider an appropriate response to what elicits them. Similarly, it is valuable to know the other's hot buttons so as to avoid pressing them and provoking disruptive emotions in the other.

The Values Underlying Constructive Conflict Resolution

The norms of cooperation and constructive conflict resolution reflect some basic values, to which people who are "profoundly divided by reasonable religious, philosophical, and moral doctrines" can adhere (Rawls, 1996, p. xxxix). A reasonable doctrine includes conceptions of the values and norms with regard to conflict that people who adhere to another reasonable doctrine (as well as those who adhere to one's own) can endorse and be expected to follow during conflict. Thus, "pro-life" and "pro-choice" advocates in the abortion conflict may have profoundly differing views, but they are both components of reasonable doctrines if the adherents to each are willing to follow common values in dealing with their conflict about abortion. Among such values are reciprocity, human equality, shared community, fallibility, and nonviolence. A brief discussion of these interrelated values follows.

Reciprocity. This is the value involved in the maxim "Do unto others as you would have others do unto you." My understanding of the maxim as it applies to conflict requires each party to treat the other with the fairness that it would normatively expect if in the other's position. It assumes reciprocity from the other—fairness to and from the other. The fairness in behavior, in process, and in outcomes expected is normative. As defined by one's culture, it is how the conflicting parties should or should not behave toward one another if they are, at a minimum, to avoid a destructive conflict or, more positively, to promote constructive management of their conflict. The norms against violence, disrespect, deceit, and irresponsibility are widespread standards for avoiding destructive conflict.

Human Equality. This value implies that all human beings are equally entitled to just and respectful treatment, with consideration for their needs, and entitled to such basic liberties as freedom of conscience, thought, and expression, as well as freedom from coercion. You are entitled to this from the other, but the other is entitled to this from you too. Human equality does not imply that people necessarily have the same status, privileges, power, needs, or wealth. It does imply that such differences not be the consequence of one's violation of the other's entitlements.

Shared Community. Implicit in constructive conflict resolution is mutual recognition of being part of a broader community that members wish to preserve, a community sharing some key values and norms; such recognition occurs despite important differences between oneself and the other.

Fallibility. The sources of disagreement between reasonable people are manifold. Disagreements may arise from such sources as the nature of the evidence, the weight to be given to types of evidence, and the vagueness of the moral or other concepts involved, as well as from differences in basic values or worldviews. Reasonable people understand that their own judgment as well as the judgment of others may be fallible.

Nonviolence. This value implies that coercive tactics are not employed, by you or the other, to obtain agreement or consent. Such tactics include physical or psychological violence (for example, humiliation), destruction of property or other valued goods, harm to one's life chances (a potential career), harm to one's loved ones, and so on.

IMPLICATIONS FOR MANAGING CONFLICT

In prior sections, discussion focused on the attitudes, norms, and values that foster cooperation. These are necessary but not in themselves sufficient. Knowledge and skills are also important in promoting constructive resolution of a conflict. This is the thesis underlying the book. Knowledge of the theory presented earlier in this chapter offers a useful framework for organizing one's thinking about the social psychological consequences of cooperation and competition as well as the conditions that lead to one rather than the other. It is a way of orienting oneself to situations not previously encountered. Along with the other theories discussed in this book, it enlarges one's knowledge of the range of conditions to be considered as one wishes to develop and maintain a constructive, cooperative process of conflict resolution and to prevent developing a destructive process.

Skills are also vitally important if one wishes to develop and implement successfully an effective, cooperative problem-solving process. There has not been much systematic discussion of the skills involved in constructive solutions to conflict. There are, I believe, three main kinds useful to the participants in a conflict as well as to third parties (such as mediators, conciliators, counselors, or therapists) who are called on to provide assistance to conflicting parties. For convenience, I label them "rapport-building skills," "cooperative conflict resolution skills," and "group process and decision-making skills."

First, there are the skills involved in establishing effective working relationships with each of the conflicting parties, and between the conflicting parties if you are the mediator; or with the other, if you are a participant. Some of the components of this broad category include such skills as breaking the ice; reducing fears, tensions, and suspicion; overcoming resistance to negotiation; establishing a framework for civil discourse and interaction; and fostering realistic hope and optimism. Thus, before negotiations begin between two individuals or groups perceiving each other as adversaries, it is often useful to have informal social gatherings or meetings in which the adversaries can get to know one another as human beings who share some similar interests and values. Skill in breaking the ice and creating a safe, friendly atmosphere for interaction between the adversaries is helpful in developing the prenegotiation experiences likely to lead to effective negotiations about the issues in dispute.

A second, related set of skills concerns developing and maintaining a cooperative conflict resolution process among the parties throughout their conflict. These are the skills that are usually emphasized in practicum courses or workshops on conflict resolution. They include identifying the type of conflict in which you are involved; reframing the issues so the conflict is perceived as a mutual problem to be resolved cooperatively; active listening and responsive communication; distinguishing between needs and positions; recognizing and acknowledging the other's needs as well as your own; encouraging, supporting, and enhancing the other; taking the perspective of the other; identifying shared interests and other similarities in values, experiences, and so on; being alert to cultural differences and the possibilities of misunderstanding arising from them; controlling anger; dealing with difficult conflicts and difficult people; being sensitive to the other's anxieties and hot buttons and how to avoid pressing them; and being aware of your own anxieties and hot buttons as well as your tendencies to be emotionally upset and misperceiving if they are pressed so that these can be controlled.

A third set of skills are involved in developing a creative and productive group problem-solving and decision-making process. These include skills pertinent to group process, leadership, and effective group discussion, such as goal and standard setting; monitoring progress toward group goals; eliciting, clarifying, coordinating, summarizing, and integrating the contributions of the various participants; and maintaining group cohesion. The third set also includes such problem-solving and decision-making skills as identifying and diagnosing the nature of the problem confronting the group; acquiring the relevant information necessary for developing possible solutions; creating or identifying several possible, alternative solutions; choosing the criteria for evaluating the alternatives (such as the "effects" on economic costs and benefits, on relations between the conflicting parties, and on third parties); selecting the alternative that optimizes the results on the chosen criteria; and implementing the decision through appropriate action.

People are not novices with regard to conflict. From their life experiences, many people have developed some of the component skills involved in building rapport, constructive conflict resolution, and effective group process and problem solving. However, some are not aware that they have the skills; nor are they aware of how and when to use them in a conflict. The fact that everyone has been a participant and observer in many conflicts from childhood on results in implicit knowledge, preconceptions, attitudes, and modes of behavior toward conflict that may be deeply ingrained before any systematic training occurs. Many of a person's preexisting orientations to conflict, and modes of behavior in it, reflect those prevalent in his or her culture, but some reflect individual predispositions acquired from unique experiences in the contexts of family, school, watching TV, and the like.

Before students can acquire explicit competence in conflict resolution, they have to become aware of their preexisting orientations to conflict as well as their typical behaviors. Awareness and motivation are developed by having a model of good performance that students can compare with their preconscious, preexisting one. Internalization comes from guided and repeated practice in imitating the model. Feedback on the students' successfulness gradually shapes their behavior to be consistent with the model, and frequent practice leads to its internalization. Once the model has been internalized, recurrence of earlier incompetent orientations to conflict is experienced as awkward and out of place because there are internal cues to the deviations of one's behavior from the internalized model. In tennis, if you have internalized a good model of serving, internal cues tell you if you are deviating from it (say, by throwing the ball too high). If self-taught tennis students have internalized poor serving models, training should be directed at making them aware of this and providing a good model. So too in conflict resolution.

In summary, the discussion in this and the preceding sections has centered on the orientation, norms, values, and skills that help to develop a cooperative, constructive process of conflict resolution. Without competence in the skills, having a cooperative orientation and knowledge of conflict processes is often insufficient to develop a cooperative process of conflict resolution. Similarly, having the skills is insufficient to develop a cooperative process, without the cooperative orientation and motivation to apply the skills, or without the knowledge of how to apply the skills in various social and cultural contexts.

IMPLICATIONS FOR TRAINING

There are, for training, several implications of the material presented in the preceding parts of this chapter. They center on the social context of learning, the social context of applying one's learning, the substantive content of the training, and the reflective practitioner.

The Social Context of Learning

The theory described in this chapter suggests that the social context of learning be one in which cooperation, constructive conflict resolution, and creative controversy are strongly emphasized. The teaching method employed should take the form of cooperative learning, and the conflictual interactions within the classroom or workshop between teacher and students and among students should model those of creative controversy and constructive conflict resolution. The social context of learning should walk the talk, and in so doing offer students the experiences that support a cooperative orientation, exemplify the values and social norms of cooperation, and model the skills involved in constructive management of conflict.

The Social Context of Application

It can be anticipated that many social contexts are unfavorable to a cooperative orientation and to use of one's skills in constructive conflict resolution. In some social contexts, an individual who has such skills may expect to be belittled by friends or associates as being weak, unassertive, or afraid. In other contexts, she may anticipate accusations of being "disloyal," a "traitor," or an "enemy lover" if she tries to develop a cooperative problem-solving relationship with the other side. In still other contexts, the possibility of developing a constructive conflict resolution process seems so slim that one does not even try to do so. In other words, if the social context leads you to expect to be unsuccessful or devalued in employing your skills, you are not apt to use them; you will do so if it leads you to expect approval and success.

The foregoing suggests that, in unfavorable social contexts, as a skilled conflict resolver you often need social support as well as two additional types of skill. One relates to the ability to place yourself outside or above your social context so that you can observe the influences emanating from it and then consciously decide whether to resist them personally or not. The other type involves the skills of a successful change agent, someone who is able to help an institution or group change its culture so that it facilitates rather than hinders constructive conflict resolution. I mention these additional skills because it is important to recognize that institutional and cultural changes are often necessary for an individual to feel free to express his or her constructive potential.

The common need for social support after training has occurred has implications for who is trained and for posttraining contacts. There are several ways to foster a social context that is supportive: train all of the participants in it, train the influential people, or train a cohort of people of sufficient size to provide effective mutual support in the face of resistance. Posttraining contacts with the training institution and its trainers may also yield the social support necessary to buttress the individual in a hostile environment.

The Substantive Content of Training

In prior parts of this chapter, I have outlined what I consider to be the attitudes, knowledge, and skills that amount to a framework for education in constructive conflict resolution. A skillful trainer fleshes out such a framework with substantive content that is sufficiently vital and intellectually compelling to engage the interest and motivation of the student, is relevant to his or her most common and most difficult conflicts, and is sufficiently diverse in content and social context to facilitate generalizing and applying the training in a variety of situations. To accomplish these objectives, a trainer must not only have a clear framework for training but must also be open and creative so that he or she can respond to the students' needs effectively.

The Reflective Practitioner

One of the important goals of education in this area is to help the student, as well as the trainer, become a reflective practitioner of constructive conflict resolution. I refer to two kinds of reflection: on managing the conflicts that you are experiencing, and on the framework of conflict resolution that you are employing. Self-reflection about how you are handling conflicts is necessary to continuing improvement and also to prevent old habits, your hot spots, social pressure, and the like from making you regress to less constructive modes of conflict resolution.

Conflict resolution as a field of study is relatively young; it is going through a period of rapid intellectual development. It is experiencing an upsurge in research, theoretical development, and practical experience that, we hope, result in improvement of the frameworks that are used for training in conflict resolution. The reflective practitioner, by reflecting on his or her practice, can learn from as well as contribute to this growing body of knowledge and reflected-on experience.

CONCLUSION

The central theme of this chapter is that a knowledgeable, skillful, cooperative approach to conflict enormously facilitates its constructive resolution. It is well to realize, however, that there is a two-way relation between effective cooperation and constructive conflict resolution. Good cooperative relations facilitate constructive management of conflict; the ability to handle constructively the inevitable conflicts that occur during cooperation facilitates the survival and deepening of cooperative relations.

References

Deutsch, M. "An Experimental Study of the Effects of Cooperation and Competition upon Group Processes." *Human Relations*, 1949a, *2*, 199–231.

Deutsch, M. "A Theory of Cooperation and Competition." *Human Relations,* 1949b, *2,* 129–151.

Deutsch, M. *The Resolution of Conflict: Constructive and Destructive Processes.* New Haven: Yale University Press, 1973.

Deutsch, M. *Distributive Justice: A Social Psychological Perspective.* New Haven: Yale University Press, 1985.

Johnson, D. W., and Johnson, R. T. *Cooperation and Competition: Theory and Research.* Edina, Minn.: Interaction, 1989.

Rawls, J. *Political Liberalism.* New York: Columbia University Press, 1996.

CHAPTER TWO

Justice and Conflict

Morton Deutsch

T hat's not fair" expresses a feeling that frequently leads to conflict. A younger brother cries out that his older brother is getting "a bigger piece of cake than I am." An applicant for a job feels that the selection procedures are biased against members of her race, gender, or ethnic group. A politician thinks the election was lost because his opponent stuffed the ballot boxes. A wife feels that her husband doesn't help sufficiently with the household chores. These all involve issues of justice, which may give rise to conflict. Conflict can lead to changes that reduce injustice; or it can increase injustice if it takes a destructive form, as in war.

TYPES OF INJUSTICE

In the scholarly literature on injustice, there are several foci of attention:

- *Distributive justice,* which is concerned with the criteria that lead you to feel you receive a *fair outcome* (the boy receives a fair share of the pie being distributed).

- *Procedural justice,* concerned with *fair treatment* in making and implementing the decisions that determine the outcome. (Is the politician being treated with dignity and respect? Has he lost the election fairly?)

- A *sense of justice,* centering on what factors determine whether an injustice is experienced as such. (If the wife does more than her fair share of

41

the household chores, what will determine whether or not she feels it is unjust?)

- *Retributive and reparative justice,* concerned with how to respond to the violation of moral norms and how to repair the moral community that has been violated (for example, in the case of job discrimination against an applicant because of race).

- The *scope of justice,* concerned with who is included in the moral community and who is thought to be entitled to fair outcomes and fair treatments. Generally, you don't include such creatures as ticks and roaches in your moral community—and some people think of other ethnic groups, heretics, or those with differing sexual orientation as "vermin" who are not entitled to justice.

I discuss each focus separately in this chapter. Recognize, though, that there is considerable overlap among them.

Distributive Justice

Issues of distributive justice pervade social life. They occur not only at the societal level but also in intimate social relations. They arise when something of value is scarce and not everyone can have what they want, or when something of negative value (a cost, a harm) cannot be avoided by all. In the schools, such questions arise in connection with who gets the teacher's attention, who gets what marks, and how much of a school's resources are to be allocated for students who are physically handicapped or socioeconomically disadvantaged. Similarly, distribution of pay, promotion, benefits, equipment, space, and so forth are common problems in work settings. Also, issues of distributive justice are involved in health care and medical practice: How is a scarce or expensive medical resource, such as a mechanical heart, to be allocated?

Scholars have identified a large number of principles that could be used in distributing grades, pay, scarce medical resources, and the like. Discussions focus on three key principles—equity, equality, and need—and their variants. The *equity principle* asserts that people should receive benefits in proportion to their contribution; those who contribute more should receive more than those who contribute less. The *equality principle* states that all members of a group should share its benefits equally. The *need principle* indicates that those who need more of a benefit should get more than those who need it less.

In any particular allocation situation, the three principles may be in conflict. Thus, paying the members of a workgroup according to their individual productivity may conflict with paying all the members of a work group equally, and these two principles may conflict with paying them according to their need (such as giving higher pay to those with more dependents). Only if all are equally productive and equally needy is there no conflict among the principles.

The principles of distributive justice may be favored differently among individuals, groups, social classes, ideologies, and so forth. For example, in a collectivist community such as an Israeli kibbutz, the members have essentially the same pay and standard of living no matter how much they differ in their individual work productivity. In contrast, in an individualistic society such as the United States, the CEO of a profit-making firm may get paid more than a thousand times what an individual worker makes. Conflict within the kibbutz arises if an individual feels that his standard of living doesn't adequately reflect his unusually valuable contribution to the community; conflict within the American firm is likely if workers feel that they are not getting a fair share of the profits.

Theory and research (Deutsch, 1985) suggest that the principles are usually salient in different social contexts. Equity is most prominent in situations in which economic productivity is the primary goal; equality is dominant when social harmony, cohesiveness, or fostering enjoyable social relations is the primary emphasis; and need is most salient in situations where encouraging personal development and personal welfare is the major goal.

Many times, all three goals are important. In such situations, the three principles can be applied in a manner that is either mutually supportive or mutually contradictory. In a mutually supportive application, the equity principle leads to recognizing individual differences in contribution and honoring those who make uniquely important contributions. In a socially harmonious honoring, no invidious distinctions are drawn between those who are honored and those who are not; the equal divine or moral value of everyone in the cooperative community is affirmed as the community honors those who give so much to it. Similarly, the equal moral worth of every individual leads to special help for those who are especially needy.

Thus, if a football player helps his team win by an unusually skillful or courageous feat, he is honored by his teammates and others in such a way that they feel good rather than demeaned by his being honored. His being honored does not imply that they have lost something; it is not a win-lose or competitive situation for them. If, in contrast, the equity principle is applied in a manner that suggests those who produce more are better human beings and entitled to superior treatment generally, then social harmony and cohesiveness are impaired. If the equality principle leads to a sameness or uniformity in which the value of unique individual contributions is denied, then productivity as well as social cohesion is impaired. It is a delicate balance that often tilts too far in one direction or the other.

The judgment that you have received a fair outcome is determined not only by whether the appropriate distributive principles are employed but also by whether your outcome is in comparative balance with the outcomes received by people like you in similar situations. If you and a coworker are equally productive, do you each receive the same pay raise? Are all members of a club invited to a party given by the club leader? If it's my turn to receive a heart transplant, is someone else—maybe a wealthy benefactor of the hospital—given higher priority?

The *theory of relative deprivation* indicates that the sense of deprivation or injustice arises if there is comparative imbalance: *egoistical* deprivation occurs if an individual feels disadvantaged relative to other individuals, and *fraternal* deprivation occurs if a person feels her group is disadvantaged relative to other groups. The sense of being deprived occurs if there is a perceived discrepancy between what a person obtains, of what she wants, and what she believes she is entitled to obtain. The deprivation is relative because one's sense of deprivation is largely determined by past and current comparisons with others as well as by future expectations.

There is an extensive literature on the determinants of the choice of other individuals or groups with whom one chooses to compare oneself. This literature is too extensive to summarize here, but it clearly demonstrates that people's feelings of deprivation are not simply a function of their objective circumstances; they are affected by a number of psychological variables. Thus, paradoxically, members of disadvantaged groups (such as women, low-paid workers, ethnic minorities) often feel less deprived than one might expect, and even less so than those who are more fortunate, because they compare themselves with "similar others"—other women, other low-paid workers. In contrast, men and middle-income workers who have more opportunities may feel relatively more deprived because they are comparing themselves with those who have enjoyed more success in upward mobility. Also, there is evidence that discontent, social unrest, and rebellion often occur after a period of improvement in political-economic conditions that leads to rising expectations regarding entitlements if they are not matched by a corresponding rise in one's benefits. The result is an increased perceived discrepancy between one's sense of entitlement and one's benefits; this is sometimes referred to as "the revolution of rising expectations."

Procedural Justice

In addition to assessing the fairness of outcomes, individuals judge the fairness of the procedures that determine the outcomes. Research evidence indicates that fair treatment and procedures are a more pervasive concern to most people than fair outcomes. Fair procedures are psychologically important for several reasons, first in encouraging the assumption that they give rise to fair outcomes in the present and also in the future. In some situations, where it is not clear what "fair outcomes" should be, fair procedures are the best guarantee that the decision about outcomes is made fairly. Research indicates that one is less apt to feel committed to authorities, organizations, social policies, and governmental rules and regulations if the procedures associated with them are considered unfair. Also, people feel affirmed if the procedures to which they are subjected treat them with the respect and dignity they feel is their due; if so treated, it is easier for them to accept a disappointing outcome.

Questions with regard to the justice of procedures can arise in various ways. Let us consider, for example, evaluation of teacher performance in a school. Some questions immediately come to mind. Who has "voice" or representation in determining whether such evaluation is necessary? How are the evaluations to be conducted? Who conducts them? What is to be evaluated? What kind of information is collected? How is its accuracy and validity ascertained? How are its consistency and reliability determined? What methods of preventing incompetency or bias in collecting and processing information are employed? Who constitutes the groups that organize the evaluations, draw conclusions, make recommendations, and make decisions? What roles do teachers, administrators, parents, students, and outside experts have in the procedures? How are the ethicality, considerateness, and dignity of the process protected?

Implicit in these questions are some values with regard to procedural justice. One wants procedures that generate relevant, unbiased, accurate, consistent, reliable, competent, and valid information and decisions as well as polite, dignified, and respectful behavior in carrying out the procedures. Also, voice and representation in the processes and decisions related to the evaluation are considered desirable by those directly affected by the decisions. In effect, fair procedures yield good information for use in the decision-making processes as well as voice in the processes for those affected by them, and considerate treatment as the procedures are being implemented.

The Sense of Injustice

Whether an injustice takes the form of physical abuse, discrimination in employment, sexual harassment, or disrespectful treatment, there will always be some people who are insensitive to the injustice and hence seemingly unaware of it. In what follows, we discuss factors that influence the sense of injustice.

Victims and Victimizers. Distributive as well as procedural injustice can advantage some people and groups and disadvantage others. Those who benefit from injustice are, wittingly or unwittingly, often its perpetrators or perpetuators, and they are usually not fully aware of their complicity. Awareness brings with it such unpleasant emotions as guilt, fear of revenge, and sometimes feelings of helplessness with regard to their ability to bring about the social changes necessary to eliminate the injustice. As one might expect, the disadvantaged are more apt to be aware of the injustice. Associated with this awareness are such feelings as anger (outrage, indignation), resentment, depression, and sense of helplessness. Positive emotions related to self-esteem, sense of power, and pride are experienced by those who are engaged in effective actions to eliminate injustice, whether they are advantaged or disadvantaged.

There seems to be a straightforward explanation for the asymmetry in sensitivity to the injustice of the disadvantaged (the victims) and the advantaged (the victimizers). The victims usually have relatively little power compared to the victimizers; the latter are more likely to set the terms of their relationship and, through their control of the state and other social institutions, to establish the legal and other reigning definitions of justice.

Thus, the victimizers—in addition to gains from their exploitative actions—commonly find reassurance in official definitions of justice and the support of such major social institutions as the church, the media, and the schools, to deaden their sensitivity to the injustices inherent in their relations with the victim. The victim may, of course, be taken in by the official definitions and the indoctrination emanating from social institutions and, as a result, lose sensitivity to her situation of injustice. However, the victim is less likely than the victimizer to lose sensitivity to injustice because she is the one who is experiencing its negative consequences. She is also less likely to feel committed to the official definitions and indoctrinations because of her lack of participation in creating them.

This explanation of differential sensitivity in terms of differential gains and differential power is not the complete story. There are, of course, relations in which the victimizer is not of superior power; even so, he avoids experiencing guilt for his actions. Consider a traffic accident in which a car hits a pedestrian. The driver of the car usually perceives the accident so as to place responsibility for it on the victim. Seeing the victim as responsible enables the driver to maintain a positive image of himself. Projecting the blame onto the victim enables the victimizer to feel blameless.

If we accept the notion that most people try to maintain a positive conception of themselves, we can expect differential sensitivity to injustice in those who experience pain, harm, and misfortune and those who cause it. If I try to think well of myself, I shall minimize my responsibility for any injustice that is connected with me, or minimize the extent of injustice that has occurred if I cannot minimize my responsibility. On the other hand, if I am the victim of pain or harm, to think well of myself I have to believe that it was not my due; it is not just desserts for a person of my good character. Thus, the need to maintain positive self-esteem leads to opposite reactions in those who cause an injustice and those who suffer from it. There is, of course, also the possibility that a victim may seek to maintain her self-esteem by denying or minimizing the injustice she is suffering; denial may not be completely conscious. Resort to denial is less apt to occur if there are other similar victims who are prepared to acknowledge and protest their own victimization.

Although the need to maintain positive self-regard is common, it is not universal. If she views herself favorably, the victim of injustice may be outraged by her experience and attempt to undo it; in so doing, she may have to challenge the victimizer. If the victimizer is more powerful than she and has the support of legal and other social institutions, she will realize that it is dangerous to act on her outrage—or even to express it. Under such circumstances, in a process that Anna Freud (1937) labeled "identification with the aggressor," the victim may control her dangerous feelings of injustice and outrage by denying them and by internalizing the derogatory attitudes of the victimizer toward herself as well as toward others who are similar to her (other women, other disadvantaged groups). Paradoxically, by identifying with the aggressor you feel more powerful as you attack or aggress against others on whom you project the "bad" characteristics in yourself that you have suppressed because of your fear of being attacked by someone with the power to harm you. We can see this phenomenon in parents who were abused as children going on to abuse their own children and in traditionally submissive women derogating independent, assertive women.

From this discussion, it is evident that for numerous reasons victims as well as their victimizers may be insensitive to injustices that are occurring. I turn now to a brief discussion of how the sense of injustice may be activated in the victim and also the victimizer. (See Deutsch and Steil, 1988, for an extended discussion.)

Activating the Sense of Injustice. The process entails falsifying and delegitimating officially sanctioned ideologies, myths, and prejudices that "justify" the injustices. I am referring to such myths as these:

- Women like men to make sexual passes at them, even at work, because it makes them feel attractive
- African Americans are morally and intellectually inferior to European Americans
- The poor deserve to be poor because they are lazy
- Everyone in the United States has equal opportunity in the competition to achieve success

The activation process also involves exposing the victims and victimizers to new ideologies, models, and reference groups that support realistic hope about the possibility that the injustice can be eliminated. Because of the anxieties they elicit, one can anticipate that the changes necessary to eliminate an injustice produce resistance from others—and sometimes in oneself. It is easier to manage resistance and anxiety by becoming aware of the value systems that support the change and of models of successful change as well as of the social support you can get from groups and individuals who support the change. You feel less vulnerable if you know that you are not alone, that others are with you.

Additionally, the process entails the work necessary to make oneself and one's group effective forces for social change. There is internally directed work, aimed at enhancing cohesiveness, trust, and effective organization among those who favor change; and there is external work, involved in building up one's political and economic strength as well as one's bargaining power. Doing so enables effective action to increase the incentives for accepting change among the advantaged who are content with the status quo, and among those who desire change but are fearful of the consequences of seeking change. However, some victims of injustice may have to free themselves from the seductive satisfaction of feeling morally superior to the victimizers before they can fully commit to and be effective in their struggle against injustice.

Retributive and Reparative Justice

In a study comparing responses to injustice and to frustration (reported in Deutsch, 1985), it was found that an injustice, whether to oneself or to another, that is experienced involves one not only personally but also as a member of a moral community whose moral norms are being violated; it evokes an obligation to restore justice. The psychology of retributive and reparative justice is concerned with the attitudes and behavior of people in response to moral rule breaking. It is reasonable to expect a person's response to be influenced by the nature of the transgression, the transgressor, the victim, and the amount of harm experienced by the victim, as well as by the person's relations to the transgressor and victim. A transgression such as murder evokes a different response than violation of customary norms of courtesy and politeness. In the United States, a white murderer is less likely to be executed than a black one. Similarly, beating and raping a black woman is less apt to result in widespread media attention than in the case of a white victim. Burning a synagogue is considered a more serious offense than painting swastikas on its walls. An Israeli Jew is less apt to be concerned about Israeli discrimination against Palestinians than Arabs are, and Arabs are unlikely to be as concerned about discrimination against Jews in their countries as Israeli Jews are.

A number of means are employed to support and reestablish the validity of moral rules once they are violated. They generally call for one, or a combination, of these actions on the part of the violator: full confession, sincere apology, contrition, restitution, compensation, self-abasement, or self-reform. They also may involve various actions by the community addressed to the violator, such as humiliation, physical punishment, incarceration, or reeducation. These actions may be addressed not just to the violator but also to others related to the violator, such as his children, family, or ethnic group.

Retribution can serve a number of functions:

- Violation of a moral code tends to weaken the code; one of the most important functions of retribution is to reassert the continuing strength and validity of the moral rule that has been violated. For example, many communities are experiencing a breakdown of the rules of courtesy and respect because children and adolescents are no longer taught these rules and there is no appropriate response when they are violated.

- Retribution can also serve a cathartic function for members of the moral community who have been affronted and angered by the transgression.

- Punishment of the violator may have a deterrent effect against future violation as well as a cathartic effect.

- Retribution may take the form of compulsory reeducation and reform of the transgressor so that he is no longer likely to engage in immoral behavior.

- Retribution in the form of restitution, in addition to its other functions, may serve to help the victim recover from the losses and damages that he or she has suffered.

There are considerable variations among cultures and subcultures with regard to both the nature of moral rules and how to respond to violations of them. Ignorance with regard to the moral rules of another culture as well as ethnocentrism are likely to give rise to misunderstanding as well as conflict if one violates the moral code of the other's group.

The Scope of Justice

The scope of justice refers to who (and what) is included in one's moral community. Who is and is not entitled to fair outcomes and fair treatment by inclusion or lack of inclusion in one's moral community? Albert Schweitzer included all living creatures in his moral community, and some Buddhists include all of nature. Most of us define a more limited moral community.

Individuals and groups who are outside the boundary in which considerations of fairness apply may be treated in ways that would be considered immoral if people within the boundary were so treated. Consider the situation in Bosnia. Prior to the breakup of Yugoslavia, the Serbs, Muslims, and Croats in Bosnia were more or less part of one moral community and treated one another with some degree of civility. After the start of civil strife (initiated by power-hungry political leaders), vilification of other ethnic groups became a political tool, and it led to excluding others from one's moral community. As a consequence, the various ethnic groups committed the most barbaric atrocities against one another. The same thing happened with the Hutus and Tutsis in Rwanda and Burundi.

At various periods in history and in different societies, groups and individuals have been treated inhumanly by other humans: slaves by their masters, natives by colonialists, blacks by whites, Jews by Nazis, women by men, children by adults, the physically disabled by those who are not, homosexuals by heterosexuals, political dissidents by political authorities, and one ethnic or religious group by another. Three central psychological questions arise with regard to moral exclusion:

1. What *social conditions* lead an individual or group to exclude others from the individual or group's moral community?

2. What *psychological mechanisms* enable otherwise moral human beings to commit atrocities against other human beings?

3. What determines *which individuals or groups are likely to be excluded* from the moral community?

Existing knowledge to answer these questions adequately is limited; their seriousness deserves fuller answers than space allows here.

Social Conditions. Studies of political, ethnic, and religious violence have identified several social conditions that appear particularly conducive to developing or intensifying hatred and alienating emotions that permit otherwise nonviolent members of a society to dehumanize victims and kill (Gurr, 1970; Staub, 1989).

The first of these conditions is emergence of, or increase in, difficult life conditions, with a corresponding increase in the sense of relative deprivation. This may happen as a result of defeat in war, economic depression, or even physical calamity. The resulting decrease in living standards often leads to a sense of insecurity and a feeling of being threatened by potential rivals for scarce jobs, housing, and the like.

The second condition is an unstable political regime whose power may be under challenge. In such situations, scapegoating may be employed by those in power as a means of deflecting criticism and of attacking potential dissidents and rivals.

Third, there may be a claim for superiority—national, racial, gender, class, cultural, religious, genetic—that justifies treating the other as having inferior moral status.

The fourth condition is when violence is culturally salient and sanctioned as a result of past wars, attention in the media, or availability of weapons.

Fifth, there may be little sense of human relatedness or social bonding with the potential victims because there is little in the way of cooperative human contact with them.

The sixth condition is social institutions that are authoritarian; there, nonconformity and open dissent against violence sanctioned by authority are inhibited.

Finally, hatred and violence are intensified if there is no active group of observers of the violence, in or outside the society, who strongly object to it and serve as a constant reminder of its injustice and immorality.

Psychological Mechanisms. There are many mechanisms by which reprehensible behavior toward another can be justified. One can do so by *appealing to a higher moral value* (killing physicians who perform abortions to discourage abortion and "save unborn children"). Or one can rationalize by *relabeling* the behavior (calling physical abuse of a child "teaching him a lesson"). Or one can *minimize* the behavior by saying it is not so harmful ("it hurts me more than it does you"). Or one can *deny personal responsibility* for the behavior (your superior has ordered you to torture the prisoner). Or one can *blame the victim* (it is because they are hiding the terrorists in their village that the village must be destroyed). Or one can *isolate oneself emotionally* or *desensitize* oneself to the human consequences of delegitimating the others (as many do in relation to beggars and homeless people in urban areas).

Selection of Targets for Exclusion. We are most likely to delegitimate others whom we sense as a threat—to anything that is important to us: our religious beliefs, economic well-being, public order, sense of reality, physical safety, reputation, ethnic group, family, moral values, institutions, and so on. If harm by the other was experienced in the past, we are apt to be increasingly ready to interpret ambiguous actions of the other as threats. A history of prior violent ethnic conflict predisposes a group to be suspicious of another's intentions. We also delegitimate others whom we exploit, take advantage of, or otherwise treat unfairly because of their deviance from normative standards of appearance or behavior. However, as indicated earlier in this chapter, there is an asymmetry such that the ability to exclude the other is more available to the powerful as compared to the weak; the powerful can do this overtly, the weak only covertly. Thus, the targets for exclusion are likely to be those with relatively little power, such as minority groups, the poor, and "sexual deviants."

Sometimes suppressed inner conflicts encourage individuals or groups to seek out external enemies. There are many kinds of internal needs for which a hostile external relationship can be an outlet:

- It may amount to an acceptable excuse for internal problems; the problems can be held out as caused by the adversary or by the need to defend against the adversary.
- It may be a distraction so that internal problems appear less salient.
- It can provide an opportunity to express pent-up hostility arising from internal conflict through combat with the external adversary.
- It may enable one to project disapproved aspects of oneself (which are not consciously recognized) onto the adversary and to attack those aspects through assault on the adversary. The general tendency is to select for projection those who are weaker, those with whom there is a prior

history of enmity, and those who symbolically represent the weaker side of the internal conflict. Thus, someone who has repressed his homosexual tendencies, fearing socially dangerous consequences for acting on them, may make homosexuals into an enemy group.

- Especially if it has dangerous undertones, conflict can serve to counter-act such personal feelings as aimlessness, boredom, lack of focus, lack of energy, and depression. It can give a sense of excitement, purpose, coherence, and unity as well as energize and mobilize oneself for strug-gle. It can be an addictive stimulant masking underlying depression.

- It may permit important parts of oneself—including attitudes, skills, and defenses developed during conflictual relations in one's formative stages—to be expressed and valued because relations with the present adversary resemble earlier conflictual relations.

IMPLICATIONS FOR UNDERSTANDING CONFLICT

There are several interrelated implications for conflict in this discussion. First of all, as indicated at the beginning of this chapter, perceived injustice is a fre-quent source of conflict. Second, if the processes or outcomes of a conflict are perceived to be unjust, the resolution of a conflict is likely to be unstable and give rise to further conflict. Third, conflict may exist about what is "just." Fourth, paradoxically, justifying as a negotiation technique—that is, blaming the other for an injustice and claiming special privilege because of the injury one has presumably suffered—is apt to lead to conflict escalation unless the other agrees that she has been unjust and takes responsibility for remedying it. "Blaming" tends to be inflaming.

Injustice as the Source of Conflict

A paradigmatic example of procedural as well as distributive injustice is two people who have to share something to which each is equally entitled (found cash, space, equipment, inherited property) and the one who gets at it first takes what he wants of it and leaves the remainder (a smaller or less valuable por-tion) to the other. Thus, if two children have to share a piece of cake and the one who divides it into two portions takes the larger one, then the other child is likely to get mad. If he is not afraid of the other, he may challenge the unfair division and try to restore equality. If he is afraid, he may be unwilling to admit to himself the injustice, but if he does he will be resentful and try to get even covertly. Thus, conflict continues even though the episode ends.

There is a clear procedural way to avoid this sort of injustice (see also the later section, "Inventing Solutions"), in which the person who divides the cake (or whatever) does not get first choice with regard to his portion of the division. There is also final-offer arbitration, a form sometimes employed when the parties cannot resolve conflict by themselves. It is based on a similar notion, namely, creating an incentive for making fair offers. Each party to a conflict agrees to binding arbitration and secretly informs the arbitrator of his or her last and best offer for an agreement; the arbitrator then selects the one that is the fairest.

Suppose two ethnic groups in a country are in conflict over how many representatives they are each allocated in the national parliament. One group wants to make the allocations in terms of the proportion of each ethnic group in the population; the other group wants to do it in terms of the proportion of the territory occupied by each ethnic population. Ethnic group A, which has fewer people but more land, makes its final offer a bicameral legislature in which one legislative body would be elected by per capita vote and the other in proportion to the size of the territory. Ethnic group B makes a final offer of a simple legislative body based on per capita vote. Most people would be inclined to endorse group A's offer.

Injustice in the Course of Conflict

Unfair procedures employed in resolving conflict undermine confidence in the institutions that establish and implement the policies and rules regulating conflict. Thus, people become alienated from political institutions if they feel that elections are not conducted fairly, or that their interests are ignored and they have no voice in affecting social policies and how they are implemented, or that they are discriminated against such that they are apt to be the losers in any political conflict. Similarly, people lose confidence in legal and judicial institutions and third-party procedures such as mediation and arbitration if the police, judges, and other third parties are biased, if they are not treated courteously, if competent legal representation is not available to them, or if they have little opportunity to express their concerns.

Trust in organizations and groups as well as in interpersonal relations is also undermined if, when conflict occurs, one is abused, not given opportunity to voice one's concerns and views, treated as an inferior whose rights and interests have legitimacy only as they are bestowed by others, or otherwise not respected as a person.

Alienation and withdrawal of commitment, of course, are not the only possible forms of response to unjust processes of conflict resolution. Anger, aggression, rebellion, sabotage, and similarly assertive attempts to remove the injustice are some other forms of response. Depending on the perceived possibilities, one may become openly or covertly active in attempting to change the institutions, relations, and situations giving rise to the injustice. Conflict is central in the functioning of all institutions and relations. If the processes involved in conflict resolution are unfair, pressures to bring about change arise; they may take a violent form if there are no socially recognized and available procedures for dealing with grievances.

Conflict About What Is Just

Many conflicts are about which principle of justice should be applied or how a given principle should be implemented. Thus, disputes about affirmative action often center on whether students (or employees) should be selected on the basis of individual relative merit as measured by test scores, academic grades, and prior work experience, or selected so as to reflect racial and ethnic diversity in the population. Each principle, in isolation, can be considered to be just. However, selection by the criterion of relative merit as measured by test score and grades often means that ethnic diversity is limited. Selection so as to achieve ethnic diversity frequently means that some individuals, from the majority group, with higher relative standing on tests, are not selected even as some minority group members with lower standing are. These results are possible even when only well-qualified applicants are chosen.

Conflict over affirmative action may not only be about principles of justice; it also concerns the justness of the procedures for measuring merit. Some claim that the standard measures of merit—tests, grades, prior work experience—are biased against individuals who are not from the dominant culture. Others assert that the measures are appropriate since selection is for performance in a setting—a college or workplace—that reflects the dominant culture.

The BTC-SBM conflict described in the preceding chapter is between two principles of justice. Should teacher representatives on the school council be selected to represent their academic department by vote of the members of the academic department? Or should they be selected to represent their academic departments but also chosen to represent the ethnic diversity of the teachers?

In dealing with conflict between reasonable principles of justice, it is well to apply the notions advanced in the previous chapter. Specifically, you want to turn the conflict into a win-win one in which it is perceived to be a mutual problem to be resolved cooperatively. In the illustration of affirmative action, there are many ways in which both claims—for diversity and for merit—can be represented in selection policies. It is better to discuss how these two principles can be combined, so that the claims of each can be adequately realized, than to create a win-lose conflict by denying the claims of one side so that the other's can be victorious.

"Justifying" as a Negotiation Tactic

"Justice" can be employed as a tactical weapon during negotiations to claim higher moral ground for oneself. Doing so claims greater morality for your position as compared to the other's. This form of justifying commonly has several effects. It hardens your position and makes it inflexible as you become morally committed to it as well as increasingly self-righteous. It leads to blaming the other and implicit denigration of the other as morally inferior. It produces a similar effect in the other and escalates the conflict into a conflict about morality.

As this happens, the conflicting parties often lose sight of the actual interests underlying their respective positions and the conflict becomes a win-lose one that is not likely to advance the interests of either side. It is not the justifying or giving reasons for your interests that is harmful but rather the claim of moral superiority, with its explicit or implicit moral denigration of the other. Whatever justifying takes place, it should be in the context of full recognition of one another's equal moral status.

IMPLICATIONS FOR TRAINING

There are several important implications here for training in constructive conflict resolution. First, knowledge of the intimate connection between conflict and injustice has to be imparted. (This chapter is an introduction to the knowledge in this area.) Second, training should help to enlarge the scope of the student's moral community so that he perceives that all people are entitled to care and justice. Third, it should help increase the empathic capacity of the student so that he can sense and experience in some measure the injustice that the victims of injustice experience. Fourth, given the nature of the many embittered conflicts between groups that have inflicted grievous harm, we need to develop insight into the processes involved in forgiveness and reconciliation. Finally, training should help to develop skill in inventing productive, conflict-resolving combinations of justice principles when they appear to be in conflict.

Many training programs deal in some measure with the first three implications, but few if any deal with the last two. Before turning to a more extended consideration of the latter implications, I briefly consider the first three.

Knowledge of Systematic Forms of Injustice in Society

Some injustices are committed by people with full realization that they are acting unjustly. Most are unwitting, as participants in a system—a family, community, social organization, school, workplace, society, or world—in which there are established traditions, structures, procedures, norms, rules, practices, and the like that determine how one should act. These traditions, structures, and so on may give rise to profound injustices that are difficult to recognize because they are taken for granted since they are so embedded in a system in which one is thoroughly enmeshed.

Illustrations of Types of Injustice

How can we help become aware of systemic injustices? I suggest taking each type of injustice (distributive, procedural, retributive, and morally exclusionary) discussed at the beginning of the chapter and using them to probe the system we wish to examine to heighten awareness of its structural sources of injustice. Illustrations for each type of injustice follow.

Distributive Injustice. Every type of system—from a society to a family—distributes benefits, costs, and harms (its reward systems are a reflection of this). One can examine such benefits as income, education, health care, police protection, housing, and water supplies, and such harms as accidents, rapes, physical attacks, sickness, imprisonment, death, and rat bites, and see how they are distributed among categories of people: males versus females, employers versus employees, whites versus blacks, heterosexuals versus homosexuals, police officers versus teachers, adults versus children. Such examination reveals some gross disparities in distribution of one or another benefit or harm received by the categories of people involved. Thus, blacks generally receive fewer benefits and more harm than whites in the United States. In most parts of the world, female children are less likely than male children to receive as much education or inherit parental property, and they are more likely to suffer sexual abuse.

Procedural Injustice. Similarly, one can probe a system to determine whether it offers fair procedures to all. Are all categories of people treated with politeness, dignity, and respect by judges, police, teachers, parents, employers, and others in authority? Are some but not others allowed to have voice and representation, as well as adequate information, in the processes and decisions that affect them?

Retributive Injustice. Are "crimes" by different categories of people less likely to be viewed as crimes, to result in an arrest, to be brought to trial, to result in conviction, to lead to punishment or imprisonment or the death penalty, and so on? Considerable disparity is apparent between how "robber barons" and ordinary robbers are treated by the criminal-justice system, between manufacturers who knowingly sell injurious products to many (obvious instances being tobacco and defective automobiles) and those who negligently cause an accident. Similarly, almost every comparison of the treatment of black and white criminal offenders indicates that, if there is a difference, blacks receive worse treatment.

Moral Exclusion. When a system is under stress, are there differences in how categories of people are treated? Are some people apt to lose their jobs, be excluded from obtaining scarce resources, or be scapegoated and victimized? During periods of economic depression, social upheaval, civil strife, and war, frustrations are often channeled to exclude some groups from the treatment normatively expected from others in the same moral community.

Enlarging the Scope of One's Moral Community

Our earlier discussion of the scope of justice suggests several additional, experientially oriented foci for training. A good place to start is to help students become aware of their own social identities: national, racial, ethnic, religious, class, occupational, gender, sexual, age, community, and social circle. Explore what characteristics they attribute to being American, or white, or Catholic, or female, and so on, and what they attribute to other, contrasting identities such as being Russian or black. Help them recognize which of these identities claim an implicit moral superiority and greater privilege in contrast to other people who have contrasting identities. Have them reverse roles, to assume an identity that is frequently viewed as morally inferior and less entitled to customary rights and privileges. Then act out, subtly but realistically, how they are treated by those who are now assuming the "morally superior and privileged" identity. Such exercises help students become more aware of implicit assumptions about their own identity as well as other relevant contrasting identities, and more sensitive to the psychological effects of considering others to have identities that are morally inferior and less privileged.

Intergroup simulations can also be used to give students an experience in which they start developing prejudice, stereotypes, and hostility toward members of other, competing groups—even as the students have full knowledge that they have been randomly assigned to the groups. Many such experiences can be employed to demonstrate how a moral community is broken down, and to illustrate the psychological mechanisms that people employ to justify this hostility toward out-group members. (Some widely used intergroup simulations are identified in the Recommended Reading section for this chapter at the back of the book.)

It is also useful to give students the experience of how their moral community can expand or contract as a function of temporary events. Thus, research has demonstrated that people are apt to react to a stranger with trust after being exposed by radio broadcasts to "good" news about people (such as acts of heroism, altruism, and helpfulness), and with suspicion after "bad" news (such as murder, rape, robbery, assault, and fraud). By helping students become aware of the temporary conditions, inside as well as outside themselves, that affect the scope of their moral community, they gain capacity to resist contracting their moral community under adverse conditions.

Increasing Empathy

Empathic concern allows you to sympathetically imagine how someone else feels and put yourself in his or her place. It is a core component of helpful responsiveness to another. It is most readily aroused for people with whom we identify, with those we recognize as people who are like ourselves and belong to our moral community. Empathy is inhibited by excluding the other from one's moral community, by dehumanizing him, and by making him into an enemy or a devil. Empathy stimulates helpfulness and altruism toward those who are in need of help; dehumanization encourages neglect, derogation, or attack.

Enlarging one's moral community increases one's scope of empathy. However, empathy can occur at different levels. The fullest level contains all of several aspects of empathy: (1) knowing what the other is feeling; (2) feeling in some measure what the other is feeling; (3) understanding why the other is feeling the way she does, including what she wants or fears; and (4) understanding her perspective and frame of reference as well as her world. Empathic responsiveness to another's concern helps the other feel understood, validated, and cared for.

Role playing, role exchanging or role reversal, and guided imagination are three interrelated methods commonly employed in training people to become empathically responsive to others. Role playing involves imagining that you are someone else, seeing the world through his eyes, wanting what he wants, feeling the emotions he feels, and behaving as he would behave in a particular situation or in reaction to someone else's behavior. Role exchange or role reversal is similar to role playing, except that it involves reversing or exchanging roles with the person with whom you are interacting in a particular situation (as during a conflict). In guided imagination, you help the student take on the role of the other by stimulating the student to imagine and adopt various relevant characteristics (not caricatures) of the role or person that is being enacted, such as how he walks, talks, eats, fantasizes, dresses, and wakes up in the morning.

Forgiveness and Reconciliation

After protracted, violent conflicts in which the conflicting parties have inflicted grievous harm (humiliation, destruction of property, torture, assault, rape, murder) on one another, the conflicting parties may still have to live and work together in the same communities. This is often the case in civil wars, ethnic and religious conflicts, gang wars, and even family disputes that have taken a destructive course. Consider the slaughter taken place between Hutus and Tutsis in Rwanda and Burundi; between blacks and whites in South Africa; between "Bloods" and "Crips" of Los Angeles; and among Serbs, Croats, and Muslims in Bosnia. Is it possible for forgiveness and reconciliation to occur? If so, what fosters these processes?

There are many meanings of *forgiveness* in the extensive and growing literature concerned with this topic. I shall use the term to mean giving up rage, the desire for vengeance, and a grudge toward those who have inflicted grievous harm on you, your loved ones, or the groups with whom you identify. It also implies willingness to accept the other into one's moral community so that he or she is entitled to care and justice. As Borris (forthcoming) has pointed out, it does not mean you have to forget the evil that has been done, condone it, or abolish punishment for it. However, it implies that the punishment should conform to the canons of justice and be directed toward the goal of reforming the harmdoer so that he or she can become a moral participant in the community.

There has been rich discussion in the psychological and religious literature of the importance of forgiveness to psychological and spiritual healing as well as to reconciliation (see for example, Minow, 1998, and Shriver, 1995). Forgiveness is, of course, not to be expected in the immediate aftermath of torture, rape, or assault. It is unlikely, as well as psychologically harmful, until one is able to be in touch with the rage, fear, guilt, humiliation, hurt, and pain that has been stored inside. But nursing hate keeps the injury alive and active in the present, instead of permitting it to take its proper place in the past. Doing so consumes psychological resources and energy that is more appropriately directed to the present and future. Although forgiveness of the other may not be necessary for self-healing, it seems to be very helpful, as well as an important ingredient in the process of reconciliation.

A well-developed psychological and psychiatric literature deals with posttraumatic stress disorders (PTSD), that is, the psychological consequences of having been subjected or exposed to grievous harm, and a growing literature is emerging from workshop experiences centering on forgiveness and reconciliation. These literatures are too extensive and detailed for more than a brief overview of the major ideas here.

Treatment of PTSD (Ochberg, 1988; Basoglu, 1992) essentially (1) gives the stressed person a supportive, safe, and secure environment (2) in which he can be helped to reexperience, in a modulated fashion, the vulnerability, helplessness, fear, rage, humiliation, guilt, and other emotions associated with his grievous harm (medication may be useful in limiting the intensity of the emotions being relived), thus (3) helping him identify the past circumstances and contexts in which the harm occurred and distinguish present realities from past realities; (4) helping him understand the reasons for his emotional reactions to the traumatic events and the appropriateness of his reactions; (5) helping him acquire the skills, attitudes, knowledge, and social support that make him less vulnerable and powerless; and (6) helping him develop an everyday life characterized by meaningful, enjoyable, and supportive relations in his family, work, and community.

PTSD treatment requires considerable professional education beyond that involved in conflict resolution training. Still, it is well for students of conflict to be aware that exposure to severe injustice can have enduring harmful psychological effects unless the posttraumatic conditions are treated effectively.

Forgiveness and reconciliation may be difficult to achieve at more than a superficial level unless the posttraumatic stress is substantially relieved. Even so, it is well to recognize that the processes involved in forgiveness and reconciliation may also play an important role in relieving PTSD. The causal arrow is multidirectional; progress in "forgiveness" or "reconciliation" or posttraumatic stress reduction facilitates progress in the other two.

There are two distinct but interrelated approaches to developing forgiveness. One centers on the victim, and the other on the relationship between the victim and the harmdoer. The focus on the victim, in addition to providing some relief from PTSD, seeks to help the victim recognize the human qualities common to victim and victimizer. In effect, various methods and exercises are employed to enable the victim to recognize the bad as well as good aspects of herself, that she has "sinful" as well as "divine" capabilities and tendencies. In other words, one helps the victim become aware of herself as a total person—with no need to deny her own fallibility and imperfections—whose lifelong experiences in her family, schools, communities, ethnic and religious groups, and workplaces have played a key role in determining her own personality and behavior. As the victim comes to accept her own moral fallibility, she is likely to accept the fallibility of the harmdoer as well, and to perceive both the good and the bad in the other.

Both victims and harmdoers are often quite moral toward those they include in their own moral community but grossly immoral to those excluded. Thus, Adolf Eichmann, who efficiently organized the mass murder of Jews for the Nazis, was considered a good family man. The New England captains of the slave ships, who transported African slaves to the Americas under the most abominable conditions, were often deacons of their local churches. The white settlers of the United States, who took possession of land occupied by native Americans and killed those who resisted, were viewed as courageous and moral within their own communities.

Recognition of the good and bad potential in all humans, the self as well as the other, facilitates the victim's forgiveness of the harmdoer. But it may not be enough. Quite often, forgiveness also requires interaction between the victim and harmdoer to establish the conditions needed for forgiving. This interaction sometimes takes the form of negotiation between the victim and harmdoer. A third party representing the community (such as a mediator or judge) usually facilitates the negotiation and sets the terms if the harmdoer and victim cannot reach an agreement. It is interesting to note that in some European courts, such negotiations are required in criminal cases before the judge sentences the convicted criminal.

Obviously, the terms of an agreement for forgiveness vary as a function of the nature and severity of the harm as well as the relationship between the victim and harmdoer. As I have suggested earlier in this chapter, the victim may seek full confession, sincere apology, contrition, restitution, compensation, self-abasement, or self-reform from the harmdoer. The victim may also seek some form of punishment and incarceration for the harmdoer. Forgiveness is most likely if the harmdoer and the victim accept the conditions, whatever they may be.

Reconciliation goes beyond forgiveness in that it not only accepts the other into one's moral community but also establishes or reestablishes a positive, cooperative relationship among the individuals and groups estranged by the harms they inflict on one another. Borris (forthcoming) has stated it very well: "Reconciliation is the end of a process that forgiveness begins."

In Chapter One, I discussed in detail some of the factors involved in initiating and maintaining cooperative relations; that discussion is relevant to the process of reconciliation. Here, I wish to consider briefly some of the special issues relating to establishing cooperative relations after a destructive conflict. Below, I outline a number of basic principles.

1. *Mutual security.* After a bitter conflict, each side tends to be concerned with its own security, without adequate recognition that neither side can attain security unless the other side also feels secure. Real security requires that both sides have as their goal *mutual* security. If weapons have been involved in the prior conflict, mutually verifiable disarmament and arms control are important components of mutual security.

2. *Mutual respect.* Just as true security from physical danger requires mutual cooperation, so does security from psychological harm and humiliation. Each side must treat the other side with the respect, courtesy, politeness, and consideration normatively expected in civil society. Insult, humiliation, and inconsiderateness by one side usually leads to reciprocation by the other and decreased physical and psychological security.

3. *Humanization of the other.* During bitter conflict, each side tends to dehumanize the other and develop images of the other as an evil enemy. There is much need for both sides to experience one another in everyday contexts as parents, homemakers, schoolchildren, teachers, and merchants, which enables them to see one another as human beings who are more like themselves than not. Problem-solving workshops, along the lines developed by Burton (1969, 1987) and Kelman (1972), are also valuable in overcoming dehumanization of one another.

4. *Fair rules for managing conflict.* Even if a tentative reconciliation has begun, new conflicts inevitably occur—over the distribution of scarce resources, procedures, values, etc. It is important to anticipate that conflicts will occur and to develop beforehand the fair rules, experts, institutions, and other resources for managing such conflicts constructively and justly.

5. *Curbing the extremists on both sides.* During a protracted and bitter conflict, each side tends to produce extremists committed to the processes of the destructive conflict as well as to its continuation. Attaining some of their initial goals may be less satisfying than continuing to inflict damage on the other. It is

well to recognize that extremists stimulate extremism on both sides. The parties need to cooperate in curbing extremism on their own side and restraining actions that stimulate and justify extremist elements on the other side.

6. *Gradual development of mutual trust and cooperation.* It takes repeated experience of successful, varied, mutually beneficial cooperation to develop a solid basis for mutual trust between former enemies. In the early stages of reconciliation, when trust is required for cooperation, the former enemies may be willing to trust a third party (who agrees to serve as a monitor, inspector, or guarantor of any cooperative arrangement) but not yet willing to trust one another if there is a risk of the other failing to reciprocate cooperation. Also in the early stages, it is especially important that cooperative endeavors be successful. This requires careful selection of the opportunities and tasks for cooperation so that they are clearly achievable as well as meaningful and significant.

Inventing Solutions

It is helpful in trying to resolve any problem constructively (as with a conflict between principles of justice) to be able to discover or invent alternative solutions that go beyond win-lose outcomes such as selecting the more powerful party's principle or flipping a coin to determine the winner. Flipping a coin provides equal opportunity to win, but it does not result in satisfactory outcomes for both sides.

For simplicity's sake, let us consider a conflict over possession of a valuable object, say, a rare antique clock bequeathed to two sons who live in separate parts of the world. Each wants the clock and feels equally entitled to it. Unlike the cake in an earlier example, the clock is not physically divisible. However, they could agree to divide *possession* of the clock so that they share it for equal periods, say, six months or one year at a time. Another solution is to sell the clock and divide the resulting money equally.

Let us assume, though, that the mother's will has prohibited sale of the clock to anyone else. Here is an alternative: the two sons can bid against one another in an auction, and the higher bidder gets the clock while the other gets half the price of the winner's bid. The auction can offer open bidding against one another or a closed, single, final bid from each person. Thus, if the winning bid is $5,000, the winner gets the clock but has to pay the other $2,500; each ends up with equally valued outcomes. The winner's net value is $2,500, but the loser also ends up with $2,500.

Another procedure employs a version of the divide-and-choose rule discussed earlier. A pool to be divided between the sons comprises the clock and an amount of money that each son contributes equally to the pool, say, $3,000. One son divides the total pool (the clock and $6,000 in cash) into two bundles of his own devising, declares the contents of the bundles, and lets the other party choose which bundle to take. Thus, if the son who values the clock at

$5,000 is the divider, he might put the clock and $500 in one bundle and $5,500 in the other. Doing so ensures that he receives a gross return of $5,500 and a net return of $2,500 ($5,500 minus $3,000), no matter which bundle the other chooses. The chooser can also obtain a net return of $2,500 if he chooses the cash bundle; presumably he would do so if he values the clock at less than $5,000. Such an outcome would be apt to be seen as fair to both sons.

The outcome of the divide-and-choose approach as well as the auction procedure seem eminently fair. Both sons win. The one who wants the clock more badly obtains it, while the other gets something of equivalent value. Other win-win procedures can undoubtedly be invented for types of conflict that at first glance seem to allow only win-lose outcomes. (See Bram and Taylor, 1996, for a very useful discussion of developing fair outcomes.) Training, I believe, creates readiness to recognize the possibility that win-win procedures can be discovered or invented. Skill in developing such procedures can be cultivated, I further believe, by showing students illustrations and modeling of this development as well as giving them extensive practice in attempting to create them.

CONCLUSION

The relationship between conflict and justice is bidirectional. Injustice breeds conflict, and destructive conflict gives rise to injustice. It is well to realize that preventing destructive conflict requires more than training in constructive conflict resolution. It also necessitates reducing the gross injustices that characterize much of our social world at the interpersonal, intergroup, and international levels. Such reduction requires changes in how various institutions of society— political, economic, educational, familial, and religious—function so that they recognize and honor the values underlying constructive conflict resolution, described in the preceding chapter (human equality, shared community, nonviolence, fallibility, and reciprocity). Adherence to these values not only eliminates gross injustices but also reduces the likelihood that conflict itself takes a destructive course and, as a consequence, gives rise to injustice.

References

Basoglu, M. (ed.). *Torture and Its Consequences: Current Treatment Approaches.* Cambridge, England: Cambridge University Press, 1992.

Borris, E. R. "Forgiveness, Reconciliation, and the Peacemaking Process." *Journal of Social Issues,* forthcoming.

Bram, S. J., and Taylor, A. D. *Fair Division: From Cake Cutting to Dispute Resolution.* New York: Cambridge University Press, 1996.

Burton, J. W. *Conflict and Communication: The Use of Controlled Communication in International Relations.* London: Macmillan, 1969.

Burton, J. W. *Resolving Deep Rooted Conflicts: A Handbook.* Lanham, Md.: University Press of America, 1987.

Deutsch, M. *Distributive Justice: A Social Psychological Perspective.* New Haven: Yale University Press, 1985.

Deutsch, M., and Steil, J. M. "Awakening the Sense of Injustice." *Social Justice Research,* 1988, *2,* 2–23.

Freud, A. *The Ego and the Mechanisms of Defense.* London: Hogarth, 1937.

Gurr, T. R. *Why Men Rebel.* Princeton: Princeton University Press, 1970.

Kelman, H. C. "The Problem-Solving Workshop in Conflict Resolution." In R. L. Merritt (ed.), *Communication in International Politics.* Urbana: University of Illinois Press, 1972.

Minow, M. "Between Vengeance and Forgiveness: South Africa's Truth and Reconciliation Commission." *Negotiation Journal,* 1998, *14,* 319–356.

Ochberg, F. *Post-Traumatic Therapy and Victims of Violence.* New York: Brunner/Mazel, 1988.

Shriver, D. W., Jr. *An Ethic for Enemies: Forgiveness in Politics.* New York: Oxford University Press, 1995.

Staub, E. *The Roots of Evil: The Origins of Genocide and Other Group Violence.* New York: Cambridge University Press, 1989.

Constructive Controversy

The Value of Intellectual Opposition

David W. Johnson
Roger T. Johnson
Dean Tjosvold

A flight crew is taking a large airliner with more than 250 people on board in for a landing. The instruments indicate the plane is still five thousand feet above the ground and the pilot sees no reason to doubt their accuracy. The copilot thinks the instruments are malfunctioning and the plane is much lower. Will this disagreement endanger the passengers and crew by distracting the pilot and copilot from their duties? Or will it illuminate a problem and thereby increase the safety of everyone on board?

THE IMPORTANCE OF INTELLECTUAL CONFLICT

We know what Thomas Jefferson would have said: "Difference of opinion leads to inquiry, and inquiry to truth." Jefferson had deep faith in the value and productiveness of constructive controversy. He is not alone. Theorists have for hundreds of years suggested that conflict has positive as well as negative benefits. Freud, for example, wrote that internal psychic conflict was a necessary (but not sufficient) condition for psychological development. Developmental psychologists propose that disequilibrium within a student's cognitive structure can motivate a shift from egocentrism to accommodation of the perspectives of others; what results is a transition from one stage of cognitive and moral reasoning to another. Motivational theorists believe that conceptual conflict can create epistemic curiosity, which motivates the search for new information and reconceptualization of the knowledge one already has. Organizational theorists insist that higher-quality problem solving depends on constructive conflict among group members. To cognitive psychologists, conceptual conflict may be necessary for insight and discovery. Educational psychologists say that conflict can increase achievement. Karl Marx believed that class conflict was necessary for social progress. From almost every social science, theorists have taken the position that conflict can have positive as well as negative outcomes.

Despite all the theorizing about the positive aspects of conflict, there has been until recently very little empirical evidence demonstrating that the presence of conflict can be more constructive than its absence. Guidelines for managing conflict tend to be based more on folk wisdom than on validated theory. Far from being encouraged and structured in most interpersonal and intergroup situations, conflict tends to be avoided and suppressed. Creating conflict to capitalize on its potential positive outcomes tends to be the exception, not the rule. In the late 1960s, therefore, building on the previous work of Morton Deutsch and others, we began a program of theorizing and research to identify the conditions under which conflict results in constructive outcomes. One of the results of our work is the theory of constructive controversy.

This chapter integrates theory, research, and practice on constructive controversy for individuals who wish to deepen their understanding of conflict and how to manage it constructively. The first part of the chapter provides (1) definitions and procedure and (2) a theoretical framework that illuminates fundamental processes involved in creating and using conflict at the interpersonal, intergroup, organizational, and international levels. The second half of the chapter aims to help readers use constructive controversy effectively in their applied situations.

WHAT IS CONSTRUCTIVE CONTROVERSY?

Constructive controversy occurs when one person's ideas, information, conclusions, theories, and opinions are incompatible with those of another, and the two seek to reach an agreement. Constructive controversies involve what Aristotle called *deliberate discourse* (discussion of the advantages and disadvantages of proposed actions) aimed at synthesizing novel solutions (*creative problem solving*). Structured constructive controversies are most commonly contrasted with concurrence seeking, debate, and individualistic learning (Table 3.1).

Debate exists when two or more individuals argue positions that are incompatible with one another and a judge declares a winner on the basis of who best presented a position. As an example of debate, suppose each member of a group is assigned a position as to whether more or less regulation is needed to control hazardous wastes; an authority then declares as the winner the person who makes the best presentation of his or her position to the group.

Table 3.1. Constructive Controversy, Debate, Concurrence Seeking, and Individualistic Processes.

Constructive Controversy	Debate	Concurrence Seeking	Individualistic Processes
Categorizing and organizing information to derive conclusions	Categorizing and organizing information to derive conclusions	Categorizing and organizing information to derive conclusions	Categorizing and organizing information to derive conclusions
Presenting, advocating, elaborating position and rationale	Presenting, advocating, elaborating position and rationale	Presenting, advocating, elaborating position and rationale	No oral statement of positions
Being challenged by opposing views resulting in conceptual conflict and uncertainty about correctness of own views	Being challenged by opposing views resulting in conceptual conflict and uncertainty about correctness of own views	Being challenged by opposing views resulting in conceptual conflict and uncertainty about correctness of own views	Presence of only one view resulting in high certainty about the correctness of own views
Epistemic curiosity motivating active search for new information and perspectives	Closed-minded rejection of opposing information and perspectives	Apprehension about differences and closed-minded adherence to own point of view	Continued high certainty about the correctness of own views
Reconceptualization, synthesis, integration	Closed-minded adherence to own point of view	Quick compromise to dominant view	Adherence to own point of view
High achievement, positive relationships, psychological health	Moderate achievement, relationships, psychological health	Low achievement, relationships, psychological health	Low achievement, relationships, psychological health

Concurrence seeking occurs when members of a group inhibit discussion to avoid any disagreement or arguments, emphasize agreement, and avoid realistic appraisal of alternative ideas and courses of action. Concurrence seeking is close to Janis's concept (1982) of *groupthink* (members of a decision-making group set aside their doubts and misgivings about whatever policy is favored by the emerging consensus so as to be able to concur with the other members). The underlying motivation of groupthink is a strong desire to preserve the harmonious atmosphere of the group on which each member has become dependent for coping with the stresses of external crises and for maintaining self-esteem.

Individualistic efforts exist when individuals work alone at their own pace and with their set of materials without interacting with each other, in a situation in which their own goals are unrelated and independent from others' (Johnson, Johnson, and Holubec, 1998).

THEORY

Rique Campa, a professor in the Department of Fisheries and Wildlife at Michigan State University, asked his class, "Can a marina be developed in an environmentally sensitive area where piping plovers have a breeding ground?" Constructive controversy begins with a strong cooperative goal for the group to achieve. The group members are to examine the two sides of the issue and come to their best reasoned judgment as to how to solve the problem. All the students must agree on the final plan.

Campa emphasizes that there are no winners or losers; only the quality of the final decision matters. He assigns students to groups of four, splits each group into pairs, and assigns one pair the "developer position" and the other pair the "Department of Natural Resources position." He then follows the structured academic constructive controversy procedure over several class periods. Participants research the issue, prepare a persuasive case for their position, present it in a compelling and interesting way, refute the opposing position while rebutting criticisms of their position, take the opposing perspectives, and derive a synthesis or integration of the positions. In conducting the constructive controversy, Campa operationalizes the theoretical process by which constructive controversy is implemented.

Campa is conducting a lesson in the process of constructive controversy. The process, which is based on cooperation, involves several theoretical assumptions (Johnson and Johnson, 1979, 1989, 1995a):

1. When individuals are presented with a problem or decision, they hold an initial conclusion from categorizing and organizing incomplete information,

their limited experience, and their specific perspective. They have a high degree of confidence in their conclusions (they freeze the epistemic process).

2. When individuals present their conclusion and its rationale to others, they engage in cognitive rehearsal, deepen their understanding of their position, and use higher-level reasoning strategies.

3. When individuals are confronted with differing conclusions based on other people's information, experiences, and perspectives, they become uncertain as to the correctness of their views. A state of conceptual conflict or disequilibrium is aroused, and they unfreeze their epistemic process.

4. Uncertainty, conceptual conflict, or disequilibrium motivates *epistemic curiosity,* an active search first for more information and new experiences (increased specific content) and second an adequate cognitive perspective and reasoning process (increased validity) in hopes of resolving the uncertainty.

5. By adapting their cognitive perspective and reasoning through understanding and accommodating the perspective and reasoning of others, individuals derive a new, reconceptualized, and reorganized conclusion. Novel solutions and decisions that, on balance, are qualitatively better are detected. The positive feelings and commitment students feel in creating a solution to the problem together is extended to each other, and interpersonal attraction increases. The competencies gained in managing conflicts constructively tend to improve psychological health. The process may begin again at this point, or it may be terminated by freezing the current conclusion and resolving any dissonance through increasing confidence in the validity of the conclusion.

The process of debate, on the other hand, derives from competition. Two sides prepare their positions, present the best case possible, listen carefully to the opposing position, attempt to refute it, rebut the opponents' attempts to refute their position, and wait for the judges to declare the winner. Although the process of debate begins the same as the process of controversy, the uncertainty created by being challenged results in a closed-minded, defensive rejection of other points of view and dissonant information. Individuals thus stay committed to their original position. Since the debate requires refutation of other points of view, however, students do learn opposing information. Moderate achievement, relationships, and psychological health may result.

The process of concurrence seeking is based on cooperation, with avoidance of conflict. Two sides prepare their positions, present the best case possible, experience uncertainty once they realize there is disagreement but immediately seek to avoid and suppress all conflict by finding a compromise position that abruptly ends all discussion, become apprehensive about the disagreement, and then seek a quick compromise to suppress the conflict. Since the differences among positions are not explored, achievement tends to be low and relationships and psychological health tend to be poor.

In individualistic situations, students study both sides of the issue but make no oral statements; their initial conclusions are never challenged, so their study tends to confirm what they initially thought. Low achievement tends to result. The absence of interpersonal interaction results in neutral relationships and no advances in psychological health.

CONDITIONS DETERMINING THE CONSTRUCTIVENESS OF CONTROVERSY

Although controversies can operate beneficially, they do not do so under all conditions. Whether controversy results in positive or negative consequences depends on the conditions under which it occurs and how it is managed: the context within which the constructive controversy takes place, the heterogeneity of participants, the distribution of information among group members, the level of group members' social skills, and group members' ability to engage in rational argument (Johnson and Johnson, 1979, 1989, 1995a).

Cooperative Goal Structure

Deutsch (1973) emphasizes that the context in which conflicts occur has important effects on whether the conflict turns out constructive or destructive. There are two possible contexts for controversy: cooperative and competitive. A cooperative context facilitates constructive controversy, whereas a competitive context promotes destructive controversy. Controversy within a competitive context tends to promote closed-minded disinterest and rejection of the opponent's ideas and information (Tjosvold, 1998). Within a cooperative context, constructive controversy induces feelings of comfort, pleasure, and helpfulness in discussing opposing positions; open-minded listening to the opposing positions; motivation to hear more about the opponent's arguments; accurate understanding of the opponent's position; and reaching integrated positions where both one's own and the opponent's conclusions and reasoning are synthesized into a final position.

Skilled Disagreement

For controversy to be managed constructively, participants need collaborative and conflict management skills (Johnson, 2000; Johnson and Johnson, 2000). The skills are necessary for following and internalizing certain norms:

- I am critical of ideas, not people. I challenge and refute the ideas of the other participants, while confirming their competence and value as individuals. I do not indicate that I personally reject them.

- I separate my personal worth from criticism of my ideas.
- I remember that we are all in this together, sink or swim. I focus on coming to the best decision possible, not on winning.
- I encourage everyone to participate and to master all the relevant information.
- I listen to everyone's ideas, even if I don't agree.
- I restate what someone has said if it is not clear.
- I differentiate before I try to integrate. I first bring out *all* ideas and facts supporting both sides and clarify how the positions differ. Then I try to identify points of agreement and put them together in a way that makes sense.
- I try to understand both sides of the issue. I try to see the issue from the opposing perspective in order to understand the opposing position.
- I change my mind when the evidence clearly indicates that I should do so.
- I emphasize rationality in seeking the best possible answer, given the available data.
- I follow the *golden rule of conflict*: act toward opponents as you would have them act toward you. I want the opposing pair to listen to me, so I listen to them. I want the opposing pair to include my ideas in their thinking, so I include their ideas in my thinking. I want the opposing pair to see the issue from my perspective, so I take their perspective.

One of the most important skills is to be able to disagree with each other's ideas while confirming one another's personal competence (Tjosvold, 1998). Disagreeing with others, and at the same time imputing that others are incompetent, tends to increase their commitment to their own ideas and their rejection of your information and reasoning. Disagreeing with others while simultaneously confirming their personal competence, however, results in being better liked and opponents being less critical of others' ideas, more interested in learning about others' ideas, and more willing to incorporate others' information and reasoning into your own analysis of the problem. You and the other protagonists are more likely to believe that goals are cooperative, integrate perspectives, and reach agreement.

Another important set of skills for exchanging information and opinions within a constructive controversy is perspective taking (Johnson, 1971; Johnson and Johnson, 1989). Information, both personal and impersonal, is disclosed when one is interacting with a person who is engaging in perspective-taking behaviors (such as paraphrasing) that communicate a desire to understand accurately. Perspective-taking ability increases one's capacity to phrase messages so that they are easily understood by others, and to comprehend their messages accurately. Engaging in perspective taking during conflict results in increased understanding and retention of the opponent's information and perspective. Perspective taking facilitates achieving creative, high-quality problem solving. Finally, perspective taking promotes positive perceptions of the information-exchange process, of fellow group members, and of the group's work.

A third set of skills involves the cycle of differentiating and integrating positions (Johnson and Johnson, 2000). Group members should ensure that there are several cycles of differentiation (bringing out differences in positions) and integration (combining several positions into one new, creative position). The potential for integration is never greater than the adequacy of the differentiation already achieved. Most controversies go through a series of differentiations and integrations before reaching a final decision.

Rational Argument

During a constructive controversy, group members have to follow the canons of rational argumentation (Johnson and Johnson, 1995a, 1995b). This includes generating ideas, collecting relevant information, organizing it using inductive and deductive logic, and making tentative conclusions based on current understanding. Rational argumentation requires that participants keep an open mind, changing their conclusions and positions when others are persuasive in their presentation of rationale, proof, and logical reasoning.

RESEARCH RESULTS: HOW PARTICIPANTS BENEFIT

The research on constructive controversy has primarily been conducted in the past thirty years by researchers in numerous settings using diverse subject populations and varied tasks within an experimental and field-experimental format. All studies randomly assigned participants to conditions. The studies, which involved elementary, intermediate, and college students, were published in journals, had high internal validity, and lasted from one to sixty hours. Taken together, their results have considerable validity. The outcomes of constructive controversy may be grouped in three broad outcomes: productivity and achievement, positive interpersonal relationships, and psychological health. For a detailed listing of the supporting studies, see Johnson and Johnson (1979, 1989, 1995a).

Productivity and Achievement

Productivity and achievement are often viewed as the "bottom line" in assessing the relative value of different methods. Consequently, we examined many measures of productivity and achievement; the results are presented here.

Achievement and Retention. Skillful participation in a constructive controversy tends to result in significantly greater mastery and retention of the material and skills being learned than do concurrence seeking, debate, or individualistic learning. Being exposed to a credible alternative view results in students' recalling more correct information, more skillfully transferring learning to new situations, and generalizing the principles they learned to a wider variety of situations.

Quality of Problem Solving. Compared with concurrence-seeking, debate, and individualistic efforts, constructive controversy tends to result in higher-quality decisions and solutions to complex problems for which differing viewpoints can plausibly be developed, including decisions that involve ethical dilemmas. An interesting question concerning constructive controversy and problem solving is what happens if erroneous information is presented by participants. Simply, can advocating two conflicting but wrong solutions to a problem create a correct one? The value of the constructive controversy process lies not so much in the correctness of an opposing position but rather in the attention and thought processes it induces. More cognitive processing may take place when individuals are exposed to more than one point of view, even if one or more of the points of view are incorrect. A number of studies with both adults and children have found significant gains in performance when erroneous information is presented by one or both sides in a constructive controversy. Thus, the resolution of the conflict is likely to be in the direction of correct performance. In this limited way, two wrongs came to make a right.

Cognitive Reasoning. Constructive controversy tends to promote significantly more higher-level reasoning than do concurrence seeking, debate, individualistic learning, and use of more complex and higher-level reasoning strategies.

Motivation to Achieve. Participants in a constructive controversy tend to be significantly more motivated to achieve and produce than do participants in concurrence seeking, debate, and individualistic learning.

Creativity. Constructive controversy tends to promote creative insight by influencing individuals to (1) view problems from new perspectives and (2) reformulate problems in ways that allow new orientations to a solution to emerge. Constructive controversy promotes significantly more accurate and complete understanding of opposing perspectives than do concurrence seeking, debate, and individualistic learning. Compared to the latter three approaches, constructive controversy increases the number of ideas; quality of ideas; creation of original ideas; use of a wider range of ideas; originality; use of more varied strategies; and the number of creative, imaginative, and novel solutions. Being confronted with credible alternative views has resulted in generation of more novel solutions, varied strategies, and original ideas. Participants tend to have a high degree of emotional involvement in and commitment to solving the problems the group was working on.

Task Involvement. In *Doctrine and Discipline*, John Milton stated, "Where there is much desire to learn, there of necessity will be much arguing, much writing, many opinions; for opinion in good men is but knowledge in the making." Increasing the clarity of one's understanding of an issue through disagreement does arouse emotions and increase involvement. *Task involvement* refers to the quality and quantity of the physical and psychological energy that individuals invest in their efforts to achieve.

Task involvement is reflected in the attitudes participants have toward the task: individuals who engaged in constructive controversies tended to *like the task* significantly better than did those engaged in concurrence-seeking discussions. Participants and observers reported a high level of student involvement in constructive controversy.

Task involvement is also reflected in participant attitudes toward the constructive controversy experience. Individuals involved in constructive controversy (and to a lesser extent, debate) *liked the procedure* significantly better than did individuals working individualistically; participating in a constructive controversy consistently promoted positive attitudes toward the experience.

Exchange of Expertise. Compared with concurrence seeking, debate, and individualistic efforts, constructive controversy tends to result in greater exchange of expertise. Participants often know varying information and theories, make different assumptions, and have differences of opinion. Within any cooperative endeavor, participants may have a wide variety of expertise and perspectives. Conflict among their ideas, information, opinions, preferences, theories, conclusions, and perspectives is inevitable. Group effectiveness is dependent on participants' skillfully exchanging their expertise. The diverse resources of group members are better used during controversy than during concurrence seeking, debate, or individualistic effort.

Attitude Change. In constructive controversy, participants reevaluate their attitudes about the issue and incorporate opponents' arguments into their own attitudes. Not only does participating in the constructive controversy procedure result in attitude change beyond what occurs when individuals read about the issue; changes in attitude also tend to be maintained after the constructive controversy ends. Thus the changes are relatively stable and not merely a response to the experience itself.

Interpersonal Attraction Among Participants

It is often assumed that the presence of constructive controversy within a group leads to difficulties in establishing good interpersonal relations and promotes negative attitudes toward fellow group members; it is also often assumed that arguing leads to rejection, divisiveness, and hostility among peers. Within constructive controversy and debate, there are elements of disagreement, argumentation, and rebuttal that could result in individuals' disliking each other and could create difficulties in establishing good relationships. On the other hand, it has been hypothesized that conflicts have the potential to create positive relationships among participants if they take a constructive course, but in the past there has been little evidence to validate such a hypothesis.

Constructive controversy tends to promote significantly greater liking among participants than do concurrence seeking, debate, or individualistic efforts. Debate fosters significantly greater interpersonal attraction among participants than individualistic efforts do. The more cooperative the context, the greater the cooperative elements in the situation, and the greater the confirmation of each other's competence as well as the resulting interpersonal attraction.

In addition to liking, constructive controversy results in significantly greater perceptions of social support from other individuals than do concurrence seeking, debate, and individualistic learning. The tendency with debate is toward significantly greater perceptions of social support than with individualistic learning. These findings corroborate previous findings that cooperative experiences produce greater perceptions of peer task support than do competitive or individualistic learning situations (Johnson and Johnson, 1989).

The combination of frank exchange of ideas coupled with a positive climate of friendship and support leads to more productive decision making and greater learning and disconfirms the myth that conflict inevitably leads to divisiveness and dislike.

Psychological Health and Social Competence

As individuals learn how to take a cooperative approach to managing conflict and constructive controversy through joint problem solving, they grow healthier psychologically and better able to deal with stress and adversity (Johnson and Johnson, 1989, 1995a, 1995b). Participants who cannot cope with the challenges they face tend not to know what to do when faced with conflict and misfortune. Having procedures and skills to derive creative syntheses that solve joint problems prepares participants to handle conflict.

The aspect of psychological health that has been most frequently examined in the research on constructive controversy is self-esteem. Constructive controversy significantly raises self-esteem more than concurrence seeking, debate, and individualistic learning do. Debate also significantly increases self-esteem compared to individualistic learning. In a series of studies on resilience in the face of adversity, Ann Mastern and Norman Garmezy at the University of Minnesota found problem-solving skills and qualities such as empathy to be directly related to individuals' long-term coping with adversity. Mastern states that both problem-solving skills and empathy can be improved through training in conflict management. Competent individuals tend to be more cooperative (as opposed to disruptive) and more proactive and involved (as opposed to withdrawn). In sum, the more individuals learn how to take a cooperative approach to managing conflicts through joint problem solving, the healthier psychologically they tend to be and the better able they are to deal with stress and adversity.

STRUCTURING CONSTRUCTIVE CONTROVERSIES

Over the past thirty years, we have (1) developed a theory of constructive controversy; (2) validated it through a program of research; (3) trained teachers, professors, administrators, managers, and executives throughout North America and numerous other countries to field-test and implement the constructive controversy procedure; and (4) developed a series of curriculum units, academic lessons, and training exercises structured for controversies. There are two formats for these materials, one for decision-making situations and one for academic learning. A detailed description of how to conduct constructive controversies may be found in Johnson and Johnson (1995a) and Johnson and Johnson (2000).

CONSTRUCTIVE CONTROVERSY AND DECISION MAKING

Let's consider an illustration of the structured use of constructive controversy to ensure high-quality decision making. A large pharmaceutical company faced the decision of whether to buy or build a chemical plant. To maximize the likelihood that the best decision would be made, the president established two advocacy teams to ensure that both the buy and the build alternatives received a fair and complete hearing. (An advocacy team is a subgroup that prepares and presents a particular policy alternative to the decision-making group.)

The buy team identified more than one hundred existing plants that would meet the company's needs, narrowed the field down to twenty, further narrowed it to three, and then selected one as the ideal plant to buy. The build team contacted dozens of engineering firms and, after four months of consideration, selected a design for the ideal plant to build.

Nine months after they were established, the two teams, armed with all the details about cost, first presented their best case and then challenged each other's information, reasoning, and conclusions. From the spirited discussion, it became apparent that the two options would cost about the same amount of money. The group therefore chose the build option because it allowed the plant to be conveniently located near company headquarters.

The purpose of group decision making is to decide on well-considered, well-understood, realistic action toward goals every member wishes to achieve. A *group decision* implies that some agreement prevails among group members as to which of several courses of action is most desirable for achieving the group's goals. Making a decision is just one step in the general *problem-solving process* of goal-directed groups—but it is a crucial one. After defining a problem or issue, thinking over alternative courses of action, and weighing the advantages and disadvantages of each, the group decides which course is most desirable to implement.

To ensure high-quality decision making, each alternative (1) must receive a complete and fair hearing and (2) be critically analyzed to reveal its strengths and weaknesses. What follows is a constructive controversy procedure that may be implemented to do just this.

First, group members propose several courses of action that will solve the problem under consideration. Whenever a group is making a decision, identify a number of alternative courses of action for them to follow.

Second, the members form advocacy teams. To ensure that each course of action receives a fair and complete hearing, assign two-member advocacy teams to present the best case possible for the position assigned to their team. *Positive interdependence* is structured by highlighting the cooperative goal of making the best decision possible (goal interdependence) and noting that a high-quality decision cannot be made without considering the information that is being organized by the other advocacy teams (resource interdependence). *Individual accountability* is structured by ensuring that each member participates in preparing and presenting the assigned position. Any information discovered that supports the other alternatives is given to the appropriate pair of advocates.

Third, members engage in the constructive controversy procedure:

1. *Each advocacy team researches its position and prepares a persuasive presentation to convince other group members of its validity.* The advocacy teams are given the time to research their assigned alternative course of action and find all the supporting evidence available. They organize what is known into a coherent and reasoned position. They plan how to present their case so that all members of the group understand thoroughly the advocacy pair's position, give it a fair and complete hearing, and are convinced of its soundness.

2. *Each advocacy team presents to the entire group without interruption the best case possible for their assigned alternative course of action.* Other advocacy teams listen carefully, taking notes and striving to learn the information provided.

3. *Open discussion proceeds, characterized by advocacy, refutation, and rebuttal.* The advocacy teams give opposing positions a "trial by fire," seeking to refute them by challenging the validity of their information and logic. They defend their own position while continuing to attempt to persuade other group members of its validity. For higher-level reasoning and critical thinking to occur, it is necessary to probe and push each other's conclusions. Members ask for data to support one another's statements, clarify rationales, and show why their position is the most rational one. Group members refute the claims being made by the opposing teams and rebut attacks on their own position. They take careful notes on and thoroughly learn the opposing positions. Members follow the specific rules for constructive controversy. Sometimes a time-out period is needed so that pairs can caucus and prepare new arguments. Members should encourage spirited arguing and playing devil's advocate. Members are instructed to "argue forcefully and persuasively for your position, presenting as many facts as you can to support your point of view. Listen critically to the opposing pair's position, asking them for the facts that support their viewpoint, and then present counterarguments. Remember," the instructions declare, "this is a complex issue, and you need to know all sides to make a good decision."

4. *Advocacy teams reverse perspectives and positions by presenting one of the opposing positions as sincerely and forcefully as they can.* Members may be told to add any new facts they know and to elaborate their position by relating it to other information they have previously learned. Advocacy pairs strive to see the issue from all perspectives simultaneously.

5. *All members drop their advocacy and reach a decision by consensus.* They may wish to summarize their decision in a group report detailing the course of action they have adopted and its supporting rationale. The chosen alternative often represents a new perspective or synthesis that is more rational than the two (or more) assigned. All group members sign the report, indicating that they agree with the decision and will do their share of the work in implementing it. Members may be given these instructions: "Summarize and synthesize the best arguments for *all* points of view. Reach a decision by consensus. Change your mind only if the facts and the rationale clearly indicate that you should do so. Write a report with the supporting evidence and rationale for your synthesis that your group has agreed on. When you are certain the report is as good as you can make it, sign it."

6. *Group members process how well the group functioned.* They can also discuss how their performance may be improved during the next constructive controversy.

Fourth, the group members implement the decision. Once it is made, all members commit themselves to implement it regardless of whether or not they initially favored the alternative adopted.

Controversies are common within decision-making situations. In the mining industry, for example, engineers are accustomed to addressing issues such as land use, air and water pollution, and health and safety. The complexity of designing the production process, balancing environmental and manufacturing interests, and numerous other factors often create the opportunity for constructive controversy. Most groups waste the benefit of such disputes, but every effective decision-making situation thrives on what constructive controversy has to offer. By their very nature, decisions are controversial, as alternative solutions are suggested and considered before agreement is reached. Once a decision is made, the constructive controversy ends and participants commit themselves to a common course of action.

CONSTRUCTIVE CONTROVERSY
AND ACADEMIC LEARNING

In an English class, participants are considering the issue of civil disobedience. They learn that in the civil rights movement, individuals broke the law to gain equal rights for minorities. In the 1970s and 1980s, prominent public figures from Wall Street to the White House have felt justified in breaking laws for personal or political gain. In numerous literary works, such as *The Adventures of Huckleberry Finn,* characters wrestle with the issue of breaking the law to redress a social injustice.

To study the role of civil disobedience in a democracy, participants are placed in a cooperative learning group of four members. The group is given the assignment of reaching their best reasoned judgment about the issue and then divided into two pairs. One pair prepares the best possible case for the constructiveness of civil disobedience in a democracy, and the other pair the case for its destructiveness.

In the resulting conflict, students draw from such sources as Thomas Jefferson and the Declaration of Independence; "Civil Disobedience," by Henry David Thoreau; a speech by Abraham Lincoln at Cooper Union in New York City; and *A Letter from the Birmingham Jail* by Martin Luther King Jr. to challenge each other's reasoning and analyses concerning when civil disobedience is, or is not, constructive.

To use constructive controversy to foster academic learning, you can implement the procedure defined by the next subsections (Johnson and Johnson, 1979, 1989, 1995a).

Structure the Task

The task must be structured cooperatively and so that there are at least two well-documented positions, pro and con. The choice of topic depends on the interests of the instructor and the purposes of the course. In math courses, controversies may focus on different ways to solve a problem. In science classes, it could be environmental issues. Since drama is based on conflict, almost any piece of literature can be turned into constructive controversy (such as having participants argue over who is the greatest romantic poet). Since most history is a recounting of conflicts, controversies can be created over any historical event. In any subject area, controversy promotes academic learning and creative group problem solving.

Make Preinstructional Decisions and Preparations

The teacher decides on the objectives for the lesson. Typically, students are randomly assigned to groups of four. Each group is then divided into two pairs. The pairs are allotted pro or con positions. The instructional materials are prepared so that group members know what position they have been assigned and where they can find supporting information. Materials that are helpful for each position are (1) a clear description of the group's task; (2) a description of the phases of the constructive controversy procedure and of the relevant social skills; (3) a definition of the positions to be advocated, with a summary of the key arguments supporting each position; and (4) relevant resource materials (including a bibliography).

Explain and Orchestrate the Task, Structure, and Procedure

The teacher explains the task so that participants are clear about the assignment and understand the objectives of the lesson. The task must be structured so that there are at least two well-documented positions (pro and con). Again, the choice of topic depends on the teacher's interests and the course objectives. Teachers may wish to help students "get in role" by presenting the issue interestingly and dramatically. Teachers structure positive interdependence by assigning two group goals, by which students are required to:

1. Produce a group report detailing the nature of the group's decision and its rationale. Members are to arrive at a consensus and ensure everyone participates in writing a high-quality group report. Groups present their report to the entire class.

2. Individually take a test on both positions. Group members must master all the information relevant to both sides of the issue.

To supplement the effects of positive goal interdependence, the materials are divided among group members (resource interdependence) and bonus points may be given if all group members score above a preset criterion on the test (reward interdependence).

The purpose of the constructive controversy is to maximize each student's learning. Teachers structure *individual accountability* by ensuring that students participate in each step of the constructive controversy procedure, by individually testing each student on both sides of the issue, and by randomly selecting students to present their group's report. Teachers specify the *social skills* participants are to master and demonstrate during the constructive controversy. The social skills emphasized are those involved in systematically advocating an intellectual position and evaluating and criticizing the position advocated by others, as well as the skills involved in synthesis and consensual decision making. Finally, teachers structure intergroup cooperation. When preparing their positions, for example, students can confer with classmates in other groups who are also preparing the same position.

As for the academic controversy procedure, the students' *overall goals* are to learn all information relevant to the issue being studied and ensure that all other group members learn the information, so that (1) their group can write the best report possible on the issue and (2) all group members achieve high scores on the test. The constructive controversy procedure is as follows.

1. *Research, learn, and prepare the position.* Students are randomly assigned to groups of four, each divided into two pairs. One pair is assigned the pro position and the other the con position. Each pair is to prepare the best case possible for its assigned position by:

   - *Researching the assigned position and learning all relevant information.* Students are to read the supporting materials and find new information to support their position. The opposing pair is given any information students find that supports its position.

   - *Organizing the information into a persuasive argument* that contains a thesis statement or claim ("George Washington was a more effective president than Abraham Lincoln"), the rationale supporting the thesis ("He accomplished A, B, and C"), and a logical conclusion that is the same as the thesis ("Therefore, George Washington was a more effective president than Abraham Lincoln").

   - *Planning how to advocate the assigned position* effectively to ensure it receives a fair and complete hearing. Make sure both pair members are ready to present the assigned position so persuasively that the opposing participants will comprehend and learn the information and, of course, agree that the position is valid and correct.

2. *Present and advocate the position.* Students present the best case for their assigned position to ensure it gets a fair and complete hearing. They need to be forceful, persuasive, and convincing in doing so. Ideally, they use more than one medium. Students are to listen carefully and learn the opposing position, taking notes and clarifying anything they do not understand.

3. *Engage in an open discussion in which there is spirited disagreement.* Students discuss the issue by freely exchanging information and ideas. Students are to (1) argue forcefully and persuasively for their position (presenting as many facts as they can to support their point of view), (2) critically analyze the evidence and reasoning supporting the opposing position, asking for data to support assertions, (3) refute the opposing position by pointing out the inadequacies in the information and reasoning, and (4) rebut attacks on their position and present counterarguments. Students are to take careful notes on and thoroughly learn the opposing position. They are to give the other position a rigorous critique while following the norms for constructive controversy. Sometimes a respite will be provided so that students can caucus with their partners and prepare new arguments. The teacher may encourage more vigorous challenging, take sides when a pair is in trouble, play devil's advocate, ask one group to observe another group engaging in a spirited argument, and generally stir up the discussion.

4. *Reverse perspectives.* Students reverse perspectives and present the best case for the opposing position. Teachers may wish to have students change chairs. In presenting the opposing position sincerely and forcefully (as if it were theirs), students may use their notes and add any new facts they know of. They should strive to see the issue from both perspectives simultaneously.

5. *Synthesize.* Students are to drop all advocacy and find a synthesis on which all members can agree. They summarize the best evidence and reasoning from both sides and integrate it into a joint position that is unique. Students are to

   • Write a group report on the group's synthesis with the supporting evidence and rationale. All group members sign the report indicating that they agree with it, can explain its content, and consider it ready to be evaluated. Each member must be able to present the report to the entire class.

   • Take a test on both positions. If all members score above the preset criteria of excellence, each receives five bonus points.

   • Process how well the group functioned and how its performance may be improved during the next constructive controversy. The specific conflict management skills required for constructive controversy may be highlighted.

- Celebrate the group's success and the hard work of each member to make every step of the constructive controversy procedure effective.

Monitor the Controversy Groups and Intervene When Needed

While the groups engage in the constructive controversy procedure, teachers monitor the learning groups and intervene to improve students' skills in engaging in each step of the constructive controversy procedure and use social skills appropriately. Teachers may also wish to intervene to reinforce particularly effective and skillful behaviors.

Evaluate Students' Learning and Process Group Effectiveness

At the end of each instructional unit, teachers evaluate students' learning and give feedback. Qualitative as well as quantitative aspects of performance may be addressed. Students are graded on both the quality of their final report and their performance on the test covering both sides of the issue. The learning groups also process how well they functioned. Students describe which member actions were helpful (and which unhelpful) in completing each step of the constructive controversy procedure and make decisions about behaviors to continue or change. In whole-class processing, the teacher gives the class feedback and has participants share incidents that occurred in their groups.

CONSTRUCTIVE CONTROVERSY AND DEMOCRACY

Thomas Jefferson believed that free and open discussion, not the social rank in which a person was born, should serve as the basis of influence within society. Based on the beliefs of Jefferson and his fellow revolutionaries, American democracy was founded on the premise that "truth" results from free and open-minded discussion in which opposing points of view are advocated and vigorously argued. Every citizen is given the opportunity to advocate for his or her ideas and to listen respectfully to opposing points of view. Once a decision is made, the minority is expected to go along willingly with the majority because its members know they have been given a fair and complete hearing. To be a citizen in our democracy, individuals need to internalize the norms for constructive controversy as well as master the process of researching an issue, organizing their conclusions, advocating their views, challenging opposing positions, making a decision, and committing themselves to implement the decision made (regardless of whether or not one initially favored the alternative adopted). In essence, using constructive controversy teaches participants to be active citizens of a democracy.

CONCLUSION

Jefferson based his faith in the future on the power of constructive conflict and the creative group problem solving that results. To keep participants from engaging in closed-minded attempts to win, which stifle and block creativity, conflicts must be structured to promote interest, curiosity, inquiry, and open-minded and creative problem solving. One way to do so is constructive controversy. In well-structured controversies, participants make an initial judgment, present their conclusions to other group members, are challenged with opposing views, grow uncertain about the correctness of their views, actively search for new information and understanding, incorporate others' perspectives and reasoning into their thinking, and reach a new set of conclusions. This process significantly increases the quality of decision making and problem solving, the quality of relationships, and improvements in psychological health.

Although the constructive controversy process can occur naturally, it may be consciously structured in decision making and learning situations. This involves dividing a cooperative group into two pairs and assigning them opposing positions. The pairs then (1) develop their position, (2) present it to the other pair and listen to the opposing position, (3) engage in a discussion in which they attempt to refute the other side and rebut attacks on their position, (4) reverse perspectives and present the other position, and (5) drop all advocacy and seek a synthesis that takes both perspectives and positions into account. Engaging in the constructive controversy procedure skillfully provides an example of how conflict creates positive outcomes.

References

Deutsch, M. *The Resolution of Conflict: Constructive and Destructive Processes.* New Haven: Yale University Press, 1973.

Janis, I. *Groupthink: Psychological Studies of Policy Decisions and Fiascoes.* Boston: Houghton Mifflin, 1982.

Johnson, D. W. "Role Reversal: A Summary and Review of the Research." *International Journal of Group Tensions,* 1971, *1,* 318–334.

Johnson, D. W. *Reaching Out: Interpersonal Effectiveness and Self-Actualization.* (7th ed.) Needham Heights, Mass.: Allyn & Bacon, 2000.

Johnson D. W., and Johnson, F. *Joining Together: Group Theory and Group Skills.* (6th ed.) Needham Heights, Mass.: Allyn & Bacon, 2000.

Johnson, D. W., and Johnson, R. "Conflict in the Classroom: Constructive Controversy and Learning." *Review of Educational Research,* 1979, *49,* 51–61.

Johnson, D. W., and Johnson, R. *Cooperation and Competition: Theory and Research.* Edina, Minn.: Interaction, 1989.

Johnson, D. W., and Johnson, R. *Creative Constructive Controversy: Intellectual Challenge in the Classroom.* Edina, Minn.: Interaction, 1995a.

Johnson, D. W., and Johnson, R. *Teaching Participants to Be Peacemakers.* Edina, Minn.: Interaction, 1995b.

Johnson, D. W., Johnson, R., and Holubec, E. *Circles of Learning: Cooperation in the Classroom.* (7th ed.) Edina, Minn.: Interaction, 1998.

Tjosvold, D. "Cooperative and Competitive Goal Approach to Conflict: Accomplishments and Challenges." *Applied Psychology: An International Review,* 1998, *47,* 285–342.

CHAPTER FOUR

Trust, Trust Development, and Trust Repair

Roy J. Lewicki
Carolyn Wiethoff

The relationship between conflict and trust is an obvious one. Most people think of trust as the "glue" that holds a relationship together. If individuals or groups trust each other, they can work through conflict relatively easily. If they don't trust each other, conflict often becomes destructive, and resolution is more difficult. Bitter conflict itself generates animosity and pain that is not easily forgotten; moreover, the parties no longer believe what the other says, nor believe that the other will follow through on commitments and proposed actions. Therefore, acrimonious conflict often serves to destroy trust and increase distrust, which makes conflict resolution ever more difficult and problematic.

In this chapter, we review some of the work on trust and show its relevance to effective conflict management. We also extend some of this work to a broader understanding of the key role of trust in relationships, and how different types of relationship can be characterized according to the levels of trust and distrust that are present. Finally, we describe procedures for rebuilding trust that has been broken, and for managing distrust in ways that can enhance short-term conflict containment while rebuilding trust over the long run.

WHAT IS TRUST?

Trust is a concept that has received attention in several social science literatures: psychology, sociology, political science, economics, anthropology, history, and sociobiology (see Worchel, 1979; Gambetta, 1988; Lewicki and Bunker, 1995,

86

for reviews). As can be expected, each literature approaches the problem with its own disciplinary lens and filters. Until recently, there has been remarkably little effort to integrate these perspectives or articulate the key role that trust plays in critical social processes, such as cooperation, coordination, and performance (for notable exceptions, see Kramer and Tyler, 1996; Sitkin, Rousseau, Burt, and Camerer, 1998).

Worchel (1979) proposes that these differing perspectives on trust can be aggregated into at least three groups (see also Lewicki and Bunker, 1995, 1996, for detailed exploration of theories within each category):

1. The views of personality theorists, who focus on individual personality differences in the readiness to trust, and on the specific developmental and social contextual factors that shape this readiness. At this level, trust is conceptualized as a belief, expectancy, or feeling deeply rooted in the personality, with origins in the individual's early psychosocial development (see Worchel, 1979).

2. The views of sociologists and economists, who focus on trust as an institutional phenomenon. Institutional trust can be defined as the belief that future interactions will continue, based on explicit or implicit rules and norms (Rousseau, Sitkin, Burt, and Camerer, 1998). At this level, trust can be conceptualized as a phenomenon within and among institutions, and as the trust individuals put in those institutions.

3. The views of social psychologists, who focus on the interpersonal transactions between individuals that create or destroy trust at the interpersonal and group levels. At this level, trust can be defined as expectations of the other party in a transaction, risks associated with assuming and acting on such expectations, and contextual factors that either enhance or inhibit development and maintenance of the relationship.

A DEFINITION OF TRUST

The literature on trust is rich with definitions and conceptualizations (see Bigley and Pearce, 1998). In this chapter, we adopt as the definition of trust "an individual's belief in, and willingness to act on the basis of, the words, actions, and decisions of another" (McAllister, 1995, p. 25; Lewicki, McAllister, and Bies, 1998, p. 440). Implicit in this definition, as in other comparable ones (Boon and Holmes, 1991), are three elements that contribute to the level of trust one has for another: the individual's *chronic disposition* toward trust (see our earlier discussion of personality), *situational parameters* (some are suggested above), and the *history of their relationship.* Our current focus is on the relationship dimension of trust, which we address throughout this chapter.

WHY IS TRUST CRITICAL TO RELATIONSHIPS?

There are many types of relationship, and it can be assumed that the nature of trust and its development are not the same in all the types. In this chapter, we discuss two basic types: professional and personal relationships. The former is considered to be a task-oriented relationship in which the parties' attention and activities are primarily directed toward achievement of goals external to their relationship. The latter is considered to be a social-emotional relationship whose primary focus is the relationship itself and the persons in the relationship (see Deutsch, 1985, for a complex treatment of types of interdependence in relationships; see also Sheppard and Sherman, 1998; and Chapters One and Three in this volume).

An effort to describe professional relationship development in a business context was proposed by Shapiro, Sheppard, and Cheraskin (1992). Those authors suggest that three types of trust operate in developing a business relationship: deterrence-based trust, knowledge-based trust, and identification-based trust. In recent papers, Lewicki and Bunker (1995, 1996) adopted these three types of trust in our work and made several major additions and modifications to the paper by Shapiro, Sheppard, and Cheraskin (1992). We briefly present these ideas below; you are encouraged to consult these papers for a richer and fuller description of each type of trust and how it is proposed that the types are linked together in a developmental sequence.

Calculus-Based Trust

Shapiro, Sheppard, and Cheraskin (1992) identified the first type as "deterrence-based trust." They argued that this form of trust is based in ensuring consistency of behavior; simply put, individuals do what they promise because they fear the consequences of not doing what they say. Like any behavior based on a theory of deterrence, trust is sustained to the degree that the deterrent (punishment) is clear, possible, and likely to occur if the trust is violated. Thus, the threat of punishment is likely to be a more significant motivator than the promise of reward.

Lewicki and Bunker (1995, 1996) called this form *calculus-based trust* (CBT). We argued that deterrence-based trust is grounded not only in the fear of punishment for violating the trust but also in the rewards to be derived from preserving it. This kind of trust is an ongoing, market-oriented, economic calculation whose value is determined by the outcomes resulting from creating and sustaining the relationship relative to the costs of maintaining or severing it. Compliance with calculus-based trust is often ensured both by the rewards of being trusting (and trustworthy) and by the "threat" that if trust is violated, one's reputation can be hurt through the person's network of friends and associates. Even if you are not an honest person, having a reputation for honesty (or trustworthiness) is a valuable asset that most people want to maintain. So even if there are opportunities to be untrustworthy, any short-term gains from untrustworthy acts must be balanced, in a calculus-based way, against the long-term benefits from maintaining a good reputation.

The most appropriate metaphor for the growth of CBT is the children's game "Chutes and Ladders." Progress is made on the game board by throwing the dice and moving ahead ("up the ladder") in a stepwise fashion. However, a player landing on a "chute" is quickly dropped back a large number of steps. Similarly, in calculus-based trust, forward progress is made by climbing the ladder, or building trust, slowly and stepwise. People prove through simple actions that they are trustworthy, and similarly, by systematically testing the other's trust. However, a single event of inconsistency or unreliability may "chute" the relationship back several steps—or, in the worst case, back to square one. Thus, CBT is often quite partial and fragile. Although CBT tends to occur most frequently in professional, nonintimate, task-oriented relationships, it can also be the first, early stage in developing intimate personal relationships.

Identification-Based Trust

A second type of trust is based on identification with the other's desires and intentions. This type of trust exists because the parties can effectively understand and appreciate one another's wants. This mutual understanding is developed to the point that each person can effectively act for the other. Identification-based trust (IBT) thus permits a party to serve as the other's agent and substitute for the other in interpersonal transactions (Deutsch, 1949). Both parties can be confident that their interests are fully protected, and that no ongoing surveillance or monitoring of one another is necessary. A true affirmation of the strength of IBT between parties can be found when one party acts for the other even more zealously than the other might demonstrate, such as when a good friend dramatically defends you against a minor insult.

A corollary of this "acting for each other" in IBT is that as the parties come to know[1] each other better and identify with the other, they also understand more clearly what they must do to sustain the other's trust. This process might be described as "second-order" learning. One comes to learn what really matters to the other and comes to place the same importance on those behaviors as the other does. Certain types of activities strengthen IBT (Shapiro, Sheppard, and Cheraskin, 1992; Lewicki and Bunker, 1995, 1996; Lewicki and Stevenson, 1998), such as developing a *collective identity* (a joint name, title, or logo); *colocation* in the same building or neighborhood; *creating joint products or goals* (a new product line or a new set of objectives); or committing to *commonly shared values* (such that the parties are actually committed to the same objectives and so can substitute for each other in external transactions).

Thus IBT develops as one both knows and predicts the other's needs, choices, and preferences, and as one also shares *some of* those same needs, choices, and preferences as one's own. Increased identification enables us to think like the other, feel like the other, and respond like the other. A collective identity develops; we empathize strongly with the other and incorporate parts of their psyche into our own identity (needs, preferences, thoughts, and behavior patterns). This form of trust can develop in working relationships if the parties come to know each other very well, but it is most likely to occur in intimate, personal relationships. Conversely, developing identification-based trust is likely to make working relationships closer and more personal.

Music suggests a suitable metaphor for IBT: the harmonizing of a barbershop quartet. The parties learn to sing in a harmony that is integrated and complex. Each knows the others' vocal range and pitch; each singer knows when to lead and follow; and each knows how to work with the others to maximize their strengths, compensate for their weaknesses, and create a joint product that is much greater than the sum of its parts. The unverbalized, synchronous chemistry of a cappella choirs, string quartets, cohesive work groups, or championship basketball teams are excellent examples of this kind of trust in action.

Trust and Relationships: An Elaboration of Our Views

In addition to our views of these two forms of trust, we need to introduce two ideas about trust and relationships. The first is that trust and distrust are not simply opposite ends of the same dimension, but conceptually different and separate. Second, relationships develop over time, and the nature of trust changes as they develop.

Trust and Distrust Are Fundamentally Different. In addition to identifying types of trust, Lewicki, McAllister, and Bies (1998) have recently argued that trust and distrust are fundamentally different from each other, rather than merely more or less of the same thing. Although trust can be defined as "confident positive expectations regarding another's conduct," distrust can indeed be "confident negative expectations" regarding another's conduct (Lewicki, McAllister, and Bies, 1998). Thus, just as trust implies belief in the other, a tendency to attribute virtuous intentions to the other, and willingness to act on the basis of the other's conduct, distrust implies fear of the other, a tendency to attribute sinister intentions to the other, and desire to protect oneself from the effects of another's conduct.

Relationships Are Developmental and Multifaceted. In discussing our views of the types of trust, we also pointed out that these forms of trust develop in different types of relationships. Work (task) relationships tend to be characterized by CBT but may develop some IBT. Intimate (personal) relationships tend to be characterized by IBT but may require a modicum of CBT for the parties to coordinate their lives together.

All relationships develop as parties share experiences with each other and gain knowledge about the other. Every time we encounter another person, we gain a new or confirming experience that strengthens the relationship. If our experiences with another person are all within the same limited context (I know the server at the bakery because I buy my bagel and juice there every morning), then we gain little additional knowledge about the other (over time, I have a rich but very narrow range of experience with that server). However, if we encounter the other in different contexts (if I join a colleague to talk research, coteach classes, and play tennis), then this variety of shared experience is likely to develop into broader, deeper knowledge of the other.

People come to know each other in many contexts and situations. Conversely, they may trust the other in some contexts and distrust in others. You may have friends you would trust to babysit your child, but not to pay back money you loaned them. A relationship is made up of components of experience that one individual has with another. Within these relationships, some elements hold varying degrees of trust, while others hold varying degrees of distrust. Our overall evaluation of the other person involves some complex judgment that weighs the scope of the relationship and elements of trust and distrust. Most people are able to be quite specific in describing both the trust and distrust elements in their relationship. If the parties teach a class together, work together on a committee, play tennis together, and belong to the same church, the scope of their experience is much broader than for parties who simply work together on a committee.

Finally, we cannot assume that we begin with a blank slate of trust or distrust in relationships. In fact, we seldom approach others with "no information." Rather, we tend to approach the other with some initial level of trust, or of caution (McKnight, Cummings, and Chervaney, 1998). In addition, we develop expectations about the degree to which we can trust new others, depending on a number of factors:

- *Personality predispositions.* Research has shown that individuals differ in their predisposition to trust another (Rotter, 1971). The higher an individual ranks in predisposition to trust, the more she expects trustworthy actions from the other, independent of her own actions.

- *Psychological orientation.* Deutsch (1985) has characterized relationships in terms of their psychological orientations, or the complex synergy of "interrelated cognitive, motivational and moral orientations" (p. 94). He maintains that people establish and maintain social relationships partly on the basis of these orientations, such that orientations are influenced by relationships and vice versa. To the extent that people strive to keep their orientations internally consistent, they may seek out relationships that are congruent with their own psyche.

- *Reputations and stereotypes.* Even if we have no direct experience with another person, our expectations may be shaped by what we learn about them through friends, associates, and hearsay. The other's reputation often creates strong expectations that lead us to look for elements of trust or distrust and also leads us to approach the relationship attuned to trust or to suspicion.

- *Actual experience over time.* With most people, we develop facets of experience as we talk, work, coordinate, and communicate. Some of these facets are strong in trust, while others may be strong in distrust. Over time, it is likely that either trust or distrust elements begin to dominate the experience base, leading to a stable and easily defined relationship. As these patterns stabilize, we tend to generalize across the scope of the relationship and describe it as one of high or low trust or distrust.

Implications of This Revised View of Trust

By incorporating the revisions just described into existing models of trust, we can summarize our ideas about trust and distrust within relationships:

- Relationships are multifaceted, and each facet represents an interaction that provides us with information about the other. The greater the variety of settings and contexts in which the parties interact, the more complex and multifaceted the relationship becomes.

- Within the same relationship, elements of trust and distrust may peacefully coexist, because they are related to different experiences with the other or knowledge of the other in varied contexts.

- Facets of trust or distrust are likely to be calculus-based or identification-based. Earlier, we defined trust as confident positive expectations regarding another's conduct, and distrust as confident negative expectations regarding another's conduct. We elaborated on those definitions in this way:

  Calculus-based trust (CBT) is a confident positive expectation regarding another's conduct. It is grounded in impersonal transactions, and the overall anticipated benefits to be derived from the relationship are assumed to outweigh any anticipated costs.

  Calculus-based distrust (CBD) is defined as confident negative expectations regarding another's conduct. It is also grounded in impersonal transactions, and the overall anticipated costs to be derived from the relationship are assumed to outweigh the anticipated benefits.

Identification-based trust (IBT) is defined as confident positive expectations regarding another's conduct. It is grounded in perceived compatibility of values, common goals, and positive emotional attachment to the other.

Identification-based distrust (IBD) is defined as confident negative expectations regarding another's conduct, grounded in perceived incompatibility of values, dissimilar goals, and negative emotional attachment to the other.

Characterizing Relationships Based on Trust Elements

Because there can be elements of each type of trust and distrust in a relationship, there are many types of relationships, varying in the combination of elements of calculus-based trust, calculus-based distrust, identification-based trust, and identification-based distrust. All of these types of relationships theoretically exist, but given the relative infancy of this theory we cannot effectively explore or discuss all of the possibilities. To simplify this framework, let us assume that we can characterize relationships as simply "high" or "low" in the number of CBT, CBD, IBT, and IBD elements. This reduces the framework to sixteen possible combinations of trust elements (see Table 4.1). Each row in this table represents a type of relationship, based on the pattern of high or low levels of CBT, CBD, IBT, and IBD. These combinations are listed in the first four columns, and a brief description of the relationship is found in the last column.

Based on our model, all sixteen types of relationship are hypothetically possible and may be found among one's friends, acquaintances, and professional associates. However, space limitations in this chapter only permit us to offer a few selective illustrations.

Relationship 1 of Table 4.1, low in all forms of trust and distrust, represents new relationships in which the actors have little prior information and no expectations about each other. Type 1 relationships may also not be new to us, but because we have had such limited interaction with the other there has been no basis for developing significant trust or distrust. Nevertheless, as we mentioned earlier, we tend to extend a modicum of trust. We walk into a new dry cleaning store chosen at random and give the attendant our favorite suit because we trust that the dry cleaner will clean it, not ruin it. The very existence of the shop's appearance as a legitimate business is sufficient to satisfy our trust.

Relationship 2 is high only in CBT. This is likely to be a business or professional relationship in which the actors have had a number of successful exchanges and transactions that are beneficial to them. Over time, each person's behavior has been positive and consistent, and the parties rely on each other to continue to act in the same way. For example, my investment counselor has

Table 4.1. Sixteen Relationship Types Based on Dominant Trust and Distrust Elements.

Type	CBT	CBD	IBT	IBD	Brief Description of the Relationship
1	Low	Low	Low	Low	Arm's-length relationship
2	High	Low	Low	Low	High CBT; good working relationship
3	Low	High	Low	Low	High CBD; working relationship characterized by cautiousness
4	Low	Low	High	Low	"Instant good chemistry" with the other based on strong perceived value compatibility but limited experience (few bands and low bandwidth)
5	Low	Low	Low	High	"Instant bad chemistry" with the other based on strong perceived value incompatibility but limited experience (few bands and low bandwidth)
6	High	Low	High	Low	Classic "high-trust" relationship, based on strong elements of CBT and IBT
7	Low	High	Low	High	Classic "high-distrust" relationship, based on strong elements of CBD and IBD
8	High	High	Low	Low	"Complex professional relationship"; strong number of CBT and CBD elements, limited experience on identification-based elements
9	Low	Low	High	High	"Love-hate relationships"; high passion and ambivalence, characterized by strong positive and strong negative attraction to the other; limited experience on calculus-based elements
10	High	Low	Low	High	"A necessary service provider"; strong CBT but also strong IBD; maintain an arm's-length relationship to benefit from the CBT aspects but minimize the IBD elements
11	Low	High	High	Low	"I love you, but you're a flake"; strong CBD (which makes us cautious) but also strong IBT (which attracts us to the other)
12	Low	High	High	High	Dominant love-hate relationship, with additional elements of CBD and few elements of CBT

Table 4.1. Sixteen Relationship Types Based on Dominant Trust and Distrust Elements (continued).

Type	CBT	CBD	IBT	IBD	Brief Description of the Relationship
13	High	Low	High	High	Dominant love-hate relationship, with additional elements of CBT and few elements of CBD
14	High	High	Low	High	Dominant high-distrust relationship, although there are some elements of CBT possible; "very distrusting, but bounded trusting transactions are possible"
15	High	High	High	Low	Dominant high-trust relationship, although there are some elements of CBD; "very trusting but takes precautions"
16	High	High	High	High	Rich, complex, highly ambivalent relationship; lots of trust and distrust along all dimensions of the relationship

Note: CBT = calculus-based trust; CBD = calculus-based distrust; IBT = identification-based trust; IBD = identification-based distrust.

made very good decisions about my money over time, and I continue to take his advice about when it is time to buy or sell.

Relationship 6, high in CBT and IBT, represents a prototypical high-trust relationship. Both parties benefit greatly from the relationship, so they seek out opportunities to be together and do things together. Continued success in these interactions enhances their trust.

Relationships 15 and 16 are high in CBT, CBD, and IBT, and low or high respectively in IBD. These relationships are characterized by a high degree of ambivalence. The parties find that there are contexts in which they can work together successfully, but they also have to regulate and limit those interactions to minimize the distrust. Additionally, the parties have some strong positive commonalities in values, goals, and interests, but they may (or may not) have strong dissimilarities in the same areas. The parties learn to manage their relationship by maximizing interaction around those areas where they have strong CBT and IBT, while regulating, controlling, or minimizing interaction in those areas with strong CBD (and perhaps IBD). However, ongoing uncertainty, coupled with the potential for strong emotional reactions to one another in a variety of circumstances, may make it difficult for the parties to sustain a stable relationship over time (Jones and Burdette, 1994).

MANAGING TRUST AND DISTRUST IN CONFLICT SITUATIONS

As we have noted, trust and distrust develop as people gain knowledge of one another. One of the benefits of our model of relationships based on trust is its clear explanation of changes in relationships over time. Relationship changes can be mapped by identifying actions that change the balance of the trust and distrust elements in the relationship or fundamentally alter the type of inter-action in the relationship. In this section, we identify behaviors that previous research suggests can change perceptions of trust and distrust.

Actions That Build Calculus-Based Trust

People who are involved in relationships with high levels of CBT and low levels of IBT (such as relationship 2 in Table 4.1) may have relatively stable ex-pectations about these relationships. Initially, CBT may be based only on the other's reputation for trustworthiness (Gabarro, 1978; Butler, 1991). Over time, CBT develops as we observe the other and identify certain behavior patterns over time. Previous research has demonstrated that effective business relation-ships are based on predictability (Jennings, 1971), reliability (McAllister, 1995), and consistency of behavior (Gabarro, 1978). In work relationships, then, CBT is enhanced if people (1) behave the same appropriate way consistently (at dif-ferent times and in different situations), (2) meet stated deadlines, and (3) per-form tasks and follow through with planned activities as promised.

In any context, if people act consistently and reliably we are likely to see them as credible and trustworthy (Lewicki and Stevenson, 1998). For example, students often want to be able to trust their faculty instructors. To the degree that faculty clearly announce their course requirements and grading criteria, use those standards consistently, follow the course outline clearly, and keep their promises, they enjoy a great deal of trust from students.

Strategies to Manage Calculus-Based Distrust

As we have noted, CBT and CBD are often founded on a cost-benefit analysis. If the costs of depending on someone's behavior outweigh the benefits, we are typically inclined to either change or terminate the relationship. This may be feasible with personal friendships, but it is often not possible to leave profes-sional relationships even when CBD is high.[2] Consequently, it is necessary to manage CBD so that the parties can continue to work together.

There are several strategies for managing CBD:

• Agree explicitly on expectations as to what is to be done, on deadlines for completion, and on the penalties for failing to comply with them. This up-front commitment by the parties to a course of action, and to the consequences for nonperformance, sets explicit expectations for behavior that may reduce the fear parties have about the vulnerabilities associated with working together.

• Agree on procedures for monitoring and verifying the other's actions. If we distrust someone, we seek ways to monitor what he does to ensure that future trust violations do not occur. Writing about disarmament during the Cold War, Osgood (1962) explicitly proposes unilateral steps that antagonistic parties can take to signal good faith and an intention to build trustworthiness.

• Cultivate alternative ways to have one's needs met. When one distrusts another (and the other's possible performance in the future), one tries to find ways to minimize future interaction or alternative ways to get needs met. Distrust can be managed by letting the other know that one has an alternative and is willing to invoke it if there are further trust violations.

• Increase the other's awareness of how his own performance is perceived by others. Workplace difficulties are sometimes alleviated when supervisors discuss performance expectations with subordinates, rather than assuming that both have the same understanding of what constitutes appropriate work behavior. Many workplace diversity efforts are actually attempts to familiarize workers from different cultures with one another. Behaviors that seemed strange or inconsistent may be explained as differences in cultural patterns of interaction. Once the parties recognize the logic inherent in each other's behavior, they are likely to view the other as consistent and predictable (Foeman, 1991), which enhances CBT.

Actions That Build IBT

Research indicates that trust is enhanced if the parties spend time sharing personal values, perceptions, motives, and goals (Gabarro, 1978). But specific time must be set aside for engaging in this activity. Parties in work relationships may do this in the course of working together, while parties in personal relationships explicitly devote time to these activities. In general, parties should engage in processes that permit them to share

- Common interests
- Common goals and objectives
- Similar reactions to common situations
- Situations where they stand for the same values and principles, thereby demonstrating integrity (Lewicki and Stevenson, 1998)

For example, Rothman (1997) has proposed a four-step framework for resolving identity-based disputes. The second key step in the framework is resonance, or the process of reflexive reframing by which parties discover common values, concerns, interests, and needs. In Rothman's framework, effective completion of the resonance step permits individuals to establish a basis of commonality (IBT) on which to build mutually acceptable solutions to managing their dispute. Moreover, studies in organizations have indicated that one component of managers' trust in their subordinates is the degree to which the employee demonstrates that she has the best interests of the manager or the organization (or both) at heart (Schoorman, Mayer, and Davis, 1996; Butler, 1995). If we believe that the other shares our concerns and goals, IBT is enhanced. IBT may also be increased if we observe the other reacting as we believe we would react in another context (Lewicki and Stevenson, 1998); however, research on the connection between similarity and perceptions of trustworthiness has produced mixed results (see Huston and Levinger, 1978).

It should be noted that IBT has a strong emotional component and is probably largely affective in nature (Lewicki and Bunker, 1995, 1996; McAllister, 1995). Despite our attempt to think logically about our relationships, how we respond to others often depends on our idiosyncratic, personal reactions to aspects of the other's physical self-presentation (Chaiken, 1986), the situation and circumstances under which we meet the person (Jones and Brehm, 1976), or even our mood at the time of the encounter. Consequently, we are likely to build IBT only with others who we feel legitimately share our goals, interests, perceptions, and values, and if we meet under circumstances that facilitate our learning of that similarity.

Strategies to Manage IBD

If we believe that another's values, perceptions, and behaviors are damaging to our own, it is often difficult to maintain even a semblance of a working relationship. However, if we anticipate that we will have a long-term relationship with someone that contains elements of IBD, and we believe we have limited alternatives, there are strategies for managing the encounter that offer both opportunities for self-protection and attainment of mutual goals. One of the most important strategies is to develop sufficient CBT so that the parties can be comfortable with the straightforward behavioral expectations that each has for the relationship.

As noted in the section on managing CBD, explicitly specifying and negotiating expected behaviors may be necessary to provide both parties with a comfort zone sufficient to sustain their interaction. It may also be helpful for the actors to openly acknowledge the areas of their mutual distrust. By doing so, they can explicitly talk about areas where they distrust each other and establish safeguards that anticipate distrustful behaviors and afford protection against potential consequences (Lewicki and Stevenson, 1998). Thus, for example, if the parties have strong disagreements about certain value-based issues (religious beliefs, political beliefs, personal values), they may be able to design ways to keep these issues from interfering with their ability to work together in more calculus-based transactions. If the costs and benefits of consistent action are clear to both parties, the groundwork for CBT may be established. This enables them to interact in future encounters with some confidence that despite deep-seated differences, they will not be fundamentally disadvantaged or harmed in the relationship.

What Happens If Trust Is Violated?

Trust violations occur if we obtain information that does not conform to our expectations of behavior for the other. Note that trust violations can occur in both directions—that is, we can expect trusting behavior and encounter distrust, or we can expect distrusting behavior and encounter trust.[3] If this disconfirming information is significant enough, or if it begins to occur regularly in ongoing encounters, we are likely to adjust our perceptions of trust dramatically and alter the type of relationship we have with the other (Lewicki and Bunker, 1996).[4]

It is likely that we have less emotional investment in relationships that are low in IBT and IBD. Thus, in those relationships violations of CBT are probably viewed as annoyances. We may need to adjust our behavior to deal with the other party, but the trust violations are not likely to affect our emotional well-being significantly. Violations of CBT can be managed by talking about the violation and attempting to find an explanation for the unexpected behavior. If the explanation is adequate to "justify" the lapse, then the high CBT relationship is likely to continue (though the violated party may be vigilant about lapses in the next few interactions). If lapses continue over time, it is likely that elements of CBD will build, and the relationship will change character to reflect low CBT or high CBD (or both).

On the other hand, if relationships are established that are high in IBT, there is also a higher level of emotional investment. In these relationships, trust violations contain both an affective and a practical component. Once a shared identity has been established, any disconfirming trust violation can be viewed as a direct challenge to a person's most central and cherished values (Lewicki and Bunker, 1995), and it may also represent conflict with the person's psychological orientation (Deutsch, 1985). The parties are likely to feel upset, angry, violated, or even foolish, if loss of face is a result of trusting the other when trusting turned out to be inappropriate. In cases where IBT is violated, we argue that the situation *must* be addressed for a high IBT relationship to continue. A number of studies have shown that when parties cannot or will not communicate about a major problem in their relationship, they are more likely to end the relationship than continue interacting (Courtright, Millar, Rogers, and Bagarozzi, 1990; Gottman, 1979; Putnam and Jones, 1982).

We envision two stages to the process of restoring IBT trust. First, the parties exchange information about the perceived trust violation (Lewicki and Bunker, 1996). They attempt to identify and understand the act that was perceived as violation. Miscommunication and misunderstandings are often cleared up at this stage. A husband might accuse his wife of admiring another man at a party, perceiving this to be an uncharacteristic violation of the IBT he has for her and the integrity of their marriage. When the wife explains that she was merely admiring the man's sweater and thinking of purchasing a similar one for her husband, it might transform the husband's perception of an IBT trust violation. An explanation that the act either was *not* what he perceived it to be, or that the motivation for the act was consistent with his expectations of his wife's commitment to their relationship, is apt to be adequate to restore the IBT relationship. (Note, however, that if this pattern persists whenever the couple is out together, the wife's explanation will cease to be adequate over time.)

In the second communication stage, the parties reaffirm their commitment to a high IBT relationship. They may affirm similar interests, goals, and actions (Lewicki and Stevenson, 1998) and explicitly recommit to the relationship. They may also explicitly realign their psychological orientations (Deutsch, 1985). They may also discuss strategies to avoid similar misunderstandings, miscommunications, or disconfirmations in the future.

However, when the parties either fail to reconcile the trust violation within their shared identity or are unable to do so, high IBT relationships may be transformed to low IBT or even IBD. If the violation is largely inconsistent with the core beliefs and values of one of the partners, and if it cannot be adequately explained within the context of the current relationship, then the parties must elect to either renegotiate their shared identity or terminate the high IBT relationship (Larson, 1993).

Naturally, not every IBT relationship is as all-encompassing as a marriage. But there are kinds of business and professional relationship where the same dynamics apply. One worker may take another into confidence and share strong dissatisfaction with the boss's behavior, only to discover that the coworker has told the boss about the negative comments. A student may ask a favorite teacher to read some poetry that the student has written, and later discover that the teacher published the poetry under his own name. Thus, no model of trust restoration can explain the idiosyncrasies of each individual relationship. Our intent is merely to explore the dynamics of trust restoration within the context of various kinds of relationship, to better understand the link between relationship and trust type.

Strategies of trust restoration necessarily differ with the kind of relationship the parties have (Bottom, Gibson, Daniels, and Murnighan, 1996). For example, research has demonstrated that people who perceive few alternatives to their existing relationship or experience a high degree of interdependence may continue the relationship with the partner despite repeated, or even violent, trust violations (Rusbult and Martz, 1995). It may also be that those who are heavily invested in high IBT relationships are actually less sensitive to trust violations (Robinson, 1996).

Despite the generally negative affect associated with distrust, we should note that trust restoration is not always a desirable alternative. Distrust is necessary when people perceive a need to protect themselves or others from possible harm, or when other parties in the relationship are not well known (Lewicki, McAllister, and Bies, 1998). Some work teams also perform better in CBD situations, perhaps because each member takes more care to ensure that the partners perform as expected. This self-policing contributes to higher product quality.

Implications for Managing Conflict More Effectively

Some of what we have said about trust we have known for a long time, but other parts are quite new and somewhat speculative. They remain to be validated through further research on how people develop and repair trust in their relationships. By way of summarizing this chapter, we would like to make some statements about trust and its implications for managing conflict.

1. *The existence of trust between individuals makes conflict resolution easier and more effective.* This point is obvious to anyone who has been in a conflict. A party who trusts another is likely to believe the other's words and assume that the other will act out of good intentions, and probably look for productive ways to resolve a conflict should one occur. Conversely, if one distrusts another, one might disbelieve the other's words, assume that the other is acting out of bad intentions, and defend oneself against the other or attempt to beat and conquer the other. As we have tried to indicate several times in this chapter, the level of trust or distrust in a relationship therefore definitively shapes emergent conflict dynamics.

2. *Trust is often the first casualty in conflict.* If trust makes conflict resolution easier and more effective, eruption of conflict usually injures trust and builds distrust. It does so because it violates the trust expectations, creates the perception of unreliability in the other party, and breaks promises that have been broken. Moreover, the conflict may serve to undermine the foundations of identification-based trust that may exist between the parties. Thus, as conflict escalates—for whatever reason or cause—it serves to decrease trust and increase distrust. The deeper the distrust that is developed, the more the parties focus on defending themselves against the other or attempting to win the conflict, which further serves to increase the focus on distrust and decrease actions that might rebuild trust.

3. *Creating trust in a relationship is initially a matter of building calculus-based trust.* Many of those writing on trust have suggested that one of the objectives in resolving a conflict is to "build trust." Yet in spite of these glib recommendations, few authors are sufficiently detailed and descriptive of those actions required to actually do so. From our review of the literature and the research we have reported in this chapter, it is clear to us that to build trust a

party must begin with those actions we outline in this chapter: act consistently and reliably, meet deadlines and commitments, and repeatedly do so over time or over several bands of activity in the relationship.

4. *Relationships can be further strengthened if the parties are able to build identification-based trust.* Strong calculus-based trust is critical to any stable relationship, but IBT (based on perceived common goals and purposes, common values, and common identity) is likely to strengthen the overall trust between the parties and enhance the ability of the relationship to withstand conflict that may be relationship fracturing. If the parties perceive themselves as having strong common goals, values, and identities, they are motivated to sustain the relationship and find productive ways to resolve the conflict so that it does not damage the relationship.

5. *Relationships characterized by calculus-based or identification-based distrust are likely to be conflict laden, and eruption of conflict within that relationship is likely to feed and encourage further distrust.* At the calculus-based level, the actor finds the other's behavior (at least) unreliable and unpredictable, and the other's intentions and motivations might be seen as intentionally malevolent in nature. At the identification-based level, the actor believes that he and the other are committed to dissimilar goals, values, and purposes and might thus attribute hostile motives and intentions to the other. Once such negative expectations are created, actions by the other become negative self-fulfilling prophecies (I expect the worst of the other and his behavior confirms my worst fears), which often leads the conflict into greater scope, intensity, and even intractability.

6. As we have noted, *most relationships are not purely trust and distrust but contain elements of both.* As a result, we have positive *and* negative feelings about the other, which produces another level of conflict: an intrapsychic conflict often called "ambivalence." States of ambivalence are characterized by elements of both trust and distrust for another; the internal conflict created by that ambivalence serves to undermine clear expectations of the other's behavior and force the actor to scrutinize every action by the other to determine whether it should be counted in the trust or the distrust column. Ambivalent relationships are often finely grained and finely differentiated (Gabarro, 1978) because the actor is forced to determine the contexts in which the other can be trusted and those in which the other should be distrusted. As noted elsewhere (Thompson, Zanna, and Griffin, 1995; Lewicki and McAllister, 1998), ambivalence can lead actors to become incapacitated in further action, or to modify strategies of influence with the other party. Thus, an actor's internal conflict between trust and distrust probably also affects how he handles the interpersonal conflict between himself and the other party. Because of the number of bands in the bandwidth of a relationship, and the ways in which trust and distrust can mix in any given relationship, we also argue that relationships holding varied degrees of am-

bivalence are far more common than relationships characterized by "pure" high trust or high distrust.

7. *Finally, it is possible to repair trust*—although it is easier to write about the steps of such repair than to actually perform it. Effective trust repair is often a key part of effective conflict resolution. In the preceding section of this chapter, we have talked about some of the steps that are necessary to repair trust.

However, as we noted, repairing trust may take a long time, because the parties have to reestablish reliability and dependability that can only occur over time. Therefore, although rebuilding trust may be necessary for effective conflict resolution in the relationship over the long run, addressing and managing the distrust may be the most effective strategy for short-term containment of conflict. By managing distrust, as noted earlier, we engage in certain activities:

1. We explicitly address the behaviors that created the distrust. These may be actions of unreliability and undependability, harsh comments and criticism, or aggressive and antagonistic activities occurring as the conflict escalated.

2. If possible, each person responsible for a trust violation or act of distrust should apologize and give a full account of the reasons for the trust violation. Acknowledging responsibility for actions that created the trust violation, and expressing regret for harm or damage caused by the violation, is often a necessary step in reducing distrust.

3. We restate and renegotiate the expectations for the other's conduct in the future. The parties have to articulate expectations about the behavior that needs to occur, and commit to those behaviors in future interactions.

4. We agree on procedures for monitoring and verifying the designated actions, to ensure that commitments are being met.

5. We simultaneously create ways to minimize our vulnerability or dependence on the other party in areas where distrust has developed. This often occurs as the vulnerable parties find ways to ensure that they are no longer vulnerable to the other's exploitation or identify alternative ways to have their needs met. If one person depends on another for a ride to work and the driver is consistently late or occasionally forgets, then even if the actor accepts the other's apology and commitment to be more reliable, the actor may also explore alternative ways to get to work.

CONCLUSION

In this chapter, we have described the critical role that trust and distrust play in relationships. We have reviewed some of the basic research on trust and elaborated on the types of trust that exist in most interpersonal relationships. We have suggested that trust and distrust coexist in most relationships, that trust and distrust can be calculus-based or identification-based, and that relationships differ in form and character as a function of the relative weight of the two types of trust in the relationship. Finally, we have suggested that managing any relationship requires us to both create trust and manage distrust effectively. These processes are most critical when trust is broken and needs to be repaired. A great deal of research remains to be done on these propositions, but we hope that the ideas proposed in this chapter serve to move this work forward.

Notes

1. In earlier work, Lewicki and Bunker (1995, 1996) identified knowledge-based trust as a separate trust. We now believe that knowledge is a dimension of relationships, along which people move from uncertainty to confidence about the other's intentions, motivations, and behaviors.

2. This is an important point. If CBD is high, we believe that parties are likely to leave the relationship—assuming the interdependence between them and the other is not required and that they have viable alternative ways of getting their needs met (Thibaut and Kelley, 1959; Fisher, Ury, and Patton, 1981; and Lewicki, Saunders, and Minton, 1999).

3. Although we do not have empirical evidence to support it at this writing, our belief is that expectation violations function much like the chutes-and-ladders process we described in discussing calculus-based trust. Thus the impact of expecting trust and experiencing distrust is *more* disconfirming and distressing than expecting distrust and encountering trust. Expecting trust and having it violated in a high-trust environment is more disruptive than encountering trust in a high-distrust environment (Lewicki and Bunker, 1996).

4. Although we indicated that trust violations can occur in both directions, we discuss only violations of trusting expectations, not violations of distrusting expectations.

References

Bigley, G. A., and Pearce, J. L. "Straining for Shared Meaning in Organization Science: Problems of Trust and Distrust." *Academy of Management Review,* 1998, *23,* 405–422.

Boon, S. D., and Holmes, J. G. "The Dynamics of Interpersonal Trust: Resolving Uncertainty in the Face of Risk." In R. A. Hinde and J. Groebel (eds.), *Cooperation and Prosocial Behavior.* Cambridge: Cambridge University Press, 1991.

Bottom, W. P., Gibson, K., Daniels, S., and Murnighan, J. K. "Rebuilding Relationships: Defection, Repentance, Forgiveness, and Reconciliation." Working paper, Washington University, St. Louis, Mo., 1996.

Butler, J. K. "Toward Understanding and Measuring Conditions of Trust: Evolution of a Conditions of Trust Inventory." *Journal of Management,* 1991, *17,* 643–663.

Butler, J. K. "Behaviors, Trust and Goal Achievement in a Win-Win Negotiating Role Play." *Group and Organization Management*, 1995, *20*, 486–501.

Chaiken, S. L. "Physical Appearance and Social Influence." In C. P. Herman, M. P. Zanna, and E. T. Higgins (eds.), *Physical Appearance, Stigma, and Social Behavior: The Ontario Symposium*. Mahwah, N.J.: Erlbaum, 1986.

Courtright, J. A., Millar, F. E., Rogers, L. E., and Bagarozzi, D. "Interaction Dynamics of Relational Negotiation: Reconciliation Versus Termination of Distressed Relationships." *Western Journal of Speech Communication*, 1990, *54*, 429–453.

Deutsch, M. "A Theory of Cooperation and Competition." *Human Relations*, 1949, *2*, 129–151.

Deutsch, M. "Interdependence and Psychological Orientation." In M. Deutsch, *Distributive Justice: A Social Psychological Perspective*. New Haven: Yale University Press, 1985.

Fisher, R., Ury, W., and Patton, B. *Getting to Yes*. Boston: Houghton Mifflin, 1981.

Foeman, A. K. "Managing Multiracial Institutions: Goals and Approaches for Race-Relations Training." *Communication Education*, 1991, *40*, 255–265.

Gabarro, J. J. "The Development of Trust Influence and Expectations." In A. G. Athos and J. J. Gabarro (eds.), *Interpersonal Behavior: Communication and Understanding in Relationships*. Upper Saddle River, N.J.: Prentice Hall, 1978.

Gambetta, D. *Trust: Making and Breaking Cooperative Relations*. Boston: Blackwell, 1988.

Gottman, J. M. *Marital Interaction: Experimental Investigations*. Orlando: Academic Press, 1979.

Huston, T. L., and Levinger, G. "Interpersonal Attraction and Relationships." *Annual Review of Psychology*, 1978, *29*, 115–156.

Jennings, E. E. *Routes to the Executive Suite*. New York: McGraw-Hill, 1971.

Jones, R. A., and Brehm, J. W. "Attitudinal Effects of Communicator Attractiveness When One Chooses to Listen." *Journal of Personality and Social Psychology*, 1976, *6*, 64–70.

Jones, W. H., and Burdette, M. P. "Betrayal in Relationships." In A. L. Weber and J. H. Harvey (eds.), *Perspectives on Close Relationships*. Needham Heights, Mass.: Allyn & Bacon, 1994.

Kramer, R., and Tyler, T. R. (eds.). *Trust in Organizations: Frontiers of Theory and Research*. Thousand Oaks, Calif.: Sage, 1996.

Larson, J. M. "Exploring Reconciliation." *Mediation Quarterly*, 1993, *11*, 95–106.

Lewicki, R. J., and Bunker, B. B. "Trust in Relationships: A Model of Development and Decline." In B. B. Bunker and J. Z. Rubin (eds.), *Conflict, Cooperation, and Justice: Essays Inspired by the Work of Morton Deutsch*. San Francisco: Jossey-Bass, 1995.

Lewicki, R. J., and Bunker, B. B. "Developing and Maintaining Trust in Work Relationships." In R. Kramer and T. R. Tyler (eds.), *Trust in Organizations: Frontiers of Theory and Research*. Thousand Oaks, Calif.: Sage, 1996.

Lewicki, R. J., and McAllister, D. J. "Confident Expectations and Reasonable Doubts: The Social Dynamics of Ambivalence in Interpersonal Relationships." Paper presented to the Conflict Management Division, Academy of Management National Meetings, San Diego, 1998.

Lewicki, R. J., McAllister, D. J., and Bies, R. J. "Trust and Distrust: New Relationships and Realities." *Academy of Management Review*, 1998, *23*, 438–458.

Lewicki, R. J., Saunders, D., and Minton, J. *Negotiation*. (3rd ed.) Burr Ridge, Ill.: Irwin/McGraw-Hill, 1999.

Lewicki, R. J., and Stevenson, M. A. "Trust Development in Negotiation: Proposed Actions and a Research Agenda." *Business and Professional Ethics Journal*, 1998, *16*, 99–132.

McAllister, D. J. "Affect-and Cognition-Based Trust as Foundations for Interpersonal Cooperation in Organizations." *Academy of Management Journal*, 1995, *38*, 24–59.

McKnight, D. H., Cummings, L. L., and Chervaney, N. L. "Initial Trust Formation in New Organizational Relationships." *Academy of Management Review*, 1998, *23*, 473–490.

Osgood, C. *An Alternative to War or Surrender*. Urbana: University of Illinois Press, 1962.

Putnam, L. L., and Jones, T. S. "Reciprocity in Negotiations: An Analysis of Bargaining Interaction." *Communication Monographs*, 1982, *49*, 171–191.

Robinson, S. L. "Trust and Breach of the Psychological Contract." *Administrative Science Quarterly*, 1996, *41*, 574–599.

Rothman, J. *Resolving Identity-Based Conflict in Nations, Organizations, and Communities*. San Francisco: Jossey-Bass, 1997.

Rotter, J. B. "Generalized Expectancies for Interpersonal Trust." *American Psychologist*, 1971, *26*, 443–452.

Rousseau, D., Sitkin, S. B., Burt, R. S., and Camerer, C. "Not So Different After All: A Cross-Discipline View of Trust." *Academy of Management Review*, 1998, *23*, 393–404.

Rusbult, C. E., and Martz, J. M. "Remaining in an Abusive Relationship: An Investment Model Analysis of Nonvoluntary Dependence." *Personality and Social Psychology Bulletin*, 1995, *21*, 558–571.

Schoorman, F. D., Mayer, R., and Davis, J. "Empowerment in Veterinary Clinics: The Role of Trust in Delegation." Paper presented to the 11th annual meeting of the Society for Industrial and Organizational Psychology, San Diego, 1996.

Shapiro, D., Sheppard, B. H., and Cheraskin, L. "Business on a Handshake." *Negotiation Journal*, 1992, *8*, 365–377.

Sheppard, B. H., and Sherman, D. M. "The Grammars of Trust: A Model and General Implications." *Academy of Management Review*, 1998, *23*(3), 422–437.

Sitkin, S. B., Rousseau, D. M., Burt, R. S., and Camerer, C. (eds.). "Special Topic Forum on Trust in and Between Organizations." *Academy of Management Review,* 1998, *23* (entire issue 3).

Thibaut, J., and Kelley, H. H. *The Social Psychology of Groups.* New York: Wiley, 1959.

Thompson, M. M., Zanna, M. P., and Griffin, D. W. "Let's Not Be Indifferent About (Attitudinal) Ambivalence." In R. E. Petty and J. A. Krosnick (eds*.), Attitude Strength: Antecedents and Consequences.* Mahwah, N.J.: Erlbaum, 1995.

Worchel, P. "Trust and Distrust." In W. G. Austin and S. Worchel (eds.), *The Social Psychology of Intergroup Relations.* Belmont, Calif.: Wadsworth, 1979.

CHAPTER FIVE

Power and Conflict

Peter T. Coleman

In the Sonagachi red-light district in Calcutta, India, prostitutes have organized to mobilize against AIDS, altering the power structure by challenging any pimp or madam who would insist on a customer's right to sex without a condom.

At a company in the United States, in an attempt to avoid layoffs, the great majority of employees agreed to cut their own salaries by 20 percent; the offer was rejected by the CEO, who chose instead to fire 20 percent of the workforce, stating that "it was very important that management's prerogative to manage as it saw fit not be compromised by sentimental human considerations" (Harvey, 1989, p. 275).

In the wilds of Wyoming, groups of ranchers and environmentalists, who historically were bitter adversaries, have teamed up to fight a proposal by the federal Department of the Interior to reintroduce wolves into their national parks.

All of these conflicts have one basic element in common: power. Power to challenge, power to resist, and power through cooperating together. Most conflicts directly or indirectly concern power, either as leverage for achieving one's goals, as a means of seeking or maintaining the balance or imbalance of power in a relationship, or as a symbolic expression of one's identity. Scholars propose that the "deep structure" of most conflicts is dictated by preexisting power relations. This structure, established through the history of relations between the parties, their differential access to resources, or the existing social norms and roles, drives the issues in their conflicts and largely influences what is considered to be important, feasible, and fair in these situations. Of course, there are also many overt conflicts about power, as for example between the haves and have-nots or between competing power seekers. Because of its ubiquity, it is paramount that when we address conflict, we consider power.

This chapter enhances our understanding of the relationship between power and conflict by drawing on useful ideas from the diverse social science literature related to power. I have organized it in three sections, beginning with a discussion of those aspects of power that are important to considering conflict and its constructive resolution. In this section, I describe some of the conceptualizations, discuss some typologies, and offer a working definition of power. I then briefly summarize some of the personal and situational factors that affect people's preferences for and responses to power in social relations. In the second section, I discuss the relevance of these ideas to conflict resolution, outlining some of the tendencies of and strategies used by members of both high-power and low-power groups when in conflict. I conclude the chapter by discussing the implications of these ideas, frameworks, and theories for training in conflict resolution.

A DISCUSSION OF POWER

Bertrand Russell wrote, "The fundamental concept in social science is power, in the same sense in which energy is the fundamental concept in physics" (1938, ch. 1). The idea of power, however, is abstract and ambiguous, even though its consequences are real. As is illustrated by the vast literature on power from philosophy, history, sociology, political science, and psychology, there are about as many conceptualizations of power as there are authors who have written on the subject. This is largely due to the fact that the presence or absence of power is an important experience in our personal lives. Our individual understanding of power is often filtered through our personal experiences (such as the relative level of power that we enjoy in our lives) and our assumptions about human nature, the nature of relations between people, and the meaning of existence. The proliferation of conceptualizations of power also stems from our training in a given area (psychology, international affairs, community activism) as it shapes our thinking through the paradigms, theories, and methodologies associated with it, which tends to orient us to specific aspects of power. But to effectively analyze, understand, and respond to power in conflict, we are in need of a practical way of approaching it.

The images that we use to understand power also have important implications for how we relate to one another personally and as members of groups. Power differences affect, profoundly or subtly, the relations between men and women, employers and employees, European Americans and African Americans, adults and children, the wealthy and the poor, and so on. Underlying and sustaining each of these differences are the root images of power that are generated by the more powerful. Thus, some feminists have argued that the images underlying and sustaining the power differences between men and women are ones generated by men: ultimate power is command-and-control power, obtained and maintained through domination and the use of threat, coercion, and force.

There are other common misconceptions about power. For example, many people assume that power and control are concentrated in some physical location in systems (as in a boardroom or behind the lectern of a classroom). This was evident in the 1960s when student activists seized the administrative offices of their schools as a means of gaining power. Another apparent tendency is to believe that power is fixed or finite and that there is only so much power to go around. A third misconception is that power flows in one direction (usually from the top down) and that individuals with differing levels of power do not mutually influence one another. Finally, there seems to be a tendency, related to these assumptions, to conceive of power in competitive terms. This is the belief that power holders gain by using their power "against" rather than "for" those with less power.

Four Perspectives on Power

In addition to these popular misconceptions, four common themes or perspectives on power are found in the social science literature:

- "Power over"
- "Power with"
- "Powerlessness and dependence"
- "Empowered and independent"

I characterize each briefly in this section.

Power Over. Morgan (1986) argued that many social theorists derive their thinking on power relations from the definition of power offered by the American political scientist Robert Dahl (1968), who proposed that power involves "an ability to get another person to do something that he or she would not otherwise have done" (p. 158). This approach to power has been termed "power over" and is akin to the widely accepted proposition on power offered by Michels (1911), who said that "every human power seeks to enlarge its prerogatives. He who has acquired power will almost always endeavor to consolidate it and to extend it" (p. 207). This conception of power was evident in the earlier example of the CEO and his response to the employees' initiative. The implicit assumption in this type of conceptualization is that power relations are inherently coercive and competitive; the more power A has, the less power available for B. Though this is sometimes the case, it is a limited perspective.

Power With. A different outlook on power was offered by Mary Parker Follett in the 1920s. She proposed that even though power was usually conceived of as power over others, it would also be possible to develop the conception of "power with" others. She envisioned this type as jointly developed, coactive, and noncoercive (Follett, [1924] 1973). This is the form of power illustrated in the vignette about partnership between ranchers and environmentalists. Follett wrote that "our task is not to learn where to place power; it is how to develop power. . . . Coercive power is the curse of the universe; co-active power, the enrichment and advancement of every human soul" (p. xii). This perspective on power is seen in the work of a few scholars today, most notably Deutsch (1973), Tjosvold (1981, 1997), Kanter (1977), and Coleman (1997).

Powerlessness and Dependence. A third perspective that has received some attention in the literature, and is particularly relevant to our discussion of conflict, approaches power from the experience and expression of powerlessness and dependence. The negative physical and psychological impact of a prolonged experience of powerlessness has been shown to be dire (Sashkin, 1984) and can lead to a tendency to become more rigid, critical, controlling of others in low power, and, ultimately, more irrational and violent (Kanter, 1977). Powerlessness and dependence are distinct though often highly correlated experiences; where you have a lack of power you tend to have some type of dependence on others. These dependent relationships can serve to meet the needs of the low-power person, but they can take many forms, from benign and supportive (as in many mentor-mentee relationships) to oppressive and abusive (as with a dictatorial parent).

Empowered and Independent. The flip side of powerlessness is, of course, having power or being empowered with a concomitant sense of independence. Scholars have referred to this view of power as having "power to" or "power from," in the sense that one has enough power to achieve one's objectives without being unduly constrained by someone or something else. Research in organizations has looked extensively at empowerment in terms of employee participation, delegation of authority, and structural decentralization and has catalogued its many positive effects for people, groups, and organizations. If individuals feel empowered in a particular situation, it reduces their need for dependence on others and opens up the possibility of acting independently, thereby bolstering their sense of self-esteem, self-efficacy, and confidence.

A Working Definition of Power

Deutsch (1973) offered a comprehensive perspective on power that can help to integrate the above perspectives. He described power as a relational concept functioning between the person and his or her environment. Power, therefore, is determined not only by the characteristics of the person or persons involved in any given situation, nor solely by the characteristics of the situation, but by the interaction of these two sets of factors. The power of the Indian prostitutes, for example, can be seen as the result of their ability to organize and mobilize their colleagues in this particular setting where demand for their services was high.

Deutsch also made an important distinction between three specific meanings of power: *environmental power,* the degree to which an individual can favorably influence his or her overall environment; *relationship power,* the degree to which a person can favorably influence another person; and *personal power,* the degree to which a person is able to satisfy his or her own desires. These three meanings for power may be positively correlated (for example, high relationship power equals high personal power), but this is not necessarily so. For example, the CEO mentioned earlier may have had more relationship power than his employees in this situation (in terms of his power over their jobs) and so could resist their attempts to influence the lay-off decision, but by doing so and firing 20 percent of the workers he undoubtedly sacrificed environmental power (his company's efficiency or market share) thanks to the effects of his actions on the morale and commitment of the remaining employees. This loss of environmental power could result in diminution of the CEO's personal power if it adversely affects his sense of self-efficacy, self-esteem, or even his personal income. The important point is that these are three distinct, but interrelated, realms of power; a shift in one type of power (relationship) may result in a gain or loss of another type (personal or environmental) depending on the people and circumstances.

Lewicki, Litterer, Minton, and Saunders (1994) offered a useful clarification in distinguishing three concepts related to power: power bases, power use, and influence strategies. Power bases are the resources for power or the tools available to influence one's environment, the other party, or one's own desires. This is potential power. There exist in the literature many typologies of the bases of power (such as wealth, physical strength, weapons, intelligence, knowledge, legitimacy, respect, affection, organizational skills, allies, and so on). These typologies can be useful for discerning different resources for power, but they should not be confused with a more specific definition of power. Following the lead of Salancik and Pfeffer (1977), I define power as the ability to bring about desired outcomes. Of course, one's outcomes or goals can be cooperative, competitive, or independent of others and can be aimed at affecting oneself, another person or persons, or one's environment.

Deutsch (1973) outlined the conditions for "effective power" as having control of the resources to generate power, motivation to influence others, skill in converting resources to power, and good judgment in employing power so that it is appropriate in type and magnitude to the situation. The distinction between access to and use of power resources on the one hand and effective power on the other is critical to a discussion of conflict, and I return to this point in the next section. Finally, strategies of influence are simply the manner in which the resources are put to use to accomplish a particular objective. Lewicki, Litterer,

Minton, and Saunders (1994) have identified such diverse strategies as persuasion, exchange, legitimacy, friendliness, ingratiation, praise, assertiveness, inspirational appeal, consultation, pressure, and coalitions.

In summary, power can be usefully conceptualized as a mutual interaction between the characteristics of a person and the characteristics of a situation, where the person has access to valued resources and uses them to achieve personal, relational, or environmental goals, often through using various strategies of influence.

Personal and Situational Factors

The definition of power that I have offered raises three central issues. First, what are the key aspects of individuals and groups that social science research has shown to be meaningful to our understanding of power and conflict? Similarly, what aspects of situations are thought to be most important to power in the mutual influence of a person with her or his environment? Third, what can we learn from the discussion about effective use of power in conflict? Figure 5.1 provides an outline of the personal and situational factors I now go on to summarize.

Psychological Orientations to Power

In his seminal work on power and motivation, McClelland (1975) presented a developmental framework for categorizing people's experiences and expressions of power that to a large degree mirrors the four perspectives on power previously

Figure 5.1. Personal and Situational Factors in Power.

Personal Factors (Power Orientations)	Situational Factors

• Cognitive
  – Ideologies: radical, pluralist, unitary
  – Implicit theories
  – Social-dominance orientation
• Motivational
  – Need for power
  – Authoritarianism
• Moral
  – Moral development
  – Egalitarianism
  – Moral scope
	• Deep structure
	  – History
	  – Roles
	  – Norms
	  – Hierarchy
	  – Distribution of wealth
	• Goal interdependence
	• Culture: power distance

summarized from the literature. He argued that people everywhere seek power by (1) obtaining support from others, often through a dependence relationship; (2) establishing one's autonomy and independence from others; (3) assertively acting on, influencing, and dominating others; or (4) becoming part of an organization or a group. He labeled these orientations support, autonomy, assertion, and togetherness.

McClelland proposed that as people mature, they progress through each of these stages of development and orientations to power, ideally moving toward the stage of togetherness. He also stressed, however, that each of the four power orientations may be useful in a given situation, and that problems typically arise for people when they become fixated on any one orientation (such as assertion or competitive), or when an individual's chronic orientation fits poorly with the particular realities or demands of a situation. From this perspective, an individual's flexibility and responsiveness to changes in his or her environment can be seen as critical to the ability to effectively respond to situations involving power.

Deutsch expanded the idea of people's psychological orientation to social situations beyond the motivational realm, to include two additional modes of human experience: the cognitive and the moral (see also Chapter Fourteen). He defined one's psychological orientation as "a more or less consistent complex of cognitive, motivational, and moral orientations to a given situation that serve to guide one's behavior and responses in that situation" (1985, p. 74). Deutsch distinguished these three modes by defining one's cognitive orientation as the "structures of expectations that help orient the individual cognitively to the situation"; one's motivational orientation as the "personal needs and motives" that are valued and potentially gratified in the situation; and one's moral orientation as the mutual obligations and rights, the "shoulds" and "oughts" with regard to all parties in the situation.

These three modes tend to cluster together and mutually influence one another, but they are distinct and therefore can help us think specifically about people's internal experiences of power in conflict. For example, the CEO in our earlier example may have been operating from a chronically competitive cognitive orientation to power (power over) and therefore interpreted the employees' offer as a competitive tactic ("they're trying to humiliate me or ingratiate themselves"), was motivated to win at all costs, and saw this as morally legitimate because of a belief that low-level employees must make sacrifices for the greater good of the organization. Ultimately, one's psychological orientation affects one's behavior through assessing the feasibility of a given action (do I have the capacity to act, and what will the consequences be?), unless the orientation is excessively chronic.

As indicated in Figure 5.1, many of the individual difference variables associated with power in the literature can be seen as operating to influence some aspect of people's psychological orientation to power through the cognitive, motivational, or moral modes. Each of these personal factors offers a potential explanation for people's chronic fixation on a given type of power orientation.

Cognitive Orientation. Burrell and Morgan (1979) have identified people's ideological frames of reference as central to their approach to power. These frames are comprehensive belief systems about the nature of relations between individuals and society. They classified three types of ideological frames: the unitary, the radical, and the pluralist. From the unitary view, society is seen as an integrated whole where the interests of the individual and society are one and where power can be largely ignored and assumed to be used benevolently by those in authority to further the mutual goals of all parties. This perspective is common in collectivist cultures and in some benevolent business organizations.

In contrast, the radical frame pictures society as comprising antagonistic class interests that are "characterized by deep-rooted social and political cleavages, and held together as much by coercion as by consent" (Morgan, 1986, p. 186). This perspective, epitomized by Marxist doctrine, focuses on unequal distribution of power in society and the significant role that this plays in virtually every aspect of our lives.

The pluralist frame views society as a space where different groups "bargain and compete for a share in the balance of power . . . to realize a negotiated order that creates unity out of diversity" (Morgan, 1986, p.185). Power is seen as distributed more or less equally among the groups, and as the primary medium through which conflicts are resolved. This pluralist view of power is prevalent in the many forms of liberal democracies.

Each distinct ideological frame engenders its own "structures of expectations" about what one can anticipate, what one should attend to, and therefore how one should respond to issues regarding power and conflict. For example, Stephens (1994) has discussed how these ideological frames lead various conflict practitioners to use conflict resolution processes to achieve vastly disparate objectives (unitary ideologies favor systems maintenance, whereas radical ideologies favor systems change) and into fundamentally different arenas for work (alternative dispute resolution to achieve community unity versus peace education and activism to produce community change).

My work on *implicit power theories* (Coleman, 1997) has focused on the effects of cognitive structures regarding power on how we automatically process social information. This approach, a social-cognitive approach, characterizes the social environment as the source of varied and complex information, and people as cognitive misers who have a limited capacity to process such information. In response to the overwhelming amount of stimuli, we often rely actively on our beliefs, stereotypes, and assumptions to help us make meaning out of unfamiliar social situations.

Implicit theories function in this manner, but they do so automatically and often out of our awareness, to focus our attention and guide how we process and comprehend information about the self and social situations. In turn, these theories contribute to developing a meaning system with regard to a specific phenomenon. My research in this area has demonstrated that individuals differ in their core assumptions regarding power: whether it is limited or expandable, competitive or cooperative, or equal or unequal. In other words, some people automatically assume that power relations are inherently antiegalitarian or win-lose, while others can see a potential for collaborative power sharing.

These differences have been shown to affect people's willingness to share power when in positions of authority. This research has also demonstrated, however, that the social environment can influence the use of these implicit theories by making these assumptions more or less cognitively salient. For example, if a child attends a school that stresses competition in most areas—for grades, for positions of leadership, and for excellence in sports—you would expect that over time the child would develop an understanding of school life as inherently win-lose. This understanding would considerably influence many of the child's decisions and choices in school and subsequent peer relations. This example highlights the importance of the interplay between people and their surrounding environment.

A related individual difference has been labeled *social dominance orientation* (Pratto, Sidanius, Stallworth, and Malle, 1994), or SDO, and is based on research predicting social and political attitudes, beliefs, and values regarding intergroup relations from an individual's SDO. SDO is defined as a very general orientation expressing antiegalitarianism; a view of human existence as zero-sum with relentless competition between groups; the desire for generalized, hierarchical relationships between groups; and a desire for in-group dominance over outgroups. The research on SDO has identified consistent gender differences in women's and men's levels of SDO (Sidanius, Pratto, and Bobo, 1994), with men having significantly higher levels of SDO than women. We could expect this type of general orientation to group relations to contribute to a chronically competitive orientation to power differences.

Motivational Orientation. Two important areas of research shed light on people's motivational orientations to power. The first is authoritarianism (Adorno, Frenkl-Brunswik, Levinson, and Sanford, 1950), which involves an exaggerated need to submit to and identify with strong authority. Originating from psychodynamic theory, this syndrome is thought to stem from early rearing by parents who use harsh and rigid forms of discipline, demand unquestioning obedience, are overly conscious of distinctions of status, and are contemptuous or exploitative toward those of lower status. The child internalizes the values of the parents and therefore is inclined toward a dominant, punitive approach to power relations. Individuals high in authoritarianism tend to favor absolute obedience to authority and resist personal freedom. These tendencies would most likely orient one toward either authoritarian or submissive orientation to power in conflict situations, depending on the relative status of the other party.

The second area of research, need for power ("nPower"; McClelland, 1975; McClelland and Burnham, 1976), has been identified as a difference of motivational orientation where people high on nPower experience great satisfaction in influencing people and arousing strong emotions in them. Individuals high on nPower seek out positions of authority. This orientation, however, is thought to interact with another personality difference, known as activity inhibition (see also Chapter Fourteen). This is, essentially, the individual's level of self-control and general orientation to others.

These two traits combine to produce two separate types of power orientation: the "personalized power orientation" and the "socialized power orientation." Individuals high on nPower and low on activity inhibition exhibit a more personalized power orientation, exemplified by a tendency to dominate others in an attempt to satisfy one's hedonistic desires. Individuals with high nPower and high activity inhibition tend to exhibit socialized power orientation, using power for the good of a cause, an organization, or an institution.

McClelland (1975) postulated that individual power orientations develop through various stages, with the personalized orientation emerging at an earlier stage of development and the socialized orientation at a later stage. The personal-social separation is a useful distinction between the destructive and constructive sides of power; it contradicts the notion of Lord Acton that all power necessarily corrupts.

Moral Orientation. Kohlberg's work on moral development (1963, 1969) has important implications for people's moral orientation to power. He, too, proposed that humans move from lower to higher levels of moral development and that the levels are attained in a fixed series of stages. At the first, preconventional, level, moral thinking is determined by the consequences of actions (punishment or rewards). In the second, the conventional level, actions are directed by a desire to conform to the expectations of others or to uphold socially accepted values and rules. The third level, the postconventional level, represents advanced moral development. Behavior at this level is directed by self-accepted moral principles. These levels result in six stages of morality:

Stage 1   Punishment orientation

Stage 2   Pleasure-seeking orientation

Stage 3   Good-boy or good-girl orientation

Stage 4   Authority orientation

Stage 5   Social-contract orientation

Stage 6   Morality of individual principles

Kohlberg argued that people advance through these stages at different rates, and that many people fail to reach the higher stages of morality. Individuals at lower levels of moral development tend to be oriented toward their own pleasure or avoidance of punishment and are therefore less concerned with obligations or the rights of the other with whom they are in conflict. Individuals in the latter stages place much higher value on justice, dignity, and equality.

Differences in the value of egalitarianism also affect one's moral orientation to power. Egalitarianism is the ideal of equality of power for all and the belief in the opportunity for people to participate equally in the decisions that control their lives (Deutsch, 1985). My research on implicit power theories found a significant positive relationship between people's implicit ideals regarding egalitarianism and their willingness to share power with people in low power (Coleman, 1997).

Even high moral development and egalitarianism may be affected by another fundamental psychosocial process, known as the scope of justice. This has been defined as "a psychological boundary for fairness . . . within which concerns with justice and moral rules govern our conduct" (Opotow, 1995, p.347). Individuals or groups within our moral boundaries are seen as deserving of the same fair, moral treatment as we deserve. Individuals or groups outside these boundaries are seen as undeserving of this same treatment. To us, their harm is of less concern, more understandable, and even justifiable. This is moral exclusion, in which we exclude individuals or members of groups from our scope of justice. Individuals vary in the narrowness of their scope of justice and in the targets of their exclusion, with some people limiting moral treatment only to members of their own race, gender, class, neighborhood, and so on. Others may extend their scope of justice to all humans or to all living things. One's scope of justice can dichotomize the moral orientation into areas of high and low moral concern, even when individuals are considered by some to be highly moral and fair (see Chapters Two and Twenty).

As in Chapter Two, Adolph Eichmann comes to mind as a cautionary example. Accused of sharing responsibility for the deaths of millions of European Jews during World War II, he was also reported to be a loyal son, a caring husband and father, a good officer, and an upstanding member of his church. The millions of prisoners and victims whose transport to death he supervised were apparently not included in what he considered to be his moral community. Eichmann explained his actions under interrogation: "In actual fact, I was merely a little cog in the machinery that carried out the directives of the German Reich. It was really none of my business. Yet what is there to 'admit'? I carried out my order" (Kohlberg, 1969).

From Kohlberg's perspective, this is clearly Stage 1 and Stage 2 moral reasoning, obedient and self-focused. Despite his higher standards for conduct within his own community, the Jewish people didn't matter.

Other individual differences—as wide-ranging as interpersonal orientation (high or low sensitivity to others), Machiavellianism, interpersonal trust, and gender—are relevant to discussing people's psychological orientation to power, but space does not allow for further elaboration (see Lewicki, Litterer, Minton, and Saunders, 1994, for discussion of these variables). Each of the cognitive, motivational, and moral differences described here can work in concert to contribute to a chronic psychological orientation and fixation on any one of the power orientations (such as powerlessness). These orientations affect how people perceive conflict, how they evaluate authority relations, and ultimately the decisions and responses they make to power differences in conflict situations. However, except for extreme cases, the influences of these individual difference factors need to be understood as operating in interaction with the individual's environment.

SITUATIONAL FACTORS: STRUCTURE, INTERDEPENDENCE, AND CULTURE

Feminists argue that power differences may begin with our images but persist through the structures and institutions of a society. Thus, power in any given situation must be understood in its historical context. History is composed of the decisions and actions, victories and defeats, justices and injustices experienced by those who came before us: members of our families, our gender, our communities, our race, our nation, and so on. These cumulative experiences have in many ways defined the rules of the power game. This historical perspective emphasizes the influences exerted on power by such factors as class and race relations, intergroup conflicts of interest and social competition, inequity between social groups on highly valued dimensions, opportunity structures and the educational systems that perpetuate them, the relative stability of status and power differences, and the perceived legitimacy of all of these factors. Understanding the historical context forces us to look beyond the current surface manifestations of power and into its deep structure. From this perspective, people are seen as agents or carriers of power relations embedded in the wider structure of history and society. They can learn to understand the rules, but perhaps do little to change them.

For example, one aspect of the structure of many conflict situations is the roles people assume. Role theory, a sociological perspective, views social processes such as power relations as if they were scripted theater. The theory holds that the roles we have in society or in our organizations (manager, laborer) often dictate the social rules or norms for our behavior. These social norms establish shared expectations among members of a system, which in most cases came into existence long before the individuals who now respond to them. It argues that we largely act out these preexisting scripts in our institutions and organizations, and that it is these roles, these shared norms and scripts, that dictate our experiences, our expectations, and our responses to power. So, for example, role theory argues that the CEO from our initial example was acting more or less consistently with what would be expected from someone in his position. Furthermore, if any one of his employees had been in the same position, they would have made essentially the same decision. It is within the underlying structure of the organization and its place in society that power relations between groups are largely predetermined and thereby constrained and perpetuated.

One of the most blatant examples of the power of roles is in the classic social psychological experiment conducted at Stanford University on the effects of deindividuated roles on behavior in institutional settings (Haney, Banks, and Zimbardo, 1973). Student subjects were recruited for this study and randomly assigned to play the role of either a guard or a prisoner in a simulated prison environment for two weeks. From the very beginning, the "guards" abused and denigrated the "prisoners," showing increasingly brutal, sadistic, and dehumanizing behavior over time. The research observations were so disturbing that the study was called off after only six days.

A related component of structure is hierarchy. Barnard (1946) argued that distinctions of status and authority are ultimately necessary for effective functioning and survival of any group above a certain size. As a result, most groups form some type of formal or informal hierarchical structure to function efficiently. Often, the greater advantages associated with higher positions lead to competition for these scarce positions, and an attempt by those in authority to maintain their status.

However, a hierarchical structure does not necessarily lead to competitive or destructive power relations within a group. In a series of studies on power and goal interdependence, Tjosvold (1997) found that variation in goal interdependence (task, reward, and outcome goals) affected the likelihood of constructive use of power between high-power and low-power persons. Cooperative goals, when compared to competitive and independent goals, were found to induce "higher expectations of assistance, more assistance, greater support, more persuasion and less coercion and more trusting and friendly attitudes" between superiors and subordinates (Tjosvold, 1997, p. 297). The abundant research on cooperative and competitive goal interdependence (see Chapters One and Three in this handbook) has consistently demonstrated the contrasting effects of these goal structures on people's attitudes and behaviors in social relations. Among other things, competition fosters "attempts to enhance the power differences between oneself and the other," in contrast with cooperation, which fosters "an orientation toward enhancing mutual power rather than power differences"

(Deutsch, 1973). In cooperative situations, people want others to perform effectively and to use their joint resources to promote common objectives. Tjosvold (1997) found that when employees feel empowered and believe they are in a cooperative relationship with their superior, it can lead to an increase in constructive controversy between the parties, resulting in achievement of more satisfying outcomes.

The culture in which we are immersed is another important influence on our experience of power. Hofstede (1980) identified *power distance* as a dimension of social relations that is determined by and varies across cultures. He defined it as the extent to which the less-powerful persons in a society accept inequality in power and consider it as normal. Hofstede argued that inequality exists within every culture, but the degree to which it is tolerated by society varies from one culture to another. So, for example, in some high-power-distance cultures (such as in parts of India) the notion of empowering employees through participation in decisions and delegation of authority is considered inappropriate and insubordinate by the employees themselves. This cultural difference regarding power not only is the source of much cross-cultural misunderstanding and conflict but it also significantly affects how individuals from different cultures respond to conflicts with others in high and low power.

IMPLICATIONS FOR CONFLICT

This discussion has several major implications for power and conflict. A sample conflict between an adolescent girl, Hannah, and her parents over weekend curfews offers a good illustration. Hannah recently turned sixteen and has argued that having reached that milestone, she should be allowed to stay out later on weekend nights than the 10:30 curfew previously established by her parents. Hannah's parents strongly disagree and have informed her that there will be no change in her curfew until she turns eighteen.

The Prevailing Approach to Power

A competitive orientation to power currently dominates the approach to power of social scientists, as well as of power holders. The majority of scholars in the social sciences investigate power through the competitive lens. Analysis of family conflict from this perspective emphasizes the imbalance of power inherent in the conflict and the various resources available to each side for purposes of altering the balance in their favor, thereby gaining the necessary leverage to prevail in the dispute. It would also be oriented to the many strategies, tactics, and countertactics that the parties could use to gain the upper hand in the situation. Although useful, this perspective ignores many other critical aspects of power, particularly the potential for the parents and adolescent to develop power with each other by approaching their dilemma as a mutual problem for the family to solve. The field of conflict resolution would be well served if scholar-practitioners developed enhanced understanding and improved methods for the cooperative, dependent, and independent approaches to power in conflict.

From a practical perspective, a chronic competitive approach to power has harmful consequences. Deutsch (1973) pointed out that reliance on competitive and coercive strategies of influence by power holders produces alienation and resistance in those subjected to the power. This, in turn, limits the power holder's ability to use other types of power based on trust (such as normative, expert, referent, and reward power) and increases the demand for scrutiny and control of subordinates. A parent who demands obedience from his adolescent in a climate of mutual distrust fosters more distrust and must be prepared to keep the youngster under surveillance. If the goal of the power holder is to achieve commitment from subordinates (rather than merely short-term compliance), excessive reliance on a power-over strategy eventually proves to be costly as well as largely ineffective. Research by Kipnis (1976) supported this contention by demonstrating that a leader's dependence on coercive strategies of influence has considerable costs in undermining relationships with followers and in compromising goal achievement.

Furthermore, it is evident that when power holders have a chronic competitive perspective on power, it reduces their chance to see sharing power with members of low-power groups as an opportunity to enhance their own personal or environmental power. From this chronic competitive perspective, power sharing is typically experienced as a threat to achieving one's goals, and the opportunities afforded by power sharing are invisible. If the father views the conflict over curfew as a win-lose power struggle, he is unlikely to reflect on the advantages of involving his daughter in reaching a solution and thereby engendering in her an improved sense of responsibility, collaboration, and trust.

The Influence of Perspective on Strategy

Our perspectives on power influence our strategies in conflict. As previously indicated, how we think about power affects how we perceive conflict and how we respond to it. Salacuse (forthcoming) applied the four power orientations to a discussion of four grand strategies for seeking power and achieving goals in international conflict resolution. Like the four orientations, these strategies, which he called dependence, autonomy, assertion, and community, can be seen as different approaches to managing power differences in conflict, each being more or less effective in a given situation.

With a dependent strategy, low-power parties seek help and support from more powerful others either by becoming dependent on them or making use of their dependence. For example, the daughter could seek support from an aunt or a family friend who shares her perspective on curfews and is willing and able to influence her parents' thinking on the subject.

This is in contrast with an autonomous strategy, where parties seek to limit their dependence on the other by restricting their interactions or by removing themselves from the conflict or the relationship altogether. One method of reducing dependence in conflict is by developing a strong BATNA (best alternative to a negotiated agreement; Fisher, Ury, and Patton, 1991). The adolescent might explore other means of getting her social needs met, such as having sleepovers at her home or organizing daytime parties during the weekend. Having these as options reduces her need to remain in conflict with her parents over the curfew.

An assertive strategy is the traditional power-over approach of the powerful. This is the unilateral attempt to use the power resources at one's disposal to impose a solution that one favors. This approach is contrasted with the community strategy, whereby a party attempts to become a member of an organization or a community that includes the other. If the curfew conflict escalates and persists, it might be useful for the family to join a parent-adolescent support group where family conflict of this sort is explored openly and normalized. Joining groups or organizations that involve the other party can put the conflict into a broader perspective and help emphasize the commonalities that both parties share. Once again, what is important is that individuals (and groups and nations) avoid becoming chronically committed to any one strategy, instead remaining skilled at each of them, particularly when trying to achieve enhanced environmental or personal power.

Cooperative Conflict and Power With

Cooperative conflict leads to power with. When conflicts occur in situations that have cooperative task, reward, or outcome interdependence structures, or between disputants sharing a cooperative psychological orientation, there is more cooperative power. In other words, in these situations conflict is probably framed as a mutual problem to be solved by both parties, which leads to an increased tendency to minimize power differences between the disputants and to mutually enhance each other's power in order to work together effectively to achieve their shared goals. Thus, if the parents can recognize that their daughter's social needs and their own needs to have a close family life are positively linked, then they may be more likely to involve her in the problem-solving and decision-making processes, thereby enhancing her power and their ability to find mutually satisfying solutions to the conflict.

Perception of Power

Perception of power matters. Saul Alinsky (1971) said, "Power is not only what you have, but what the enemy thinks you have." Often, initial assessments of another's power are erroneous because they are based on aggregates of relative power (the sum total of another's power in comparison to my own), and not on the other's *relevant* power resources or on the other's efficacy in implementing the strategies relevant to the conflict at hand (Salacuse, forthcoming). This typically leads to a sense of overconfidence on the part of the power holders and to a sense of helplessness for those in low power. In fact, Hannah could have considerable power and influence in terms of the harmony, cohesion, and stress level of the family.

Effective Power

The most critical questions to ask in any conflict situation are: "What do I really want or need in this situation?" and "How can I use the power available to me effectively here?" This may mean restraining one's chronic impulses and stopping to assess such things as short-term and long-term objectives, the realm of power that is of primary concern to oneself (personal, relational, environmental), the types of power resource available that are relevant to a given situation, the best strategy given one's objectives, and the likely responses of the other party to using such strategies. If the mother's desire is to improve her strained relationship with her daughter by spending more time together on the weekends, then using a coercive strategy to keep her at home is sure to prove largely ineffective.

Context and Power

The context drives the person, who drives the context. It is critical to bear in mind that power is typically context-dependent and that even the most powerful people are powerless under certain conditions. In these situations, it is the norms, roles, policies, structures, and cultures that are also responsible for power differences and must also be targeted for change. Hannah's parents may be responding in a nonnegotiable manner due to the way their own parents behaved or the way friends of theirs act or because of some unexamined assumptions about what constitutes "good parenting" in our society. This could lead them into responses and decisions that they themselves, upon reflection, may disagree with.

Tendencies and Strategies for Members of High-Power Groups

The overwhelming evidence seems to indicate that the powerful tend to like power, use it, justify having it, and attempt to keep it. The powerful also tend to be more satisfied and less personally discontent than those not enjoying high power; they have a longer time perspective and more freedom to act and therefore can plan further into the future. These higher levels of satisfaction lead to vested interests in the status quo and development of rationales for maintaining power, such as the power holders' belief in their own superior competence and superior moral value. Kipnis (1976) argued that much of this may be the result of the corrupting nature of power itself. He proposed that having power and exercising it successfully over time lead to acquired "taste for power," inflated sense of self, devaluing of those of lesser power, and temptation to use power illegally to enhance one's position.

Fiske (1993) has demonstrated that powerful people tend to pay less attention to powerless people since they view them as not affecting their outcomes, they are often too busy to pay attention, and they are often motivated by their own high need to dominate others. Inattention to the powerless makes powerful people more vulnerable to use of stereotypes or implicit theories when interacting with the powerless. Mindell (1995) explained the state of unawareness that having privilege often fosters in this way: "Rank is a drug. The more you have, the less aware you are of how it effects others negatively" (p. 56).

Thus, in conflict situations high power holders and members of high-power groups (HPGs) often neglect to analyze—as well as underestimate—the power of low power holders and members of low-power groups (LPGs; Salacuse, forthcoming). Additionally, they usually attempt to dominate the relationship, to use pressure tactics, to offer few concessions, to have high aspirations and to use contentious tactics. HPGs, therefore, make it difficult to arrive at negotiated agreements that are satisfactory to all parties.

When met with a substantial challenge to their power from LPGs, the common responses of members of HPGs fall into the categories of repression or ambivalent tolerance (Duckitt, 1992). If the validity of the concerns of the LPG are not recognized, HPGs may use force to quell the challenge of the LPG. But if the challenges are acknowledged, HPGs may respond with tolerant attitudes and expressions of concern—though ultimately with resistance to implementing any real change in their power relations (Duckitt, 1992).

In light of their unreflective tendency to dominate, it becomes critical for members of HPGs to be aware of the likelihood that they will elicit resistance and alienation (from members of LPGs with whom they are in conflict) through using illegitimate techniques, inappropriate sanctions, or influence that is considered excessive for the situation (Deutsch, 1973). The cost to the HPG is not only ill will but also the need to be continuously vigilant and mobilized to prevent retaliation by the LPG.

Tendencies and Strategies for Members of Low-Power Groups

Not surprisingly, the tendencies for members of LPGs are opposite to those of members of HPGs, with one exception. LPG members tend to be dependent on others, to have short time perspectives, to be unable to plan far ahead, and to be generally discontent. Often, the LPG members attempt to rid themselves of the negative feelings associated with their experiences of powerlessness and dependence (such as rage and fear) by projecting blame onto even less powerful groups or onto relatively safe in-group targets. The latter can result in a breakdown of LPG in-group solidarity (Kanter, 1977). Intense negative feelings may also limit the LPG members' capacity to respond constructively in conflict with HPGs and impel such destructive impulses as violent destruction of property (Deutsch, 1973).

Several tactics can enhance the power of LPGs. The first is for the group to amass more power for assertion—either by increasing their own resources, organization, cohesion, and motivation for change or by decreasing the resources of (or increasing the costs for) the HPGs. The latter can be accomplished through acts of civil disobedience, militancy, or by what Alinsky (1971) described as "Jujitsu tactics": actually using the imbalance of power in the relationship against the more powerful. Another approach available to LPG members is to attempt to appeal to the better side of the members of the HPG, say, trying (through such tactics as ingratiation, guilt, and helplessness) to induce them to use their power more benevolently or by trying to raise the HPG's awareness of any injustice that they may be party to (see Deutsch's discussion in Chapter Two of awakening the sense of injustice). LPGs can also develop skills in implementing the strategies of autonomy, dependence, and community.

IMPLICATIONS FOR TRAINING IN CONFLICT RESOLUTION

In conclusion, we offer a few propositions from this chapter for use in designing training approaches for power and conflict. The general goals of such training are to enhance people's understanding of power, to facilitate reflection of their own tendencies when in low or high power, and to increase their ability to use it effectively when in conflict.

- Training should help students understand and reflect critically on their commonly held images of and assumptions about power, as well as the sources of these assumptions and images.

- Students should become aware of their own chronic tendencies to react in situations in which they have superior or inferior power to others.

- Students should become emotionally and cognitively aware of the privileges or injustices they and others experience as a result of their skin color, gender, economics, class, age, religion, sexual orientation, physical status, and the like.

- In a conflict situation, students should be able to analyze for the other as well as themselves the resources of power, their orientation to power, and the strategies and tactics for effectively implementing their available power. Students should also be able to identify and develop the necessary skills for implementing their available power in the conflict.

- Students should also be able to distinguish between conflicts in which power with, power from, and power under, rather than power over, are appropriate orientations to the conflict.

Here is an exercise, developed by Susan Fountain, showing the type of training that gives students simple yet rich experience useful for exploring and examining many of the principles I have just described.

Participants are asked to leave the training room momentarily. It is then organized into two work areas, with several tables grouped to accommodate four or five people per group in each area. In one work area, the tables are filled with markers, colored pencils, paste, poster board, magazines, scissors, and other colorful and decorative items. In the other work area, the tables receive one piece of white typing paper and two black lead pencils. The participants are then randomly assigned to two groups and allowed into the room and seated.

The groups are then told that their objective is to use the materials they have been given to generate a definition of power. They are informed that once each group has completed its task, they will display their definition and everyone will vote on the best definition generated from the class. The groups then begin their work on the task. The trainers actively support and participate in the work of the high-resource group, while attempting to avoid contact with members of the low-resource group. When the work is complete, the class votes on the best definition of power. The participants are then brought into a circle to debrief.

In my experience with this exercise, many useful learning opportunities present themselves. For example, the types of definition generated can differ greatly between the high-resource and low-resource groups. The former tend to produce definitions that are mostly positive, superficial, and largely shaped by the mainstream images from the magazines (beauty, status, wealth, computers, and so on). The low-resource group definitions may be more radical and rageful, often challenging the status quo—and even the authority of the trainers. One image listed a series of negative emotions and obscenities circled by pencils that were then jabbed into the paper like daggers. These starkly contrasting definitions often lead to discussion that identifies the source of these differences.

It is also fairly common in this exercise for many members of the high-resource group to remain completely unaware of the disparity in resources until it is explicitly pointed out to them at the conclusion of the exercise. Members of the low-resource groups, in contrast, are all very aware of the discrepancies. This can be a very powerful moment. Again, the actual difference in resources is minor, but it is symbolic of more meaningful ones, and the participants begin to make the connection to other areas in their lives where they are often blind to their own privilege.

Finally, members of the low-resource group often attempt during the exercise to alter the imbalance of power. Various strategies are employed, including demanding or stealing resources, ingratiation, playing on the guilt of high-resource group members, appealing to higher authorities (the trainers), or challenging the legitimacy of the exercise. Of course, there are also members of the low-resource group who simply accept their lot and follow the rules. These choices are all opportunities to (1) explore what sort of strategies and tactics can be useful when in low power, (2) have participants reflect on their own inclinations and reactions in the situation (whether in low or high power), and (3) examine the beliefs and assumptions on which many of the strategies were based.

CONCLUSION

Rosabeth Kanter once said that power is the last dirty word. I have attempted to challenge that notion in this chapter, and to emphasize the potential for an expansive approach to power in conflict. The realists of the day may remain skeptical, for the world is filled with evidence to the contrary: evidence of coercive power holders, of power hoarding, and of the defensiveness and resistance of the powerful under conditions that cry out for change. Perhaps the time is ripe for a new approach to power.

References

Adorno, T. W., Frenkl-Brunswik, E., Levinson, D. J., and Sanford, R. N. *The Authoritarian Personality.* New York: HarperCollins, 1950.

Alinsky, S. D. *Rules for Radicals: A Practical Primer for Realistic Radicals.* New York: Random House, 1971.

Barnard, C. I. "Functions and Pathology of Status Systems in Formal Organizations." In W. F. Whyte (ed.), *Industry and Society.* New York: McGraw-Hill, 1946.

Burrell, G., and Morgan, G. *Sociological Paradigms and Organizational Analysis.* Portsmouth, N.H.: Heinemann, 1979.

Coleman, P. T. "Psychological Resistance to and Facilitation of Power-Sharing in Organizations." *Dissertation Abstracts,* 1997.

Dahl, R. A. "Power." In D. L. Sills (ed.), *International Encyclopedia of the Social Sciences.* Vol. 12. Old Tappan, N.J.: Macmillan, 1968.

Deutsch, M. *The Resolution of Conflict: Constructive and Destructive Processes.* New Haven: Yale University Press, 1973.

Deutsch, M. *Distributive Justice: A Social Psychological Perspective.* New Haven: Yale University Press, 1985.

Duckitt, J. H. *The Social Psychology of Prejudice.* New York: Praeger, 1992.

Fisher, R. J., Ury, W., and Patton, B. *Getting to Yes: Negotiating Agreement Without Giving In.* (2nd ed.) New York: Penguin, 1991.

Fiske, S. T "Controlling Other People: The Impact of Power on Stereotyping." *American Psychologist,* 1993, *48,* 621–628.

Follett, M. P. "Power." In E. M. Fox and L. Urwick (eds.), *Dynamic Administration: The Collected Papers of Mary Parker Follett.* London: Pitman, 1973. (Originally published 1924.)

Haney, C., Banks, C., and Zimbardo, P. "Interpersonal Dynamics in a Simulated Prison." *International Journal of Criminology and Penology,* 1973, *1,* 69–97.

Harvey, J. B. "Some Thoughts About Organizational Backstabbing." *Academy of Management Executive,* 1989, *3,* 271–277.

Hofstede, G. *Culture's Consequences: International Differences in Work-Related Values.* Thousand Oaks, Calif.: Sage, 1980.

Kanter, R. M. *Men and Women of the Corporation.* New York: Basic Books, 1977.

Kipnis, D. *The Powerholders.* Chicago: University of Chicago Press, 1976.

Kohlberg, L. "Moral Development and Identification." In H. Stevenson (ed.), *Child Psychology (62nd Yearbook of the National Society for the Study of Education).* Chicago: University of Chicago Press, 1963.

Kohlberg, L. "The Cognitive-Developmental Approach to Socialization." In D. A. Goslin (ed.), *Handbook of Socialization Theory and Research.* Skokie, Ill.: Rand McNally, 1969.

Lewicki, R. J., Litterer, J. A., Minton, J. W., and Saunders, D. M. *Negotiation.* (2nd ed.) Burr Ridge, Ill.: Irwin, 1994.

McClelland, D. C. *Power: The Inner Experience.* New York: Irvington, 1975.

McClelland, D. C., and Burnham, D. H. "Power Is the Great Motivator." *Harvard Business Review,* 1976, *54*(2), 100–110.

Michels, R. *Political Parties: A Sociological Study of the Oligarchical Tendencies of Modern Democracy.* New York: Dover, 1911.

Mindell, A. *Sitting in the Fire: Large Group Transformation Using Conflict and Diversity.* Portland, Ore.: Lao Tse Press, 1995.

Morgan, G. *Images of Organization.* London: Sage, 1986.

Opotow, S. "Drawing the Line: Social Categorization, Moral Exclusion, and the Scope of Justice." In B. B. Bunker and J. Z. Rubin (eds.), *Cooperation, Conflict, and Justice: Essays Inspired by the Work of Morton Deutsch.* New York: Russell Sage Foundation, 1995.

Pratto, F., Sidanius, J., Stallworth, L. M., and Malle, B. F. "Social Dominance Orientation: A Personality Variable Predicting Social and Political Attitudes." *Journal of Personality and Social Psychology,* 1994, *67,* 741–763.

Russell, B. *Power: A New Social Analysis.* New York: Norton, 1938.

Salacuse, J. W. "How Should the Lamb Negotiate with the Lion?" In *Power in International Negotiations.* Cambridge, Mass.: Harvard University Press, forthcoming.

Salancik, G. R., and Pfeffer, J. "Who Gets Power and How They Hold On to It: A Strategic Contingency Model of Power." *Organizational Dynamics,* 1977, *5,* 3–21.

Sashkin, M. "Participative Management Is an Ethical Imperative." *Organizational Dynamics,* 1984, *12*(4), 4–22.

Sidanius, J., Pratto, F., and Bobo, L. "Social Dominance Orientation and the Political Psychology of Gender: A Case of Invariance?" *Journal of Personality and Social Psychology,* 1994, *67,* 998–1011.

Stephens, J. B. "Gender Conflict: Connecting Feminist Theory and Conflict Resolution Theory." In A. Taylor and J. B. Miller (eds.), *Gender and Conflict.* Cresskill, N.J.: Hampton Press, 1994.

Tjosvold, D. "Unequal Power Relationships Within a Cooperative or Competitive Context." *Journal of Applied Social Psychology,* 1981, *11,* 137–150.

Tjosvold, D. "The Leadership Relationship in Hong Kong: Power, Interdependence, and Controversy." In K. Leung, U. Kim, S. Yamaguchi, and Y. Kashima (eds.), *Progress in Asian Social Psychology.* Vol. 1. New York: Wiley, 1997.

CHAPTER SIX

Communication and Conflict

Robert M. Krauss
Ezequiel Morsella

Battle, n. A method of untying with the teeth
a political knot that would not yield to the tongue.
—Ambrose Bierce, *The Devil's Dictionary* (1911)

When neighbors feud, lovers quarrel, or nations war, the predictable remedy prescribed by the voices of reason is communication. The prevailing view is that, faced with conflict, communicating is always the right thing to do: the U.N. Security Council encourages hostile countries to "hold talks," and marriage counselors advise quarreling couples to "express their feelings." So commonplace is the prescription that advice to the contrary seems anomalous; it's difficult to imagine the Secretary General imploring hostile nations to refrain from dialogue. The positive role of communication in ameliorating conflict seems so obvious that the premise is seldom given serious examination. Why should communicating be so helpful? Under what conditions does communication reduce conflict?

An attempt to answer such questions is the main burden of this chapter. In large part, the answers derive from considering what communication entails and what its instantiation precludes, that is, what it brings to, and demands of, particular situations. To understand the complex interplay between communication and conflict, we describe four paradigms of communication—four models of the communication process—and consider how each relates to conflict.[1] We briefly examine communicative mishaps that are potential sources of conflict and consider how and why communication can ameliorate conflict. Finally, we discuss some inherent limitations of communication as a peacemaker, limitations that result from the realization that understanding, the cardinal goal of communication, does not imply agreement, as Bierce's definition illustrates.

FOUR COMMUNICATION PARADIGMS

Before we begin discussing the intricate interplay of conflict and communication, it is important to specify what we mean by the latter term. The concept of communication is an important focus for fields as diverse as cell biology, computer science, ethology, linguistics, electrical engineering, sociology, anthropology, genetics, philosophy, semiotics, and literary theory, each of which employs the term in its unique way. Indeed, *communication* has been used in so many ways and in so many contexts that, as sociologist Thomas Luckman observes, it "has come to mean all things to all men."

Common to all conceptualizations of communication is the idea of information transfer. Information that originates in one part of a system is formulated into a message that is transmitted to another part of that system. As a result, information residing in one locus comes to be replicated at another. In human communication, the information corresponds to what are loosely referred to as ideas, or more scientifically, mental representations. In its most elemental form, human communication may be construed as the process by which ideas contained within one mind are conveyed to other minds. Though attractive because of its simplicity, this description fails to capture the true richness and subtlety of the process by which humans communicate, an enterprise that involves far more than automatically transferring ideas.

The Encoding-Decoding Paradigm

The most straightforward conceptualization of communication can be found in the *encoder-decoder* paradigm, in which communication *is* described as transferring information via codes. A code is a system that maps a set of signals onto a set of meanings. In the simplest kind of code, the mapping is one-to-one: for every signal there is one and only one meaning, and for every meaning there is one and only one signal. Such is the case for Morse Code. The sequence *dot dot dot dot* signifies the letter *H,* and only *H*; conversely, the letter *H* is uniquely represented by the sequence *dot dot dot dot,* and only that sequence.

Much of the communication in nonhuman species is based on the encoding-decoding principle. For example, vervet monkeys have two distinctive vocalizations for signaling the presence of their main predators: eagles and snakes. When one or the other signal is sounded, the vervets respond quickly and appropriately, scanning the sky in the first case, and scanning the grass around them in the second. Just as the Morse *dot dot dot dot* invariably designates the letter *H,* the vervet "aerial predator call" unambiguously signals the presence of predacious eagles.

Viewing human communication as encoding and decoding assumes a process in which an abstract proposition is (1) encoded in a message (that is, transformed into a signal whose elements have a one-to-one correspondence with the elements of the proposition) by the sender, (2) transmitted over a channel to the receiver, and (3) decoded into an abstract proposition that, it is believed, is isomorphic with the original one. For example, a speaker may formulate the proposition [John] [give book] [Mary] and thus transmit the message, "John, please give Mary the book." After receiving and processing the message, John presumably understands that he has been asked to give a particular book to someone named Mary.

One reason the received message may not be identical to the transmitted one is that all communication channels contribute some degree of noise (any undesired signal) to the message. The more signal there is relative to the amount of noise (the signal-to-noise ratio), the closer the transmitted message is to the received message; hence the more similar the received proposition is to the original one. A low signal-to-noise ratio can distort the meaning of a message, or even render it incomprehensible.

Noise, of course, has a deleterious effect on all communication, but its effect in the arena of conflict can be especially pernicious because it forces the recipient of a message to "fill in" information the noise has distorted. Given the antagonistic interpersonal orientation that parties in such situations often have, the filled-in information is more likely to worsen conflict than reduce it.

As an example of how noise may be introduced into communication, consider what happens when using third (or fourth or fifth) parties to transmit messages, in contrast to direct communication. As in the children's game of Telegraph, each party's successive retelling of a message is likely to introduce some distortion, so that when it arrives at the ultimate destination it may bear little resemblance to the original. There may be times when discussing delicate subjects is inadvisable in environments where misunderstanding is likely to occur. Also, whenever distortion is likely redundancy (multiply encoded messages) can be helpful. Restating the same idea in different forms does not guarantee its acceptance, but it should increase the probability of correct understanding.

Principle 1: **Avoid communication channels with low signal-to-noise ratios; if that is impossible, increase redundancy by restating the same idea in various forms.**

But noise is not the only factor that can compromise communication. Even if the transmitted and received messages are identical, the retrieved proposition may vary significantly from the original. Speaker and listener may be employing codes that differ subtly, and this may lead to misunderstanding. For example, lexical choice often reflects a speaker's implicit attitude toward the subject of the utterance. In a given situation, any one of several closely related terms (*woman, lady; Negro, black, African American; crippled, handicapped, disabled, physically challenged*) might serve adequately to designate or refer to a particular individual, yet each term may be associated with a somewhat different conceptualization of its referent, as part of a complex ideology or network of attitudes and values. If such ideologies or values are not shared, application of a term may be construed as antagonistic.

For example, at the height of the Cold War, an offhand comment made by Soviet Premier Nikita Khrushchev to a British diplomat was translated as "We will bury you." According to linguist Alan K. Melby, Khrushchev's remark, made in the context of a conversation about the competition between communism and capitalism, was essentially a restatement (in considerably more vivid language) of Marx's claim of communism's historic inevitability. Although "we will bury you" is an acceptable literal rendering of Khrushchev's words, an equally accurate, and contextually more appropriate, translation would have been, "We will be present at your burial." Such a rendering is consistent with Khrushchev's comment later in the same conversation that communism did not need to go to war to destroy capitalism, since the latter would eventually self-destruct. In the United States, the common interpretation of "we will bury you" was that *we* referred to the USSR, *you* meant the United States, and *bury* denoted *annihilate*. For many, especially those who viewed communism as a malign doctrine, the phrase became prima facie evidence of the USSR's malevolent intentions toward the United States.

The controversy over proper translation of Khrushchev's remark reveals a serious shortcoming of the encoder-decoder account of human communication: although language is in some respects a code, in other respects it is not. The fact that "we will bury you" could yield two equally "correct" renderings that differed so radically underscores the fact that humans do not use language simply as a set of signals mapped onto a set of meanings.

The Intentionalist Paradigm

The Khrushchev episode dramatically illustrates why encoding and decoding is not a good characterization of human communication. There was no question about the specific words Khrushchev had uttered, nor did competent translators differ on the ways the Russian utterance might be rendered in English. At issue was a more complicated question: What had Khrushchev *intended* the utterance to mean?

The view of communication implicit in the encoder-decoder position is that meanings of messages are fully specified by their elements—that meaning is encoded, and that decoding the message is equivalent to specifying its meaning. However, it's easy to demonstrate that this is often not the case. Unlike the vervet's aerial-predator call, which has an invariant significance, in human communication the same message can be understood to mean different things in different circumstances, and this fact necessitates a distinction between a message's literal meaning and its intended meaning. "Do you know what time it is?" is literally a question about what the addressee knows, but it is usually understood as a request. Although its grammatical mood is interrogative, it is conventionally taken to be an imperative; a reasonable paraphrase might be "Tell me the time." However, not all sentences of the form *Do you know X?* are intended as requests; "Do you know C++?" is likely to be understood as a question about familiarity with a programming language.

Understanding consists of recognizing communicative intentions—not the words used, but rather what speakers intend those words to mean. The intentionalist paradigm highlights the danger of participants' misconstruing each other's communicative intentions.

Principle 2: **When listening, try to understand the intended meaning of what your counterpart is saying.**

What might be called the Humpty Dumpty approach to communication ("When I use a word, it means just what I choose it to mean—neither more nor less") is a formula for disaster. In fact, communicators in a conflict situation should assume precisely the opposite of what Humpty Dumpty's maxim advises.

Principle 3: **When formulating a message, consider what the listener will take your words to mean.**

Had Khrushchev prefaced "We will bury you" with an allusion to Marx's claim of communism's historic inevitability, it's unlikely that the remark would have fanned the flames of the Cold War.

In conflict, misconstruals are especially likely because individuals interpret utterances to be consistent with their own attitudes. More than half a century ago, Solomon Asch (1946) demonstrated that the same message ("I hold that a little rebellion, now and then, is a good thing, and as necessary in the political world as storms are in the physical") would be interpreted quite differently depending on whether it was attributed to V. I. Lenin or to Thomas Jefferson (its actual author). The word *rebellion* can be interpreted in more than one way. Respondents' knowledge of the purported author was an important determinant of their interpretation of the word, and hence of the message's intended meaning.

The problem can become considerably more problematic when the parties to the conflict use different languages to communicate, as the furor caused by Khrushchev's remark illustrates. The translator had provided a literal English rendering of a Russian phrase that was intended to be understood figuratively. Nonliteral usage is a pervasive feature of language use. It adds enormously to our ability to formulate colorful and nuanced messages, but it does pose particular problems for a translator. In the first place, correctly apprehending the intended meaning of a nonliteral expression often requires cultural knowledge that goes beyond just technical mastery of the language. Understanding the significance of Ronald Reagan's challenge to Soviet Premier Leonid Brezhnev—"Go ahead, make my day!"—requires at least a vague awareness of the Clint Eastwood film it echoes, *Dirty Harry*. It can require considerable cognitive effort to apprehend a speaker's communicative intention, but the effort must be expended if the parties are to understand each other. In the absence of this effort, communication can become bogged down in a cycle of misinterpretation and denial:

PARTY 1: You said *X*.

PARTY 2: Yes, but it should have been obvious that I meant Y.

PARTY 1: Well, how was I to know you didn't mean *X*?

Given the flexible relationship between the literal and intended meanings of an utterance, it is remarkable how well we understand each other. Utterances that are intended to be understood nonliterally are a common feature of everyday language use. Although some canonical forms of nonliteral usage are so salient that they have names (irony, metaphor, hyperbole), more mundane examples of nonliteral usage pervade everyday talk. When we say that we understand what others say, we are implicitly claiming to comprehend what they intend for us to understand. The decoded meaning of the utterance certainly contributes to that intended meaning, but it is only part of it. Occasionally, misunderstandings do occur (as when an addressee interprets an ironic statement literally), but for the most part, we understand nonliterally intended utterances correctly, usually without being consciously aware of possible meanings that such an utterance could have in other contexts.

Despite facility in accomplishing this, the process by which a listener constructs the intention of an utterance is exceedingly complex and a matter of some contention among psycholinguists. In large part, it depends on the existence of knowledge that is shared between speaker and addressee, or common ground, as it is often called.

The most elemental kind of common ground communicators rely on is knowledge of the language they are speaking. But, as many an embarrassed tourist has discovered, much of the common ground that underlies language use derives from a complex matrix of shared cultural knowledge. Without this knowledge, many utterances are incomprehensible, or perhaps worse, interpreted incorrectly. This point is particularly relevant to use of language in conflict situations, especially when the conflict stems from differences in intention, goal, value, and ideology. To the extent that such variations derive from a lack of mutually shared knowledge, communication suffers. Understanding the importance of common ground in interpreting utterances points to one of the drawbacks of relying too heavily on an intentionalist interpretation of communication: the addressee cannot derive the intended meaning from a message if the meaning resides outside the realm of shared knowledge. Moreover, since what is common ground for a given speaker varies as a function of the addressee (that is, it varies from addressee to addressee), the speaker is obliged to generate only those utterances that he believes the addressee is capable of understanding.

Of course, it is within participants' power to make this easy or less easy to accomplish. Not only can addressees try to look beyond the speakers' words to the underlying communicative intention, but speakers can seek to express themselves in ways that will lead to the desired interpretation on their addressees' part. This, of course, requires one to see the world through the eyes of another.

The Perspective-Taking Paradigm

Perspective taking assumes that individuals perceive the world from differing vantage points, and that because the experiences of each individual are to some degree dependent on his or her vantage point, messages must be formulated with this perspective in mind. The late Roger Brown put the essential idea succinctly: "Effective coding requires that the point of view of the auditor be realistically imagined" (1965, p. 242). However, apart from the general admonition that the addressee's perspective be taken into account, it is not always clear how one should go about implementing what is sometimes referred to as the principle of audience design—the idea that messages should be designed to accord with an addressee's ability to comprehend them. In the best of circumstances, it is difficult to take the perspective of another accurately; the more unlike oneself the other happens to be, the more difficult the task becomes.

In conflict situations, even more problematic than the absence of common ground may be the misperception of common ground—incorrect assumptions that communicators make about what their partners know. It is well established that people's estimates of what others know, believe, or value tend to be biased in the direction of their own beliefs—what they themselves know. As a result, comprehending the intended meaning of an utterance may require knowledge one lacks, and this is particularly likely if the cultural situations of the parties involved are markedly different. In all probability, it would never have occurred to so confirmed a Marxist as Nikita Khrushchev that the context for the interpretation of his ill-received remark would be anything other than the doctrine of Marxism's historic inevitability.

Such misperceptions are common in conflict for two reasons. First, the magnitude of the perspectival differences that communicators must accommodate may itself be an important source of conflict. For an ardent pro-life activist, it may be difficult to conduct a discussion about abortion that is not grounded in the position that abortion is a kind of murder; messages grounded in this premise, directed at the activist's pro-choice counterpart, are unlikely to ameliorate conflict.

Second, conflict tends to make perceived distinctions among participants more salient, and in so doing heighten the tendency to categorize them as members of in-groups or out-groups. The language people use in such situations reflects these distinctions. One manifestation of this is what Maass, Semin, and their colleagues have termed the *linguistic intergroup bias* (Maass and Arcuri, 1992; Maass, Salvi, Arcuri, and Semin, 1989). Any interpersonal act can be characterized at various levels of generality. For example, an observer might remark, "John carried Mary's suitcase," or "John helped Mary," or "John is a helpful person," all in reference to the same incident. A well-established research finding is that people describe the actions of in-group and out-group members with systematic differences. For an action that is negatively valent, the behavior of out-group members tends to be characterized at a relatively high level of abstraction, while that of in-group members is characterized more concretely. For positively valent behaviors, however, the pattern is reversed. Positively valent behavior of out-group members is characterized as a specific episode, while that of in-group members is characterized abstractly.

One consequence of the linguistic intergroup bias is to make stereotypes resistant to disconfirmation, since behavior that is congruent with a negative out-group stereotype tends to be characterized as a general property ("Smith is aggressive"), while behavior that is inconsistent with the stereotype tends to be characterized in quite specific terms ("Smith gave CPR to an accident victim"). The enhanced salience of stereotypes in conflict situations enormously complicates the process by which, again in Brown's words, "the point of view of the auditor [can be] realistically imagined," and by so doing undermines the effectiveness of communication.

Principle 4: **When speaking, take your listener's perspective into account.**

Just as the speaker must take pains to be aware of the possible constructions listeners may place on an utterance, listeners have to be sensitive to the alternative constructions an utterance might yield. Although we habitually respond to what others say as though it could mean one and only one thing, this is seldom the case.

How insensitivity to this principle can affect communication is illustrated in a recent controversy involving Washington, D.C., public advocate David Howard's use of the word *niggardly* in a conversation with two aides. The aides, both African Americans, were unfamiliar with the obscure synonym for *stingy* and took it to be a form of a similar-sounding racial epithet, to which it is in fact etymologically unrelated. The ensuing flap (Howard, who is Caucasian, initially resigned, but was then reinstated by Mayor Anthony Williams) polarized activists on both sides of the political spectrum. Although Howard was correct philologically, he was mistaken in assuming the word *niggardly* was in common ground. In retrospect, it seems clear that his choice of words was injudicious. Because the word was obscure, there was a good chance that at least some people would not know its meaning; and because of its similarity to a taboo word, the likelihood was great that it would be misinterpreted. Especially in situations where the addressee's interpretation is consequential, an effective communicator tries to view his or her own utterances from the other's perspective.

A serious complication of perspective taking in conflict situations derives from what is called the multiple audience problem. It is not uncommon for a communication to be designed to simultaneously convey different messages to different listeners, and this seems particularly likely to occur in conflict situations. For example, a mayor negotiating a salary increase with the teachers' union may feel it's necessary to "send a message" to other municipal unions that he is willing to run the risk of a strike. Or the leader of the union may go to great lengths to assure that a reasonable concession, part of the normal give-and-take of negotiation, is not seen by union members as a sign of weakness. The number of different (and sometimes contradictory) perspectives that a speaker may feel obliged to take into account can make public or open negotiations extremely difficult. Other things being equal, participants would be well advised to reduce the number of audiences to which their messages are addressed.

Of course, another person's perspective is not always self-evident. It probably is in the best interests of the parties to expend some effort ascertaining what is and is not in common ground, and if necessary enlarging its contents. Such mutually cooperative efforts to ensure coordination on meaning is the essence of a dialogic approach to communication (discussed next). Participants deeply enmeshed in an acrimonious and apparently intractable conflict may find it difficult to achieve the degree of sensitivity to the other that such an approach requires. But without it there can be no communication of any consequence.

The Dialogic Paradigm

Thus far, our discussion has depicted communication as an unremittingly individualistic process—the product of contributions by what Susan Brennan has called "autonomous information processors." Speakers and addressees act with respect to one another, but they act as individual entities. Communication consists of a set of discursively related, but independent, episodes. This kind of depiction may be appropriate for certain communications, such as the process by which writers communicate with their readers and broadcasters with their audiences; but it seems to miss the essence of what happens in most of the situations in which people communicate.

Participants in conversations and similar highly interactive communicative forms behave less like autonomous information processors and more like participants in an intrinsically cooperative activity. Brennan and Herbert Clark have made the point nicely: "It takes two people working together to play a duet, shake hands, play chess, waltz, teach, or make love. To succeed, the two of them have to coordinate both the content and process of what they are doing. . . . Communication . . . is a collective activity of the first order" (Clark and Brennan, 1991, p. 127).

What we call the dialogic paradigm focuses on the collaborative nature of communicative activity. Perhaps the most fundamental respects in which the other three paradigms we have discussed differ from the dialogic is where they locate meaning. For the encoding-decoding paradigm, meaning is a property of messages; for the intentionalist paradigm, it resides in speakers' intentions; for the perspective-taking paradigm, it derives from the addressee's point of view.

In dialogic perspective, communication is regarded as a joint accomplishment of the participants, who have collaborated to achieve some set of communicative goals. Meaning is "socially situated"—deriving from the particular circumstances of the interaction—and the meaning of an utterance can be understood *only* in the context of those circumstances. Because the participants are invested in understanding, and being understood by, each other, speakers and addressees take pains to ensure that they have similar conceptions of the meaning of each message before they proceed to the next one.

An encoding-decoding approach to communication puts the listener in the role of a passive recipient whose task is to process the meaning of the transmitted message, but a participant in a communicative interchange is not limited to this role. Active listeners raise questions, clarify ambiguous declarations, and take great pains to ensure that they and their counterpart have the same understanding of what has been said. It is instructive to observe the person who is not speaking in a conversation in which the participants are deeply involved. Typically, such listeners are anything but inactive. They nod, interject brief comments ("uh-huh," "yes," "right, right," "hmmm"), and change their facial expressions to mirror the emotive content of what is being said. These actions—sometimes called communicating in the back channel—are one means by which participants demonstrate their involvement in the interaction, and their understanding of what has been said. Considerable research has shown that the absence of back-channel responses makes communication significantly more difficult (Krauss, 1987). Effective communication requires that listeners be responsive.

Principle 5: Be an active listener.

This recommendation seems to ask parties involved in an unresolved conflict to behave cooperatively; indeed, that is precisely what they do. Communication is intrinsically a cooperative activity. As the dialogic perspective makes clear, in communication the participants must collaborate to create meaning, and one reason that communication between conflicting parties so often is unavailing is that the parties are unable to collaborate to that degree. As Bismarck might have remarked, communication becomes a continuation of conflict by verbal means. Of course, the cooperation necessary for effective communication is of a minimal sort, and participants may collaborate to express (one hopes regretfully) their inability to see a resolution that is mutually acceptable. Nevertheless, that communication can be a first step, and developing lines of communication can be the foundation on which a solution ultimately rests. A paradoxical fact about human nature is that few things are as effective in inducing conflicting parties to cooperate as a common foe. In communication, the common foe is misunderstanding, and in collaborating to vanquish this enemy the parties to a conflict may be taking the first step toward reducing their differences.

Principle 6: Focus initially on establishing conditions that allow effective communication to occur; the cooperation that communication requires, once established, may generalize to other contexts.

FORM VERSUS SUBSTANCE: BOTH MATTER

Each of the four paradigms reveals pitfalls that an effective communicator should avoid (noise, third-party transmitters, multiple audiences, and so on). Our discussion thus far has mainly focused on the inherent complexity of communication, and how its misuse can engender or exacerbate conflict. At first glance, the picture it presents is bleak. Tallying all the ways a communicative interchange can go awry leads one to wonder whether communication can ever have an ameliorative effect. Nevertheless, we all know that at least some disputes do get resolved peacefully, that long-standing adversaries can become allies, and that even seemingly irresolvable conflicts can be isolated, allowing parties to "agree to disagree." In this section, we consider some simple behaviors that can enhance (though not guarantee) the ameliorative effects of communication.

Given a genuine desire to resolve the conflict, communication, artfully employed, can help achieve that end. Obviously, what is most critical is the substance of the communication—the quality of the proposals and counterproposals that each participant makes. It would be foolish to expect others to accept solutions not in their best interests just because of "good communication." However, quite apart from substance, the form that messages take can have (sometimes unintended) consequences. The very flexibility that makes communication so adaptable a tool also allows for more and less effective ways of achieving the same ends. For example, "Shut the door," "Would you mind closing the door?" and "I wish we could leave the door open, but it's so noisy" could (in appropriate contexts) be instances of utterances understood to have the same intended meaning. Although they differ in grammatical type and in the particular words they employ, all are understood as directives—attempts to induce the addressee to do something.

Utterances often are described in terms of the *speech acts* (Austin, 1962) they represent. Like physical actions, the things we say are intended to accomplish certain purposes; but unlike physical actions, they accomplish their purposes communicatively rather than directly. As we have just illustrated, the same speech act can be accomplished by a variety of utterances. Nevertheless, although "Shut the door" and "Would you mind closing the door?" both represent directives to close the door, they differ in another respect. The latter is an indirect speech act (one whose literal and intended meanings differ), while the former is a direct speech act that represents its meaning literally. Generally speaking, indirect speech acts are perceived as more polite than direct ones, probably because the two kinds of directive have implications for the status or power differential of requester and requestee. Although different versions of the same speech act may be identical insofar as the message's explicit content (construing that term narrowly) is concerned, it behooves a communicator to ensure that the form of the message does not undermine the information it conveys.

Principle 7: Pay attention to message form.

CONCLUSION

We conclude this discussion with a point we alluded to earlier. Communication is not a panacea, and in the absence of genuine desire to resolve conflict it is as likely to intensify the parties' disagreement as to moderate it. Although the point may seem too obvious to warrant mentioning, conflicts often serve multiple functions, and the parties may approach resolution with some ambivalence. They may find that the perceived benefits of continuing conflict outweigh its costs. In such cases, communication aimed at resolving the conflict may be unavailing—and could conceivably make things worse.

In a study published more than thirty years ago, Krauss and Deutsch (1966) provided subjects in a bargaining experiment with an opportunity to communicate. The bargaining problem they confronted in the experiment was a relatively simple one to solve. However, allowing participants the means by which they could obstruct each other's progress complicated matters considerably, typically resulting in poorer outcomes for both. The means of obstruction transformed participants' focus from jointly solving a simple coordination problem to devising individual strategies that would defeat the other. Giving them a verbal communication channel did not materially improve matters; indeed, in some cases it made things worse.

The results of this experiment underscore the naïveté of regarding communication as the universal solvent for conflict, one whose application is certain to improve matters. More realistic is a view of communication as a neutral instrument—one that can be used to convey threats as well as offers of reconciliation, to put forth unreasonable offers as well as acceptable ones, to inflame a tense situation as well as to defuse it.

Given a genuine desire to resolve a conflict, communication can facilitate achieving this goal. Although we can affect others (and be affected by them) through communication, we can affect them (and be affected by them) only so much. The fruit of communication is to establish understanding, but beyond this, communication can do little (directly) to change the state of affairs or sway the outcome of a conflict based on irreconcilable goals. Good communication cannot guarantee that conflict is ameliorated or resolved, but poor communication greatly increases the likelihood that conflict continues or is made worse.

Note

1. In this chapter, we try to summarize very briefly a large body of theory and research on the social psychology of communication as it relates to conflict. Space limitations prevent us from doing much more than skimming the surface, and in so doing we present a picture that is distorted in certain respects. Detailed treatments of these issues can be found in Krauss and Fussell (1996) and Krauss and Chiu (1998).

References

Asch, S. E. "Forming Impressions of Personality." *Journal of Personality and Social Psychology,* 1946, *41,* 258–290.

Asch, S. E. *Social Psychology.* Upper Saddle River, N.J.: Prentice Hall, 1952.

Austin, J. L. *How to Do Things with Words.* Oxford: Oxford University Press, 1962.

Brown, R. *Social Psychology.* New York: Free Press, 1965.

Clark, H. H., and Brennan, S. E. "Grounding in Communication." In L. B. Resnick, J. M. Levine, and S. D. Teasley (eds.), *Perspectives on Socially Shared Cognition.* Washington, D.C.: American Psychological Association, 1991.

Krauss, R. M. "The Role of the Listener: Addressee Influences on Message Formulation." *Journal of Language and Social Psychology,* 1987, *6,* 81–97.

Krauss, R. M., and Chiu, C. Y. "Language and Social Behavior." In D. T. Gilbert, S. T. Fiske, and G. Lindzey (eds.), *Handbook of Social Psychology.* Vol. 1. (4th ed.) New York: McGraw-Hill, 1998.

Krauss, R. M., and Deutsch, M. "Communication in Interpersonal Bargaining." *Journal of Personality and Social Psychology,* 1966, *4,* 572–577.

Krauss, R. M., and Fussell, S. R. "Social Psychological Models of Interpersonal Communication." In E. T. Higgins and A. W. Kruglanski (eds*.), Social Psychology: A Handbook of Basic Principles.* New York: Guilford Press, 1996.

Maass, A., and Arcuri, L. "The Role of Language in the Persistence of Stereotypes." In G. R. Semin and K. Fiedler (eds.), *Language, Interaction, and Social Cognition.* Thousand Oaks, Calif.: Sage, 1992.

Maass, A., Salvi, D., Arcuri, L., and Semin, G. R. "Language Use in Intergroup Contexts: The Linguistic Intergroup Bias." *Journal of Personality and Social Psychology,* 1989, *57,* 981–993.

CHAPTER SEVEN

Persuasion in Negotiations and Conflict Situations

Shelly L. Chaiken
Deborah H. Gruenfeld
Charles M. Judd

The focus of this chapter is on persuasion and attitude change in negotiation, bargaining, and conflict resolution. We define persuasion as the principles and processes by which people's attitudes, beliefs, and behaviors are formed, are modified, or resist change in the face of others' attempts at influence. These attempts are designed to convince targets of persuasion to accept a position on some policy issue or plan of action that is typically contrary to their existing attitudes, beliefs, or practices.

Although many participants in negotiation bring an impressive amount of implicit knowledge to the conflict resolution setting, there is a vast amount of theory and research on persuasion of which even expert negotiators may be unaware. We believe that knowledge of the principles and processes that underlie persuasion can increase negotiators' competence and success. Our main goal in this chapter is therefore to offer an integrative discussion of contemporary persuasion theory and research that is important to understanding the practice of negotiation and conflict resolution. We have a secondary goal as well, to stimulate research on the role of persuasion processes in negotiation settings.[1]

AN OVERVIEW OF PERSUASION THEORY AND RESEARCH

Although basic theory and research on persuasion have been brought to bear on the study of negotiation, bargaining, and conflict resolution, our perusal of recent reviews (Levine and Thompson, 1996; Pruitt, 1998) suggests that conflict researchers may be largely unaware of current advances in understanding persuasion. We begin by illustrating the research paradigm that has guided both historical and contemporary approaches to persuasion. We then discuss a broad theoretical perspective on persuasion that distinguishes between two means of processing persuasive appeals: an effortful "systematic" mode, and a cursory "heuristic" mode.

Dual-process perspectives have dominated persuasion theory and research for over a decade; they are increasingly influential in numerous such other domains of social psychology as prejudice, stereotyping, and decision making (see Chaiken and Trope, 1999). In the second portion of the chapter, we describe the prototypical negotiation paradigm and examine the implications of a dual-process theoretical approach for understanding persuasion in such settings.

The Paradigmatic Persuasion Experiment

The prototypical persuasion study takes place in a university laboratory and investigates what effect exposure to persuasive messages has on an audience's attitudes, beliefs, or intentions. Most notably, such studies examine the extent to which message recipients' attitudes, beliefs, and intentions change by moving toward the position advocated in the message. Such messages are designed to convey not only the specific position advocated by the source but also a series of arguments that support the truth, desirability, or reasonableness of that position. In most studies, a single message, attributed to a single source, is presented to one or more recipients, whose responses to the message are assessed. Responses measured typically include recipients' attitudes toward the issue discussed, perceptions of the source, memory of the arguments presented, and freely generated thoughts or ideas about the issue.

The issues addressed in such paradigmatic persuasion studies are wide ranging, including foreign affairs (for example, should Israel yield the Golan Heights to Syria?), racial issues (affirmative action, policing policies), business and government proposals (retirement benefits, universal health coverage, corporate mergers), and a host of more mundane issues of relevance to targeted audience members' work, school, or personal lives (maternal or paternal leaves of absence, increasing college tuition, union dues, taxes).

In addition, numerous variables of critical importance to understanding persuasion have been examined in the traditional paradigm. For example, much is known about source factors such as communicator credibility (trustworthiness and expertise) and likability, and the psychological mechanisms by which these source factors have an impact on persuasion. Other variable types that have been well researched include recipient characteristics such as self-esteem and mood, contextual factors such as modality of presentation (television versus print) and the relevance of the message topic to audience members' own lives, and message variables such as the amount and style of persuasive argumentation.

Despite the range of issues and variables studied in persuasion research, the essential paradigm is somewhat constrained in its portrayal of natural persuasion settings. A unidirectional, source-to-audience model of persuasion probably maps directly onto only a subset of the contexts in which social influence occurs. Although it might afford an accurate picture of persuasion through exposure to public media such as television, radio, newspaper, and magazines, or in public forums such as political, religious, and professional rallies, it is unlikely to capture the dynamic processes of persuasion that occur in the kinds of interpersonal interaction that characterize negotiations.

When persuasion theorists and researchers contemplate complex social settings, they traditionally do so by adding layers of complexity to the basic paradigm. This involves introducing new variables that capture essential features of particularistic settings. For example, researchers have explored the role of multiple persuasion sources by varying whether persuasive messages are attributed to a single source or to multiple sources. The consequences of direct interpersonal influence have been examined by instructing experimental participants to anticipate interacting with the message source, or by exposing participants to a message whose position is endorsed (or opposed) by a person or group with whom they expect to interact. As a final example, in research on majority and minority influence, participants are led to believe that the message they receive is endorsed by many, as opposed to few, other "persons" and also by leading participants to believe that their own positions on issues are either anonymous or will be known to these other persons (for reviews, see Eagly and Chaiken, 1993; and Petty and Wegener, 1998).

So, although the prototypical persuasion paradigm serves as the underlying framework for theory and research, it has been treated only as a skeletal framework on which variables and processes are added to understand more fully the complex processes of persuasion. At the same time, it is clear that the framework represents in some ways a simplification of social influence in real-life settings. As we discuss later, negotiation-conflict settings pose serious challenges to persuasion theorists and researchers both because of the inherent complexities of these settings and because the settings themselves vary so widely (mediated divorce settlements, labor-management negotiations, international conflicts). Thus, it is probably the case that no one experimental paradigm in persuasion can ever address all the inherent complexities of persuasion in these conflict situations with complete success. Nevertheless, we believe that the study of persuasion, using variations of its basic paradigm, can be informative about social influence processes in a wide range of negotiation and conflict settings. The basic paradigm and its modifications permit us to address a host of issues manageably. The leap from there to real-world negotiation settings is sizeable but manageable, given good theory about both conflict and persuasion.

The Heuristic-Systematic Model

Before discussing the implications of contemporary persuasion theorizing for negotiation and conflict resolution contexts, we must describe our theoretical perspective. As indicated earlier, this perspective is known as the heuristic-systematic model (Chaiken, Giner-Sorolla, and Chen, 1996; Chen and Chaiken, 1999). It is one of a set of dual-process models proven to be important in contemporary social psychology (see Chaiken and Trope, 1999). We treat this model simply as a perspective, borrowing terms and insights from other dual-process models wherever it is useful to do so. Our goal is to acquaint the reader with dual-process models in general and exploit the general perspective these models offer for understanding conflict and negotiation.

Modes of Information Processing. Like other dual-process theories, the heuristic-systematic model proposes two distinct modes of information processing. Systematic processing involves attempts to thoroughly understand any information encountered through careful attention, deep thinking, and intensive reasoning about relevant stimuli (such as arguments, sources, and the causes of their behavior), and to integrate this information as a basis for subsequent attitudes, judgments, and behaviors. A systematic approach to processing information about the Israeli-Palestinian conflict might entail reading as many magazine and newspaper reports as possible to learn and develop an opinion about the "best" course of U.S. action. Not surprisingly, such systematic information processing entails much mental effort, requiring both deliberate attention and allocation of mental resources. Thus, systematic processing is unlikely to occur unless a person is both able and motivated to do it.

Relative to systematic processing, heuristic processing is much less demanding in terms of the mental work required and much less dependent on adequate levels of personal or situational capacity for such work (knowledge, time). In fact, heuristic processing has often been characterized as relatively automatic insofar as it requires little cognitive effort and capacity (Chaiken and Trope, 1999). Heuristic processing involves focusing on salient and easily comprehended cues in the persuasion context such as a source's credentials, the number of people endorsing a position, or the number of arguments presented. These cues activate well-learned, routinized decision rules, known as heuristics. Examples include "experts' statements can be trusted," "consensus implies correctness," and "argument length implies argument strength." These simple rules allow judgments, attitudes, and intentions to be formed quickly and efficiently, with little additional cognitive processing. A heuristic approach to the Israeli-Palestinian conflict might involve adopting the opinion of a noted Middle-East political expert with little expenditure of mental effort and regardless of any personal or situational capacity constraints. Put simply but abstractly, heuristics are the *ifs* in an if-then rule structure, and the judgments (such as adopting this expert's Mideast opinion) are the *thens* ("If expert, then agree").

Cognitive Consequences of Processing Modes. Our description of these two modes of information processing could be interpreted to mean that heuristic processing is superficial and irrational, while systematic processing is detailed and optimal insofar as it guarantees good, rational, accurate judgments. There is truth to depicting heuristic processing as superficial, and systematic processing as involving greater depth of detail. Yet neither mode is necessarily more or less rational than the other, and nonoptimal, poor, or biased judgments can ensue from either mode.

In the case of heuristic processing, many of the mental rules of thumb we have learned and stored in memory are decent guides to good judgment. Experience and culture have taught us that experts are usually more credible than novices, so what's wrong with agreeing with a recognized expert's opinion on some issue or policy? In general, most of the heuristics that people use in navigating their way through life's many demands to make a judgment or come to a conclusion have proved useful and reliable in the past and should presumably remain so in the present. Moreover, in a world that offers abundant information but too little time or opportunity to think in a detailed, systematic way about every decision, heuristic processing can be highly functional.

Yet heuristic processing is obviously fallible. Experts can sometimes be wrong. Majorities are not always right. Numerous reasons are not always good reasons. Thus, although heuristic processing can and often does produce reasonable judgments that people hold with relatively high confidence, it can sometimes produce judgments that are different—and subjectively poorer—than what people would reach if they processed information more systematically. This is because systematic processing of persuasive appeals can increase both the breadth and depth of a recipient's issue-relevant knowledge in ways that heuristic processing does not. Systematic processing, though not guaranteeing an optimal judgment, constitutes an opportunity to adjust habitual responses if they are not suited to a particular situation.

As noted earlier, one potential advantage of systematic processing is that it involves sustained attention and information search. This can increase the depth of understanding about a particular issue, or at least about a particular point of view. Moreover, when driven by a need for accuracy, systematic processing can involve more objective and evenhanded thought about message-relevant stimuli than heuristic processing, which tends to be biased in favor of prior judgments and the cognitive routines on which they are based. This kind of controlled, objective, systematic thought can increase the breadth of understanding about the issue at hand and, more important, about the alternative perspectives from which it can be viewed and understood.

For example, systematic processing can lead to complex thought patterns that involve examining issues from alternative viewpoints and weighing the pros and cons of opposing perspectives. Research on cognitive complexity has established that a number of advantages are associated with this kind of reasoning, among them diminished susceptibility to overconfidence and bias from belief perseverance, and superior performance in both group problem-solving and managerial decision tasks (for example, Gruenfeld and Hollingshead, 1993; Tetlock, 1992). Of special relevance to conflict settings, cognitive complexity has been associated with increasing tolerance for alternative viewpoints, facilitating political compromise, identifying integrative solutions to conflict, and avoiding war (for example, Gruenfeld and Kim, 1998; Pruitt and Lewis, 1975; Tetlock, 1988; Tetlock, Armor, and Peterson, 1994). Hence, individuals who process information in cognitively complex ways are often more effective, especially in conflict and decision-making settings, than those who do not.

There are some disadvantages that are worth keeping in mind when it comes to complex reasoning in social situations. Decision makers who discuss alternatives in terms of trade-offs can appear indecisive and unprincipled (Suedfeld, 1985). Complex thinkers can also be perceived as antagonistic and narcissistic (Tetlock, Peterson, and Berry, 1993), presumably because they continue to seek new information and raise alternatives even as others are approaching consensus. Both of these factors can undermine the credibility of someone making a complex decision and his or her likability as a communicator, thus reducing the capacity to persuade others (Gruenfeld and Fan, 1999).

Importantly, systematic processing is more likely to lead to deep, pervasive cognitive restructuring than heuristic processing is. This means that the cognitive changes that occur as a consequence of systematic processing are likely to persist, and thus affect future judgments, intentions, and behavior, relative to the changes that accompany heuristic processing (see Eagly and Chaiken, 1993; Petty and Wegener, 1998). Hence, in actuarial terms, systematic processing may well produce more optimal judgments than heuristic processing does (Creyer, Bettman, and Paine, 1998).

Sources of Bias. Although enduring, systematic processing is far from foolproof. This is because the cognitive effort associated with systematic processing does not always increase the breadth of one's knowledge. In fact, sometimes systematic processing simply strengthens prior conceptual pathways. Systematic processing can be biased by both "cool" cognitive factors (such as a message recipient's existing attitudes and knowledge structures) and, as discussed later, "hotter" motivational factors (say, a recipient's strategic goals or ideological commitments).

It is well known that people's attitudes can exert a selective effect at virtually all stages of information processing (attending to information in the environment, interpreting this information, remembering it). It is also well known that for most people on most issues, knowledge is skewed so that it is evaluatively consistent with their attitudes. The fact that knowledge about an issue (or some other entity) is evaluatively skewed in this way means that when people engage in systematic processing they are cognitively predisposed to find the merits in proattitudinal information and the flaws in counterattitudinal information (see Eagly and Chaiken, 1993, 1998). Thus, through the cool, purely cognitive process of critically processing a source's arguments, perceivers may find themselves genuinely swayed by arguments that fit their preexisting attitudes and beliefs.

As for situationally based cognitive factors that may bias systematic processing, a particularly important one is heuristic processing itself. That is, even if perceivers go beyond heuristic processing and engage in modest-to-high amounts of systematic processing, there is the possibility that heuristic processing could bias their systematic processing.

Consider, for example, the possible impact of listening to President Clinton propose and argue for a new welfare policy versus listening to the (current) democratic minority leader, Richard Gephardt, present the very same proposal and arguments. Perhaps you like both sources, but you think Clinton is more expert than Gephardt—that is, a more credible source. Before hearing either speaker, you have probably already formed the tentative, heuristic-based expectancy that Clinton's arguments will be more compelling and valid than Gephardt's.[2] In turn, this differential expectancy about the validity of the two sources' arguments may guide systematic processing in a way that verifies your initial expectancies. As you attend to and think about Clinton's arguments you may (truly) perceive them to be more compelling than Gephardt's (same) arguments, had you heard them. And you may think about, or elaborate, Clinton's arguments in ways that make them even more convincing ("I can see that making welfare recipients work would help the economy not just in terms of decreasing total welfare payments but also in terms of decreasing health care costs, because working has positive health consequences"). In contrast, as you would be less inclined to expect Gephardt's arguments to be persuasive, you may not perceive them as highly credible and may elaborate his arguments in ways that make them even less plausible ("I can see that making welfare recipients work would help the economy in terms of decreasing welfare payments, but in the long run it seems that the economy suffers because those who cannot work or find real work will never be able to contribute to the economy").

Motives for Processing

The motivation to attain accurate judgments is pervasive in everyday life since effective behavior requires understanding our environment and the causal relations underlying what we observe. When accuracy concerns are present but not particularly great, information processors may look for heuristic cues that signal accuracy, such as source credibility. Indeed, to enhance their persuasive power, communicators (among them political candidates and negotiators) actively behave or portray themselves so as to enhance others' perceptions of them as experts in the topic of their communications, and as trustworthy, likable individuals. If accuracy motivation increases, heuristic processing may be accompanied by systematic processing. Why? According to the heuristic-systematic model, heuristic processing alone is not likely to provide sufficient judgmental confidence at higher levels of accuracy motivation. Thus, systematic processing is also undertaken in the interests of maximizing confidence in one's judgments and decisions.

How much processing occurs, and thus whether heuristic or systematic processing dominates judgment, depends primarily on (1) the extent to which judgment-relevant heuristics are accessible to perceivers (see Chen and Chaiken, 1999); (2) the extent to which personal and situational capacity for systematic processing is adequate; and, most important here, (3) the level of judgmental confidence a perceiver desires and (4) the perceived self-efficacy of systematic processing (the belief that systematic processing does confer better judgments). Assuming that factors (1) and (2) are in place and that our perceiver believes in the efficacy of systematic processing, factor (4), our theoretical perspective, predicts that people will process heuristically, but in addition they will engage in more systematic processing as the level of desired judgmental confidence increases—that is, as they feel the need to make more accurate judgments.

Research supports this proposition. When accuracy motivation is modest (or when capacity is inadequate), heuristic cues such as source expertise, consensus opinion, and people's own attitudes and ideologies have been shown to exert a powerful influence on judgment—regardless of persuasive arguments or other particularistic information that, if processed, might temper or reverse the heuristic-based judgment (for relevant experiments, see Chaiken, Wood, and Eagly, 1996; Petty and Wegener, 1998). Only if accuracy motivation is higher—for example, if the issue is of great personal importance or the perceiver is accountable to others—do judgments that reveal ample systematic processing occur.

Although accuracy motivation is pervasive, other motivations may often supplant or at least compete with it (Chaiken, Giner-Sorolla, and Chen, 1996). Research has identified two additional broad motives, referred to as defense motivation and impression motivation, that can activate either heuristic or systematic processing (or both). Defense motivation compels message recipients to process information in ways that protect and validate beliefs, images, and interests that are important to their sense of self. For instance, these beliefs could be about one's own valued qualities ("I'm intelligent and socially sensitive"), one's fundamental underlying value commitments ("Anyone can make it in our society if they're sufficiently motivated"), or one's identity in valued groups ("Being Jewish is important to who I am and what I value"). These self-interests or self-definitional beliefs are defended because the perceiver feels, at least subliminally, that if they were challenged, overall personal integrity and well-being would be threatened.

When defense motivation is present but moderate, then heuristic processing dominates judgment—but defensively, or selectively. Thus, a defense-motivated target might accept the position of a source whose position reinforced his or her cherished values and social identity without considering the validity of the specific arguments presented. Alternatively, a source whose position was inconsistent with the target's core values and interests might be heuristically dismissed without consideration of any specific arguments (see Chaiken, Giner-Sorolla, and Chen, 1996). If, however, a target's motivation is strong, systematic processing can also have a defensive slant. Thus, people can be defensively selective—that is, more critical in their evaluation of arguments supporting non-preferred positions and more generous in their evaluation of arguments supporting preferred positions—if uncongenial heuristic cues are made available in the influence setting (such as when consensus information opposes your self-interests). Theoretically, this greater level of defensively biased systematic processing occurs because heuristic processing of the uncongenial heuristic information could actually undermine subjective confidence in one's preferred position. To attain sufficient confidence, then, the person for whom defense motivation is high enough engages in more (albeit biased) systematic processing of persuasion information.

The third broad motivational concern addressed by our perspective is impression motivation. Impression motives (of which there are many specific instances) entail considering the interpersonal consequences of expressing a particular judgment in a given social context (such as in a dyadic interaction, during a negotiation). Here, the perceiver's goal is to express attitudes and other judgments that satisfy his or her current social goals. Like defense-motivated processing, impression-motivated processing is not necessarily engaged in self-consciously and is also marked by a selective bias. However, the selectivity of heuristic and systematic processing in the service of impression motivation is specifically aimed at satisfying social goals, rather than preserving existing, self-definitional attitudes and beliefs.

Impression-motivated heuristic processing entails selective application of heuristics. For example, the heuristic "moderate judgment minimizes disagreement" may be applied to serve the (conscious or unconscious) goal of ensuring a smooth interaction with a person or group whose own views on the issue are unknown or vague. On the other hand, when others' views are known, "go along to get along" may be a useful heuristic to serve the same goal. With sufficient personal and situational capacity and higher levels of impression motivation, people may also process systematically, in similarly selective ways. Thus, a party to a negotiation who is motivated not only to be well liked by other participants but also to appear forceful and expert may systematically process information from other participants so as to be prepared to counterargue their issue positions and arguments.

Illustrating the importance of impression-motivated processing, Chen and colleagues (see Chen and Chaiken, 1999) led participants to anticipate a discussion about a social issue with an alleged partner who held a favorable, or unfavorable, opinion on the issue. Before this discussion, participants read "imagination scenarios" subtly designed to arouse (or prime) the accuracy goal of determining a valid opinion, or the impression goal of getting along with another person. After this task, participants familiarized themselves with the discussion issue by reading an evaluatively balanced essay concerning this issue (in this case, whether election returns should be broadcast while polls are still open). Participants then listed the thoughts that had occurred to them as they read the essay and indicated their own issue attitudes. Finally, they learned that there would be no actual discussion and were excused.

Impression-motivated participants expressed attitudes that were much more congruent with their alleged partners' attitudes than accuracy-motivated participants' were; when the partner favored one side of the issue, they favored the same side, whereas when the partner opposed it, they opposed it. Interestingly, accuracy-motivated and impression-motivated participants exhibited the same amount of systematic processing (as indexed by the number of issue-relevant thoughts). Yet although accuracy-motivated participants' systematic processing was openminded and unbiased by their partners' attitudes, impression-motivated participants' systematic processing of the essay arguments was biased in a direction that cohered with their partners' attitudes; for example, when the partner favored allowing broadcasts of election returns while the polls were still open, these participants' thought listings revealed much more favorable thinking about arguments favoring the broadcasting of returns and more unfavorable thinking about arguments opposing it.

Although accuracy motivation, defense motivation, and impression motivation may sometimes operate in isolation from one another, it is likely the case that multiple motives may be relevant in any given setting. Thus, both heuristic and systematic processing may be influenced by more than a single motivation. To examine contexts in which multiple motives are operative, Zuckerman and Chaiken (1997, cited in Chen and Chaiken, 1999) replicated the same experiment but replaced the earlier study's manipulation of motivation arousal with a mood manipulation designed to influence the relative importance of various motivations. Participants in the "good mood" condition watched a comedy routine by Jerry Seinfeld, while "neutral mood" participants watched a videotape concerning housebuilding. It was hypothesized that placing participants in a good mood would mitigate the assumed greater arousal of impression motivation (compared to accuracy motivation) as participants anticipated discussing their opinion, because a positive mood generally increases people's confidence in their own abilities and hence their tolerance for interpersonal conflict.

Consistent with the idea that impression motivation would tend to be higher than accuracy motivation in the basic get-acquainted discussion, participants who were in a neutral mood engaged in impression-motivated processing, favoring the issue more when their alleged partner did so. In contrast, consistent with the idea that being in a positive mood increases one's toleration for disagreement, or self-confidence in expressing one's own attitude, positive-mood participants expressed attitudes that showed little alignment with the partners' attitudes. Moreover, their attitudes were arrived at through unbiased, accuracy-motivated systematic processing.

CONCLUSIONS REGARDING THE TWO MODES OF COGNITIVE PROCESSING

The heuristic-systematic model distinguishes between two modes of cognitive processing, which reflect two means of persuading others. Whereas heuristic processing involves reliance on superficial stimulus cues that activate automatic cognitive responses and have direct effects on judgment, systematic processing involves more careful and controlled attention to multiple stimulus dimensions and controlled attempts to actively derive judgments based on their complex implications.

Both processing modes have advantages. Heuristic processing is easier and more efficient than systematic processing, which requires greater effort and hence greater motivation. Heuristic processing therefore tends to dominate unless both the motive and the capacity for systematic processing are sufficiently great. The motivations for accuracy, defense, and impression management can activate either type of processing, and neither type is necessarily more closely associated with judgment accuracy, nor the likelihood of attitude change. However, because systematic processing entails thorough perusal of the available evidence, it is more likely to lead to deep, long-lasting cognitive change than heuristic processing. Because it entails active attempts to control the encoding and evaluation of available evidence, systematic processing can increase the breadth and depth of the information processed, which increases the chances that message recipients learn something new.

Although this dual-processing framework focuses primarily on the motivational and processing mechanisms that govern *recipients'* responses to persuasive communications, it also has important implications for those who seek to persuade. Educated guesses about the motivational goals of message recipients (in particular settings and on particular issues) can enable persuasive communicators to incorporate in their messages information intended to enhance recipients' concerns about accuracy (as opposed to defense or impression motivation). If systematic processing is desired, communicators can implement any of a number of treatments that research has shown to enhance motivation, or capacity, for extensive information processing (emphasizing the personal relevance of the issue to recipients, or using rhetorical questions in one's message; see Petty and Wegener, 1998).

Finally, communicators' awareness of the role played by cognitive heuristics in persuasion should enable them to include heuristic cues in their messages or in the contexts in which they deliver their messages. Communicators should, for example, behave or portray themselves so as to maximize others' perceptions that they are expert, trustworthy, and likable. In addition, they can also build into their persuasion attempt other heuristic cues (such as noting that consensus opinion supports their viewpoint, or that many more arguments exist in support of their viewpoint than in opposition).

PERSUASION IN NEGOTIATION AND CONFLICT SETTINGS

One of the great challenges in thinking about persuasion in conflict and negotiation settings comes from the realization that persuasion in such settings is a much more complicated, multifaceted affair than it is in the typical persuasion scenario.

Complexities of Negotiation and Conflict Settings

As noted earlier, the paradigmatic research approach to persuasion typically involves a single source of the persuasive message and a single target who is to be persuaded. Persuasion episodes are conceived as one-shot interactions in which the source has unidirectional influence on the target, with regard to a single unidimensional issue. In most studies using this paradigm, the source and target are autonomous, rather than interdependent actors. They have had no prior interactions, and with the exception of anticipated-interaction manipulations in which possible consequences are introduced but do not materialize, they cannot affect one another's future outcomes. In fact, the source is neither present nor personally identifiable in many persuasion studies, and it is therefore perceived at a distance rather than through firsthand experience and interpersonal exchange. Persuasive messages in this research are regularly processed in terms of their intrapsychic consequences, but they are rarely processed in terms of their interpersonal or social consequences.

As we have already stated, this basic paradigm can be and has been elaborated in a variety of ways, including having multiple sources and multiple targets.

But the negotiation setting introduces an additional level of complexity that, to our knowledge, has never been studied closely from a persuasion point of view. In contrast to the one-shot, unidirectional message transmissions that characterize the persuasion paradigm, negotiations and conflicts involve dynamic, repeated interactions between sources and targets who together are simultaneously the senders and recipients of persuasive messages. In other words, parties in negotiation engage in bidirectional, mutual-influence attempts at persuasion. Additionally, attempts at influence can be directed not only at one's opponent but also at the groups or constituencies each party represents—and at any mediators who might be present. Finally, the messages exchanged during negotiation often address multiple, related issues and the relations among them (such as order of priority), rather than single, independent ones.

Perhaps the most important difference between persuasion and negotiation contexts is that in negotiations the source and the target of attempts at influence are interdependent; their outcomes depend on one another's actions (Neale and Bazerman, 1991). In fact, interdependence is the impetus for negotiation. If parties were autonomous, decisions could be made independently without interaction, and negotiation would not be necessary. However, interdependence pervades social systems because resources are distributed unevenly among the groups and individuals within them. This creates opportunities for social exchange, but also the potential for conflict. Moreover, the asymmetric distribution of resources in such systems creates power differences among members. This means that influence in negotiation contexts can be exercised through coercion, as well as through persuasion (see Lawler, 1993).

These complexities can be clarified by considering the paradigmatic negotiation setting. In the simple case, two parties face a joint decision about how to share some kind of resource, perhaps money, property, or access to such things. Often there are multiple issues at stake, and though the parties' preferences are by definition incompatible with regard to some of these issues, they are also often compatible with regard to others. Moreover, whereas some conflicts can only be resolved by a distributive outcome (in which one party's gain is the other party's loss), many conflicts can be resolved through various forms of problem solving. Ideally, parties can reach integrative outcomes by discovering compatible issues and trading off concessions. Integrative outcomes allow both parties to win on some important issues, and they permit opportunities to maximize joint profits. However, a quintessential feature of this paradigm, and of most naturally occurring conflict resolution scenarios, is that a party is not always aware of the specific preference structure that underlies its public stance.

In the actual negotiation, representatives of conflicting parties exchange information in attempts to reach an agreement that maximizes their individual outcomes, while taking joint outcomes into consideration to some extent. For example, if opponents have an ongoing relationship, they are likely to prefer an outcome that actually resolves the conflict by satisfying both parties, as opposed to an outcome sure to lead to future retaliation by the loser. In the process of negotiation, both parties attempt to construct these outcomes using a wide range of strategies that include, but are not limited to, persuasive appeals. Parties might attempt to persuade one another by offering specific arguments and some kind of logical rationale for a particular outcome. But they can also appeal to outside sources, make threats, lie, and use other forms of strategic misrepresentation to coerce opponents into accepting outcomes that they do not actually believe are acceptable.

The distinction between coercion and persuasion has a long history in social psychology. Research on social influence has established that if public compliance is not accompanied by private acceptance, the outcomes of influence are typically ephemeral and unstable across social situations. Yet our perusal of the literature on conflict and negotiation (for example, Pruitt, 1998) suggests that research on the process and outcomes of negotiation has only rarely considered the differential effects of tactics that are designed to persuade versus those designed to coerce another party into complying with a request.

Coercion involves attempts to influence another person to behave in a certain way (to concede self-interests, say, or to accept a suboptimal resolution) without any concern for whether the influence target genuinely endorses the proposed outcome and accepts its consequences. In other words, if someone complies with influence as a function of behavioral coercion, then he or she does so in spite of private beliefs and attitudes that remain uncommitted to the compliance.

On the other hand, as persuasion is typically defined by social psychologists it involves influence designed to change beliefs, in addition to simply eliciting behavioral compliance. Persuasion involves changing another person's mind about what is in his or her best interests in the context of a particular conflict. If persuasion is successful, then the old beliefs and attitudes are in fact changed and new ones internalized, so that the behavioral change that ensues is in fact consistent with one's beliefs and attitudes.

In sum, studies of persuasion have tended to emphasize the conditions that lead people to change their minds (with less concern for whether they ultimately change their behavior), but studies of negotiation have tended to emphasize the conditions that lead people to change their behaviors (with little regard for whether they have ultimately changed their minds).

The distinction between persuasion and coercion in conflict situations has clear implications for the ultimate success of a negotiated agreement. Negotiated settlements most typically fall apart if the parties to the settlement do not truly believe that it is in their self-interest. For a negotiated settlement to stand the test of time, both parties have to be persuaded that the settlement is in some sense optimal. Simple behavioral compliance with the terms of the settlement, without the private commitment that is the goal of persuasion, all too often means that the settlement eventually breaks down and that further conflict ensues. Thus coercion is a viable tactic for parties with the power to use it; however, it is likely to produce relatively unstable agreements (Lawler, 1993).

These considerations illustrate a central theme of this chapter. By examining the role and processes of persuasion in conflict and negotiation, our purpose is to illustrate that successful conflict resolution (in the sense of arriving at a mutually agreeable solution) necessarily must involve social influence that goes beyond attempts at coercion and relies increasingly on persuasion. We believe that persuasion, rather than coercion, is a necessary prerequisite for successful conflict resolution for two important reasons. First, persuasion is an opportunity for opponents to increase the breadth and depth of their knowledge about the conflict and one another's interests, which can increase the probability of identifying integrative outcomes. Second, persuasion can lead to deep, cognitive changes that increase internalization of agreement and hence the probability that agreements are stable across time and situation. To elaborate these arguments, we now turn to discussion of motives for information processing in conflict and negotiation settings, and how they can change as the negotiation process proceeds.

Processing Motives in Negotiation and Conflict

As discussed earlier, processing motives determine how persuasive appeals are dealt with. In negotiation, when important outcomes are at stake, motives are likely to be intense. Partisans are undoubtedly vigilant in their processing of one another's verbal and nonverbal communications. Thus, although heuristic cues may influence information processing, messages in the conflict situation are sure to be processed systematically. This is not to say, however, that the dominant motivation for processing is typically accuracy motivation. In fact, we suspect that in the initial stages of negotiation, accuracy motivation plays a very small role and that both impression and defense motives dominate systematic perusal of information from others in the setting. As noted earlier, message senders can attempt to decrease such domination by communicating information designed to reduce defensive or impression concerns among their recipients, before focusing on critical persuasive arguments.

As partisans in conflict approach a negotiation, position differences are initially salient, but the odds are actual interests—and especially mutual interests—remain hidden. Generalized conflict schemas suggest that parties' interests will be diametrically opposed; that the pool of available resources is a "fixed pie" (Neale and Bazerman, 1991); and that therefore only distributive, zero-sum outcomes are possible. These presumptions activate a defensive motive in processing information received from the other side. Specifically, parties typically assume that their opponents are intractably self-interested and that their overtures and messages, and even their concessions, reflect attempts at manipulation, deception, and coercion. As noted earlier, persuasion research indicates that if systematic processing is activated by a defense motivation, parties seek out and attend to information that supports the desire to dismiss, resist, and reject an opponent's overtures, and they resist attending to information that supports the appropriateness of cooperative responses.

Social psychologists know a fair amount about what happens when messages are processed in some detail from a defensive posture. With this as the primary motivation, one's goal in processing is to resist influence; to maintain prior beliefs, commitments, and interests; and to look for confirmation of those interests in the messages that are processed. This sort of motivated processing has been shown to lead to overestimating divergence between the opposing parties (Judd and Johnson, 1981), so that each party to the conflict actually overestimates the degree to which the opposing party has adopted an extreme and opposing position on the issues under dispute. Additionally, when objectively neutral or ambiguous information is processed by disputing parties from a defensive standpoint, each party may see the information as confirming its own previous point of view (see Eagly and Chaiken, 1993). Finally, concessions offered by one party to the conflict are typically devalued, that is, interpreted by the other party as minimal concessions, offering no real benefits toward conflict resolution. As a result of defensive processing of messages in the conflict, these various effects all suggest that conflict should escalate, that positions become polarized and entrenched, and that actual interests and potentially mutual interests remain hidden.

In addition to defense motives, impression motives may also operate in the early stages of negotiation, since parties are eager to create a specific impression vis-à-vis various audiences. For example, when face-to-face with an opponent, negotiators might communicate their power to control their own outcomes, their authority to act on behalf of constituents, and their confidence in their own judgment. But when communicating to their constituents, they may want to emphasize their loyalty and credibility as negotiators. The former case may lead to focusing on information that supports characterizations of the other party as extreme, threatening, and untrustworthy. In the latter case, negotiators may focus on the most important of constituents' interests and ignore information that creates opportunities for trading off concessions.

In sum, both defense and impression motives are potent in negotiation settings, and these motives certainly activate systematic information processing. But they probably reduce the likelihood of the opponents being open to persuasion. If one's goal is primarily to present a good impression as a tough negotiator—one who stands up for the interests of the party represented and is respected by the other side in the dispute as a formidable opponent—then similar sorts of oppositional bias should occur in processing influence attempts from that opponent. One should be motivated to resist those attempts as attempted coercion, look for confirmation of this tactic in the opponent's evidence and arguments, and phrase one's own influence arguments in language that convinces others of the legitimacy of one's position and the strength of one's commitment to that position. If negotiators cannot move beyond these initial motives, conflict surely escalates, positions become rigidified, and resolution seems more remote.

Research in negotiation has established that a critical turning point in this process occurs when and if the negotiators turn away from their public positions and find compatible issues within opponents' underlying interests (Neale and Bazerman, 1991). Initially, negotiators start out with positions that they publicly espouse and defend. They tend to portray the conflict as a divergence in these positions, and they may attempt to coerce the opposition into accepting an outcome that fails to achieve the latter's own stated position. Talking about real underlying interests, as opposed to publicly stated positions, makes it increasingly possible to persuade the other party to sacrifice some things of lesser interest in favor of gaining other things of more interest. It is only through this sort of persuasion—rather than coercion—that successful resolution can be achieved with both parties committed to it.

This can only occur, however, if opponents are both willing and able not only to transmit but also to receive information. That is, negotiators must be willing and able to persuade and be persuaded. Moreover, they must want to search for information that *disconfirms,* as well as information that confirms, their prior beliefs about their opponents' interests. If parties in negotiation begin to change one another's minds about the nature of the conflict, the issues at stake, and the compatibility of interests, then cooperation can ensue.

From a persuasion perspective, then, the key to successful conflict resolution is movement away from attempts at coercion, toward attempts at persuasion. Specifically, this depends on cognitive and motivational changes. Persuasion occurs more when parties are motivated to be accurate in their information processing than when they are motivated to be defensive, or to make a particular kind of impression. This is because the first motive (accuracy) increases the desire to take information in, while the latter motives increase the desire to put information out. Persuasion cannot occur in negotiation if both parties are more interested in transmitting information than in receiving it. Individuals are more flexible, cognitively speaking, when they are prepared to receive information than when they are prepared to transmit information (Zajonc, 1960). Cognitive flexibility is necessary for change. Hence, an important objective for effective negotiation is to increase cognitive flexibility in both parties.

As noted earlier, however, the extent to which cognitive change is helpful in negotiation depends on the motives it is meant to serve. Defense and impression motives ensure that any new information processed confirms prior beliefs, but an accuracy motive increases the willingness to consider information that disconfirms prior beliefs. Thus factors that increase negotiators' receptivity to information—especially information that disconfirms prior beliefs—increases the chances of parties being persuaded to reconsider prior interpretations of the conflict and discover invisible preference structures that are an opportunity for an integrative outcome.

Facilitating Persuasion in Negotiation and Conflict

To the extent that cognitive flexibility and an accuracy motive can improve negotiation outcomes, an important question for both researchers and practitioners is how to facilitate these changes. We propose that there are two possible approaches to achieving this goal. On the one hand, negotiators can attempt to change the motivations underlying systematic processing in the negotiation setting. This involves initiating changes in the norms that govern communication and information exchange, to discourage defensive and impression motivated behavior and encourage behaviors that serve the motive for accuracy. On the other hand, negotiators can change their own influence strategy from a coercion approach to one of persuasion. This involves attempting to facilitate internalization of new beliefs in one's opponent. Let us discuss each approach in turn.

Facilitating Motivational Changes. We have argued that the primary motivations underlying systematic processing in the initial stages of the negotiation setting are defense and impression maintenance. In the presence of such motivations, even though the opponent's messages are systematically attended to, there is very little chance that the quality of the arguments offered by the opponent can actually lead to persuasion and influence. This is the case because the arguments are processed not for the merits of what they have to say but rather to confirm defense- and impression-related concerns. Only when the parties to the conflict can reflect more or less accurately on the merits of the arguments the other puts forward, only when they truly begin to listen to each other with the goal of evaluating more or less impartially what the other has to say, can the negotiation process move away from a purely competitive situation to one where mutually satisfactory outcomes can result. The question is how this transition is made (for a related discussion, see the section on reframing in Chapter One).

One obvious tactic is to offer arguments that run counter to expectations in that it is not easy to interpret them as being motivated solely by one's own self-interest. In essence, one says to the opposition, "Listen to what I have to say, because I really am not what you think I am"; one does this by offering unexpected concessions, by talking about the other's interests rather than one's own, and by focusing on gains that the other can accrue from settlement rather than the losses that loom if a suboptimal settlement is adopted. Initially, the opposition might meet such tactics with great suspicion, since defensive motives are apt to be strong and the belief that communications are motivated by something other than self-interest is unlikely. Nevertheless, with persistence, this sort of tactic should gradually induce the opposition to adopt more of an accuracy motivation orientation, at which point true persuasion rather than mutual coercion is possible.

Another tactic that can be adopted to enhance accuracy motivation and move toward persuasion and away from coercion is for the negotiating parties to focus on interests rather than stated positions. Thus one can begin the process of honestly communicating to the opponent which things matter more in a settlement and which matter less. Instead of advocating a position contrary to what the opponent states, one can begin to talk about the various dimensions along which potential settlements may vary, and the relative importance of these various dimensions to each party. By revealing interests in this way, and not focusing just on stated positions, one can begin the process of jointly identifying mutually satisfactory outcomes or truly integrative solutions. In so doing, information processing should become more complex and arguments should be heard for what they say rather than interpreted simply as reflecting self-interests.

Persuasion is also more likely if the negotiating parties begin to individuate each other, to see the other not as a representative of a constituency with stated positions but as a person who has individual points of view and individual interests. This implies some dissociation from each party's constituency, not in the sense of inadequately representing their true interests but in the sense that one makes clear that one is more than a spokesperson, that one has personal points of view and arguments that deserve to be listened to. Perhaps hand in hand with this, one may begin to point out that both negotiators, even though they are each representing constituencies with opposing interests, have some common interests separate from those of their constituents.

According to research on persuasion, instilling an accuracy motive is one of the most direct means of inducing objectivity in the processing of information. According to research on negotiation, greater objectivity about the true structure of mutual and individual interests is critical for the problem solving necessary in developing satisfactory outcomes. Hence, in addition to addressing parties' motives, it can be useful to have strategies for increasing objectivity that address the desired cognitive changes directly.

Facilitating Cognitive Changes. As noted earlier, parties in negotiation often approach one another prepared to transmit rather than receive information. This effectively precludes the possibility of learning anything new about the opponent's interests, motives, and willingness to cooperate. Internalizing new information—especially if it disconfirms prior beliefs—is critical if persuasion is to have a positive effect on negotiation outcomes. There are three types of cognitive changes that can be usefully addressed.

First, parties can attempt to increase cognitive flexibility by asking questions and seeking information, rather than making assertions, requests, threats, and demands. Posing questions or puzzles that require logical thought may help enlighten both parties about the tacit beliefs and preferences that underlie their positions. Questioning is also a less threatening form of communication than assertion, which may facilitate unfreezing cognitive structures (for extensive discussions of communication and unfreezing, see Chapters Six and Twenty-Four).

Information seeking offers other cognitive benefits as well. The process of posing questions and answering them may also induce each party to learn about their own interests and priorities in addition to those of their opponent. There is some evidence that in attempting to persuade others, one becomes open to persuasion oneself (Downing, Judd, and Brauer, 1992). Parties in negotiation may be persuaded by the arguments they hear themselves making as much as they are by arguments made by their opponents. To the extent that answering questions creates opportunity for the parties to learn more about their own interests and priorities, and the concessions they are willing to make, it may lead to agreements based on cognitive changes that have an especially good chance to persist.

Finally, in light of the importance of evidence that disconfirms prior schemas and beliefs, questions can be strategically designed to seek disconfirming evidence. Doing so may begin the process of changing norms and perceptions that maintain defense and impression motivations.

CONCLUSION

We have two primary goals in this chapter. First, we want to give a theoretical overview of current social psychological research and theory in the area of persuasion. The first half of the chapter is devoted to this goal, presenting in some detail a dual-process model arguing that persuasion happens as a result of two types of information processing, one based on heuristics and the other involving systematic processing. Additionally, we argue that there are three sorts of motivation (from accuracy, defense, and impression concerns) that may influence information processing, and hence persuasion. Each of these can be associated with both heuristic and systematic processing; as a result it is the level of motivation, not the specific type, that influences the degree to which systematic processing occurs.

The goal in the second half of the chapter is to show the relevance of the considerations that persuasion research raises for negotiation and conflict resolution. Here we suggest that people in conflict may often confuse coercion with persuasion. Additionally, we argue that for a negotiated settlement to be integrative and long-lasting, the negotiating parties must move from attempts at coercion to persuasion, and motives for information processing should shift from defensive and impression-management concerns toward an accuracy orientation.

Our hope is that the considerations raised by persuasion research can encourage new insights into the process of negotiation and how to achieve both integrative and long-lasting settlements.

Notes

1. Some readers might think that this book, oriented as it is to practitioners, is the wrong place to make contact with relevant scientists. We believe, though, that the interplay between theory and practice is bidirectional, so that practice benefits theory just as much as theory benefits practice. Our second goal, to influence scientists as well as practitioners, can thus be well served by communicating most directly with practitioners of negotiation and conflict resolution.

2. You do not necessarily do this self-consciously. In fact, heuristic processing often proceeds without any awareness among perceivers that they have been heuristic, or superficial, or somehow incomplete in their processing (see Chen and Chaiken, 1999).

References

Chaiken, S. L., Giner-Sorolla, R., and Chen, S. "Beyond Accuracy: Multiple Motives in Heuristic and Systematic Processing." In P. M. Gollwitzer and J. A. Bargh (eds.), *The Psychology of Action: Linking Motivation and Cognition to Action.* New York: Guilford Press, 1996.

Chaiken, S. L., and Trope, Y. (eds.). *Dual-Process Theories in Social Psychology.* New York: Guilford Press, 1999.

Chaiken, S. L., Wood, W., and Eagly, A. H. "Principles of Persuasion." In E. T. Higgins and A. W. Kruglanski (eds.), *Social Psychology: A Handbook of Basic Principles.* New York: Guilford Press, 1996.

Chen, S., and Chaiken, S. L. "The Heuristic-Systematic Model in Its Broader Context." In S. L. Chaiken and Y. Trope (eds.), *Dual-Process Theories in Social Psychology.* New York: Guilford Press, 1999.

Creyer, E. H., Bettman, J. R., and Paine, J. W. "The Impact of Accuracy and Effort Feedback and Goals on Adaptive Decision Behavior." *Journal of Behavioral Decision Making,* 1998, *3,* 1–16.

Downing, J. M., Judd, C. M., and Brauer, M. "Effects of Repeated Expressions on Attitude Extremity." *Journal of Personality and Social Psychology,* 1992, *63,* 17–29.

Eagly, A. H., and Chaiken, S. L. *The Psychology of Attitudes.* Orlando: Harcourt Brace, 1993.

Eagly, A. H., and Chaiken, S. L. "Attitude Structure and Function." In D. T. Gilbert, S. T. Fiske, and G. Lindzey (eds.), *The Handbook of Social Psychology.* Vol. 1. (4th ed.) New York: McGraw-Hill, 1998.

Gruenfeld, D. H., and Fan, E. T. "What Newcomers See and What Oldtimers Say: Discontinuities in Knowledge Exchange." In L. Thompson, D. Messick, and J. Levine (eds.), *Cognition in Organizations: The Management of Knowledge.* Mahwah, N.J.: Erlbaum, 1999.

Gruenfeld, D. H., and Hollingshead, A. B. "Sociocognition in Work Groups: The Evolution of Group Integrative Complexity and Its Relation to Task Performance." *Small Group Research,* 1993, *24,* 383–406.

Gruenfeld, D. H., and Kim, P. H. "Interdependence and Reasoning in Supreme Court Justices." Working paper, Northwestern University, 1998.

Judd, C. M., and Johnson, J. T. "Attitudes, Polarization, and Diagnosticity: Exploring the Effect of Affect." *Journal of Personality and Social Psychology,* 1981, *41,* 26–36.

Lawler, E. J. "From Revolutionary Coalitions to Bilateral Deterrence: A Non-Zero-Sum Approach to Social Power." In J. K. Murnighan (ed.), *Social Psychology in Organizations: Advances in Theory and Research.* Upper Saddle River, N.J.: Prentice Hall, 1993.

Levine, J., and Thompson, L. "Conflict in Groups." In E. T. Higgins and A. W. Kruglanski (eds.), *Social Psychology: A Handbook of Basic Principles.* New York: Guilford Press, 1996.

Neale, M. A., and Bazerman, M. *Cognition and Rationality in Negotiation.* New York: Free Press, 1991.

Petty, R. E., and Wegener, D. T. "Attitude Change: Multiple Roles for Persuasion Variables." In D. T. Gilbert, S. T. Fiske, and G. Lindzey (eds.), *The Handbook of Social Psychology.* Vol. 1. (4th ed.) New York: McGraw-Hill, 1998.

Pruitt, D. G. "Social Conflict." In D. T. Gilbert, S. T. Fiske, and G. Lindzey (eds.), *The Handbook of Social Psychology.* Vol. 2. (4th ed.) New York: McGraw-Hill, 1998.

Pruitt, D. G., and Lewis, S. A. "Development of Integrative Solutions in Bilateral Negotiation." *Journal of Personality and Social Psychology,* 1975, *31,* 621–633.

Suedfeld, P. "APA Presidential Addresses: The Relation of Integrative Complexity to Historical, Professional, and Personal Factors." *Journal of Personality and Social Psychology,* 1985, *49,* 1643–1651.

Tetlock, P. E. "Monitoring the Integrative Complexity of American and Soviet Policy Statements: What Can Be Learned?" *Journal of Social Issues,* 1988, *44,* 101–131.

Tetlock, P. E. "Good Judgment in International Politics: Three Psychological Perspectives." *Political Psychology,* 1992, *13,* 517–540.

Tetlock, P. E., Armor, D., and Peterson, R. S. "The Slavery Debate in Antebellum America: Cognitive Style, Value Conflict, and the Limits of Compromise." *Journal of Personality and Social Psychology,* 1994, *66,* 115–126.

Tetlock, P. E., Peterson, R. S., and Berry, J. M. "Flattering and Unflattering Personality Portraits of Integratively Simple and Complex Managers." *Journal of Personality and Social Psychology,* 1993, *64,* 500–511.

Zajonc, R. B. "The Process of Cognitive Tuning in Communication." *Journal of Abnormal and Social Psychology,* 1960, *61,* 159–167.

CHAPTER EIGHT

Intergroup Conflict

Ronald J. Fisher

Intergroup conflict is expressed in many forms and settings, in every society. In an organization, poorly managed differences between departments or factions within the same unit can dampen morale, create animosity, and reduce motivation and productivity. In a community setting, schisms between interest groups on important social issues can lead to polarization and hostility, while low-intensity conflict between ethnic, racial, or religious groups finds expression in prejudice, discrimination, and social activism intended to reduce inequity. At the societal level, high-intensity conflict between identity groups on a broad scale can break out into ethnopolitical warfare, which engages the international community as well as local actors. At every level of human interaction, poorly handled conflict between authorities and constituents or between majorities and minorities can lead to frustration and alienation on both sides. In fact, wherever important differences exist between groups, there is the potential for destructive intergroup conflict.

It is important to note that destructive intergroup conflict is only one major form of relationship in the wider domain of intergroup relations, that is, interactions among individuals that occur in terms of their group identification. Intergroup relations is concerned with all manner of relationship among groups, including both cooperative and competitive interaction as well as constructive intergroup conflict. In most ongoing intergroup relationships in countless settings, cooperative relations exist and conflict is handled more or less constructively, to the satisfaction of the parties involved. But if this does not occur around incompatible goals or activities, and the parties work to control or frustrate each other adversarially and antagonistically, the scene is set for destructive intergroup conflict. Given that such conflicts can be very costly to the parties involved as well as the wider system, especially at the intercommunal and international levels, it is essential to understand them and to look for ways of managing and resolving them, which is the focus of this chapter.

From the point of view generally held in the social sciences, intergroup conflict is not simply a matter of misperception or misunderstanding; instead, it is based in real differences between groups in terms of social power, access to resources, important life values, or other significant incompatibilities. However, these realistic sources of conflict are typically exacerbated by the subjective processes individuals employ in seeing and interpreting the world, and in how groups function in the face of differences and perceived threat. As individuals and as groups, human beings are not well equipped to deal with important differences among themselves and others, and they often engage in behaviors that make the situation worse, unless social processes and institutions are available to them to manage their incompatibility effectively. If differences are handled constructively, such conflict can be a source of learning, creativity, and social change toward a pluralistic, harmonious, and equitable world.

Although intergroup conflict finds innumerable expressions, this chapter focuses on the general processes of causation, escalation, and resolution that apply to these many forms. Still, it needs to be understood that each organizational, community, cultural, political, and societal setting requires further analysis to truly understand the intergroup conflicts at that level of interaction and within that particular setting, prior to suggesting avenues for handling them constructively. In addition, the general concepts and principles available from Western social scientific research and practice have to be interpreted, modified, and augmented with cultural sensitivity to be useful in varied cultural settings. In some cases, general prescriptions are inappropriate and counterproductive, and application has to await further developments in theory and practice, both locally and globally.

Although compatible with much theory and research in the social sciences on intergroup conflict, this chapter draws especially on work in social psychology, an interdiscipline between sociology and psychology that seeks to integrate understanding of individual processes, especially in perception and cognition, with knowledge of social processes, particularly those at the group and intergroup levels. Studies of the development and resolution of intergroup conflict over time—for example, with boys camp groups (Sherif, 1966), management personnel in training workshops (Blake and Mouton, 1961), volunteers in a prison simulation (Haney, Banks, and Zimbardo, 1973), and university students in a simulated community conflict over resources and values (Fisher, Grant, Hall, and others, 1990)—have illuminated our understanding of the processes and outcomes that can arise from realistic group incompatibility. Much of this understanding has been captured in general treatments of conflict—its sources, tendency to escalate, and general strategies directed toward managing it (see, for example, Deutsch, 1973, 1983, 1991; Fisher, 1990, 1993, 1997; and Rubin, Pruitt, and Kim, 1994). Knowledge is also drawn from theories of social identity (Tajfel and Turner, 1986), ethnocentrism (Levine and Campbell, 1972), and intergroup relations (Taylor and Moghaddam, 1994). In addition, social and organizational psychologists have contributed to developing methods to manage and resolve intergroup conflict in various settings (Blake and Mouton, 1984; Blake, Shepard, and Mouton, 1964; Brown, 1983; Fisher, 1994, 1997).

From these and other sources, one can deduce a social psychological approach to addressing intergroup conflict that is phenomenological (stressing the subjective reality of the groups), interactive (emphasizing the behavioral interaction of the groups in expressing, maintaining, and resolving their conflict), and multilevel (realizing that understanding is necessary at numerous levels of analysis from various disciplines within a systems orientation). Thus, the ideas that are covered in this chapter come from many sources that are further identified in the references given above, and that need to be combined with the fruits of the other social sciences to gain the necessary context and greater meaning. Therefore, the interested reader is requested to search the literature for concepts and practices that are identified here, rather than referring to this chapter as the primary source.

INTERGROUP CONFLICT: SOURCES AND DYNAMICS

The essence of intergroup conflict lies in three elements: incompatibilities, behaviors, and sentiments. A broad definition of destructive conflict sees it as a social situation in which there are perceived incompatibilities in goals or values between two (or more) parties, attempts by the parties to control one another, and antagonistic feelings toward each other. When the parties are groups, individuals are acting and reacting toward members of the other group in terms of their social identification with their group (which forms an important part of their social identity) rather than as individuals. The definition stresses that incompatibility by itself does not constitute conflict, since the parties could live in peaceful coexistence. However, when there are attempts to control the other party to deal with the incompatibility, and when such interactions result in and are fueled by antagonistic emotions, destructive conflict exists.

This definition is in line with an approach to studying conflict known as "realistic group conflict theory," which stresses that objective conflicts of interest cause conflict. In contrast, "social identity theory" holds that simply categorizing individuals into groups (in a minimally competitive social context) is enough to create differentiation between groups and some amount of bias in favor of one's in-group and discrimination against out-groups. In real life, both contributions are typically in play, and it is not easy to know which is primary, although the bias here is to put more weight into real differences of interest.

Sources of Intergroup Conflict

What are some areas of incompatibility that can give rise to destructive intergroup conflict? One useful typology, proposed by Daniel Katz, identifies economic, value, and power differences as primary drivers. Economic conflict is competition over scarce resources; it can occur in any setting and over any desired goods or services. Resources are typically in finite if not short supply, and groups understandably often approach this "distributive situation" with a fixed-pie assumption that what one gains, the other loses. The stage is thus set for competitive strategies and behaviors to obtain one's fair share (which is seen as unfair by the other group) and in so doing to frustrate the other group's goal-directed behavior. Reciprocal interaction along this line usually generates a perception of threat and feelings of hostility.

Value conflicts involve differences in what groups believe in, from minor variance in preference or principle to major cleavage in ideology or way of life. Conflict can arise over valued means or valued ends, that is, over how goals are achieved or what their nature or priorities are. Organizations often comprise groups in conflict over how decisions should be made (autocratically or democratically) and over the outcomes to be prized (say, highest-quality service or highest return on investment). Societies and the world at large are composed of cultural and religious groups, with myriad variations in preference, practice, and priority that can place them in situations of incompatibility. Again, the question is how the groups, particularly the dominant group(s), choose to deal with these differences—for example, by forcing their cultural norms on other groups or by supporting intercultural respect and harmony.

Power conflict occurs when each group wishes to maximize its influence and control in the relationship with the other. At base, this is a struggle for dominance, whether in a corporate office or a region of the globe. As such, it is often not resolvable quickly. The resulting struggle may lead to victory and defeat or a tense stalemate and deadlock. Power conflict often recycles through various substantive issues, and over time the dynamic of a mutual win-lose orientation becomes apparent. This, however, is not to be confused with inherent use of power in all types of conflict in which parties work to influence each other. Power conflict is often distinguished by use of negative power (through behaviors such as threat, deception, or manipulation) as opposed to tactics of positive power (such as persuasion, use of valid information, and consideration of the pros and cons of alternative actions); see also Chapter Five.

To this typology can be added contemporary concern with needs conflict, that is, differences in the degree to which the basic human needs of groups, and the individuals within them, are being frustrated or satisfied. This line of theorizing comes partly from the work of psychologist Abraham Maslow and sociologist Paul Sites; it has been brought into the conflict domain by international relations specialists John Burton, Edward Azar, and others. Basic needs are seen as fundamental requirements for human development; proposed lists include the need for security, identity, recognition of identity, freedom, distributive justice, and participation. Identity groups are seen as the primary vehicle through which these necessities are expressed and satisfied, thus leading to intergroup conflict if one group's basic needs are frustrated or denied. It is proposed that the most destructive and intractable conflicts on the world scene between identity groups—that is, racial, religious, ethnic, or cultural groups—are due to need frustration. However, identity groups also exist in organizations and communities, wherever groups form around a common social identity, and if needs for recognition of that identity or for distributive justice based on identity are denied, then conflict is similarly predicted.

An important qualification is that many times conflict is a mixture of these sources, rather than a pure type. This can be true in the initial causation, as when power and economic competition are simultaneously expressed, or over time, as when value differences or need frustrations are addressed through increasing use of negative power. The typology also does not rule out misperception and miscommunication as potential sources of conflict, but it is unlikely that serious intergroup conflict could sustain itself for any period of time based solely on these subjective aspects. This is not to deny that misperceptions can produce behaviors that give rise to serious conflict, as when one group launches a preemptive strike against another from the mistaken fear that the other is about to attack. Destructive conflict, though, is typically over real differences, poorly managed.

Perceptual and Cognitive Factors

Regardless of the source, conflict between groups often engages perceptual, cognitive, emotional, and behavioral mechanisms at both the individual and group levels that exacerbate the initial incompatibility. Social identity theory tells us that the simple perceptual act of group categorization in a minimally competitive context sets in motion a process of group differentiation with resulting ingroup favoritism. This is apparently because individuals must attain and maintain a positive social identity, which they do by first engaging in social categorization of groups, and then by making favorable social comparisons of their own group in relation to others. Thus, there is pressure to gain distinctiveness for one's own group and to evaluate it positively in comparison with other groups, thereby leading to discrimination against them.

The concept of ethnocentrism captures how identity groups tend to be ethnically centered, to accept and even glorify those who are alike (the in-group), and to denigrate, discriminate against, and reject those who are unlike (out-groups). Realistic group conflict theory sees ethnocentrism as an outcome of objective conflicts of interest and competitive interactions by groups to obtain their goals, a process in which perceived threat plays a key role by heightening in-group solidarity and engendering hostility toward the threatening out-group, especially if there is a history of antagonism between them.

In contrast, research supporting social identity theory demonstrates that intergroup discrimination can occur without any clear conflict of interest or any intergroup interaction. Here, discrimination is limited to in-group favoritism rather than out-group derogation and hostility. Both theories predict that individuals in intergroup conflict engage in misperceptions that accentuate intergroup differences. However, realistic group conflict theory provides a much richer treatment of the interplay of perceptions and interactions in producing destructive intergroup conflict.

Groups in conflict tend to develop negative stereotypes of each other: oversimplified, inaccurate, rigid, and derogatory beliefs about the characteristics of the other group that are applied indiscriminately to all the individuals in that group. They come about partly through the processes of group categorization, which exaggerate the differences between groups and the homogeneity of the out-group. But they also come about through selective perception and memory retrieval, by which qualities and behaviors that fit the stereotype are accepted and retained, while those that do not are rejected. Mutual stereotyping leads in part to a mirror image, in which each group sees the other negatively (as aggressive, untrustworthy, manipulative) and itself positively (as peaceful, trustworthy, cooperative). Through the process of socialization, these simplified pictures are passed on to new group members (children, recruits, new employees) so that they can take their rightful place in defending the interests of their in-group against out-group enemies.

Cognitive biases also complicate intergroup conflict through the attributions that individuals make about the behavior of others, that is, how they make judgments about the causes of behaviors or events. In intergroup relations, there is a tendency to see out-group members as personally responsible for negative behavior ("He's sadistic"), rather than this being due to situational factors ("He was ordered to do it"). In addition, the personal characteristics that are the focus of attribution tend to be group qualities that are embodied in the negative stereotype ("They're all monsters"). In contrast, undesirable behavior by an in-group member tends to be attributed to external conditions for which the member is not responsible ("What else could the poor man do?"). Thus, attribution perpetuates and strengthens stereotypes and mirror images, as well as fueling hostility between conflicting groups as each holds the other largely responsible for the shared mess they are in.

Group-Level Factors

The individual processes of perception and cognition make important contributions to understanding intergroup conflict, but its complexity and intractability are also due to group-level forces. Like individuals, social groups do not usually respond constructively to differences that appear to threaten the identity or well-being of the group. The functioning of each group, in terms of identity, cohesiveness, conformity pressures, and decision making, has a significant impact on how conflict is played out and ultimately resolved or terminated. In addition, the structure and culture of the organization, community, or society in which intergroup conflict occurs influence its expression and management. Unfortunately, these latter areas are not so well explored as they should be, and space limitations here preclude consideration of these higher-level influences.

All individuals are members of social groups, by birth or by choice, and the group identifications that one carries form the central element of one's social identity. Many theorists, including those who developed social identity theory, believe that an individual's self-esteem is linked to group membership, in that a positive self-concept requires favorable evaluation of one's group(s) and invidious comparison with other groups. Thus, the seeds are sown for ethnic groups to display ethnocentrism, and national groups to exhibit nationalism—pride and loyalty to one's nation and denigration of other nations. However, we do not need to be at the level of large collectives to see the functioning of group identity. Professional groups, scientific disciplines, political parties, government departments, lobby groups, businesses, sports teams, street gangs—all have their sense of group identity, and it affects their relations with other groups. The dark side of social identity is that in expressing commitment and affection to in-groups, there is a tendency to devalue and disrespect out-groups, thus contributing to intergroup conflict in a situation involving incompatibility.

Along with identity, groups tend to develop cohesiveness, essentially a shared sense of attraction to the group and motivation to remain in it. Along with fostering satisfaction and productivity, cohesiveness acts powerfully in heightening conformity to the group; thus it has important implications for intergroup conflict. Cohesive groups are more effective in striving toward their goals; furthermore, it is also generally accepted that intergroup conflict increases cohesiveness within the competing groups, primarily through the effects of threat. Thus, the interplay between group cohesiveness and competition is a significant factor in sustaining intergroup conflict.

Groups in conflict are notorious for pressuring members to conform, to toe the line and support the cause. Group norms (standards of acceptable behavior) and related social influence processes dictate both the stereotypes and the discriminatory behavior held to be appropriate with respect to out-groups. Members who deviate from these norms are called to task and may be ridiculed, punished, ostracized, or eliminated, depending on the severity of the conflict and the deviant behavior. Holding polarized opinions is characteristic of cohesive groups under threat, and insidious and powerful influences are brought to bear on members who voice disagreement with the majority.

Cohesiveness is the main factor behind the phenomenon of groupthink, as articulated by Irving Janis (1982), by which an insulated group of decision makers under stress pushes concurrence seeking to the point that it overrides realistic and moral appraisal of alternatives. Janis identifies a number of U.S. foreign policy fiascoes (among them the Bay of Pigs invasion and the bombing of Cambodia) as instances in which independent critical thinking was replaced by a decision to engage in irrational and dehumanizing action toward an out-group. Groupthink is characterized by symptoms showing overestimation of the group's power and morality, closed-mindedness, and severe pressure toward uniformity. This is compatible with a large body of theory and research demonstrating that decision making in general is not a rational, orderly process, but indeed involving cognitive bias, group liability, and organizational constraint that produce less-than-optimal outcomes (see also Chapter Nine). The sobering thought with regard to intergroup conflict is that groups on both sides may be making faulty decisions that exacerbate rather than alleviate the situation.

The role of group leadership in intergroup conflict is also an important element of decision making, given that leaders and other high-status members hold more power than the rank and file. A common phenomenon in situations of competition and conflict is that aggressive leaders tend to come to the fore, while cooperative or accommodating leaders tend to lose power or position. Janis postulated that lack of impartial leadership is also an important condition of groupthink, in that directive leadership that is committed to a particular direction or decision tends to influence cohesive groups toward concurrence seeking. In addition, groups in conflict tend to influence leaders in an aggressive direction, and this constituent pressure supports militant leaders' use of contentious tactics in interactions with the out-group.

Escalation Dynamics

All of the individual and group factors described so far have one thing in common: they tend to influence conflict interaction in the direction of escalation, that is, the process by which conflict becomes intense and hostile. Escalation involves increasing use of heavier methods of influence, especially coercive or punishing tactics, by each group to reach its goals in opposition to those of the other group. Escalation also typically results in proliferating issues, not just the basic ones that the conflict is perceived to be about (say, wages or benefits in union-management conflict) but also process issues that arise from how the two parties treat each other (perhaps use of deception in negotiation). Escalation feeds largely on fear and defensiveness, in which a threat by one party to gain its objectives is met by a counterthreat from the other, and the reciprocal interaction moves to a higher level of cost each time around in a climate of increasing mistrust. The self-fulfilling prophecy (first identified by Robert Merton, 1952) comes into play in a specific manner: defensiveness and mistrust motivate a cautious or controlling move, which elicits a defensive and hostile counteraction, which is then perceived as justifying the initial action, etc. This type of interaction, for example, led Ralph White to characterize the Cold War as partly due to "defensively motivated aggression."

Our understanding of the escalatory process has been enhanced by Deutsch's work (see Chapter One) on the difference between cooperative and competitive interaction. The modal approach that parties take in terms of perception, attitude, communication, and task orientation tends to show a consistency that is very powerful in determining the nature of their interaction over time. Deutsch's Crude Law of Social Relations (again, see Chapter One) captures a great deal of the reality of intergroup conflict; the characteristic processes and effects elicited by a type of social relationship (cooperative or competitive) tend also to elicit that type of social relationship. As Deutsch points out, cooperative processes of problem solving are similar to constructive processes of conflict resolution, while competitive processes are similar to destructive ones in addressing conflict.

The competitive-destructive dynamic has also been captured by Deutsch in his elucidation of the "malignant social process," which describes the increasingly dangerous and costly interaction of high-intensity intergroup conflict. Through a combination of cognitive rigidity and bias, self-fulfilling prophecy, and unwitting commitment to prior beliefs and action, parties are drawn into an escalating spiral wherein past investment justifies increasing risk, and unacceptable losses foreclose a way out. Thus, it is understandable how groups get locked into destructive conflict and appear unable to deescalate or resolve the situation on their own.

Resistance to Resolution

The downside of escalation is found not only in the pain and cost that the parties endure but as well in the resistance to deescalation and resolution that negative interaction creates. Dean Pruitt, Jeffrey Rubin, and their colleagues have been at the forefront of studying and theorizing how parties get locked into conflict. At the individual level, they see psychological changes, among them negative attitude and perceptions that first encourage escalation (through the biases noted above), but then support the persistence of escalatory interaction (through similar biases). To these they add the process of deindividuation (by which outgroup members are seen not as individuals but as members of a category who are dehumanized and deserve inhumane treatment).

Structural change at the group level also results from escalation. Hostile perception of the out-group and destructive motives toward them become cemented in group norms; pressure is brought to bear on the group members to accept these norms as right. As we have mentioned, increased cohesiveness and militant leadership tend to support contentious tactics and aggressive objectives. In addition, a militant subgroup, benefiting from the conflict in terms of status, power, or wealth, develops strong vested interest in its continuation. At the level of the larger social system—the organization, community, or global society—intense conflict induces polarization by which other players, initially outside the conflict, are drawn into coalitions that ultimately fracture the system into two opposing camps. This increases the intensity of the conflict and eliminates neutrals who could serve a useful third-party role in its resolution.

The final contributors to deescalation resistance are the phenomena of overcommitment and entrapment. Psychological and group changes tend to strengthen the commitment made to contentious behavior, such that it becomes self-reinforcing, partly through the act of rationalization. Whatever was done in the past is seen as necessary, and the barrier to conflict termination is the other party's intransigence. Commitment to a destructive and costly course of action is increased further by entrapment, in which costs already incurred are justified by continuing expenditures in pursuit of victory. Even though irrational by outside judgment, each party pursues its goals, believing that the ultimate reward is just around the corner and that only attaining it can justify what has already been expended. The longer mutual intransigence persists, the more the parties feel compelled to justify their positions through continued intransigence.

IMPLICATIONS FOR UNDERSTANDING AND PRACTICE

The complexity and intractability of destructive, escalated intergroup conflict boggles the mind and depresses the spirit of those who would deign to do anything about it, members of the conflicting groups and outsiders alike. This is true whether the conflict involves factions within an organization that have crossed each other off, interest groups in a community that can only yell at each other about the issues that divide them, or ethnic groups that believe total eradication of the enemy is the only viable solution. Nonetheless, this horrendous social problem is a phenomenon that can be understood and rendered amenable, over time, to action and intervention that transform seemingly intractable incompatibility into a workable relationship. The task is not easy, and civilization is far from having the knowledge and expertise required. But from what we now know, some implications for addressing intergroup conflict can be discerned.

A number of implications take the form of broad orientations to approaching resolution of intergroup conflict, orientations that must be further operationalized as specific strategies and tactics. First among these is the premise that intense intergroup conflict is both an objective and a subjective phenomenon, and that attempts to address only one set of factors or the other are doomed to failure, either immediate or long-term. Thus, methods are required that settle substantive interests *and* that address psychological, social, and cultural aspects—the stuff of identity conflict. Given this complexity and its attendant intransigence, it is typically the case that members of the parties themselves are unable to engage in the analysis and interaction required. This implies that involving third parties outside the conflict—perceived to be impartial, competent, and trustworthy—is usually required to deescalate and resolve the situation. In doing so, third parties must realize that deescalation is not simply the reverse of escalation, because of the residue and resistance built up through a history of antagonistic interaction.

A further implication of the objective-subjective mix is that various methods of intervention may be required at different stages of escalation to deescalate the conflict to a level where subsequent interventions can work. For example, interventions that focus on perceptual, attitudinal, and relationship issues may be required before third-party efforts at mediating agreement on substantive matters can be successful. This form of contingency modeling has been put forward by Loraleigh Keashly and myself, as well as other scholar-practitioners in the field, including Dean Pruitt and Paul Olzack (see Chapter Twenty-One).

A related implication is that intervention in intergroup conflict must start with thorough analysis of the situation before an intervention is designed and implemented. Such analysis should involve not only the third party but also members or representatives of the groups themselves, because each phase of deescalation and resolution is dependent on earlier ones. For example, analysis, understanding, and dialogue are necessary for reconciliation to occur, and developing alternative solutions must be based on diagnosis of each party's motivations, aspirations, and constraints.

Finally, the objective and subjective mix of conflict also implies that change is required in both process or relationship qualities and substantive or structural aspects for intergroup conflict to come to enduring resolution. That is, clearing up misattributions and rebuilding trust, for example, need to go hand in hand with developing decision-making procedures and resource-allocation systems that address the basic incompatibility. Thus, conflict resolution is prescribed not simply as a mechanism for dealing with difficult differences within an existing social system but also as an approach that can facilitate constructive social change toward a responsive and equitable system.

Elsewhere, I have delineated a set of generic principles for resolving intergroup conflict (see the Recommended Reading list for this chapter) that embody implications flowing from the ideas and implications given above. I summarize these principles below, organized into three major phases of addressing intergroup conflict: analysis, confrontation, and resolution.

Implications for Analyzing the Conflict

As noted earlier, conflict analysis should be the lead activity in moving into a field of incompatibility and destructive interaction. Unlike the analysis that parties usually engage in (which identifies political, economic, legal, or military strategies and resources they can use to prevail), conflict analysis carried out by third parties in a facilitative role focuses on the sources and dynamics of the conflict that have brought it to its present state of intractability. Of course, this involves identifying the parties and factions as well as the issues they insist the conflict is about. However, it also goes beneath the surface issues to identify the underlying interests, values, and needs that relate to the position each party takes, that is, its demands and offers. In addition, this work must entail a process analysis, surfacing and discussing the perceptions, thoughts, goals, fears, and needs of each party, and a trust-building process that allows the parties to exchange clarification, acknowledgment, assurance, and possible contributions to rebuilding their relationship.

It is implied in these activities and outcomes that the parties are engaging in intense, face-to-face interaction involving genuine communication and development of realistic empathy for each other. It is further implied that this form of analysis must be carried out by a skilled, impartial, and trusted third party having knowledge of conflict processes and skills in group dynamics and intergroup relations. It is conceivable that members of the parties can form a balanced team to undertake this consulting role, but this is doubly difficult because of group identification. Given that the third party also requires knowledge of the system and culture in which the conflict is embedded—be it organizational, community, societal, or international—it is also implied that the intervenor should be a multiskilled team of diverse individuals, since it is unlikely that any one person will have the varied knowledge and skills required to facilitate a constructive discussion about the complex issues in conflict.

The stage of conflict analysis may reveal that objective interests predominate, and that the parties are motivated to settle their differences and either ignore subjective elements or defer considering them to a future time. In this case, the parties may shift to a negotiation mode and move toward mutually satisfactory agreement; more likely, they have to engage the services of a mediator to assist them in crafting a settlement.

It is also possible that the parties agree to engage and accept a binding third-party judgment by a superior authority—a higher manager or body in the organization, an arbitrator appointed for the purpose, or a legal adjudicator who is available to them. Unfortunately, it is often the case that in intense intergroup conflict these options are either not engaged (because each party fears losing and believes it can still win) or not successful in the long run (because the set-tlements do not deal with the underlying sources and subjective aspects that drive the conflict to such a high level of escalation and intractability). In these cases, continuing involvement by a third party in a consultative role is often re-quired, although it is not readily available in many settings.

Implications for Confronting the Conflict

When third-party assisted interaction *is* possible, after analysis comes the stage of productive confrontation, in which the parties directly engage one another on the issues dividing them and work toward mutually acceptable solutions through joint problem solving. It is essential that this process be carried out under norms of mutual respect, shared exploration, and commitment to the problem-solving process, rather than fixation on positions. It is implied that the "facilitative con-ditions of intergroup contact" (articulated by social scientists starting with Gordon Allport) are in place for these interactions: equal-status participants from each group; positive institutional supports for the process; a cooperative reward and task structure; good potential for participants to get to know each other as persons; and involvement of respected, competent, and well-adjusted individu-als. Thus, it is further implied that intergroup engagements must be well de-signed, with appropriate selection of individual participants and identification of both formal and informal activities and goals. Again, this is a role best left to knowledgeable, skilled, and trusted third-party consultants.

Equally challenging is facilitation of the engagement sessions themselves, which need to incorporate such qualities as open and accurate representation of group perception; recognition of intergroup diversity, including gender and cultural differences; and persistence to attain mutually acceptable outcomes. A strong implication is that the parties must be encouraged to follow a strategy of collaboration rather than competition. That is, they have to engage in a combi-nation of assertive behavior (stressing one's own needs) and cooperation (show-ing concern for the other party's needs). This two-dimensional approach or dual-concern model is well represented in the conflict resolution field, building on the early work of Robert Blake and Jane Mouton with elaborations by Kenneth Thomas, Afzalur Rahim, and others. The parties must also engage in a joint problem-solving process that carries them to a shared solution. Knowl-edge of group problem solving is a starting point, but it was the pioneering ef-forts of Blake, Mouton, and their colleagues that led to developing a social technology of intergroup problem solving. They have articulated how this tech-nology can be applied by consultants or by members of the groups themselves, at least in organizational settings.

Implications for Resolving the Conflict

Conflict resolution refers to both the collaborative process by which differences are handled and the outcomes that are jointly agreed to by the parties. As distinct from conflict management, mitigation, or amelioration, conflict resolution involves transforming the relationship and situation such that solutions developed by the parties are sustainable and self-correcting in the long run. Future incompatibility will occur, of course, and further problem solving toward social change is required, but the manner of approaching differences and the quality of the outcome are different.

Thus one implication of this approach is that conflict and the relationships in which it is embedded must be transformed in an enduring fashion, as opposed to simply settling disputes or, worse yet, suppressing differences. To accomplish this, the resolution process and outcomes must address basic human needs for development and satisfaction to some acceptable degree. Needs for security, identity, recognition, participation, distributive justice, and so on must be identified in the analysis, and mechanisms to address them ("satisfiers") must be built into the outcomes. Relations between identity groups can then be built around each group having a satisfactory degree of recognition and autonomy (power), so that it can freely enter into an interdependent relationship that is mutually beneficial.

A further implication related to outcomes necessary for resolution is that mechanisms and procedures for dealing with differences assertively and cooperatively must be built into decision making and policy making. If all parties concerned with a situation of conflict are meaningfully involved, and if procedures that work to achieve consensus (not unanimity) are implemented, the chances of incompatibility escalating into destructive conflict are markedly reduced. This assertion is built on humanistic and democratic values, which of course are not in play in many institutions, cultures, and societies; this is why conflict resolution must be seen as part of the slow march of civilization toward a participative and egalitarian world. Each social unit (organization, institution, community, society) has choices to make regarding the benefit and cost of social control (oppression in the extreme), versus the benefit and ultimately reduced cost of moving in a democratic direction.

Therefore, at the far end of conflict resolution, it is implied that institutions and societies must create political and economic structures that support equality and equity among different groups as well as individuals (see also the discussion of the values and norms underlying constructive conflict resolution in Chapter One). At the societal level, democratic pluralism and multiculturalism are policies that reduce destructive intergroup conflict. Depending on the geographical distribution of groups, political arrangements involving power sharing or federalism are congruent with a conflict resolution approach. Recognition of and respect among distinct identity groups in cultural and political terms must go hand in hand with equality of opportunity in economic terms. Conflict resolution thus does not imply assimilation or homogenization, although members of distinct identity groups may share a political or national identity as well; but it does imply a mosaic of integrated social groups, cooperating interdependently for mutual benefit.

IMPLICATIONS FOR TRAINING

All of these implications cry out for new roles, innovative practice, and transformed policy and institutions to deal creatively with differences among diverse groups. Whether one is a member or representative of a group in conflict, or a third party charged with facilitating conflict resolution, the challenge in terms of the qualities and skills required is daunting. At the same time, there is now a welcome proliferation of education and training opportunities at all levels (elementary and secondary schools, colleges and universities, undergraduate and graduate programs, professional development workshops) in relevant areas such as interpersonal communication, problem solving, consensus building, conflict management, and so on. The question to be addressed here is, What are the basic skills required to build on the understanding outlined in this chapter to operationalize conflict resolution processes? I can give only a rudimentary answer because of space limitations, but I hope it is a useful starting point. These comments share some points made by Deutsch (in Chapters One and Two) on the skills required for maintaining a cooperative conflict resolution process and a productive group problem-solving process.

The list of analytical (and especially behavioral) skills desired in enacting the facilitation role in resolving intergroup conflict is a long one indeed. It is drawn from multiple areas of professional practice: human relations training, counseling, cross-cultural communication, community development, organizational consulting, intergroup relations, and international diplomacy. No one intervenor can aspire to develop the full skill set required to facilitate productive confrontation at the intergroup level; it is therefore assumed that such work involves teams of professionals, often from disparate but complementary disciplines relevant to the particular context of the conflict (organization, urban community, international region, and so forth). Teams are also required since it is common at certain points to work with the groups separately as well as at the interface of their relationship.

Analytical skills from many domains of understanding are useful, but at the core of this practice is the ability to apply knowledge about social conflict; its causes; forms of expression; processes of escalation; and mechanisms for deescalation, management, and resolution. The task of the intervenor is to offer theoretical interpretation and insight at apparently useful points. These inputs often illuminate the functioning of groups in conflict (such as normative pressure toward aggressive action) or dynamics of the interface between the groups (such as the typical manner in which majorities and minorities relate to each other). Further understanding of the context in which the intergroup conflict occurs is essential, whether one is working in an urban American community, a human-service organization, or a particular region of the globe. In this regard, facilitators who are from the context in question—perhaps even from the groups in conflict—can play an especially illuminating role if they are able to rise above their biases and preconceived notions about the conflict and its resolution.

At the personal level, intervenors require many of the qualities and skills of any professional, reflective practitioner, notably integrity and detachment. Self-confidence and assuredness (although not too much) is necessary to step into the cauldron of intergroup conflict. A high level of self-awareness is essential in terms of how one is affected by the criticism, attack, and similar behavior from others, and how one's own behavior is perceived by and affects them. One needs the capacity to tolerate ambiguity and to respond constructively to defensiveness or resistance to one's efforts. Sensitivity to gender, cultural, and other differences must be coupled with respect for and capacity to work well with the wide variety of individuals to be encountered. Finally, the intervenor needs genuineness, caring, and strength of character to build meaningful and authentic relationships with others, and to persevere with them in difficult times and over the long run.

In terms of interpersonal functioning, capable facilitators of interpersonal conflict develop many of the commonly trained communication and relationship-building skills of the helping professions. The ability to speak genuinely and respectfully and to convey concise, organized messages is coupled with the skill of reflective, empathic listening. It is also vital to give and receive feedback on behavior, and to be able to productively discuss differences in perception that often arise.

Advanced skills of relating are also often useful—especially confrontation (sensitivity to inconsistency in another's behavior and the capacity to describe it clearly and nonjudgmentally) and immediacy (the ability to relate another's implied statements to your relationship or the situation at hand). In short, a good team of facilitators can respond constructively and respectfully to whatever messages members of antagonistic groups bring forward, so as not to antagonize individuals or escalate differences.

The third-party role at the group level is that of a facilitative leader who has the capacity to help the antagonistic groups work together toward their shared goals in the intervention and in the long run. This requires deep knowledge of group process and the capacity to facilitate group interaction. With regard to task leadership, the facilitator designs and implements agendas that engage conflicting parties in productive confrontation and keeps them on track as necessary. On the socioemotional side of leadership, the facilitator provides encouragement and support, releases tension at certain points, and harmonizes misunderstanding. The intervenor has to be capable of dealing with disruptive or aggressive behavior that challenges the work of the group. In essence, the facilitation team works to model and uphold the norms of analytical and respectful interaction. The team member's role is thus a combination of discussion moderator, human relations trainer, dialogue facilitator, and process consultant.

Another important role for the intervenor involves managing the problem-solving process toward deescalation and resolution. Although steeped in models of group problem solving, the process at the intergroup level has additional challenges and pitfalls. The capable facilitator understands that at best only an uneasy coalition can be built between members or representatives of identity groups. This is because in-groups are constantly pulled in an ethnocentric direction, including all of the cognitive and social biases noted above. Thus, moving the groups through the problem-solving process is a shared and mutually accepted experience at all stages. If any one stage, such as initial diagnosis or creation of alternatives, is imbalanced through the domination of one group or biased in the interests of one group, the outcomes are not sustainable. Mutuality and reciprocity are the keys; the parties are constantly reminded that only through joint involvement and shared commitment can they be successful in dealing with their conflict.

The final set of skills for individuals who intend to orchestrate intergroup confrontation revolves around the ability to manage difficult interactions at the interface of two or more groups. Building on all the previous skills, this challenge requires that facilitators design and implement constructive interchanges between individuals from the conflicting groups to move them toward resolving their difficulties and toward a renewed relationship. The ability to control disruptive interaction (argument, debate, mutual accusation, recrimination, attack on the third party or the process) is combined with the skill to manage a charged agenda over time, stay on track, and move toward accomplishment and closure.

At all times, the facilitator is working toward increasing mutual understanding and inducing joint problem solving. Sometimes the best that can be done is for the parties to agree to disagree, but if it is done with full understanding and a sense of respect, it is a far cry from the usual antagonism and blaming. The skills of the human relations trainer are especially useful at this level of interaction. However, when working with intergroup conflict resolution, the focus of the trainer is not on individuals as they interact with other individuals in the group, but on how individuals interact *in terms of their group identity* with members of the other group.

This approach to intergroup conflict resolution sees it as a form of professional consultation, wherein the help giver uses his or her expertise to facilitate the problem solving of the client system. Thus, skills and ethical practices that are necessary to implement the process and attain the outcomes of consultation are the final requirement for this line of work.

The skills of consultation revolve around the capacity to initiate and manage the phases of consultation, from contact to closure. Contact with the groups in conflict should come from a base of credibility, legitimacy, and impartiality, even in the case of a facilitation team composed of members of the two groups, where intervenors are respected within and outside their communities and balance on the team ensures overall impartiality. In the entry process, the consultant needs to assess the antagonists' perception of these qualities, and all parties need to assess how good a fit there is between the intervenor's values and capabilities and the client system's need for consultation. If entry is successful, the consultant next concentrates on the critical process of contracting, wherein expectations of all parties are clarified and ground rules for the intervention are specified. Thus, the consultant must spell out the rationale, methods, and objectives of the proposed intervention and seek the agreement of the parties.

Diagnostic skills are central to the next phase of consultation, in which the intervenor gathers information about the current state of the client system—in this case, the intergroup conflict—and about the preferred state as perceived by the parties. This phase of implementation then invokes many of the skills already noted, wherein the consultant delivers the activities at the intergroup interface that are intended to increase the capacity for joint problem solving.

Evaluation is the last phase prior to exit; it requires the methodological skills of the social scientist in order to judge how the intervention was carried out and what its effects were, both intended and unintended. In exiting the client system, the consultant hopes that the parties now have the understanding and skills to manage their future relations by themselves. In all phases of consultation, the successful intervenor functions with a high degree of ethical conduct, including the ability to deal with ethical issues as they arise. Thus, casting this work as professional consultation adds another challenging layer to the training requirements for would-be intervenors.

CONCLUSION

Intergroup conflict occurs frequently and is often handled poorly at all levels of society and between societies. It is based in numerous sources and involves a complex interplay of individual perception, attitude, and behavior as well as group factors that have a built-in tendency toward escalation. There is considerable need for skilled intervenors and social roles and institutions to support their practice. A wide range of knowledge, much of it from a social psychological base, yields implications for analyzing, confronting, and resolving intergroup conflict. One of the greatest challenges is to train diverse professionals in the knowledge and skills required to facilitate productive resolution of intergroup conflict. Through a combination of skills in interpersonal communication, group facilitation, intergroup problem solving, and system-level consulting, outside third parties or balanced teams of representatives can help groups confront their differences effectively and build long-term partnerships.

References

Blake, R. R., and Mouton, J. S. *Group Dynamics: Key to Decision-Making.* Houston: Gulf, 1961.

Blake, R. R., and Mouton, J. S. *Solving Costly Organizational Conflicts.* San Francisco: Jossey-Bass, 1984.

Blake, R. R., Shepard, H. A., and Mouton, J. S. *Managing Intergroup Conflict in Industry.* Houston: Gulf, 1964.

Brown, L. D. *Managing Conflict at Organizational Interfaces.* Reading, Mass.: Addison-Wesley, 1983.

Deutsch, M. *The Resolution of Conflict: Constructive and Destructive Processes.* New Haven: Yale University Press, 1973.

Deutsch, M. "The Prevention of World War III: A Psychological Perspective." *Political Psychology,* 1983, *4,* 3–32.

Deutsch, M. "Subjective Features of Conflict Resolution: Psychological, Social, and Cultural Influences." In R. Vayrynen (ed.), *New Directions in Conflict Theory.* London: Sage, 1991.

Fisher, R. J. *The Social Psychology of Intergroup and International Conflict Resolution.* New York: Springer-Verlag, 1990.

Fisher, R. J. "Developing the Field of Interactive Conflict Resolution: Issues in Training, Funding, and Institutionalization." *Political Psychology,* 1993, *14,* 123–138.

Fisher, R. J. "Generic Principles for Resolving Intergroup Conflict." *Journal of Social Issues,* 1994, *50,* 47–66.

Fisher, R. J. *Interactive Conflict Resolution.* Syracuse, N.Y.: Syracuse University Press, 1997.

Fisher, R. J., Grant, P. R., Hall, D. G., and others. "The Development and Testing of a Strategic Simulation of Intergroup Conflict." *Journal of Psychology,* 1990, *124,* 223–240.

Haney, C. C., Banks, C., and Zimbardo, P. "Interpersonal Dynamics in a Simulated Prison." *International Journal of Criminology and Penology,* 1973, *1,* 69–97.

Janis, I. L. *Groupthink.* (2nd ed.) Boston: Houghton Mifflin, 1982.

Levine, R. A., and Campbell, D. T. *Ethnocentrism: Theories of Conflict, Ethnic Attitudes, and Group Behavior.* New York: Wiley, 1972.

Merton, R. K. *Social Theory and Social Structure.* (Rev. ed.) New York: Free Press, 1952.

Rubin, J. Z., Pruitt, D. G., and Kim, S. H. *Social Conflict: Escalation, Stalemate, and Settlement.* (2nd ed.) New York: McGraw-Hill, 1994.

Sherif, M. *In Common Predicament: Social Psychology of Intergroup Conflict and Cooperation: The Robber's Cave Experiment.* Norman: University of Oklahoma Book Exchange, 1966.

Tajfel, H., and Turner, J. "An Integrative Theory of Intergroup Conflict." In S. Worchel and W. G. Austin (eds.), *The Social Psychology of Intergroup Relations.* Chicago: Nelson-Hall, 1986.

Taylor, D. M., and Moghaddam, F. M. *Theories of Intergroup Relations.* (2nd ed.) New York: Praeger, 1994.

CHAPTER NINE

Problem Solving
and Decision Making
in Conflict Resolution

Eben A. Weitzman
Patricia Flynn Weitzman

One way to think about what people do when they resolve conflict is that they solve a problem together. Another way to think about it is that they make a decision—again, together. Sometimes, in the scholarly literature, problem solving and decision making are treated as synonymous. For convenience, we distinguish between the two, even though the processes are intermingled in the course of conflict resolution. Under the heading "Problem Solving," we discuss diagnosis of the conflict and also the development of alternative possibilities for resolving a conflict. Under "Decision Making," we consider a range of the kinds of decisions people involved in resolving conflict have to make, both individually and together, including choice among the alternative possibilities and commitment to the choice that is made. When faced with the necessity for commitment and choice, the parties may decide that the alternatives are inadequate and reiterate the process of diagnosis and development of alternatives (problem solving); there may be repeated cycles of such reiteration before a conflict is resolved.

It is thus possible to think about problem solving and decision making as components of a broader conflict resolution process. Research and practice over the past few decades have shown these ways of thinking about conflict to be profitable both for understanding conflict and for developing constructive approaches to resolving it. We begin by suggesting a simple model of the interaction between problem-solving and decision-making processes in conflict resolution. This model introduces a framework and guide for the remainder of the chapter.

A SIMPLE MODEL

In Figure 9.1, we suggest an integrated model of problem solving and decision making in conflict resolution (for simplicity, we refer to it as the PSDM model). When people are unable to resolve conflict constructively, they are in some way unable or unwilling to reach a resolution that is to all parties—at the least—acceptable. There are many potential sources of such stuckness. Their interests might appear to be (or actually be) incompatible; they might be too angry with one another to talk constructively; they might have fundamental differences in values about the subject of their conflict or about processes for resolving it; they may hold different versions of "the truth" about what has already happened, what will happen, or about any of the "facts" involved; they may have different views of, or desires for, the nature of their relationship; or they may have deep misunderstandings that are hard to sort out. (Since the word *interests* is often understood as a reference to the tangible outcomes people may be seeking, we use the term *concerns* to encompass not only interests but also values, emotional investments, views of reality, and so on.)

We could say, then, that there is a complex puzzle, or problem, to be solved: putting together the various interests, values, preferences, realities, emotional investments, and so on, of the parties involved, and finding a solution that accounts for these at least well enough. In that sense, problem solving needs to take place. Along the way, there are many decisions to be made, both individually and together (see Figure 9.1). The private decisions include prioritizing concerns, evaluating proposals, figuring out whether to offer or seek more; and deciding whether to trust, to name a few. Decisions to be made together may concern processes to be used, whether and when to get help from a third party, choices from among the options generated during problem solving, and whether to enter into an agreement. Some of these decisions are made *during* the course of problem solving, and some *after* the problem-solving process has yielded a set of alternatives to consider. One possible decision to be made afterward is whether the options generated are inadequate, and the parties must return to another round of problem solving. So the process may be *iterative,* necessitating repeated return to the problem-solving stage until parties decide to agree.

The rest of this chapter aims to move us through this outlined process. To do so, we must understand the parts of the process, and how they work.

PROBLEM SOLVING

Broadly speaking, problem-solving approaches to understanding and resolving conflict deal with conflict as a puzzle, or interpersonal dilemma, to be worked out. There are two fundamental parts to the problem-solving process:

Figure 9.1. An Integrated Model of Problem Solving and Decision Making in Conflict Resolution.

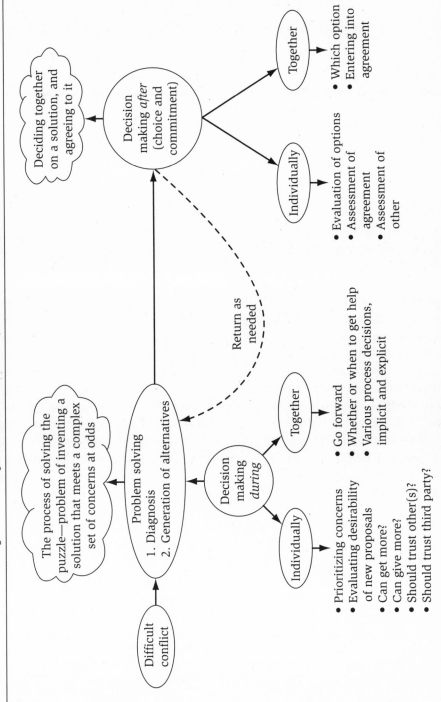

Note: The lists of decisions to be made are intended to be illustrative, not exhaustive.

1. Diagnosing the conflict (figuring out what the cause of the stuckness is, or identifying the problem)
2. Developing alternative solutions to the problem

In this section, we give an overview of some problem-solving approaches to conflict resolution. We also discuss some of the research that supports the use of problem-solving approaches, as well as research that helps us understand the conditions under which problem solving is more or less likely to be undertaken. We also consider some of the major critiques of problem-solving approaches, both in the literature and out in the field.

Problem Solving as the Search for Good, Constructive, Mutually Satisfying Solutions

An important part of the motivation to engage in problem solving is a desire to take some of the heat out of the process—to move people away from being stuck in their anger, their desire for revenge, and so on, and focus them on finding a way out.

One view of how problem-solving approaches attempt to do this is in terms of what the word *problem* means. One sense of the word is as dilemma, obstacle, difficulty, or predicament—generally, a bad thing. Another is as puzzle, enigma, riddle, or question—often seen as a challenge, and even an opportunity for growth. Conflicts are often felt to be problems in the first sense of the word: as difficulties or predicaments. Problem-solving approaches to conflict resolution attempt to recast the conflict as a problem in the second sense—as puzzles or riddles—and attempt to engage the parties in solving those puzzles. In a training or intervention, we might hear the notion put something like this: "We're in conflict. We can fight it out, or work it out. If we're going to work it out, let's figure out what that would take." (See Chapters One and Twenty-Four for further discussion of reframing a conflict as a mutual problem to be solved cooperatively.)

Along these lines, Rubin, Pruitt, and Kim suggest that "problem solving can be defined as any effort to *develop a mutually acceptable solution to a conflict*" (1994, p. 168; emphasis added). *Developing mutually acceptable solutions* is the hallmark of problem-solving approaches.

A Discussion of Problem-Solving Approaches. In their book *Social Conflict*, Rubin and colleagues (1994) offer one of the best, most useful discussions available of problem-solving approaches. So it seems worthwhile to devote a few paragraphs to their work at the outset of this chapter.

Although the phrase *any effort* in the quote just above might leave the definition a bit broad, those authors go on to clarify the highest aspirations of problem solving approaches: "At its best, problem solving involves a joint effort to find a mutually acceptable solution. The parties or their representatives talk freely to one another. They exchange information about their interests and priorities, work together to identify the true issues dividing them, brainstorm in search of alternatives that bridge their opposing interests, and collectively evaluate those alternatives from the viewpoint of their mutual welfare" (Rubin, Pruitt, and Kim, 1994, p. 169).

In describing problem-solving approaches, the same authors describe three broad classes of outcomes that can be sought: compromise (meeting in the middle through a process of sacrifice on both sides); agreeing to a fair procedure for determining a winner; and integrative solutions (those in which all parties' needs are considered and met).

This last type of solution, the integrative, is the hoped-for goal in problem-solving approaches, though it may not always be realistically possible (more on this later). Rubin, Pruitt, and Kim (1994) review a variety of forms for finding such solutions:

- *Expanding the pie* (finding ways to work together to create more of a resource to be divided)

- *Nonspecific compensation* (finding new ways to compensate a party for yielding on an issue)

- *Logrolling* (each side concedes on issues it believes are less important, building momentum toward agreement and goodwill)

- *Bridging* (new options are created that satisfy critical underlying interests, if not the initial demands that were put on the table)

To illustrate, imagine the case of a hypothetical labor negotiation in which management and a union are divided over a range of issues, including wages, medical insurance, disability, workplace safety conditions, and productivity goals. The first approach, expanding the pie, might entail raising prices to bring in more revenue to support the compensation desired by the union, while also providing more profit for the company. The second, nonspecific compensation, might oblige management to offer, say, additional vacation time or a flex-time arrangement to compensate for a concession on wage demands. The parties might also engage in the third approach, logrolling: the union concedes on a minor change in productivity goals (which union representatives view as less important in this case), and management concedes on an issue of work-safety conditions that is relatively inexpensive to fix. The combination of agreements builds momentum toward reaching agreement on some of the more difficult issues. Finally, the parties might find a bridging solution, in which moderate redesign of the facility and work flow (1) eliminates the safety issue (union interest) and (2) increases productivity (management interest) without imposing an unacceptable burden on the workers, (3) thereby generating the revenue to pay for increased wages and benefits (union interest) as well as profits (management interest). What makes this bridging solution different from the price-raising, expanding-the-pie example is that it makes use of a new option (redesign) that integratively addresses the various underlying interests on both sides of the table.

A key component, not only to the approach described by Rubin, Pruitt, and Kim but to most of the problem-solving approaches, is analyzing underlying interests, those often-unspoken real needs that produce the publicly stated demands in the first place. In addition, Rubin and colleagues suggest pushing further to look for interests under those interests, and so on, in an effort to find interests that are bridgeable—that is, satisfiable in newly created, mutually acceptable ways.

Rubin, Pruitt, and Kim (1994) offer a good description of a problem-solving process for conflicts of interest. They suggest (1) determining whether there is a real conflict of interest; (2) determining one's own interests, setting high aspirations, and sticking to them; and (3) seeking a way to reconcile both parties' aspirations. Note that steps 1 and 2 are part of the diagnosis phase of problem solving, while step 3 represents the phase of generating alternatives. If step 3 is particularly difficult, it may be necessary to lower aspirations and search some more. Steps 2 and 3 represent the core of many problem-solving approaches: developing clarity as to the real issues and interests, and developing *mutually satisfactory* solutions.

Evidence of Better Outcomes with Problem-Solving Approaches. There is evidence for the effectiveness of problem-solving approaches, in both the short term (reaching agreements, short-term satisfaction) and the long term (long-term satisfaction with, adherence to, and quality of agreements).

In a key study, Kressel and his colleagues (1994) compared the effectiveness of mediators using a problem-solving style (PSS), focused on good problem solving rather than settlement itself, with those using a settlement-oriented style (SOS), focused on the goal of getting an agreement, "more or less independent of the quality of the agreements" (p. 73), in child custody cases. They found overwhelmingly that disputants working with mediators using PSS more frequently reached settlement and were more satisfied with their agreements. They also found that the PSS settlements tended to be more durable, produce long-term outcomes of higher quality, leave disputants with more favorable attitudes toward the mediation, and be more likely to have a lasting positive impact on the relationship between parties. It is also important to note that there were some consistent exceptions: for example, when one party "bargained in bad faith" or was psychologically disturbed, PSS did not produce workable agreements.

Although Kressel and colleagues focused on long-term outcomes, Zubek and her colleagues (1992) looked at short-term benefits of problem-solving behavior in mediation in community mediation centers. They demonstrated a greater likelihood of short-term success in mediation (STSM) with joint problem solving, and less STSM with hostile and contending behavior by the conflicting parties. They then looked at the mediator behaviors that led to STSM and found them to include those that stimulate thinking and structure discussion. In addition, the more mediators applied pressure on disputants to reach agreement, the *lower* the rates of reaching agreement and goal achievement, satisfaction with the agreement, and satisfaction with the conduct of the hearing, which lends further support for the PSS versus SOS findings of Kressel and colleagues above.

In yet another context, van de Vliert, Euwema, and Huismans (1995) found that problem solving tended to enhance effectiveness in conflict for police sergeants, with both superiors and subordinates. This is the type of traditional, hierarchical context many critics point to as one in which a problem solving approach is unlikely to gain acceptance or be effective. The second is that it tended to enhance the sergeants' effectiveness in conflicts with both their subordinates and their superiors (though the latter effect represented a nonsignificant trend).

Finally, Carnevale and Pruitt (1992) reviewed a wide range of both experimental and field research on problem solving in negotiation and mediation. They concluded that problem solving is much more likely than other approaches to lead to win-win solutions to conflicts. In addition, they found that problem solving is more likely both to be engaged in, and to be effective, when disputants are concerned about the other party's welfare than when they are focused solely on their own.

Research That Predicts Use of Problem Solving. If we accept the premise that problem solving is something to strive for, it is helpful to know about the conditions under which disputants are more, or less, likely to engage in problem-solving behavior.

Some information is available. Strutton, Pelton, and Lumpkin (1993) found that if the psychological climate of an organization was characterized by higher levels of (1) cohesion, (2) fairness, (3) recognition of success, and (4) openness to innovation, members were more likely to choose problem-solving and persuasion strategies and less likely to engage in bargaining and politicking. In a study pointing to factors that might inhibit problem solving, Dant and Schul (1992) found that a group making frequent use of integrative problem-solving conflict resolution strategies among its members still preferred directive third-party intervention when stakes were high, issues were complex, there were significant policy implications, and dependence on the organization was high.

Carnevale and Pruitt (1992) as well as Pruitt and Rubin (1986) argue that disputants' relative levels of concern for their own and each other's interests predict the conflict resolution strategy that is adopted. Thus, when disputants do not care about their own or the other's outcomes, they are likely to adopt a strategy of *inaction*; when they are concerned with the other's outcome, but not their own, they are likely to *yield*; and when they are primarily concerned about their own interests, they tend to adopt *contending* strategies. But when disputants are concerned *both* about their own interests and the other's as well (holding a *dual concern*), they are more likely to engage in problem solving. This suggests that strategies and techniques that help to cultivate a concern for the other's interests and outcomes help to promote problem solving in conflict situations. (See also, in Chapter One, the section on initiation of cooperation.)

Individual and Social Interaction Perspectives on Problem Solving

Consistent with the viewpoint put forth by Carnevale and Pruitt (1992), another angle on problem solving in conflict has come from the social cognitive literature, particularly from developmental researchers interested in the development of social understanding, and its relationship to thought processes during conflict and other social interactions. Within cognitive psychology, problem solving is viewed as a cognitive process, very much in the sense of working through puzzles (solving a math problem, stacking crates to get the banana, and so on). Social cognition theorists have tended to look at conflict resolution as a particular kind of cognitive problem solving, that of solving *interpersonal* problems.

Two complementary ways of looking at interpersonal conflict have arisen from this distinction. One takes an information-processing approach, where each phase of the interpersonal problem-solving process is analyzed against an ideal standard (for example, Dodge, 1980; Spivack and Shure, 1976). The individual goes through an internal problem-solving process in determining how to engage with the other. More effective strategies are equated with success at achieving some predetermined outcome. The phases include identifying the problem, generating alternative strategies, evaluating consequences, and using new or different strategies for resolution. It is important to note that these phases may be executed well or poorly and may lead to a decision to engage in contentious, collaborative, or any other type of tactics. Although these phases have been drawn from cognitive psychology, research has shown them to be applicable to the realm of social problems (see review by Rubin and Krasnor, 1986). If collaborative tactics are chosen by both parties, a joint problem-solving process may then occur that can be described with the same four phases.

The other approach emphasizes general social competencies such as communication skills, skills in finding common ground, and other social skills that are discussed in various chapters in this book. From this perspective, one of the primary social cognitive tasks that conflict presents to the individual is *social perspective coordination*. In other words, how do I understand the other's perspective, and develop an understanding of the situation that accounts for both that perspective and my own? Within this framework, a model of interpersonal negotiation strategies (INS) has been described that depicts a developmental progression in the ability to coordinate social perspectives in conflict, ranging from an egocentric inability to differentiate subjective perspectives (that is, mine from yours) to the ability to coordinate the self's and the other's perspectives in terms of the relationship between them, or from a third-person viewpoint (Selman, 1980; Yeates, Schultz, and Selman, 1991). The functional steps of the INS model are similar to the steps articulated in information-processing approaches—that is, defining the problem, generating alternative strategies, selecting and implementing a specific strategy, and evaluating outcomes—but the INS model integrates additional developmental levels of perspective taking (egocentric, unilateral, reciprocal, and mutual) that underlie each of the functional steps (Selman, 1980). Here are descriptions adapted from Selman (1980) and Weitzman and Weitzman (forthcoming):

• At the *egocentric* level, which is characterized by impulsive, fight-or-flight thinking, the other is viewed as an object and the self is seen as being in conflict with the external world. The types of behaviors that might be seen at this level are whining, fleeing, ignoring, hitting, cursing, or fighting.

• At the *unilateral* level, which is characterized by obeying or commanding the other person, although the other is now understood to have interests, the self is seen as the principal subject of the negotiation, with interests separate from the other. The types of behaviors typically seen at this level are threatening the other person, going behind the other's back, avoiding the problem, or waiting for someone else to help.

• At the *reciprocal* level, which is characterized by exchange-oriented negotiations and attempts at influence, the needs of the other are appreciated but considered after the needs of the self. Typical behaviors are accommodation, barter, asking for reasons, persuasion, giving reasons, and appealing to a mediator.

• At the *mutual* level, which is characterized by collaborative negotiations, the needs of both the self and the other are coordinated, and a mutual, third-person perspective is adopted in which both sets of interests are taken into account. The types of behaviors that might be seen at this level are various forms of collaboration to develop satisfaction of mutual goals simultaneously.

In our work, we have used the INS model to explain the nature of everyday conflict in the lives of adults (Weitzman, Chee, and Levkoff, forthcoming; Weitzman, forthcoming; Weitzman and Weitzman, forthcoming). Our research has revealed some discontinuity between strategy choice and its social cognitive foundation. For example, in a study with elderly women, we found that although many women articulated reciprocal or mutual social perspective-taking skills, many of these same women opted for strategies associated with the unilateral level (Weitzman and Weitzman, forthcoming). Similarly, Yeates, Schultz, and Selman (1991) have shown that although the essential sequence of problem-solving steps is stable across conflict contexts, perspective taking often is not. Cultural norms (for example, where older women are socialized to yield, particularly to men, rather than press to get their needs met), perceived power differentials between the parties in conflict, and other contextual factors may lead to the use of less sophisticated strategies, regardless of perspective-taking ability.

So even though the basic steps of individual problem solving remain fairly constant across situations, good, collaborative outcomes do not. The key issue this research brings to light is that an individual's decision whether or not to coordinate his or her perspective with that of the other person is a central aspect of the conflict resolution process, one that may be highly relevant for training.

Critiques

There are also some serious critiques of problem-solving approaches to conflict resolution, and they deserve some attention here as well. For simplicity, we summarize them here as "the Bush and Folger critique" and "the skeptic's critique."

The Bush and Folger Critique. Bush and Folger (1994) argue that problem solving, an orientation they see as underlying a "satisfaction story" of mediation (focusing only on satisfying the disputants, and not taking advantage of the broader opportunities inherent in mediation), is narrow and mechanistic in that it assumes that conflict is a problem. This is seen as at odds with widely held values in the dispute resolution field to the effect that, because of its capacity for stimulating growth and leading to change, conflict is a good thing.

We happen to share those values, but we believe there is a fundamental error in this critique. That is, Bush and Folger (1994) cast what the problem-solving mediator does as looking to solve problems in the first of the two senses we offered at the beginning of this chapter: problems as obstacles, difficulties or predicaments, that is, "bad things." The result is that their argument frames problem-solving approaches to mediation as more or less equivalent to the settlement-oriented style described by Kressel and colleagues (1994), apparently missing the fact that the work of Kressel and colleagues, Zubek and colleagues (1992), and others has found substantial differences between such approaches. However, cooperative problem-solving approaches are *not* working from such a definition in mediation any more than they are in one-on-one approaches; rather, they are working on a problem-as-puzzle model, which is very much consistent with the values of conflict as opportunity. If conflict is to be taken as an opportunity for change and growth, it is imperative that disputants move beyond fighting and take full advantage of the power of collaboration to develop new and better alternatives. That is the essence of problem-solving approaches. They can lead to transformation and empowerment of others as this approach becomes a general, personal orientation to resolving conflict.

The Skeptic's Critique. There is a skeptic's critique often heard out in the field—during training or in conversation among practitioners—that says "This is fine on paper, but it isn't realistic." In detail, it goes something like this. People are angry and don't want to solve problems, work with each other, or talk to each other. What may help to persuade those holding this view of problem solving is that research and practical experience are firm in their conclusions. People *do* respond better to problem-solving approaches than settlement-oriented ones, they reach agreement more often and faster, they report being more satisfied, and both agreements and satisfaction hold up better in the long run.

Another critique argues that people often don't know what actually constitutes "the problem," and even when they think they do know, each side often has a very different problem in mind. Perhaps the most helpful way to respond to this critique is to quote again from Rubin, Pruitt, and Kim (1994). Essential to their definition is that parties "work together to identify the true issues dividing them, brainstorm in search of alternatives that bridge their opposing interests, and collectively evaluate those alternatives from the viewpoint of their mutual welfare" (p. 169). That is, problem-solving approaches attempt to get the parties to focus on identifying the issues at the heart of their quarrel (in other words, to diagnose the nature of their conflict) and do not assume that those central, underlying issues are already known. They then ask the parties to treat the collection of issues (or needs or interests or other types of concern) on the table as a mutual problem to be solved collectively. Note that there is no assumption here that the parties have the same basic issues in mind as they approach the negotiating table, nor that they define their conflict in terms similar enough even to give it the same name. The core of problem-solving approaches is helping parties see their own interest in finding solutions that meet not only their needs but those of the other as well. That is often hard to do, so is this challenge: What kind of solution can we come up with such that my needs, which are A, B, and C, and your needs, which are X, Y, and Z, can all be met at least acceptably well? It is *this* puzzle that is the problem to be solved.

DECISION MAKING

Consider again, briefly, our simple PSDM model (Figure 9.1). We suggested that decision making is going on both during and after the problem-solving process. At both of those points, there are decisions that each party makes individually and decisions made by the parties together. We will now discuss the individual as decision maker and then group decision making.

First, a broad summary. Many of the theorists whose work is mentioned here define the negotiation process itself in decision-making terms (for example, Bazerman and Neale, 1986; Kahneman, 1992; Zey, 1992). Some taking this view conceptualize each party as a decision maker (for example, Kahneman, 1992; Mann, 1992), while others focus on the conflict resolution process as one of joint decision making (for example, Bennett, Tait, and Macdonagh, 1994; Brett, 1991). It is possible, on the one hand, to think of the negotiator as someone with a series of decisions to make in the course of a negotiation, ultimately leading to the problem of whether to agree to a particular solution. On the other hand, one can also think about the process of negotiation as one of *joint* decision making, in which two or more parties with differing interests must jointly reach a decision—the resolution they ultimately agree to. In fact, many clients, when engaging a third-party mediator, describe their conflicts precisely as decision-making problems in which a group of people are having a hard time making a decision together.

The Individual as Decision Maker

The emphasis in this section is on the problem of *choice* among alternatives, be they alternative agreements or alternative actions to take along the way. Many theories of decision making emphasize the notion of *rational* choice and are built on the notion of expected utility. The expected-utility principle has been traced as far back as the eighteenth-century theorist Bernoulli (Abelson and Levi, 1985). The idea is that risky decisions involve choices in which we cannot be certain of what will happen as a result of our choice (as when a negotiator decides to hold out for a larger concession). For each option, we have to consider (1) the likelihood (expectation) that making this choice will get us what we hope it will and (2) the value, or utility, we attach to that outcome. Assuming that both the probability and the utility can be expressed as numbers, the expected utility for each option, then, is the product of probability and the associated utility. Thus "the expected-utility principle says that preferences between options accord with their relative expected utilities" (Abelson and Levi, 1985, p. 244).

Various limits to this approach have been discovered, however, and they have led to a number of useful ideas. Here we briefly summarize a few of the key findings and theories.

Anchors, Frames, and Reference Points. It turns out that anchors, frames, and reference points can influence decision-making processes in such ways that people do not make the kinds of choices that the "rational" decision-making model predicts. The description here follows Kahneman (1992), whose excellent review is recommended to those interested in pursuing these ideas in detail.

The *reference point* in a negotiation is the point above which the party considers an outcome to be a gain, and below which any outcome is considered a loss. In a given negotiation, several reference points might be available to a party: the status quo, the party's opening offer, the other side's initial offer, a settlement reached in a comparable case, and so on. Depending on which reference point a party has in mind, a given outcome might be seen (or *framed*) as a gain or a loss. The central finding here is that people tend to be *loss-averse:* avoiding loss is more important than achieving gain, and "concessions that increase one's losses are much more painful than concessions that forgo gains" (Kahneman, 1992, p. 298). As a result, when faced with a possible loss, people become more willing to take risks (say, refusing to make a better offer and thus *risking* impasse) rather than accept a large loss. By contrast, if there is a possibility of gain, people tend to be less willing to take the risk (perhaps of impasse) in the hope of yet larger gains. If a decision is framed negatively (as one between losses), then people tend to be more risk-prone than if it is framed positively (as one between gains). There is an important exception to this effect: if the goods being lost or gained are desirable only, or mainly, to be used in exchange (money kept for spending, goods kept for trading), then giving them up may not be viewed as a loss, and concessions may not be as painful (Kahneman, 1992).

Anchors are salient values that influence our thinking about possible outcomes, much like reference points. The difference is that whereas reference points define the neutral point between gains and losses, anchors may be anywhere along the scale and are often at the extremes. One of the most striking of anchoring effects is that negotiators are often unduly influenced by an anchor that they clearly know to be irrelevant—such as an outrageously low offer. Kahneman defines anchoring effects as "cases in which a stimulus or message that is clearly designated as irrelevant and uninformative nevertheless increases the [perceived] normality of a possible outcome" (1992, p. 308). There are a great many subtleties to the effects of anchors. The critical point for conflict resolution is recognizing their existence and developing methods for coping with their influence.

Impact of Stress. Conflict often produces psychological states such as stress, and affective (emotional) reactions that include anxiety, anger, and elation (Mann, 1992), thus introducing another set of barriers to "rational" decision making. From the perspective of Janis and Mann's conflict theory of decision making (1977), there are important linkages among stress, conflict, and coping patterns (Janis, 1993; Mann, 1992); according to Mann, "the model is founded on the assumption that decisional conflict is a source of psychological stress. The task of making a vital decision is worrisome and can cause anxiety reactions such as agitation, quick temper, sleeplessness or oversleeping, loss of appetite or compulsive overeating, and other psychosomatic symptoms" (p. 209).

From this perspective come a number of interesting findings. Cognitive functioning in decision making declines under stress; time pressure increases stress and thus negatively affects decision making, as well as reduces the willingness to take risks; and mood has predictable effects on risk taking: when in a good mood (compared to a neutral mood), people are more risk seeking when the risk is low but less risk seeking when risk is high. This pattern appears to reflect the fact that in a good mood, people think more about loss under high-risk situations, but they think less about loss when risk is low (Mann, 1992).

Another View of Risk. In the previous sections, we have discussed some of the impact of framing, stress, emotion, and mood on risk taking. Taking a slightly different view, Hollenbeck and his colleagues have argued that much of the research on risky decision making is limited in that it uses decisions that are static: they involve a one-shot decision with no future implications, no effect of past performance, and a high degree of specificity about outcomes and probabilities (Hollenbeck, Ilgen, Phillips, and Hedlund, 1994). By contrast, most decisions in conflict situations do not meet these conditions. Hollenbeck and colleagues conducted an experiment in which they varied these conditions and found that giving a general do-your-best goal instead of a specific goal actually reversed the framing effect described by Kahneman and Tversky (1984). Hollenbeck and colleagues conclude that to better understand the conditions that lead to risk taking, we need to know more about dynamic contexts, and we cannot freely generalize findings from static settings.

An Applied Approach. Approaches such as that of Janis and Mann (1977) are close in flavor to problem-solving approaches in being analytical and depersonalizing the conflict. In this approach, a decision maker fills out a "decisional balance sheet," listing all outcomes, weighting and summing costs and benefits, and thus analyzing the relative costs and benefits of each choice in order to make a decision. If the parties are willing to undertake the process together, they may be able to arrive at a decision they can agree to accept. But this approach makes some serious errors (as do others like it). In particular, it assumes that preferences on all issues can be translated into a common currency. This may be workable in some circumstances, as in a divorce mediation, for weighing relative preferences for the pots and pans on the one hand and a painting on the other. But it may be much less workable for weighing relative preferences for the house on the one hand and custody of the children on the other, since the house and the children do not readily convert into a common currency.

Group Decision Making and Commitment

Viewing negotiation as joint decision making opens up the possibility of exploring such decisional biases as overconfidence and lack of perspective taking—processes about which there is knowledge in the decision-making domain—that may alter performance and dispute resolution behavior (Bazerman and Neale, 1986).

Behavioral Decision Making. One prominent, and particularly helpful, approach to understanding group decision making is known as behavioral decision making (BDM). BDM emphasizes rational negotiation, with the goal of making decisions that maximize one's interests (Bazerman and Neale, 1992). Bazerman, Neale, and their colleagues have conducted an extensive program of research based on this approach (Bazerman and Neale, 1986; Loewenstein, Thompson, and Bazerman, 1989; Mannix and Neale, 1993; Neale and Bazerman, 1992; Thompson and Loewenstein, 1992; Valley, White, Neale, and Bazerman, 1992). Their findings are informative in terms of understanding conflict and working to resolve it. From a behavioral decision-theory perspective, negotiation is seen as "a multiparty decision making activity where the individual cognitions of each party and the interactive dynamics of multiple parties are critical elements" (Neale and Bazerman, 1992, p. 157). The approach aims at being both descriptive and prescriptive, and it works with such concepts as the perceptions of the negotiators, their biases, and their aspirations.

Bazerman and Neale (1992) offer a list of seven pervasive decision-making biases that interfere with the goal of negotiating rationally to maximize one's interests. The first is "irrationally escalating your commitment to an initial course of action, even when it is no longer the most beneficial choice" (p. 2). Possible causes of this bias include the competitive irrationality that can ensue when winning becomes more important than the original goal, and also the biases in perception and judgment resulting from our tendency to seek information that confirms what we are doing and avoid information that challenges us.

The second bias is "assuming your gain must come at the expense of the other party, and missing opportunities for tradeoffs that benefit both sides" (Bazerman and Neale, 1992, p. 2). Earlier, we discussed some of the benefits of approaching mixed-motive conflict as potentially integrative rather than purely distributive. Bazerman and Neale argue that "parties in a negotiation often don't find these beneficial trade-offs because each *assumes* its interests *directly* conflict with those of the other party" (p. 16). They call this mindset the *mythical fixed pie.*

The third bias is "anchoring your judgments upon irrelevant information, such as an initial offer" (Bazerman and Neale, 1992, p. 2). For more on anchoring, see our earlier discussion under "Anchors, Frames, and Reference Points."

The fourth is "being overly affected by the way information is presented to you" (Bazerman and Neale, 1992, p. 2). This refers to the effect of framing, discussed earlier. Bazerman and Neale suggest that a mediator who wants to encourage parties to compromise should work to help the parties see the conflict in a positive frame, one emphasizing gains rather than losses.

The fifth bias, "relying too much on readily available information, while ignoring more relevant data" (Bazerman and Neale, 1992, p. 2), has obvious implications for the quality of decisions. Bazerman and Neale urge negotiators to work to counteract this bias. Similarly, we urge mediators to be on the lookout for this tendency, both in disputants and in themselves.

The sixth bias, "failing to consider what you can learn by focusing on the other side's perspective" (Bazerman and Neale, 1992, p. 2), takes a somewhat different slant on perspective taking from those presented earlier. In their version, emphasis is on gaining information about the other side's motives by paying attention to their actions and taking their perspective into account.

The final bias, "being overconfident about attaining outcomes that favor you" (Bazerman and Neale, 1992, p. 2), is a particularly important one. Through anchoring on one's own initial proposal, failing to learn from considering the other side's perspective, distorting one's perceptions of the conflict situation in order to feel better about oneself, and focusing too strongly on information that supports one's position and ignoring information that challenges it, parties to a dispute often become overconfident in their ability to win; as a result, they miss out on opportunities to create integrative solutions. Thus mediators in court-connected mediation programs may be faced with two parties, each absolutely certain that if they fail to settle the dispute, the judge or jury will find in their favor.

Let us now briefly discuss a number of other findings from the work of Bazerman, Neale, and their colleagues.

Power Imbalance. In an experimental study of the effects of power imbalance and level of aspiration, Mannix and Neale (1993) found that in a negotiation with integrative potential (1) higher joint gains were achieved when power was equal than when unequal; (2) higher joint gains were achieved when aspirations were high rather than low; and (3) when power was unequal, higher joint-gain solutions tended to be driven by the offers of the low-power party. That is, in unequal power situations the high-power party was less likely to initiate a joint-gain solution. As a result, the onus of generating and selling a joint-gain solution appeared to fall on the low-power party.

Interpretations of Fairness. Thompson and Loewenstein (1992) found a tendency among negotiators, in a simulation of a collective bargaining process, to make "egocentric interpretations of fairness." That is, participants tended to assess fairness with a bias toward their own interests. This led to discrepancies between what each party saw as fair, each side tending to an interpretation benefiting themselves. Further, "the more people disagreed in terms of their perception of a fair settlement wage, the longer it took them to reach a settlement" (p. 184). Perhaps more surprisingly, providing the subjects with more background information, which might be expected to reduce bias, served only to exacerbate the self-serving nature of fairness assessments. (For more on biases, see Chapter Ten.)

Preferences in Different Types of Relationships. Finally, in a study that bears directly on our earlier discussion of problem solving, Loewenstein, Thompson, and Bazerman (1989) found that people's preferences for doing better than the other in disputes depended strongly on the nature of the relationship between the parties. The researchers manipulated two aspects of the dispute relationship: whether it was a business or personal dispute; and whether the relationship between the parties was positive, negative, or neutral. They found that although parties (across combinations of dispute type and relationship) did not like outcomes in which they did more poorly than the other, there were substantial differences in how much parties preferred an outcome in which they did better than the other. First, in a negative relationship disputants tended to like doing better than the other, while in a positive or neutral relationship disputants tended to *dislike* doing better than the other (up to a certain high amount of gain, after which their preferences begin to rise again). Similarly, in business disputes, participants liked doing better than the other, but in personal disputes they disliked doing better than the other (again, up to a point). Significantly, these two tendencies reinforced each other; in business disputes, the preference for doing better was substantially enhanced in a negative relationship.

This study may have profound implications for the problem-solving approaches we have discussed. In particular, it tells us that in certain situations (such as a business dispute or negative relationship) people may be highly motivated to create a large difference between what they and their negotiating partners receive. Such motivation runs directly counter to the goal of the cooperative problem-solving approaches: to engage parties in maximizing mutual gain.

UNDERSTANDING PROBLEM SOLVING AND DECISION MAKING IN CONFLICT SITUATIONS

Our simple model of the interaction of problem solving and decision making in conflict resolution (Figure 9.1) offers a framework for integrating what we know about these processes. In this section, we take a brief walk through the PSDM model, illustrating some of the ways these findings and perspectives can be used to enhance our understanding of conflict.

The PSDM Model Revisited

We have proposed that problem solving and decision making be viewed as integral parts of the cooperative conflict resolution process. We have also suggested that decision making takes place both *during* and *after* problem solving, and that at each point some decisions are made by the parties as individuals and some by the parties together.

Both problem-solving and decision-making approaches to conflict resolution, be they conscious designs of the professional mediator or spontaneous behaviors by the most naïve of disputants, fundamentally work with the basic dynamics of cooperation and competition, as discussed at greater length in other parts of this book (see Chapter One). Briefly, if conflict is approached as a cooperative endeavor in which the parties see their outcomes as positively correlated, people tend to work hard to create a resolution that maximizes both parties' outcomes. The goal becomes to *do as well as possible for both self and other*, rather than to engage in the kind of destructive win-lose struggle that exemplifies competitive, contentious conflict.

In the kind of integrated view we are taking, cooperative conflict resolution consists of four general phases: (1) diagnosing the conflict, (2) identifying alternative solutions, (3) evaluating and choosing a mutually acceptable solution, and (4) committing to the decision and implementing it. The left-hand part of the PSDM model (Figure 9.1) is concerned primarily with phases 1 and 2, with both problem solving and decision making taking place. The right-hand part of the model, labeled "Decision making *after,*" is concerned primarily with phases 3 and 4, where the solutions generated must be selected and committed to. As indicated in the model, if it becomes clear during phases 3 or 4 that an adequate solution has not been generated, it is necessary to return to the problem-solving process, looking for further solutions and, if necessary, reconsidering the original diagnosis.

Diagnosis

Diagnosis is the first part of the problem-solving process. Perhaps the first step in diagnosis involves an important decision: determining what kind of conflict you're in. A fundamental problem in conflict resolution in applied work is determining those few conflicts that really are *not* amenable to a constructive, integrative approach.

Determining What Kind of Conflict You're In. Often, we are working to convince our students and those we train that most of the conflicts initially appearing to be unalterably competitive, zero-sum situations by their nature are in fact at worst mixed-motive. Many of us even take an initial, dogmatic stance with students that there are virtually no cases in which collaborative approaches are impossible, in an effort to break them of the common tendency to respond competitively (Bazerman and Neale, 1992). (At least the first author of this chapter knows he's guilty of this.) Yet we know from practical experience, as well as some of the research findings discussed earlier, that this is not the case. It would seem naïve to deny that there *are* situations in which power-wielding, contentious tactics are warranted. Books such as Bazerman and Neale's that alert readers to common biased misperceptions and urge them to look more closely are an important start. A set of empirically and theoretically justified principles, guidelines, or frameworks are badly needed to help identify those cases that really *are* immutably contentious.

This would serve at least two aims. It would be an indispensable tool for conflict resolution efforts both in the first person and by a third-party intervenor. It would also give us the ability to say to our students, "Here's how you know a case that really *can't* be transformed into a 'mutual problem to be solved collaboratively.' If it doesn't meet these criteria, the potential is in there somewhere. Now let's work on how to find it."

Identifying the Problem or Problems. The next step in diagnosis is to develop an understanding of what the conflict is about—whether in substantive interests, values, or other types of concerns—that lends itself to problem solving. This involves identifying each side's *real* concerns (getting past initial positions or bargaining gambits), and developing a common understanding of the joint set of concerns of each party. Some concerns that might be asked or investigated at this stage include

What do I want?

Why do I want it?

What do I think are the various ways I can satisfy what I want?

What does the other want?

Why?

What are the various ways the other believes he or she can satisfy his or her wants?

Do we each fully understand one another's needs, reasons, beliefs, and feelings?

Is the conflict based on a misunderstanding, or is it a real conflict of interests, beliefs, preferences, or values?

What is it about?

In our earlier discussion of decision making, we emphasized research concerned with decision making under conditions of risk. Risk taking is important in this context in at least two ways. The research we have reported focused on the willingness to hold to a position and risk impasse—a risky decision that works against cooperative conflict resolution. But there are other kinds of risks where such a course of action is desirable. For example, offering a concession (or an apology!) can feel like a risk if you are not sure it will be reciprocated. In building trust where it is lacking between parties in conflict, it is often necessary to get one of the parties to take a risk and demonstrate trust in order to persuade the other party to begin trusting.

Finally, during the diagnosis phase, social perspective coordination is important. To arrive at a joint diagnosis, parties have to be willing and able to appreciate the other as a person with concerns of his or her own, and coordinate these concerns with the party's perspective so as to create the joint diagnosis.

Identifying Alternative Solutions

Once the parties have reached a joint diagnosis, the next step is to begin generating alternative solutions that may meet each party's goals at least acceptably well. One of the most commonly mentioned approaches to doing this is brainstorming. Here, the emphasis is on generating as many creative ideas as possible, hoping to encourage parties to think of the kinds of mutually acceptable solutions that have eluded them. Most brainstorming sessions employ a "no evaluation" rule: during the brainstorming session, no comments on proposed ideas are allowed, in the hope of encouraging parties to think of as many ideas as they can, no matter how silly or impractical. Once a list of alternatives is on a blackboard or newsprint, parties are often able to begin sorting through them and find options that are workable.

A list of other techniques is suggested by Treffinger, Isaksen, and Dorval (1994). For example, they recommend "idea checklists," lists of idea-stimulating questions such as "What might you do instead?" or "What might be changed or used in a different way?" (p. 43). They also recommend using metaphors or analogies to stimulate creativity, and blending active strategies (like brainstorming) with reflective strategies (such as built-in down time, for thinking things over).

Social perspective coordination is important here as well. To create viable solutions that meet each party's concerns, it is helpful—if not essential—for parties to be able to grasp and appreciate the importance of the other's perspective, and choose to engage in the search for solutions that satisfy the other's concerns.

Evaluating and Choosing

Once a set of possible alternative solutions has been identified, the next task is to evaluate the various options and choose among them. This involves a variety of individual decisions: about preferences among the advantages the options offer, about which seem fairer, which are likely to last, and so on. As the parties make these decisions, such factors as stress, anchors, frames, and reference points may all play a role in interfering with reasonable, rational decision making. Procedures like Janis and Mann's decisional balance sheet exercise (1977) may be helpful here, as may the recommendations offered by Bazerman and Neale (1992) for overcoming biases.

There are also, at this stage, group decisions to be made, primarily as to which option is chosen. Several of the behavioral decision-making findings are important here, largely as things that negotiators as well as mediators and other third parties should look out for. Integrative solutions, for example, are more likely if power is relatively equal, and they tend to be driven by the low-power party if it is not (Mannix and Neale, 1993). There is a tendency to egocentric interpretations of fairness (Thompson and Loewenstein, 1992). Also, people are less interested in doing better than the other (a competitive goal) when the relationship is personal, and when it is positive (Loewenstein, Thompson, and Bazerman, 1989). Again, procedures such as that of Janis and Mann (1977) may be helpful.

Committing to a Choice

Finally, once a mutually agreeable solution has been found, the decision must be made to enter into agreement. Trust, and the attendant risks, are important factors. It is critical that parties be willing to put mutual satisfaction before the goal of "doing better than the other." Social perspective coordination is important again, and here the issue of choosing to act on the social understanding gained is crucial; it is not enough just to understand—understanding must be translated into willingness to act. Among the key factors suggested here by our work with elderly women (Weitzman and Weitzman, forthcoming) are beliefs that the agreement will really work, and be abided by; and that the costs, emotional and otherwise, will not be too high.

IMPLICATIONS FOR TRAINING AND PRACTICE

We suggest that rather than being taught separately, in different training programs, problem-solving and decision-making approaches to cooperative conflict resolution should be taught together in integrated fashion. In the previous section, we have made an argument for considering the conflict resolution process in roughly four phases, incorporating problem solving and decision making throughout. We also recommend the development of training programs that approach the process in the same way. In this section, we briefly highlight a few factors that should be part of such training.

Conditions That Encourage Problem Solving

Training in problem-solving approaches should include information about the conditions that are likely to lead to parties' willingness to engage in problem solving. We know for example, that a psychological climate characterized by cohesion, fairness, recognition of success, and openness to innovation encourages people to choose problem-solving and persuasion strategies, and less likely to engage in bargaining and politicking (Strutton, Pelton, and Lumpkin, 1993). Training for mediators, designs for organizational alternative dispute resolution

(ADR) programs, and conflict resolution programs for high schools, to name a few, could all make use of this information.

In addition, encouraging problem solving through cultivating concern for the other can be important (for example, Carnevale and Pruitt, 1992; Rubin, Pruitt, and Kim, 1994). One common approach is to engage parties in perspective taking to help them see the other's concerns as legitimate. Our work on social perspective coordination (Weitzman and Weitzman, forthcoming) suggests not only that people must learn to take the perspective of the other but also that attention must be paid to translating perspective-taking ability into the choice of conflict resolution strategy. (See Chapters One and Three for more on the conditions that encourage conflict resolution.)

Teaching the Lessons from the Decision-Making Literature

The information from the aforementioned decision-making literature that would be particularly helpful if built into conflict resolution training includes the concepts of anchors, frames, and reference points. Kahneman (1992) suggests what he calls the Lewinian prescription, based on the concept of loss aversion: concessions that eliminate losses are more effective than concessions that improve on existing gains. Mediators as well as negotiators could learn to look for these opportunities.

Earlier, we presented selected information about the decision-making phenomena that help explain and predict disputant behavior. Such information is often incorporated into negotiation training aimed at "winning" in competitive negotiations, but it seems, at least anecdotally, much less often to be a part of mediation training. Yet understanding issues such as the impact of stress, power imbalance, disclosure of information, egocentric interpretations of fairness, and preferences for relative outcomes, as well as the role of issues of risk taking and the factors that influence risk-taking propensity, would seem to be of enormous value for mediators.

One more approach from the decision-making literature needs introduction here. Building on the sort of literature described earlier, Brett argues for "transforming conflict in organizational groups into high quality group decisions" (1991, p. 291) and prescribes techniques for doing so. Her approach is based in the assumption that by harnessing negotiation and decision theory, one can bring conflict to a constructive outcome through a decision-making approach. Her prescriptions include

- Criteria for determining if a high-quality decision has been reached
- Guidelines for improving the decision-making process
- Methods for integrating differing points of view
- Tactics for creating mutual gain, coalition gain, and individual gain

- Choosing decision rules that maximize integration of information
- Guidelines about when to use mutual gain, individual gain, and coalition gain approaches

This approach offers concrete, structured advice, based solidly in the research literature, for applying decision-making techniques to resolving group conflict.

In a similar vein, Janis and Mann's approach (1977) suggests that parties sit down together and analyze their conflict as a difficult decision. Their book offers devices such as the decisional balance sheet, a form for listing choice criteria (the things that matter to each party), assigning numerical values and valences (+ or −) to each, and manipulating the results. In this approach, disputants sit down together with a decisional balance sheet, carefully consider their own and the other's concerns, and look for a solution that maximizes each side's benefit and minimizes cost.

Approaches such as those of Brett (1991) and Janis and Mann (1977) represent formalized, detailed technologies that can and should be taught more widely than they currently are. Though we have criticized some underlying assumptions of some of these approaches (questioning, for example, the common-currency assumptions in the Janis and Mann approach), they remain tools that can be of great value if applied appropriately, and as tools integrated into a problem-solving and decision-making approach. Our training programs would benefit from offering students more in the way of such concrete, specified techniques for incorporation into their toolkits.

CONCLUSION

We have suggested that problem solving and decision making are processes interwoven in many cooperative conflict resolution procedures. Both training and practice could benefit from approaching the conflict resolution process as one in which diagnosis, development of alternatives, choice, and commitment take place, and in which problem solving and decision making both play a critical part.

References

Abelson, R. P., and Levi, A. "Decision Making and Decision Theory." In G. Lindzey and E. Aronson (eds.), *The Handbook of Social Psychology*. Vol. 1. (3rd ed.) New York: Random House, 1985.

Bazerman, M. H., and Neale, M. A. "Heuristics in Negotiation: Limitations to Effective Dispute Resolution." In H. R. Arkes and K. R. Hammond (eds.), *Judgment and Decision Making: An Interdisciplinary Reader*. Cambridge: Cambridge University Press, 1986.

Bazerman, M. H., and Neale, M. A. *Negotiating Rationally.* New York: Free Press, 1992.

Bennett, P., Tait, A., and Macdonagh, K. "Interact: Developing Software for Interactive Decisions." *Group Decision and Negotiation,* 1994, *3,* 351–372.

Brett, J. M. "Negotiating Group Decisions." *Negotiation Journal,* 1991, *7,* 291–310.

Bush, R.A.B., and Folger, J. P. *The Promise of Mediation: Responding to Conflict Through Empowerment and Recognition.* San Francisco: Jossey-Bass, 1994.

Carnevale, P. J., and Pruitt, D. G. "Negotiation and Mediation." *Annual Review of Psychology,* 1992, *43,* 531–582.

Dant, R. P., and Schul, P. L. "Conflict Resolution Processes in Contractual Channels of Distribution." *Journal of Marketing,* 1992, *56,* 38–54.

Dodge, K. A. "Social Cognition and Children's Aggressive Behavior." *Child Development,* 1980, *51,* 162–170.

Hollenbeck, J. R., Ilgen, D. R., Phillips, J. M., and Hedlund, J. "Decision Risk in Dynamic Two-Stage Contexts: Beyond the Status Quo." *Journal of Applied Psychology,* 1994, *79,* 592–598.

Janis, I. L. "Decision Making Under Stress." In S.B.L. Goldberger (ed.), *Handbook of Stress: Theoretical and Clinical Aspects.* (2nd ed.) New York: Free Press, 1993.

Janis, I. L., and Mann, L. *Decision Making: A Psychological Analysis of Conflict, Choice, and Commitment.* New York: Free Press, 1977.

Kahneman, D. "Reference Points, Anchors, Norms, and Mixed Feelings." *Organizational Behavior and Human Decision Processes,* 1992, *51,* 296–312.

Kahneman, D., and Tversky, A. "Choices, Values, and Frames." *American Psychologist,* 1984, *39,* 341–350.

Kressel, K., and others. "The Settlement-Orientation vs. the Problem-Solving Style in Custody Mediation." *Journal of Social Issues,* 1994, *50,* 67–84.

Loewenstein, G. F., Thompson, L., and Bazerman, M. H. "Social Utility and Decision Making in Interpersonal Contexts." *Journal of Personality and Social Psychology,* 1989, *57,* 426–441.

Mann, L. "Stress, Affect, and Risk Taking." In J. F. Yates (ed.), *Risk-Taking Behavior.* New York: Wiley, 1992.

Mannix, E. A., and Neale, M. A. "Power Imbalance and the Pattern of Exchange in Dyadic Negotiation." *Group Decision and Negotiation,* 1993, *2,* 119–133.

Neale, M. A., and Bazerman, M. H. "Negotiator Cognition and Rationality: A Behavioral Decision Theory Perspective." *Organizational Behavior and Human Decision Processes,* 1992, *51,* 157–175.

Pruitt, D. G., and Rubin, J. Z. *Social Conflict: Escalation, Stalemate, and Settlement.* New York: Random House, 1986.

Rubin, J. Z., Pruitt, D. G., and Kim, S. H. *Social Conflict: Escalation, Stalemate, and Settlement.* New York: McGraw-Hill, 1994.

Rubin, K. H., and Krasnor, L. R. "Social-Cognitive and Social Behavioral Perspectives on Problem Solving." In M. Perlmutter (ed.), *Minnesota Symposia on Child Psychology.* Vol. 18. Mahwah, N.J.: Erlbaum, 1986.

Selman, R. L. *The Growth of Interpersonal Understanding.* Orlando: Academic Press, 1980.

Spivack, G., and Shure, M. *The Social Adjustment of Young Children.* San Francisco: Jossey-Bass, 1976.

Strutton, D., Pelton, L. E., and Lumpkin, J. R. "The Influence of Psychological Climate on Conflict Resolution Strategies in Franchise Relationships." *Journal of the Academy of Marketing Science,* 1993, *21,* 207–215.

Thompson, L., and Loewenstein, G. "Egocentric Interpretations of Fairness and Interpersonal Conflict." *Organizational Behavior and Human Decision Processes,* 1992, *51,* 176–197.

Treffinger, D. J., Isaksen, S. G., and Dorval, K. B. *Creative Problem Solving: An Introduction.* (Rev. ed.) Sarasota, Fla.: Center for Creative Learning, 1994.

Valley, K. L., White, S. B., Neale, M. A., and Bazerman, M. H. "Agents as Information Brokers: The Effects of Information Disclosure on Negotiated Outcomes." *Organizational Behavior and Human Decision Processes,* 1992, *51,* 220–236.

van de Vliert, E., Euwema, M. C., and Huismans, S. E. "Managing Conflict with a Subordinate or a Superior: Effectiveness of Conglomerated Behavior." *Journal of Applied Psychology,* 1995, *80,* 271–281.

Weitzman, P. F. "Young Adult Women Resolving Conflicts: An Examination of Context and Strategies." *Journal of Adult Development,* forthcoming.

Weitzman, P. F., Chee, Y. K., and Levkoff, S. E. "An Examination of the Strategies Used by African-American and Chinese-American Caregivers to Resolve Family Conflicts." *American Journal of Alzheimer's Disease,* forthcoming.

Weitzman, P. F., and Weitzman, E. A. "Interpersonal Negotiation Strategies in a Sample of Older Women." *Journal of Clinical Geropsychology,* forthcoming.

Yeates, K. O., Schultz, L. H., and Selman, R. L. "The Development of Interpersonal Negotiation Strategies in Thought and Action: A Social-Cognitive Link to Behavioral Adjustment and Social Status." *Merrill-Palmer Quarterly,* 1991, *37,* 369–403.

Zey, M. (ed.). *Decision Making: Alternatives to Rational Choice Models.* Thousand Oaks, Calif.: Sage, 1992.

Zubek, J. M., and others. "Disputant and Mediator Behaviors Affecting Short-Term Success in Mediation." *Journal of Conflict Resolution,* 1992, *36,* 546–572.

PART TWO

INTRAPSYCHIC PROCESSES

Judgmental Biases
in Conflict Resolution
and How to Overcome Them

Leigh Thompson
Janice Nadler

A common fallacy held by negotiators and dispute resolution professionals is that conflict escalation, negotiation impasse, and unsatisfactory agreement are driven by intransigence and self-interested motivation. Whereas self-interest and opposing motivation do interfere with productively resolving conflict, there are a host of seemingly benign beliefs and cognitions that also interfere with effective conflict resolution but often go undetected. Unfortunately, these beliefs are not easily corrected during the process of conflict resolution itself because it is difficult for negotiators to monitor them. Furthermore, third-party intervention is no guarantee that erroneous belief and cognition are adequately identified and eliminated. In fact, the mere presence of a third party may exaggerate the tendency of these faulty and erroneous beliefs to disturb the otherwise effective resolution of conflict. Further, third parties, and other self-proclaimed neutrals, often fall prey to similar cognitive bias.

We argue in this chapter that identifying and challenging such bias can do much to effectively resolve dispute and conflict of interest. Unfortunately, most negotiators are not aware of the existence of cognitive biases and their deleterious effects. In the first section, we lay out our basic framework and key assumptions. In the second section, we provide illustrative examples of the effects of cognitive bias on conflict management. Finally, we examine methods for eliminating or reducing cognitive bias at the bargaining table.

COGNITIVE BIASES AND THEIR EFFECTS
ON CONFLICT MANAGEMENT

In conflict and negotiation, as in all social interaction, we are bombarded with stimuli from outside ourselves as well as inputs from within. From outside, there is the other's physical appearance, what she says and her nonverbal behavior, the social situation and the physical environment in which the behavior occurs, and so on. From inside, there is one's bodily state; one's emotions, needs, values, expectations, cultural assumptions, cognitive schemas, implicit theories, and plans, and one's self-conception. Only a small percentage of this information is consciously noticed.

Our perceptual and cognitive apparatus generally does a good job of selecting and organizing, from this flood of data, the relevant information to help us understand what is going on and how to act appropriately in terms of our self-requirements and the requirements of the situation we are in. The information people work with as a result of what they perceive in any situation is a function not only of who and what they are studying but also of the surrounding context. Further, in contrast to perception of external physical events (which usually can be directly observed), much of the information we need to know about people is not directly accessible; rather, we must infer it on the basis of their behavior and spoken words. As is easily imagined, this can lead to misperception and misunderstanding because of differences in background (gender, class, culture, ethnicity, social roles, etc.) between the actor and the perceiver.

Given the complexity of the task, it is not surprising that misunderstanding, error, and bias in judgment occur naturally even under favorable circumstances. In conflict, bias is apt to occur because conflict often leads to inadequate communication between the negotiating parties; arousal of emotional tensions that constrict thinking to stereotypes and to black-and-white viewpoints; primary focus on opposed interests; and anxiety, which may propel one to deny the conflict or flee into agreement before thinking through its consequences.

This tendency to use shortcuts, or heuristics, when we process information is an extremely cost-effective strategy, and much of the time heuristic processing provides us with accurate information. Whereas it may seem peculiar that heuristics, which are cognitive shortcuts, are cost-effective if our basic argument is that they lead to biases and hinder effective conflict resolution, our point is that much of the time, these heuristics may be effective when used in nonconflict situations because they can lead to an answer or solution that is acceptable and efficient. For example, in forming an impression of a new next-door neighbor, one could do an extensive search (interviewing friends and relatives, perhaps even hiring a private investigator); or one could simply rely on gut impression. The former strategy is obviously costly and time consuming, and even if more accurate it is unclear what the gain is.

In competitive encounters such as negotiation, though, the heuristic-based judgments we make are often wrong. Furthermore, the nature of our errors is not random but instead systematic. For the purposes of our discussion, we focus on systematic error and patterned fallacy; these are known as *biases.* Biases come in many forms and shapes. For instance, people can be biased about other people, as when they use stereotypes (I might perceive all New Yorkers as pushy). People can also be biased about situations (the gambler's fallacy—that he has lost so many times in a row that he is "due" to win). Paradoxically, people can also be biased about themselves (the vast majority of people judge themselves to be above average on many positive characteristics and abilities, even though it is logically impossible for most people to be above average).

Table 10.1 lists some common types of bias in judgment that occur in social cognition of ourselves, of other people, of other groups, and so on. In this chapter, we focus on four key biases selected for special emphasis because of their fundamental pervasiveness in many kinds of conflict situations. Thus, we regard these biases to be at the core of others that may crop up in conflict situations. In describing each bias, we offer relevant examples from empirical research and set forth some implications for conflict management. The four biases are

1. The need to simplify conflict
2. The tendency to perceive opposing forces
3. The perception of a false dichotomy between competition and cooperation
4. Egocentrically tainted judgment, particularly regarding the fairness of a decision or outcome

The first step in effectively managing conflict is to be aware of the existence of these particular biases.

Need to Simplify Conflict

It may often seem that parties interlocked in conflict at the bargaining table are purposefully attempting to complicate matters. In fact, people tend do the opposite: they dramatically *oversimplify* situations. At the negotiating table, as in many other situations, people tend to form judgments and attitudes without much deliberation and without the benefit of complete evidence. There are a number of reasons, notably that the human mind—though highly evolved—is simply not a computer, capable of endless processing of full information. Rather, people tend to focus on one or two salient points in a situation. In this sense,

Table 10.1. Core Biases and Their Effects.

Core Bias	Effects
Need to simplify conflict situations	Stereotyping
	Ignoring inconsistent information
	Confusing cause and effect relations
Perception of opposing forces	Fixed-pie perception
	Lose-lose outcomes
	Exaggeration of conflict
	Reactive devaluation
False dichotomy between cooperation and competition	Overly tough (escalatory) strategies
	Overly concessionary strategies
	Suboptimal solutions
Egocentric judgment	Biased judgments of fairness
	Invalid perceptions of control
	Higher likelihood of impasse

people do not pay attention to every detail; rather, they look for a few salient cues and then make an assumption about how to act.

For example, when meeting someone for the first time, the impression I form shapes my future perceptions of that person. If I meet Sarah and decide that she seems unfriendly, then henceforth I will probably interpret anything she does in this light. We tend to use first impressions as a way of understanding what other people are like, but we often give first impressions extra weight without realizing it.

In addition to the general problem of stereotyping (which we discuss further in this chapter), the need to simplify the conflict situation also can result in other biases or poor gathering of crucial information needed to optimally resolve conflict. The desire to simplify the situation leads us to ignore information that is inconsistent with our initial beliefs, and in some cases, to interpret ambiguous information as being consistent with them. For example, we often associate the color black with negative ideas: death, evil, "bad guys" wearing black hats. As an illustration of how prior beliefs about the color black can influence perception, consider two groups of trained referees who were shown videotapes of the same aggressive play in a football game (Frank and Gilovich,

1988). One group of referees viewed a version of the tape where the aggressive team wore white uniforms, whereas the other referees saw the aggressive team wearing black. The referees who watched the black-uniformed version rated the play as much more aggressive and deserving of a penalty than did referees who judged the white-uniformed team. Perhaps it is not surprising, then, that in professional football and hockey, teams that wear black uniforms are penalized significantly more than average (Frank and Gilovich, 1988). If our initial beliefs about the color black are negative, then we tend to interpret ambiguous information as being consistent with those beliefs.

Further, the need to simplify a conflict situation can lead to faulty perception about cause-and-effect relationships. People may falsely infer a relationship where none exists, or they may assume that a given action by one person results in an action by the other person. This effect, known as the "biased punctuation of conflict," occurs when people interpret interaction with their adversaries in other-derogating terms (Kahn and Kramer, 1990). Actor A perceives the history of conflict with another actor, B, as a sequence of B-A, B-A, B-A, in which the initial hostile or aggressive move was always made by B, obliging A to engage in defensive and legitimate retaliatory action. Actor B punctuates the same history of interaction as A-B, A-B, A-B, however, reversing the roles of aggressor and defender. Disagreement about how to punctuate a sequence of events in a conflict relationship is at the root of many disputes. When each side to the dispute is queried, they explain their frustrations and actions as defenses against the acts of the other party. As a result, conflict escalates unnecessarily.

Opposing Forces

In very general terms, people in negotiation and conflict situations tend to assume that the degree of opposition between themselves and other parties is greater than it actually is. A classic root cause of most ill-fated negotiations is the fixed-pie perception, the belief that the other party's gain comes at our expense, and our gain at theirs (Bazerman and Neale, 1992; Thompson and Hastie, 1990). The fixed-pie perception simply means that most negotiators work under the assumption that the other party's gain is one's own loss, and vice versa. In one investigation, for example, more than two-thirds of the negotiators assumed that the amount of available resources was fixed, even though this was not the case (Thompson and Hastie, 1990).

A close cousin of the fixed-pie perception is the lose-lose outcome (Thompson and Hrebec, 1996). The possibility of lose-lose negotiations often goes unchecked, since most people tend to view the opposite of win-win as win-lose; however, lose-lose negotiations do exist (Thompson, 1990). They occur if both parties settle for something that both prefer less than what they can readily have. Here are sample lose-lose situations:

- Two countries have been in conflict for decades. Each would benefit from peaceful coexistence. But their attempts at peace talks never achieve substantive progress, and the conflict rages on.

- The management and labor representatives for a local industry embroiled in contract-renewal talks both realize that, if the union goes on strike, company owners and union membership alike will suffer. But no agreement is reached by the time the contract expires.

False Dichotomy: Choosing Between Cooperation and Competition

If you view the world through the lens of a fixed-pie vision, the choices are pretty clear: either hold out to protect your own interests, which are by definition opposed to the other's, or cooperate with the other party so that some kind of compromise can be reached. Cooperation and competition are thought to be the yin and yang of conflict resolution, and it is true that most conflicts are mixed-motive in the sense that we are motivated to get as much of the pie as we can for ourselves, but at the same time motivated to work together with the other person to ensure we reach mutual agreement. We argue, though, that this is a false dichotomy in most instances, because we need *not* choose to behave purely cooperatively or purely competitively. There is a third, enlightened strategy, which we call strategic creativity (Neale and Bazerman, 1991; Thompson, 1998).

Strategic creativity involves using both cooperation and competition. Specifically, cooperation is needed to reach some kind of mutual agreement with the other party. Fundamentally, cooperation implies concern for your own interests as well as those of the other party. Furthermore, pure cooperation also implies that the other party feels the same way about you. This, of course, is the basis for trust. Yet it is often unrealistic or inappropriate to assume that people are concerned with the other party's interests. This is true in conflict situations, as when two neighbors have a dispute about a fallen tree on the property line; it is also true in negotiation situations, as when an employer and an employee discuss the terms of employment. In most cases, the primary objective of the parties is to further their own interests. Thus, we do not encourage parties to expect that others have their best interests in mind. Rather, we suggest that parties to conflict and negotiation situations attempt to discover points of mutual interest and use them to leverage mutually acceptable resolutions.

In addition, strategic creativity takes things a step further by assuming that parties' interests, though partially opposed, are not fully so. The strategically creative negotiator does not fall into the trap of baring his soul (and interests) to the other party, hoping not to be taken advantage of; this is unrealistic and perhaps downright foolhardy. Yet, neither does the strategically creative negotiator adopt a strictly competitive stance. Rather, she searches for an opportunity to satisfy the other party's interests beneficially for herself as well.

One way to accomplish this is to identify the issues at hand, and then assess which are important to you, and which are important to the other person. Suppose Eileen is returning for her third interview at a medical software company. The company's representatives have already told her that they would like to offer employment, and they want to meet to work out the details. Eileen has decided that for her the most important issue is the signing bonus, while the company representative has decided that an annual raise is most important. During the meeting, Eileen and the representative construct a deal that involves a relatively high signing bonus and relatively low annual raise. Note that this arrangement meets the needs of both parties; each concedes on an unimportant issue and receives the preferred option on an important issue. Furthermore, both Eileen and the company consider this arrangement superior to a simple compromise (a deal in which Eileen receives a medium-sized bonus and a medium-sized annual raise).

Egocentric Judgment: "I Only Want What's Fair (for Me)"

Underlying all of the biases we have discussed thus far is a basic tendency for people to protect their own egos and interests. Our psychological immune system is so efficient that we do not even realize our judgments are tainted with self-interest. For example, consider a husband and wife reflecting on their perceptions of responsibility for cleaning dishes, shopping, child care, and other household and relationship activities. Imagine asking each spouse independently to score who does what percentage of the work, using a 100 percent scale. In such a case, both partners generally assume themselves to be more responsible than the other (Ross and Sicoly, 1979). When both spouses' contributions are totaled for a "couple" score, the perceived contributions frequently amount to more than 100 percent! The same pattern can occur in product development teams and numerous other settings. Such differences in perception undoubtedly exacerbate conflict, at home, in the workplace, and elsewhere.

Yet despite the egocentric bias, most negotiators describe themselves as wanting to be "fair" (Loewenstein, Thompson, and Bazerman, 1989). Most people also prefer to divide resources "fairly" (Messick, 1993). The problem is that self-interest tinges otherwise fair allocation of resources. This is because fairness is not an absolute construct, but highly subjective. What is fair to one person may not be fair in the eyes of another. Multiple interpretations of fairness are equally valid in various situations.

Summary

The findings we have described represent four important and pervasive biases that occur in negotiation and conflict resolution. They are based on a review of fifteen years of research. In a sense, these four findings are enemies that theorists and practitioners must fight to eliminate. In the next section, we further elaborate on the biases that threaten successful dispute resolution in negotiation, focusing specifically on their impact on conflict management.

IMPLICATIONS FOR CONFLICT MANAGEMENT

Practitioners and laypersons have neither the time nor the inclination to read the vast body of empirical research literature on negotiator bias and cognition. In this section, we distill years of research into a few key principles that are best illustrated in the form of stories. We deliberately focus on the research literature that has proved to be reliable (replicable and generalizable across a variety of conflict situations, people, and domains) and valid (causal relationships, not just post hoc observation or intuition). We review the four key findings on bias already outlined in the context of conflict situations. At the end of each review, we describe what we think are the key implications for practitioners.

Exaggeration of Conflict

People involved in social or political conflict tend to overestimate the extremity of the other side's beliefs, a reflection of the first, opposing-forces, bias.

Consider the reactions to the real-life conflict commonly referred to as the Howard Beach incident, in which a young black man, Michael Griffith, was struck and killed by a passing car as he attempted to escape a group of white pursuers in the Howard Beach neighborhood of Brooklyn. In one study, people who characterized themselves as liberals or conservatives were asked to rate the extent to which they believed in the truth of certain statements about the case ("The white pursuers deliberately chased Michael Griffith into the path of oncoming traffic"; "Michael Griffith had consumed cocaine on the night in question"; Robinson, Keltner, Ward, and Ross, 1995). The same people were then asked to predict how "the other side" would rate the truth of the same statements. That is, conservatives were asked to predict liberals' ratings for each question, as were liberals asked to predict conservatives' ratings. Both liberals and conservatives overestimated the difference between their side and the other. Liberals overestimated the extent to which conservatives believed in the truth of statements favoring the white perpetrators; conservatives overestimated the extent to which liberals believed in the truth of statements favoring the black victim. Thus, the partisans in this case believed that the distance between their positions was greater than it really was.

Perhaps most surprising, neutrals (people who described themselves as neither liberal nor conservative) also succumbed to this mistake; they too overestimated the gap between liberals' and conservatives' beliefs about the Howard Beach incident. All three groups (liberals, conservatives, and neutrals) exaggerated the extent of conflict: all three groups overestimated first the extent to which conservatives would interpret the events in ways that blamed the black victim, and second the extent to which liberals would interpret events in ways that favored the black victim.

The pattern of results is not unique to this incident. Exaggeration of perceived conflict has been shown to exist in many other domains: abortion, the death penalty, the arms race, and even the "Western canon debate" (the dispute among educators about the choice of books in introductory college civilization and literature courses).

It is important to consider the implications of the tendency for people to exaggerate conflict. If the partisans in a conflict perceive their differences as greater than they really are, then they might be overly pessimistic about finding common ground. If people hold erroneous assumptions about the gap between their own position and that of the other side, then people might decide that it is not worth even sitting down at the bargaining table on the grounds that any discussion is fruitless (Robinson, Keltner, Ward, and Ross, 1995).

The fact that we exaggerate the extent of conflict means that information exchange among parties is crucial. Unless both sides to a conflict discuss the nature of their beliefs, assumptions, and concerns, each side continues to perceive the other as unreasonable and extreme. Because neutral third parties also tend to exaggerate conflict, these results have important implications for mediators as well. To be effective, mediators must understand the true nature of each side's position. If a mediator relies on her preconceived assumptions about each party's position, she is likely to overestimate the extremity of each party's position, and to overestimate the gap between the parties.

In addition to forming an accurate understanding of the conflict, mediators have an important role to play in helping parties overcome their own perception of exaggerated conflict. Exaggeration of conflict comes in two forms: each side tends to see the other side's position as more extreme than it really is, and one's own side is also seen as more extreme than it really is. Mediators can help parties see that their own position need not be as extreme as they think it needs to be.

Lose-Lose Outcomes

Sometimes all of the people in an interdependent decision-making situation prefer one settlement to another but nevertheless fail to achieve it.

Consider a case where two colleagues are interviewing several people for a junior management position in their division. They both prefer to hire the same person, but failing to realize this they end up hiring another. This is called a lose-lose agreement, because the people involved settle for an outcome that is clearly worse for both than another just as readily available.

The frequency with which lose-lose agreements occur is both surprising and alarming. One statistical analysis involving more than five thousand participants revealed that lose-lose agreements occurred 20 percent of the time (Thompson and Hrebec, 1996). That is, in cases where the parties have compatible preferences with regard to a particular issue, fully one time in five they agree on an alternative that both prefer less than another outcome.

Moreover, it is unlikely that the lose-lose agreement is an artifact of the laboratory, with no real-world significance. Balke, Hammond, and Meyer's examination (1973) of labor-management negotiations at Dow Chemical is a case in point. Analysis of that dispute revealed that labor and management both preferred the same wage increase; yet neither party realized it until after a costly two-month strike.

Another example is illustrated in Walton and McKersie's analysis (1965) of the Cuban missile crisis, which stemmed from the Soviet Union's buildup of missile bases in Cuba during the Cold War. The crisis had reached dangerous proportions when the United States threatened to retaliate against the Soviet Union when Cuba fired on American airplanes. Meanwhile, the Soviet Union, unbeknown to the United States, also preferred that Cuba refrain from provoking the United States, because there was a danger that Cuba's behavior would incite a war over issues not important to Soviet interests. The parties that had come to the brink of nuclear war shared compatible interests, without realizing it.

Why does this happen? As discussed earlier, people sometimes adopt a fixed-pie perception in which they believe that the other person's interests are completely opposed to their own. This belief is established at the outset, before people even have the opportunity to meet or talk with each other. In addition, the fixed-pie perception is remarkably durable; it remains even when people have high incentives and ample feedback is available to challenge the perception.

But sometimes people who do realize their preferences are compatible with the other party's still fail to capitalize on shared interests. Political pressures, situational norms, and organizational constraints can prevent people from optimizing their compatible interests. A vacation rental company with a weeklong rental policy gets a call, late in the week, from a renter requesting a midweek stay. If would be better for both parties to rent the property. But this means that company policy would be broken, so the agency refuses. Parties may face similar kinds of social pressure in other situations, and the desire to save face may prevent a person from settling on what is obviously a better deal (Rubin, Pruitt, and Kim, 1994).

Invalid Perceptions of Control

We all like to think that we have control over our environment. To some degree, this is certainly true; when we pull on a door it usually opens, and when we say hello to a colleague we usually receive a hello in response. Theorists from several domains conclude that this sense of personal control is necessary to a healthy self-concept; without some sense of control over outcomes in our environment, we would feel helpless and worthless. But we easily become so accustomed to feeling in control that we automatically, egocentrically assume we have causal influence over certain events in our environment when in fact, we have no such influence. As an intriguing example, craps players act as though they control the dice by throwing them softly to produce low numbers or throwing hard for high numbers (Henslin, 1967). As another, a baseball player on a hitting streak might wear the same pair of socks in every game for fear of jinxing the streak.

Inflated perceptions of control generally stem from the same sort of egocentric bias that we described earlier. In short, people are acutely aware of their own actions, thoughts, and feelings and less aware of those of others. Moreover, we have a poor memory for contingency information, and our judgments are biased by self-serving motivations. Although people who are given a lottery ticket with a preassigned number gladly accept the opportunity to trade the ticket for one from a different lottery with a better chance of winning (Langer, 1975), those who choose their own number prefer to hold on to the ticket and forgo the opportunity to enter a lottery with a better chance of winning. Why? Because picking our own lottery number gives us an illusion of control; we try to choose a "good" number because we think it's more likely to win, even though in reality all numbers have equal likelihood. Thus, when it comes to causal relationships between events, people often falsely believe they exert more control than is actually the case.

Conflict situations often present circumstances that encourage people to adopt invalid perceptions of control. In one study, negotiators faced an opponent who was (unbeknown to the negotiator participating in the study) actually a confederate of the experimenter. During the negotiation, the confederate strictly follows a preset schedule of concessions. When the preprogrammed schedule calls for the confederate to make an extreme initial demand followed by retreats to a moderate demand, the participants feel they have control over the opponent and the final settlement. But when the schedule calls for the confederate to make a moderate initial demand and then refuse to retreat, negotiators react unfavorably because they feel they have no causal influence on the outcome of the negotiation (Benton, Kelley, and Liebling, 1972).

In another study, participants play a game where they have a choice of cooperating or competing with the other party. The other party faces a similar choice. The worst outcome for a player is to cooperate while the opponent competes. The best outcome for both players together is if both cooperate. As a player in this game, you are told either that your opponent has already made a choice, or that your opponent will make a choice at the same time you do. In either case, you do not know your opponent's choice before making your own, and your opponent does not know your choice before making his own. Faced with this situation, people are more likely to cooperate if their opponent's decision is made at the same time as their own (Morris, Sim, and Girrotto, 1995).

In this situation, you have the causal illusion that you can influence an opponent who has not yet decided by "showing" him that you are cooperating. On the other hand, if the opponent has already made a decision, you know there is no way of influencing it, since causation cannot work backward in time. Of course, in either case, the opponent has no way of knowing your choice until after making his own, so you are unable to show him anything about your choice.

These results suggest a tactic for concession making during conflict resolution: tell your opponent that you will make a concession simultaneously with or just after he makes a concession. This fosters the illusion of control in your opponent; he reasons that by showing you he is making a generous concession, you will reciprocate and do the same. In the meantime, regardless of what you decide to do, you can benefit from the opponent's generous concession. Similarly, mediators can suggest to each party that the other party is ripe for influence—and suggest that a concession will greatly influence the other party.

Biased Judgments of Fairness

People involved in conflict usually think that the outcome they advocate is fair. But what does it mean for an outcome to be fair? We have made the point that fairness is not an absolute construct; instead, it is socially defined. What is fair to one person may not be fair in the eyes of another. Consider a group of three people who go out to dinner. One orders a bottle of expensive red wine, an appetizer, and a pricey main course. The second abstains from drinking and orders two inexpensive side dishes. The third orders a moderately priced meal. Then the bill arrives. The wine drinker immediately suggests that the group split the bill into thirds, explaining that equality is the simplest approach. The teetotaler winces and suggests that the group ask the waitress to bring three separate checks. The third group member argues that, because he is an impoverished graduate student, the two others should cover the bill. This example illustrates that in any situation, there are as many interpretations of fairness as there are parties involved. Here, equality, equity, and need are all plausible principles on which a decision can be made. Hence, in conflict resolution, two people may both truly want a fair settlement, but they may have very different and equally justifiable ideas about what is fair.

Although people generally want what is fair, their assessments of fairness are often self-serving (Messick and Sentis, 1979). Moreover, the fact that we have little or no self-awareness of this influence on our otherwise sound judgment heightens the intransigence of our views. Suppose you have worked for seven hours and have been paid $25. Another person has worked for ten hours doing the same work. How much do you think the other person should get paid? If you're like most people, you believe the other person should get paid more for doing more work—about $30, on average (Messick and Sentis, 1979). This is hardly a self-serving response. Now, consider the reverse situation: the other person has worked for seven hours and been paid $25. You have worked for ten hours. What is a fair wage for you to be paid? Messick and Sentis found the average response to be about $35. The difference is about $10, and it illustrates the phenomenon of egocentric bias: people pay themselves substantially more than they are willing to pay others for doing the same task.

Consider another example. You are told about an accident in which a motorcyclist was injured after being hit by a car. After learning all the facts, you are asked to make a judgment of how much money you think is a fair settlement to compensate the motorcyclist for his injuries. Then, you are asked to play the role of either the injured motorcyclist or the driver of the car and to negotiate a settlement. Most of the time, people in this situation have no trouble coming to an agreement (Babcock, Loewenstein, Issacharoff, and Camerer, 1995).

Now imagine doing the same thing, except that your role assignment comes first. That is, first you are asked to play the role of the motorcyclist or the driver, and then you learn all the facts, decide on a fair settlement, and finally negotiate. In this situation, the only thing that changes is that you learn the facts and make a fair settlement judgment through the eyes of one of the parties, instead of from the standpoint of a neutral observer. As it turns out, this difference is crucial. Instead of having no trouble coming to an agreement (as do the people who do not know their roles until just prior to the negotiation), people who know their roles from the beginning have a very difficult time coming to an agreement (Babcock, Loewenstein, Issacharoff, and Camerer, 1995). The high impasse rate among people who know their roles from the beginning is linked to self-serving judgments of fairness. The more biased the prenegotiation fair-settlement judgment, the more likely the later negotiation will result in impasse. Thus, a person who knows she is playing the role of motorcyclist before making a fair-settlement judgment is likely to assess a large damage award (in her own favor). A person who knows he is playing the role of the car driver before making a fair-settlement judgment is more likely to assess a small damage award (in his own favor). The end result is that these two people have quite a hard time negotiating an agreement, because their assessments of what is fair are so far apart.

In conflict situations, there are often as many proposed solutions as there are parties. Each party sincerely believes its own proposed outcome is fair for everyone. At the same time, each party's conception of fairness is tainted by self-interest, so that each solution is most favorable to the party proposing it.

Liking, Respect, and Collective Interests

Negotiations in organizational settings often take place in the context of collective decision making. Negotiation among group members is necessary for many common but important group decisions, such as hiring, promotion, dismissals, and capital expenditures. These decisions often pose a social dilemma, because members must decide between self-interest and group interest. As a manager, I prefer on the one hand to have members of my team devote 100 percent of their time to the current team project; but on the other hand, I want all managers to contribute to the success of the organization by assigning their team members to work on organizationwide tasks. If each manager contributes some of his or her own resources to organizationwide tasks, then the organization as a whole benefits—but each manager has fewer resources to devote to that team's project. On the other hand, if each manager refuses to contribute any resources to the organizationwide tasks, then the organization as a whole suffers (and perhaps eventually collapses), even though each manager benefits individually.

This classic problem of choosing between furthering one's own interests and those of the larger group or collective is at the heart of many conflicts. Our earlier discussion of egocentric judgment processes revealed that people tend to serve their own interests not necessarily because they are selfish and greedy, but because their own interests are immediately accessible to them. Thus, even people who truly desire to be evenhanded often behave in what may seem to a neutral observer self-interest. The question, of course, is how to mitigate this undesirable impulse. Merely telling people to monitor their own behavior is surely insufficient—and it may even increase self-interested behavior. Rather, to the extent that people can develop and enhance a sense of social identity—that is, derive meaning and identity from relationships with others—the egocentric effect may be mitigated.

The importance of social relationships in curbing self-interested behavior was illustrated in a study in which people were asked to decide between keeping resources for themselves or contributing to the organization as a whole (Thompson, Kray, and Lind, 1998). Not surprisingly, the better the relationship among the decision makers (the more they knew and liked each other) the more likely they were to agree to contribute resources to the organization as a whole. Remarkably, there was another important factor that affected people's decisions to contribute to the organization: how much respect was bestowed by organizational authorities. People who were granted high respect from relevant organizational authorities (and who also knew and liked their fellow decision makers) contributed the most resources to the organization as a whole. Thus, in the team management example considered earlier, a group of managers who know and like each other, and who also feel that upper management respects and carefully considers their decisions, contributes the most team resources for the good of the organization as a whole. On the other hand, if managers do not know and like each other, or if they are not accorded respect from upper management, they are likely to contribute the least to organizationwide concerns.

I'm Happy Only If You're Sad

When a conflict is resolved, the parties often assess how satisfied they are with the outcome of the resolution. But parties to a conflict do not measure their outcomes on an absolute scale. Instead, success is a socially determined construct, measured by many factors, including comparison with similar others, views of significant others, and the outcomes of one's opponent. In fact, there is little or no relationship between how good people feel and their actual outcomes. In conflict situations in which parties' interests are not completely aligned, how good people feel is a converse function of the emotions displayed by the other person: when the other is sad, we feel good; when they are happy, we feel bad (Thompson, Valley, and Kramer, 1995).

Consider a situation involving a car accident. Jim's car collides with Mike's, and both cars are damaged. The parties' insurance companies cannot agree on a settlement, so the case goes to arbitration. After hearing the evidence, the arbitrator awards Mike $2,000 for the damage to his car. After the decision, Jim hears Mike tell his lawyer, "I'm really happy with the arbitrator's decision—I got more than I expected." Upon hearing this, Jim feels very dissatisfied with the arbitrator's decision.

Now imagine the same situation, except this time Jim hears Mike tell his lawyer, "I'm not very happy with the arbitrator's decision—I got less than I expected." In this situation, Jim is likely to feel quite satisfied with the arbitrator's decision. Notice that Jim is more satisfied when Mike is disappointed than when Mike is happy, even though the outcome of the dispute is exactly the same in both situations. Thus, feelings of satisfaction are often relative, especially in competitive situations; they are inversely related to how the other party feels about the outcome.

Our feeling of satisfaction after the fact is not the only way we are affected by our opponent. Our preferences *during* an ongoing dispute can also be affected by the opponent's expressed preferences. Consider the case of Susan, who has been working as a data-entry clerk but a while ago slipped and fell, injuring her back. Because of her back injury, she has trouble sitting in front of the computer entering data for long periods of time. Susan's employer decides that because she can't do her work, she should take a leave of absence without pay. Months go by, with Susan requesting to return to her job, and her employer refusing to let her return unless she can prove that she has no trouble doing her data-entry job. Susan explains that she can do the job so long as she can take frequent breaks to get up and walk around, but her employer feels this makes it impossible for her to get all her work done. Instead, the employer tries placing her in other positions—the mail room, the copy room, and finally the reception desk—but these all prove worse for her back condition than her original job.

As time goes on, Susan becomes angry and suspicious toward her employer, eventually becoming convinced that her supervisors are purposely trying to make her life miserable. Finally, her employer relents and tells her that she can have her data-entry job back, and that she can take breaks as needed for her back condition. But now Susan refuses to accept the offer, reasoning that since they're making the offer there must be "something in it" for them, so it must therefore be bad for her. Instead, she stays on unpaid leave of absence and decides to take her employer to court.

Susan's case is an example of reactive devaluation, the tendency for a party to value an offer less just because it was the other party who offered it (Oskamp, 1965; Ross and Stillinger, 1991). The reasoning behind reactive devaluation is that my opponent wouldn't make this offer unless it's good for him. But if it's good for him, then it's probably bad for me, so I'll refuse to accept it. The examples of Susan's employment dispute and Jim and Mike's car accident illustrate that our preferences and our evaluation of a dispute can be determined by the other party's preferences and reactions. When the other party is happy, we are sad; when the other party seems to favor a particular outcome, we devalue it.

The Schmooze Effect

When people negotiate face-to-face, they rely on subtle behavior cues—posture, intonation, facial expression—to understand what the opponent is thinking and feeling. In fact, research indicates that the credibility of a message is much affected by whether the nonverbal cues are consistent or inconsistent with the verbal message. We understand our opponent's behavioral synchrony cues automatically; this is not something we are necessarily aware of. Yet this subtle process helps negotiators build rapport and trust, which can lead to favorable agreements for all parties.

When behavioral synchrony cues are absent—as when negotiators communicate via some method other than face-to-face contact—then rapport and trust must be built in some other way. In the absence of any rapport-building mechanism, negotiators endure strained and tense interactions, and they attribute their own feeling of ill ease to the malevolent intentions of the other party.

In recent years, changing organizational structures have created social networks composed of organization members who are physically separated, as in multinational corporations. Members of these organizations come to rely increasingly on electronically mediated communication methods (e-mail, fax, and phone) to conduct negotiations. But unless negotiators make a conscious effort to develop mutual cooperation and rapport, the absence of social cues in electronically mediated negotiations can lead to uncertainty about social norms and increased risk taking.

In one investigation, managers negotiated via e-mail with another manager whom they did not know (Moore, Kurtzberg, Thompson, and Morris, 1998). Some negotiators were instructed to develop a personal exchange prior to the negotiation through (electronic) exchange of pictures, talk of interests, and get-acquainted remarks; other negotiators were given no such instructions.

In the end, negotiators who were instructed to "schmooze" were much more successful than the others: they felt good about both the negotiation and their negotiating partner; they expressed it during the negotiation; and as a result, their impasse rate was very low, and their negotiated outcome was quite good. On the other hand, negotiators who did not establish rapport on a personal level in the beginning were much less successful: they felt bad about the negotiation and their opponent, and they expressed it during the negotiation by taking unwise risks. For example, negotiators without established rapport often made threats, such as telling the opponent "This is my final offer." These negotiators also expressed a tendency to "flame" or insult their opponent. As a result, negotiators who had not schmoozed reached an impasse in a large proportion of cases, and when agreement was reached, the negotiated outcome tended to be less favorable compared to outcomes of negotiators who had schmoozed.

Thus, the absence of social cues in electronically mediated negotiation can be compensated for by schmoozing. Doing so allows trust to develop between negotiators, leading to positive feelings about the opponent and the negotiation, and in the end, a low chance of impasse and better outcomes for both parties.

IMPLICATIONS FOR TRAINING PEOPLE

As contributors to the body of scientific empirical research on negotiation and conflict resolution, we admit with some embarrassment that much more thought goes into examining the nature of bias and error at the bargaining table than to solutions as to how to eliminate or reduce it. Perhaps this reflects the fundamental tension between basic and applied research. However, we are not content to naïvely suggest that mere awareness of bias is sufficient to deal with it. Thus, we have undertaken a line of empirical investigation that asks how negotiators learn and apply principles at the bargaining table; we review the highlights here. Our conclusion about learning to reduce cognitive bias and error at the bargaining table is based on three principles: feedback, analogical reasoning, and behavioral skills.

The Importance of Feedback

Most people do not get timely or accurate feedback about their performance. Thus they continue to make the same mistakes time and again. To return to the fixed-pie perception, we enter the negotiation assuming that the other party's gain comes at our expense, and vice versa. Even if this assumption is false (as it often is), chances are good that we do not realize it and enter our next negotiation with the same fixed-pie assumption. Even if people receive feedback, it is often incomplete or misconstrued, whether by the sender or the recipient. This, of course, is completely consistent with the egocentric biases we discussed earlier.

As a way of combating bias, Thompson and De Harpport (1994) examined the effects of three feedback situations: process feedback, outcome feedback, and no feedback. Negotiators who received no feedback knew nothing about the other party or the underlying structure of the negotiation. They were given a blank sheet of paper and asked to write some comments about the nature of their experience in the negotiation they had just completed. Negotiators who received outcome feedback were told the value of the overall package to the other party in the completed negotiation. This feedback provided important information about the underlying structure of the negotiation. Finally, negotiators who received process feedback were given complete information about their opponent's preferences for each issue negotiated. As an example, for a company representative who negotiated an employment contract, process feedback imparted information about how the employee subjectively valued the various issues discussed (salary, vacation, annual raise, and so on).

Negotiators who received process feedback were most likely to abandon the pervasive fixed-pie assumption in subsequent negotiations, and to recognize trade-offs that were mutually beneficial for both parties. Suppose two negotiators have just received process feedback after negotiating a job contract. Assume these same parties are to negotiate again about a completely different set of issues, say, a house rental. Having received process feedback, they are likely to assume correctly that not every gain for the other party constitutes an equal loss for themselves. Furthermore, they recognize that mutually beneficial exchanges can be made: if the landlord is to concede on an issue important to the tenant (say, monthly rent), then in exchange the tenant can concede on an issue important to the landlord (lease length). In this way, negotiators who receive process feedback reach agreements that are satisfactory to both parties. By contrast, negotiators who receive only outcome feedback are not as successful in recognizing this integrative potential, and those who receive no feedback are the least successful of all.

Analogical Reasoning

One of the most effective means by which people solve problems is analogical reasoning (Gick and Holyoak, 1983). Analogy is the process of mapping the solution for one problem into a solution for another problem. This involves noticing that a solution to a problem from the past is relevant, and then mapping the elements from that solution to the target problem. For example, a student learning about the structure of the atom enhances her understanding by drawing on her prior knowledge of the structure of the solar system.

In many instances, experienced negotiators have occasion to reason by analogy from a previous negotiation experience but often fail to do so. This problem of failing to capitalize on opportunities to learn by analogy is not limited to negotiators; in general, people's ability to take full advantage of prior experience is highly limited (Loewenstein, Thompson, and Gentner, forthcoming). Having solved one problem does not always help in solving an analogous problem if the two come from different contexts. We do not always access prior knowledge, given an analogous situation.

In a study of learning by analogy (Gick and Holyoak, 1983), students were given a problem about how to use radiation to destroy a patient's tumor, given that the stream of rays at full strength will destroy the healthy tissue en route to the tumor. The solution is to converge on the tumor with low-strength radiation from multiple directions. Having been given this problem and learned the solution, people are then given an analogous one: a general needs to capture a fortress but finds he cannot use his entire army to make a frontal attack. One solution is to divide the army and converge on the fortress from many directions. Even when the tumor problem and the fortress problem are presented in the same session, only about 41 percent of students spontaneously applied the convergence solution to the radiation problem. Though they retained the knowledge about the first solution, they failed to access it. Yet, when simply told to "think about the earlier [tumor] problem," a full 85 percent of students applied the convergence solution to the new problem. Simply reminding people of an analogous problem helps them map the solution onto the new problem.

The good news for negotiators is that analogy training can substantially improve negotiation performance. In one study, managers who received analogy training were nearly three times as likely to recognize and apply the appropriate principle in future negotiations (Loewenstein, Thompson, and Gentner, forthcoming). As a result, negotiators with analogy training outperformed those without. For example, in negotiating a deal for a Broadway production, negotiation dyads with analogy training gained an average of $21,000 over their untrained counterparts, who made suboptimal agreements and left large amounts of money on the bargaining table—wasted, as far as both parties were concerned.

In another study of negotiator training, four other learning principles were compared to learning by analogy (Nadler, Thompson, and Van Boven, 1999): (1) learning observation (watching other negotiators), (2) textbook learning (reading about negotiation principles), (3) learning by feedback (process feedback, as described in the previous section), and (4) learning by experience only (no explicit training). The greatest improvement in negotiator performance was seen with negotiators who had analogy training or observation training. Performance also improved, albeit to a lesser extent, when negotiators learned through feedback. Those exposed to textbook learning or to learning by experience alone showed no measurable improvement in performance. Thus, the picture emerging from this research is that training programs teaching negotiators how to make relevant comparisons between prior and current negotiation experiences is an extremely effective method for improving outcomes.

Behavioral Skills

To be effective at conflict resolution, people need to have strategies that work. Further, the strategies need to be general enough to apply to varying situations. Yet they cannot be so general as to be useless. In this subsection we identify and discuss five key strategies in the bargaining literature that withstand the difficult test of empirical investigation.

Build Trust and Share Information. In long-term relationships, people learn to build trust as a way of responding to uncertainty. Even though we lack a close relationship with someone, we might expect to have future interactions: a car dealer who makes a sale might expect the customer to refer friends or engage in repeat business; a job candidate negotiating terms with an interviewer expects to interact with the same person once on the job; two managers from different divisions working together toward an organizational goal know they will inevitably have future contact. In all of these situations, opportunity for deceit exists because of informational uncertainty or asymmetry. One way of dealing with this uncertainty is by building trust through sharing information of the sort that clearly indicates an interest in mutual well-being. Sharing such information helps ensure that the parties can continue to develop good working relations for the future.

Ask Questions. Building trust is not always possible. Sometimes negotiations are a one-shot deal, where the parties are aware they will never see one another again. Even where future interaction is possible, building trust is still difficult. If trust is absent or unclear, one of the most important strategies to pursue is to ask questions—specifically, to gather information about the opponent's preferences to ascertain which issues the opponent values most, which option is most preferred on each specific issue, and whether the opponent's expectations regarding the future differ from your own. Ideally, the issue most valued by your opponent is different from yours, in which case both parties can get what is most wanted by giving up something considered less valuable. But it is difficult to achieve trade-offs without asking about the opponent's priorities.

Provide Information. If the opponent is reluctant to answer any questions, there is an alternative strategy available: share some information first. Offering information is usually an effective strategy because it invariably triggers the reciprocity principle. We often feel obligated to return in kind what others have offered or given to us. Reciprocity is a powerful behavioral tendency observable in all human societies. People feel upset and distressed if they receive a favor—or a slight—from another person but are prevented from returning it.

Negotiators who extend information about their own interests or priorities are likely to receive some information in return. Although they may not want to reveal their reservation price (the minimum for which they will settle) or their best alternative option, they can still offer information about the relative importance of the issues as they see them. The goal is to exchange just enough information so that the final agreement is maximally beneficial for both parties and divides all resources available without leaving anything left over on the bargaining table.

Make Multiple Offers Simultaneously. Sometimes, negotiators are disappointed to find that their attempts to obtain and seek information are not effective. There is an alternative strategy: make one offer, and wait to hear the opponent's response. Little can be learned, though, about the opponent's interests and preferences simply from a single offer that is rejected. A more productive strategy is to make multiple offers. This involves presenting the other party with two (or more) proposals of equal value to oneself. The other party is asked to indicate which of the proposals he prefers. This can reveal valuable information about which issues are important to him. Thus the negotiator plays detective by drawing conclusions based on the opponent's response to the multiple offers.

Search for Postsettlement Settlements. Sometimes, parties may decide to renegotiate after a mutually agreeable settlement has been reached. It may seem counterintuitive or counterproductive to resume negotiations after a deal has been struck. But the strategy of postsettlement settlements is remarkably effective in improving the quality of negotiated agreements. Negotiators using this strategy agree to explore other options, mindful that the goal is to find another agreement that both prefer to the current one—with the understanding that they are bound by the initial agreement if another is not found. The postsettlement settlement strategy allows both parties to reveal their preferences without fear of exploitation, because they can safely revert to their previous agreement.

CONCLUSION

We believe that the marriage between practitioners and theorists should be much more solid than it is. Theorists have identified a host of rather benign-looking beliefs and cognitions that hinder effective negotiations, but they have failed to produce a systematic body of research aimed at reducing cognitive biases that hinder effective dispute resolution. Unfortunately, most negotiators are not aware of the existence of cognitive bias and its deleterious effects. In this chapter, we have identified four key biases that conflict theorists, and practitioners in particular, must fight to eliminate. We have also examined use of performance feedback and analogy training, and named five specific behavioral skills that meet the test of empirical investigation. We hope that theorists and practitioners continue to identify and examine new methods by which to eliminate or reduce cognitive bias at the bargaining table.

References

Babcock, L., Loewenstein, G. F., Issacharoff, S., and Camerer, C. "Biased Judgment of Fairness in Bargaining." *American Economic Review,* 1995, *85,* 1337–1343.

Balke, W. M., Hammond, K. R., and Meyer, G. D. "An Alternate Approach to Labor-Management Relations." *Administrative Science Quarterly,* 1973, *18,* 311–327.

Bazerman, M. H., and Neale, M. A. *Negotiating Rationally.* New York: Free Press, 1992.

Benton, A. A., Kelley, H. H., and Liebling, R. M. "Effects of Extremity of Offers and Concession Rates on the Outcomes of Bargaining." *Journal of Personality and Social Psychology,* 1972, *24,* 409–415.

Frank, M. G., and Gilovich, T. "The Dark Side of Self and Social Perception: Black Uniforms and Aggression in Professional Sports." *Journal of Personality and Social Psychology,* 1988, *54,* 74–85.

Gick, M. L., and Holyoak, K. J. "Schema Induction and Analogical Transfer." *Cognitive Psychology,* 1983, *15,* 1–38.

Henslin, J. M. "Craps and Magic." *American Journal of Sociology,* 1967, *73,* 316–330.

Kahn, R. L., and Kramer, R. M. *Untying the Knot: Deescalatory Processes in International Conflict.* San Francisco: Jossey-Bass, 1990.

Langer, E. J. "The Illusion of Control." *Journal of Personality and Social Psychology,* 1975, *32,* 311–328.

Loewenstein, G. F., Thompson, L., and Bazerman, M. "Social Utility and Decision Making in Interpersonal Contexts." *Journal of Personality and Social Psychology,* 1989, *57,* 426–441.

Loewenstein, G. F., Thompson, L., and Gentner, D. "Analogical Encoding Facilitates Knowledge Transfer in Negotiation." *Psychonomic Bulletin and Review,* forthcoming.

Messick, D. M. "Equality as a Decision Heuristic." In B. A. Mellers and J. Baron (eds.), *Psychological Perspectives on Justice.* New York: Cambridge University Press, 1993.

Messick, D. M., and Sentis, K. P. "Fairness and Preference." *Journal of Experimental Social Psychology,* 1979, *15,* 418–434.

Moore, D. A., Kurtzberg, T. R., Thompson, L. L., and Morris, M. W. "Long and Short Routes to Success in Electronically Mediated Negotiations: Group Affiliations and Good Vibrations." *Organizational Behavior and Human Decision Processes,* 1998, *77,* 22–43.

Morris, M. W., Sim, D. S., and Girrotto, V. "Time of Decision, Ethical Obligation, and Causal Illusion: Temporal Cues and Social Heuristics in the Prisoner's Dilemma." In R. M. Kramer and D. M. Messick (eds.), *Negotiation as a Social Process.* Thousand Oaks, Calif.: Sage, 1995.

Nadler, J., Thompson, L., and Van Boven, L. "The Role of Learning in Negotiation." Unpublished manuscript, Northwestern University, 1999.

Neale, M. A., and Bazerman, M. H. *Cognition and Rationality in Negotiation.* New York: Free Press, 1991.

Oskamp, S. "Attitudes Toward U.S. and Russian Actions: A Double Standard." *Psychological Reports,* 1965, *16,* 43–46.

Robinson, R. J., Keltner, D., Ward, A., and Ross, L. "Actual Versus Assumed Differences in Construal: 'Naïve Realism' in Intergroup Perception and Conflict." *Journal of Personality and Social Psychology,* 1995, *68,* 404–417.

Ross, L., and Stillinger, C. "Barriers to Conflict Resolution." *Negotiation Journal,* 1991, *7,* 389–404.

Ross, M., and Sicoly, F. "Egocentric Biases in Availability Attribution." *Journal of Personality and Social Psychology,* 1979, *8,* 322–336.

Rubin, J. Z., Pruitt, D. G., and Kim, S. H. *Social Conflict: Escalation, Stalemate, and Settlement.* New York: McGraw-Hill, 1994.

Thompson, L. "The Influence of Experience on Negotiation Performance." *Journal of Experimental Social Psychology,* 1990, *26,* 528–544.

Thompson, L. *The Mind and Heart of the Negotiator.* Upper Saddle River, N.J.: Prentice Hall, 1998.

Thompson, L., and De Harpport, T. "Social Judgment, Feedback, and Interpersonal Learning in Negotiation." *Organizational Behavior and Human Decision Processes,* 1994, *58,* 327–345.

Thompson, L., and Hastie, R. "Social Perception in Negotiation." *Organizational Behavior and Human Decision Processes,* 1990, *47,* 98–123.

Thompson, L., and Hrebec, D. "Lose-Lose Agreements in Interdependent Decision Making." *Psychological Bulletin,* 1996, *120,* 396–409.

Thompson, L., Kray, L. J., and Lind, E. A. "Cohesion and Respect: An Examination of Group Decision Making in Social and Escalation Dilemmas." *Journal of Experimental Social Psychology,* 1998, *34,* 289–311.

Thompson, L., Valley, K. L., and Kramer, R. M. "The Bittersweet Feeling of Success: An Examination of Social Perception in Negotiation." *Journal of Experimental Social Psychology,* 1995, *31,* 467–492.

Walton, R. E., and McKersie, R. B. *A Behavioral Theory of Labor Relations.* New York: McGraw-Hill, 1965.

CHAPTER ELEVEN

Anger and Retaliation in Conflict

The Role of Attribution

Keith G. Allred

I t's early Friday evening, the end of a long week. At least Margaret thought the workweek would be over by now. Her supervisor, Robin, has just told her—as she was going out the door—to come into the office at 8:00 Saturday morning to help with a report. The only reason Margaret doesn't have to stay late tonight is that she and Dan, her husband, already have tickets to a show. She rushes home to make it to the show on time. It's now twenty minutes past the time Dan promised to be home, and Margaret is sure they'll be late. She can sense being on the verge of conflict with both her boss and her husband.

What determines whether a conflict in fact ensues, and what course it takes? Attribution theory, one of the dominant paradigms in social psychology in the last three decades, suggests that Margaret's beliefs about why her husband and her boss behave as they do exert a critical influence. Let us consider contrasting scenarios of Margaret's interactions with her boss and spouse to illustrate the role that attribution plays in conflict.

First, imagine that Dan arrives home late and explains that he got wrapped up in a new game on his computer at work and lost track of time. Margaret and Dan begin a heated argument about his irresponsibility and thoughtlessness, which continues as they drive frantically to the show. The next morning, as she drives to work, she finds herself thinking about how disorganized her boss is and how often she has to pay the price for it. Robin seems to expect that other people's dedication should compensate for her lack of organization. Margaret feels her anger rising. When she arrives at work, she confronts Robin immediately. Within a few hours, Margaret becomes involved in two heated arguments.

Now, imagine by contrast that Dan comes home and explains that there was an accident on the highway that backed up traffic for miles. Margaret tells him not to worry about it. She enjoys the evening with him in spite of the somewhat frantic drive to the show. The next morning, as Margaret heads into work, she finds herself thinking about her boss's situation. Robin is struggling to succeed at her job while meeting the demands of being a single mother; though a very competent person, she nevertheless finds it impossible sometimes to juggle everything to her complete satisfaction. Just this week, her daughter had another serious asthma attack, requiring a brief stay in the hospital. Her daughter's attack has left Robin unable to complete a report and now requiring Margaret's help. Although Margaret obviously would enjoy having the weekend off, she finds herself feeling quite sympathetic toward her boss and willing to help.

The critical difference between the two scenarios is not what the other person does, but *why* Margaret thinks the other person does it. If Margaret thinks her husband is late because he is playing computer games, or thinks Robin needs her to come in on Saturday because Robin is too disorganized to complete her report on time, Margaret tends to become angry and feel an impulse to strike back. If she thinks Dan is late because of unusually slow traffic or that Robin has her come in on Saturday because Robin's daughter is going through another bout with asthma, Margaret tends to feel sympathy and willingness to be understanding and helpful.

Social psychologists describe the difference in Margaret's interpretations of why the other party acts as he or she does as a matter of *attribution*. Margaret attributes Robin's request that she come in on Saturday to either her boss's disorganization or to her daughter's asthma. Similarly, she attributes Dan's tardiness to either his choosing to play computer games at the office or being caught in traffic delays. This chapter reviews insights that research on attribution offers into conflict dynamics.

Attribution research can be divided into two main categories (Kelley and Michela, 1980). One has investigated how people arrive at attributions; it identifies some of the sophisticated and rational processes by which people accurately identify the causes of their own and other people's behavior. This category also identifies certain common inaccuracies in attribution. The second body of attribution research examines the implications of attribution. It focuses on the emotions, such as anger or sympathy, that result from attributing a person's behavior to various causes. This line of attribution research also investigates the behavioral consequences of these emotions, such as retaliation or helping. After reviewing these two branches of attribution research, I discuss their implications for understanding conflict dynamics. The chapter concludes with a discussion of strategies for conflict management training and mediation, as suggested by the insights generated by attribution research.

ATTRIBUTIONS: EXPLAINING OTHER PEOPLE'S BEHAVIOR

Fritz Heider (1958), considered to be the first attribution theorist, suggested that people strive to understand the causes of events around them, particularly other people's behavior, because accurate understanding of these causes helps people make appropriate and adaptive responses to those events. If Margaret can accurately understand why her boss requests that she come to work on Saturday, she is better able to respond appropriately. Heider's work investigated why, on some occasions, we attribute other people's behavior to their dispositions (such as their personality traits, attitudes, or abilities) while on other occasions we attribute it to the external circumstances in which they find themselves.

Jones and Davis (1965) and Kelley (1967) extended Heider's work. As seen in Figure 11.1, Jones and Davis proposed that the process of attributing another person's behavior to disposition rather than the situation involves two stages. In the first stage, one considers whether the other person's act was intentional. The act is considered intentional to the extent that the person knows that the behavior will produce the consequences observed (stage 1A) and the person has the ability to achieve the consequences he or she intends (stage 1B). For example, imagine that Margaret thinks Dan doesn't know, because of the unforeseen traffic, that leaving work when he does will result in his arriving home late (stage 1A), and that in traffic Dan can't overcome the obstacle to his intention of arriving home on time (stage 1B). In this case, Margaret concludes that his late arrival isn't intentional and therefore doesn't result from disposition. However, if Margaret perceives that Dan knows that by continuing to play with the computer he'll arrive home late (stage 1A) and that he can choose not to continue playing but plays anyway (stage 1B), then she concludes that Dan's behavior is intentional.

In the event you conclude that the other person's behavior is intentional, Jones and Davis suggest, you enter the second stage: considering whether the act results from the person's disposition. The more the act has a strongly positive or negative effect on you, the more likely you are to attribute the behavior to a corresponding disposition (stage 2A). Additionally, the more you perceive a positive or negative effect to be the intended result of the act, the more you attribute the behavior to disposition (stage 2B). Since Dan's intentional behavior has a negative effect on Margaret—she's going to be late to the show—she'll probably infer that Dan's behavior results from disposition (stage 2A). She might, for example, attribute his behavior to his thoughtlessness. If Dan's behavior doesn't affect her because she arrives home late herself, then she is less likely to attribute his

Figure 11.1. Jones and Davis's Two-Stage Process for Making Dispositional Attributions.

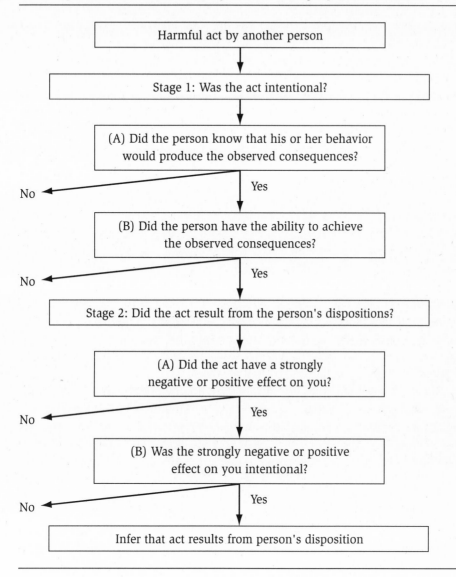

behavior to disposition. Finally, if Margaret perceives that Dan's behavior has the negative effect of making her late for the show and that Dan *intends* this negative consequence, Margaret is even more likely to infer that his behavior results from a disposition, such as his meanness (stage 2B).

Following soon after Jones and Davis (1965), Kelley (1967) suggested that people consider three kinds of information when attempting to determine whether a person behaved in a certain way because of disposition or because of external circumstances. According to Kelley, an attributor looks to see if (1) the person behaves the same way only in a particular kind of circumstance (distinctiveness information), or (2) across many circumstances (consistency information). Margaret may notice that Dan is always late, not just when he's coming home in unusually heavy traffic (low distinctiveness and high consistency). An attributor, according to Kelley, also considers whether the person's behavior is (3) unique in the situation or whether other people also behave this way in the same circumstances (consensus information). Margaret may realize that other people in the neighborhood who work near Dan typically arrive home on time (low consensus). With this combination of the three types of attributional information, Margaret tends to attribute Dan's behavior to something internal to him. However, if she recognizes that he only arrives home late when an accident slows traffic (high distinctiveness), is generally quite punctual rather than late (low consistency), and that everyone else working in the same area arrives home late when traffic is slow (high consensus), she is more likely to attribute his behavior to external circumstances.

Heider, Jones and Davis, and Kelley describe the process by which one arrives at a causal explanation as sophisticated and rational. In fact, they describe people as "lay scientists," searching systematically for the causes of other people's behavior. A substantial body of research supports this view (for reviews, see Kelley and Michela, 1980, and Ross and Fletcher, 1985).

However, attribution researchers have also discovered important exceptions to people's attributional rationality. Research indicates that when people err in attributing other people's behavior, they do so on the side of inferring too quickly and easily that a given behavior is the result of disposition while largely ignoring information indicating that circumstances cause the behavior (for reviews, see Gilbert and Malone, 1995; Gilbert, Miller, and Ross, 1998; McArthur, 1972; Ross, 1977; Ross and Nisbett, 1991). For example, research indicates that in observing a person at an airport yelling at an airline agent, one tends to overattribute the behavior to bad temper and underattribute it to circumstances, such as having recently been the victim of recurring unfair treatment by the airline. Our tendency to overattribute behavior to dispositions and underattribute it to circumstances is known as the *fundamental attribution error* (Ross, 1977).

Although we tend to err toward attributing other people's behavior to disposition, we tend to attribute our own behavior to our circumstances (for reviews, see Kelley and Michela, 1980; Watson, 1982). This tendency is referred to as the *actor-observer bias* (Jones and Nisbett, 1972). It should be noted that the actor-observer bias appears to be less pronounced in Asian cultures than in European and American cultures because Asians are less prone to the fundamental attribution error, emphasizing disposition less in attributing the cause of other people's behavior than Europeans and Americans do (Choi and Nisbett, 1998).

Just as there are differences in how we attribute our own and other people's negative behavior, there are also differences in how we attribute the negative behavior of people who are or are not members of our own social group. Research on the *intergroup attributional bias* indicates that one frequently attributes an out-group member's negative behavior to the person's character or disposition more than one does an in-group member's behavior (for a review, see Hewstone, 1990). For example, we attribute an out-group member's failure to keep an appointment to laziness rather than bad weather or heavy traffic more often than we do for an in-group member. Recent research indicates that the intergroup attributional bias may be less pervasive than originally thought. It may occur mostly between groups having strongly conflicting interests or a long history of pronounced conflict, as with Protestants and Catholics in northern Ireland or Arabs and Israelis in the Middle East (Flippen, Hornstein, Siegal, and Weitzman, 1996; Hewstone, 1988, 1990). Nevertheless, in a situation of conflicting interest or long-standing conflict, the intergroup attributional bias can be a powerful source of conflict between members of social groups.

THE EMOTIONAL AND BEHAVIORAL
IMPLICATIONS OF ATTRIBUTIONS

As Heider first suggested, people presumably concern themselves with the cause of other people's behavior for the purpose of responding to the behavior appropriately. Research examining the role of attribution in shaping behavioral response has found that emotion is a critical link between an attribution and a behavioral response; certain kinds of attribution arouse discrete emotions, such as anger or sympathy. It is these emotions, in turn, that elicit such responses as retaliation or helping behavior.

Bernard Weiner (for reviews, see Weiner, 1986, 1995) proposes the most fully developed and tested theory of the emotional and behavioral implications of attribution. Once a person arrives at an attribution, Weiner suggests, it can be characterized according to two dimensions beyond that of how internal or external the cause is to the actor. First, Weiner suggests that the causes to which people attribute behavior vary in how stable or unchanging they are over time. For example, Margaret might attribute Robin's request to work on Saturday to her boss's lack of effort to get her report done on time. On the other hand, she may think that Robin did not finish the report because Robin is incapable of performing the high-level quantitative reasoning required for this report. Lack of innate ability in quantitative reasoning is a relatively stable or unchanging cause of Robin's failure to finish the report.

However, lack of effort is likely to be a relatively unstable cause, one much more likely to change over time. A second dimension that Weiner identifies beyond the internal-external dimension is how much control the person has over the cause. Although the internal-external and controllable-uncontrollable dimensions may often be related, they are not the same. Both lack of effort and lack of quantitative ability in Robin's failure to complete her report are attributions internal to Robin. But she would be able to control lack of effort, while lack of quantitative reasoning ability may be largely beyond her control.

Weiner (1986, 1995) and his colleagues offer further evidence that these underlying dimensions of attribution are important because an attribution's location on each dimension determines which emotions a person feels. Because research indicates that the controllability dimension influences other-directed emotions such as anger and sympathy, it is perhaps the most relevant one for understanding conflict dynamics. The scenarios at the start of the chapter describe interpretations Margaret can make of her boss's and her husband's negative behaviors. According to Margaret's first interpretations, Dan comes home late because of his forgetfulness and thoughtlessness and Robin needs her to come in on the weekend because she is too disorganized to meet a deadline. In these instances, the cause of the negative behavior is under the volitional control of the other person; Margaret's spouse and her boss can choose to behave otherwise. Research confirms that Margaret's reactions, given these controllable attributions, are typical. Attributing another person's negative behavior to causes within his or her control tends to arouse anger toward the person.

In the contrasting interpretations, Margaret attributes Dan's lateness to traffic and Robin's need for her to work over the weekend to her daughter's asthma attack. In both of these cases, the other has less control over the cause of the negative behavior. Again, research confirms that Margaret's reactions are typical. Attributing another person's negative behavior to causes beyond the person's control tends to elicit sympathy rather than anger.

According to a number of studies, it is the emotional response aroused by attribution that drives a person's behavioral response (de Rivera, 1984; Roseman, Spindel, and Jose, 1990; Smith and Lazarus, 1993; Weiner, 1986, 1995). Anger, resulting from a controllable attribution for another person's negative behavior— whether it negatively affects oneself or other people—has been linked with punishing behavior in general (Averill, 1982; de Rivera, 1984; Roseman, Spindel, and Jose, 1990; Smith and Lazarus, 1993; Weiner, 1995). Recent research has examined the particular case in which the other person's behavior negatively affects oneself. The anger that results from attributing such a behavior to a controllable cause arouses specifically retaliatory impulses, impulses to harm the other person (Allred, 1999). In these studies, 59 percent of the managers who were asked to recall an occasion when they held someone else responsible for a behavior that harmed them personally reported actually retaliating against the other party. In just over half of the occasions in which managers retaliated, the retaliatory acts took an overt form, often manifesting itself in heated verbal confrontation and, occasionally, in a violent or malicious act. In just under half of the cases, their retaliation was covert; managers often reported fabricating a reason they could not give the harmdoer the help he or she sought on a subsequent occasion.

The attribution-to-emotion-to-behavior sequence identified in attribution research constitutes a process that equips human beings with the ability to detect and respond to other people's harmful behavior. First, they make a judgment about whether the person acting harmfully did so for a reason beyond his or her control. If Dan is late because of traffic and if Robin doesn't finish her report because of her daughter's asthma, there is little point in Margaret's becoming angry and retaliating since neither her spouse nor her boss have the power to act otherwise. If, however, Dan is late because of thoughtlessness and Robin hasn't finished her report because she's disorganized, Margaret's resulting anger and retaliation raise the cost of the others' harmful behaviors. In these instances, Margaret's angry retaliation may prevent Dan and Robin, who have control over their behavior, from acting in that way again.

IMPLICATIONS FOR CONFLICT DYNAMICS

Until recently, researchers have paid very little attention to the role that emotion plays in conflict (Barry and Oliver, 1996; Bartunek, Kolb, and Lewicki, 1992; Greenhalgh and Chapman, 1995; Kolb and Putnam, 1992; Thomas, 1992). By identifying both the causes and consequences of anger in conflict, attribution research is beginning to address this oversight. It has identified a psychological mechanism by which people detect and respond to others' harmful behaviors. On many occasions, anger-driven retaliation may be successful in arresting a person's harmful behavior and preventing it in the future.

However, part of the usefulness of the attributional perspective on conflict is that it reveals some of the psychological sources of many particularly destructive conflicts. Anger-driven conflict is often maladaptive in at least two respects. First, it is particularly destructive because, once angered at each other, parties in a conflict become less effective at solving the problems between them. One study found that negotiators who held each other responsible for harmful behavior in a previous interaction felt greater anger and less compassion toward each other than those who did not hold each other responsible for the same harmful behavior (Allred, Mallozzi, Matsui, and Raia, 1997). Consequently, the angry negotiators had less positive regard for each other's interests in the negotiation. As a result, the negotiators who were angry with each other discovered fewer mutually beneficial solutions than the participants who were not angry with each other.

A second reason that angry, retaliatory conflicts are especially maladaptive is because they are frequently rooted in misperceptions that tend to escalate the conflict. Research on the actor-observer bias seems to suggest that a harmdoer attributes his or her behavior to external causes while the harmed party attributes the behavior to a disposition of the harmdoer. However, most actor-observer bias research has not examined situations in which the actor's behavior has a direct and negative impact on the observer. For example, many actor-observer bias studies investigate situations in which one person observes another in conversation or offering an opinion on a topic, rather than the situation Margaret faces in which Robin's and Dan's behaviors have direct and negative impact on her.

A recent study investigated these situations in which the actor's behavior negatively affects the observer (Allred, Chiongbian, and Parlamis, 1999). Because the controllability dimension drives anger, the study also investigated bias in attributing behavior to a cause controllable by the actor, rather than investigating only bias in attributing behavior to a cause internal to the actor as previous actor-observer bias research has done. The results of the study indicated the presence of an *accuser bias,* the tendency for an observer negatively affected by an actor's behavior to attribute the behavior to causes under the control of the actor. For example, given that Margaret is negatively affected by Robin's request that she come to work on Saturday, she is more likely to attribute the request to Robin's lack of organization than to her daughter's asthma attack. Consequently, Margaret is likely to feel greater anger and a stronger impulse to retaliate than she otherwise would. The accuser bias thus tends to make anger-driven conflict especially destructive because such conflicts are often rooted in exaggerated judgments of responsibility that lead to excessive anger and retaliation.

The destructive effects of the accuser bias are greatly exacerbated because the person who acts negatively falls victim to the opposite bias. The study documenting the accuser bias also revealed a *bias of the accused,* a tendency to attribute one's own harmful behavior to circumstances beyond one's control (Allred, Chiongbian, and Parlamis, 1999). In our example, Robin is likely to overattribute her need to have Margaret come in to her daughter's asthma attack, and underattribute it to her own lack of organization.

On many occasions, the cause of a behavior, such as Robin's, cannot be solely attributed to the situation or the person but is instead the result of some combination of the two. Robin's daughter's asthma may contribute to her failure to complete her report on time, but she might also have been behind on the report before her daughter's asthma attack because of her own lack of organization. The point of the research on the accuser bias and the bias of the accused is that, of the contributing causes of a harmful behavior, the accused tends to focus on those beyond her control, while the accuser focuses on those within the control of the accused. Consequently, the accuser holds the accused more responsible for the harmful behavior than the accused holds herself accountable (Weiner, 1995).

It is this difference in judgment of the harmdoer's responsibility that can lead to the most destructive kinds of anger-driven conflict (Allred, 1999). Anger-driven conflict is only likely to proceed very far if the harmed party holds the harmdoer more responsible than the harmdoer does himself. As seen in Figure 11.2, there are four possible combinations of the harmdoer's and harmed party's judgments of the harmdoer's responsibility.

Figure 11.2. Combinations of Harmdoer's and Harmed Party's Judgments of Responsibility.

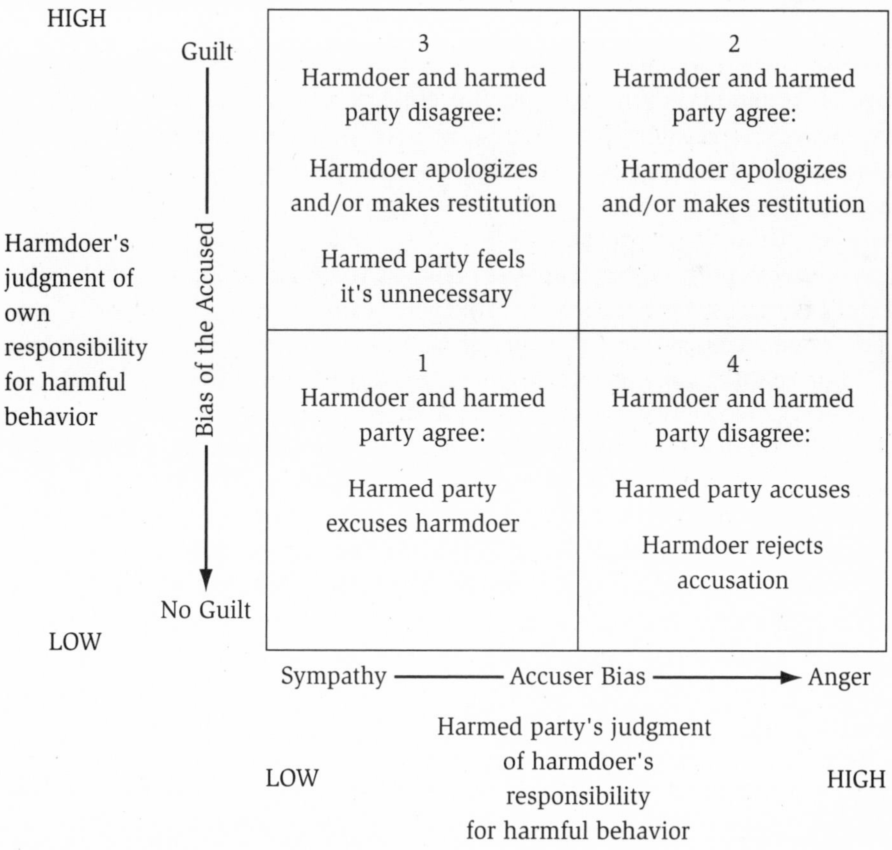

First, if the harmdoer and the harmed party agree that the harmdoer is not responsible, then the conflict may not proceed very far because the harmed party is likely to excuse the harmdoer's behavior.

Second, if the harmdoer and the harmed party agree that the harmdoer is responsible, then the conflict may not go very far because the harmdoer might feel guilty, apologize, and make amends.

Third, even if the harmdoer and harmed party disagree over how responsible the harmdoer is, the conflict is unlikely to continue if the harmdoer holds himself more responsible for the behavior than the harmed party does. In this case, the harmdoer tends to feel guilty, apologize, and offer to make amends and the harmed party tends to think that this response is unnecessary.

In the fourth combination, however, if the harmed party holds the harmdoer more responsible than she holds herself, the harmed party tends to feel an impulse to demand that the harmdoer make amends or face retaliation. The harmdoer, on the other hand, tends to reject demands to make amends and to see retaliation as unjustified.

Of course, reasonable people can honestly disagree about many things, including judgments about how responsible one party is for behavior that harms another party, without necessarily revealing bias. Nevertheless, given the accuser bias and bias of the accused, this latter direction of disagreement about the level of responsibility is probably the result of one or both parties' bias. In other words, if the parties could be freed of the biases peculiar to being either on the giving or the receiving end of the harmful behavior, the angry, retaliatory conflict might disappear.

The difference in judgment of responsibility created by the accuser bias and the bias of the accused is destructive not simply because it tends to elicit angry conflicts based on misperception. It can also be the fuel for a self-perpetuating and escalating spiral of anger-driven conflict (Allred, 1999). Returning to Margaret's experience, imagine the scenario depicted in Figure 11.3. As Margaret drives in to help Robin with the report on Saturday morning, she thinks about Robin's disorganization while overlooking her daughter's asthma attack. This accuser bias focus arouses in Margaret greater anger than she would feel if she had a more accurate view of the causes of Robin's behavior. When she walks in the door, her anger compels her to say, "You and everyone else would be better off if you'd try to get a little more organized so these emergencies didn't happen as often."

As Robin hears this, her thoughts are drawn to how her daughter's asthma attack kept her from completing the report on time. In focusing on her daughter's asthma attack, she tends to ignore that she, in fact, isn't very organized and that she might not have been able to finish the report on time without help even if her daughter hadn't had an attack. Because of this bias of the accused, Robin concludes that she is less responsible for Margaret's having to come in than she actually is. Because she feels she is not as responsible for the lost Saturday as Margaret thinks she is, she views the comment as unjustified.

Figure 11.3. Self-Perpetuating Cycle of Angry Conflict.

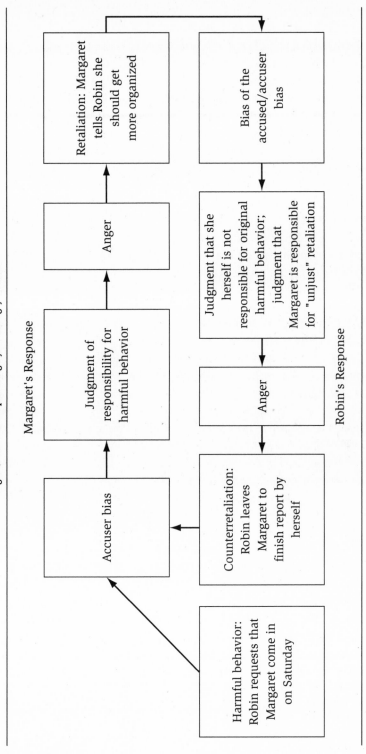

In fact, from Robin's perspective the comment is itself a harmful act by Margaret against Robin. Now it's Robin's turn to fall victim to the accuser bias. Having already overlooked her own culpability for Margaret's lost Saturday, Robin concludes that only a selfish, insensitive person would fail to understand her situation and make such a comment. Consequently, Robin is more angered by Margaret's criticism than she otherwise would be and feels justified in letting Margaret have it. She responds: "I can't believe you could be so selfish and insensitive—you know the situation with my daughter. You're going to have to learn to help others on the team when it's needed, and I'm giving you an opportunity to learn that lesson right now." Robin hands Margaret the file and, before walking out the door, says, "I expect the report on my desk first thing Monday morning. Have a nice weekend."

At this point, the cycle depicted in Figure 11.3 has come full circle. Margaret is even more certain to fall victim to the accuser bias as she attributes the cause of Robin's leaving her to do the weekend's work herself. As a result, she becomes overly angry and finds some way to retaliate. Thus the cycle continues, manifesting a particularly pernicious form of Deutsch's Crude Law of Social Relations (1973; see also Chapter One of this book), which suggests that competitive and destructive (as well as cooperative and constructive) social processes tend to perpetuate themselves.

In fact, research suggests that once these mutually derogating attributional patterns give rise to such dynamics they can become so entrenched that they define not only a unique and especially destructive type of conflict but an especially destructive type of relationship as well. Research on attributional patterns in close relationships is instructive because it captures attributional dynamics between interdependent parties over longer periods of time than has been true of most of the research reviewed so far. Stimulated by the initial work of Orvis, Kelley, and Butler (1976), dozens of studies investigating differences in attributional patterns among people in close relationships, mostly marital couples, have found similar results (for reviews, see Baucom, 1987; Bradbury and Fincham, 1990; Harvey, 1987; Sillars, 1985). In stressed or dissatisfied relationships, the parties consistently attributed each other's negative behavior to internal, controllable causes and attributed each other's positive behavior to external, uncontrollable causes. Consequently, people in stressed relationships felt negative emotions toward each other and had difficulty solving the problems that arose between them.

People in satisfied relationships, by contrast, tended to exhibit no such derogating pattern of attribution. In fact, people in some satisfied relationships exhibited a reversal of typical derogating attribution, attributing each other's negative behavior to external, uncontrollable causes and positive behavior to internal, controllable causes. Consequently, in satisfied relationships people experienced positive emotions toward each other and were successful at solving the problems that arose between them.

Once established, both the stressed and satisfied marital patterns are self-fulfilling and self-perpetuating. That is, at some point the bias actually becomes an accurate perception. In a distressed relationship, the parties purposely behave negatively toward each other, although each sees his or her own negative behavior as the other person's just desserts for a prior negative act by that person (Bies, Tripp, and Kramer, 1997; Sillars, 1981). In a satisfied relationship, the parties intentionally act kindly toward each other. Nevertheless, Bradbury and Fincham (1990) say the evidence suggests that attributional bias is the ultimate causal agent. In other words, the pattern is largely set in motion in the first place by the difference in attributional pattern. The research on attributional patterns in close relationships thus suggests that once Margaret and Robin begin to exchange angry, retaliatory behavior—fueled by offsetting biases in judging how responsible each is for these behaviors—they face more than simply the destructiveness of a single angry conflict. They also run the risk of transforming their relationship into one characterized by chronic angry conflict.

IMPLICATIONS FOR CONFLICT
MANAGEMENT AND INTERVENTION

Are there ways of preventing or more effectively managing these destructive, anger-driven conflicts? The increased understanding of anger in conflict that comes with attribution research suggests possible approaches. The attributional perspective on anger in conflict also explains why existing approaches to anger management have proved counterproductive.

It has become popular, even in works that receive considerable attention in scholarly circles, to advise people to "vent" their anger (Fisher, Ury, and Patton, 1991; Rubin, Pruitt, and Kim, 1994). This advice draws on a metaphor that compares anger to a gas whose pressure in a sealed vessel is building and can only be dissipated by releasing it. Those who follow the existing advice to vent their anger typically do so by describing the other party's harmful effect on themselves and the reasons for holding the other responsible for that harmful effect. For example, Fisher, Ury, and Patton conclude that "people obtain psychological release through the simple process of recounting their grievances" (1991, p. 31). Venting is thus an exercise in rehearsing the very attributions that arouse anger in the first place. As a consequence, rather than giving psychological relief from the anger, research indicates that venting actually makes the individuals even angrier (for reviews, see Averill, 1982; Berkowitz, 1970; Bushman, Baumeister, and Stack, 1999; Lewis and Bucher, 1992; Tavris, 1984, 1989). Training programs that teach people to vent and mediators who encourage disputants to vent are thus likely to be counterproductive in reducing anger.

Does research on anger then suggest that grievances should not be discussed? Not necessarily. Although little research investigates the question directly, whether a frank discussion of grievances is productive or not probably depends largely on the discussants' primary motivations. If their focus is on the act of venting itself—the act of unleashing their angry venom on the other person for the purpose of dissipating that anger—greater anger is likely to result. For the reasons discussed, the conflict might become more destructive and intractable as a result of the heightened anger. If their intent in discussing grievances is to get the problems out on the table for the purpose of solving them, the discussion may, in fact, be productive, even as it runs the risk of an angry exchange of remarks.

Attributional research suggests alternatives to venting for anger management. Specifically, people can seek to correct the common biases in judging another's responsibility for a harmful behavior that arouses anger, rather than rehearsing those often-inaccurate judgments. Research indicates that two training approaches, which can be easily combined, are effective in reducing these biases and the anger that results from them (for reviews, see Tavris, 1984, 1989). First, training programs should aim to educate people about attributional bias and instruct them in full, rational processing of information regarding the causes of other people's behavior, particularly information regarding situational causes. One experiment found that participants who were educated about the fundamental attribution error and taught how to use attributional information in the way that Kelley (1967) prescribed were significantly less prone to that error (Chen, Froehle, and Morran, 1997).

Second, training programs should aim to increase participants' skills and motivation to empathically take the perspective of the other person in gaining an appreciation for factors beyond his control that may influence him to behave as he does. Regan and Totten (1975) found that the fundamental attribution error was significantly reduced for participants who were instructed to empathize with another person they observed, relative to those participants instructed simply to observe the other person. Allred (1999) found that people retaliate less frequently, and more frequently engage in responses to another's behavior that are oriented to problem solving, if they consider the other party's perspective. The study that tested an attributional retraining intervention also tested a perspective-taking training intervention and, similarly, found that the latter significantly reduced attribution of other people's behavior to the person's dispositions (Chen, Froehle, and Morran, 1997).

Mediators can also intervene when they detect an accuser bias at work in an angry conflict. The mediator can help the accuser take the perspective of the accused for the purpose of taking stock of those mitigating factors beyond the control of the accused.

Even after seeking out mitigating factors, one may still correctly conclude that the other person is indeed responsible, at least to some degree, for harmful behavior. Of course, not all judgments that another person is responsible for harmful behavior are the result of bias. The anger that results from accurate attribution is, in some sense, justified. But attribution research on anger in conflict suggests that anger is a blunt instrument that often does more damage than good. It may be advisable to treat justified anger as a signal that one needs to take some measures to arrest or prevent harmful treatment by that person, even as one tries to restrain the accompanying retaliatory impulse. Consequently, conflict management training or mediation may aim to help people learn to act on justified anger in a manner in which solving the problem, rather than harming the other person, is the chief goal.

The insights afforded by attributional research on anger also suggest approaches to responding to other people's anger. First, the bias of the accused indicates that if we are accused of harmful behavior, we often fail to acknowledge, to ourselves and others, the extent to which we actually are responsible for harming other people. Consequently, training programs can also focus on making people aware of the bias of the accused and giving them strategies for overcoming it. Such strategies should encourage individuals to seek out the factors within their control that lead them to act harmfully. Mediators can play a similar role. If, as a result of searching for factors within their control, individuals conclude that they do bear some responsibility for the harm done, they can acknowledge that responsibility and apologize. The primary purpose of the anger-driven retaliatory response is to get the other person to stop acting harmfully. An effective apology generally includes communicating that one will not repeat the same harmful behavior. Accordingly, an apology signals that the purpose of the anger has been fulfilled. Attributional research confirms that apologies are effective at diffusing anger (Weiner, Graham, Peter, and Zmuidinas, 1991).

Sometimes, even after seeking out factors within your control that lead you to act harmfully toward another person, you may still accurately conclude that you have no choice but to act that way, or that the negative effect is inadvertent or unintended. On such occasions, it may be wise to offer an explanation of your behavior. Given the research on the accuser bias, you cannot assume that the other person is cognizant of the mitigating factors that are apparent to you, even though such an assumption often seems to be made. By explaining the circumstances, you may prevent or undo the effects of the accuser bias.

However, it is not entirely clear to what extent, or when, explanations are effective. Even though considerable research indicates that an explanation—particularly emphasizing that the cause of one's negative behavior is external or uncontrollable—is effective in reducing anger and punishment behavior (Bies, 1987; Bies and Shapiro, 1987; Shapiro, 1991; Scott and Lyman, 1968; Weiner,

1992), these effects may be limited to certain situations or settings that researchers do not as yet fully understand. For example, Lee and Robinson (1996) found that explanations emphasizing an external or uncontrollable cause of harmful behavior were actually counterproductive among managers operating in for-profit organizations, particularly when offering explanations to subordinates. Lee and Robinson also found that explanations that emphasized an unstable cause, or one that would not remain true in the future, were effective. More research is therefore needed as a sound basis for training initiatives and mediation strategies regarding the effect of explaining one's own negative behavior.

In conclusion, many a prolonged and destructive conflict lasts as long and causes as much damage as it does because the disputants are driven by anger to retaliate against each other. Attribution research reveals that anger-driven retaliation is aroused by a judgment that the other person is responsible for harmful action. Conflict management training programs and mediation strategies that help the parties overcome their biases in judging responsibility can go far toward preventing or dissipating the anger driving destructive conflict.

References

Allred, K. G. "Anger and Retaliation: Toward an Understanding of Impassioned Conflict in Organizations." In R. J. Bies, R. J. Lewicki, and B. H. Sheppard (eds.), *Research on Negotiations in Organizations*. Vol. 7. Greenwich, Conn.: JAI Press, 1999.

Allred, K. G., Chiongbian, V., and Parlamis, J. "Judgment, Anger, and Retaliation: A New Perspective on Conflict in Organizations." Unpublished manuscript, International Center for Cooperation and Conflict Resolution, Teachers College, Columbia University, 1999.

Allred, K. G., Mallozzi, J. S., Matsui, F., and Raia, C. P. "The Influence of Anger and Compassion on Negotiation Performance." *Organizational Behavior and Human Decision Processes*, 1997, *70*, 175–187.

Averill, J. *Anger and Aggression*. New York: Springer-Verlag, 1982.

Barry, B., and Oliver, R. L. "Affect in Dyadic Negotiation: A Model and Propositions." *Organizational Behavior and Human Decision Processes*, 1996, *67*, 127–143.

Bartunek, J. M., Kolb, D. M., and Lewicki, R. J. "Bringing Conflict out from Behind the Scenes: Private, Informal, and Nonrational Dimensions of Conflict in Organizations." In D. M. Kolb and J. M. Bartunek (eds.), *Hidden Conflict in Organizations*. Thousand Oaks, Calif.: Sage, 1992.

Baucom, D. H. "Attributions in Distressed Relations: How Can We Explain Them?" In S. Duck and D. Perlman (eds.), *Intimate Relationships: Development, Dynamics, and Deterioration*. Thousand Oaks, Calif.: Sage, 1987.

Berkowitz, L. "Experimental Investigations of Hostility Catharsis." *Journal of Consulting and Clinical Psychology*, 1970, *35*, 1–7.

Bies, R. J. "The Predicament of Injustice: The Management of Moral Outrage." In L. L. Cummings and B. M. Staw (eds.), *Research in Organizational Behavior.* Greenwich, Conn.: JAI Press, 1987.

Bies, R. J., and Shapiro, D. L. "Interactional Fairness Judgments: The Influence of Causal Accounts." *Social Justice Research,* 1987, *1,* 199–218.

Bies, R. J., Tripp, T. M., and Kramer, R. M. "At the Breaking Point: Cognitive and Social Dynamics of Revenge in Organizations." In R. A. Giacalone and J. Greenberg (eds.), *Antisocial Behavior in Organizations.* London: Sage, 1997.

Bradbury, T. N., and Fincham, F. D. "Attributions in Marriage: Review and Critique." *Psychological Bulletin,* 1990, *107,* 3–33.

Bushman, B. J., Baumeister, R. F, and Stack, A. D. "Catharsis, Aggression, and Persuasive Influence: Self-Fulfilling or Self-Defeating Prophecies?" *Journal of Personality and Social Psychology,* 1999, *76,* 367–376.

Chen, M., Froehle, T., and Morran, K. "Deconstructing Dispositional Bias in Clinical Inference: Two Interventions." *Journal of Counseling and Development,* 1997, *76,* 74–81.

Choi, I., and Nisbett, R. E. "Situational Salience and Cultural Differences in the Correspondence Bias and Actor-Observer Bias." *Personality and Social Psychology Bulletin,* 1998, *25,* 949–960.

de Rivera, J. "The Structure of Emotional Relationships." In P. Shaver (ed.), *Review of Personality and Social Psychology.* Thousand Oaks, Calif.: Sage, 1984.

Deutsch, M. *The Resolution of Conflict: Constructive and Destructive Processes.* New Haven: Yale University Press, 1973.

Fisher, R. J., Ury, W., and Patton, B. *Getting to Yes: Negotiating Agreement Without Giving In.* (2nd ed.) New York: Penguin, 1991.

Flippen, A. R., Hornstein, H. A., Siegal, W. E., and Weitzman, E. A. "A Comparison of Similarity and Interdependence as Triggers for In-Group Formation." *Personality and Social Psychology Bulletin,* 1996, *22,* 882–893.

Gilbert, D. T., and Malone, P. S. "The Correspondence Bias." *Psychological Bulletin,* 1995, *117,* 21–38.

Gilbert, D. T., Miller, A. G., and Ross, L. "Speeding with Ned: A Personal View of the Correspondence Bias." In J. M. Darley and J. Cooper (eds.), *Attribution and Social Interaction: The Legacy of Edward E. Jones.* Washington, D.C.: American Psychological Association, 1998.

Greenhalgh, L., and Chapman, D. I. "Joint Decision Making: The Inseparability of Relationships and Negotiation." In R. M. Kramer and D. M. Messick (eds.), *Negotiation as a Social Process.* Thousand Oaks, Calif.: Sage, 1995.

Harvey, J. H. "Attributions in Close Relationships: Research and Theoretical Developments." *Journal of Social and Clinical Psychology,* 1987, *5,* 420–434.

Heider, F. *The Psychology of Intergroup Relations.* New York: Wiley, 1958.

Hewstone, M. "Attributional Biases of Intergroup Conflict." In W. Stroebe (ed.), *The Social Psychology of Intergroup Conflict: Theory, Research, and Applications.* New York: Springer-Verlag, 1988.

Hewstone, M. "The 'Ultimate Attribution Error'? A Review of the Literature on Intergroup Causal Attribution." *European Journal of Social Psychology,* 1990, *20,* 311–335.

Jones, E. E., and Davis, K. E. "From Acts to Dispositions: The Attribution Process in Person Perception." In L. Berkowitz (ed.), *Advances in Experimental Social Psychology.* Vol. 2. Orlando: Academic Press, 1965.

Jones, E. E., and Nisbett, R. E. "The Actor and the Observer: Divergent Perceptions of the Causes of Behavior." In E. E. Jones (ed.), *Attribution: Perceiving the Causes of Behavior.* Morristown, N.J.: General Learning Press, 1972.

Kelley, H. H. "Attribution Theory in Social Psychology." In D. Levine (ed.), *Nebraska Symposium on Motivation.* Morristown, N.J.: General Learning Press, 1967.

Kelley, H. H., and Michela, J. L. "Attribution Theory and Research." *Annual Review of Psychology,* 1980, *31,* 457–501.

Kolb, D. M., and Putnam, L. L. "The Dialectics of Disputing." In D. M. Kolb and J. M. Bartunek (eds.), *Hidden Conflict in Organizations.* Thousand Oaks, Calif.: Sage, 1992.

Lee, F., and Robinson, R. J. "Explaining Negative Events: Attribution Theory and the Effectiveness of Social Accounts." Paper presented at the annual meeting of the International Association of Conflict Management, College Park, Md., 1996.

Lewis, W. A., and Bucher, A. M. "Anger, Catharsis, the Reformulated Frustration Aggression Hypothesis, and Health Consequences." *Psychotherapy,* 1992, *29,* 385–392.

McArthur, L. A. "The How and What of Why: Some Determinants and Consequences of Causal Attribution." In E. T. Higgins, C. P. Herman, and M. P. Zanna (eds.), *Social Cognition: The Ontario Symposium.* Vol. 1. Mahwah, N.J.: Erlbaum, 1972.

Orvis, B. R., Kelley, H. H., and Butler, D. "Attributional Conflict in Young Couples." In J. Harvey, W. J. Ickes, and R. F. Kidd (eds.), *New Directions in Attribution Research.* Vol. 1. Mahwah, N.J.: Erlbaum, 1976.

Regan, D. T., and Totten, J. "Empathy and Attribution: Turning Observers into Actors." *Journal of Personality and Social Psychology,* 1975, *32,* 850–856.

Roseman, I. J., Spindel, M. S., and Jose, P. E. "Appraisals of Emotion-Eliciting Events: Testing a Theory of Discrete Emotions." *Journal of Personality and Social Psychology,* 1990, *59,* 899–915.

Ross, L. "The Intuitive Psychologist and His Shortcomings: Distortions in the Attribution Process." In L. Berkowitz (ed.), *Advances in Experimental Social Psychology.* Vol. 10. Orlando: Academic Press, 1977.

Ross, L., and Nisbett, R. E. *The Person and the Situation.* New York: McGraw-Hill, 1991.

Ross, M., and Fletcher, G.J.O. "Attribution and Social Perception." In G. Lindzey and E. Aronson (eds.), *Handbook of Social Psychology,* Vol. 2: *Special Fields and Applications.* (3rd ed.) New York: Random House, 1985.

Rubin, J. Z., Pruitt, D. G., and Kim, S. H. *Social Conflict: Escalation, Stalemate, and Settlement.* New York: McGraw-Hill, 1994.

Scott, M. B., and Lyman, S. M. "Accounts." *American Sociological Review,* 1968, *5,* 46–62.

Shapiro, D. "The Effects of Explanations of Negative Reactions to Deceit." *Administrative Science Quarterly,* 1991, *36,* 614–630.

Sillars, A. L. "Attributions and Interpersonal Conflict Resolution." In J. H. Harvey, W. J. Ickes, and R. F. Kidd (eds.), *New Directions in Attribution Research.* Vol. 3. Mahwah, N.J.: Erlbaum, 1981.

Sillars, A. L. "Interpersonal Perception in Relationships." In W. J. Ickes (ed.), *Compatible and Incompatible Relationships.* New York: Springer-Verlag, 1985.

Smith, C. A., and Lazarus, R. S. "Appraisal Components, Core Relational Themes, and the Emotions." *Cognition and Emotion,* 1993, *7,* 233–270.

Tavris, C. "On the Wisdom of Counting to Ten: Personal and Social Dangers of Anger Expression." In P. Shaver (ed.), *Review of Personality and Social Psychology.* Thousand Oaks, Calif.: Sage, 1984.

Tavris, C. *Anger: The Misunderstood Emotion.* New York: Simon & Schuster, 1989.

Thomas, K. W. "Conflict and Negotiation Processes in Organizations." In M. D. Dunnette and L. M. Hough (eds.), *Handbook of Industrial and Organizational Psychology.* Vol. 3. (2nd ed.) Palo Alto, Calif.: Consulting Psychologists Press, 1992.

Watson, D. "The Actor and the Observer: How Are Their Perceptions of Causality Different?" *Psychology Bulletin,* 1982, *92,* 682–700.

Weiner, B. *An Attributional Theory of Motivation and Emotion.* New York: Springer-Verlag, 1986.

Weiner, B. "Excuses in Everyday Interaction." In M. L. McLaughlin, M. J. Cody, and S. R. Reed (eds.), *Explaining One's Self to Others.* Mahwah, N.J.: Erlbaum, 1992.

Weiner, B. *Judgments of Responsibility: A Foundation for a Theory of Social Conduct.* New York: Guilford Press, 1995.

Weiner, B., Graham, S., Peter, O., and Zmuidinas, M. "Public Confession and Forgiveness." *Journal of Personality,* 1991, *59,* 281–312.

CHAPTER TWELVE

Self-Regulation in the
Service of Conflict Resolution

Walter Mischel
Aaron L. DeSmet

A mong the most frustrating conflicts are those that people fight within their own heads, as they struggle with the dilemmas and temptations they encounter and create. This has been chronicled ever since Adam was tempted by Eve and Paradise was lost forever. In everyday life, we see these internal wars when, after resolving to skip the dessert, we are faced with the pastry tray, or when the tobacco addict, choking with emphysema, battles with himself not to light the next cigarette. Such conflicts are omnipresent—as people try to pursue a difficult achievement goal, or follow through on a health regimen (adhering to diets, exercise schedules, medications), or maintain a close relationship—activities that all require more than habit and routine to stay on course as conflict becomes inevitable and the difficulty and frustration of the effort escalates.

In this chapter, we consider some of the main findings from psychology that address these internal battles. We do so on the assumption that understanding what makes intrapsychic conflict easier to negotiate constructively is also relevant to the diverse types of conflict that characterize the human condition, at every level from the interpersonal to the international. Our primary goal is to capture what psychological research and theory tell us about willpower, and to examine the potential implications for conflict resolution.

UNDERSTANDING SELF-REGULATION

The facet of willpower that is of particular concern here is the ability to inhibit impulsive, automatic, "hot" emotional responses, which conflict with and threaten to undo the more valued but distant future goals one is trying to pursue (trying to bypass the pastry, or continue studying for an exam rather than turn on the TV, or forgo alcohol, or save for retirement rather than buy the sports car, or settle a long-standing border dispute with one's neighbor).

A Prototypic Conflict Within the Self: The Marshmallow Dilemma

The "delay of gratification" paradigm (Mischel, Shoda, and Rodriguez, 1989) is more widely known as the "marshmallow test" in recent media versions and best-selling advice volumes. Popularization notwithstanding (Goleman, 1995), in psychological research this method has been a prototype for the study of willpower in pursuit of difficult goals and a cornerstone for the concept of emotional intelligence (EQ). It has been researched extensively, both in experiments and in longitudinal studies that follow the same individuals for many years.

In this method, a young child is presented with some consumable that she desires, for example a food treat. A dilemma is posed: wait until the experimenter returns and get two of the desired treats, or ring a bell and the experimenter returns immediately but brings only one treat. The child clearly prefers the larger outcome and commits herself to wait for it. Soon, though, the delay becomes very difficult as waiting for the chosen goal drags on in the face of conflict, frustration, and temptation to ring the bell and take the immediately available treat. Though simple in its structure, this method has been shown to tap the type of skill and self-regulatory strategy fundamental for impulse control and for sustaining willpower, or strength in the face of temptation.

A choice between waiting for two marshmallows or settling for one now may seem artificial and far from the choices adults confront in their worlds. But for the young child, this type of problem, when carefully structured in age-appropriate ways, creates a genuine conflict as involving to her as many dilemmas of life are to adults. It provides a route to study the underlying processes systematically. Early studies of the delay situation revealed large individual differences in children's willingness and ability to delay. Years later, the time spent waiting for two marshmallows later versus one now proved to be remarkably indicative of important outcomes in later life. As examples, the number of seconds a preschooler is willing to wait for the bigger treats, rather than settling for the lesser one available immediately, significantly predicts diverse adaptive cognitive and social outcomes decades later, notably SAT scores (Mischel, 1996).

Given that behavior in this situation is not of trivial interest, it becomes important to understand what is happening psychologically that makes some children ring quickly and others wait for what seems forever. This problem has driven an extensive research program (Mischel, 1996), addressing the question, If humans initially are driven by impulses, pressing for immediate release, ruled by a pleasure principle and largely indifferent to reason—as has long been assumed—how do they become able to control their actions and feelings, overcoming the power of stimuli to elicit automatic reactions, and exerting the self-control strategies or willpower essential for executing their difficult-to-achieve intentions?

It is tempting to interpret the marshmallow-test results to support the view that how people manage to persist and exert self-control reflects basic character traits such as ego control or conscientiousness, traits that may already be visible quite early in life. Such constructs can be useful in characterizing broad individual differences in predisposition to self-control and ability to negotiate difficult conflicts without losing the long-term goal that one seeks, but at best they offer incomplete explanations. They overlook, for example, the finding that the same preschooler who was unable to wait even a minute under some conditions was able to wait twenty minutes when the situation was represented or framed in other terms or when the conditions changed in even seemingly minor ways. So we need to understand what people can do when they try to persist in goal pursuit, to deal effectively with conflict without succumbing impulsively to the immediate temptations and impulses to quit.

The Self-Regulatory Process

In recent years, research has gone beyond folk wisdom and speculation to begin demystifying willpower. The findings speak to why at least some people under some circumstances are able to turn their good intentions into effective behavior as they cope with the conflicts most important to them. Much of this research focuses on the processes of self-regulation that make it extremely difficult—or relatively easy—for people to deal effectively with seemingly mundane but potentially life-threatening conflicts and the conditions that can make such inevitable challenges manageable. Beginning in the early years of life, ineffective self-regulation predicts many adverse outcomes: subsequent school failure, poor academic and social competence, conduct disorders, and various forms of addictive and antisocial behavior. Conversely, individuals who can effectively self-regulate and cope with conflict in pursuing their goals can at least partially shape their lives and futures in constructive directions. It is therefore important to understand the processes that enable self-regulation and willpower in the service of constructive conflict resolution.

Effective self-regulation, or its failure, depends on a sequence of closely connected and interacting mental and emotional processes. These include how the individual *encodes* or construes the situation in which self-regulation is attempted, the *expectancies* and *beliefs* that become activated, the *feelings* and emotions triggered and experienced, and the *goals* and *values* engaged. Although these are essential preliminaries for even attempting to exert effortful control, nevertheless successful effort depends on the self-control *skills* and *strategic competencies* that are employed in trying to pursue them.

The motivation to try to self-regulate tends to increase to the extent that the activity or situation is encoded as personally meaningful and self-relevant. New mothers, for example, cope better with the often-exhausting and conflict-provoking chores and routines of parenting an infant if they view those tasks as fulfilling important self-obligations rather than as taking time away from other modes of self-fulfillment, such as a career. Even if events and situations are perceived as highly self-relevant, however, the person does not necessarily consciously attempt to self-regulate. On the contrary, such situations easily and automatically trigger the enduring behavior patterns that characterize an individual's personality. These are exactly the reaction patterns that have become well established and then are enacted with little or no control, thought, or awareness. One example of such an automatic reaction is the anger and abusiveness readily triggered in rejection-sensitive men who are quick to perceive it from a romantic partner even if it has not occurred. Their maladaptive reaction pattern of uncontrolled hostility may be essentially reflexive, bypassing conscious control and preventing purposeful self-intervention effort. In such a case, the person applies encodings even if they do not fit and maintains them regardless of contradictory evidence. The ironic and often tragic result is that the outcome the man most fears and expects—rejection by the romantic partner—is precipitated by his own behavior in a self-fulfilling prophecy.

Expectancy and belief that one is able to exert control and successfully execute necessary action is also an essential prerequisite for self-regulation. It supports one's efforts and guides whether, where, when, and how one attempts to self-regulate (Mischel, Cantor, and Feldman, 1996). To even try purposeful self-regulation requires a representation of the self as a causal agent capable of executing an intended action. Perceived self-efficacy—the belief that "I can do it"—is a foundation for successfully pursuing a difficult goal, or for changing and improving one's situation or oneself. Its psychological opposite, perceived helplessness, is the route to giving up, apathy, and depression. Even when the self-regulatory task is something aversive that has to be endured and cannot be controlled—say, a painful dental procedure—the belief that one can predict or control the stress is an important ingredient for coping. Generally, most people tend to become less upset if they think they can predict and control stressful or painful events, even if the perception is illusory.

Whereas expectation of efficacy and control enhances the potential for self-control and goal pursuit, anxious feelings and self-preoccupying thoughts undermine such efforts. The thought *I'm no good at this; I'll never be able to do it* in the test-anxious person competes and interferes with task-relevant thoughts (*Now I have to recheck my answers*). Interference from self-preoccupying thoughts tends to be greatest when the task to be done is complex and requires many competing responses, as is always the case when the problem and conflict to be solved are complex and difficult. As the motivation to do well increases (as when success on the task is especially important), anxiety and the tendency to catastrophize become particularly maladaptive, interfering with attention to the task and concentration on how to master it effectively.

Persistence in goal pursuit is also bolstered, or undermined, by outcome expectancies about the likelihood that the effort, cost, and time spent on the task will or will not actually result in the desired outcome. People base outcome expectations both on information in the current situation and on expectations generalized from previous similar situations. In short, expectancy has a substantial impact on self-regulatory choices: people are likely to choose to perform an action that requires effort if they believe that they can perform the action (they have high self-efficacy expectancy) and expect it to lead to favorable consequences.

Affects: Hot Reactions and the Emotional Brain

The situations in which people most need and want to self-regulate and control their impulses as they struggle to resolve conflict tend to be those in which it is most difficult for them to do so. These are the situations that elicit hot emotional reactions such as intense fear and anxiety, or strong appetites or craving. In such a situation, the person may be subject to what is called "stimulus control"—namely, situations in which the stimulus triggers a virtually uncontrollable automatic response. The central challenge for effort at self-regulation is how to overcome such reflexive, automatic stimulus control with reflective self-control.

Consider, for example, the dilemma of the addict who is trying to quit but is tempted with heroin, or the starving dieter faced with the ultimate chocolate cake, or the test-anxious student facing an important examination. This kind of hot situation tends to automatically trigger a hot reaction, rapidly generating the associated feelings of fear or desire and the urge to respond impulsively, bypassing self-regulatory controls just when it is most important to have them. Such hot, reflexive reactions may be part of the overall arousal state that helps initiate quick adaptive action, as in an emergency response to a fire alarm or sudden danger that mobilizes the body's resources. However, the arousal state makes thoughtful self-regulation and planful action and reflection most difficult (Metcalfe and Mischel, 1999).

Crucially important in emotional reactions, particularly fear, is a small almond-shaped region in the forebrain, called the amygdala (which means "almond" in Latin). The central nucleus of this brain structure reacts almost instantly to signals that warn of danger, immediately sending out behavioral, physiological (autonomic), and endocrine responses. It mobilizes the body for action, readying it to fight or flee in response to a perceived threat. This reflexive emergency reaction is useful for adaptation: there is evolutionary survival value in reacting automatically to a snake in the grass without taking time to reflect on it, or to fight an opponent who is ready to strike when flight is not possible. But these automatic reactions are only a quick fix and can become destructive if they persist (Ledoux, 1996). Unlike lower animals in the evolutionary ladder, human beings have the capacity to eventually take control with high-level brain centers (the prefrontal cortex) and to start thinking and planning their way through the problem that the amygdala has already begun to respond to automatically and emotionally. The trick in achieving effective self-regulation is to move from the automatic, hot, emotional response that can quickly become maladaptive to cool, reasoned, reflective action that makes use of the vast cognitive resources that give humans their advantage.

From Hot to Cool: Essentials of Willpower

To understand the processes that enable willpower in executing one's intentions, two closely interacting systems have been proposed: a hot system and a "cool" one (Metcalfe and Mischel, 1999). The cool system is a "know" system: it is cognitive, complex, contemplative, slow, rational, strategic, integrated, coherent, and emotionally neutral. It is the basis of self-regulation and self-control. In contrast, the hot one is a "go" system: emotional, simple, reflexive, fast. The hot system develops early in life and is dominant in the first few years. It is accentuated by stress, whether in the immediate situation or from chronic stress. It is tuned biologically to be responsive to innate releasing stimuli, both negative and positive, that elicit automatic, aversive, fear-and-flight reactions, or appetitive and sexual approach reactions. Impulsive and reflexive, the hot system is the basis of emotionality, fears as well as passions; it undermines rational attempts at self-control.

The two systems are interconnected and interact with one another. Analysis of the interactions between these systems allows prediction and explanation of diverse findings on the nature of willpower from decades of research. Although the processes involved in these interactions are quite complex, the implications for conflict management are straightforward. Namely, the essential ingredient for effective self-regulation and willpower is to strategically cool the hot system and its impulsive reaction tendencies—reaction that is readily activated in a conflict situation—and instead mobilize the cool system in pursuit of the long-term goal.

The balance between the hot and cool systems depends on several factors, the first of which is developmental level. The hot system develops and dominates early in life, whereas the cool system develops later (by age four) and becomes increasingly dominant over the course of development. These developmental differences are consistent with evidence on the differential rates of development of the relevant brain areas for these two systems.

In the context of conflict resolution, the most important determinant of hot-system, cool-system balance is stress. At high levels, stress deactivates the cool system and creates hot-system dominance. At low levels of stress, complex thinking, planning, and remembering are possible. When stress levels jump from low to very high, as in life-threatening emergency conditions, responding tends to be reflexive and automatic—hardly the time for cognitive complexity and rumination. Under conditions in which an animal's life is threatened, quick response driven by innately determined stimuli may be essential. At the same time, such automatic reactions undo rational efforts at constructive conflict resolution.

The effects of chronic stress are evident even at a physical level. For example, exposure to prolonged stress has correlated with decreases in the volume of the hippocampus (Sapolsky, 1996), a brain structure that is basic for the functioning of the cool system. Severe and chronic stress (as in war conditions) may result in dominant activation of the hot system as opposed to the cool system in ways that become relatively stable and difficult to reverse. In short, conflict and stress are intimately linked and feed each other so as to easily and automatically undermine rational problem solving and escalate irrational and self-defeating hot behavior. In this cycle, stress increases the potential for conflict, which in turn escalates the level of stress, producing a pernicious cascade of impulsive hot-system responses and consequences that further undermine any chance for rational and effective conflict resolution. Fortunately, in recent years diverse strands of research from several fields have converged that speak directly to this dilemma and point to new directions—or at least metaphors—for dealing constructively with conflict.

Consider again the marshmallow test. For this situation, delay of gratification and frustration tolerance is enhanced if the person can transform the aversive waiting period into a pleasant, nonwaiting situation. This can be done by diverting attention and thoughts away from the frustrative components of delay of gratification and thinking instead about other, pleasant things. Such distractions can be achieved by engaging in activities, overtly or mentally, during the delay period that help to suppress or decrease the aversiveness of waiting for the desired outcome, while retaining the goal and continuing to persist for it.

In short, voluntary delay of reward can be aided by any overt or covert activity that serves as a distracter from the reward and thus from the aversiveness of wanting it but not having it. Through such distraction, it is possible to convert the frustrating delay-of-reward situation into a psychologically less aversive condition. Children waited much longer for a preferred reward if they were distracted cognitively from the goal objects than they did while directly attending to them.

Whereas the children's reward-directed thoughts or cognitions during the wait greatly reduced, rather than enhanced, the length of time they were able to delay gratification, distracting oneself from the rewards, overtly or cognitively (for example, by thinking of "fun things") made it possible to wait longer. These results contradicted the notion that willpower requires one to maintain directed attention to things that are aversive, difficult, or boring. Rather than trying to maintain an aversive activity such as delay of reward through an act of will or focused attention, effective self-control is helped by transforming the difficult into the easy, the aversive into the pleasant, and the boring into the interesting, while still maintaining the task-required activity on which the ultimate reward depends. Rather than willing oneself to heroic bravery, one needs to enact the necessary "difficult" response while engaging in another one cognitively.

Doing this effectively when the task is complex may require extensive rehearsal and planning for implementing the necessary action when it is needed. Thus, in effective delay of gratification the child tunes out the hot properties of the reward stimulus while strategically cooling through self-distraction to sustain waiting behavior. Similarly, distracting and relaxation-induced activity, such as listening to music, reduces anxiety in the face of uncontrollable shocks and helps people cope with chronic pain (such as from rheumatoid arthritis, and even with severe life crises). Cooling strategies generally can help one transform potentially stressful situations to make them less aversive. For example, if surgical patients are encouraged to reconstrue their hospital stay as a vacation from the stresses of daily life, they show better postoperative adjustment, just as chronically ill patients who reinterpret their conditions positively also show better adjustment.

IMPLICATIONS FOR UNDERSTANDING INTERPERSONAL CONFLICT

These findings also have direct implications for analyzing interpersonal conflicts constructively.

Self-Regulatory Failure in Interpersonal Conflict

Interpersonal conflict often involves complex, mixed-motive situations, where the relationship between one's own set of goals and another's are simultaneously *positively interdependent* and *negatively interdependent* (see Chapter One). Sayings like "You always hurt the ones you love" indicate the common wisdom that the interdependence coming from interpersonal closeness creates the very situation where emotions are strong and the tendency to react impulsively in hurtful, damaging ways is greatest. Although people may attempt to control the hot, emotional responses that intensify conflict and damage relationships, they often find that their good intentions are not enough to refrain from blowing up, making personal attacks, or otherwise doing things they later regret.

Regulating expression of negative feelings is not easy to do in the heat of conflict. The conflict situation itself creates a general level of stress that may shift the balance of power from cool-system to hot-system dominance. In addition, specific things are often said and done during conflict that push specific psychological buttons, which in turn trigger hot, emotional reactions. Failure to exert self-control over such reactions can instigate similarly hot responses from the other party, thus intensifying the conflict; further undermining efforts at self-control; and making cool, collaborative responses even more difficult.

People fail to self-regulate during conflict for countless reasons, among them ambivalence or lack of firm resolve to accomplish a particular goal. As mentioned earlier, one's motivation to self-regulate increases if the situation or activity in question is considered personally relevant and meaningful. Specifically, when pursuit of constructive conflict resolution is personally meaningful, people are likely to muster the willpower to act accordingly. When the focus of one's intentions is on "getting my way" rather than on maintaining the relationship or constructive resolution, people are more likely to follow habitual routines and their impulsive urges. In conflict, this translates into uncontrolled aggression or reflexive conflict avoidance (fight or flight).

Another reason for self-regulatory failure is lack of mental, emotional, or physical resources to do so. Since self-regulation and self-control require a certain amount of psychological and physiological energy, it comes as no surprise that when people are emotionally stressed, mentally drained, distracted, busy with other things, or just plain tired, they find it all the more difficult to overcome a powerful emotional impulse. Anxiety and rumination, in particular, tend to drain and distract, diverting precious psychological resources that might otherwise be used in self-regulation.

Anxiety, rumination, and preoccupation undermine self-regulation, particularly if the conflict is a complex one that requires abundant mental resources for successful resolution. As the perceived stakes increase, however, the anxiety level and the propensity to catastrophize also increase, interfering with the ability to self-regulate and solve a complex problem. The very nature of a conflict situation—emotional and stress-inducing—thus undermines self-control. This suggests the importance of avoiding potential conflict situations when one is busy, anxious, stressed, or physically tired. To illustrate, consider a couple driving home late at night after a long day. It would be prudent for them to avoid or postpone even a mildly contentious discussion, because if the discussion leads to a full-blown argument, the presence of physical exhaustion and at least one participant's preoccupation with the task of driving are likely to leave far fewer resources available to focus on the problem and to exert self-control while doing so.

One of the lessons learned in research on the marshmallow test was that self-regulatory strategies, rather than pure power of will, are important determinants of success or failure. For example, thinking about how great two marshmallows are going to taste tends to undermine the ability to self-regulate. Even as this strategy stresses that two is better than one, it highlights the very stimuli that are likely to provoke hot, appetitive responses. Instead, children who distract themselves or think of their desired reward in cooler terms are better able to wait. Aggression can be similarly managed. The strategies by which people cope may dictate success or failure at controlling aggressive or violent reactions. For instance, a violent act is often committed because the aggressor has become immersed in the immediate situation, which creates intense anger, arousing emotion and hot-system reaction. Domestic violence is a good example. As a parent or spouse becomes immersed and totally focused on the irritating or frustrating acts of a family member, it creates a narrow focus on the intolerable aspects of the present situation. This leads to a hot-system reaction and creates a cycle: narrow focus on the present tends to accentuate frustration and anger, and anger tends to impair the ability to transcend the immediate situation and activate more rational, cool, problem-solving strategies.

If people become immersed in the immediate situation, without directing any thought or attention to themselves or their own behavior, their conduct can easily stray from their basic goals and intentions. As stimulating features of the environment monopolize one's attention, self-regulation becomes increasingly difficult. For this reason, becoming absorbed in the hot, provocative aspects of a conflict situation tends to undermine attempts at self-regulation. This appears to be a key factor in mob behavior, where people lose their sense of self, become absorbed in a larger group experience, and are no longer inhibited by a sense of morality or appropriateness. People in mobs lose the ability to restrain impulses they would normally hold in check. Some of the atrocities perpetrated in Los Angeles following the acquittal of officers who had beaten Rodney King illustrate the nature of mob behavior. Intense group experiences charged with anger lead to a spiral of intensifying, thoughtless aggression, an oblivious frenzy that ultimately ends in violence (or riots, or gang rape, or lynch mobs).

Since stress makes self-control difficult, coping with stress can be an effective strategy in bolstering one's ability to self-regulate. Poor coping skills, however, can have the opposite effect. Using alcohol, for instance, may alleviate the psychological experience of distress and may have a calming effect physiologically, but it also tends to impair judgment and erode inhibitions that might otherwise keep inappropriate or aggressive responses in check. Alcohol also tends to narrow one's focus of attention to the immediate situation and away from the self, which may have disinhibition effects similar to those seen in mob behavior. Transcendence, on the other hand, represents an effective coping skill that facilitates self-control. When people are engaged in conflict, they need to pay attention to their own feelings and to what the other is saying, but this can lead to intense arousal and hot responses that are difficult to control. By maintaining focus on these things but transforming them symbolically, abstracting, and focusing on informative rather than arousing features, one may effectively transcend the aggravation, offensiveness, and immediacy of the intolerable present.

Understanding Escalatory Spirals in Conflict

Because conflicts escalate easily, it is important to understand and prevent inadvertent snowballing effects.

Snowballing in Intrapersonal Conflict. Everyone has seen an instance in which one little step crosses an imaginary line, leading to more frequent and more severe transgression. The dieter who cheats a little for a special occasion, the ex-smoker who sneaks just one little cigarette to help calm his nerves, or the alcoholic who takes one tiny sip to feel more at ease at the annual holiday party—these are the first steps to ruin. Hence such idioms as "falling off the wagon." A minor lapse often snowballs into a much larger transgression for several reasons. First, we may soften our commitment to a behavior standard that has been violated. If we can cross a line just this one time, and nothing terrible results, then there is less reason not to cheat "just this once" the next time.

Another reason is that crossing the line may negatively affect our efficacy beliefs. Even if we feel terrible about the lapse (or perhaps especially if we feel terrible about it), failure to meet a goal or standard may result in a damaged sense of self-efficacy. In short, when a person thinks she just can't do something, she will not try as hard to do it, so crossing a line may lead to the sense that even trying to adhere to the standard is pointless, and the goal is abandoned.

A final reason is that initial lapses may open emotional floodgates. Research indicates that emotions seem not so much to cause initial lapses but to be *triggered by the lapse.* The emotional arousal makes it that much more difficult to restrain subsequent impulses, which again leads to snowballing. This is not so surprising if we consider that the lapse itself (one slice of pie for a dieter) tends to be attention-consuming and emotionally arousing, which works against efforts at self-control.

Escalation in Interpersonal Conflict. After an initially minor transgression during a conflict, the parties may goad each other and themselves into ever-larger transgressions. Violent altercation, for instance, typically begins with relatively innocuous acts, followed by an escalating spiral of reciprocal provocation. An initial aggressive act leading to violence is almost never seen at the time as a first step in an escalating conflict that may ultimately lead to viciousness, violence, hospitalization, or even death. Instead, the initial aggressive act tends to be viewed at the time as essentially harmless. But it elicits a hostile response that seems to justify an even more aggressive countermove, and so on, eventually snowballing into violence. Zillman (1993) has documented physiological evidence for this effect. Each provocation triggers an emotional and physiological response ("arousal"), which takes time to dissipate. If another aggressive act triggers further psychological-physiological excitation before the original response has worn off, the arousal triggered by the second provocation builds on the first, and the arousal state is heightened even further. A third or fourth act in rapid succession then amplifies arousal even further, and so on.

Most people are familiar with divorced couples who simply cannot be in the same room together without the slightest provocation triggering a series of aggressive reactions that quickly spiral out of control. Such habitual escalatory reactions between parties in a protracted conflict follow some of the same rules as all kinds of habitual response. To illustrate, consider Pavlov's dogs, who were exposed to food that made them salivate. The food was repeatedly paired with a distinctive bell, so that when the bell rang, food was shown, and the dogs salivated. Eventually, the dogs learned to anticipate food whenever they heard a bell, and would salivate merely at the sound of the bell, regardless of whether food was ever presented.

Habitual responses can have similar effects in human behavior. In a prolonged conflict characterized by escalation and a spiral of increasing intensity and hostility, the overpowering trigger that leads to an automatic, habitual response can become simply the presence of the other party! Harmful acts by another person (the other) can trigger a complex set of cognitive, emotional, and behavioral responses, and when the pairing of the other with intense negative responses is repeated many times, the emotional-behavioral reaction may become automatic. Note that what originally triggers an angry response is the other's behavior and its perceived harmful consequences (see Chapter Eleven). Over time, however, the trigger can become the paired stimulus, the other person himself who now triggers a hostile, retaliatory response automatically. This presents quite a difficult problem, because anger and hostility may have become such a strong conditioned response that the other person need not do anything (except be there) to trigger them.

When rapidly escalating intensity becomes the typical mode of interaction between opposing parties in a protracted conflict, the parties increasingly tend to respond automatically to the other with hostile aggression. Thus, the automatic emotional snowballing we have just described at the intrapersonal level can extend to the relationship itself. If this happens, escalatory spirals are likely to be the norm. Escaping such a cycle requires that the conflicting parties use cooling strategies to counteract the hot responses fueling the fire of the intensifying conflict.

Cooling Strategies

Between six and eighteen months of age, infants begin to learn to regulate their emotions. Six-month-olds approached by a stranger tend to cope with their fear and anxiety by averting their eyes and "fussing." Twelve- and eighteen-month-olds, on the other hand, use other strategies, such as self-distraction and self-soothing, to deal with an anxiety-producing stranger. These more sophisticated cooling strategies allow children to effectively cope with their hot fear and anxiety reactions. Because conflict elicits similar fight-or-flight emotional responses, self-distraction, self-calming, and other cooling strategies are equally important skills for adults.

Taking a Time-Out. People who have stressful jobs are able to reduce conflict and improve their family relationships by taking brief time-outs after returning home from work. Without a time-out, going straight from a stressful workday to family interaction often leads to argument and dispute. But spending part of an hour by themselves enables these stressed-out wage earners to calm down prior to dealing with their families, and subsequent family interactions are therefore much more pleasant.

In the middle of a conflict, calling for a time-out, or even just stopping and counting to ten, can allow people the extra time they need to calm down and cool off. If people take an extended time-out, they should take care not to engage in other arousing or anxiety-producing activities. They should also avoid "silent seething" (Baumeister, Heatherton, and Tice, 1993), where the time-out is used to nurse the angry feelings and plot the next counterattack. Instead, people should use a time-out to do quiet, relaxing, distracting things. Those who have a difficult time setting the conflict aside, as when snide comments and slammed doors continue to goad one or the other party back into the conflict, may need to physically separate themselves and remain incommunicado for a period of time.

One word of caution is that a time-out should not be used to avoid conflict; it is only meant to provide a brief respite for charged-up individuals to cool off. Be careful not to use the time-out as an avoidance mechanism by setting a specific time to come back to the discussion and resolve the conflict.

Another way to apply the concept of a time-out is to communicate in writing rather than face-to-face. This allows people to continue working on interpersonal problems and conflict resolution, and it can have several cooling effects compared to communicating in person. For one, it can help slow the process down so people have more time to react, consider their thoughts and feelings, take the other's perspective, and control their own level of arousal and emotional expression. By offering personal time to think through issues, conflicting parties can devote more time and energy not only to message sending and receiving but also to message creation and message interpretation.

Those who use a time-out to put a message in writing should think carefully about the message they wish to send and about whether or not they wish to send it at all. If a letter or e-mail message is written hastily and then sent without a second glance, it may prove no better than face-to-face communication. Instead, the message sender should write a thoughtful message, put the letter away, reread it later, try to examine it from the other's point of view, and let others check the message for provocative or ambiguous elements. Even if the message is ultimately delivered face-to-face, such exercises can help prompt a controlled response to hot aspects of the conflict that might otherwise trigger regrettable words and actions that only enflame the conflict and damage the relationship.

Self-Regulatory Plans and Implementation Strategies. If the other person is getting more and more upset, one can do several things to try to cool the other off. Face-saving strategies, for example, can offer the other person a way out of a previous threat or commitment. Humor can be used to add levity to the situation. People can defuse an intensifying conflict by exhibiting a surprisingly positive behavior, such as ingratiation, to interrupt the cycle of provocation. The important thing is to find a way to intervene and deescalate the conflict. Coming up with specific deescalation strategies helps make using those strategies more likely and effective.

For people who themselves tend to get increasingly aggravated during a conflict, where it becomes difficult to control one's own emotional expression, it is especially important to create specific self-regulatory strategies for cooling off and reacting to hot stimuli. Implementation strategies connect general goals ("Resolve conflict constructively") to a specific implementation intention ("If she says I'm rude, I'll ask her to cite specific examples; I won't lose my temper and start calling her names"). This helps ensure a preferred response by tying a hot trigger event to the *intended* response rather than the *habitual* response. For instance, translating the goal of "health and physical fitness" into an intention to "exercise regularly" is not an effective plan of action because it is too broad. An effective plan of action specifies the how, when, and where rather than just the what of the action steps needed to accomplish the goal (Gollwitzer, 1996). A better plan for the person seeking a healthier lifestyle might be "I'll go to the park and jog two miles every weekday evening as soon as I get home from work." This is a better plan because it specifies the exact action (jogging two miles), where and when it happens (every weekday in the park), and the situation that triggers the action (as soon as I get home from work). A similarly detailed plan of action can help ensure that specific conflict resolution strategies are initiated at the right time and place, and with the appropriate people.

Stress and Stress Management. Managing stress plays a surprisingly important role in conflict resolution. Managing and reducing stress improves not only self-cooling and self-control but also one's ability to generate and assess possible solutions to the conflict. Because a high level of stress can shift the balance from cool-system dominance to hot, managing stress effectively can mean the difference between suppressing hot impulses and lashing out uncontrollably. But stress also tends to decrease one's ability to solve complex problems. So people who argue when they are stressed and fatigued often find that they lack the self-control they might otherwise have. Their problem-solving ability is also impaired, so stress doubly undermines any attempt to resolve the conflict constructively.

Third Parties. If conflicting parties must interact to make a joint decision or negotiate an agreement, communicating through an intermediary helps avoid the spontaneous hostility triggered by the other person. It is important for the intermediary to be considered neutral by both parties and to be an appropriately skilled diplomat for the task. If the value of a third party is simply to discourage inappropriate behavior, then conflicting parties can meet in a public place where there are strict norms and social sanctions against aggressive behavior, or they can meet in the presence of a mutual friend who is unlikely to put up with either party's abuse or maltreatment of the other.

Framing and Reframing Goals. Since the actions required to achieve a long-term goal are elaborate and must be executed over time despite uncertainty, unforeseen difficulty, distraction, competing interests, and intermittent setbacks, there is a need for tenacity in the pursuit of long-term goals. However, it is under these very conditions that one must also remain flexible, being open to unexpected opportunities and recognizing potential discrepancies between desired outcomes and actual capabilities and constraints (Mischel, Cantor, and Feldman, 1996).

Although self-regulatory strategies and implementation plans should be concrete and specific, goals and goal pursuit need not be rigid. What is needed is tenacious but *flexible* goal pursuit. Tenacity refers to perseverance in pursuit of a goal, while flexibility refers to adaptive goal adjustment and creative modification of action plans and strategies.

One way to maintain tenacity and flexibility is to alter lower-level goal intentions by finding new routes toward achieving the bigger goals they serve. Think of the tasks one performs at a job, which often represent intermediate goals ("finishing the report that is due at the end of the week"). Such an intermediate goal is not necessarily intrinsically desired in and of itself. Rather, it is valued because of its utility in accomplishing other goals, such as not getting fired or reprimanded, earning a promotion or a pay raise, having an impact through one's work, pursuing a meaningful career, being considered competent by oneself and others, and so on. It is not so hard to be flexible about finishing a report on time if one can pursue other equally efficacious strategies for achieving the equivalent ends. So whenever an intermediate goal cannot be accomplished, people can maintain perseverance even as they modify their goals and action plans.

When a goal appears impossibly daunting or the action to attain it seems too difficult or effortful, flexibility allows one to adjust the goal or plan without abandoning it. Instead, by finding a different path or intermediate goal for achieving a similar overarching goal, by breaking a goal down into manageable chunks, or by changing the goal to an outcome that is slightly less desired but more attainable, one can maintain tenacious but flexible goal pursuit.

Staying creative and flexible while doggedly pursuing important goals is not always so easy to do. When people get stuck and are unable to think about or frame their situations and their goals broadly and flexibly, they may need to make themselves aware of the normally unconscious assumptions and perceptual filters that constrain flexible framing and problem-solving approaches. One way to open up creative, flexible thinking is a technique called *backcasting* (a twist on forecasting). In backcasting, a facilitator or mediator describes a future situation (say, the aftermath of a constructive resolution to the conflict) and participants are expected to flesh out the scenario and describe the sequence of actions and events that lead to that point. Participants start by visualizing themselves in the prescribed future as if it were the very real present. Then they write down a vivid description of the future scenario and explain how the situation came to be. By describing an ideal future in the present tense, and explaining a plausible route by which it comes to pass, participants can broaden their thinking and solve problems creatively. A related Adlerian counseling methodology is called the "as if" technique, which aims to change beliefs and perceptions of the problem, facilitate reframing, encourage change in efficacy beliefs, and redirect problematic behavior. Just as with scenario backcasting, the basic idea is to use pretending and visualization of possible futures to facilitate insight and problem resolution. Variations include role playing, role-reversal exercises, or combining standard as-if or backcasting techniques with other procedures such as guided imagery or hypnotic age progression.

IMPLICATIONS FOR TRAINING

We next consider how the foregoing methods and insights can be used in training efforts.

Modeling

People do not learn new response patterns solely through direct experience. They can also learn adaptive responses to conflict from observing others. Aggressive or assaultive children and adolescents, in particular, can profit immensely from training intervention that teaches them nonviolent techniques for handling interpersonal conflict. By expanding their repertory of skills, they achieve greater freedom in responding to present and future problems. Modeling desired behaviors is a means by which children and adults can acquire new skills. The method of modeling that has yielded the most impressive results with diverse problems contains three major components. First, alternative modes of appropriate and effective response are repeatedly modeled by several people in a variety of aggression-provoking situations. Second, learners receive the necessary guidance along with ample opportunity to practice the new behavior until they can respond to a problem situation skillfully and spontaneously. Third, a simulated problem situation starts out easily to ensure success, and these success experiences are rewarded.

Live or videotaped demonstrations can be an excellent way to role-model appropriate behaviors. Videotapes can be especially useful. First, they can show a variety of realistic situations and contexts. In addition, voice-over narration can direct attention to what is important and specify the action plan of which the model is merely an example. Demonstration can also be used to contrast good and poor performance, and to show the positive outcomes associated with good performance and the potential negative consequences of poor performance.

If done correctly, demonstration can symbolically model internal processes of self-control by showing what people are thinking and feeling. By having people talk out loud and explain what they are thinking and feeling, demonstration can model internal dynamics as well as observable behavior. On an instructional video, voice-overs can be used to represent what people are thinking to themselves and the cognitive-affective strategies they are using to help manage themselves during the conflict.

Rehearsing and Role Playing

Practicing a newly learned behavior helps in two ways. First, repetition helps establish and strengthen activation pathways in cognition, facilitating acquisition and retention of the new behavior. In short, by practicing, people become skillful and remember more about what they learn. If enactive rehearsal is not feasible (something cannot actually be rehearsed in action), then cognitive rehearsal can be used. Top athletes, for example, often use visualization techniques to help inculcate their intended behavior by imagining in detail the precise sequence of actions they will execute. Even in enactive rehearsal, it may help for people to visualize themselves in the specific situation where the desired behavior will take place.

The second benefit of rehearsal is that it makes certain ways of thinking and doing natural and automatic. Rehearsal forces people to think through not just what they will do but precisely how they will do it. Even cognitive rehearsal has been shown to speed up a learned behavior, so that one responds to an anticipated situation with an immediate, fluid response, rather than a slow, awkward one.

Role plays simulating everyday experience can be used to make enactive rehearsal complex, dynamic, and realistic so that a general response pattern is learned and applied. This gives the learners practice translating the general strategy into appropriate responses so that they learn not just the behavior but also how to "train the brain" to think in ways that produce constructive conflict resolution, even in novel, unexpected conflict situations. Unscripted simulations help prevent novel events in real life from disrupting a learned response. Such disruption is exactly what occurs if the learned behavior set is based on a discrete, narrowly contrived stimulus situation and a static behavioral script that one is not used to modifying to take into account differing situations.

Role plays should start with easy situations and become progressively more surprising and difficult as an individual masters rudimentary skills. You can start, for example, with specific skills that require little adaptation to novel situations, such as how to paraphrase in active listening.

Feedback

Practice in simulation and role play is intended to help learners master a repertoire of basic skills and behaviors that can then be tested in uncertain, dynamic situations. Role models help set the standard for desired behavior, and a simulation can create a realistic environment in which to practice one's own behavior. In addition, performance feedback that accurately reflects the discrepancy between the desired behavior and *one's actual behavior* is needed to facilitate learning. Videotapes, along with constructive feedback and helpful advice by a skilled observer, can help point out how body language, tone of voice, word choice, mannerism, and other behavior are either more or less effective in dealing with a particular conflict situation. Simulation can be designed to confront learners with increasingly complex or difficult situations, perhaps where they must begin to resist insults and goading, resolve complex interpersonal problems, and bring multiple skill sets to bear on difficult conflicts. (See also Chapter Twenty-Four.)

Self-Instruction and Self-Reward

When performed in real-life situations, even well-rehearsed behavior may seem awkward at first. One way to maintain a newly learned behavior and bolster self-confidence in executing it is to self-instruct and self-reward. In training, provide learners with helpful self-instruction messages: things they can tell themselves to better control their impulses. Verbalizing these instructions, out loud or covertly, can be especially helpful. In one study, young children committed themselves to finishing a task of putting pegs into a pegboard before they could play with a desired toy, Mr. Clown Box. They knew before they started on the peg task that after they began, Mr. Clown Box would likely try to tempt them by asking them to look at him and play with him. Children who were given highly specific plans about how to react to Mr. Clown Box—such as "When Mr. Clown Box says to look at him and play with him, then you can just say, 'No, I'm not going to look at Mr. Clown Box'"—spent more time performing the peg box task than those who were told something general, on the order of "Just think of something to say out loud that will help you not look at Mr. Clown Box."

CONCLUSION

Constructively negotiating and resolving conflict with others requires self-regulation to strategically modify one's own thoughts and actions so as to allow progress toward important shared goals. An essential ingredient is to cool hot impulses, emotions, and automatic fight-or-flight reactions that are easily triggered by the stress inherent in conflict. The cooling strategies that can help one to effectively manage internal conflict (as in goal-directed delay of gratification), for example through selective attention, have been identified and help to demystify the essentials of willpower. The same principles also can be harnessed for dealing strategically and rationally with diverse interpersonal and intergroup dilemmas. This chapter has discussed findings that illustrate just such strategies.

References

Baumeister, R. F., Heatherton, T. F., and Tice, D. M. "When Ego Threats Lead to Self-Regulation Failure: Negative Consequences of High Self-Esteem." *Journal of Personality and Social Psychology,* 1993, *64,* 141–156.

Goleman, D. *Emotional Intelligence.* New York: Bantam Books, 1995.

Gollwitzer, P. M. "The Volitional Benefits of Planning." In P. M. Gollwitzer and J. A. Bargh (eds.), *The Psychology of Action: Linking Cognition and Motivation to Behavior.* New York: Guilford Press, 1996.

Ledoux, J. *The Emotional Brain.* New York: Simon & Schuster, 1996.

Metcalfe, J., and Mischel, W. "A Hot/Cool System Analysis of Delay of Gratification: Dynamics of Willpower." *Psychological Review,* 1999, *106,* 3–19.

Mischel, W. "From Good Intentions to Willpower." In P. M. Gollwitzer and J. A. Bargh (eds.), *The Psychology of Action: Linking Cognition and Motivation to Behavior.* New York: Guilford Press, 1996.

Mischel, W., Cantor, N., and Feldman, S. "Principles of Self-Regulation: The Nature of Willpower and Self-Control." In E. T. Higgins and A. W. Kruglanski (eds.), *Social Psychology: Handbook of Basic Principles.* New York: Guilford Press, 1996.

Mischel, W., Shoda, Y., and Rodriguez, M. L. "Delay of Gratification in Children." *Science,* 1989, *244,* 933–938.

Sapolsky, R. M. "Why Stress Is Bad for Your Brain." *Science,* 1996, *273,* 749–750.

Zillman, D. "Cognition-Excitation Interdependencies in the Escalation of Anger and Angry Aggression." In M. Potegal (ed.), *Escalation of Aggression: Biological and Social Processes.* Mahwah, N.J.: Erlbaum, 1993.

PART THREE

PERSONAL
DIFFERENCES

Process and Outcome Goal Orientations in Conflict Situations

The Importance of Framing

Tal Y. Katz
Caryn J. Block

In this chapter, we suggest a new framework to approach conflict situations. Since conflict is broadly defined as perceived divergence of interests, or belief that the parties' current aspirations cannot be achieved simultaneously (Rubin, Pruitt, and Kim, 1994), a critical issue in resolving a conflict is the process through which people change these beliefs, or their perception that they can only achieve their goals at the expense of the other party. In fact, it has long been demonstrated that when people reframe conflict situations so they are not seen as zero-sum, conflicts are resolved productively, with both parties increasing their outcomes (Deutsch, 1973). This chapter provides a motivational framework to explain how conflict situations can be framed such that the parties to the conflict are more likely to perceive the conflict as not zero-sum.

In the first part of the chapter, we use a framework that has been applied in other settings to explain *how* people differentially perceive achievement situations, moral dilemmas, and social judgments. Then we explain *why* people tend to perceive conflict situations in a certain way, using the framework, which is based on a motivational theory developed by Dweck and others (Ames and Archer, 1988; Dweck, 1986, 1999; Dweck and Leggett, 1988). We also explain how people with differing goal orientations are likely to perceive conflict, and why and what course of action they try to follow to resolve their conflict. Our explanation is based on the types of achievement goal individuals pursue, and the underlying perceptions that lead them to pursue these goals. Finally, we suggest conflict resolution techniques, to be used by the parties or by mediators, based on this theoretical framework.

FRAMING ACHIEVEMENT SITUATIONS

We base our discussion on the premise that how a situation is framed or labeled influences how people behave. Thus, if an achievement or conflict situation is framed as a test of ability, people behave differently than if the situation is labeled as a learning and self-development opportunity. For example, in a laboratory setting, when people worked on an activity labeled as an assessment activity (a test of their ability to perform on the task), they were more anxious, and produced lower-quality work and a smaller quantity of it compared to people who worked on the same activity when it was labeled as a self-development or learning activity (Block and others, 1995). Why does framing the situation as assessment versus learning have this type of effect in an achievement situation?

To answer this question, we rely on the theory developed by Dweck and her colleagues. According to this theory, individuals may frame achievement situations in two general ways: as a performance goal or a learning goal. With a performance goal, individuals focus mainly on the outcome of the situation, on gaining favorable judgment of their competence, and on avoiding unfavorable judgment of their competence. Other people may frame achievement situations as a learning or self-development opportunity, focusing on the processes that lead them to the desired outcome and on increasing their competence to master the task. Thus, the motivation to perform a given task is a function of these achievement goal orientations. Individuals with a performance goal orientation are primarily motivated to demonstrate their level of competence on a given task, whereas individuals with a learning goal are primarily motivated to improve their level of competence.

Approaching a situation with a learning or process goal, the individual usually chooses a mastery-oriented response pattern. This pattern has certain characteristics:

- It increases the person's positive affect
- It leads to a high level of effort on the task
- It encourages individuals to seek challenge because they are eager to learn
- It enables them to perceive failure and mistakes as an opportunity to learn more effective strategies to perform the task

On the other hand, outcome goals have been found to produce challenge avoidance and learned-helplessness responses, since expending effort and failing are perceived to be from lack of ability; this has the effect of undermining the person's self-image. Thus, a process orientation (as compared to an outcome orientation) is likely to lead to more interest in the task, greater effort, less anxiety in the face of challenge, better performance, and higher self-esteem.

The characteristics or attributes of the achievement situation itself may influence how the person perceives the situation and, as a result, his or her goal orientation. The situation can make various types of goals salient and consequently affect how people think about themselves, their task, and others. Thus, in several studies, researchers assigned specific types of goals to the participants (Elliott and Dweck, 1988; Block and others, 1995). By assigning process or outcome goals, the researchers actually structured the situation for the participants, and in doing so influenced their behavior. Assigned goal orientations, for instance, have been shown to influence the level of difficulty of the task that children choose to work on. Children choose to work on more difficult tasks when assigned a process rather than outcome goal (Elliott and Dweck, 1988).

In an organizational setting, a work unit may have a specific climate that encourages process orientation by emphasizing learning and improvement, while other work unit climates may encourage end-state results, without emphasizing improvement or development of strategies to improve performance. Katz, Block, and Pearsall (1997) found that situational goal orientation, as perceived by employees, influenced performance such that a work climate emphasizing the process enhanced performance (as rated by managers), while a climate emphasizing outcomes did not.

Assigned goal orientations have also been shown to influence the type of feedback both children (Butler, 1992) and adults (Butler, 1993) prefer. Feedback can impart information about how a person performs on a given task in comparison with others, or it can provide information about how much the person has learned or improved in performing the given task. The latter is more helpful in the process of mastering a complex task since it reveals effective strategies for performing the task. On the other hand, comparative feedback tends to introduce anxiety by adding a sense of competition, and it does not yield the information needed for successful performance. Research has found that individuals seek task-related as opposed to comparative feedback when assigned a process goal, and they seek comparative (as opposed to task-related) feedback when assigned an outcome goal.

Although the situational cues are clearly important determinants of goal orientation, individuals do have a predisposition to adopt a process or outcome orientation. One reliable predictor of the type of goal orientation adopted in an achievement situation is one's conception of ability as either a *fixed entity* or a *malleable quality*. One may perceive the ability to perform a given task as an inborn, unchangeable quality or as a quality that can be improved through learning, practice, and experience. Research with children and adults has demonstrated that those who consider their ability fixed and unchanging are prone to behave as if they were pursuing an outcome goal, which focuses them on demonstrating the adequacy of their ability. Those who consider their ability malleable and incremental are likely to behave as if pursuing a process goal, which focuses them on increasing their ability and developing better ways to master their task.

Related research has also examined the effect of manipulating the individual's view of ability as fixed or incremental for a given task. In a study by Matrocchio (1994), subjects who were in the incremental-ability condition were told that the skills required to perform well on this task would develop as they were practiced, that mistakes were a normal part of this task, and that the more practice they had, the more capable they would become. In contrast, subjects in the fixed-ability group were told that the skills required to perform well on this task were based on skills they already possessed, and that mistakes should serve as a reminder to work smart, not hard. Results of this study showed that the incremental-ability subjects were more confident in their ability to perform well on the training task and less anxious after the training than the fixed-ability subjects. However, there were no differences in the amount learned as a result of the training program.

In a study using similar manipulation of the belief regarding ability as fixed or malleable, Wood and Bandura (1989) found that subjects who were told that ability on a complex managerial decision-making task was fixed reported a sense of lower self-efficacy, set lower goals for themselves, and were less efficient in using strategies; as a consequence, they exhibited lower levels of decision making on the task. On the other hand, subjects who were told that ability on this task was malleable maintained their original levels of self-efficacy, set challenging goals for themselves, and were more efficient in their use of strategies, resulting in better decision-making outcomes.

In sum, achievement situations can be framed as process-focused or outcome-focused by way of emphasizing a specific type of goal, seeking certain feedback, and perceiving ability as dependent on either effort or ability. Next, we see how we can use this framework in a conflict situation.

APPLYING THE THEORY TO CONFLICT SITUATIONS

So far we have discussed a theory that explains how situational cues and the person's perception of ability as a fixed or malleable trait affect how an individual frames an achievement situation. How does this theoretical framework apply to conflict situations?

We note that this theory is mainly concerned with individual behavior, although a conflict is always an interaction between two or more individuals. Nevertheless, we shall assume that the behavior of people involved in a conflict is much influenced by which goal orientation (process or outcome) and which conception of ability (malleable or fixed) they hold as they approach the conflict.

Conflicts inherently involve some type of achievement motivation, since in a conflict situation people are motivated to achieve a certain *goal* so as to satisfy their needs, interests, or aspirations. As is true for other achievement situations, people may perceive their goals in a conflict situation in terms of outcome or process. People who are oriented toward an *outcome goal* mainly concentrate on the final result or outcome; as a consequence, they are preoccupied with their *position*. According to Fisher, Ury, and Patton (1991), people who focus on their positions tend to lock themselves into those positions. The more they clarify their position and defend it, the more committed they become to it, and the more attention they pay to their own position, the less attention they devote to meeting the underlying concerns of the parties. In contrast, people who are oriented toward a *process goal* focus mainly on formulating and mastering the best *strategy* leading to successful resolution of the conflict. They tend to focus on constructive processes to resolve the conflict. Initial preoccupation with achieving a positional goal and final outcome is less likely to lead to constructive conflict resolution than an initial focus on process and strategy, which identifies basic needs and interests. The latter focus facilitates developing the strategies, the trust, good communication, and effective problem solving necessary to resolve difficult conflicts.

The advantage of one goal orientation over the other in a conflict situation lies in the behavior patterns each orientation elicits as predicted by the theory. First of all, if people approach a conflict situation with a process goal, it usually leads them to the mastery-oriented response pattern. Thus, they probably experience positive affect. For example, people who approach a conflict situation with the goal of working with the other party on how to develop a mutually agreed solution, as opposed to those who see the situation as a win-lose struggle, are more apt to have positive feelings and be less anxious about the situation. Second, they put a high level of effort into the cooperative resolution process. Their process orientation promotes challenge-seeking behavior. They are more likely to take risks and offer goodwill gestures.

In contrast, people who approach the conflict with an outcome goal and direct their effort toward achieving their own position are less aware and responsive to the other's needs, tend to avoid a challenging solution, and perceive any failure to achieve exactly what they wanted as lack of personal ability to achieve their goal. However, this does not necessarily mean that the people who focus on outcomes are not completely involved in the conflict. They may invest deeply in it, but they tend to use maladaptive strategies in solving it.

Additionally, we suggest a parallel to the differences found by Dweck and her colleagues between the fixed and malleable views of ability. We propose that people who tend to perceive positions as fixed rather than malleable also tend to perceive conflict as zero-sum, or a competitive situation, which has to be won by one party at the expense of the other. Conversely, people who perceive their position to be malleable see a conflict situation as not zero-sum, or cooperative. They are more likely to try to work on a creative solution, to expand the pie of possible alternatives such that each party is able to satisfy its needs.

We also suggest that fixation on positions leads to a tendency toward cognitive rigidity during the conflict. Cognitive rigidity is characterized by limited range of thought and inability to envision alternative possibilities for resolving the conflict (Deutsch, 1973). Such rigidity often leads to an oversimplified, black-and-white view of the issues in conflict and further contributes to a win-lose or competitive orientation among the parties to a conflict.

Kelley and Stahelski (1970) have reported research, from the theory of Dweck and her colleagues, that is relevant to the implications we have drawn for conflict. They found that a person's behavior in a specific situation probably depends on what she or he thinks the other person will do, which in turn is likely to reflect what she or he thinks the other person is trying to accomplish in the relationship—in particular, whether the other is trying to satisfy a joint interest or merely his or her own interests. People who are inflexibly competitive in their behavior judge others to be the same way, regardless of the others' actual behavior. Kelley and Stahelski (1970) state that "cooperative and competitive persons are likely to develop different views of what 'other people' are like with respect to cooperativeness versus competitiveness. Specifically, it seemed probable that competitors would tend to believe that other people are also and uniformly competitive, whereas cooperators would believe other people are heterogeneous in this respect, some being cooperative and others, competitive" (p. 69). It seems that "uniformly competitive" people perceive the situation as zero-sum and engage in the maladaptive pattern of behaviors that are characteristic of people who pursue outcome goals; they mainly try to demonstrate their ability to achieve their goals.

Process goals lead to a mastery-oriented response pattern under conditions psychologically similar to conflict. Since every conflict is unique, the individual usually encounters a novel situation. In a conflict, the information one has is often ambiguous; thus people face obstacles and challenges to achieving their goal and satisfying their interest. Furthermore, failure to achieve one's goal or to negotiate effectively is not an uncommon experience. This is particularly the case in the early stages of a conflict. It takes time to build trust among the parties and to communicate so that they understand one another's needs. People with a process goal tend to interpret a negative reaction from the other as information regarding the success of their current conflict resolution strategy, and they will use this information as an impetus to analyze and change their strategy. In contrast, people with an outcome goal are likely to interpret a negative reaction from the other as information regarding their ability to solve the conflict. Thus, when faced with a challenge in a conflict, people with an outcome goal are apt to become anxious and less cognitively flexible in dealing with the conflict.

SITUATIONAL DETERMINANTS OF GOAL ORIENTATION IN CONFLICT RESOLUTION

Several situational factors predict whether a person adopts a process or an outcome goal in a conflict situation. They may be managed in a conflict situation to promote strategy development and constructive resolution.

The conflict situation itself can emphasize goals that focus on a particular outcome or on the conflict process. A person approaching a conflict situation with an outcome goal emphasizes social comparison. Thus, one tries to do better than one's opponent or other people who have been in a similar situation before. The parties tend to focus on their outcomes and freeze themselves into positions, which gives them a comparative advantage. On the other hand, if absolute standards and self-improvement are emphasized, people focus on efforts to develop a better strategy for resolving the conflict.

The attributes of the situation may be emphasized in a conflict so as to promote constructive resolution. This can be done through self-awareness or through help from a third party. One way is to stay focused on the processes involved in constructive conflict resolution, which are described in many chapters in this book, rather than on the outcome of the conflict; and to cultivate awareness of the type of goal one is pursuing. Second, conflict resolution training is often necessary for people to develop self-awareness of the type of goal pursued. Finally, a third party or mediator can help the parties pursue process goals, as opposed to focusing on solutions.

A mediator can help the parties set process goals for themselves and also emphasize that they are capable of mastering the situation through learning about the processes that facilitate constructive interaction during a conflict. A mediator may frame the situation on the one hand to emphasize what each side is trying to achieve or its position. By doing so, she encourages the sides to focus on the end-state result and to ignore the possible strategies to get to the desired solution. On the other hand, the mediator can encourage the sides to focus on such processes as finding common ground, developing mutual understanding, empowering one another, and understanding the other's needs and emotions. Doing so encourages using fair tactics and constructive strategies to resolve the conflict.

Burgess and Burgess (1996) suggest a transformative approach to intractable conflicts, which they call constructive confrontation. They write that mediators or conflict specialists would do better confronting difficult or intractable conflict if they moved away from the unrealistic goal of resolution and focused instead on how such conflicts can be conducted constructively—in other words, focus on the processes not on the outcomes, especially when it looks impossible to reach a final solution. Bush and Folger (1994) suggest a similar framework in which mediators should focus less on resolution and more on empowerment and recognition of the parties (see Bush and Folger for a discussion of their approach, as well as Chapters Nine and Twenty-Five in this volume). We suggest that these techniques of focusing on process instead of outcome can be beneficial in any conflict (not only intractable ones) and that in less complex conflicts the parties can do it themselves, without the help of a mediator, if they are trained to do so.

Another situational factor that plays an import role in determining which orientation is adopted is the type of feedback the individual receives. He or she is likely to assume a process orientation if the feedback received during a conflict is process-focused, and an outcome orientation if receiving normative feedback as to where he or she stands compared to others.

In relation to feedback, a mediator can give the conflicting parties useful feedback information about progress toward building trust (improving communication so it is easier for them to understand each other's needs) and suggest alternatives to help them focus on process. Or the mediator can focus on outcomes and tell the sides of better results (say, quick agreement) other negotiators in similar situations have achieved, and thus stimulate them to be outcome-oriented.

Finally, it is necessary to pay attention to one's assumption about the malleability of the situation. The parties must be constantly aware that positions are malleable (one's own as well as the other's) rather than fixed, and that a successful outcome for oneself is not contingent on ability but rather on the effort involved in developing an effective process for dealing with the conflict. Recognizing that the situation is malleable leads to a creative search to find a new, mutually congenial way of satisfying the needs underlying one's own position and the other's. Mediators can also help the parties be metacognitive—self-aware of the conflict process, their assumptions about the malleability of positions, and their own goal orientation.

It is naïve to believe that people will completely give up their initial outcome goal and position in a conflict situation. However, it is important to understand that they need to engage in a constructive process to achieve the outcome. They need to perceive that they are more likely to achieve satisfaction of their underlying needs if in addition to the outcome they also focus on developing a constructive process responsive to the other's needs as well.

CONCLUSION

We have presented a framework suggesting that orientation to the processes involved in an achievement situation, rather than to outcomes, leads to learning and effective performance as well as to a favorable attitude toward tasks and a greater sense of self-efficacy. These goal orientations are related to naïve theories about the nature of ability, one that it is a fixed quality and the other that it is malleable. However, such goal orientations can also be influenced and modified by how the situation is framed, the goal set, and the feedback received.

We have applied the foregoing framework to conflict situations and have suggested that an orientation to conflict that focuses on the process involved in constructively resolving conflict, rather than on obtaining one's desired outcome, is likely to lead to constructive resolution as well as to better outcomes. We also suggest that a malleable rather than fixed conception of a conflict situation is more apt to stimulate creative search for new alternatives and a way of satisfying the needs underlying both sides' positions. Finally, we have suggested strategies to frame a conflict situation so that the parties can foster a process orientation.

References

Ames, C., and Archer, J. "Achievement Goals in the Classroom: Students' Learning Strategies and Motivation Processes." *Journal of Educational Psychology,* 1988, *80,* 260–267.

Block, C. J., and others. "The Influence of Learning and Performance Goal Orientations on Anxiety, Motivation, and Performance on Complex Tasks." Paper presented at conference of the Academy of Management, Vancouver, B.C., June 1995.

Burgess, H., and Burgess, G. "Constructive Confrontation: A Transformative Approach to Intractable Conflicts." *Mediation Quarterly,* 1996, *13,* 305–322.

Bush, R.A.B., and Folger, J. P. *The Promise of Mediation: Responding to Conflict Through Empowerment and Recognition.* San Francisco: Jossey-Bass, 1994.

Butler, R. "What Young People Want to Know When: Effects of Mastery and Ability Goals on Interest in Different Kinds of Social Comparisons." *Journal of Personality and Social Psychology,* 1992, *62,* 924–943.

Butler, R. "Effects of Task- and Ego-Achievement Goals on Information Seeking During Task Engagement." *Journal of Personality and Social Psychology,* 1993, *65,* 18–31.

Deutsch, M. *The Resolution of Conflict: Constructive and Destructive Processes.* New Haven: Yale University Press, 1973.

Dweck, C. S. "Motivational Processes Affecting Learning." *American Psychologist,* 1986, *41,* 1040–1048.

Dweck, C. S. *Self-Theories: Their Role in Motivation, Personality, and Development.* Philadelphia: Psychology Press, 1999.

Dweck, C. S., and Leggett, E. L. "A Social-Cognitive Approach to Motivation and Personality." *Psychological Review,* 1988, *95,* 256–273.

Elliott, E. S., and Dweck, C. S. "Goals: An Approach to Motivation and Achievement." *Journal of Personality and Social Psychology,* 1988, *54,* 5–12.

Fisher, R. J., Ury, W., and Patton, B. *Getting to Yes: Negotiating Agreement Without Giving In.* (2nd ed.) New York: Penguin, 1991.

Katz, T., Block, C., and Pearsall, S. "Goal Orientation in the Workplace: Dispositional and Situational Effects on Strategies and Performance." Paper presented at the conference of the Academy of Management, Boston, Aug. 1997.

Kelley, H. H., and Stahelski, A. J. "Social Interaction Basis of Cooperators' and Competitors' Beliefs About Others." *Journal of Personality and Social Psychology*, 1970, *16*, 66–91.

Matrocchio, J. "Effects of Conceptions of Ability on Anxiety, Self-Efficacy, and Learning in Training." *Journal of Applied Psychology*, 1994, *79*, 819–825.

Rubin, J. Z., Pruitt, D. G., and Kim, S. H. *Social Conflict: Escalation, Stalemate, and Settlement.* New York: McGraw-Hill, 1994.

Wood, R. E., and Bandura, A. "Impact of Conceptions of Ability on Self-Regulatory Mechanisms and Complex Decision-Making." *Journal of Personality and Social Psychology*, 1989, *56*, 407–415.

CHAPTER FOURTEEN

Personality and Conflict

Sandra V. Sandy

Susan K. Boardman

Morton Deutsch

Throughout literary history, many novelists and playwrights have defined personality as "destiny," poignantly illustrating the "inevitability" of their protagonist's fate as a consequence of character traits that relentlessly determine his or her choices in life. But even as naïve observers, if we look deeply enough within ourselves we are often surprised by the extent to which we are ruled by needs and strivings that defy commonsense logic. Although many social scientists agree with the fiction writers on the power of personality to shape the course of our lives, scientists focus on predictability rather than inevitability. The task of science is to observe and document any reliable association between specific character traits and the likelihood of varying life choices, patterns of behavior, and consequences of the behavior for oneself and others.

Parties involved in a conflict they are attempting to resolve constructively must strive to understand each other despite any difference in ethnic and gender identities, family and life experiences, and cultural perspectives. Although conflict resolution practitioners and theorists recognize the potentially important effects that individual differences have on the negotiation process and its outcome, research in this area has been piecemeal and few guidelines exist for practical application. At this stage, a synthesis of cross-discipline information concerning personality can offer additional tools to benefit practitioners and prove useful to theorists wishing to conduct future investigation in this area. Awareness of how personal characteristics predispose an individual to respond within the negotiation setting equips all parties more effectively to (1) uncover and understand the psychological as well as substantive interests underlying conflict—particularly those interests that would normally remain unrecognized or unarticulated if personality is not considered, (2) respond so as to facilitate a constructive resolution process avoiding escalation and deadlock, and (3) generate a satisfying solution to meet the priority needs of both parties.

The first section of this chapter reviews some of the ideas relevant to conflict from several major theoretical approaches to personality: psychodynamic theory, need theory, social-learning theory, and situation-person interaction theory. *Our review of these theories is not intended to be comprehensive.* It is limited to selecting several ideas from each theory that are useful to understanding personal reaction and behavior in a conflict situation. In the second section, we discuss the trait approach to personality and assessment. First, we briefly indicate some of the individual traits thought to be related to conflict behavior and then discuss some of the limitations of this approach. Next, we discuss more fully a multiple-trait approach, as well as a method for assessing personal conflict orientations that seem to have considerable promise for evaluating personality style, reaction, and behavior as they relate to conflict. In the final section, we discuss how one can use personality theory and assessment to enhance conflict resolution in practice.

REPRESENTATIVE MODELS OF PERSONALITY

There are two major approaches to the study of personality: *idiographic,* the belief that human behavior cannot be broken down into its constituent parts; and *nomothetic,* the view that some general dimension of behavior can be used to describe most people of a general age group (Martin, 1988, p. 10). To illustrate, let us begin by noting that one of the most influential models of personality, the psychodynamic, relies on idiographic use of case-history studies to reach conclusions about human nature.

Psychodynamic Theories

The work of Sigmund Freud, during the period from the late 1880s to the late 1930s, marks the beginning of the psychodynamic study of human personality. His intellectual descendants are numerous: Carl Jung, Alfred Adler, Karen Horney, Anna Freud, Erik Erikson, Erich Fromm, Harry S. Sullivan, Melanie Klein, W.R.D. Fairbairn, Donald Winnicott, Heinz Hartmann, Jacques Lacan, and Heinz Kohut.

Inevitably, Freud's descendants have modified, revised, extended, and in other ways changed his original ideas. The changes have mainly been to place greater emphasis on the social (cultural, class, gender, familial, and experiential) determinants of psychodynamic processes, to develop detailed characterization of the structural components involved in the dynamic intrapsychic processes, and to seek adequate conceptualization of the cognitive and self-processes that are central to the individual's relation to reality. Despite the changes, there are some key elements that characterize most of the psychodynamic approaches.

An Active Unconscious. People actively seek to remain unaware (unconscious) of those of their impulses, thoughts, and actions that make them feel very disturbing emotions (for example, anxiety, guilt, shame).

Internal Conflict. People may have internal conflict between desires and conscience, desires and fears, and what the "good" self wants and what the "bad" self wants; the conflict may occur outside of consciousness.

Control and Defense Mechanisms. People develop tactics and strategies to control their impulses, thoughts, actions, and realities so that they won't feel anxious, guilty, or ashamed. If their controls are ineffective, they develop defense mechanisms to keep from feeling these disturbing emotions.

Stages of Development. From birth on to old age, people go through stages of development. Most current psychodynamic theorists accept the view that the developmental stages reflect both biological and social determinants, even though they may differ in their weighting of the two as well as in their labeling of the stages, and how they specifically characterize them. Freudian theory focuses mainly on the three earliest stages of development—the oral, anal, and phallic—because it was believed that the main features of personality development were set early in childhood. Freud employed these anatomical terms to characterize the early stages because he thought these bodily zones were successively infused with libidinal energy.

Later psychoanalysts were apt to characterize them psychosocially in terms of the social situation confronting the developing child. In the oral stage, infants are primarily concerned with receiving feeding and care from a parenting figure; in the anal stage, they are faced with the need to develop control over their excretions as well as other forms of self-control; and in the phallic stage, they face the need to establish a sexual identity as a boy or girl and to repress their sexual striving toward the parent of the opposite sex. Associated with these stages are normal frustrations, a development crisis, and typical defense mechanisms. However, certain forms of psychopathology are likely to develop if severe frustration and crisis face the child during a particular stage, with the result that the child becomes "fixated" at that stage; in addition, some adult character traits are thought to originate in each given stage.

Table 14.1 presents, in summary form, some of the features that Freud and the earlier psychoanalysts associated with the three early stages.

Table 14.1. Normal Frustrations, Typical Defense Mechanisms, Developmental Crises, Psychopathology, and Adult Character Traits with Several Early Stages of Psychosexual Development.

Stages of Development	Normal Frustrations	Developmental Crisis	Defense Mechanisms	Psychopathology	Adult Character Traits
I. Oral (0 to 18 months)					
A. Oral erotic period (from birth to about 6 months)	Lack of continuous availability of caretaker to satisfy infant's needs	Trust versus mistrust	Apathy, withdrawal, denial, introjection, hallucinatory gratification	Schizophrenia, manic-depression, depressive states, schizoid personality	Passivity, dependence, restlessness, receptivity, curiosity, generosity, compliance, optimism
B. Oral sadistic (from about 6 to 18 months)	Teething, weaning, and the birth of a new sibling		Withdrawal, denial, introjection, projection		Demandingness, clingingness, explorativeness, ambivalence, cynicism, pessimism, sarcasm

II. Anal (8 to 48 months) A. Anal-erotic (from about 8 to 24 months)	Onset of toilet training and other demands for self-control	Autonomy versus shame and	Projection	Paranoia, psychopathy, sadomasochism, obsessive-compulsive disorders	Bossiness, hostility, disorderliness, irresponsibility, dirtiness, assertiveness
B. Anal-sadistic (from about 12 to 48 months)	Toilet training and other demands for self-control	guilt	Reaction-formation, undoing, intellectualization, rationalization		Stubbornness, parsimony, punctuality, cautiousness, pedantry, righteousness, indecision
III. Phallic (2 to 6 years)	Transformation of the pregenital child into a "boy" or "girl" with internalization of key values concerning future adult and sex roles, with renunciation of the opposite-sex parent as an object of sexual strivings	Initiative versus guilt	Repression, displacement, conversion, histrionics	Hysteria, amnesia, anxiety states, phobias	Impulsiveness, naïveté, fickleness, conformity, shallowness, opportunism, haughtiness, assertiveness, arrogance

The Layered Personality. How someone has gone through the stages of development determines current personality. One can presumably discover the residue of earlier stages of development in current personality and behavior. Thus, a paranoid/schizoid adult personality supposedly reflects a basic fault in the earliest stage of development in which the infant did not experience the minimal love, care, and nurturance that would enable him to feel basic trust in the world. The concept of layered personality does not imply that earlier faults cannot be repaired. However, it does imply that an adult personality with a repaired fault is not the same as one that did not need repair. Under severe frustration or anxiety, such a personality is apt to regress to an earlier stage. Also, the concept of layered personality does not imply that an unimpaired adult personality is able to completely resist becoming temporarily or permanently suspicious and paranoid if the current social environment is sufficiently dire and hostile for a prolonged period. It is natural and adaptive to become hypervigilant and suspicious if one is immersed in a dangerous hostile environment.

In this section, we discuss several important ideas, deriving from the work of psychodynamic theorists, that are particularly relevant to the conflict practitioner. Undoubtedly, many more ideas could be expressed in a detailed and comprehensive exposition of psychodynamic viewpoints than we attempt to present in this chapter.

Conflict with Another Can Lead to Intrapsychic Conflict and Anxiety. People may feel anxious because they sense they are unable to control their destructive or evil impulses toward the other in a heated conflict. Or the conflict may lead to a sense of helplessness and vulnerability if they feel overwhelmed by the power and strength of the other. Freud called the first type of internal conflict id-superego conflict (between a primitive impulse and conscience) and the second type an ego-reality conflict (between an immature self and a threatening reality). Later psychoanalysts used somewhat different language, speaking of a conflict among "internal objects" or between internalized images of self and of significant adults (as between an evil self and a harsh or punitive parent; or a weak self and an overwhelming, controlling parent).

If the anxiety aroused by the conflict with another is intense, the individual may rely on unconscious defense mechanisms to screen it out in an attempt to reduce the anxiety. Anxiety is most apt to be aroused if one's basic security, self-conception, self-worth, or social identity is threatened. Defense mechanisms are pathological or ineffective if they create the conditions that produce anxiety, thus requiring continued use of the defense. For example, a student who may be anxious about his intellectual abilities avoids studying and as a consequence does poorly in his course work. He rationalizes his poor grades are due to lack of motivation and effort. His grades further his anxiety about his ability, which in turn fuel his defenses of avoidance and rationalization. The defenses would not be pathological if, in fact, external circumstances prevented him from studying and, given the opportunity, he put much effort into his studies.

The defense mechanisms that people use are determined in part by their layered personality, which may have given rise to a characterological tendency to employ certain defense mechanisms rather than others, and also in part by the situation they confront. Psychoanalysts have identified many defense mechanisms; they are usually discussed in relation to intrapsychic conflict. We believe that they are also applicable in interpersonal and other external conflict. We have space to discuss only a number of the important ones for understanding conflict with others (see Fenichel, 1945, and Freud, 1937, for fuller discussions).

Denial occurs when it is too disturbing to recognize the existence of a conflict (as between husband and wife about their affection toward one another, so they deny it—repressing it so that it remains unconscious, or suppressing it so they don't think about it).

Avoidance involves not facing the conflict, even when you are fully aware of it. To support avoidance, you develop ever-changing *rationalizations* for not facing the conflict ("I'm too tired," "This is not the right timing," "She's not ready," "It won't do any good").

Projection allows denial of faults in yourself. It involves projecting or attributing your own faults to the other ("You're too hostile," "You don't trust me," "You're to blame, not me," "I'm attacking to prevent you from attacking me"). Suspicion, hostility, vulnerability, hypervigilance, and helplessness, as well as attacking or withdrawing from the potential attack of the other, are often associated with this defense.

Reaction formation involves taking on the attributes and characteristics of the other with whom you are in conflict. The conflict is masked by agreement with or submission to the other, by flattering and ingratiating yourself with the other. A child who likes to be messy but is very anxious about her mother's angry reactions may become excessively neat and finicky in a way that is annoying to her mother.

Displacement involves changing the topic of the conflict or changing the party with whom you engage in conflict. Thus, if it is too painful to express openly your hurt and anger toward your spouse because he is not sufficiently affectionate, you may constantly attack him as being too stingy with money. If it is too dangerous to express your anger toward your exploitative boss, you may direct it at a subordinate who annoys you.

Counterphobic defenses entail denial of anxiety about conflict by aggressively seeking it out—by being confrontational, challenging, or having a chip on your shoulder.

Escalation of the importance of the conflict is a complex mechanism that entails narcissistic self-focus on your own needs with inattention to the other's, histrionic intensity of emotional expressiveness and calling attention to yourself, and demanding needfulness. The needs involved in the conflict become life-or-death issues, the emotions expressed are very intense, and the other person must give in. The function of this defense is to get the other to feel that your urgent needs must have highest priority.

In *intellectualization and minimization of the importance of the conflict,* you do not feel the intensity of your needs intellectually but instead experience the conflict with little emotion. You focus on details and side issues, making the central issue from your perspective in the conflict seem unimportant to yourself and the other.

The psychoanalytical emphasis on intrapsychic conflict, anxiety, and defense mechanisms highlights the importance of understanding the interplay between internal conflict and the external conflict with another. Thus, if an external conflict elicits anxiety and defensiveness, the anxious party is apt to project onto, transfer, or attribute to the other characteristics similar to those of internalized significant others who, in the past, elicited similar anxiety in unresolved earlier conflict. Similarly, the anxious party may unconsciously attribute to himself the characteristics he had in the earlier conflict. Thus, if you are made very anxious by a conflict with a supervisor (you feel your basic security is threatened), you may distort your perception of the supervisor and what she is saying so that you unconsciously experience the conflict as similar to unresolved conflict between your mother and yourself as a child.

If you or the other is acting defensively, it is important to understand what is making you or her anxious, what threat is being experienced. The sense of threat, anxiety, and defensiveness hamper developing a productive and cooperative problem-solving orientation toward the conflict. Similarly, transference reactions—for example, reacting to the other as though she were similar to your parent—produces a distorted perception of the other and interferes with realistic, effective problem solving. You can sometimes tell when the other is projecting a false image onto you by your own countertransference reaction: you feel that she is attempting to induce you to enact a role that feels inappropriate in your interactions with her. You can sometimes become aware of projecting a false image onto the other by recognizing that other people don't see her this way, or that you are defensive and anxious in your response to her with no apparent justification.

Summary and Critique of the Psychodynamic Approach. In the preceding pages, we do not attempt to present an exposition of the specific theories of the many contributors to the development of psychoanalytical theory, from Freud to the present day. Rather, we seek to abstract from these theories some of the major ideas that are useful to a conflict practitioner and that can be briefly presented. Psychoanalysis has been criticized—particularly the earlier Freudian version, which no longer seems appropriate in light of the changes made by later theorists: it is too biologically deterministic, too sexist, too pessimistic, and too focused on sex and aggression as the motives of behavior, as well as not oriented at all to positive motivations, to learning and development of cognitive functions, or to the broader societal and cultural determinants of personality development. Nevertheless, it is a useful framework for understanding issues that we all confront during development (security, control and power, sexual identity, transformation from childhood to adulthood) and the problems and personality residues that may result from inadequate care and harsh circumstances during our early years.

Psychoanalysis is not a scientific theory that was developed and tested in a scientific laboratory, as is the case for most of the theories presented elsewhere in this book. Rather, it is a mosaic of subtheories mainly developed in clinically treating psychopathology. Many of its concepts are not defined so as to indicate how they can be observed and measured. It is instead an encompassing intellectual framework for thinking about personality and its development, one that has given rise to a variety of useful subtheories and ideas, many of which are testable and indeed have been tested in research.

Need Theories

Under this heading, we consider some of the ideas of Henry A. Murray and Abraham Maslow, the most influential of the need theorists.

Murray's Need Theory of Personality. Murray's approach to personality was much influenced by the work of Jung, Freud, and their successors, and he was one of the first psychologists to translate psychodynamic concepts and ideas into testable hypotheses. Unlike their concern with the abnormal, Murray's focus was on the normal personality. The most distinctive feature of his theory is its complex system of motivational concepts. In his theory, needs arise not only from internal processes but also from environmental forces.

Murray's most influential contribution to personality theory is the concept of the individual as a striving, seeking being; his orientation reflects primarily a motivational psychology. As he states it, "the most important thing to discover about an individual . . . is the superordinate directionality (or directionalities) of his activities, whether mental, verbal, or physical" (1951, p. 276). This concern with directionality led him to develop the most complete taxonomy of needs ever created.

Need is a force in the brain region that organizes perception, thought, and action so as to change an existing unsatisfactory condition. Needs can be evoked by environmental as well as internal processes. They vary in strength from person to person and from situation to situation. Murray hypothesized the existence of about two dozen needs and characterized them in some detail. He insisted that adequate understanding of human motivation must incorporate a sufficiently large number of variables to reflect, at least in part, the tremendous complexity of human motives.

Working from Murray's theory, McClelland and his colleagues (McClelland, Atkinson, Clark, and Lowell, 1953; McClelland, 1971) did extensive research on four basic needs: achievement, affiliation, power, and autonomy. Those high in need of achievement are concerned with improving their performance, do best on a moderately challenging task, prefer personal responsibility, and seek performance feedback. Persons rated high in the need for affiliation are concerned with maintaining or repairing relationships, are rewarded by being with friends, and seek approval from friends and strangers. Those in need of power are concerned with their reputation and find themselves motivated in a situation presenting hierarchical conditions. In their desire to attain prestige, they are likely to engage in competition more than the other types do. Finally, those having high autonomy needs want to be independent, unattached, and free of restraint.

Murray's theory is a rich and complex view of personality. It can help practitioners become aware of the diversity of human needs and their expression as well as the external circumstances that tend to evoke them and the childhood experiences that lead individuals to varied life striving. Its major deficiency is the lack of a well-defined learning and developmental theory of what determines the acquisition and strength of an individual's needs.

Maslow's Hierarchy of Needs. Although Maslow, early in his professional career, coauthored an excellent textbook on abnormal psychology with a psychoanalyst, he came to feel that a psychology based on the study of the abnormal was bound to give a pessimistic, limited view of the human personality and not take into account altruism, love, joy, truth, justice, beauty, and other positive features of human life. Maslow was one of the founders of the humanistic school of psychology, which emphasizes the positive aspects of human nature.

Maslow is best known for his postulation of a hierarchy of human needs; our discussion in this chapter is limited to this area of his work. In order of priority, he identified these types of needs:

- *Physiological needs*: for air, water, and food, and the need to maintain equilibrium in the blood and body tissues in relation to various substances and the type of cell. Frustration of these needs leads to apathy, illness, disability, and death.

- *Safety needs*: for security, freedom from fear and anxiety, shelter, protection from danger, order, and predictable satisfaction of one's basic needs. Here, frustration leads to fear, anxiety, rage, and psychosis.

- *Belongingness and love needs*: to be part of a group (a family, a circle of friends), to feel cared for, to care for someone, to be intimate with someone, and so forth. Frustration produces alienation, loneliness, and various forms of neurosis.

- *Esteem needs*: for self-esteem (self-confidence, mastery, worth, strength, and the like) and social esteem (respect, dignity, appreciation, and so on). Feelings of inadequacy, inferiority, helplessness, incompetence, shame, guilt, and the like, are associated with frustration of these needs.

- *Self-actualization needs*: to become the kind of person one is most suited to become; to realize one's full potential in relatedness to others, in developing talents, and in participating in one's community. The need for self-actualization also includes such meta-needs as truth, curiosity, justice, beauty, aliveness, playfulness, and the like.

Maslow considered the first four in this list to be deficiency needs, arising from a lack of what is needed. Once these basic needs are all reasonably satisfied, we get in touch with our needs for self-realization and pursue their satisfaction. Although Maslow initially postulated needs as hierarchically ordered, he later accepted the view that in reality some people violate the hierarchy—say, putting themselves in danger and going hungry to protect someone they love or a group with whom they identify.

Maslow's theory, or a variation of it, is the foundation of the "human needs" theory of John Burton (1990) and his colleagues and students. The fundamental thesis of this approach is that a conflict is not resolved constructively unless the parties' basic human needs are brought out and dealt with to the satisfaction of each party. The application of this idea to conflict is called the "problem-solving workshop." Burton initially developed it while he was serving as a consultant in the Cypress conflict between the Greeks and Turks; subsequently, it was systematically developed by Kelman (1986) and his colleagues. It entails creating conditions that enable the participants to express their real needs openly and honestly, and then try to work out a resolution that meets the basic needs of both sides. (See also mention of this in Chapter Eight.)

Social Learning Theory

In Bandura's interactionist approach to personality (Bandura, 1986), the individual is a thinking person who can impose some direction on the forces from within and the pressures from the external environment. Bandura asserts that behavior is a function of a person in her environment; cognition, other personal traits, and the environment mutually influence one another. People learn by observing the behavior of others and the differential consequences attending these behaviors. Learning requires that the person be aware of appropriate responses and value the consequences of the behavior in question.

Unlike a number of other theorists, Bandura does not believe that aggression is innate. Through imitation of social models, people learn aggression, altruism, and other forms of social behavior as well as constructive and destructive ways of dealing with conflict. The ability to imitate another's behavior depends on the characteristics of the model (whether the model makes his behavior unambiguous and clearly observable), the attention of the observer (whether the observer is sharply focused on the model's behavior), memory processes (whether the observer is intelligent and able to recall what has been observed), and behavioral capabilities (whether the observer has the physical and intellectual capability to reproduce the behavior observed).

Assuming that one has the capability, readiness to reproduce the behavior of the model is determined by such factors as whether the model has been perceived to obtain positive or negative consequences as a result of behavior, the attractiveness and power of the model, the vividness of the behavior, and the intrinsic attractiveness of the behavior that has been modeled. Thus, a boy may be predisposed to engage in aggressive behavior (using a handgun to threaten a rival) if he has seen a prestigious older figure (his father, older brother, a group leader, a movie star) engage in such behavior and feel good about doing so. He is capable of doing so (as well as predisposed) if he has access to a handgun.

Developing a sense of self-efficacy or confidence in these competencies requires one to (1) use these skills to master tasks and overcome the obstacles posed by the environment, (2) cultivate belief in the capacity to use one's competencies effectively, and (3) identify realistic goals and opportunities to use one's skills effectively. Realistic encouragement to achieve an ambitious but attainable goal promotes successful experience, which in turn, aids developing the sense of self-efficacy; social prodding to achieve unattainable goals often produces a sense of failure and undermines self-efficacy.

We selectively emphasize Bandura's concepts of observational learning and self-efficacy because of their relevance to conflict. Given that most people acquire their knowledge, attitudes, and skills in managing conflict through observational learning, some people have inadequate knowledge, inappropriate attitudes, and poor skills for resolving their conflicts constructively while others are better prepared to do so. It is very much a function of the models they have been exposed to in their families, schools, communities, and the media. It is our impression that many people have been exposed to poor models. Change in how they deal with conflict requires much relearning.

Relearning involves helping people become fully aware of how they currently behave in conflict situations, exposing them to models of constructive behavior, and extending repeated opportunities in various situations to enact and be rewarded for constructive behavior. In the course of relearning, people should become uncomfortable and dissatisfied with their old, ineffective ways of managing conflict and also develop a sense of self-efficacy in new, constructive methods of conflict resolution.

Social Situations and Psychological Orientations

Although Deutsch is not classified as a personality theorist, his concept of situationally linked psychological orientations is a useful and somewhat different perspective. He employs the term *psychological orientation* to refer to a more-

or-less consistent complex of cognitive, motivational, and moral orientations to a given situation that serve to guide one's behavior and response in that situation. He assumes that the causal arrow between psychological orientation and social situation is bidirectional; a given psychological orientation can lead to a given type of social relation or be induced by that type of social relation (Deutsch, 1982, 1985). With Wish and Kaplan (Wish, Deutsch, and Kaplan, 1976), he identified five basic dimensions of interpersonal relations:

1. *Cooperation-competition.* Such social relations as "close friends," "teammates," and "coworkers" are usually on the cooperative side of this dimension, while "enemies," "political opponents," and "rivals" are usually on the competitive side. See Chapter One for further discussion.

2. *Power distribution (equal versus unequal).* "Business partners," "business rivals," and "close friends" are typically on the equal side, while "parent and child," "teacher and student," and "boss and employee" are on the unequal side. See Chapter Five for further discussion.

3. *Task-oriented versus social-emotional.* Such interpersonal relations as "lovers" and "close friends" are social-emotional, while "task force," "negotiators," and "business rivals" are task-oriented.

4. *Formal versus informal.* Relations within a bureaucracy tend to be formal and regulated by externally determined social rules and conventions, while the relationship norms between intimates are informally determined by the participants involved.

5. *Intensity and importance.* This dimension has to do with the intensity or superficiality of the relationship. Important relationships, as between parent and child or between lovers, are on the important side, while unimportant relationships, as between casual acquaintances or between salesperson and customer, are on the superficial side.

The character of a given social relationship can be identified by locating it on all the dimensions. Thus, an intimate relationship between lovers is typically characterized in the United States as relatively cooperative, equal, social-emotional, informal, and intense. Similarly a sadomasochistic relationship between a bully and his victim is usually identified as competitive, unequal, social-emotional, informal, and intense. Deutsch indicates that a distinctive psychological orientation is associated with the particular location of a social relationship along the five dimensions. Positing that there are three components of a psychological orientation that are mutually consistent, he describes them as follows.

Cognitive orientation consists of structured expectation about oneself, the social environment, and the people involved. This makes it possible for one to interpret and respond quickly to what's going on in a specific situation. If your expectation leads to inappropriate interpretation and response, then the expectation is likely to be revised. Or if the circumstances confronting you are sufficiently malleable, your interpretation and response to them may help to shape their form. Thus, what you expect to happen in a situation involving negotiations about your salary with your boss is apt to be quite different from what you expect in a situation where you and your spouse are making love.

Motivational orientation alerts one to the possibility that in the situation certain types of need may be gratified or frustrated. It orients you to such questions as "What do I want here, and how do I get it? What is to be valued or feared in this relationship?" In a business negotiation, you are oriented to satisfaction of financial needs, not affection; in a love relationship, the opposite is true.

Moral orientation focuses on the mutual obligations, rights, and entitlements of the people involved in the relationship. It implies that in a relationship you and the other(s) mutually perceive the obligations you have to one another and mutually respect the framework of social norms that define what is fair or unfair in the interactions and outcomes of everyone involved.

To illustrate Deutsch's ideas, we contrast the psychological orientations in two relations: friend-friend and police officer–thief. Because of space limitations, we limit our discussion to the cooperative-competitive, power, and task-oriented versus social-emotional dimensions.

Friends have a cooperative cognitive orientation of "We are for one another"; the motivational orientation is of affection, affiliation, and trust; and the moral orientation is one of mutual benevolence, respect, and equality. In contrast, the police officer and thief have a competitive cognitive orientation (what's good for the other is bad for me); the motivational orientation is of hostility, suspicion, and aggressiveness or defensiveness; the moral orientation involved is that of a win-lose struggle to be conducted either under fair rules or a no-holds-barred one in which any means to defeat the other can be employed.

Friends are of equal power and employ their power cooperatively. Their cognitive orientation to power and influence relies on its positive forms (persuasion, benefit, legitimate power); their motivational orientation supports mutual esteem, respect, and status for both parties; their moral orientation is that of egalitarianism. In contrast, the police officer and thief are of unequal power. The officer is cognitively oriented toward using negative forms of power (coercion and harm), with a motivational orientation to dominate, command, and control. Morally, the officer feels superior and ready to exclude the thief from the former's moral community (those who are entitled to care and justice). In cognitive response to the low-power position, the thief either tries to improve power relative to the police officer or submits to the role as one who is under the officer's control. Thus the thief's motivational orientation may be rebellious and resistant (expressing the need for autonomy and inferiority avoidance) or passive and submissive (expressing the need for abasement). This moral orientation is either to exclude the officer from the thief's own moral community or to "identify with the aggressor" (A. Freud, 1937), adopting the moral authority of the more powerful for oneself.

The friends have a social-emotional orientation, while the police officer and thief have a task-oriented relationship to one another. In the latter, one is cognitively oriented to making decisions about which means are most efficient in achieving one's ends; the task-oriented relationship requires an analytical attitude to compare the effectiveness of various means. One is oriented to the other impersonally as an instrument to achieve one's ends. The motivational orientation evoked by a task-oriented situation is that of achievement, and the moral orientation toward the other is utilitarian. In contrast, friends have a cognitive orientation in which the unique personal qualities and identity of the other are of paramount importance. Motivations characteristic of such relations include affiliation, affection, esteem, play, and nurturance-succorance. The moral obligation to a friend is to esteem the other as a person and to help when the other is in need.

Deutsch's view of the relation between social situation and psychological orientation is not only that particular situations induce a particular psychological orientation, but also that individuals vary in their psychological orientation and personality. Based on their life experiences, some people tend to be cooperative, egalitarian, and social-emotional in their orientation, while others tend to be competitive, power seeking, and task-oriented. For example, in many cultures, compared to men, women tend to have relatively strong orientations of the former type (cooperative and so on), while men have relatively stronger orientations of the latter (competitive) type.

Personality disposition influences the choice of social situation and the social relations that one seeks out or avoids. Given the opportunity, people select social relations and situations that are most compatible with their dominant psychological orientations. They also seek to alter or leave a social relation or situation if it is incompatible with their disposition. If this is impossible, they employ the alternative, latent psychological orientations within themselves that are compatible with the social situation.

Knowledge of the dimensions of social relation can be helpful to a conflict practitioner in analyzing both the characteristics of a situation as well as the psychological orientations the parties are apt to display in the circumstances. It is also useful in characterizing individuals in terms of their dominant psychological orientations to social situations. It should be noted, however, that Deutsch's ideas are not well specified about what happens if the individual's disposition and the situational requirements are incompatible.

TRAIT APPROACHES

The second major approach to the study of personality is the nomothetic, exemplified by "trait" research and its application to behavior. Traits can be defined as words summarizing a set of behaviors, or describing a consistent response to relationships and situations as measured through an assessment instrument (Martin, 1988). It is assumed that, in well-designed and tested assessment instruments, many individuals can validly report social-emotional responses and behaviors that are broadly consistent across situations (some characteristics are less stable across situations than others). Measurement of individual characteristics is widespread and has proved to be quite useful in a number of situations, as when a clinical psychologist or psychiatrist diagnoses a patient and prescribes treatment based on the results of a battery of trait-assessment instruments in addition to a diagnostic interview. Research studies frequently use personality measures to predict behavior under designated situational constraints. Personality assessment may also be extremely useful in placing children or adults in the most effective educational settings or in identifying a cognitive mediator that affects behavior, such as an individual's attribution of intentionality as a reaction to imagined hostility from another.

Since our interests center on multitrait measurement, we briefly mention single-trait approaches and refer the reader to other sources for in-depth discussion.

Single Traits

In this section, we describe the single-trait approach to studying conflict process and outcome. This approach, which seeks to understand social behavior in terms of relatively stable traits or dispositions residing within the individual, is now considered to have limited usefulness unless the characteristics of the situation as well as the nature of the personal dispositions are taken into account. The trait approach typically focuses on one or more enduring predispositions of specific types: motivational tendencies (aggression, power, pride, fear), character traits (authoritarianism, Machiavellianism, locus of control, dogmatism), cognitive tendencies (cognitive simplicity versus complexity, open versus closed mind), values and ideologies (egalitarianism-nonegalitarianism, cooperative-competitive, traditional-modern), self-conceptions and bases of self-esteem, and learned habits and skills of coping. (See Bell and Blakeney, 1977; Neale and Bazerman, 1983; Rotter, 1980; and Stevens, Bavetta, and Gist, 1993, for discussions of some single-trait measures.)

There are several ways in which personality research on individual traits has failed to offer useful and replicable information (Lewicki, Litterer, Minton, and Saunders, 1994). One explanation for the disparate results is that a personality assessment instrument may be too crude to detect subtle effects when other variables affecting the conflict (such as power or cultural differences between the parties) are very strong. Second, research instruments and methods differ widely across studies, leading to inconsistent findings. Third, a considerable portion of the existing personality research has been conducted on college samples—individuals whose personalities are still flexible and changing. Finally, studies have often so limited the choices available to the participants in the conflict that it would be difficult for the participant's behavior to reveal personality differences.

The now-dominant approach to explaining social behavior is one that seeks to understand its regularity in terms of the interacting and reciprocally influencing contribution of both situational and dispositional determinants. There are several well-supported propositions in this approach:

1. Individuals vary considerably in terms of whether they manifest consistency of personality in their social behavior across situations—for example, those who monitor and regulate their behavioral choices on the basis of situational information show relatively little consistency (Snyder and Ickes, 1985).

2. Some situations have "strong" characteristics, in which little individual variation in behavior occurs despite differences in individual traits (Mischel, 1977).

3. A situation can evoke dispositions because of their apparent relevance to it; subsequently, the situation becomes salient as a guide to behavior and permits modes of behaving that are differentially responsive to individual differences (Bem and Lenney, 1976).

4. A situation can evoke self-focusing tendencies that make predispositions salient to the self, and as a consequence, these predispositions can also become influential determinants of behavior in situations where such a self-focus is not evoked.

5. There is a tendency for a congruence between personal disposition and situational characteristics (Deutsch, 1982, 1985) such that someone with a given disposition tends to seek out the type of social situation that fits the disposition; people tend to mold their dispositions to fit a situation that they find difficult to leave or alter. That is, the causal arrow goes both ways between situational characteristics and personality disposition.

Multitrait Measures of Personality

Given the importance of creating clearer definitions and comprehensive measures of personality, a number of researchers over the past two decades have worked to develop reliable multidimensional personality assessment instruments.

Measures of Conflict Style. A number of similar approaches to measuring individual styles of managing conflict have been developed (Blake and Mouton, 1964; Kilmann and Thomas, 1977; Rahim, 1986). Although the early model of Kilmann and Thomas was named "the MODE," these models are now commonly called "dual concern models" (Rubin, Pruitt, and Kim, 1994). They have their origins in Blake and Mouton's two-dimensional "managerial grid," in which a manager's style was characterized in terms of the two separate dimensions of having a "concern for people" and a "concern for production of results."

The dual-concern model of conflict style also has two dimensions: "concern about other's outcomes" and "concern about own outcomes." High concern for the other as well as oneself is linked to a *collaborative problem-solving* style. High concern for self and low concern for the other is connected with a *contending, competitive* approach. High concern for the other and low concern for self is associated with *yielding or submission*. Low concern for both self and the other is linked with *withdrawal, inaction,* or *avoiding* behavior. Pruitt and Carnevale (1993) suggest that *compromise* is associated with a strong conciliatory tendency coupled with moderate concern for self.

There has not yet been much research on the measures of conflict style. As we have suggested in our five propositions, there is reason to believe that conflict behavior is determined by both situational and dispositional influences. Thus, research by Rahim (1986) indicates that a manager in conflict with a supervisor resorts to yielding, while with peers the manager employs compromising, and with subordinates problem solving.

The Five-Factor Model. In an attempt to describe personality more completely than is afforded by individual traits, Costa and McCrae (1985) developed a five-factor model (FFM) of personality, comprising five independent dimensions: neuroticism, extroversion, openness, conscientiousness, and agreeableness.

Neuroticism is a tendency to experience unpleasant emotions. It encompasses six subscales: anxiety, hostility, depression, self-consciousness, impulsiveness, and vulnerability (for example, panic in emergencies). People with strong neurotic tendencies may engage in several problem behaviors during a negotiation. Obsessive compulsives might get so bogged down in detail that it becomes difficult to reach a decision. Histrionics may stay so globally focused that the necessary details of achieving settlement are ignored. People with low neurotic tendencies are less likely to interpret the situation in terms of their own emotional distortion.

Differences in the desire for social activity are incorporated in the *extroversion* scale, which includes such interpersonal traits as warmth, gregariousness, assertiveness, activity, excitement seeking, and positive emotions. An extrovert might be likely to gain attention by attempting to control the negotiation. An introvert is less secure and therefore might avoid a conflict situation.

Openness to experience denotes receptiveness to ideas and experiences, with subscales of openness to fantasy, aesthetics, feelings, actions, ideas, and values. Since feelings are very important to open individuals, they may get overwhelmed by their feelings in negotiation; conversely, they might excel in perspective-taking ability because of their sensitivity. Avoidant subjects are unlikely to be open to feelings.

The dimension of *conscientiousness* refers to achievement striving, competence, and self-discipline. Those low on this scale may be disorganized or lazy,

negligent, and prone to quitting rather than persevering. Th[...]
of this dimension are well prepared, well organized, and st[...]
These characteristics can be useful in constructive negotiation[...]
scientiousness can lead to destructive preoccupation with per[...]

Agreeableness refers to persons who are trusting, generous,[...]
natured. High agreeableness in individuals leads them to ha[...]
concern for others but also may inhibit assertiveness or cause[...]
others. In a conflict situation, this may result in decisions that[...]
own best interests. Low scorers are suspicious, antagonistic,[...]
and self-centered. These individuals are prone to express anger[...]
ations, to be guarded in expressing their own feelings, and to[...]
than cooperate with other people.

Critique of Five-Factor Model. Although the FFM has its share[...]
it has also attracted criticism:

- It is not a scientific description of personality since it doe[...]
  from a priori theory and hypotheses; its terms reflect soci[...]
  scientific evaluations of personality (Block, 1995).

- Personality structure is a property of the individual that is[...]
  organized around the individual's motivation and persona[...]
  structed cognition and values and that varies considerably[...]
  ation (Mischel, 1968). A factor-analysis approach to perso[...]
  represent its dynamic structure.

- The dimensions of the five-factor model are too broad to [...]
  behavior (Mershon and Gorsuch, 1988). Proponents of the[...]
  several studies showing that these factors account for a si[...]
  portion of the variance in personality disorder (Dyce, 1997[...]

However, the FFM dimensions have been reliably demonstra[...]
an impressive number of groups, including children, women and[...]
and white respondents, and in people from such varied lingual an[...]
grounds as Dutch, German, Japanese, Chinese, and Filipino. Fu[...]
personality-trait constructs of the FFM reflect many of the person[...]
used in psychotherapy, the difference being that the FFM dimen[...]
testable in research and cover a fuller range of human behavior[...]
butes of personality emerging from the study of psychopathology[...]

We focus here on the five-factor trait model to offer informat[...]
resolution because it is

- More comprehensive than other trait models of personality[...]
  rating a wide range of human response and behavior—mo[...]
  ventories can be subsumed within its dimensions

ormal behaviors as well as the extremes to be found in
isorder

ariety of languages and cultures

approach that is straightforward and fairly easily understood

h nonpersonality factors as cognitive distortion, dysfunctional
valuation, intelligence, and situational demands need to be ex-
th the five personality factors to fully account for behavior.
sing the multitrait approach would be to lose sight of its merit
sons without an advanced degree in personality psychology or
In methodologically appropriate use, the FFM appears to offer
ation about the conflict resolution process for practitioners. As
ow, Sandy and Boardman (1999) conducted research on the ef-
ality on conflict resolution behavior using the subscale break-
M.

d Conflict Resolution Strategies. For our research, 165 gradu-
ith no conflict resolution training experience, were asked to fill
I-R five-factor model questionnaire (Costa and McCrae, 1985;
, and Dye, 1991). Following this, subjects were asked to select
they had experienced during the previous three months. Each
successive weeks, they were given a comprehensive question-
be one conflict (open-ended questions) and report the strategies
andle it (using both open-ended questions and the MODE in-
ey also characterized their relationship with the other person in
d, using five-point rating scales, indicated the size and impor-
nflict. In addition, they reported whether or not the conflict was
whether the conflict strengthened or weakened their relationship.
f conflict reported included relationship issues, another person's
own expectations, discourteous or annoying behavior, disagree-
what should be done, one's own failure to meet another's expec-
eing offended by what another person said. Conflicts were with
ficant others, friends, acquaintances, and people in the workplace
s or subordinates).

reliability analyses of the MODE (Kilmann and Thomas, 1977) in-
subjects used four strategies for handling conflict: problem solv-
ng, avoidance, and manipulation. Problem solving consisted of
s as "I sought a mutually beneficial solution" and "I tried to un-
or her." Contending strategies included "I used threats" and "I
n my sense of humor." Avoidance covered items such as "I tried
subject" and "I denied that there was any problem in the con-
manipulation included "I criticized an aspect of his or her per-

sonality" and "I told him or her how to behave in the future." The manipulation scale items were unrelated to specific personality traits or the closeness of the relationship, but they were significantly associated with what the conflict was about: it was used to a significant degree when the conflict was about the other person's failure to meet one's own expectations.

Type of relationship had an effect on use of avoidance. It occurred frequently with family or friends. (This pattern was also obtained in a recent study on latent conflict in the workplace; Boardman and Sandy, 1999.) Contending was used to a greater extent with significant others than with supervisors or subordinates. Finally, conflicts over the relationship and what to do in a situation occurred to a great extent with people one is close to; annoying behavior was frequent with people with whom one is not particularly close.

Personality "facet" scales from the FFM dimensions formed "predictive clusters" of individual characteristics that tended to be associated with the dominant strategy used in the conflict reported. For example, those who used problem-solving strategies scored high on "positive emotions" (extroversion) and "order" (conscientiousness). The problem-solving strategy occurred most frequently in close relationships when the incidence of conflict was low. As might be expected, a problem-solving approach led to a greater number of resolved conflicts than did other strategies and significantly strengthened the relationship. A combination of low openness, low agreeableness, and low conscientiousness was significantly related to use of contending as a conflict resolution strategy, which would be predicted by theory. A combination of high neuroticism, low openness, high agreeableness, and low conscientiousness was significantly related to use of avoidance as a conflict resolution strategy, also predicted by theory. These findings provide empirical support for the importance of personality theory in studying conflict resolution.

USING KNOWLEDGE OF PERSONALITY AT THE BARGAINING TABLE

Few would contest the need for continued research on personality. Yet the consistency with which personality types have already been identified in literature and psychology should afford some confidence in their validity. Specific personality types frequently show similar problems in conflict management, in their unconscious motivation, and in the type of conflict resolution strategy they use to handle a conflict situation (Heitler, 1990). Awareness of these patterns helps the conflict resolution practitioner anticipate problems in the negotiation process, intervene effectively, build better communication between negotiating parties, and assist negotiators to a satisfactory and lasting settlement. This knowledge helps the conflict resolution practitioner uncover the driving forces behind certain locked positions, such as inability to make or commit to an agreement. Understanding personality needs may be a key factor in resolving some supposedly intractable conflicts and in creating a stable, long-term solution.

"SUBSTANTIVE NEED" AND "PERSONALITY NEED"

Frequently, conflicts are initiated and perpetuated by two types of underlying need: conscious, substantive conflict needs (what the conflicting parties want to get out of the negotiation) underlying the positions being taken; and psychological needs of personality (who the person is—the subconscious or unconscious forces that we refer to as "personality needs").

Little is usually said about the underlying personality needs that may initiate the conflict or block a negotiated settlement. Substantive conflict need is often quite amenable to negotiation, but personality need may remain unrecognized by all parties. Fundamentally, a conflict always reflects both types of need, that is, the substantive issues involved in the conflict as well as the issues relating to personality (such as the identity that the individual is seeking to maintain and protect in the conflict situation).

Personal identity is the subjective sense of who one really is and how one wants other people to see oneself (Erikson, 1968). It is also inextricably bound with one's communal culture or social identity and represents the important affiliations one has. Identity conflict, as compared to interest conflict, may be described as relatively intangible and based in the history, psychology, culture, values, and beliefs of the group with which one identifies (Rothman, 1997). Through identification with their groups, individuals often obtain a feeling of security and recognition.

Identity issues frequently arise as a result of insensitive behavior during conflict that unwittingly challenges the individual's cherished self-identity and that of his cherished group(s). Prenegotiation dialogue to establish respect between disputants and maintain individual dignity may be helpful in increasing sensitivity to one another's psychological needs and to prevent unwitting challenges to the other's self-identity. Knowledge of personality can help disputants become aware of one another's psychological needs.

Table 14.2 shows predictable resolution strategies in conflict situations for dominating personality characteristics, presenting for each psychodynamic personality descriptor its most relevant corresponding level on the FFM dimensions of personality that we have discussed.

In addition, the table indicates the likely underlying psychological needs motivating each personality as well as a variety of potential negotiation problems that may result with each one. As previously described, note that someone

Table 14.2. Potential Negotiation Problems as a Function of Personality.

Conflict Resolution Strategy	Therapeutic Personality	NEO Personality	Psychological Needs	Potential Negotiation Problems
Fight (contend)	Paranoia	Low agreeableness Low openness High neuroticism	Respect; safety from blame or criticism	Projection of own feelings onto others; rigid black-and-white thinking; anger; difficulty accepting new ideas; withholds information
	Narcissism	Low agreeableness High extroversion	Attention; special privileges	Self-centered; lack of empathy; demandingness; tendency to control or coerce others
	High extroversion Histrionic	Low conscientiousness High openness	Attention	Escalation of feelings to be heard, dominate, or gain control
Flight (withdraw)	Addictive	Low extroversion High agreeableness Low openness Low conscientiousness	Safety/security	Usually unaware of extent of engaging in escape maneuvers to avoid conflict; may change topic, physically withdraw, and so on; tries to avoid making decisions

Table 14.2. Potential Negotiation Problems as a Function of Personality (continued).

Conflict Resolution Strategy	Therapeutic Personality	NEO Personality	Psychological Needs	Potential Negotiation Problems
	Obsessive-compulsive	Low extroversion Low openness High conscientiousness	To be correct	May be stuck in details through dutifulness and deliberation; high in harm avoidance
Flight or inaction	Avoidant or anxious	Low extroversion High agreeableness High neuroticism	Protection from anxiety; fear of rejection	Fear of being shamed or blamed; may be emotionally overreactive; may have tendency to catastrophize problems; tendency to avoid making decisions
Submit	Dependent	High neuroticism Low extroversion Low conscientiousness	To be taken care of; love and attention	Easily gives up what is wanted; feels resigned and negative toward self and others
Problem solving	Integrated	Moderate scores on NEO scales	Expressed in conflict "need"	May become frustrated by difficult negotiator

Note: The set of attributes that define each FFM domain can be grouped in a variety of ways to allow comprehensive interpretation of personality in an individual case. Since in-depth understanding such as is required in psychotherapy is not the goal in conflict resolution, it is sufficient for our purposes to pay attention to the five broadly reliable dispositions that are included in the table. High or low scores on one or more of these dimensions can facilitate a practitioner's understanding of a disputant in a conflict. We can use any especially dominant traits to forewarn of potential problems and to alert the need for prevention intervention, before the negotiation or mediation becomes bogged down in differences of personal style.

falling on the high or low end of the five specific dimensions is most likely to present a predictable type of problem during the negotiation process. For example, an individual very high in conscientiousness, and who works very earnestly in the early stages of negotiation, may have difficulty making choices in the decision-making stage of problem solving, particularly someone falling into the "obsessive" category. Parties who have a very low degree of conscientiousness, on the other hand, may be agreeable throughout the process and quickly come to settlement terms, prior to having their priority needs understood and met. Consequently, they may leave the negotiation without a sense of commitment to the solution since their personality needs have not been met and their natural tendency is to be somewhat lax in follow-through. The traits making up personality frequently lead to a tendency to use specific strategies in handling conflict. This helps explain the surprise of a negotiation that has been going well suddenly seeming to fall apart. It must be remembered, however, that more than one personality dimension may be strongly influencing the individual's decision process.

CONCLUSION

From our presentation in this chapter, it is obvious that individual differences in personality can strongly affect behavior in a conflict situation. The substantial amount of knowledge acquired by students of personality is potentially relevant to conflict practitioners. However, the fact that the field of conflict has reflected primarily a social psychological perspective has led to neglect of the existing knowledge and to only sparse attempts to develop new knowledge through systematic study of the effects of personality on conflict style and behavior.

We draw two implications. First, if the field of conflict study and conflict training is to progress, much more research is necessary on the effects of personality on conflict management and on learning how to manage conflict constructively. Second, systematic study of the existing knowledge of personality should become a component in training conflict practitioners. With such knowledge, practitioners could develop differentiated strategies for training people with various dispositions as well as for managing those who have the dysfunctional personality patterns that often lead to destructive conflict. However, it should be clearly recognized that such training does not equip the conflict practitioner to provide psychotherapy to disputants, a task that falls in the domain of a qualified psychotherapist.

References

Bandura, A. *Social Foundations of Thought and Action: A Social Cognitive Approach.* Upper Saddle River, N.J.: Prentice Hall, 1986.

Bell, E. C., and Blakeney, R. N. "Personality Correlates of Conflict Resolution Modes." *Human Relations,* 1977, *30,* 849–857.

Bem, S. L., and Lenney, E. "Sex Typing and the Avoidance of Cross-Sex Behavior." *Journal of Personality and Social Psychology,* 1976, *33,* 48–54.

Blake, R. R., and Mouton, J. S. *The Managerial Grid.* Houston: Gulf, 1964.

Block, J. "A Contrarian View of the Five-Factor Approach to Personality Description." *Psychological Bulletin,* 1995, *117,* 187–215.

Boardman, S. K., and Sandy, S. V. "The Effects of Power, Personality, and Gender on Conflict Resolution: Sustaining Latent Conflict in Organizations." Unpublished manuscript, 1999.

Burton, J. W. *Conflict: Human Needs Theory.* New York: St. Martin's Press, 1990.

Costa, P. T., Jr., and McCrae, R. R. *The NEO Personality Inventory Manual.* Odessa, Fla.: Psychological Assessment Resources, 1985.

Costa, P. T., Jr., McCrae, R. R., and Dye, D. A. "Facet Scales for Agreeableness and Conscientiousness: A Revision of the NEO Personality Inventory." *Personality and Individual Differences,* 1991, *12,* 887–898.

Deutsch, M. "Interdependence and Psychological Orientation." In V. J. Derlaga and J. Grzelak (eds.), *Cooperation and Helping Behavior: Theories and Research.* Orlando: Academic Press, 1982.

Deutsch, M. *Distributive Justice: A Social Psychological Perspective.* New Haven: Yale University, 1985.

Dyce, J. A. "The Big Five Factors of Personality and Their Relationship to Personality Disorders." *Journal of Clinical Psychology,* 1997, *53,* 587–593.

Erikson, E. H. *Identity: Youth and Crisis.* New York: Norton, 1968.

Fenichel, O. *The Psychoanalytic Theory of Neurosis.* New York: Norton, 1945.

Freud, A. *The Ego and the Mechanisms of Defence.* London: Hogarth, 1937.

Heitler, S. M. *From Conflict to Resolution: Strategies for Diagnosis and Treatment of Distressed Individuals, Couples, and Families.* New York: Norton, 1990.

Kelman, H. C. "Interactive Problem Solving: A Social Psychological Approach to Conflict Resolution." In W. Klassen (ed.), *Dialogue Toward Interfaith Understanding.* Jerusalem: Ecumenical Institute for Theological Research, 1986.

Kilmann, R. H., and Thomas, K. W. "Developing a Forced-Choice Measure of Conflict-Handling Behavior: The Mode Instrument." *Educational and Psychological Measurement,* 1977, *37,* 309–325.

Lewicki, R. J., Litterer, J. A., Minton, J. W., and Saunders, D. M. *Negotiation.* (2nd ed.) Burr Ridge, Ill.: Irwin, 1994.

Martin, R. P. *Assessment of Personality and Behavior Problems: Infancy Through Adolescence.* New York: Guilford Press, 1988.

McClelland, D. C. *Assessing Human Motivation.* New York: General Learning Press, 1971.

McClelland, D. C., Atkinson, J. W., Clark, R. A., and Lowell, E. L. *The Achievement Motive.* New York: Appleton-Century-Crofts, 1953.

Mershon, B., and Gorsuch, R. L. "Number of Factors in the Personality Sphere: Does Increase in Factors Increase Predictability of Real-Life Criteria?" *Journal of Personality and Social Psychology,* 1988, *55,* 675–680.

Mischel, W. *Personality and Assessment.* New York: Wiley, 1968.

Mischel, W. "On the Future of Personality Measurement." *American Psychologist,* 1977, *32,* 246–254.

Murray, H. A. *Explorations in Personality.* New York: Oxford University Press, 1951.

Neale, M. A., and Bazerman, M. H. "The Role of Perspective-Taking Ability in Negotiating Under Different Forms of Arbitration." *Industrial and Labor Relations Review,* 1983, *36,* 378–388.

Pruitt, D. G., and Carnevale, P. J. *Negotiation and Social Conflict.* Buckingham, England: Open University Press, 1993.

Rahim, M. A. (ed.). *Managing Conflict in Organizations.* New York: Praeger, 1986.

Rothman, J. *Resolving Identity-Based Conflicts in Nations, Organizations, and Communities.* San Francisco: Jossey-Bass, 1997.

Rotter, J. B. "Interpersonal Trust, Trustworthiness, and Gullibility." *American Psychologist,* 1980, *35,* 1–7.

Rubin, J. Z., Pruitt, D. G., and Kim, S. H. *Social Conflict: Escalation, Stalemate, and Settlement.* (2nd ed.) New York: McGraw-Hill, 1994.

Sandy, S. V., and Boardman, S. K. "The Influence of Personality on Conflict Resolution Styles and Choices." Unpublished manuscript, 1999.

Snyder, M., and Ickes, W. "Personality and Social Behavior." In G. Lindszey and E. Aronson (eds.), *The Handbook of Social Psychology,* Vol. 2: *Special Fields and Applications.* (3rd ed.) New York: Random House, 1985.

Stevens, C. K., Bavetta, A. G., and Gist, M. E. "Gender Differences in the Acquisition of Salary Negotiation Skills: The Role of Goals, Self-Efficacy, and Perceived Control." *Journal of Applied Psychology,* 1993, 78, 723–735.

Wish, M., Deutsch, M., and Kaplan, S. J. "Perceived Dimensions of Interpersonal Relations." *Journal of Personality and Social Psychology,* 1976, *33,* 409–420.

CHAPTER FIFTEEN

The Development of Conflict Resolution Skills in Children

Preschool to Adolescence

Sandra V. Sandy

Kathleen M. Cochran

Anna Hall considered manners more important than feelings, and beauty most important of all. From the beginning, she made Eleanor feel homely and unloved, always outside the closed circle that embraced her two younger brothers. Anna mocked her daughter's appearance and chided her manner, calling her "Granny" because she was so serious, even at the age of two. Before company Eleanor was embarrassed to hear her mother explain that she was a shy and solemn child. And Eleanor wrote, "I never smiled."
—Cook (1992)

I n early childhood, feelings and emotions are the primary intellectual puzzles that children are required to solve before they can successfully maneuver through the complicated cognitive tasks of later development. If the emotional components of learning are improperly laid in the brain's pathways, a variety of problems may result. Although Eleanor Roosevelt managed, through a loving father, caring teachers, and a privileged social position, to overcome her mother's put-downs and lead an extraordinarily productive life, she suffered emotional pain and struggled against feelings of insecurity most of her life. Consistent, small put-downs often have sizable negative emotional and motivational consequences for young children, who, during this period of their lives, need to be acquiring confidence in their own ability to influence the environment.

THE IMPORTANCE OF SOCIAL-EMOTIONAL LEARNING AND CONFLICT MANAGEMENT

Poor grades and dropping out of school can frequently be traced to lack of social-emotional skills. Social competence and appropriate behavior are strong and consistent predictors of academic outcomes, and the social climate of the classroom appears to be a powerful motivator of academic as well as cooperative classroom behavior. In fact, social and emotional variables predict achievement as well as or better than intellectual ability, sensory deficits, or neurological factors (Horn and Packard, 1985). Recent research shows a strong interlinkage among social-emotional and conflict resolution skills, traditional intellectual skills (reading, writing, and math), and success in the adult workplace (Deutsch, 1993; Gardner, 1993; Goleman, 1998; Gottman, 1997; Jensen, 1998; Shore, 1997). Social-emotional and conflict resolution skills are based in cooperation, communication, sense of community, appreciation of diversity and values, empathy, perspective taking, self-control, concentration, self-efficacy, creativity, and problem solving (Jensen, 1998).

As described in this chapter, the pedagogical approach to social-emotional learning emanates from a multidisciplinary perspective that integrates the most compelling findings from the fields of neuroscience, education, and psychology concerning developmental, cognitive, and individual personality traits. One conclusion, however, clearly stands out from the converging evidence on social-emotional skills development: *early childhood is the time when the building blocks for all later development and intellectual growth are set in place.* Since most conflict resolution programs for children concentrate on middle childhood or adolescence, our primary emphasis here is on early childhood and the need for a broader and different instructional perspective for children at this stage of development.

We present the rationale for developing social-emotional skills in children within the framework of conflict resolution training, a social skill of particular importance for children and adults. Conflict is a desirable opportunity for learning in a classroom since its effective resolution requires successfully acquiring all the skills usually defined within the social-emotional learning lexicon. How we learn to handle conflict determines the positive or negative role it has in constructing our feelings, our intellect, and our personality.

Although there are a variety of ways to settle a conflict (litigation, arbitration, distributive bargaining, integrative negotiation, and the like), we refer to constructive or principled negotiation throughout this chapter. This reflects our view that this type of conflict interaction best promotes emotional and cognitive growth in children and adolescents.

Most people are well aware of the general differences among preschoolers, elementary school-age children, and adolescents; however, not everyone has a solid understanding of all the important cognitive, emotional, and physical capabilities that differentiate these groups. In addition to our discussion of early childhood, we also briefly cover developmental issues and conflict management in middle childhood (ages six to twelve) and adolescence (ages twelve or thirteen to adulthood). The discussion at each level focuses on how developmental differences should guide our approach to teaching children age-appropriate skills.

In each section, we discuss conflict resolution programs that are useful for the relevant age group. The final section assesses how well we are doing currently in our efforts to reach children effectively and suggests future directions in children's conflict resolution programs as well as improvements to be made in terms of curricula and systematic evaluation.

EARLY CHILDHOOD

First, we refer to representative developmental theorists (Piaget, Kohlberg, Selman, Erikson) to guide us through the classic stage theories concerning social cognition and emotional development. Although recent research suggests children may know more than they tell us and that some stages may appear earlier or show more inconsistency than previously thought, there is still much that is useful in these theories. Second, we cover comparatively recent work on neo-Piagetian theories: minor modification of Piaget's theory (De Vries and Zan, 1994; Flavell, 1990); major modification of Piaget's stages in the form of social-emotional competence domains (Elias and others, 1997); and biosocial-behavioral shift, a move from set stages to developmental advancement allowing the characteristics of various stages to coexist (Fischer, Bullock, Rotenberg, and Raya, 1993). Other important influences include theoretical perspectives concerning social context (Ceci, 1990), social cognition (Mize, 1995; Siegler, 1991), and neuroscientific discoveries regarding synaptic connections in the brain (Jensen, 1998; Shore, 1997).

There are other theorists and researchers who have influenced the design of our curriculum activities, for example, Vygotsky and Bronfenbrenner, but we mention them only briefly because of space limitations. These postclassic theorists add significantly to knowledge about the fundamental elements of school readiness and conflict management: innate temperament and individuality, emotional control, role taking, empathy, perspective taking, moral reasoning, problem solving, and the interconnection between social-emotional learning and academic achievement.

Both classic and postclassic theorists have been of great help in creating the Peaceful Kids ECSEL Program at the International Center for Cooperation and Conflict Resolution, Teachers College, Columbia University, in 1998. For example, our research supports a fluid sequence in cognition and learning; we find stagelike changes in early childhood are rarely straightforward. The context and emotional state of children at particular times determine whether they act according to a new stage or reflect characteristics of an earlier one. This fluidity appears to be true at later developmental stages as well. Finally, a brief outline of the latest neurological discoveries regarding the brain's functioning offers information about the critical timing and most effective methods of learning during early childhood.

Stage Theories of Early Childhood Development

Kohlberg called early childhood the stage of heteronomous morality, a time referred to by Piaget as the preoperational stage of development, or morality of
constraint (see Tables 15.1 and 15.2). Children in this stage are subject to externally imposed rules and adhere unquestioningly to rules and the directives
of powerful adults. Their motives and those of other children and adults are dis-
regarded; only outcomes are important.

Developing a "Self." In a Piagetian, and neo-Piagetian, constructivist approach
(De Vries and Zan, 1994), a critical developmental task for a young child is decentering, that is, constructing a self separate from others and developing the

Table 15.1. Piaget's Social Cognitive Approach to Children's Development.

Stage	Description
Sensorimotor (birth to age 2)	Centration describes this stage. Children focus on the most salient aspect of an event. It is most evident in their egocentrism, seeing the world in terms of their own point of view.
Preoperational (2 to 6)	Children can now use symbols, words, and gestures to represent reality; objects no longer have to be present to be thought about. On the other hand, children have diffi-culty differentiating their perspective from another's point of view and are unsure about causal relations. Emotions: 4-year-olds can usually distinguish between real and displayed feelings but are unable to provide justi-fications for their judgments.
Concrete operational (6 to 12)	Operational thought enables children to combine, sepa-rate, order, and transform objects. However, these opera-tions must be carried out in the presence of the objects and events.
Formal operational (12 to 19)	Adolescents become capable of systematic thought. They are interested in abstract ideas and the process of thought itself.

Note: One of the major critiques of Piaget is that researchers are finding evidence that children are actually more competent in a number of ways than Piaget thought. Neo-Piagetians retain Piaget's theories
of stage but criticize the postulation of an invariant sequence in stages. On the basis of information-
processing theory and cognitive science perspectives, many developmentalists agree that cognition develops in varying domains over a period of time rather than in separate stages.

Table 15.2. Comparison of Social Cognitive Approaches to Development.

Kohlberg: Moral Stages	Damon: Justice in Dividing Resources	Selman: Perspective Taking
Level 1: Preconventional		
Early childhood (heteronomous morality) *Stage 1 (End of early childhood to beginning of middle childhood)*	*Level 0-A (4 and under)*	*Egocentric impulsive level (0)* *(Ages 3 to 6)*[a]
The morality of obedience: adherence to rules backed by punishment	Justice is getting what one wishes: "I should go because I want to."	Negotiation through unreflective physical means (fight or flight); shared experience through unreflective imitation
	Level 0-B (ages 4 to 5) Justifications are based on external factors such as size and gender: "I should get more because I'm bigger."	
Middle childhood (instrumental morality) *Stage 2 (ages 7 to 10 or 11)*	*Level 1-A (ages 5 to 7)*	*Unilateral one-way level (1)* *(Ages 5 to 9)*
Justice is seen as an exchange system: you give as much as others give you	Justice is always strict equality, everyone gets the same.	Negotiation through one-way commands or orders or through automatic obedience
	Level 1-B (ages 6 to 9) A notion of reciprocity develops: people should be paid back in kind for doing good or bad things	Shared experience through expressive enthusiasm without concern for reciprocity

Level II: Conventional

Stage 3 Social-relational morality
(10 or 11 to beginning of adolescence)
Children believe that shared feelings and agreements are more important than self-interest.

Adolescence
Stage 4 Law and order

Laws govern what is right.

Level III: Principled
Stages 5 and 6
(Adolescence to adulthood)
Principled, postconventional understanding

Level 2-A
(ages 8 to 10)
Moral relativity—learning how different persons can have different yet equally valid claims for justice

Level 2-B
(ages 10 and up)
Choices take account of two or more people's (as well as situational) demands. There is feeling that all persons should be given their due (does not necessarily mean equality in treatment)

Reciprocal reflective level (2)
(Ages 7 to 12)
Negotiation through cooperation using persuasion or deference; shared experience through mutual reflection on similar perceptions and experiences

Mutual third-person level (3)
(Beginning in adolescence)
Negotiation through strategies integrating needs of self and other.
Shared experience through empathic reflective process

Societal perspective taking level (4)
(Late adolescence to adulthood)
Individuals are capable of taking a generalized perspective of morality.

Sources: Adapted from Kohlberg, 1976; Damon, 1980; Selman, 1980. Damon contests the idea of stages as an invariant sequence since children regress in level and show inconsistent levels of performance from one testing time to the next.

[a] Recent research suggests that preschoolers may know more than they can tell us and so this level may need revision.

capacity to think in terms of other people's attitudes toward oneself. Within this theoretical framework, as in others, *well-managed conflict is one of the most important factors in overcoming egocentrism and acquiring new knowledge about oneself and others.* Naturally occurring conflict is an opportunity for children to develop social, emotional, intellectual, and moral skills by working through their disagreements.

The Influence of Friends. Contrary to what was previously believed, peer relationships in early childhood are now seen as an important factor in promoting perspective taking (the ability to analyze a situation in terms of emotions, intentions, and reasons from both sides of an issue) and moral development. Equal peer relationships give children a chance to experience reciprocity, which greatly assists them in perspective taking and problem solving.

Friends influence children through their attitudes, behavior, and personal characteristics. The quality of the friendship is important: positive, mutually supportive, and cooperative relationships are, not surprisingly, more constructive than those characterized by put-downs and hostile rivalry. Friendships positively affect a child's school adjustment in three ways:

1. Attitude toward classes (cooperative students value classes, teachers, and what they are learning)

2. Classroom behavior (cooperative students are rarely disruptive)

3. Academic achievement (cooperative students learn what is taught and receive high grades and test scores)

Role of Conflict. During early childhood, the parent often pleads: "How do I change my child's behavior so that she is more agreeable?" The answer is to recognize that oppositional, conflict-provoking behavior usually represents an important developmental step. What needs to be changed is how the child's behavior is viewed, and in particular how it is handled by the parent.

Conflict serves different purposes according to the level of early childhood development. During the second and third years, it corresponds with children's developing autonomy. The increasing assertiveness of the child is to be desired rather than socialized into compliance with parental demands. Between the ages of three and seven, constructive conflict management helps to coordinate play. According to the theorists in Table 15.2, there is, in early childhood, little full-scale perspective taking. However, incipient perspective taking is readily apparent in the child's empathic response to others, and a number of current theorists believe young children are more capable of perspective taking than classic stage theories allowed (see the later section "Empathy and Perspective Taking"). Children are often seen comforting friends who are upset or mirroring the emotion of others around them. Skills training in recognizing emotion in self and others encourages development of empathy, a precursor to perspective taking.

Selman (see Table 15.2) refers to the "egocentric, impulsive stage" of development as representing the primitive foundation of social perspective taking. According to this view, young children may recognize that other children display different preferences, but they lack the capacity to distinguish between their own perception of an event or person and that of another child. Neither do preschoolers see the cause-effect relationship in other people between thinking and behaving. This often leads to confusion over cause-effect relationships, such as whether punishment following misbehavior is the effect of misbehavior or its cause. Without guidance, children are likely to feel that they did something wrong *because* they are punished but fail to understand precisely what they did wrong. (Note that some modern theorists feel young children are more capable of perspective taking than stated above.)

The egocentric stage of social perspective taking corresponds to Kohlberg's level 1 (preconventional heteronomous morality) and Damon's level 0-A (justice is getting what one wishes) and level 0-B (justifications are based on external factors such as size or gender). Children at stage 0 view a conflict situation as being an event where *one cannot do what one wants because of how the other person is behaving.* Conflict resolution thus consists of fight ("Hit her!") or flight ("Go play with another toy or do something else").

Developmental Abilities and Neural Activity

Recent research in neuroscience has made significant progress in mapping how a child's mind develops and learning takes place (Jensen, 1998; Shore, 1997). There is no longer any question about the fundamental role of nurture in learning. Children get smarter as they interact with their environment; stimulation from important others promotes essential brain activity. The interplay between neural activity and learning builds personality and temperament. Negative patterns can be interrupted during the brain's high-activity stage in early childhood, and patterns promoting the child's emotional, social, and cognitive well-being can be "automatized" by learning and frequent practice. Neuroscientific research shows that

- The first forty-eight months of a child's life are more important to brain development than previously thought. In fact, much of the brain's infrastructure is in place by age four. By this age, children have already mapped out, through repetition, significant aspects of their cognitive and behavioral repertoire.

- Early experience at home and school critically influences the ability to learn and the capacity to regulate emotion.

- Across all ethnic groups, *the human brain benefits significantly from good experience and teaching,* particularly during the first four years.

- Children learn in the context of important relationships. Caregiving and stimulation help children develop capacity for empathy, perspective taking, emotional regulation, behavioral control, problem solving, and optimal cognitive functioning.

- There are key emotional milestones that children must pass at specific developmental points, particularly in early childhood.

Regarding this last point, those children who do not pass the milestones appropriately are at risk of retaining such negative traits as impulsivity, immature emotional functioning, behavioral problems, and even propensity to violence. Instruction in early childhood must be flexible to take into account a wide range of individual differences in temperament, personality, environment, interests, and variation across developmental levels.

Individual Differences That Affect Socioemotional Competence

Every child is born with a certain temperament, or characteristic way of responding emotionally to the world. It is important to accept temperament for what it is and to focus the skills development involved in conflict resolution toward helping each child make the most effective use of his innate characteristics.

Temperament. Conflict resolution is often helpful for so-called difficult children; however, a child with a serious behavior or emotional problem may often require an intensive, therapeutic approach to manage the difficulty. In any case, labeling a child (for example, as a troublemaker or a pushover) is to be strictly avoided since the label may stick and be difficult to change even if the child learns to cope with the temperamental traits that cause trouble. Another factor to consider is the considerable difference in significance of a temperamental trait depending on the age level. A child's so-called negative traits at one developmental stage (for example, hyperactivity) may turn into positive characteristics at a later stage (such as a high energy level in adulthood). The critical point is to accept the child's temperament *as it is,* without labeling it or being judgmental, while working to help the child to grow and develop in a positive direction.

Temperamental differences are seen in such traits as activity level; fearfulness; persistence; shyness; positive or negative mood; regularity of eating and sleeping; sensitivity to bright light, loud noises, or touch; adaptability to new situations; distractibility; irritability and anger level; and impulsivity.

Emotion. Emotion influences most of our behavior. A threatening situation (a hostile look from a classmate) may trigger intense emotion, which creates action that occurs without thinking. This is why students need to be taught emotional-management strategies (stop and think before responding, for example) repetitively, so they can become automatic responses. Achieving socioemotional competence requires children to develop awareness of both their own emotional states and those of others. The key to developing this awareness is acquiring the communication skills involved in clearly expressing one's own emotions as well as in effective listening and attending to the other's verbal and nonverbal emotional expression. Such skills are fostered by constructive conflict experiences.

Although emotion in Western cultures has often been considered irrational in relation to cognition, neuroscientists now believe that *emotions provide information in much the same way logic does.* Emotions also direct attention and create meaning using their own memory pathways. In addition to music, games, drama, or storytelling, there are other ways to engage emotion in learning, such as ritual clapping, cheers, chants, or songs to mark the beginning or completion of a project. It is important for adults to model a love of learning, letting children share the ideas and activities that excite them. It is also important for students to show and discuss their work with one another and tell what they like and dislike about it. Whenever emotions are involved following a learning experience, there is greater recall and accuracy about the information learned (McGaugh and others, 1995).

Empathy and Perspective Taking. As rage fuels aggression, so empathy inspires understanding, sharing, helping, and cooperation. Empathy first begins in infancy, when even a two-week-old child may cry upon hearing another child cry. Many believe empathy at this stage is an innate reflex. The second stage in developing empathy is *comforting behavior,* which occurs during the second year of life. At this age, children begin to understand that it is the other person who is distressed; this understanding may lead them to engage in efforts to comfort. Since a two-year-old is not skilled at recognizing the other person's point of view, the child's attempt usually reflects what he himself finds comforting, such as giving Mommy a toy or his blankie if he sees that his mother is distressed. The third stage occurs roughly at three to five years of age: at this age, a child shows more empathy to the distress of a friend than to another (Farver and Branstetter, 1994). Also at this age, increasing language skills enable children not only to empathize with people in stories, pictures, or film but also to take into account differences between their level of knowledge and that of younger children. This indicates less egocentrism than presumed by Piaget. In fact, current knowledge of children's competencies in early childhood leads us to suspect that they are far more capable of perspective taking than they have been given credit. Developmental capabilities appear to have a much wider age variation than previously thought.

Two important ways to promote social-emotional learning of empathy and perspective taking as well as other prosocial behaviors include *explicit modeling* by adults and *induction.* Modeling refers to adults behaving in ways they desire the child to imitate. Induction refers to parents and teachers giving explanations that appeal to the child's pride, desire to be grown up, and concern for others.

Motivation and Personality

Dweck (1996) has demonstrated that major patterns of adaptive or maladaptive behavior (such as a mastery orientation or a helplessness orientation to tasks) are affected by children's implicit theories or self-conceptions about their ability. For example, some children believe their intelligence is a fixed entity; others believe it can be increased by effort. Those holding an entity theory are oriented toward proving the adequacy of their performance in order to win approval of their intelligence. The latter group, adhering to an incremental theory, are more interested in pursuing learning goals whereby they can increase their ability. These latter children, who focus on such controllable factors as effort, are likely to persist when experiencing setback or failure (for further discussion, see Chapter Thirteen). Implicit motivational theories do not exist only in the intellectual realm; as we have already mentioned, they are paralleled in social interaction as well. School adjustment depends on both social and academic goals and abilities: having prosocial goals and successful peer relationships are critical factors in promoting interest and achievement in school.

In addition to implicit theories about ability, several other factors influence the choice of a goal: its importance, the interpretation of an event (attribution), knowledge of strategies for reaching the goal, and environmental variables. For example, aggressive children are bound by the importance of control and dominance. They have more confidence than other children that they can master events involving aggression. In social situations, they interpret the actions of their peers, even when accidental or ambiguous, as being hostile; thus, the behavior of others becomes provocative and inspires a need for retaliation. Frequently, these children lack strategies for interacting successfully with peers. They do not know that it is important to show interest in what a peer is doing or that they need to cooperate with other people in playtime activities. Similarly, children who fear or experience rejection by others are caught up in the importance of avoiding rejection. These children are handicapped by lack of group entry skills, such as knowing how to express interest in others' activities and to suggest cooperative ways of joining the ongoing group process. Environmental variables refer primarily to the atmosphere established in the home or classroom and whether it promotes adaptive or maladaptive behavior.

Parents, teachers, and other adults play a major role in determining what kind of theories children develop about their personality characteristics. They do this mainly in two ways. One is by the implicit theories and explicit explanations that adults offer for their own behavior and personality; children imitate adults and internalize these explanations for their own personality and behavior. The second way is to explain the child's behavior and personality characteristics. Thus, a parent who explains the child's behavior by presumably fixed characteristics such as genes, ability, or temperament rather than malleable characteristics such as knowledge, effort, or mood often stimulates the child to use similar explanations. As we have already stated, the type of theory that children develop about their personality and behavior greatly affects their academic learning and emotional development.

Adults also need to consider the environmental or context variables that may be changed to help children, especially those who are socially isolated or aggressive. An effective way of doing this involves decreasing competition among children and promoting cooperative learning activities (Johnson and Johnson, 1991). In the classroom, having children work cooperatively in small groups promotes common achievement goals and enhances the motivation to learn through group acceptance and support. Children require coaching in the various strategies that can be used to achieve their goals. Teaching these strategies is a step-by-step process that involves instruction and many practice sessions.

Self-Control. Self-control is a critical skill that enables a child to inhibit his initial impulses; an example mentioned earlier is to stop and think before acting. (See also Chapter Twelve.) Basically, there are four forms of inhibition to be mastered (Maccoby, 1980):

1. *Movement:* prior to age six or seven, children have difficulty in stopping an action already in progress
2. *Emotions:* before age four, young children have little control over the intensity of their emotion
3. *Reflection:* before age six or so, children commonly fail to engage in the reflection necessary to perform well
4. *Gratification:* children under twelve often have difficulty in refusing immediate gratification to wait for a better choice later

Summary. Differentiating cause and effect, empathy, and perspective taking, along with self-regulation and problem solving, are among the key elements of positive conflict management. Modern theorists and researchers find the young child to be far more capable of learning these skills than did their classic predecessors. However, children do not learn skills merely by observation; they require instruction in cause-and-effect sequences before they can separate right from wrong, or unintentional from intended harm. Equally important, children must learn empathy and perspective taking before they can become aware of the effects their actions have on others. These lessons need to be conveyed through gentleness and kindness; turning an amoral child into a moral one need not include lifelong guilt. The most effective, long-lasting, and pervasive acquisition of these skills occurs in early childhood, a time when the brain is most receptive to learning (that is, from birth until the child is four or so).

The Peaceful Kids ECSEL Program

In the Peaceful Kids Early Childhood Social-Emotional Learning (ECSEL) curriculum (Sandy and Cochran, 1998), we work to achieve emotional, social, and intellectual growth through an integrated approach involving parents, day care staff, and children in a shared learning venture.

The ECSEL staff do extensive role modeling and assist parents and teachers in doing the same at home and in the classroom. We encourage parents and teachers to set rules and discuss them with children before actual implementation. We also help them plan cooperative discipline techniques that, in the long run, are far more effective than angry yelling or rote punishment. Cooperative discipline is based on mutual affection and trust between teachers, parents, and children. Thus, the accent is on helping the child understand both her own and the other person's feelings and perspective, as well as the consequences of her action, rather than simply getting the child to obey.

The goal is to help parents and teachers promote the child's internalization of standards of right and wrong. Internalization depends on consistency about clearly stated rules, consistent and appropriate praise for following rules, and consistent, appropriate discipline when rules are broken. Most important, internalization depends on loving parents who are loved in turn by the child; discipline has a much greater positive effect from a loving parent than from a distant or unloving one. If a child is thus motivated through love to adopt his parents' standards, he is likely to remember the rules prior to potential misbehavior and, anticipating his parents' disappointment if he breaks the rules, resist engaging in that behavior. But if punishment is used as the primary deterrent to misbehavior, the child learns that the objective is not to get caught.

When stressful methods of discipline (arguing, yelling, and overly harsh punishment) are used with preschoolers, the brain becomes rewired so as to make children prone to impulsiveness, overarousal, and aggressiveness. Children exposed to such harsh methods are often especially in need of remedial help to acquire the emotional literacy skills necessary to understand the nonverbal behavior of others correctly (Jensen, 1998).

Although children appear to have innate capacity for certain social-emotional responses such as empathy and perspective taking, these are frequently hit-or-miss skills unless the child is effectively tutored by an adult. Since interpersonal understanding is influenced more by experience than by age, a three-year-old can be at a higher developmental level than a six-year-old. Accordingly, the ECSEL conflict resolution program uses a spiraling effect to review or teach older preschoolers what the younger preschoolers are taught in their basic program. We never finish with a topic, but revisit it at other levels of complexity according to the child's ability to understand. Scaffolding (a process whereby an adult creates a supportive guideline for thinking about problems through a series of questions) is a process we model and encourage parents and teaching staff to use at every possible opportunity in real-life problem solving and conflict resolution.

In ECSEL, we introduce preschoolers to vocabulary related to feelings, cooperation, and problem solving. This vocabulary is amplified and extended to various situations and emotional contexts. It begins with four basic emotions: sad, angry, scared, and happy. Children learn to sense and label these emotions in themselves through pantomime, stories, puppet shows, discussions about situations in which these emotions occur, and role plays involving both adults and children. Simultaneously, children learn to understand both verbal and nonverbal cues as to how other people feel in various situations.

The four basic emotions are later amplified to include complex feelings such as disappointment, embarrassment, joy, and excitement. Parents are encouraged to read extensively to their children; the program provides stories, games, and word exercises as take-home activities for parents to enjoy with their children. We also instruct parents on how to turn storybook time into an expanded emotional and cognitive learning experience for their children, for example, by questioning the child about the feelings of a character in the book, what the character may be thinking, other actions the character might have taken, and how to evaluate actions and their consequences.

One particularly popular scaffolding activity involves using three sets of picture cards (large ones in the classroom and a smaller version for take-home use) illustrating a situation. The sets involve and are labeled as feelings, consequences, and problem solving. As with other activities and learning tasks, the picture cards are designed for relevance to the children's interests and experiences, since this facilitates the brain's making a connection with existing neural sites, thus maintaining the information efficiently in memory.

Children learn about cooperative skills through motor tasks such as creating group drawings, building structures together with materials such as Legos and blocks, and problem-solving activities involving balance (two children carrying a small object on a board or using sticks to lift a small box into a larger one). As frequently as possible, we engage the teaching staff in leading small groups of children in such activities as communication go-rounds, pantomime, puppetry, and structure role plays and skits to build children's group skills and support prosocial, cooperative behaviors such as listening, sharing, and taking turns. Teacher-facilitated group work also provides modeling and skill development that can help aggressive or shy children learn and practice strategies for group entry and constructive play.

Problem solving is presented in our STAR model: *stop* and think, *tell* how you feel, *ask* what we can do, and *resolve* the situation. We enact puppet scenarios to show ways of achieving a goal, demonstrating positive and negative behavior. As examples, aggressive behavior such as two children fighting may lead to both of them failing to achieve their goals. Shy or fearful behavior could end in the child's failing to even attempt to achieve a goal. The best approach is to assertively ask for or work toward one's goals. If this fails, then it is time to think of another way to attain what is wanted or needed. Including negative consequences is essential since children do not intuitively know which actions are likely to lead to a negative outcome. However, in modeling or demonstrating negative behaviors, it is important to assume a quiet, understated manner, since children are often attracted to loud, rude behavior and will imitate it. Positive behavior is best shown in a lively, celebratory way, since children are drawn to noisy, action-filled events.

To get and maintain the attention of the preschooler, we create strong, frequent contrasts in activity. Sustaining continuous high-level attention for more than ten minutes is difficult (even for adults). Knowledge of children's capacity for concentration must guide any expectation for sustaining attention in early childhood; a rough guideline is to involve preschoolers in four to six minutes of direct instruction (Jensen, 1998). Following this, they need time to create meaning, which is accomplished through internal rather than external attention. Internal attention is largely carried out unconsciously while the child is playing or engaged in an apparently mindless activity. External attention is the direct listening that occurs during instruction. Last but not least, time is required for the learning to take. Activities and practice sessions are repeated with the children in a variety of situations and over many weeks for enduring internalization of these lessons. Obviously, parental support and assistance in conducting at-home practice sessions is an integral component of this process.

Since stress is deleterious to learning, we consciously work with our teachers and parents to reduce stress for children. The outcome of stress is activation of defense mechanisms, which may be useful for surviving physical danger but interfere with learning. Stressors range from a rude classmate to a tense parent overreacting to the child's behavior or a teacher who, perhaps unwittingly, embarrasses a student in front of peers.

The aim of ECSEL is to help each child not only succeed in school (and eventually the workplace) but also have a fulfilling personal life characterized by respectful communication, creative problem solving, and regard for the feelings of others and unburdened by thoughtless put-downs or other avoidable, limiting experiences. The teachers and families who have participated in this program over the past three years unequivocally affirm its usefulness in directing preschoolers toward these ultimate goals.

Involving parents along with children and day care staff produces the greatest increase in children's social-emotional learning. For example, in comparison to classrooms where only teaching staff were engaged in skills development, we found that parent involvement resulted in significant gains in children's assertiveness, cooperation, and self-control. Children in the parent-involvement groups also showed significant decline in externalizing (aggressive) and internalizing (withdrawn, moody) behaviors. In classrooms with parent participation, day care staff and parents were in agreement concerning positive effects for the children. Staff in these classrooms were also likely to integrate the ECSEL curriculum throughout the day's activities. Parents themselves increased in authoritative (as opposed to authoritarian) parenting practices; they remained in control while respecting their children and recognizing that the youngsters, too, were entitled to a number of rights. For example, parents explained rules and decisions to children while also considering the child's point of view—whether or not that view was accepted in the end result. Authoritarian practices (obedience to strict rules) and permissive practices (low control over children) also diminished among parents in the ECSEL program.

MIDDLE CHILDHOOD

Although early childhood is the optimal time to begin teaching the skills described in the first section of this chapter, learning must continue through the later developmental periods. Motivations, interests, and influences change dramatically from early childhood to middle childhood and, later, adolescence. Each developmental age has its own external influences and unique problems, which require their own type and level of instruction to sustain skills. A lesson learned within the context of one age must be revisited and revised to meet the needs of another.

Entering Middle Childhood

One of the major differences between early childhood and middle childhood is that children dramatically reduce the amount of time they spend with parents and other adults and increase the time they spend with peers. As a consequence of decreased adult supervision, children find themselves with greater personal responsibility for their behavior and often need to work out disputes for themselves. These conflict management experiences are an opportunity for children to master new cognitive and social skills. Other differences include expanded social context in which to function and increased responsibility for participation in their own education.

Stage Theories of Middle Childhood

Piaget observed that from age seven or eight to approximately nine to eleven, the imaginary play of early childhood gives way to play with largely unquestioned rules. Rule-based games are an opportunity for the child to experience the give-and-take of negotiation, settling disagreements, and making and enforcing rules. In this way, the child comes to understand that social rules provide a structure for cooperating with others. (See Selman's reciprocal reflective level in Table 15.2.) Erikson viewed this time of life as the period when children confront the task of learning to be competent at activities valued by adults and peers; success in this endeavor creates a sense of industry, and failure results in a sense of inferiority (see Table 15.3). Successful conflict management in middle childhood helps children create and maintain peer friendships, thus promoting a sense of competence and industry.

Sense of Self. The sense of self acquired in early childhood must now be further developed or revised to fit the new context. In addition to spending more time with many other children and with far fewer adults involved, the child in the elementary classroom is primarily engaged in structured learning tasks. The

Table 15.3. Erikson's Psychosocial Stages in Development.

Stage	Development Themes and Challenges
First year	"Trust versus mistrust" Infants learn to trust or mistrust others to care for their basic needs.
Second year	"Autonomy versus shame and doubt" Two-year-olds learn to exercise their will and to control themselves. Otherwise they become unsure of themselves, doubting that they can do things for themselves.
Third to sixth year	"Initiative versus guilt" Children learn to initiate their own activities, to become purposeful, and to enjoy their accomplishments. When they are frustrated by adults in their attempts to initiate activities, they feel guilty for their attempts to become independent.
Seventh year through puberty	"Industry versus inferiority" Children are learning to be competent at activities valued by adults and peers; when they do not, they feel inferior.
Adolescence	"Identity versus role confusion" The primary task of adolescence is to establish a sense of personal identity as part of a social group. Failure to do this results in confusion about who they are and what they want to do in life.

Source: Adapted from Erikson, 1963.

change from an adult-centered to a peer-centered environment requires the child to reconcile the sense of self-identity acquired within the family context with the new self-concepts being formed as a consequence of different relationships. The child's relationship with parents also changes as the parents begin to rely on discussion and explanation of cause and consequence to influence the child's behavior.

Influence of Friends. Around age ten or eleven, children change to a "social-relational moral perspective" (see Table 15.2), wherein shared feelings and harmony with people close to them are more important than individual self-interest. This perspective marks growth of the inclination and the ability to interact with other children without adult supervision. One problem with this growing ability is that children now depend more on peers to define right and wrong and less on such authorities as parents and teachers.

Self-Esteem. Social acceptance is an important goal of middle childhood. At this age, children become aware of their relative status among peers and have concerns about rejection. They also use gossip as a means of finding out about the group's norms; once they know what their friends value and approve, they can shape their own behavior to achieve peer acceptance. Children already competent in group-entry skills achieve peer acceptance easily and are likely to resist unwelcome pressure from the group.

There is evidence that social comparison affects a child's self-evaluation more strongly with increasing age. This fits well with the decreasing self-esteem that occurs during middle childhood, as children begin to compare their performance with that of their peers and to define themselves accordingly. They also begin to think of the interpersonal implications of their own characteristics ("I always do my homework and know the answers in class, so other kids call me nerdy").

Children of all ages whose friendships have positive, cooperative features are high in self-esteem and prosocial behavior, are popular with peers, have few emotional problems, are well behaved, and experience good academic adjustment, including positive attitudes toward school. Despite greater reliance in middle childhood on peer opinion and values, parents remain an important influence on the child. In fact, high self-esteem has been linked to authoritative parenting. This approach to parenting includes a close affectionate relationship, which makes the child feel important; clearly defined limits and consequences for transgression, to give the child the sense that norms are real and significant; and respect for individuality, because the child needs to express individuality. Parents show respect for their children by reasoning with them and taking their point of view into account. The key to a child's high self-esteem is the feeling, transmitted in large part by the family and valued teachers, that she has the ability to control her own future by controlling both herself and her environment.

Conversely, a child with negative friendship relationships (characterized by rivalries and put-downs) is likely to be a low achiever both academically and socially. He also displays disruptive behavior and may suffer depression and anxiety. In contrast to a child with high self-esteem, this child is more likely to have had authoritarian or permissive parents and less parental acceptance, fewer clearly defined limits, and less respect for individuality. Low self-esteem may also result if a preadolescent fails at attempted tasks. Unlike younger children, a preadolescent is prone to attribute her failure to innate ability and not to situational factors such as effort. This failure experience results in reduced expectations for success, negative feelings, and low persistence (Dweck, 1996).

Perspective Taking. With rule-based games, children must keep in mind an overall set of task conditions as well as engage in social perspective taking. Thus, they must take into consideration the wishes, thoughts, and actions of other children along with their own. At this age, children make inferences about the perspectives of other people and are aware that other people can do the same about them. But they often have difficulty in simultaneously focusing on their own perspective while trying to assume the perspective of another. As a result, they frequently adhere to the correctness of either their own view or that of an authority (adult or older child seen as an authority). Becoming skilled in negotiating conflictful social interaction with peers while playing a game depends on a child's growing ability to understand how others think (social perspective taking) and feel (socioemotional competence).

Cooperation. In middle childhood, children begin wrestling with such issues as morality and rules of fairness (see Table 15.2). According to Kohlberg (1976), children around the age of seven or eight enter the stage of development called "instrumental morality," or self-regulation, which includes cooperative behavior. In this sense, cooperating means working toward a common goal while coordinating one's own feelings and perspective with another's. The motive for cooperation is mutual affection and trust, which develops into the ability to take the perspective of another. Given that children may show characteristics of earlier stages of development depending on the circumstance, middle childhood youngsters may still have a somewhat egocentric point of view, in which they have difficulty distinguishing between their own interests and those of other children.

Middle childhood also sees emerging belief in equity: if a group member works harder and contributes more to a project, that member deserves more of the rewards. This is justice as an exchange system, in which you should receive as much as you give. Sometimes the temptation of an appealing reward, however, causes even older children to attempt to get as much as they can from the outcome without regard to how much they contribute (Damon, 1977).

Self-Control. To encourage a child's self-regulation, the goal of the adult (parent or teacher) should be to increasingly appeal to the child's cooperation rather than obedience. Although adult-child relationships are not equal in power, an adult who respects the child's thoughts, opinions, and endeavors can permit and encourage the child to think about and question causes, potential outcomes, and general explanations.

The Role of Conflict

If a relationship is threatened (on the playground, for example), preadolescents engage in fewer conflicts with friends than with acquaintances. However, in the classroom or places where continued interaction is not at risk, the preadolescent disagrees more with friends than nonfriends. The type of conflict most commonly occurring depends on gender: boys' disagreements often involve power issues, whereas for girls the subject of disagreement is usually interpersonal matters. Children who are aggressive also engage in conflicts that differ according to gender: boys have goals of instrumentality (getting what they want, whether it be a material object or a privileged position) and dominance, whereas girls are likely to engage in relationship aggression; they are displaying behavior intended to damage another child's friendship or feeling of inclusion by the peer group.

Preadolescents commonly believe that one person is responsible for any given conflict, and they feel that resolution should come from that person. Thus, it becomes important for adults to engage both (or all) participants in a dispute in what Shure and Spivack (1978) refer to as problem-solving dialoguing—a form of questioning, similar to scaffolding, that helps a child develop an alternative solution and consequential thinking. This process results in clearly defining the problem, searching for the original problem (one child's version of the conflict may not include the first action that occurred), and emphasizing the child's ability (not the adult's) to solve the problem.

The Creative Response to Conflict Program. A well-respected conflict resolution program widely used with children in middle childhood is the program developed by Creative Response to Conflict (CRC) in Nyack, New York.[1] CRC employs age-appropriate classroom activities in five thematic areas: affirmation, communication, cooperation, problem solving, and bias awareness. In addition, CRC emphasizes the importance of actively training and involving school staff, parents, and other community members as part of a holistic approach to changing culture and climate.

For middle-years children, advances in development allow for the use of more complex and collaborative approaches to skill development—for instance, asking students to respond to a conflict scenario by brainstorming and problem solving in cooperative groups. Unlike young children, who have trouble getting outside their own identities, middle-years children can engage easily and independently in role plays, which require them to separate their own thoughts and actions from those of the characters they play.

This movement away from egocentrism also makes the middle years a time when children can be introduced to mediation. CRC trains children beginning in the third grade to be peer mediators who help other children work out conflicts on the playground. Solutions to conflict are not imposed; rather, mediators help disputants work out their own agreements. This approach, which further promotes perspective-taking and problem-solving skills, is particularly successful with middle-years students because it meshes with their growing reliance on peers for affirmation and their need for autonomy and self-direction.

ADOLESCENCE

The defining developmental task of adolescence is identity formation (see Table 15.3). Rapid and dramatic changes, physical and psychosocial, occur in almost all aspects of adolescent life. Consequently, adolescents too are confronted with the stressful necessity of reworking earlier developmental tasks to respond to their new problems and needs. Building an identity requires integrating sexual drives and social demands into a healthy personality.

Stage Theories of Adolescence

According to Erikson's psychosocial stages in development (see Table 15.3), the transition from childhood to adulthood requires a return to earlier developmental issues that emerge with age-related complexity:

- Adolescents revisit the attachment phase of infancy as they search for *trust,* as with trustworthy and admirable friends. In early adolescence, this task focuses on same-sex friends; later, it turns toward finding partners of the opposite sex. As they begin to function as members of society rather than only family, classroom, or other small groups, adolescents seek to establish trust through political and social causes and trustworthy leaders.

- Expression of *autonomy* begins with the two-year-old's insistence on "doing it myself." In adolescence, autonomy refers to learning to make one's own decisions and choices in life rather than accepting those of parents or friends.

- In early childhood, *initiative* was demonstrated through pretend play. Its counterpart in adolescence is establishing one's own goals rather than simply accepting what others plan.

- *Industry* in middle childhood focuses on tasks set by the teacher or parent. In adolescence, industry means taking responsibility for one's own ambitions and the quality of work produced.

Friends and Self-Esteem. In adolescence, high school students spend an average of twenty-two nonschool hours a week with their peers, approximately twice as much time as with adults (Csikszentmihalyi and Larson, 1984). Despite the importance of peers in an adolescent's life, the amount of time spent with peers is influenced by how parents respond to the child's developmental changes. The adolescent frequently responds to strict, authoritarian behavior from parents by turning to peers for support and behavioral guidance. Authoritative parents accept their child's growing up, continue to include her in family decision making, support her self-expression, *and* monitor her behavior (ask her to call when she will be late coming in at night). As a consequence, adolescents of authoritative parents become competent in school and are less likely to cause trouble. Their friends also enjoy the indirect benefits of improved school performance and behavior (Steinberg and Darling, 1994).

For adolescents, friendship goes beyond reciprocal action and is viewed within the context of a long-term series of interactions. Conflict is seen as a natural occurrence within this relationship. The adolescent also realizes that working through and resolving a conflict usually strengthens a relationship if constructively managed.

Although the extent to which friends may negatively influence the adolescent appears to be exaggerated, friends have considerable influence because of the need for social approval. Praise from friends rewards specific behaviors and makes it likely they will occur again. Friends seek to be like their friends for two reasons: (1) friends have characteristics the individual wishes to have (intrinsic motivation), and (2) the individual judges her own competence by comparing her performance with that of classmates (social comparison). Prosocial and responsible classroom behavior has been related directly to classroom grades and test scores even when the effects of academic behavior, teacher preference among students, IQ, family structure, sex, ethnicity, and days absent from school were taken into account (Wentzel, 1993).

Loyalty and intimacy are valued and expected in adolescent friendships; the self-disclosing conversations that occur between close friends, especially among girls, help teenagers shape their identity. However, by the late teen years, the adolescent is capable of tolerating friends with different likes, dislikes, values, and beliefs. Selman's stages 3 and 4 illustrate this change (see Table 15.2). Boys, though, usually form relationships with a group, and it helps them assert their independence from authority figures between the ages of fourteen and sixteen. For boys, validation of worth occurs through action rather than personal disclosure between friends. Like attachment in infancy, adolescent boys and girls use friends to make sense of ambiguous or anxiety-provoking situations. Among both boys and girls in some countries, a clique (a peer group of adolescents small enough to allow regular interaction) becomes part of the social environment.

Friendship and Cooperation. Conformity to peer pressure increases between ages nine and fifteen but decreases thereafter. It is likely that middle adolescence is when conventional standards of behavior are least followed. On the whole, adolescents are perceived to engage in high levels of behavior that poses risks to their health, safety, and well-being. However, antisocial behavior is more common among boys than girls and is much higher when peer groups are organized around competition, as with gangs. Contrary to common belief, adolescents are no more likely than other age groups to feel invulnerable (Quadrel, Fischoff, and Davis, 1993). Sensation seeking, or the need for novel experiences, has also been found wanting as a viable hypothesis for this behavior. At present, there exists no generally accepted explanation for risk-taking behavior in adolescence.

Students often establish borders between their group and other groups during early adolescence. Students of other races are frequently seen as possessing different values and orientations. Teachers and other adults too often fail to pay attention to the effect of peer-group dynamics in forming students' attitudes about others. This may be due, in part, to the fact that adolescents are likely to keep their activities unobserved by parents and other adults in authority.

Perspective Taking. Erikson's model of the identity crisis of adolescence fits well with Piaget's ideas of formal operational thought as well as empirical studies exploring the development of self-understanding in adolescents. Adolescents' thinking about themselves grows more abstract and self-reflective. They also work to integrate their past selves with the self they hope to achieve in the future (Selman, 1980).

Younger adolescents (approximately nine to fifteen) develop friendships for intimacy and support. Since the adolescent at this age is capable of stepping outside the interaction and taking the perspective of a third party, friendships survive run-of-the-mill conflict. However, adolescent relationships at this age are frequently tinged with possessiveness and jealousy.

Although still recognizing the need for the support and sense of identity provided by friends, older adolescents (approximately age twelve to adulthood) are capable of accepting their friends' needs to have other relationships as well. They are able to view events from the perspective of the law, morality, and society as a whole.

The Role of Conflict

The adolescent is able to see parties in a conflict from a generalized third-person perspective, that is, to step outside the conflict as a neutral third person and simultaneously consider both his own perspective and the other's. He can view the conflict interaction from the vantage point of the disinterested average spectator.

Conflict in adolescence occurs more frequently with parents than siblings or peers—presumably because individual autonomy has become the developmental issue at this age. The most common conflict issues between parents and adolescents are authority, autonomy, and responsibility (Smetana, 1989). Adolescents report an average of seven disagreements daily (Collins and Laursen, 1992). However, the parent's response to differences of opinion with the adolescent can help the young person's developing sense of identity, ego formation, and social-cognitive skills. The most helpful parental response takes the form of a supportive but challenging discussion about the issue. Adolescents from families that openly and constructively express their conflict are significantly better able to resolve conflict with their peers than those whose parents cut off disagreement unilaterally. As at younger ages, conflict in adolescence is likely to occur in close relationships. Conflict with same-sex friends declines in later adolescence but increases with romantic partners.

Naïve Conflict Resolution Strategies. Without specific skills development in conflict resolution, the resolution strategies the adolescent uses with friends commonly involve submission (one person gives in to the other's demands), compromise (both parties make concessions), third-party intervention (parties accept a resolution suggested by an uninvolved person), standoff (parties change the topic or divert their attention to a different activity), and withdrawal (one person refuses to continue the conflict exchange). More than 50 percent of adolescent conflicts are resolved by standoff or withdrawal. Unilateral power assertion is used more frequently than negotiation, which is the least-used method of resolution (Vuchinich, 1990).

The San Francisco Community Board Program. An example of a conflict resolution program that is responsive to adolescent developmental needs is the curriculum prepared by the San Francisco Community Board (Sadalla, Henriquez, and Holmberg, 1987). The Community Board Program (CBP) develops problem-solving skills, such as negotiation, in students who normally would avoid conflict and those who become aggressive to get what they want in a conflict situation. Like ECSEL, the CBP works to ensure development of age-appropriate skills; it takes both natural physical development as well as effective nurturing to create children who become emotionally and academically proficient.

Unlike programs for young children like ECSEL, the CBP must take into account students who have well-established negative patterns of conflict resolution. Unlearning old habits can be a long and difficult process, particularly once a student gains a reputation for particular behavior or characteristics. (Peers make it difficult for a student to change a negative reputation even as early as the middle school years.) The CBP also builds on the adolescent's greater capacity for dealing with complex cognitive issues, greater independence from parental constraint, and a growing sense of evolving self that is largely absent in the preschooler and underdeveloped in the preadolescent.

CONCLUSION

The theory and practice of conflict resolution is a young but active field. New developments occur as we establish rigor and discipline in our approaches to this area. It is encouraging that we now have a fully evaluated program available for preschoolers, a group previously ignored or given only cursory service. As many theorists and practitioners have said, it is extremely important that conflict resolution skills be taught as early as possible. Early skills become old habits; we need to teach very young children good habits, ones that help them develop fulfilling lives. Instruction does not stop with preschoolers, though; it must be continued to help children resolve the problems and levels of complexity that occur with developmental advancement.

There are several directions for research to improve our practice. One involves investigating the effects of conflict resolution skills development in children from preschool to adolescence. We need to quantify the amount of training that is necessary for most effective skills development. Second, we need to explore how personal traits and characteristics affect our methods of instruction and training. Does one approach work for all? Obviously not, since some children lack assertiveness and require a great amount of work in this area, while others have impulsive or self-control issues that may increase their level of aggression in a conflict situation. Finally, we need to be policy-minded and work hard to influence society's decision makers. Development in conflict resolution and social-emotional learning skills is so critical to the education of our children that we must actively support infusion of this instruction throughout each child's educational experience, both in school and at home.

Note

1. For information, contact Priscilla Prutzman, executive director, Creative Response to Conflict, Inc., Box 271, 521 North Broadway, Nyack, NY 10960; phone (914) 353–1796; fax (914) 358–4924; e-mail ccrcnyack@aol.com

References

Ceci, S. J. *On Intelligence . . . More or Less: A Bio-Ecological Treatise on Intellectual Development.* Upper Saddle River, N.J.: Prentice Hall, 1990.

Collins, W. A., and Laursen, B. "Conflict and Relationships During Adolescence." In C. U. Shantz and W. W. Hartup (eds.), *Conflict in Child and Adolescent Development.* New York: Cambridge University Press, 1992.

Cook, B. W. *Eleanor Roosevelt.* Vol. 1. New York: Viking, 1992.

Csikszentmihalyi, M., and Larson, R. *Being Adolescent: Conflict and Growth in the Teenage Years.* New York: Basic Books, 1984.

Damon, W. *The Social World of the Child.* San Francisco: Jossey-Bass, 1977.

Damon, W. "Patterns of Change in Children's Social Reasoning: A Two-Year Longitudinal Study." *Child Development,* 1980, *51,* 1010–1017.

Deutsch, M. "Educating for a Peaceful World." *American Psychologist,* 1993, *48,* 510–517.

De Vries, R., and Zan, B. *Moral Classrooms, Moral Children: Creating a Constructivist Atmosphere in Early Education.* New York: Teachers College Press, 1994.

Dweck, C. S. "Social Motivation: Goals and Social-Cognitive Processes. A Comment." In J. Juvonen and K. R. Wentzel (eds.), *Social Motivation: Understanding Children's School Adjustment.* New York: Cambridge University Press, 1996.

Elias, J., and others. *Promoting Social and Emotional Learning: Guidelines for Educators.* Alexandria, Va: Association for Supervision and Curriculum Development, 1997.

Erikson, E. H. *Childhood and Society.* (2nd ed.) New York: Norton, 1963.

Farver, J. M., and Branstetter, W. H. "Preschoolers' Prosocial Responses to Their Peers' Distress." *Developmental Psychology,* 1994, *30,* 334–341.

Fischer, K. W., Bullock, D. H., Rotenberg, E. J., and Raya, P. "The Dynamics of Competence: How Context Contributes Directly to Skill." In R. H. Wozniak and K. W. Fischer (eds.), *Development in Context: Acting and Thinking in Specific Environments.* Mahwah, N.J.: Erlbaum, 1993.

Flavell, J. H. "Perspectives on Perspective Taking." Paper presented at the 20th annual symposium of the Jean Piaget Society, Philadelphia, June 1990.

Gardner, H. *Multiple Intelligences: The Theory in Practice—A Reader.* New York: Basic Books, 1993.

Goleman, D. *Working with Emotional Intelligence.* New York: Bantam Books, 1998.

Gottman, J. *Raising an Emotionally Intelligent Child: The Heart of Parenting.* New York: Fireside, 1997.

Horn, W. F., and Packard, T. "Early Identification of Learning Problems: A Meta-Analysis." *Journal of Educational Psychology,* 1985, *77,* 597–607.

Jensen, E. *Teaching with the Brain in Mind.* Alexandria, Va.: Association for Supervision and Curriculum Development, 1998.

Johnson, D. W., and Johnson, R. *Teaching Students to Be Peacemakers.* Edina, Minn.: Interaction, 1991.

Kohlberg, L. "Moral Stages and Moralization: The Cognitive-Developmental Approach to Socialization." In J. Likona (ed.), *Moral Development Behavior: Theory, Research and Social Issues.* Austin, Tex.: Holt, Rinehart and Winston, 1976.

Maccoby, E. E. *Social Development: Psychological Growth and the Parent-Child Relationship.* Orlando: Harcourt Brace, 1980.

McGaugh, J. L., and others. "Involvement of the Amygdala in the Regulation of Memory Storage." In J. L. McGaugh, F. Bermudez-Ratton, and R. A. Prado-Alcala (eds.), *Plasticity in the Central Nervous System: Learning and Memory.* Mahwah, N.J.: Erlbaum, 1995.

Mize, J. "Coaching Preschool Children in Social Skills: A Cognitive–Social Learning Curriculum." In G. Cartledge and J. F. Milburn (eds.), *Teaching Social Skills to Children and Youth: Innovative Approaches.* (3rd ed.) Needham Heights, Mass.: Allyn & Bacon, 1995.

Quadrel, M. J., Fischoff, B., and Davis, W. "Adolescent (In)vulnerability." *American Psychologist,* 1993, *48,* 102–116.

Sadalla, G., Henriquez, M., and Holmberg, M. *Conflict Resolution: A Secondary School Curriculum.* San Francisco: Community Board Program, 1987.

Sandy, S. V., and Cochran, K. M. *Peaceful Kids ECSEL: Conflict Resolution Skills for Preschool Children (Program Guide).* New York: International Center for Cooperation and Conflict Resolution, 1998.

Selman, R. L. *The Growth of Interpersonal Understanding: Developmental and Clinical Analysis.* Orlando: Academic Press, 1980.

Shore, R. *Rethinking the Brain: New Insights into Early Development.* New York: Families and Work Institute, 1997.

Shure, M. B., and Spivack, G. *Problem-Solving Techniques in Childrearing.* San Francisco: Jossey-Bass, 1978.

Siegler, R. S. *Children's Thinking.* (2nd ed.) Upper Saddle River, N.J.: Prentice Hall, 1991.

Smetana, J. G. "Adolescents' and Parents' Reasoning About Actual Family Conflicts." *Child Development,* 1989, *60,* 1052–1067.

Steinberg, L., and Darling, N. E. "The Broader Context of Social Influence in Adolescence." In R. K. Silbereisen and E. Todt (eds.), *Adolescence in Context.* New York: Springer-Verlag, 1994.

Vuchinich, S. "Sequencing and Social Structure in Family Conflict. *Social Psychology Quarterly,* 1990, *47,* 217–234.

Wentzel, K. R. "Does Being Good Make the Grade? Relations Between Academic and Social Competence in Early Adolescence." *Journal of Educational Psychology,* 1993, *14,* 168–291.

PART FOUR

CREATIVITY AND CHANGE

CHAPTER SIXTEEN

Creativity and Conflict Resolution

The Role of Point of View

Howard E. Gruber

First conundrum: educators often view conflict as the problem child, the practitioner's task as elimination of conflict. On the other hand, students of creativity often view conflict as its necessary companion: (1) novelty engenders conflict and/or (2) creativity requires conflict.

Second conundrum: conflict resolution requires collaboration, if not as the goal then at least as the means. Creative work has been treated, by and large, as an individual effort, sometimes painfully isolated.

As an undergraduate at Brooklyn College, I learned from Solomon Asch, my teacher, about two interesting lines of research: his work on group pressures and his work with Witkin on frames of reference. Both of these bear on the issue of point of view, which is the major focus of this chapter. It has become clear to me, as to others, that an essential and almost omnipresent aspect of creative work is posing good questions. In studying Darwin's notebooks and correspondence (Gruber, 1981) one sees that he gloried in discovering questions. He wrote many letters to scientists and naturalists around the world, posing challenging questions. His contemporaries were often mystified: Where did his

The shadow box research, part of which is presented here, was supported by a grant to Howard E. Gruber from Le Fonds National Suisse de la Recherche Scientifique, project nos. 1.043–084 and 1.738–087. Collaborators were Danielle Maurice, Emiel Reit, Isabelle Sehl, and Anastasia Tryphon. Some of the work was done while at the Institute for Advanced Study in Princeton. I thank all of them and also thank Doris Wallace for her part in this project.

The material on the shadow box was liberally adapted from Gruber (1990).

questions come from? As a student, I adopted the position that having a novel point of view is the main thing. After all, among the contemporaries in question, then as now, were many good problem solvers—but where do their problems come from? Novel problems stem from a novel point of view. Then the central question becomes: How is a novel point of view constructed?

In his 1996 book, *Human Judgment and Social Policy,* Kenneth Hammond distinguishes between theories of truth, which center on the correspondence of ideas with facts, and theories that look inward for coherence of ideas with other ideas. The latter, coherence theories, do not offer definite procedures for making judgments and consequently must rely on wisdom and intuition. Correspondence theories do so provide, but in a world teeming with uncertainties there is a triple price to be paid—which Hammond sums up beautifully in the subtitle of his book: "irreducible uncertainty, inevitable error, unavoidable injustice." In both existing and historically experienced circumstances, this view casts a pretty dark shadow. My chosen topic, however, is not judgment but its necessary prelude, discovering or inventing the alternatives to be judged and among which to choose. Here, what is needed is not so much accuracy or logic but creative imagination and construction.

In this chapter, I give a brief account of the evolving systems approach to creative work, with special emphasis on point of view and social aspects of creativity. In addition, I explore some possible relations between creativity and conflict resolution, presenting experimental work with a "shadow box" designed to illuminate collaborative synthesis of disparate points of view.

EVOLVING SYSTEMS APPROACH

This approach is predicated on the uniqueness of each creative person as he or she moves through a series of commitments, problems, solutions, and transformations. These aspects of the creative process are not fixed, and they are not universal. Rather, they constantly evolve, and they differ from one creator to another. The system as a whole is composed of subsystems that are loosely coupled with each other. This looseness provokes the emergence of disequilibrium and the finding of new questions; consequently, it opens the way to unpredictable innovation.

Our task is to describe how a given creator actually works. It is not our task to measure the amount of creativity or to find factors that apply in the same way to all creators. What is necessary for one creative person confronting a problem may be unnecessary or even ill-advised for another.

The creative individual described here, interested in creativity in the moral domain, is only a first approximation. People who take responsibility want to make something happen. For this, they need allies, who must be persuaded, recruited, trained, and supported. Moreover, a full expression of morality would bring together moral thought, moral feeling, and moral action. Beyond these components, there must be creative integration. Although this last is rarely discussed, Donna Chirico has made an interesting effort in her integrative article, "Where Is the Wisdom? The Challenge of Moral Creativity at the Millennium" (forthcoming). And of course, Erich Fromm's whole oeuvre is a reflection on such a synthesis (see Fromm, 1962, for example).

In her case study of Niebuhr, Chirico shows how the quest for integration of thought, feeling, and action can lead to surprising results, can even go astray. She shows how Niebuhr achieved such an integration, but at a price. As he grew in influence, he gained new opportunities to move to the plane of moral action. But this brought him into collaborative interaction with a largely conservative establishment. In a series of such contacts, he became more conservative. Chirico (forthcoming) writes, "As Niebuhr became involved increasingly in the political power structure as an insider, his radical views about the role of government shifted toward those of the authority figures he had previously denounced. Niebuhr moved from speaking as an independent thinker, whose ideology was informed by the Christian message, to acting as an advocate for the prevailing opinions of the United States government."

Chirico stresses the difficulty, the need for the hard and steady work required, if we want to contribute to social transformation. She writes, "In a postmodern world where all is relative anyway, it is easier to accept inequity in the guise of personal or cultural differences than to take a moral stand . . . without moral creativity there can be no attempt. This involves self-sacrifice so that a community of concerned selves can come together and provoke change. It starts with taking a moral stand."

Each creative case presents different aspects for study. These evolving opportunities may be grouped under three major headings: knowledge, purpose, and affect. All of them apply in the first instance to the creative individual at work. In addition, there are aspects that apply to the creator as a social being: social origins and development; relations with colleagues, mentorships, and so on.

Since each creative person is unique, if collaboration is needed it must be collaboration among people who differ (in style, background, ability profile, and the like). Collaboration and similar relationships may take many forms: working together on a shared project where both members of a pair do work that is essentially the same (as Picasso and Braque did in inventing cubism); working together in a teamlike setting where participants complement each other (as in the production of a film, an opera, or a ballet); and sharing ideas either face-to-face or in written correspondence (as Vincent van Gogh and his brother, Theo, did through the medium of thousands of letters mostly about Vincent's actual work, his plans for future work, and his sensuous experiences).

Networks of Enterprise

It is well established that creative work evolves over long periods of time. Some writers even speak of the ten-year rule. Whether this duration is two years or twenty or simply highly variable, it is certainly a far cry from the millisecond flashes vaunted by the devotees of sudden insight and mysterious intuition as the essence of creative effort.

If creative work takes so long, we must have an approach to motivation that recognizes the time it takes. I have found that one important aspect of creative work is the way each creator organizes a life so that diverse projects don't become obstacles to each other. I use the term *enterprise* to make room for the typical situation in which a person who completes one project does not abandon the line of work it entailed but picks up another that is part of the same set of concerns. I use the term *network* to accommodate the finding that creators are often simultaneously involved in several projects and enterprises linked to each other in complex ways.

Time and Irreality. One of the most persistent myths about creative work is the allegation that novelty comes about through lightninglike flashes of insight. To the contrary, serious studies reveal accounts in which the time taken is on the order of years and decades. Even when a moment of sudden transformation occurs, it is the hard-won result of a long developmental process.

Engagement and commitment for such long periods of steady work require appropriate organization of the task space. One the one hand, the creator must fashion a network of enterprise that can withstand the challenges of distraction, fatigue, and failure. On the other hand, one of the chief instruments of creative persistence is a well-developed fantasy life: what cannot be done (yet) on the plane of reality is attainable in the world of dreams, fantasy, half-baked notebooks (Darwin) and private discussions (Einstein). Play becomes the midwife of creative change.

Play Ethic. We teach and preach the work ethic, but from time to time the play ethic rears its head, especially among creators. But there is no inescapable conflict between work and play. There is fusion of work and play as well, as transformation of activity from playlike to worklike and vice versa, in an endless cycle.

Once we take account of this constructive, collective, perdurably patient character of creative work, it follows that some of the miasmal mystery surrounding thought about creativity can evaporate. To work together, people must communicate. For this they must share a common language—which sometimes means that one must teach others the language to be shared. A striking example of this process is how the physicist Freeman Dyson deliberately set about working with

Richard Feynman, bent on learning to understand "Feynman diagrams" so that he could teach the wider community of physicists to do likewise (see Schweber, 1994).

Extraordinary Moral Responsibility and Creativity in the Moral Domain

These are closely linked ideas. For the most part, research on moral development has been limited to the plane of judgment. When all that is required of the subject is to make a moral judgment, he or she is free to choose any position, from the mundane to the fanciful, from the craven to the courageous. But if morally guided conduct must follow from judgment, many if not most subjects disappear into the cracks. Indeed, these judgmental interstices are seen as normal and necessary for maintaining an orderly society. "Who will bell the cat?" is experienced as a threatening question.

The expression

$$\text{Ought} \rightarrow \text{Can} \rightarrow \text{Create}$$

is shorthand for a somewhat complex idea, to wit, that one "ought" to do some particular thing, or that there "ought to be a law" only makes sense if the predicated *ought* is possible. So *ought* implies "can." But situations occur in which it is urgent to make the passage from "cannot" to *can* and where this can only be done by discovering and taking some new, unexplored path. This is when creative work becomes the moral imperative.

THE SHADOW BOX EXPERIMENTS

In Plato's parable of the cave, the prisoners are chained to a single station and see nothing but shadows on the wall. They have no way of distancing or decentering themselves from this one limited view of the world. Limited and distorted as it may be, it is their reality. Plato's point is that this is the normal situation of ordinary mortals, leaving them vulnerable to the distortions of group pressure. Sherif's work on the formation of social norms and Asch's work on group pressures have important points in common with the prisoners in Plato's cave. The subjects in the experiments of both researchers are all looking at the scene to be judged in essentially the same way and from the same point of view. Thus, a difference in reports of what is seen must mean a disagreement. There is no opportunity for dialogue among the observers. The subjects are limited to looking and listening; they have no chance for an active exploratory or manipulative approach. Finally, the situation invites only judgment on a single variable, not the construction of a complex idea or object.

Under such conditions, intersubjective differences become disagreements that can only be solved by yielding, domination, and compromise—all of which occur.

In contrast, it is possible to imagine conditions in which observers have different information about the same reality but no need to disagree with each other. They may even be able to transcend their individual limitations and together arrive at a deeper grasp of the reality in question than would be possible for each alone. Our research grew out of the conviction that people can be vigorously truthful.

We have embodied this possibility in the microcosm of a shadow box (see Figure 16.1). In this arrangement, an object concealed in a box casts two differing shadows on two screens at right angles to each other. The subjects' task is to discover the shape of the hidden object by discussing and synthesizing the two shadows of which each sees only one. Although our main interest was the process of collaboration of subjects with different viewpoints, to study that we also looked at the performance of single subjects shuttling back and forth between two screens.

Figure 16.1. The Shadow Box.

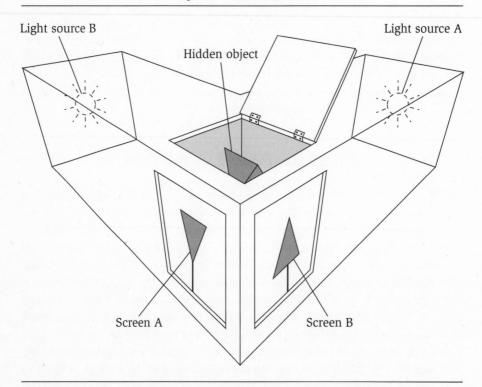

Note: The task is to use the two shadows to work out the shape of the hidden object.

Source: Gruber, H. E. "The Cooperative Synthesis of Disparate Points of View." In I. Rock (ed.), *The Legacy of Solomon Asch: Essays in Cognition and Social Psychology.* Mahwah, N.J.: Erlbaum, 1990. Reprinted with permission.

Cooperative synthesis of such disparate points of view in the shadow box situation is not a simple matter. Each subject is asked to make an a priori assumption that the other participant's observations represent the same entity. Each participant must convey what he or she sees clearly and correctly to the other. This may require inventing a suitable scheme for representing the information in question. When difficulties of communication arise, the problem of trusting the other must be dealt with. Often, too, the subjects must overcome a common tendency to ignore or underemphasize the other person's contribution and to center attention on one's own point of view.

When we compare one person shuttling between two station points with a pair of people each of whom sees only one screen, sometimes the single person is superior, and sometimes the pair. Over a wide range of situations, the individual perceptual apparatus is admirably organized for synthesizing disparate inputs: binocular vision, the kinetic depth effect, and all sorts of intermodal phenomena testify to the capability. On the other hand, there are at least some situations in which two heads are better than one.

From a practical point of view, the question of one head or two may not always be germane. There are real-world situations in which shuttling back and forth between station points in not feasible, so there must be an observer at each point. In negotiating situations, the number of heads is determined by sociopolitical realities. Going beyond the shadow box, the processes involved in cooperative synthesis of points of view are interesting in their own right.

Experiment One: Interaction of Social and Cognitive Factors

The subjects were first shown how the setup worked: two lamps, two screens, and a stalk on which to mount the object (see Figure 16.1). They were shown how two shadows could be generated, one on each screen, and it was suggested to them that they could figure out what the object was by talking to each other or drawing pictures (material supplied). We compared subjects working in pairs with subjects working alone. In the pair situation, they were asked not to look at the other person's screen. The subjects were children (ages seven to nine), adolescents (fourteen to sixteen), and adults (twenty to fifty-three). The pairs were asked to communicate with each other about what they saw, and to work together to come to an agreement as to the shape of the concealed object that would account for the two shadows. Each single subject or each pair of subjects worked on two Lego objects and two geometrical objects, as shown in Figure 16.2.

The subjects almost invariably found the task challenging and interesting and worked on it for as long as an hour. Among children, the majority failed to solve (correctly synthesize) any of the objects, and among the adolescents and adults there were a few who failed completely.

The main difference between adolescents and adults was that the latter often hit spontaneously on the idea that there might be more than one solution to a

Figure 16.2. Objects and Shadows in Experiment One: Geometrical Objects and Lego Objects.

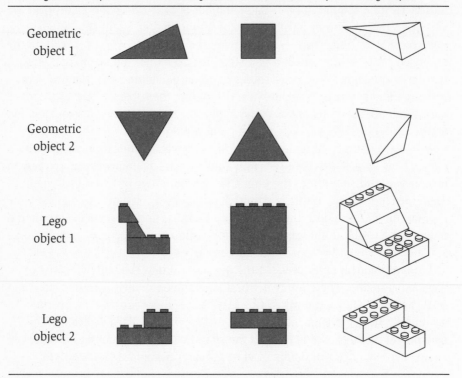

Geometric object 1

Geometric object 2

Lego object 1

Lego object 2

Source: Gruber, H. E. "The Cooperative Synthesis of Disparate Points of View." In I. Rock (ed.), *The Legacy of Solomon Asch: Essays in Cognition and Social Psychology.* Mahwah, N.J.: Erlbaum, 1990. Reprinted with permission.

problem, sometimes even recognizing the possibility of an unlimited number of solutions. To our surprise, in a number of experiments there was little difference in problem-solving success between singles and pairs. In only one respect was the pair condition clearly superior to the single: frequency of multiple solutions. This superiority was more pronounced in adult pairs than in adolescents.

Experiment Two: Comparison of Cooperative and Individualistic Orientations

Our goal was to examine the effect of social orientations within pairs on the synthesis of points of view. We used three kinds of instruction to the pairs. The *cooperative* instruction encouraged the pair to work together throughout the experiment, indicating that their performance would be evaluated as a pair compared with other pairs. The *individualistic* instruction asked the subjects to exchange information as to their respective shadows and then to work alone in solving the problem, indicating that their performance would be evaluated as individuals. The *neutral* instruction did not specify any mode of working together and did not mention evaluation. The subjects were twenty-four pairs of adolescents (ages fourteen to sixteen) and twenty-four pairs of adults (twenty-three to fifty-eight). There were no consistent or striking differences between the sexes, so that variable is ignored in this discussion.

Each pair was given a single problem, a tetrahedron fixed on an edge in such a position that each subject saw a triangular shadow, one with apex up, the other with apex down (see Figure 16.1). We chose this rather difficult task to avoid the possibility that most subjects would solve the problem easily and to keep the subjects working long enough for us to make the observations we were interested in.

The resulting patterns of social behavior could be classified as individualistic, cooperative, or competitive. Subjects by no means followed the instructions we gave them. Surprisingly, among the adults the predominant behavior was cooperative, even when the instructions were neutral. Furthermore, even in the group given individualistic instructions, almost half the subjects were cooperative. It seemed as though the structure of the shadow box situation, presenting two perspectives bearing on a single object, naturally evoked cooperation as the appropriate response mode.

Most of the successful adult pairs were ones in which both members were cooperative. Moreover, in six of eight such pairs, the partners had different problem-solving strategies, one working mainly by adding planes and the other by constructing volumes. In exchanging information, the adults were more precise and detailed than the adolescents, giving information not only about shape but also about orientation, size, and position on the screen. The adults gave equal weight to both shadows, while the adolescents tended to focus on their own viewpoint. Adults were attentive to their partner's suggestion, and they duly profited from their differences by improving the quality of their solutions and their comprehension of the tasks. The adolescents were less interested in the other's ideas. They were also more concerned about whose solution was correct, as if only one were possible.

THE IMPORTANCE OF POINT OF VIEW

The importance of point of view emerges explicitly in many settings: Plato's cave, the anthropologist's relativism (which need not be despairingly total), postmodern nihilism, and so forth. Under conditions in which subjects are not able to explore and communicate freely, intersubjective differences become disagreements that are difficult to resolve. Techniques of conflict resolution that are successful under some conditions may lead only to fiasco in other circumstances, such as change in scale or change of mood. For example, sharing the commons requires civility and negotiation, and such conditions may sometimes be unattainable.

From our work with the shadow box, it becomes clear experimentally that under certain conditions taking the point of view of the other (POVO) is essential for collaborative work and that some problems absolutely require the synthesis of disparate points of view (POVOSYN). But such synthesis, like all creative work, is a delicate plant and may fail if conditions change.

The classic studies of conformity by Sherif (1936) and by Asch (1952) stemmed from rather different perspectives about the truth value of beliefs. Sherif thought that the development of social norms could be readily studied in a highly ambiguous stimulus situation, notably the autokinetic effect, and that this ambiguity corresponds well to real-world conditions. Asch objected to this image of human nature as passively yielding to group pressures; he believed that if confronted with clearly discriminable and unambiguous stimuli, observers would resist conformity.

Does the epistemology of the shadow box, especially recognizing multiple solutions, mean that anything goes, that we are no further than when we started in our quest for paths to truth? I think not. Even though there are multiple solutions, at least some are always excluded. The existence of multiple solutions does not open the way to unregulated relativism. To take only one example, a stationary cube can cast a variety of shadows, depending on its orientation, but it can never cast a circular shadow. By the same token, a stationary sphere can never cast a square shadow.

The importance of point of view is concisely expressed in a remark often attributed to Isaac Newton: "If I have seen farther, it is by standing on the shoulders of giants" (reported by Catherine Drinker Bowen in Merton, 1985). Merton's book-length exploration of this aphorism is a pleasure to read. When all is said and done, a stationary sphere can never cast a square shadow.

References

Asch, S. E. *Social Psychology.* Upper Saddle River, N.J.: Prentice Hall, 1952.

Chirico, D. M. "Where Is the Wisdom? The Challenge of Moral Creativity at the Millennium." *Psychohistory,* forthcoming.

Fromm, E. *Beyond the Chains of Illusion.* New York: Simon & Schuster, 1962.

Gruber, H. E. *Darwin on Man: A Psychological Study of Scientific Creativity.* (2nd ed.) Chicago: University of Chicago Press, 1981.

Gruber, H. E. "The Cooperative Synthesis of Disparate Points of View." In I. Rock (ed.), *The Legacy of Solomon Asch: Essays in Cognition and Social Psychology.* Mahwah, N.J.: Erlbaum, 1990.

Hammond, K. R. *Human Judgment and Social Policy: Irreducible Uncertainty, Inevitable Error, and Unavoidable Injustice.* New York: Oxford University Press, 1996.

Merton, R. K. *On the Shoulders of Giants: A Shandean Postscript.* Orlando: Harcourt Brace, 1985.

Schweber, S. S. *QED and the Men Who Made It.* Princeton, N.J.: Princeton University Press, 1994.

Sherif, M. *The Psychology of Social Norms.* New York: HarperCollins, 1936.

CHAPTER SEVENTEEN

Some Guidelines for Developing a Creative Approach to Conflict

Peter T. Coleman
Morton Deutsch

I n his stimulating essay on creativity and conflict resolution in Chapter Sixteen, Howard Gruber raises a number of important questions, which we discuss briefly before presenting some guidelines to creative conflict resolution.

CREATIVITY RESULTING FROM CONFLICT

The first question is, if "creativity requires conflict," under what conditions of conflict is creativity likely to emerge?

One of the creative functions of conflict resides in its ability to arouse motivation to solve a problem that might otherwise go unattended. A scholar who exposes his theories and research to the scrutiny of his peers may be stimulated to a deeper analysis if a colleague confronts him with conflicting data and theoretical analysis. Similarly, individuals and groups who have authority and power and who are satisfied with the status quo may be aroused to recognize problems and be motivated to work on them as opposition from the dissatisfied makes the customary relations and arrangements unworkable and unrewarding, or as they are helped to perceive the possibility of more satisfying relations and arrangements. Accepting the necessity for change in the status quo (rather than rigid, defensive adherence to previously existing positions) is most likely, however, when the circumstances arousing new motivation suggest courses of action that pose minimal threat to the social or self-esteem of those who must change.

Thus, although acute dissatisfaction with things as they are and motivation to recognize and work at problems are necessary for creative solutions, these things are not sufficient. The circumstances conducive to creatively breaking through impasses are varied, but they have in common that "they provide the individual with an environment in which he does not feel threatened and in which he does not feel under pressure. He is relaxed but alert" (Stein, 1968). Threat induces defensiveness and reduces both tolerance of ambiguity and openness to the new and unfamiliar; excessive tension leads to primitization and stereotyping of thought processes. As Rokeach (1960) has pointed out, threat and excessive tension lead to the closed rather than open mind. To entertain novel ideas that may at first seem wild and implausible, to question initial assumptions of the framework within which the problem or conflict occurs, the individual needs the freedom or courage to express herself without fear of censure. Much research (see, for example, Carnevale and Probst, 1998, and Chapter Three of this volume) has demonstrated that a competitive, as opposed to cooperative, approach to conflict leads to restricted judgment, reduced complexity, inability to consider alternative perspectives, and less creative problem solving.

NOVEL POINT OF VIEW

The second question is, how is a novel point of view developed and constructed?

Gruber rightly stresses the importance to creativity of a novel point of view that stimulates new questions. Throughout this handbook, there is stress on the fact that a novel perspective regarding conflict is to view it as a mutual problem the conflicting parties can work on together, cooperatively, in an attempt to discover mutually satisfactory solutions. As Chapter One emphasizes, reframing the conflict so that the conflicting parties see themselves as being in a collaborative rather than oppositional relation with regard to resolving their conflict is crucial to creative resolution. It not only produces an atmosphere conducive to creativity but vastly expands the range of potential solutions as well.

Although reframing makes a conflict more amenable to a solution, the ability to reformulate the reframed mutual problem so that, in turn, one can find a solution to it is dependent on the availability of cognitive resources. Ideas are important to creative resolution of conflict, and any factors that broaden the range of ideas and alternatives available to the participants in a conflict are useful. Intelligence, exposure to diverse experiences, interest in ideas, preference for the novel and complex, receptivity to metaphors and analogies, the capacity to make remote associations, independence of judgment, and the ability to play with ideas are some of the personal factors that characterize creative problem solvers. The availability of ideas is also dependent on such social conditions as the opportunity to communicate with and be exposed to other people who may have relevant and unfamiliar ideas (such as experts, impartial outsiders, people facing similar or analogous situations); a social atmosphere that values innovation and originality and encourages exchanging ideas; and a social tradition that fosters the optimistic view that, with effort and time, constructive solutions to problems that initially seem intractable can be discovered or invented.

TIME AND CONFLICT RESOLUTION

The third question is, do creative solutions emerge only after extensive time and effort are focused on the problem, or are there conflicts that permit solution in a relatively short time?

Gruber is surely correct to emphasize that such profound, intellectual problems as those addressed by Darwin and Einstein require extended time and effort. Similarly, one can assume that such complex conflicts as those in the Middle East and the Balkans—or in an embittered dysfunctional family—also involve prolonged creative effort. But not all problems are profound, and not all conflicts are deeply enmeshed in difficult personal, social, economic, and political conditions.

PLAY AND CREATIVITY

Fourth, why is play the midwife of creative change?

Almost all students of creativity emphasize the importance of playfulness to the creative process. As Gruber points out, the play ethic permits one to engage in fantasy and to consider fantastic and unreal ideas, which sometimes can be transformed into workable solutions. It also permits fun, humor, and relaxation of internal censors that inhibit expression of challenging, unconventional, far-out ideas. Families, groups, and organizations as well as individuals who have the play ethic are apt to discover novel solutions to the problems and conflicts they experience.

INDIVIDUAL WORK AND COLLABORATION

Fifth, what are the differences between creative individual work and creative collaboration?

Gruber's fascinating experiments bring this question sharply into focus. From his research, as well as that of others, it is evident that an individual is not at a disadvantage, compared to a collaborating pair of people, if she has access to the different perspectives (which are available within the pair) necessary to constructing an appropriate integrated picture of the reality with which she is dealing. However, the individual could reasonably assume that, if she is limited to her own perspective, it would be much more difficult or perhaps impossible to do so. On the other hand, a pair of subjects, each with his or her own perspective concerning the reality being perceived (but with sufficient information between them), is also able to construct a valid picture of the reality if they are cooperative. In fact, they are able to generate more such pictures than the individual problem solver is.

One can generalize by stating that collaborative (as compared to individual) problem solving—when the collaboration is effectively cooperative—usually provides more resources, more diversity in ideas, and more social support for the work involved in creative problem solving. On the other hand, individual as compared to collaborative work does not require the skills and attitudes involved in effective cooperation, which include communication, perspective taking, trust, empathy, control of egocentricity, and the like (see Chapter One for fuller discussion of the skills and attitudes involved in effective cooperation). Thus, individual work is apt to be more creative if it is difficult to establish effective cooperation, while collaborative work is apt to be so if there is effective cooperation and the collaborators have more resources available to them than are available to an individual.

The Egg Drop Exercise

As Gruber and we have emphasized, constructive resolution of conflict often requires that the disputants be able to see old things in new ways. Here we describe an innovative training experience, developed by Kenneth Sole, for exploring conflict and creativity under conditions of cooperation and competition. We also outline several guidelines for conflict resolvers for use in facilitating a creative process in conflict situations.

The Egg Drop

This is an exercise in intragroup creative problem solving conducted under conditions of intragroup and intergroup competition and conflict. The participants are put into teams of five to ten individuals and informed of the task. A coat hanger has been hung from the ceiling, and one dozen raw eggs are suspended from it by strands of cotton thread. A ladder leads to the structure. The teams are then instructed that the objective of the activity is to be the *first team* to build a freestanding "apparatus" that successfully catches and holds a falling raw egg, unbroken, six inches above the floor.

Each team is furnished with an identical kit of "stuff" (string, tape, cupcakes, instant soup, hairpins, and so on), and instructed to build an apparatus to catch the egg of their choice. The eggs are each numbered sequentially. The teams are informed that they may use only the materials in their kit to build the apparatus.

In addition, each team is asked to select a member of their group to sit on a panel of judges. They are instructed not to consult with any of their prior team members regarding the creative process. In addition to the rules provided, the judges may decide (unilaterally) to impose additional rules for the teams to follow. These rules are delivered to the teams via formal proclamation.

When the judges begin the competition, each team member suits up in garbage bags and rubber gloves and then begins work on designing the apparatus. As soon as a team is ready, one member is required to call "Ready." At that time they must announce (within fifteen seconds) the number of the egg they wish to catch. From the time the team declares the egg they plan to catch, they have three minutes to position their apparatus for catching the egg. By the end of the three-minute period, one of the team members must cut the thread that holds the chosen egg. Each team is limited to two egg attempts per apparatus.

No member of a team may touch any egg, suspension threads, or hanging structure at any time. A judge noticing violation of any of these rules imposes the penalty of confiscation. The other team(s) confiscate one item from the kit of the offending team. Teams have thirty seconds to select the item they wish to confiscate. If a team member informs the judges (or a judge) of violations, the penalty is doubled. Decisions of the judges are final.

This exercise gives participants a rich (and ridiculous) opportunity to explore creative problem solving under conditions of competition and conflict. The experience can be particularly useful for intact workgroups or for other groups experiencing conflict, because it allows exploration of conflict dynamics under relatively benign circumstances. During the exercise, conflicts typically emerge between the teams, between the panel of judges and the teams, and within a team between individuals with differing ideas and styles of problem solving. All of these conflicts have implications for the creative problem-solving process.

General Guidelines for Creativity and Conflict

The discussions that follow the exercise can cover many of the themes outlined in the guidelines we offer here. The ideas and processes summarized here have been informed by the work of many scholars and practitioners, among them Howard Gruber, Kenneth Sole, John Cleese, Donald Treffinger, Scott Isaksen, Brian Dorval, and Peter Carnevale.

Challenge the Myths about Creativity. Treffinger, Isaksen, and Dorval (1994) identified four common myths that many people hold about creativity:

1. "I'm not a creative person" (creativity is a rare and special quality possessed by only a few).
2. "Creativity is too mysterious to be taught" (creativity is a supernatural and uncontrollable phenomenon).
3. "Creativity equals arts" (creativity only exists in relation to artistic endeavors).
4. "Creativity is madness" (creativity is associated with eccentricity and insanity).

The egg drop exercise often puts people face-to-face with these and other assumptions that they hold about the creative process and their own capacity to be creative. These myths negatively influence people's approach to problem solving under many conditions, but particularly under conditions of perceived threat that are associated with many conflict situations. Training should support people in exploring these assumptions and in broadening their understanding of the creative process to include how they solve conflicts and other problems in their lives.

Use Time and Space Arrangements to Create an Oasis for Creative Problem Solving. John Cleese, who first found fame in *Monty Python's Flying Circus* and has been a consultant to many organizations on creativity, coined *time-space oasis* to depict a situation where the most basic conditions are met for functioning creatively (Cleese, 1991). The condition of time has two dimensions, length and endurance. People must have a sufficient amount of time to open up and see things flexibly and creatively, particularly if working in a conflict situation where they are operating primarily in a critical mode. Thus, the competition to be the *first* to complete the egg drop apparatus reduces the group's time and usually stresses their ability to innovate. Once in a creative mode, disputants need ample time to create, but not so much time that they tire and become discouraged. Cleese recommends ninety minutes as a good amount of time for a working session (thirty minutes to open up and sixty minutes to work constructively).

The other component of time is the need for disputants to persist and endure, even after a marginally acceptable solution presents itself. Research has shown that humans tend to be poor decision makers because they often choose the first acceptable solution to a problem that emerges, even if it is far from being the best that could be developed. Truly creative solutions are usually discovered only after persisting in exploring the problem and its potential solutions. Prolonged and deep engagement with a problem can lead not only to a high level of innovation but also to deep and enduring satisfaction among the disputants with the agreement they produce.

The second dimension of the time-space oasis is having access to a different space. It is often useful for disputants to remove themselves from their customary environments to be able to think afresh. The many demands and distractions of one's usual environment, whether related to the conflict or not, draw one back into habitual or standard ways of seeing a problem and responding to it. A new environment (particularly a confidential one) can allow disputants some degree of freedom to try out new perspectives, behaviors, or ways of working with a problem. This is a primary reason that exercises such as the egg drop, which are removed from actual work or conflict settings, can be useful in helping disputants explore relational or conflict dynamics.

Develop a Serious but Playful Atmosphere. As Howard Gruber indicated, play-fulness is often central to a creative process. Humor, play, and a sense of fun can all contribute to releasing tension and opening up one's view of things, ultimately leading to development of a novel point of view. The egg drop exercise captures this relationship between play and a new perspective. The rules of the exercise are always presented in the most formal of manners, but the task, the uniforms, and the objects involved belie this formality and communicate a high degree of silliness. This climate is experienced by the participants as especially conducive to experimenting, making mistakes, and attempting the uncommon or ridiculous.

But humor, playfulness, and fun are tricky endeavors when working with difficult conflicts. Particularly in escalated conflicts, disputants often approach their problems grimly. Having a conflict resolver introduce humor or play could easily offend or enrage in these situations. If introduced, it must be done with sensitivity and artistry. To establish a climate that allows for humor or play, Cleese (1991) recommends that we separate the idea of seriousness from that of solemnity. He claims that it is rarely useful to be solemn, and that serious topics can often be approached with a touch of humor. Conflict-resolving practitioners could greatly benefit from training to develop the social skills useful in creating a serious but playful problem-solving atmosphere.

Foster "Optimal" Tension. Tension is the primary link between conflict and creativity. Conflict signals dissatisfaction with something or someone. This dissatisfaction brings tension into the system. If standard approaches to reducing tension are ineffective, it increases. This increase can eventually motivate people to seek new means of reducing the tension (or to keep hammering away with the old means), which can lead to adaptation or innovation and eventual reduction in tension. However, too much tension in a system can impair people's capacity to think creatively to envision a new approach.

The egg drop exercise introduces many sources of tension. The intergroup competition over winning, the limited and obscure resources that the teams are asked to work with, the constant evaluation of the judges, and even the request that the members wear trash bags and rubber gloves all increase tension. The tension works to engage the participants, but it also adversely affects their ability to think creatively, even if there is only minimal intergroup competition. Optimal tension, therefore, is a state where there isn't too little tension regarding the problem being faced in a conflict (where the disputants are not sufficiently motivated to deal with the issues and the conflict remains unresolved) or too much tension (which can lead either to conflict avoidance because it is so threatening or to conflict escalation as the tension limits one to an oversimplified black-and-white perception of the issues).

Thus, it becomes critical for conflict resolvers to develop the skills necessary to assess the level of tension in a conflict system, to diagnose what level is optimal for a given system, and to discover levers for increasing tension (such as through using open confrontation or empowering members of low-power groups) or decreasing it (such as through using humor or temporarily separating disputants from one another).

Foster Confidence to Take the Risk of Being Outlandish. Self-confidence is an individual characteristic that can affect a person's ability to take the risk involved in developing a novel point of view. However, a person's confidence level can also be significantly affected by the situation and by those in power (or perceived to be so) in the situation. Conflict specialists who emphasize their expertise and knowledge in a problem-solving session tend to elicit dependence and less confidence from the disputants, with the consequence that fewer novel ideas and recommendations are generated by the parties. A conflict specialist who supports and encourages the ideas of the disputants, highlighting those aspects of their ideas that are particularly useful or innovative, is likely to draw out a flow of ideas that expand the menu of perspectives and alternatives. It is important for facilitators to remember that the open flow of ideas and information is a dynamic responsive to the support (and playfulness) of the facilitator.

Have Appropriately Phased Open (Divergent) and Closed (Convergent) Thinking. This is the yin and yang of the creative problem-solving process. Creativity is most often associated with openness of ideas, a free-flowing of thoughts, images, symbols and so on. Decision making, though, is most often associated with moving toward closure: converging on the alternative or set of alternatives that best address the problem. A creative problem-solving approach to conflict requires both. Disputants must have the capacity and opportunity to open up to understand a problem from various perspectives and to generate many, perhaps novel, ideas or solutions, *as well as* the chance to (eventually) reach closure by taking a good, hard look at those perspectives and ideas and determining if they are any good and if they will work in a particular situation.

The open and closed modes of experience are in opposition to each other, in that it is difficult to remain open to new alternative possibilities while trying to close in on a final decision. It is therefore useful to alternate from one mode to another during the problem-solving process. Alternating between the open and closed modes can be useful during various phases of the problem-solving process, such as when defining or redefining the issues, generating solutions, or planning methods of implementation or achieving constituent buy-in. It is useful to defer judgment (delayed evaluation of the alternatives) when in the open mode, and then weigh both the strengths and weaknesses of the alternatives when moving into the closed mode for decision making.

Typically, conflict moves people into the closed mode and produces rigid thinking with restricted judgment, reduced complexity, and narrower range of attention.

Exactly why this occurs is unclear, but scholars have speculated that it may be due to a number of factors: the conflict triggering a negative affect such as anxiety, a competitive orientation overloading cognitive functioning and leading to preoccupation with formulating strategies and tactics to prevail in the conflict, or simply providing too much cognitive stimulation. If this occurs, conflict resolvers must find the means to reorient disputants, at least temporarily, into an open mode.

Recent research by Carnevale and Probst (1998) has identified an important qualifier to the causal chain of "conflict equals tension equals impaired cognitive functioning." The research found that people's cognitive functioning does become more rigid and restricted if they either anticipate or engage in competitive conflicts, but not when they expect or engage in cooperative conflict. People in a cooperative experience are better able to combine categories, see commonalities in their positions, and better locate integrative solutions than those in competitive conflicts.

The exact reasons for this difference are as yet unclear, but the implications for practice are important. Conflict resolvers who effectively reframe the conflict as a mutual problem to be solved cooperatively by the parties also open up the disputants' capacity to think creatively about the problem and the solution.

Adequately Define the Problem. Adequate definition is the aspect of creative conflict resolution that is most often shortchanged. The uncomfortable experience of tension associated with many conflicts often moves people to try to solve the problem *quickly.* This tendency puts them prematurely into the closed mode of decision making around the nature of the problem, before they take the time to open up and examine the problem from alternative perspectives. Ultimately, this can lead to superficial or even incorrect understanding of the problem-at-hand, and much time wasted generating and implementing solutions to the wrong concerns.

Ironically, this approach can take more time than if the problem is examined thoroughly up front. For example, what is the egg drop problem? Is it to build an apparatus quickly? Is it to keep the other teams from building an apparatus? Or is it to stop the egg six inches from the ground? Each of these definitions of the problem leads to a distinct strategy for solving it. Spending some time exploring the problem, and perhaps identifying the pervasive concerns behind the presenting problem, can lead to satisfying, long-lasting, and even efficient solutions.

TECHNIQUES FOR STIMULATING NOVEL IDEAS

It is important to recognize that most creative artists, writers, and scientists produce many ideas before they find a good, novel, creative one. In the preceding guidelines, we discuss some of the conditions fostering openness of the free flow of thought necessary to produce many ideas. Brainstorming (see Osborn, 1953) is a technique widely used to generate ideas. In conflict situations, it may be employed to come up with ideas about the problem or conflict, its potential solution, and action to be taken (Fisher, Ury, and Patton, 1991). In a brainstorming session, whether as an individual or as a group, one is encouraged to use imagination to come up with as many varied ideas as possible, without censoring or judging them, whether produced by oneself or by another. In a group setting, others are encouraged to free associate with, elaborate, and build on the ideas of others.

To encourage novelty as well as quality in ideas, people are encouraged to use metaphors (Lakoff and Johnson, 1980) and analogies. (For example, what new ideas might be developed about a conflict between ethnic groups by using the metaphor of family feud?) Other techniques for stimulating novelty include "synectics," or joining together opposites (Gordon and Poze, 1977); raising questions about ways of changing the situation (Eberle, 1971); substituting, separating, adding, combining, reducing, magnifying, deleting, or otherwise rearranging elements.

As the chapters on change processes (Chapter Eighteen), on intractable conflict (Chapter Twenty-One), and on large-group methods (Chapter Twenty-Six) indicate, another way of getting out of a rut and creating new ideas is to try imagining a desirable future. Beckhard and Reuben (1987), Blake and Mouton (1984), Boulding (1986), and others have used various terms—"envisioning the desired future state," "social imaging," "future search"—to characterize the process by which individuals, groups, or organizations are encouraged to free themselves from the constraints of current reality to develop an image of a better future. In practice, this procedure has been useful in helping people develop awareness of new possibilities and new directions. One could expect such a procedure to be helpful in a conflict situation: the parties are aided in imagining desirable relations in the future and to start the process of thinking how they can get there from the present situation.

A third party, such as a mediator, can bring new thinking into a stuck conflict. She may help the conflicting parties become aware of new possibilities for agreement other than win-lose or lose-lose resolution of their conflict. Thus, as Rubin, Pruitt, and Kim (1994) have pointed out, mutually satisfactory agreements may be reached by (1) expanding the pie, so that there is enough for both sides; (2) nonspecific compensation, which involves having one party receive its best alternative and compensating the other in some other way; (3) logrolling, by having the parties make mutually beneficial trade-offs among the issues; (4) cost cutting, by reducing or eliminating the costs to the party not getting its way; or (5) bridging, by finding an option that satisfies the interests of both parties (recall the discussion in Chapter Nine).

Also, by making the parties aware of their potentially "creative" differences in what they value, their expectations, their attitude toward risk, their time preferences, and the like (Thompson, 1998), we help them see that their differences can facilitate mutually satisfactory agreement.

CONCLUSION

Betty Reardon, a noted peace educator, once said, "The failure to achieve peace is in essence a failure of imagination" (personal communication). Throughout our history, a considerable amount of human and economic resources have been invested in creating new and deadlier means to wage war. The time has come to invest the energy and resources necessary to innovate and create new and livelier means to wage peace.

References

Beckhard, R., and Reuben, H. T. *Organizational Transitions.* (2nd ed.) Reading, Mass.: Addison-Wesley, 1987.

Blake, R. R., and Mouton, J. S. *Restoring Trust Between Groups in Conflict.* San Francisco: Jossey-Bass, 1984.

Boulding, E. "Enlivening Our Social Imagination." In D. Carlson and C. Comstock (eds.), *Citizen Summitry: Keeping the Peace When It Matters Too Much to Be Left to Politicians.* Los Angeles: Tarcher, 1986.

Carnevale, P. J., and Probst, T. M. "Social Values and Social Conflict in Creative Problem Solving and Categorization." *Journal of Personality and Social Psychology,* 1998, *74,* 1300–1309.

Cleese, J. "And Now for Something Completely Different." *Personnel,* Apr. 1991, pp. 13–15.

Eberle, B. *SCAMPER.* Buffalo, N.Y.: DOK, 1971.

Fisher, R. J., Ury, W., and Patton, B. *Getting to Yes: Negotiating Agreement Without Giving In.* (2nd ed.) New York: Penguin, 1991.

Gordon, W.J.J., and Poze, T. *The Metaphorical Way of Learning and Knowing.* Cambridge, Mass.: Porpoise Books, 1977.

Lakoff, R., and Johnson, M. *Metaphors We Live By.* Chicago: University of Chicago Press, 1980.

Osborn, A. F. *Applied Imagination.* New York: Scribner, 1953.

Rokeach, M. *The Open and Closed Mind.* New York: Basic Books, 1960.

Rubin, J. Z., Pruitt, D. G., and Kim, S. H. *Social Conflict.* (2nd ed.) New York: McGraw-Hill, 1994.

Stein, M. "The Creative Individual." Unpublished manuscript, 1968.

Thompson, L. *The Mind and Heart of the Negotiator.* Upper Saddle River, N.J.: Prentice Hall, 1998.

Treffinger, D. J., Isaksen, S. G., and Dorval, K. B. *Creative Problem Solving: An Introduction.* (Rev. ed.) Sarasota, Fla.: Center for Creative Learning, 1994.

CHAPTER EIGHTEEN

Change Processes and Conflict

Eric C. Marcus

*Change means movement. Movement means friction. Only in the
frictionless vacuum of a nonexistent abstract world can movement
or change occur without that abrasive friction of conflict.*
—Alinsky (1971, p. 21)

I n this chapter, I consider the relationship between change processes and conflict. If we define conflict as incompatibility—of ideas, beliefs, behaviors, roles,
needs, desires, values, and so on—then resolving such incompatibility leads,
in some way, to change: in attitude, perception, belief, norms, behavior, roles,
relationship, and so forth. I examine how conflict influences change, and vice
versa—how change influences the conflict process. Last, I discuss some of the
implications these influences have on training people in skills for productive conflict resolution.

I make the assumption that the process of change is, at its core, a process of
conflict resolution. Therefore, one can think of change as an outcome of a constructive or destructive conflict resolution process, and the process of change as a
series of conflict resolution activities that lead to some new (changed) end state.
Thus, the process of planned change gives rise to conflict; conversely, conflicts
and how they are resolved exert a strong influence on the success of planned
change. A second assumption I make is that there is a conceptual similarity in the
process of change for individuals, groups, and organizations.

In this chapter, I look at common theoretical notions regarding the process
of change and focus on three critical psychological components involved in any
change process: motivation, resistance, and commitment to change. I start by
clarifying the types of change to which I am referring. What do I mean by change?
I rely on a dictionary definition: "To cause to be different; to give a completely
different form or appearance to; transform." For my purposes, this discussion cen-

ters on change affecting individuals and groups within a social context. By social change, I refer to changes in the social systems of which we are part: a dyad (a marital relationship), small groups we belong to (the fundraising committee of the PTA), and larger groups (the organization where we work). My interest is in looking at change as it occurs in such social systems, as distinct from changes in weather patterns and other types occurring outside of our individual or social realm.

THEORETICAL CONCEPTIONS OF THE CHANGE PROCESS

Although there are many psychological theories of individual change (notably the psychodynamic and learning theories), few have been applied to understand change as it occurs in social systems. On the other hand, Lewin, Beckhard, Bridges, and others offer theoretical conceptions to help us understand the process of change occurring in organizations and groups as well as individuals. Lewin provides an overall theoretical framework for understanding the process of change in these types of systems. Beckhard, Harris, Bridges, and others apply the concepts to understanding planned change. I briefly review some of these conceptualizations and then explore key aspects of each and their related dynamics of motivation, resistance, and commitment during the process of change.

Lewin: The Process of Change

Much of the theorizing on the change process is rooted in Lewin's original concepts of unfreezing, movement, and refreezing (Lewin, 1947). This is a linear description much applied to understanding change both in individuals and social systems:

$$\text{Unfreezing} \rightarrow \text{Movement} \rightarrow \text{Refreezing}$$

Unfreezing. In Lewin's conceptualization, the first step toward change is unfreezing, or developing openness toward something different, a melting of the solidity of the current state. Unfreezing may involve numerous methods, depending on the specific area of change. For example, to enable a group to attain higher-level productivity, one might use social comparison processes (such as productivity data) to show how other groups are already attaining such levels. This part of the change process has also been referred to as developing awareness of the need for change (Lippitt, Watson, and Westerley, 1958). The critical psychological process involved in unfreezing is concerned with creating the motivation for becoming different.

Driving and Restraining Forces. Lewin's application of force field analysis to characterize human social behavior is relevant to understanding the process of unfreezing. Force field analysis is a useful method for portraying the array of forces acting on a system at any given time, and it serves to illustrate the current state of the system. Among these forces are those that promote the change goal (driving forces) and those working in opposition to it (restraining forces). Further, the forces may differ in strength in facilitating or hindering movement. These driving and restraining forces, along with their relative strengths, together identify a quasi-stationary equilibrium, which reflects the current state.

Driving forces are those motivations, attitudes, behaviors, or other characteristics of a situation that help move toward the goal, or unfreeze from the present situation. In an example of someone trying to get in better physical shape, some of the forces might be seeing that one's clothes are getting too tight, tiring easily when climbing stairs, increasing difficulty getting around a tennis court, or desire to feel better. Restraining forces are the opposite: they are the constellation of forces working against change, working to keep the status quo. Again, with the goal of getting in better shape, some examples of restraining forces are low willpower and motivation, enjoyment of eating as a social experience, a preference for sloth, and finding oneself often in the presence of lots of unhealthy food.

To begin the process of change, or unfreezing, the driving forces must be relatively stronger than the resisting forces, and a certain level of tension must be created. Increasing tension is a key factor in unfreezing and creating motivation to change. It is the fuel that powers the beginning of the change process. To illustrate the role of tension, think of a system as an ice cube; heat from a candle can represent tension. As we move the heat (tension) closer to the frozen state, the ice cube begins to melt; this begins the process of unfreezing. For the tension to be productive, it must be experienced at an optimal level. If the candle is brought too close to the ice cube, or for too long, it produces too much tension. If it is kept too far away, not enough unfreezing occurs, and not enough tension. Some feelings associated with tension include stress, discomfort, and anxiety.

A useful construct for understanding a system's ability to handle tension is tolerance for ambiguity, or the unknown. This refers to one's ability to handle the feelings generated by the tension productively. It is a construct cited as a core quality associated with creativity and good management, as well as productive conflict resolution and change.

As an example, the legal order to breakup the Bell system and AT&T to create competition in long-distance phone service created tension in that system (AT&T) to change (Tunstall, 1985). In this case, an external event (a federal court order) stimulated (actually forced) a process of unfreezing from the status quo. A situation that once worked—that was comfortable, successful, and stable—now becomes uncomfortable, doesn't work so well any longer, and forces people to look at something in a new way.

Movement. Once openness has been achieved, the next step involves movement: taking some action that changes or moves the social system to a new level. Some examples of this movement in our get-in-shape example are eating better foods (to lose weight), walking to work rather than taking the bus (to get oneself in shape), and involving all family members in setting up for dinner (to reduce preparation time). Additional examples in other realms are reorganizing employees' job responsibilities (to increase organizational efficiency) and engaging in acts of civil disobedience (to improve the social, economic, or political conditions of a particular group).

Although these activities signifying movement seem rather straightforward, complex processes are operating that make such movement difficult. Primary among these are restraining forces, which are also a form of resistance to change. This resistance is a key psychological component playing a strong role in the transition process. Resistance is mobilization of energy to protect the status quo in the face of real or perceived threat to it. Resistance may be thought of as behavior intended to protect one from the effect of real or imagined change (Zander, 1950). It is a key factor influencing the intensity of the conflicts that arise during change, and the ability to resolve them productively. Early on, the degree of resistance has an impact on the ease of unfreezing. The stronger the resistance, the more difficult it is to unfreeze from the present state.

Refreezing. Refreezing involves establishing actions or processes that support the new level of behavior and lead to resilience against those resistant forces encouraging old patterns and behaviors. In other words, deliberate steps must be taken to ensure that the new behaviors "stick," or remain relatively permanent in the system. This is often a process of restabilizing a system to its new or changed level of behavior. For example, a group whose members are trying to embrace a norm of not talking about members behind their backs might adopt a process of frequent group meetings, or avoiding discussion of personal issues if all are not present. Refreezing may also be understood in terms of the degree of commitment to the new, changed, state that exists in the system.

Commitment is a psychological construct that has received much empirical attention as a predictor of key organizational phenomena such as retention and performance. According to Salancik (1977), commitment is a state in which we become bound by our actions, where our beliefs about those actions keep us doing them. Salancik defines three aspects of committing behavior. It is visible, observable to oneself and others; it is irrevocable and cannot be taken back; and it is behavior undertaken of one's own volition, or by choice. This is linked to personal responsibility: we usually accept responsibility for behavior we enact by choice.

This last component of commitment, volition, makes evidence for it ambiguous; it is not observable and can only be attributed. It is this element that distinguishes commitment from compliance. Here, I use *compliance* to refer to behavior whose origin lies outside of oneself and is based on the perceived values of the system. Argyris (1998) refers to this as external commitment, where the desired state is one of internal commitment. Many strategies for refreezing a system end up achieving compliance to change because the methods used to bring about change do not offer choice for those whose commitment is needed. On the surface, compliance looks like commitment because both kinds of behavior are public, or visible, and may be irrevocable.

There are often many opportunities to tempt the system to move back to behaviors associated with the prechange state. This process is referred to as commitment testing (Marcus, 1994). It occurs when we are faced with the choice of reverting to old behaviors. For example, once we change our eating habits to be healthier, commitment testing occurs as we see the pastry carousel at the local diner, or smell butter cookies baking in the kitchen, or are invited to have a piece of seven-layer cake at a birthday party. Our response to these situations is an opportunity to test as well as renew our commitment to our new behavior.

Often, commitment testing engenders conflict. In the dietary example, the conflict is intrapersonal. The desire to support the changed state is incompatible with the desire to revert to old habits. The resolution of this conflict affects the level of success of the change. To the extent that this conflict is resolved in support of the changed state, the change is likely to be successful. That is, the refrozen state is likely to stay frozen.

Beckhard: Managing Planned Change

Beckhard and Harris (1987) and others (such as Bridges, 1980, 1986) have applied these concepts to understand and manage planned organizational change; they use slightly different terms when applying Lewin's concepts. Beckhard's model can be represented as follows:

Current state → Transition state → Desired future state

When this model is applied to organizational change, it often helps members develop a deeper understanding of the process and phases of planned change. Though linear, Beckhard suggests beginning with the end. The first step for those involved is to *envision a desired future state*. This helps to establish a goal for the change and serves the purpose of beginning the process of unfreezing, as well as being open to something different. Similarly, it has been found that starting with what people desire in the future generates energy, enthusiasm, motivation, and commitment to the plan and its implementation (Lindaman and Lippitt, 1979). Once this is undertaken, the next step is to move backward and *assess the current state* of the organization or entity—its current capabilities, capacities, and so forth. With the envisioned future, and assessment of current state, the next phase is to *create a transition state*. This is based, in part, on the gaps between the current state and the desired future state. These gaps create tension, which serve as a motivating force in the transition state. The larger the gap, or discrepancy, the greater the tension. The transition state is a way for a system to balance or modulate its own need for stability with its need for change.

Although this model is most often used in large, complex organizational change, the concepts are applicable on both the individual and small-group levels. Indeed, the model has been used successfully in managing many types of change, such as future search (Weisbord, 1992; on future search, see also Chapter Twenty-Six). This is a methodology for gathering together all key elements of a group or organization to identify and plan a desired future together. It takes place over a relatively short period of time (several days) and is intended to generate motivation, overcome resistance, and strengthen commitment to the agreed-on change plan.

Lewin's and Beckhard's models are linear conceptions of a sequential process of change. The models imply ordering of the phases one goes through in the change process. There is little empirical work examining the factors that may facilitate or hinder moving from one stage to the next. For example, what might be some of the conditions conducive to unfreezing? In other words, what conditions motivate unfreezing? How can resistance be weakened or overcome? What factors make refreezing difficult? How is commitment to change maintained? We turn now to a discussion of these and related questions.

Motivation and Unfreezing

Whenever a change is contemplated in any social system, a key question that is often raised among the leaders of the change is, how can we get people to buy in to a new state of affairs? The key psychological process these leaders are grappling with concerns generating the motivation to change, to unfreeze from the current state.

Creation of conflict is inherent in the process of unfreezing. The nature of the conflict, though differing with the situation, may be expressed as follows: "Our desire to do things as we've been doing them is incompatible with our need and desire to do things differently, in the future." In other words, the present state is incompatible with the desired or necessary future state. The prospect of change spurs this conflict. Beckhard's model brings out this conflict in identifying gaps between the current state and the desired future. Bartunek (1993) refers to this as a conflict of cognitive schemas—our beliefs and expectations about ourselves and our environment. The original schema is no longer adequate and a new schema is not yet apparent. The experience of this conflict often gives rise to resistance, those forces working to protect the status quo.

Conflict creates the tension or motivating forces that call into question the status quo; it contributes to the process of unfreezing from the current state.

Therefore, a curious question to consider is how to create conflict that increases the level of tension to unfreeze from the current state. I briefly focus on two areas: feedback and social support.

A common method used to generate motivation to change centers on providing feedback to the system. This can occur in many forms. The intent is to identify and make salient discrepancies between the current state and the desired or ideal state. Feedback, or information obtained about a system from outside of the system, is a common way to increase people's understanding of the need for change. Information constituting feedback is intended to stimulate the kind of conflict that motivates change. Nonetheless, the conflict that might be generated by the feedback can be handled in a variety of ways, not all of which increase the motivation to change.

There is often ample feedback available from our social environment. Unfortunately, though, such social feedback is rarely unambiguous; that is, it can be interpreted in multiple ways. Further, our interpretation is strongly influenced by factors such as our own needs and experiences, the context within which it occurs, the sender or source of the feedback, and so on. Meaningful, accurate feedback can be most useful as a motivator of change when it occurs in a context of support.

Earlier, I described the process of unfreezing as generating the energy to change, and tolerating the ambiguity that unfreezing can foster. What contributes to the ability of an individual or group to tolerate ambiguity? One element concerns the perception that one possesses or has access to the resources needed to manage the unknown. Social support is often cited as one of those critical resources in managing significant personal change. Approaches using a "twelve-step" model (for example, Alcoholics Anonymous) rely on social support as a way to strengthen people's tolerance for the stressful, anxious state that accompanies ambiguity during change. Social support can derive from many sources. In these programs, it comes from working in a group with individuals who share a common personal goal and who often have had similar personal experiences outside of the context of the twelve-step meetings. Social support may also stem from a benevolent leader, or a person who contributes to the social climate in a way conducive to individuals' being able to tolerate the ambiguity of change.

It is my contention that feedback and social support can create the conditions to motivate individuals and groups to unfreeze from the current state.

Movement and Resistance

I stated earlier that resistance serves a protective function in any change. At the same time, resistance is cited as a key factor working against successful change. This presents a curious paradox: resistance is a necessary part of change yet can be its undoing. Our interest is in looking at two aspects of resistance: how to identify and diagnose resistance when it emerges, and how to find ways to weaken it rather than strengthen it. Is change possible without resistance? Is the goal of a successful change effort to prevent forces of resistance from emerging? What factors weaken or strengthen resistance to change?

Many approaches to organizational change view resistance similarly to conflict. That is, it is something to get rid of, stamp out, push down, and in any other manner treat as an undesirable force that needs to be eradicated. Or it may be seen merely as a nuisance that one must "get past." If the resistant forces are linked to specific people or groups (with such language as "troublemakers," "naysayers," "malcontents"), a common tactic used by the larger part of the system is to try to get rid of those people—and by implication any resistance.

This orientation may sometimes lead to successful change, but it overlooks the potentially constructive role that resistance plays in the change process. In other words, resistance is a naturally emerging part of the change process, or any movement away from the status quo (Connor, 1992). As Klein notes, "a necessary prerequisite of successful change is the mobilization of forces against it" (1966, p. 502). Change without resistance is akin to premature conflict resolution; the parties involved manage to avoid those necessary parts of the process that lead to real change (or real resolution).

It is likely that the conflict expressed by individuals or groups labeled as "resisters" is a type of misattributed conflict, where the true conflict is about the planned change. In other words, conflict that emerges as expression of resistance is between the wrong parties and, in turn, over the wrong issues. Such conflicts can be viewed as an *expression* of the central conflict in any change—between what we want to be (a desired future) and what we are (the current state). Thus, in using Beckhard's model, we uncover this central conflict early on, when we highlight the gaps between where we are and where we want to be.

It is useful to consider the observation (K. Sole, personal communication) that resistance to change may be manifested in an infinite number of creative ways. Often, though, it is difficult to understand how particular behaviors or actions manifest resistance.

As an example, consider a patient's decision to change therapists just as he is about to make significant progress in his therapeutic situation. This can be understood as a legitimate desire for the patient to seek better therapy. Another possibility is to view this as a form of resistance to the patient's movement toward greater psychological health. The therapist can handle this situation in a variety of ways. The most constructive might be for the therapist to support the patient at this stage. This may involve reminding him that therapeutic progress is sometimes very difficult. Or it may mean suggesting to the patient that he is here by his own choice, and if he feels he would be better served by another therapist he should do so. Properly diagnosing such actions takes great skill on the part of the therapist.

Resistance and Conflict. It is my contention that a system cannot change without experiencing conflict. How it is handled profoundly determines the success of the effort to change. Furthermore, there is a strong similarity between the process involved in successful change effort and that involved in constructive conflict resolution.

The goal of change efforts is not necessarily to prevent forces of resistance from emerging, but rather to manage them productively, to weaken rather than strengthen them. Doing so is a complex and fascinating challenge. Further, there is a reciprocal relationship between handling resistance appropriately (in ways that weaken it) and the process of constructive conflict resolution. The same process used to weaken forces of resistance may also promote constructive conflict resolution. Conversely, if inappropriate strategies are used in handling resistance, it is likely that destructive processes will be used to deal with the emerging conflict, and vice versa.

With this in mind, what factors might serve to strengthen or weaken resistance? Though little empirical work exists in this area, some common theoretical notions are available. One of the key variables influencing the strength of resistance occurs among those most affected by change. It concerns increasing this group's understanding of the need for change and participation in its planning. To the extent that there is little understanding of the need for change and little participation in planning among those affected by it, the stronger the forces of resistance are likely to be (Zander, 1950). Conversely, if there is a high degree of understanding of and participation in the planned change, the resisting forces become weaker (Coch and French, 1948).

It can be hypothesized that the strongest forces of resistance are expressed by those with the greatest interest in preserving the status quo. Furthermore, resistance is aggravated and hence strengthened as more energy is directed to eradicating it. The more we try to push against the forces of resistance (through persuasion, logic, coercion) in an attempt to weaken or abolish them, the stronger they become, and the more likely they are to manifest themselves in a multitude of ways. Zander (1950) and Deutsch (1973) identify several other factors likely to increase resistance:

- Basing the logic for the change on personal reasons rather than objective reasons
- Disregarding already established group or organizational norms
- Lack of uniformity or agreement in the rationale for the change
- Using illegitimate techniques that fall outside of the boundaries and norms of interaction
- Negative sanctions such as punishments and threats

- Sanctions that are inappropriate in kind (such as reward of money for agreeing to support a group's strategic direction)
- Influence that is excessive in magnitude

Efforts to diminish resistant forces through coercion or other means of force may lead to temporary compliance rather than lasting change (Deci, 1995).

As an example, consider the decision to close down a plant manufacturing a product that is no longer profitable. This action has varying impact depending on how the resistance is handled. A common way of handling this type of change is to anticipate the resistant reactions of those most affected and respond to them with persuasive, convincing, well-thought-out, rehearsed, logical statements about such things as the financial need to take the action. Similarly, another approach occurs when those responsible for the decisions make every attempt to avoid the employees most affected—to lay low, disappear, or hide after the announcement is made. If those affected are denied the opportunity to express their feelings and thoughts (especially feelings of loss), strong negative attitudes are likely to emerge, along with the potential to sabotage the best interests of the organization. In other words, these actions often strengthen the forces of resistance.

Constructively Handling Resistance. We identify several factors that may strengthen resistance. What, though, are some of the conditions that may weaken resistance and foster a constructive resolution process? Some of them are a smaller change, keeping parts of the system stable, giving all parties a chance to mourn the loss that any change entails, making abundant resources available during change, and involvement by those most affected in planning their own fate. Let us consider each of these in some detail.

The first condition is a smaller change (or amount of deviation from the status quo). It is not necessary, though, to assume that only small conflicts can be resolved productively and thereby yield small change. It is useful to apply Fisher's notions on fractionating conflict (1964): break a larger conflict down into manageable pieces and work on resolving the smaller pieces first. This allows participants to experience constructive resolution. This can enhance the parties' confidence as they progress to working on resolving larger issues, which thereby may produce greater change.

Another condition for weakening resistance involves keeping parts of the system stable. This is related to issues concerning the size of the change. Here, though, it is important to pay attention to the balance between stability and change. If there is too much change going on (simultaneously moving to a new house, becoming a parent, switching jobs), this may increase the tension to too high a level for change to be productive. Keeping parts of the system stable can reduce the level of stress and tension the parties experience and therefore foster constructive resolution.

Giving parties the chance to mourn the loss that any change entails is another critical influence that may serve to weaken forces of resistance. In any change, there is loss. If parties are able to recognize and express feelings of loss associated with change, they can move forward in the change process (Bridges, 1986). Many cultures, including our own, have elaborate rituals for mourning the death of a person. They enable the mourners to accept the loss and move on. Similarly, in any change process opportunities to mourn the loss of the past play a valuable role in helping people move toward a desired future.

Moreover, these opportunities may allow the parties to then engage in a cooperative resolution process. One difficulty in this concerns our natural tendency to avoid thinking about the past as we move toward a desired future. This is especially apparent in many organizational change efforts. There is often a taboo against speaking about or holding on to symbols of the past. A primitive assumption implies that the past is bad, negative, to be forgotten, and all of the hopes and dreams become bound up in the desired future. Thus, it is important to examine our assumptions about the past in order to successfully move toward the future.

It appears that one ingredient that might lower resistance is abundant availability of resources (time, money, people) to support change. However, there is a paradox here as well. Abundant resources, under some conditions, may serve to undermine the change by lowering the necessary degree of tension and therefore weaken the motivation needed to move change forward. (For further relevant discussion, see Chapter Seventeen.)

One last factor, written about extensively in the field of organization development, is to involve those most affected by change in its planning and implementation (see, for example, Burke, 1987). Participation in planning one's future can have beneficial effects on one's future! Involving people affected by change in planning and implementation serves to increase their commitment to any change.

With reference to handling a plant closing, I suggest that one alternative strategy is stronger presence by the leaders of the change effort among those most affected by it. The leaders of the operation could meet with employees and encourage them to express their reactions and concerns. This type of action, though understandably difficult, may serve to weaken the resistant forces productively. Further, having a chance to candidly express one's attitudes, concerns, and biases, where they can be heard by those with power to change the situation (regardless of whether they do change it), often serves to weaken those forces. Engaging those groups most affected in planning (how to make the transition in closing the plant, as well as reducing or redeploying the workforce) can have productive benefits. There are many possibilities other than simply closing the plant and making immediate mass layoffs. It should be noted, though, that mere participation, though it may lower resistance, does not ensure a cooperative process of resolving the inevitable conflicts that emerge in such a situation.

Gaining Commitment

Commitment by a critical mass of people is the sufficient condition needed to sustain any change. It is the force that refreezes a system to its new, changed state. There are methods that may serve to increase the level of commitment to a new, changed state. Several strategies are similar to those methods useful for weakening forces of resistance. A common one, just discussed, is to involve those affected by the change in planning and implementing it. Participation and involvement play a powerful role during change. It is widely accepted that meaningful participation and involvement enables those affected to commit to the change; participation leads to commitment.

In a conflict situation, several types of action may lead to increased commitment to bring about constructive changes: recognizing that both parties are engaged by choice, acknowledging that either can walk away at any time, making unilateral statements of one's own commitment to a mutually productive resolution, and placing oneself in a situation where avoidance of the conflict is less likely.

We can influence our own and others' level of commitment by telling the party we are in conflict with about our commitment to constructive resolution during the early stages of the conflict: "I'm determined to work this out in a way that we can both be satisfied with" or "I'll persist until we're both comfortable." Such statements are public, cannot be taken back, and intend to give both parties an opportunity to commit to engaging in constructive conflict-handling skills.

Another type of action is to place oneself in a situation where avoidance of the conflict is less likely. By voluntarily doing so, we force ourselves to take action that we might not otherwise take. If I'm angry at a colleague for some action he took but concerned about letting him know I'm angry, I might avoid contact with him and therefore the prospect of telling him about my feelings. If, though, I voluntarily place myself in closer proximity to him, I increase the likelihood that we must work on the conflict, which is a more constructive course than continued avoidance.

It is important to further differentiate processes that might increase commitment from those that increase compliance. From the preceding discussion we can understand that it is difficult to discern when a group or individual is complying with someone else's wishes, and when the behavior reflects true change. In any system where there is a power hierarchy, gaining commitment to change becomes especially tricky. Although the outcome (committing to change versus complying with another's wishes) looks the same on the surface, understanding the methods used is one way to see which outcome we are headed for. That is, when those higher in the authority structure use methods of coercion (methods likely to feed forces of resistance), in a context where two-way communication between the hierarchy levels is not supported, the desired behaviors are surely meant to comply with the wishes of those in higher authority. Further, the long-term effect of compliance is that behaviors revert to the prechange state, whenever the people above are not around. Conversely, if those with greater power use methods that diminish forces of resistance (such as relying on high participation and involvement among those lower in the hierarchy, active listening, opportunities to mourn the loss of what people are giving up), they are likely to see greater commitment to the changes being sought. This is visible as the behaviors stick even when no one is around to police the behavior.

SOME IMPLICATIONS FOR TRAINING

Several implications for training emerge from this discussion. Let us briefly explore how the newly trained conflict resolver may act as a change agent within her own social system. Here I am referring to the issue of finding ways to change the system to which the newly trained conflict resolver returns.

The question I address is, how can the trained conflict resolver be an effective change agent? A difficulty that people often experience after receiving training in a particular skill area is how to practice the new skills back in a setting that does not necessarily support developing those skills in the first place. How can we apply what we know about the change process to encourage changing a system to be more supportive of constructive conflict resolution skills?

With this question in mind, we can apply the same three psychological principles involved in change to this application: create the motivation to change systemic conflict management skills, overcome people's resistance to changing those skills, and generate commitment to constructive conflict resolution skills in future conflicts in the system.

Thus, the person trained in skills of effective conflict resolution can be seen as a representative of the system whose conflict skills need strengthening. The person's role is twofold: first, to acquire conflict skills and, second, to transfer those skills to the system that offered the resources for the individual to attend the training. This second role involves becoming a change agent.

Generating Motivation

To become a change agent after conflict training, one needs to identify where the system is in relation to strengthening its conflict resolution skills. We can assume that the act of undertaking training in this area is a sign of unfreezing from the current state. However, we must not confuse this sign with the system's motivation to change. It is seductive to believe that by providing training to members an organization will, upon completion, believe that it has become skilled in the area of training. We must also consider how to change the system that endorses the training. To begin this process, it is useful for the change agent to reflect on the nature of his own changes—how he may have moved closer to his desired future state with regard to conflict-handling skills.

Further, the skilled conflict resolver must work at making salient to the system some desired future state, or a change goal. This can be done by reflecting on the initial reasons for undertaking the training. These may include, for example, the desire to reduce divisiveness between professional staff and support staff. A way to create tension, then, would be to highlight the gaps between the current state of divisiveness and the desired future state, say, by articulating a sense of introspection about where the system currently is, or posing questions about the current state to groups of stakeholders (perhaps the leadership of the organization, the two groups with a history of divisiveness, or one's peers). From these activities, it is important to identify a group that, in the change agent's judgment, demonstrates sufficient readiness for change.

Identifying and Handling Resistance

Many forces operate to move the social system back to the pretraining state, among them using the hierarchy and power structure to resolve conflict, leaders' modeling of poor conflict-handling skills, and using verbal or physical threats or abuse to resolve issues. It is an important first step for the conflict resolver merely to be aware of the power of those forces working to maintain the status quo. Further, it is difficult to anticipate all the manifestations of resistance that may arise. Nonetheless, the key idea to keep in mind is not how to prevent resistance from developing but rather how to recognize and handle it productively.

One idea for doing this is to focus on how the conflict resolver himself is changing, rather than focusing on how the other, or the system, needs to change. Second, change agents often devote too much attention and resources to those most resistant to a change, underemphasizing the degree of attention and support needed by those individuals and groups who are least resistant. Another way to look at this is to increase the level of support, attention, and resources to those whose motivation for change is already high. To some, preaching to the converted is redundant or a waste of energy. It can, though, play a valuable role in helping to spread the positive energy for change rather than trying to weaken the negative energy against change.

Fostering Commitment

Several ideas can be applied to generating commitment to changing a system's conflict-handling skills. First, the change agent must create opportunities for key members of the system to participate in planning how their skills are to be strengthened. If, for example, the change agent must reduce intergroup conflict, she might engage members of both groups in strategizing effective ways of bringing parties together. Under the guidance of the conflict resolver, this type of session might serve both to model effective conflict-handling skills and to build some of the commitment needed for further strengthening the skills in the system.

A related idea about generating commitment has to do with free choice. Allowing people to choose the level of involvement they wish to pursue in the change effort contributes to commitment. Furthermore, reminding people that they are free to participate or not is often a useful strategy for reducing resistance. In many social systems, especially in work settings, we come to believe that we are in an unpleasant situation *by force*. This is rarely the case. Reminding people about their choice in these matters can be freeing, both reducing resistance and generating commitment. Thus, if people don't want to participate in strengthening their conflict skills, the change agent should not mandate or force their participation. Such action merely leads to compliance and other increases in resistance.

CONCLUSION

It was my intent, in this chapter, to look at some of the linkages and interrelationships between conflict processes and change. I have discussed the bidirectional nature of the processes involved in change and conflict. My view is that any change process—at the individual, group, organizational, community, or societal level—finds conflict inherent in the process. Similarly, any conflict resolution process brings about change in some form, between or within the parties in conflict.

I have highlighted three important psychological components of the change process and how they influence the course of conflict. Motivation, resistance, and commitment are by no means the only psychological dynamics involved in change. It is my contention, though, that they are important enough to warrant further theorizing and empirical study as they relate to conflict and change. Furthermore, it would behoove the conflict resolution practitioner to work with these dynamics as they relate to creating change in the system within which any conflict training takes place.

References

Alinsky, S. *Rules for Radicals.* New York: Vintage Books, 1971.

Argyris, C. "Empowerment: The Emperor's New Clothes." *Harvard Business Review,* 1998, *76,* 98–105.

Bartunek, J. M. "The Multiple Cognitions and Conflicts Associated with Second Order Organizational Change." In J. K. Murnighan (ed.), *Social Psychology in Organizations,* Upper Saddle River, N.J.: Prentice Hall, 1993.

Beckhard, R., and Harris, R. *Managing Organizational Transitions.* (2nd ed.) Reading, Mass.: Addison-Wesley, 1987.

Bridges, W. *Transitions.* Reading, Mass.: Addison-Wesley, 1980.

Bridges, W. "Managing Organizational Transitions." *Organizational Dynamics,* Summer 1986, pp. 24–33.

Burke, W. W. "Organization Development: A Normative View." Reading, Mass.: Addison-Wesley, 1987.

Coch, L., and French, J.R.P. "Overcoming Resistance to Change." *Human Relations,* 1948, *11,* 512–532.

Connor, D. R. *Managing at the Speed of Change.* New York: Villard, 1992.

Deci, E. *Why We Do What We Do: Understanding Self-Motivation.* New York: Penguin, 1995.

Deutsch, M. *The Resolution of Conflict: Constructive and Destructive Processes.* New Haven: Yale University Press, 1973.

Fisher, R. "Fractionating Conflict." In R. Fisher (ed.), *International Conflict and Behavioral Science: The Craigville Papers.* New York: Basic Books, 1964.

Klein, G. "Some Notes on the Dynamics of Resistance to Change: The Defender Role." In G. Watson (ed.), *Concepts for Social Change.* Washington, D.C.: National Training Laboratories, 1966.

Lewin, K. "Group Decision and Social Change." In E. E. Maccoby, T. Newcomb, and E. Hartley (eds.), *Readings in Social Psychology.* Austin, Tex.: Holt, Rinehart and Winston, 1947.

Lindaman, E., and Lippitt, R. *Choosing the Future You Prefer.* Washington, D.C.: Development Publications, 1979.

Lippitt, R., Watson, J., and Westerley, B. *The Dynamics of Planned Change.* Orlando: Harcourt Brace, 1958.

Marcus, E. C. "Measuring Change in Evolving Organizational Cultures." Paper presented at the ninth annual conference of the Society for Industrial and Organizational Psychology, Nashville, Tenn., 1994.

Salancik, G. "Commitment Is Too Easy." *Organizational Dynamics,* 1977, *6,* 62–80.

Tunstall, B. *Disconnecting Parties: Managing the Bell System Break-Up.* New York: McGraw-Hill, 1985.

Weisbord, M. R. *Productive Workplaces: Organizing and Managing for Dignity, Meaning, and Community.* San Francisco: Jossey-Bass, 1992.

Zander, A. "Resistance to Change: Its Analysis and Prevention." *Advanced Management Journal,* 1950.

CHAPTER NINETEEN

Learning Through Reflection

Victoria J. Marsick
Alfonso Sauquet

In this chapter, we introduce a model for learning from experience through reflection (Marsick and Watkins, 1990; Watkins and Marsick, 1993; Cseh, Watkins, and Marsick, 1999). We discuss its roots in adult learning theory and action science, and we draw out implications for use of the model. We then illustrate how a conflict participant can apply these ideas to effectively achieve objectives before, during, or after a conflict. Finally, we speak to implications for what a trainer or teacher can do to help a student learn to become a reflective practitioner of conflict, before drawing some conclusions about the value and limitations of this model for conflict resolution.

OUR MODEL OF LEARNING THROUGH REFLECTION ON EXPERIENCE

Many models of learning from experience have their roots in the thinking of John Dewey (1938), who examined how past actions guide future actions (Boud, Cohen, and Walker, 1993; Jarvis, 1992; Kolb, 1984; Schön, 1987). Dewey observed that if people do not get desired results, they attend to the resulting "error" or mismatch between intended and actual outcomes. He described learning as a somewhat informal use of what is known as the scientific method. People collect and interpret data about their experiences. They develop and test their hunches even though they may not do so very systematically. Dewey summed up learning from experience: "It involves (1) observation of surrounding conditions; (2) knowledge of what has happened in similar situations in the past, a knowledge obtained partly by recollection and partly from the information, advice, and warning of those who have had a wider experience; and (3) judgment which puts together what is observed and what is recalled to see what they signify" (1938, p. 69).

People make meaning of situations they encounter by filtering them through impressions they acquire over time from past experiences. They determine whether they can rely on past interpretations, or whether they need a new response set. They may need to search for new ideas and information, or reevaluate old ideas and information. Learning takes place as people interpret and reinterpret their experience in light of a growing, cumulative set of insights and then revise their actions to meet their goals. Learning results in new insights and a relatively new set of what Dewey called "habits" of new behavior.

Figure 19.1 depicts a model for learning through experience that Marsick and Watkins (1990) have developed, based on Dewey's work as applied to problem solving. The circle in the center represents encountering a new experience. New experiences are always potentially problematic, even though people may simplify them by emphasizing what is familiar, whether or not this is accurate. In our model, people use reflection to become aware of the problematic aspects of the experience, to probe these features, and to learn new ways to understand and address the challenge they encounter. Problem-solving steps are located at the vertical and horizontal axes and are labeled (clockwise) as N, E, S, and W— the cardinal compass points north, east, south, and west. Learning steps are located in between problem-solving steps; they are labeled (beginning clockwise just before north) with the letters denoting northwest, northeast, southeast, and southwest (NW, NE, SE, and SW).

Problem solving begins with diagnosing a problem as people encounter a new experience (north, or N). They frame the new experience based on what they learned from past experience (NW). They assess similarities or differences and use their interpretation to make sense of the new situation. People often make these judgments quickly, without much conscious reflection. Reflection slows down the diagnosis, but it also helps a person become aware of the complexity of the situation and the assumptions used to judge the new challenge.

After diagnosing a new experience (N), people learn more about the context of the problem (NE). They find out what other people are thinking and doing; they try to understand the politics of what is going on. They may gather information from other people or social groups that are affected by the problem, and they might test their thinking with others or conduct mini-experiments before they choose a course of action. Reflection can play a key role in this phase by opening up lines of thinking that would otherwise remain unexplored. Interpretation of the context leads to choice as to alternative action, guided by recollection of past solutions and by one's own search for other potential models for action.

Figure 19.1. Marsick and Watkins's Informal and Incidental Learning Model.

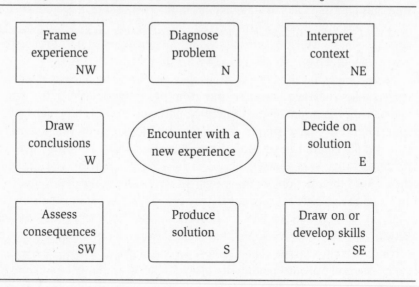

Source: Adapted from Marsick and Watkins, 1990.

Once a decision has been made about a course of action (E), a person develops or gathers what is needed to implement the decision (SE). Reflection might be anticipatory, and lead to developing new capabilities so as to implement the solution. Reflection often occurs while the action is being implemented over time. When people reflect-in-action (Schön, 1987), they typically do so if they are taken by surprise in the course of action. Because they are learning as they implement, they may make quick judgments based on partial information. They may also seek further information during action.

Once an action is taken (S), people assess consequences and decide whether or not outcomes match their goals (SW). Reflection after the fact allows for a full learning review. It is relatively easy to assess *intended* consequences if goals are reasonably explicit and data are available to make sound judgments. It is harder to recognize *unintended* consequences, although reflection can lead one to ask questions of a range of people and explore sources of information that might otherwise be ignored. A learning review leads to conclusions about results (W) and lessons learned that can be of help in planning future actions. Reflection at this point brings a person full circle to the new understanding (NW) drawn in preparing for another iteration of the cycle.

Reflection is central to every phase of learning from experience, although not everyone always uses reflection consciously to its fullest potential. Reflection sensitizes people to surprises and mismatches that signal the inadequacy of their prior stock of knowledge. Through reflection-in-action (Schön, 1987), people adjust their course of action and learn while they are carrying out the solution. Reflection after the fact helps to draw out lessons learned that are useful for the next problem-solving cycle.

In situations of conflict, people may be forced into making quick sense of many complex factors that influence how they interpret the context and identify unintended consequences. Studies of informal learning highlight the fact that when contexts are highly variable and surprise-rich, as is certainly the case under conditions of conflict, their interpretation assumes large significance (Cseh, 1998; Cseh, Watkins, and Marsick, 1999). Our model calls for refocusing attention on a variety of contextual factors that influence how people frame what is problematic about a conflict, think about alternative actions, and look for unintended consequences.

At the heart of this model is the dynamic interaction of action—having an experience—and reflection that helps a person interpret and reinterpret experience. The quality of reflection is central to how a person makes meaning of what is occurring. We are often guided in reflection by internalized social rules, norms, values, and beliefs that have been acquired implicitly and explicitly through socialization. These internalized perspectives can distort our interpretation of an experience. To learn deeply from experience, people must critically reflect on the assumptions, values, and beliefs that shape their understanding. To gain insight into how people engage in deep, critical reflection, we turn to work by Jack Mezirow (1991, 1995, 1997) and Chris Argyris and Donald Schön (1974, 1978).

CRITICAL REFLECTION

Adults shape their understanding of a new situation by looking through the lens of tacit, often unconscious belief systems, which Mezirow (1991, 1995, 1997) calls meaning perspectives (or, more recently, habits of mind) and meaning schemas (more recently, points of view). Mezirow defines *meaning perspectives* as "a general frame of reference, set of schemas, worldview, or personal paradigm. A meaning perspective involves a set of *psychocultural* assumptions, for the most part culturally assimilated but including intentionally learned theories, that serve as one of three sets of codes significantly shaping sensation and de-limiting perception and cognition: *sociolinguistic* (e.g., social norms, cultural and language codes, ideologies, theories), *psychological* (e.g., repressed parental prohibitions which continue to block ways of feeling and acting, personality traits) and *epistemic* (e.g., learning, cognitive and intelligence styles, sensory learning preferences, focus on wholes or parts)" (1995, p. 42; italics added).

Meaning perspectives are broad, guiding frames of mind that influence development of focused meaning schemas, "the specific set of beliefs, knowledge, judgment, attitude, and feeling which shape a particular interpretation, as when we think of an Irishman, a cathedral, a grandmother, or a conservative or when we express a point of view, an ideal or a way of acting" (Mezirow, 1995, p. 43).

Meaning perspectives or schemas are the containers that shape our experience. These containers are taken for granted and therefore hard to see, let alone question. That is why it is so difficult, for example, for a white person to see how she is racist, or a male to understand how his actions could be seen as sexist. In addition, through this questioning a person also challenges the basic assumptions of one's group and culture. Mezirow's work points to the need for critical reflection, but he does not give us much practical advice about how to probe deeply into assumptions. Action science provides these tools.

Action Science

Chris Argyris and Donald Schön (1974, 1978) developed action science to explore the gap between what people say they want to do, and what they are actually able to produce. They hypothesize that people are guided by a theory of action, which is cognitive in nature. Argyris and Schön (1978) argued against the behaviorists' belief that people act somewhat blindly in response to their external environment: "human learning . . . need not be understood in terms of the 'reinforcement' or 'extinction' of patterns of behavior but as the construction, testing, and restructuring of a certain kind of knowledge" (p. 10).

Theories of action predict that people act in certain ways under certain conditions, when guided by certain values, to achieve desired consequences. Argyris and Schön explain that when things go wrong, people first change their tactics. They call this single-loop learning. For example, if a peer rejects another employee's opinion, the employee might decide that he did not phrase his argument effectively. He might try to state the same viewpoint differently, or he might gather more information to build a stronger case. If the reasons for resistance do not lie in the format of the argument, these tactical changes do not remedy the mismatch. Instead, the employee must reconsider how he has framed the problem. Argyris and Schön (1974, 1978) call this deeper level of analysis double-loop learning about assumptions, values, beliefs, or norms that influence action. In our example, double-loop learning might take place if the employee recognizes that his definition of *effective* or of *participative decision making* is fundamentally different from that of his colleague. Single-loop learning is not, in and of itself, "bad." Learning to change tactics often yields valuable gains, but such learning may not go far enough.

People often believe that they act according to one set of beliefs (espoused theory), but because of tacitly held assumptions, values, and norms, in fact they act in ways that often contradict their espoused theories (theory-in-use). The employee in our example might believe in participatory decision making (his espoused theory), but in this case he wants to exclude some stakeholder groups that hold highly divergent views (theory-in-use).

Argyris and Schön identified a core set of values that control many of the interactions they studied. These values underlie what they describe as a behavioral-social world, or culture, that they call "Model I." Model I values lead to actions that often engender conflict. These values include the need to exert unilateral control over the interaction, a drive to win at all costs, and a tendency to act as if one is rational even when emotions run high.

Argyris and Schön describe an alternative learning culture that they call Model II. Its values include committing to valid information even if it contradicts opinions held by powerful others or oneself, ensuring that agreements are based on free and informed choice, and finding solutions based on internal commitment rather than external persuasion or coercion. Model II cultures cannot be developed without engaging in some double-loop learning. Decisions often take longer because more information is considered and people are encouraged to advocate for their viewpoint while also remaining open to contradictory information. In Model II, people probe for the reasoning that leads others to the conclusions and judgments they reach. Employees are encouraged to raise divergent views even if, by doing so, they generate controversy. Leaders in a Model II culture manage the resulting conflict because they see that this helps them avoid mistakes and generate innovative thinking.

Model I values lead people to control outcomes toward their own respective goals. In Model II, people value learning about the best solution more than achieving goals that might be incomplete, inaccurate, or inappropriate. Model I cultures encourage blaming because someone has to be right, whereas Model II cultures recognize that problems are complex and co-created. In a Model II culture, people who subscribe to action science take responsibility for finding and correcting behaviors that contribute to results not really desired even when others in the situation do not.

A Model I culture may not be supportive of double-loop learning practices, such as willingness to change an opinion if it turns out to be based on faulty reasoning, or interest in generating evidence to support alternative viewpoints that might be superior to one's own thinking. Individuals can practice double-loop learning in a Model I culture, but if they do so they are clearly going against norms they might, or might not, be able to change. Hence, double-loop learners carefully choose when and how to use these skills. (For a related discussion from a different theoretical perspective, see Chapter Fourteen.)

Experiential Learning

It is seldom possible to probe deeply into our beliefs without confronting many facets of our psychological makeup that we may find difficult to name, face, and change. Others may not want us to think or act differently either, even if the relationship is dysfunctional. For these and other reasons, engaging in critical reflection can evoke powerful feelings that seem at odds with instrumental, rational ways of learning from experience. Ironically, focusing on reflection can lead to an exclusive cognitive emphasis. Some educators rebel against this limited focus. Boud, Cohen, and Walker (1993), for example, describe learning as a holistic process that involves thinking, feeling, and the will to action. They note that in English-speaking cultures "there is a cultural bias towards the cognitive and conative aspects of learning. The development of the affect is inhibited and instrumental thinking is highly valued" (p. 12).

Those same authors emphasize the affective side of learning from experience. Postle (1993), for example, draws on the work of John Heron (1992) on multi-modal learning. The base of learning is affective, contends Heron—as does David Kolb (1984). By affective, they both mean that people learn from experience through a direct encounter with life that involves total immersion, with all its attendant sensations and feelings. The affective dimension to learning includes emotions and also a deeper, nonrational understanding of the situation.

Boud, Cohen, and Walker (1993) legitimate feelings as grist for the mill of reflection. They do not shrink from feelings, as might be so in a Model I world, where the value placed on rationality can leave people ashamed or embarrassed about emotions. Some experiential educators, such as Heron (1992), go a step further. Feelings precede rational explanations and therefore can point the way to fresh insights as people revisit and reinterpret these feelings.

Sometimes, experiential educators help learners get in touch with insights they normally filter out of their awareness. In essence, feelings are opened up through anticipatory reflection and learning about future possible states. People are helped to forge new experiences, and to use the feelings these situations evoke to challenge prior viewpoints. They are helped to reframe fundamental viewpoints based on new feelings that are triggered by seeing, feeling, hearing, touching, or otherwise sensing the world in new ways. They are freed from the bonds of having to name and rationally explain what they may sense but have not yet fully experienced.

Using Reflection and Critical Reflection to Learn from Experience

Our model in Figure 19.1 integrates reflection and critical reflection. We also recognize that powerful feelings often arise as people learn from experience. We recommend that feelings be recognized and used to reassess mental models, and to get in touch with new interpretations of present and future events.

Simple reflection involves reviewing attendant thoughts, feelings, and actions without questioning one's interpretation or meaning of the experience. But people can be misled by their interpretation of experience. They might frame the experience or solutions inaccurately, especially if they miss information or signals about the nature of the new challenge. Prior assumptions and beliefs can lead to partial, limited, or incorrect assessment of a situation. Simple reflection in our model is stimulated by questions such as

- What did I intend?
- What actions, feelings, or results surprised me?
- How is this experience alike or different from my prior experiences?
- What does this experience tell me about worldviews other than my own?

Critically reflective questions do more. They probe the context, or the person's assumptions, and how this has an impact on their judgments. Such questions look more like these:

- What else is going on in the environment that I might not have considered but that has an impact on how I understand the situation?
- In what ways could I be wrong about my hunches?
- In what way might I be using inapplicable lessons from my past to frame problems or solutions, and is this framing accurate?
- Are there other ways to interpret the feelings I have in this situation?

It is not easy to engage in critical reflection during a conflict, although it can be done with practice. Critical reflection demands an open mind and heart, willingness to question one's interpretations of the situation, suspension of blame, as well as the ability to slow things down and probe for alternative viewpoints. Critical reflection is more easily carried out before or after the fact, in the cooler light of day and with time to learn new skills in order to change one's customary response patterns.

ILLUSTRATING THE MODEL

What would it look like if we were to use this model of learning from experience in working through conflict? We show how a person can do so, with or without assistance from a facilitator, by introducing a hypothetical example that is a composite of situations we have seen in practice.

Let us imagine a normal work conflict that seems exacerbated by perceptions of gender difference. Although the focus in this example is on male-female relationships, it is not hard to imagine an analogous situation for race, class, or other dimensions of power. This example is set in a financial services company. Women form about 10 percent of the senior staff. They often find that they are left out of information loops, or that when they come into the room men grow quiet, ignore them, or tell jokes that the women find demeaning.

Use of Reflection During Conflict

Imagine a marketing manager, named Sue, who has been appointed as the only female on a task force put together to take certain financial services out to new markets using data-based delivery systems. Several meetings have already been held. As Sue walks into her third meeting, she decides to take the lead in pulling things together. She summarizes what she thinks the group has agreed to, identifies where they have disagreements, and makes a suggestion about how to move forward. The roadblock is whether or not they can gain market share with their targeted group of consumers by using the commercial outlet they have selected.

Sue suggests that they use a consulting group, called ThinkRight, to gather more information. One of her team members, Bob, strongly disagrees and accuses Sue of trying to railroad a decision. He half jokes about how Sue is trying to impose her choices on the group. The other men nod in agreement. This seems a no-win situation; Sue cannot easily let their challenge to her pass without feeling as though she is giving up the ability to influence the situation. Yet any action she takes might, she thinks, appear as even more aggressive.

If Sue engages in single-loop learning about her conflict with Bob, she might reflect on the tactics she used in addressing the roadblock. She might consider that she and Bob share the same goal and simply disagree on tactics—for example, whether they need more data, whether ThinkRight is the best consultant group, or whether there is a better way to check out the group's assumptions. She might also reimmerse herself in her gut feelings about the experience, and check her intuition. She can look at her style of presentation, nonverbal cues about how her peers perceive her, and a holistic sense of what she thinks is taking place.

If Sue engages in double-loop learning, she might wonder if she has framed the problem correctly in the first place: Is there a more fundamental disagreement in the group than the choice of the delivery system for financial services? She might probe her level of comfort and skill in managing power dynamics. She can ask herself whether she is, indeed, railroading a decision. She might raise the question of her gender, perhaps also somewhat jokingly as Bob did, but not try to ignore the comment. She might throw it back on the group by stating how she feels and ask others how they feel. She might ask people to consider the way their group had been working together, and thus open up a discussion of underlying group dynamics that might be affecting their interactions.

If Sue probes into assumptions and beliefs, she opens up further avenues for discussion that others might not consider, or that they might consider to be not discussable. Doing so can open up the group to new ways of thinking about the problem, or it can exacerbate the conflict, depending on how Sue addresses the issues and how others interact with her in pursuing their analysis.

Use of Reflection After Conflict

Let us further imagine that Sue has the conversation with her team members that we present in Table 19.1. In this conversation, Bob challenges Sue. She is not happy with the conversation, so she meets with some colleagues who are using action science to develop skills in handling conflict by analyzing their experiences after they happen.

Table 19.1. Sue's Dialogue with Her Teammates.

What Sue Felt or Thought but Did Not Say	What Sue and Teammates Said
"These guys! We've been chewing on this question ever since we began meeting. Someone must know something about this situation that I don't know."	*Sue:* "So, that summarizes what we have agreed to. I think we disagree about whether we think that the people we want to reach actually shop in the kind of convenience store we have targeted. I suggest that we hire ThinkRight Consultants to do focus groups to check out our assumptions on this one."
"What's Bob up to now?! This is coming from left field."	*Bob:* "You've been pushing those people from the moment we met. What's in it for you to use these guys?"
"Here we go again. These guys are trying to make me look like I don't know what I'm doing."	*Sue:* "Huh? I'm just trying to move us forward. We've been circling around this question ever since we began meeting. I want us to move forward."
"What do I do with this one . . . he's made it look like, if I confront him, he's right . . . the jerk! He's not really joking."	*Bob (said somewhat mockingly, as if in humor):* "Yeah, yeah. I know how you women work. Give you an inch and you take a mile!" *(laughter all around from others)* "You're just trying to railroad your decision through." *(Others nod in agreement; no one else speaks up.)*

An action science consultant works with Sue by helping identify her explicit and implicit intentions for this interaction. Sue might first identify her goal as trying to get the best solution to the roadblock, but eventually she might also become aware of conflicting goals—such as to win in her confrontation with Bob. Sue might also realize that she values looking good in front of her teammates, especially in light of the gender discrimination at the company, and she wants to be respected as a professional. The consultant helps Sue recognize the mismatch between her intentions and outcomes. This mismatch may stimulate a desire to learn a new way of addressing conflict.

As they review the conflict, the consultant draws out explicit assumptions that Sue might be holding about her teammates and her interactions with them in this situation. The consultant uses the ladder of inference to help Sue see how she makes sense of the conflict. This device helps reveal the reasoning people use in coming to conclusions and taking action. Using the ladder of inference, Sue can begin to see how she uses her own meaning schemas (to use Mezirow's language) to filter and interpret what she sees in the experience. Table 19.2 illustrates hypothetical ladders of inference for Sue and Bob.

If these ladders bear any relationship to reality, we can see that Bob and Sue are on a collision course. Their respective framing of the situation makes it very

Table 19.2. Dueling Ladders of Inference.

Steps on the Ladder of Inference	Sue's Ladder	Bob's Ladder
Actions that I take	"I'll just joke a bit too, so I don't look foolish, but I'll be darned if I'm going to give this one up. . . . I'll show him I'm right!"	"I'll just put Sue in her place here . . . that should stop her from pursuing her agenda."
Conclusions that I draw	"I'd better get some data out on the table to see what's going on here so I won't get duped."	"Sue's using ThinkRight as a 'screen' to cover up her real motives."
Assumptions that I make	"I'll bet that Bob is just trying to make me look bad."	"Sue has a hidden agenda. . . . She wants to grab control here."
Meanings that I add	"This seems like a no-brainer. . . . These guys must know something that I don't."	"In my life, when women take the lead, they don't let me have any say in the matter."
Data I select from what I observe	"This decision shouldn't be so hard. . . . Maybe an outside perspective would help us get past this roadblock."	"Once again, Sue's in charge."
Directly observable data	"I suggest that we hire ThinkRight Consultants to do focus groups."	"I suggest that we hire ThinkRight Consultants to do focus groups."

difficult to look for common goals. They are each influenced by deeply held beliefs and values they have not consciously explored—and that may also bring out strong feelings sure to affect their decisions. Their choices may lead them to take action that actually creates the consequences they say they do not wish to experience.

The consultant helps Sue map the links between her assumptions and how they shape her actions, to see this chain of consequence. Table 19.3 illustrates this kind of mapping. The consultant knows it takes time to map causal links with any degree of accuracy. To prevent projecting meaning schemas on Sue, the consultant must test whether various interpretations actually represent Sue's viewpoint. In this way, the consultant can help Sue see that her interpretations are likely to lead her to the gap she says she wants to avoid, between her various stated intentions and the likely outcomes from the interaction.

Underlying beliefs and values—Sue's, Bob's, the other teammates', and the company's—are not easily changed even if they can be recognized as unproductive. Using Mezirow's framework, the consultant can help Sue look in greater depth at the kind of assumptions that might be influencing her action. People's responses often reflect views in the dominant culture. By mapping out responses and discussing them with others, they can identify deeper patterns that cause conflict, and they may be able to produce a change in the cultural patterns that otherwise make it difficult to act in new ways.

Recently, for example, Karen Watkins taught a graduate course in action science at the University of Georgia (Marsick and Watkins, 1999). Two individuals from different organizations had brought in cases in which sexual harassment was an underlying theme. In the group discussion that ensued, many individuals agreed that this was a significant societal concern. The class mapped the themes from the point of view of common responses, and how these responses would have to change in order to allow greater learning to occur. These maps are shown in Table 19.4. Action science can help make public many issues that otherwise cannot easily be addressed because of potential repercussions.

Table 19.3. Mapping One Possible Set of Causal Links in Sue's Case.

Sue's Intentions	Sue's Assumptions	Sue's Actions	Sue's Outcomes
To be taken seriously as a professional	"Bob's trying to make me look bad."	"I'll stick to my guns and push to hire ThinkRight."	Sue's teammates thinks she is too wedded to her own solution and thus not professional.

Table 19.4. Action Science Map of Sexual Harassment in the Workplace.

Individual Level			
Contextual Cues	Action Strategies	Consequences	System Consequences
When sexually harassing behavior occurs . . .	I make a joke of it, pretend it didn't happen, and say nothing . . .	which guarantees that the behavior will escalate . . .	and neither I nor the others affected by the behavior (i.e., perpetrators, managers, and learners) learn how to define limits of acceptable behavior in the workplace.

System Level			
When sexually harassing behavior occurs . . .	managers and others ask victims to "just handle it," tease and make light of it, and expect victims to confront it alone without upsetting the system . . .	which guarantees that the behavior will escalate . . .	and a sexually harassing culture will be tolerated or encouraged and victims are doubly victimized.

The Learning Alternative			
When sexually harassing behavior occurs . . .	I recognize that others and I are affected and ask that all concerned become involved in remedying the situation . . .	which guarantees that the behavior that is acceptable will be publicly discussed and consensus may emerge about what is and is not acceptable . . .	and the system will either publicly admit that it tolerates this behavior or begin to engage in explicit conversations to help both victims and perpetrators make meaning of "sexually harassing behavior."

Source: Marsick, V. J., and Watkins, K. E. *Facilitating the Learning Organization.* Aldershot, England: Gower Publishing Limited, 1999, p. 154, Table 9.2. Reprinted with permission.

Use of Reflection Before a New Conflict

The consultant can help Sue create and role-play alternative ways of addressing the situation. Sue needs to practice these alternatives to gain the skills required to address conflict differently. She probably finds it difficult to act in new ways, given that her current behavior has been shaped by past successes, and given the reality of the politics in her company. Getting all the information on the table may mean that Sue has to give up some of her beliefs. For example, other people in the group might have information about the use of ThinkRight that suggests focus groups are not the right way to test these market assumptions. Or, even though Sue might have the capability to take charge of this situation, the resistance she is experiencing might make it difficult for her to get the same results as a male executive could obtain.

By redesigning and practicing new responses, Sue can learn how to work with conflict constructively in the future. Redesigns take the form of what action scientists label productive reasoning skills. Sue can be helped to lay out her position clearly, whatever it might ultimately be, and then talk to the team about her reasoning and the actual data that support it. Sue can then ask the team what they think of her position, and if they have any information that she is missing that ought to be considered. Redesigns usually do not include saying all that is in "one's left-hand column" (of Table 19.3). However, the consultant encourages Sue to acknowledge and work through the feelings she has about the situation so that she can reassess and reintegrate them into her view about the action she should take.

An action science consultant often helps people identify signals that cause them to act defensively and create a self-fulfilling prophecy that may also be self-defeating. Oscar Mink (in Marsick and Watkins, 1990) developed a formula to help people new to action science to identify their theory-in-use patterns (see Exhibit 19.1). One begins by identifying the undesired consequences that one seems to produce. Patterns begin to emerge that show when and how one engages in behavior that produces these consequences.

For example, it might be that the person acts in a certain way only with authority figures, or when he feels he is not given choices, or when he feels judged. By paying attention to these circumstances, the person can anticipate a likely response and change his behavior accordingly. A theory-in-use proposition for Sue, for example, might read like this: "When I'm confronted with a man who makes light of my contribution, I'm afraid that I won't be taken seriously as a professional; so I dig in and hold on to my position, even if I was not initially wedded to it, which guarantees that I won't be taken seriously as a professional."

Theory-in-use propositions often speak to values and beliefs that are particularly significant to a person. This also means that, in conflict situations, people find it difficult to set them aside in their negotiations and responses.

Exhibit 19.1. Mink's Formula for Constructing Theory-in-Use Propositions.

When _____ happens, I am afraid that
　　　　　　　　(triggering situation)

_____ will happen, so I
　　　　(what I don't want to happen)

_____, which guarantees that
　　　　　　(what I do)

_____ will happen.
　　　(what I don't want to happen)

Source: Marsick, V. J., and Watkins, K. E. *Facilitating the Learning Organization.* Aldershot, England: Gower Publishing Limited, 1999, p. 151, Figure 9.3. Reprinted with permission.

USING THE MODEL TO FACILITATE LEARNING THROUGH REFLECTION

Facilitators can help people reflect on both the cognitive and noncognitive dimensions of conflict. The challenge may be greatest when conflict emerges unexpectedly. On the one hand, the element of surprise makes working with conflict challenging. On the other hand, the impact of any such work is great because need is so apparent and results so immediately tangible. Learning from past experience can help facilitators build skills to better address conflict in the moment.

Facilitating Reflection During the Experience of Conflict

One step that can help people address conflict in the moment is to put in place a learning review process that becomes routine, as well as a structure to assist in reflection. Learning reviews help people become aware of goals, outcomes, contextual factors that influence how they understand a situation, assumptions that influence actions, and feelings that they cannot articulate but recognize are operative. Facilitators can identify ways to do such learning reviews, help people gain skills in carrying them out, and encourage them to articulate their viewpoints and discuss them openly with others. They can create a culture where conflict is expected and recognized for the value it brings to results.

The U.S. Army, for example, developed the after-action review (AAR) for this purpose (Sullivan and Harper, 1997). AARs are typically held in battle environments, but they are also being used in noncombat situations. The learning review is guided by four questions: What did we intend to happen? What happened? Why did it happen that way? How can we improve what happened? AARs focus attention on goals, which in itself can increase conscious learning. Data are collected to track actions and results so that the discussion can be based on what is called "ground truth," that is, accurate data-based reports of what took place on the battleground. Ground truth in the army is collected by using computer-based technology for detailed information on moves that were made. About 75 percent of the time spent in an AAR involves focused reflection on why things occurred and how people can improve their actions next time. Ground rules are set for dialogue and reflection, which include freedom to speak up, regardless of one's rank; a norm of honesty rather than sugarcoating or holding back for fear of reprisal; and strict avoidance of blame.

After-action reviews are being adapted by corporations for use in noncombat situations, where the enemy may not be as easily identified, the motivation for working together not as clear, and the consequences of a mistake not as obvious. Conflicts in civilian life also might not resolve in a clear-cut win-loss outcome. The four steps of reflection, however, are similar to steps in our model and show how this framework can be made operational.

Facilitators can also help people attend to the noncognitive dimensions of conflict. Perhaps the most powerful first step for doing so is to make space for naming and working with feelings. Shame and stigma are often associated with showing feelings, at least with Model I cultural values. The facilitator can help to create a respectful, safe environment for feelings to be expressed. She may well have to stand tough if others wish to avoid feelings or, even worse, "punish" someone else for showing feelings. To do so, she often needs to use double-loop learning skills to identify and address the underlying values and beliefs that influence cultural norms.

Facilitating Reflection Before or After Conflict

People are often blind to their own views. Mezirow (1991, 1997) recommends discourse as a means of identifying and considering preferred ways of acting. The conditions for discourse seem to be an unattainable ideal at first glance, but action science dialogue groups show that they can be created: "those participating have full information; are free from coercion; have equal opportunity to assume the various roles of discourse (to advance beliefs, challenge, defend, explain, assess evidence, and judge arguments); become critically reflective of assumptions; are empathic and open to other perspectives; are willing to listen and to search for common ground or a synthesis of different points of view; and can make a tentative best judgment to guide action" (Mezirow, 1997, p. 10).

It is easier to help a person identify, name, and vent powerful feelings before or after a real or perceived threat occurs. The facilitator can more easily create a safe environment in which to extract and address fears, separate real from imagined consequences, and help a person develop both single-loop and double-loop approaches to working with the conflict.

An action science consultant facilitates dialogue about a situation, or a "case," in which a person charts both what was said (in the right column of the case), and what was thought or felt but not said (in the left column). The consultant helps the case writer identify mismatches between intentions and actual consequences, drawing up a ladder of inference, identify assumptions, and map links between assumptions and actions. The case writer and the consultant design and role-play alternative actions.

Facilitators can also engage people in anticipatory reflection of alternative worldviews, to step outside of current mental models that restrict new insights and skill development. Some examples might illustrate this approach. Richard Leachman (1999) uses abstract paintings along with word descriptions to help people create, populate, visit, and experience new worlds. He then invites people to revisit a problem through the lens of experience created by their foray into this new world. Other experiential educators engage people in dance, poetry, metaphor, guided imagery, or painting. Bruce Copley designs learning that uses all of the senses. He devises exercises that connect people to their physical world and then enable them to see how this connection opens up new points of view. He helps people learn from other humans, animals, plants, and inanimate objects: "through this 'whole person' involvement the mind, the body, the feelings, the spirit, the experience, the idea and the meaning become one" (1999, pp. 4–5).

CONCLUSION

We have introduced, described, and illustrated a model for learning through reflection on experience that we believe holds potential for those who help others address and learn from conflict. The value of reflection is that it is available to everyone. At the same time, as Ellen Langer (1989) observes about a similar capacity for mindfulness, its very availability may make people discount its usefulness or take it for granted.

To learn from experience, people have to slow down their thinking process so that they can critically assess it. They need to get in touch with deeper feelings, thoughts, and factors that lie outside of their current mental and sensory models for taking in and interpreting the world they encounter. They have to step outside of the frameworks by which they understand experience, which can be disconcerting and at times difficult to do. Reflection can lead to new insight, but it can also cause frustration because people then have to develop new capabilities for double-loop learning and skillful conversation.

References

Argyris, C., and Schön, D. A. *Theory in Practice: Increasing Organizational Effectiveness.* San Francisco: Jossey-Bass, 1974.

Argyris, C., and Schön, D. A. *Organizational Learning: A Theory of Action Perspective.* Reading, Mass.: Addison-Wesley, 1978.

Boud, D., Cohen, R., and Walker, D. (eds.). *Using Experience for Learning.* Briston, Pa.: Society for Research into Higher Education and Open University Press, 1993.

Copley, B. "Cogmotics: Breathing Life into Education and Learning Through the Fine Art of Holistic Animation." Presentation at the annual conference of the Management Institute, Lund, Sweden, May 1999.

Cseh, M. "Managerial Learning in the Transition to a Free Market Economy in Romanian Private Companies." Unpublished doctoral dissertation, University of Georgia, Athens, 1998.

Cseh, M., Watkins, K. E., and Marsick, V. J. "Reconceptualizing Marsick and Watkins' Model of Informal and Incidental Learning in the Workplace." In K. P. Kuchinke (ed.), *Proceedings, Academy of Human Resource Development Conference.* Vol. 1. Baton Rouge, La.: Academy of Human Resource Development, 1999.

Dewey, J. *Experience and Education.* New York: Collier, 1938.

Heron, J. *Feeling and Personhood: Psychology in Another Key.* London: Sage, 1992.

Jarvis, P. *Paradoxes of Learning: On Becoming an Individual in Society.* San Francisco: Jossey-Bass, 1992.

Kolb, D. A. *Experiential Learning.* Upper Saddle River, N.J.: Prentice Hall, 1984.

Langer, E. J. *Mindfulness.* Reading, Mass.: Addison-Wesley, 1989.

Leachman, R. "Experiential Simulations of World Views and Basic Assumptions." Presentation at the annual conference of the Management Institute, Lund, Sweden, May 1999.

Marsick, V. J., and Watkins, K. E. *Informal and Incidental Learning in the Workplace.* New York: Routledge, 1990.

Marsick, V. J., and Watkins, K. E. *Facilitating the Learning Organization: Making Learning Count.* Aldershot, England: Gower, 1999.

Mezirow, J. D. *Transformative Dimensions of Adult Learning.* San Francisco: Jossey-Bass, 1991.

Mezirow, J. D. "Transformation Theory of Adult Learning." In M. R. Welton (ed.), *In Defense of the Lifeworld: Critical Perspectives on Adult Learning.* Albany: State University of New York Press, 1995.

Mezirow, J. D. "Transformative Learning: Theory to Practice." In P. Cranton (ed.), *Transformative Learning in Action: Insights from Practice.* New Directions for Adult and Continuing Education, no. 74. San Francisco: Jossey-Bass, 1997.

Postle, D. "Putting the Heart Back into Learning." In D. Boud, R. Cohen, and D. Walker (eds.), *Using Experience for Learning.* Briston, Pa.: Society for Research into Higher Education and Open University Press, 1993.

Schön, D. A. *Educating the Reflective Practitioner: Toward a New Design for Teaching and Learning in the Professions.* San Francisco: Jossey-Bass, 1987.

Sullivan, G. R., and Harper, M. V. *Hope Is Not a Method: What Business Leaders Can Learn from America's Army.* New York: Broadway Books, 1997.

Watkins, K. E., and Marsick, V. J. *Sculpting the Learning Organization: Lessons in the Art and Science of Systematic Change.* San Francisco: Jossey-Bass, 1993.

PART FIVE

DIFFICULT CONFLICTS

CHAPTER TWENTY

Aggression and Violence

Susan Opotow

Two million children have been killed in wars over the past decade; fifteen million more have been seriously injured, permanently disabled, or traumatized (Renner, 1998; Renner, 1997; Novicki, 1996; Dellums, 1996).

Five hundred million military-style handheld weapons are currently in circulation. Millions more are produced each year. In the United States, gun violence kills thirty-eight thousand people each year. Worldwide, gun violence accounts for 90 percent of the injuries and deaths in wars and criminal violence. Teens are more likely to die from gunshot wounds than from all diseases (Worldwatch Institute, 1997; Sheppard, 1999; Fingerhut, 1993; Renner, 1998).

More than one hundred million land mines scattered across sixty-four countries kill or maim fifteen thousand people each year; 80 percent are civilians, and many are children (Bills, 1996).

Three to four million women are battered by husbands and boyfriends each year in the United States. A woman is nine times more likely to be killed by her husband than by a stranger (Frist, 1998; Venne, 1995).

More than three million children in the United States witness domestic abuse each year; more than half develop posttraumatic stress disorders. These child witnesses are themselves at high risk of being abused at home (University of Michigan, 1997; Frist, 1998).

All of these statistics undercount the prevalence and destructiveness of violence in innumerable lives, communities, and nations. In addition, weapons of mass destruction developed over the past sixty years threaten violence of immense proportions. Not all forms of violence are increasing, however. In the largest cities in the United States, interpersonal violence is at its lowest level in three decades (U.S. Dept. of Justice, 1999). Slavery is now uncommon and abhorred throughout the world, no longer accepted and prevalent as it was in the past. Clearly, forms and prevalence of violence undergo change over time.

FORMS OF AGGRESSION

In popular usage, aggression can be viewed as positive and confused with assertion, which is the bold, energetic pursuit of one's goals. This chapter employs a psychological definition of aggression as "any form of behavior directed toward the goal of harming or injuring another living being who is motivated to avoid such treatment" (Baron, 1977, p. 7). Aggression is not (1) mere thinking, but physical or verbal action or inaction; (2) accidental or helpful intent gone awry, but deliberately intended harm; or (3) consensual behavior between aggressor and victim, but directed at a living target wishing to avoid harm.

Aggression takes many forms:

- *Physical,* in assault and sexual abuse, or *symbolic,* in verbal, psychological, or emotional abuse
- *Vigorous* attack, or *passive* withholding or diverting of needed resources
- *Instrumental,* as a means for obtaining valued goods or goals, or *emotional,* as an end in itself in sadistic or dominating behavior
- *Sanctioned* or *unsanctioned* by those in power
- Intended to *preserve the status quo,* as by governmental militia, or intended to *change the status quo,* as by revolutionaries
- *Prosocial* or *antisocial* in its goals

Direct and Structural Violence

Aggression and violence take direct and structural forms. *Direct violence* is concrete, evident, and committed by and on particular people, such as assault, drive-by shooting, torture, and war. In contrast, *structural violence* is gradual, imperceptible, and diffused in society as the way things are done, as a matter of whose voice is systemically heard or ignored, and who gets particular resources and who goes without. Structural violence is often hidden, chronic, and institutionalized. It occurs at all levels of society—locally, regionally, nationally, and internationally—when basic resources needed for human well-being and dignity are distributed unfairly. Subpoverty wages and dangerous, substandard housing are symptoms of structural violence when "some, the topdogs, get much more out of the interaction in the structure than others, the underdogs"

(Galtung, 1969, p. 198). Structural violence maims and kills as the by-product of increased exposure to risk, hardship, and dangers. Because structural violence can be imperceptible and its agency diffused, victims of structural violence, such as poor people, can be seen as causing their own debilitation.

Levels of Analysis

Aggression and violence occur at every societal level. In individuals, aggression and violence can occur as suicide and self-mutilation; in interpersonal relationships, as rape and deliberately passing on infectious disease; within and between families, communities, regions, ethnic groups, nations, and allied nations, as struggle for political control and liberation.

Envisioning these societal levels as points along a linear dimension of increasing size and social complexity does not capture the strong influence that larger social levels, such as ethnic, national, or religious communities, exert on such smaller levels. Like handcrafted, wooden Russian *matryoshka* dolls, smaller units—an individual, family, or community—are nested within larger-identity communities that are themselves nested within regions and nations. This model (see Figure 20.1) captures how culture, expectancies, and socially shared constructions of reality from one level infuse and influence other levels. Individual aggression is more likely when one's peer group, family, community, or society encourages or expects aggression. Although this influence among levels is bidirectional, an individual is usually less able to influence the cultural norms of larger social groups, such as her society, than vice versa.

The nested model captures the contextual influences on aggressive and violent behavior, but it is highly simplified. Some levels are "thicker" and more influential than thinner, less influential others. Multiple sources of influence often characterize each level. Individuals are nested in families as well as other close groups, such as friends and teams, each influencing beliefs, attitudes, and behavior. These influences may be congruent or discrepant. As the next section describes, aggression also results from internal as well as social influences.

THEORIES OF AGGRESSION

Is aggression innate, or is it nurtured by social context? Some theories emphasize the biological origins of aggression, while others emphasize its environmental, social, and contextual origins. In aggression research, simpler theories have given way to multicausal, contingent analyses that consider both nature and nurture, including biological, motivational, cognitive, emotional, and social causes of aggression. This chapter describes influential aggression research and theory. Its order runs from theories that are biologically centered, to those

Figure 20.1. Model of Nested Social Contexts.

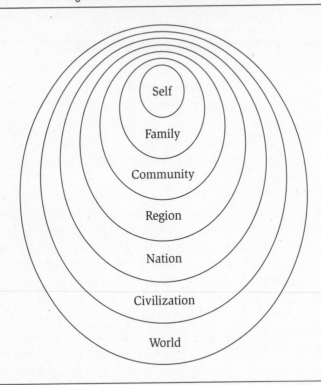

incorporating both biological and contextual factors, to those that are predominantly context-centered. The emphasis of this chapter is on social context, which can ameliorate or exacerbate individual tendencies and is more amenable to intervention than biological predisposition. Social context also influences the form and prevalence of aggression. As a later section on moral theories describes, morals and norms exert a significant influence on social context and expression of aggression.

Evolution and Physiology

Instinctivist and sociobiological approaches describe human aggression as a physiological predisposition that has evolved over the millennia to foster species survival. This theoretical perspective depicts aggression as ineradicable and "hard-wired" into our biological makeup. Sociobiological research examines homologous aggressive behavior among such animals as insects, fish, birds, and humans. Among nonhuman animals, aggression is largely pragmatic, activated for obtaining food, acquiring or maintaining leadership, protecting a flock or young, and facing threat. For both animals and humans, aggression is sensitive to context. It is elicited or repressed depending on particular social and physical conditions. Young children, lion cubs, and the young of other species inhibit aggression when circumstances make it prudent for them to do so.

The physiological predisposition for aggression is readily aroused in adverse environmental conditions. In Shakespeare's play of four hundred years ago, *Romeo and Juliet,* Benvolio warns Mercutio that on "hot days is the mad blood stirring." Research concurs. Interpersonal and mob violence increase during hot spells, in extremely low temperatures, and when foul odors, excessive noise, and crowding make life unpleasant. Alcohol and drugs also facilitate aggression. Alcohol intoxication is implicated in domestic abuse, vehicular deaths, and more than half of reported homicides. Although adverse environmental conditions, alcohol, and drugs do not inevitably result in violence, they reduce self-restraint. Reduced restraint along with frustration, misperception, and poor communication can lead to violence. (See also Chapters Twelve and Thirteen.)

Though there is little doubt that people have inherited the potential for aggression, they also inherit the potential for altruism and cooperation. Most important, they inherit the potential for thoughtful problem solving, which enables them to choose behaviors suitable for attaining their goals. Thus, the human potential for aggression does not unthinkingly lead to destructive behavior without regard for an individual's social context or capacity for choice and decision making.

Deviance

Predisposition for aggressive behavior is associated with a number of abnormal physiological conditions, including neurological deficits, abnormal levels of the neurotransmitters serotonin and monoamine oxidase (MAO), hormonal imbalance, birth trauma, brain tumors, exposure to such toxic substances as lead, and various medical disorders. Compared with nonviolent offenders, criminally violent individuals are more likely to have experienced significant head injuries and exhibit neurological impairment. Physiological deviance can cause aggressive behavior, but aggression can also cause physiological deviance. For example, high levels of testosterone, a male hormone, are a consequence as well as a cause of domineering behavior (American Psychological Association, 1996). Physiological deviance does not invariably cause violent behavior. Early experiences and environmental factors are also influential and modify effects of physiological functioning.

Psychological deviance, such as schizophrenia and antisocial personality disorder, are sometimes associated with violent behavior. Antisocial personality disorder describes individuals who lack guilt, who are grossly selfish, callous, irresponsible, and impulsive—characteristics that frequently lead to destructive conflict and violence. Mental illness does not inevitably lead to violence. Even though some mentally ill people are violent toward themselves and others, they are no more likely to be violent than people in the general population. Like normally functioning people, they are sensitive to situational facilitators and constraints on aggressive and violent behavior. Nor does deviance account for most violence. Many violent individuals have neither physiological nor psychological disorders, as exemplified by Holocaust bureaucrats and slave owners who were highly regarded in their own society and responsible and loyal to their family, group, or cause. This sense of responsibility and loyalty can itself instigate violence.

Disposition

Disposition (also called "personality" or "temperament") influences how individuals respond to events and how they perceive and handle conflict. Some people are unflappable, while others are easily irritated. Although a hostile environment might provoke aggressive responses in anyone, people we label "aggressive" see hostility in ambiguous circumstances, have the stable tendency to react offensively to minimal provocation, and are likely to initiate overt aggression when the opportunity exists to do so (see Chapter Fourteen).

In recent school-related murders by youths, explanations describing the young people as being severely troubled, having feelings of inferiority or suicidal impulses, harboring pent-up grudges, and holding explosive anger identify disposition as a crucial determinant. In retrospect, the statement "I'm at my point of no return" (Egan, 1998, p. 22)—written in a poem by a boy who subsequently killed two students and the teacher of his ninth grade algebra class—gives voice to a desperate internal state. Contextual explanations, in contrast, emphasize elements of the social environment as a crucial determinant: the availability of semiautomatic weapons; an adult culture that ignores or is insensitive to adolescent needs and warning signs; a pop culture of violent rap lyrics, video games, television, and Internet sites; and a culture in which violence is an attractive and acceptable option for resolving conflict (Fainaru, 1998). Both disposition and context are clearly important. Troubled youths with easy access to weapons, lax supervision, and a violent culture are a lethal and tragic combination.

Dispositional explanations of aggression are not limited to individuals. In intergroup, institutional, interregional, and international conflict, such explanations of aggression simplify a conflict conceptually by focusing on the malevolence of an aggressor's culture. But whether individual or societal, dispositions only partly explain violence. The Third Reich's policy of genocide only partly resulted from Adolf Hitler's pathological but effective mix of demagogy, charisma, and anti-Semitism and, at the institutional level, the Reich's virulent, supremacist ideology. Their policy of genocide was successful because many ordinary people, groups, and institutions supported Hitler and the Third Reich. Psychologically, it is easier to see violent individuals or groups as sole causal agents than to see the larger context, which is characterized by prevailing and anticipated economic conditions; political institutions; available and scarce resources; conflict resolution practices; and the degree to which a society is open or closed to new groups, traditions, and ideas. Conceptually complex explanations implicate ordinary people, who are harder to label as purely evil.

Motivation

Motivational theories describe aggression as resulting from blocked human needs. Maslow's hierarchy (1970) proposes that some needs are more basic than others (see Chapter Fourteen). These needs must be satisfied before higher needs become salient. *Biological needs* for food, water, oxygen, and rest are the most basic. Failure to meet these fundamental needs can lead to desperate behavior, including aggression. The next levels of needs are *safety needs* for security and freedom from fear and danger; *attachment needs* for social belonging, affiliation, and loving and being loved; and *esteem needs* for a sense of confidence, self-worth, and respect from others. Higher-level needs are next: *cognitive needs* for knowledge, understanding, and novelty; *aesthetic needs* for order, creativity, and beauty; *self-actualization* needs for fulfilling one's potential and having socially meaningful goals; and finally, *transcendence and spiritual needs* for a higher state of consciousness.

Maslow describes needs as inborn, but family and cultural values shape how they are expressed and met. Though frustrated needs can result in anger, hostility, and aggression, they can also motivate constructive behavior. Frustrated biological or safety needs can mobilize community cooperation, or war; frustrated love needs can spur other creative energies, or lead to stalking or self-destructive behavior. Motivation theory focuses on an individual's needs, but larger social levels also have needs for basic environmental resources, security, and a sense of identity. These needs are at the heart of many protracted, deadly intranational and international conflicts.

Frustration and Arousal

In 1939, a group of psychologists sparked considerable controversy when they asserted that frustration causes aggression (Dollard and others, 1939). Building on earlier psychoanalytic ideas, they defined *frustration* as the state that emerges when circumstances interfere with a goal response. Their work spurred considerable research, which examined the relationship between frustration and aggression. This research found that although frustration activates readiness for aggression, it does not inevitably cause aggression; frustration also generates constructive problem solving. Nor is aggression always the result of frustration; aggression also results from competition, greed, and fear. The effect of frustration on aggression is mediated by perceptions about what is happening and who is to blame, by past events, by negative or positive feelings, and by displaced hostility (Berkowitz, 1993). Stimuli in the immediate environment, such as guns, knives, or axes, not only have destructive potential in their own right but are also powerful cues that can spark violent behavior. As Leonard Berkowitz (1968) quips, "The finger pulls the trigger, but the trigger may also be pulling the finger" (p. 22).

Frustration and arousal can lead to *relative deprivation,* the sense of injustice that emerges when individuals or groups size up their lot with that of comparable others (see Chapter Two for further discussion). If the comparison reveals that social and economic trends have benefited some groups but not one's own, frustration and the belief that norms of fairness have been violated can, in turn, precipitate political unrest and violence (Gurr, 1970).

Gender

Are men more aggressive and violent than women? Ninety percent of murderers are male. But when context, intensity, and type of violence are considered, the relationship between gender and violence is more complex. Women are becoming more violent in some spheres but less in others (Hien and Hien, 1998). In the United States between 1982 and 1991, offenses against family and children increased by 196 percent for females and 63 percent for males. Perpetrators of domestic violence against children are 71 percent female and 58 percent male. Women, however, spend far more time with children than men, while men inflict more severe violence. Among adults, male-to-female and female-to-male violence assault rates are similar, with females inflicting less physical injury (unless weapons are used). Over the past twenty years, the 30 percent decline of intimate-partner violence is primarily the decline of women killing men. It coincides with gains for women, among them improvements in their economic status and greater availability of such resources as legal advocacy and shelters.

Active, direct, in-your-face aggression is more typical of males, while indirect, verbal, or self-directed aggression such as self-defeating behavior and depression are more common among women. Research with children identifies gender differences in aggression style. Among boys and girls, direct and physical aggression toward peers is common until age two. Direct aggression then declines steadily as children mature, but it remains more common among boys. As direct aggression declines, indirect and relational aggression such as bad-mouthing, gossip, smear campaigns, and socially isolating peers becomes common for both boys and girls but remains more common among girls. Indirect aggression inflicts subtle but long-lasting psychological and social damage.

Children learn gender role expectancies in conflict by watching adults. In *Bone Black,* bell hooks (1996) describes violence and gender role from her perspective as a child:

Out of nowhere he comes home from work angry. He reaches the porch yelling and screaming at the woman inside—yelling that she is his wife, he can do with her what he wants. They do not understand what is happening. He is pushing, hitting, telling her to shut up. She is pleading—crying. . . . Yelling, screaming, hitting: they stare at the red blood that trickles through the crying mouth. They cannot believe this pleading, crying woman, this woman who does not fight back, is the same person they know. The person they know is strong, gets things done, is a woman of ways and means, a woman of action. They do not know her still, paralyzed, waiting for the next blow, pleading. They do not know their mama afraid [pp. 146–147].

Anger

Anger is a felt, internal state arising from such cognitive and neurophysiological sources as memories, thoughts, arousal, and facial changes. Anger results from the cognition that someone is responsible for one's suffering, the belief that a negative occurrence would not have happened otherwise, and that someone acted in a socially unjustified manner (Berkowitz and Heimer, 1989). Though anger can accompany aggressive behavior, aggression occurs without anger, and aroused anger does not necessarily lead to aggressive responses or destructive outcomes. Anger can prompt nonviolent conflict resolution by stimulating people to be aware of others' feelings and beliefs about injustice, by motivating them to make amends, and by restoring feelings of self-efficacy.

Behavioral Origins

From a behavioral perspective, aggression is not a genetically predetermined response but a conditioned response to stimuli that have been rewarded or punished in the past. Past reinforcement of aggression—praise, satisfaction, or other rewards—increases the likelihood of an individual continuing to use aggressive responses; punishment decreases the likelihood. In the most primitive sense this behavior is learned, but it is learned behaviorally rather than cognitively.

Criminal-justice systems explicitly link violence and its punishment. Punishment, however, is an effective deterrent only under specific circumstances: if the salience and certainty of punishment is high, if it occurs quickly after the offensive behavior, and if it is of considerable magnitude. In one social experiment, police officers in Minneapolis responded to domestic violence with either on-the-spot arrest or counseling. Their response was randomly assigned. Arrest (the punitive response) more effectively deterred further domestic abuse, even when the length of arrest was brief (Sherman and Berk, 1984). Execution, commonly viewed as an effective deterrent to violent crime, inhibits homicide only briefly. Following an execution, the homicide rate shows an immediate decrease but then rises above the previous baseline rate. Executions may advertise killing as an effective problem-solving strategy more than deter violence (Phillips and Hensley, 1984).

Social Learning

Aggression as a way of interacting with others and solving social problems is learned directly from personal experiences and vicariously from watching influential role models enact aggressive behavior. Observations segue into behavioral imitation (Bandura, 1983). Media violence is a form of social learning that desensitizes viewers to violence by conveying norms, attitudes, and beliefs that justify violence and by teaching viewers aggressive scripts for dealing with problems. Social learning is evident in copycat crimes, following films or news with grotesque content.

Growing up in a violent home strongly predicts that a boy later enacts violence in his intimate teen and adult relationships (Peled, Jaffe, and Edleson, 1995). Children also look to older peers as admired role models from whom they can learn essential survival skills, social expectancies, and attunement to nuance. Social skills, including violence, are acquired in a learning process: "If you wonder how a fourteen-year-old can shoot another child his own age in the head, or how boys can do a 'drive-by-shooting' and then go home to dinner, you need to know you don't get there in a day, or week, or month. It takes years of preparation to be willing to commit murder, to be willing to kill or die for a corner, a color, or a leather jacket. Many of the children of America are conditioned early to kill and, more frighteningly, to die for what to an outsider might seem a trivial cause" (Canada, 1995, p. 35).

Using nonviolent conflict resolution processes, such as negotiation, also requires apprenticeship. Talking out a conflict is a finely honed communication and interpersonal skill. Unskilled talking may not only fail to resolve conflict but also risk rapid conflict escalation. Nonviolent conflict processes are likely to be appropriately and effectively employed if they are modeled at home, at school, in the workplace, in the community, in the media, and in the larger society.

Social Cognition

Social cognition helps us make sense of other people, ourselves, and our experiences. It includes our subjective interpretations, how we label people and circumstances, if-then scripts describing causality, and our information-processing strategies when making decisions and solving problems. From a cognitive perspective, aggression results from hostile thoughts, fantasies, imagery, and imagined intentions, and from considering a limited rather than a full range of behavioral options. (See Chapters Eleven and Twelve.) Less destructive behavior can emerge from new ways of thinking about oneself, others, the context, and behavioral possibilities.

Social cognitions are the attributions and inferences based on observation, reinforcement, and personal experience stored in memory as cognitive scripts. Once an experience is encoded as benign or threatening, a potential response is deemed acceptable or not by applying rules acquired during socialization and from past experience. A behavioral response is ultimately selected and enacted. Cognitive bias, deficiency, and error can occur throughout this process, from erroneously encoding cues to inadequately searching for responses, ineptly applying social mores, and bungling selected responses. As the next section describes, flaws in this process result in two kinds of aggression.

Social Competence

Research on social competence in children differentiates between reactive and proactive aggression (Dodge and Coie, 1987). *Reactive aggression* is striking back in response to perceived provocation. Its behavioral symptoms include short-tempered volatility, overreacting to accidental annoyances or affronts, and misreading intention. Reactive aggression can result from chronic exposure to such life-threatening dangers as recurring domestic or social violence and traumatic loss of loved ones. These experiences disrupt a child's sense of security and can lead to hypervigilance, unwarranted fear response, and hostile attribution when faced with a minor provocation or ambiguous statement. Treatment includes increasing the child's awareness of situations that trigger aggressive response; increasing the ability to understand others' behaviors and intentions accurately; anger-control training; and exposure to admired, competent role models who handle challenge without resorting to aggression or violence. Close, satisfying relationships characterized by reciprocity, cooperation, communication of feelings, respect, and trust can help children use assertive but less aggressive responses to challenges they face.

A second type of aggressive behavior, *proactive aggression,* is oriented, purposive, instigating behavior (such as bullying, dominating, and initiating verbal and physical aggression). Proactive aggression results from social experience in which violence is reinforced as a preferred, appropriate response to social challenge. Coercive child-rearing practice and observing successful and socially endorsed aggression in the media, the community, and among family members can lead to proactive aggression. Proactively aggressive children may accurately perceive others' behavior and intentions but evaluate an aggressive response positively ("This will show them that I can take care of myself"), have a limited response repertoire (fight or flee), or attempt a nonaggressive response but encounter difficulty in enactment and bumble into aggression. Treatment options include learning nonaggressive problem-solving strategies, receiving consistent punishment for aggression and reinforcement of nonaggressive responses, and raising awareness of the long-term negative outcomes of aggression and positive outcomes of nonaggression.

Culture and Social Context

Culture influences how we think about aggression. Aggression can be admired for leading to victory and attainment of important goals; it is applauded in many forms of entertainment and recreation. Roman gladiator contests, now seen as depraved and cruel, have given way to such contemporary events as boxing; wrestling; and cock, bull, or dog fighting. In some sports, playing dirty, brawls, and fan violence are part of the thrill. Aggression is a key ingredient of such participatory recreational activities as hunting—and its playful, high-tech analog, laser tag: "Why just daydream about demolishing your competitors? You may find more satisfaction in rubbing out rivals for sport at one of the increasingly popular places where you can wage war games for a modest fee. More and more business managers and employees act out their aggression these days at the country's 500 laser-tag arenas, where opponents in sci-fi-style gear shoot at each other with laser guns" (Berman, 1998, p. 22).

There is significant cross-cultural variation in acceptable kinds and levels of aggression. Domestic violence is more prevalent and acceptable in patrilocal as compared with matrilocal societies in which women are isolated from their biological families and their own supportive social networks (Baumgarten, 1993). Societies characterized by war also tend to show multiple forms of aggression, including homicide, theft, competition at work, strict child-rearing practices, sexual repression of women, and punitive orientation toward human needs at all periods of an individual's life from infancy to adulthood. In contrast, peaceful societies are characterized by tolerance in child rearing, acceptance of self-expression, and support for institutionalizing humanistic values (Russell, 1972). Thus social contexts shape biological propensities by valuing particular behaviors, customs, and institutions; these in turn influence the form and prevalence of aggression and violence. Among the many social influences exerted, moral influences are extremely potent. They determine the kinds of aggression that are noticed or ignored as well as those that are deplored, accepted, or applauded.

MORAL THEORIES OF AGGRESSION AND VIOLENCE

In his *Theory of Interdependence and Psychological Orientation,* Morton Deutsch (1982) has emphasized that psychological orientations to social situations contain cognitive and motivational components as well as moral components. From this standpoint, it is apparent that theories of aggression primarily emphasize biology, cognition, and motives while neglecting moral aspects. *Morals* are the norms, rights, entitlements, obligations, responsibilities, and duties that shape our sense of justice and guide behavior with others. Morals are an important aspect of aggression and violence because feelings of injustice charge conflict with great intensity and ratchet up the stakes rapidly (see Chapter Two).

Cognitions, motivations, and morals entwine in conflict, aggression, and violence. Cognition about social identity, such as gender ("male," "female"), ethnicity, sexual orientation, and age, underlies such volatile moral issues as "Who deserves to get what?" in terms of power, privilege, material resources, and legal justice. Anger is predominantly described as cognitive and physiological, but it is fundamentally moral as well. The cognition that someone acted unfairly and is the cause of one's suffering is essentially a moral judgment that focuses on responsibility and violation of social norms. Morals and motives are also closely connected. *Blame* is based on perception of prevailing norms. It identifies particular people as responsible for one's failure to achieve an important goal. Blame can incite a sense of injustice that can be highly motivating and justify aggression. Moral theories concerning violation of norms, social judgment, disengagement of moral control, and moral exclusion describe the considerable influence that morals have on social perception, relations, and behavior underlying aggression and violence.

Norm Violations

Social norms guide behavior and dictate our responsibilities, entitlements, and obligations. Social norms guide our behavioral expectancy about how people should behave with and respond to each other. These norms can be transient, or they can be long-lived and survive for generations as traditions. Social norms are assumed to be widely known, shared, and respected within a group. Because norms nurture social coordination and communication, violation is socially disruptive and often punished through formal, informal, and folk-justice systems. Violating a norm can set in motion a chain of linked attributions focusing on malevolent motives and highlighting antagonistic interests, resulting in hostile reaction, conflict escalation, and violence. Norm violations are less likely to trigger this negative cycle if they are seen to result from transient rather than stable factors, from unintentional rather than intentional behavior, and when parties to a conflict (friends, community groups, or nations) have developed *norms of redress*. Norms of redress are procedures for bringing about retributive or reparative justice. They can effectively avert conflict escalation if they are in place and well established before the violation occurs (De Ridder and Tripathi, 1992).

Moral Reasoning and Judgments

Research on sociomoral reasoning examines how people judge their own and others' behavior, including such norm-violating behavior as aggression or theft. Sociomoral judgments of aggression consider an actor's intentions; the appropriateness, intensity, justification, and nature (proactive or reactive) of the aggression; and the harm done. These judgments can be accurate or faulty, and they are influenced by gender, age, ideology, and the perceiver's feelings of affinity for the victim or the aggressor (Rule and Nesdale, 1976).

As children mature, their ability to take multiple perspectives increases with their progress from simple, self-oriented thinking to complex and abstract analyses. Some theorists see moral development and reasoning as occurring in an orderly progression of increasingly sophisticated reasoning, while others propose that it is reactive to social context. Danger and threat, for example, can cause people capable of sophisticated social reasoning to engage in simple, egocentric thinking.

Domain theorists point out that moral reasoning can be sidestepped by viewing behavior in nonmoral terms. Instead of concentrating on the *moral domain,* in which fairness, responsibility, and deserving are pertinent, behavior can be construed as occurring within the *conventional domain,* in which social conventions and structures to maintain norms are salient, or in the *personal domain,* in which personal discretion and privacy are salient. Understanding others' behavior depends on knowing whether they view that behavior in moral or nonmoral terms. Adolescents, for example, can view smoking or drug use as a moral issue (right or wrong), as socially conventional behavior (hanging out with friends), or as a personal issue that is up to their own taste, preferences, and discretion (Berkowitz, Guerra, and Nucci, 1991). Similarly, abortion can be viewed as a matter of personal discretion, or it can be viewed as immoral violence (Smetana, 1982).

Domain theory has chilling implications for aggression and violence. Domestic abuse is rendered nonmoral by abusers invoking the personal domain: "This is a family matter. Why do you want to make a big deal of it?" (Quindlen, 1994, p. A21). Hate-crime perpetrators, too, invoke prevailing homophobic, misogynistic, or racist norms to cloak violence in social convention while denying that it is a violation of human dignity and rights.

Disengagement of Moral Controls

Norms deterring or subduing aggression and violence come from within the individual as well as from formal and informal societal norms. They can be weakened in a process of habituation to violence during war, strife, and conflict, gradually lessening scruples and distress about performing formerly abhorrent acts. Brutality is further facilitated by construing it as serving moral purposes and viewing targets as belonging to social categories without merit (Bandura, 1991). Moral disengagement occurs during war, but as well as in everyday discrimination that reduces restraints against harming or exploiting certain "kinds" of people. Everyday structural violence flourishes when people preserve their self-esteem and sense of moral worthiness by keeping themselves uninformed and by avoiding questions that would reveal answers they do not want to know, such as the advantages that race confers on white people at the expense of people of color, or the advantages that gender confers on men at the expense of women.

Moral Exclusion

Moral considerations guide our behavior with those individuals and groups who are inside our scope of justice or moral community. Aggression and violence result not only from underdeveloped norms, or from sidestepping and gradual disengagement of norms but also from failing to view others as included within our scope of justice. *Moral inclusion* means that considerations of fairness apply to others, they are entitled to a share of community resources, and they are helped, when appropriate, even at considerable cost to oneself (Opotow, 1990, 1993). *Moral exclusion,* in contrast, dispenses with these considerations as irrelevant and views those excluded as outside the community in which norms apply, and therefore as expendable, undeserving, and eligible targets of exploitation, aggression, and violence. Those excluded can be viewed as benign or helpful, but nevertheless inferior, undeserving, or simply as property (as children, slaves, and women have been over time). Those excluded can also be viewed as posing an active threat, as "evil," "heretics," "perverts," "criminals," and "vermin."

Aggression and violence, justified by moral exclusion, can be seen as deserved, fair, and furthering the greater good. In its most virulent and widespread form, moral exclusion justifies institutionalizing torture, slavery, and genocide. Aggression and violence can occur without moral exclusion if adversaries respect each other and abide by fair rules of combat, as in conflicts among equals. Aggression and violence also occur without moral exclusion when people fall victim to mayhem, accidents, or natural disasters. Structural violence, however, influences which groups experience higher risk simply by, say, living in areas prone to flooding, neighborhoods abutting toxic hazards, or in unsafe housing.

Some kinds of social injustice are inevitably normalized within a society. Because it is difficult to see oneself or one's society as fundamentally unjust, moral exclusion helps conceal injustice by using denial about the social contexts, the other, and oneself: (1) denying harmful outcomes by minimizing their duration or effects; (2) denying others' humanity and deservingness by derogating them; and (3) denying one's own role in direct or structural violence by victim blaming and seeing one's own contribution as negligible (Opotow, Weiss, Lemler, and Brown, 1997). If the violence statistics described at the start of this chapter seem to depict a social reality that is quite removed from your own, it may illustrate the pervasiveness of denial and its self-protective function.

IMPLICATIONS FOR PRACTICE

This chapter has described numerous causes of aggression and violence. Clearly, many are interrelated and part of a complex system. Therefore, effective conflict resolution initiatives include interrelated efforts aimed at systemic change. This change process includes four steps: (1) accurate diagnosis, (2) strategies and plans for implementation, (3) implementing solutions, and (4) ongoing evaluation.

Diagnosis

Accurate diagnosis considers the issues, parties' motivations to change, and the cultures in which aggression and violence occur. Diagnosis identifies the presenting and underlying issues in a conflict system, including basic needs, fears, and the stated positions of the parties engaged in a violent relationship. Conflict resolution initiatives require involving relevant parties. Mistreatment, exploitation, and injury can be sufficiently aversive to motivate parties to rethink their destructive attitudes, processes, outcomes, and their willingness to engage in constructive change. Accumulated injuries resulting from aggression and violence as well as those that may yet occur can prod conflict participants to begin the difficult work of relational, cognitive, and behavioral change.

Diagnosis also identifies those affected by aggression and violence. In aggression and violence, there may be secondary victims and more distant parties affected by violence (including those outside the scope of justice, such as aged people and children who depend on primary victims for their well-being) as well as victims of structural violence. Understanding how violence ripples out from larger to smaller levels (as well as vice versa) is essential. Diagnosis also needs to transcend the immediate cultural context that may render some kinds of violence invisible, inevitable, or innocuous. Myths such as "violence is a natural part of life" or "I saw lots of violence as a kid and I turned out OK" denies the way that violence enacted in relationships, in the culture, and in the media actively shape expectancies, mores, and behavior.

Strategies and Plans for Implementation

The multiple, complex, interconnected causes of aggression and violence are effectively countered with comprehensive, coordinated multiparty efforts. Conflict resolution training programs that work in conjunction with mental health and community agencies, medical services, and schools can approach aggression and violence with a wide array of resources. Domestic violence deterrence, for example, is more effective when representatives from advocacy groups, health resources, social service agencies, and the justice system cooperate. At larger social levels, dispute resolution programs can collaborate with medical societies, police leadership, elected officials, the media, and school systems. Collaboration among key, influential, and visible players is important, as is working closely with community members having subtle forms of influence. Forward-looking conflict resolution interventions and programs collaborate closely with youth. Unless children are involved as partners, hopes for a future culture of constructive conflict resolution and nonviolence are dim.

Effective intervention considers appropriate processes and venues for conflict resolution. Conflicts characterized by violence and coercion may not lend themselves to informal, consensual dispute resolution methods. Informal methods of dispute resolution can introduce practical and ethical difficulties in relationships characterized by inequality and violence. Emphasis on rational problem solving, making informed choices, win-win outcomes, and present rather than past grievances—all characteristic of many conflict resolution approaches—may unwittingly serve to keep victims enmeshed in violent relationships (Maxwell, 1998). Societal biases supporting racial or gender discrimination can subtly pervade dispute resolution processes and replicate power imbalances. They are particularly problematic in informal dispute resolution venues that lack such legal safeguards as appeals and public scrutiny (Grillo, 1991).

Community-based antiviolence programs emphasize four main approaches: conflict management skills training, youth-operated programs, psychoeducational strategies, or family-based strategies (Greene, 1998). Regardless of their main emphasis, successful programs

- Are tailored to the unique issues and resources of the community
- Listen to youths and community members to appreciate their knowledge and coping skills
- Include conflict management skills training that help youngsters learn nonviolent means to resolve conflict, instill nonviolence as a social norm, and recognize warning signs of escalating conflict
- Include youth-operated programs that teach young people the dire consequences of violent behavior ("Been there, done that")
- Include development of trusting relationships with key adults, such as parents and staff members at youth programs
- Include such psychoeducational resources as mentoring programs, family cohesion efforts, and counseling

Multiple approaches are evident in an ambitious, nationwide bullying-prevention program that targeted individuals, families, classes at school, and school systems throughout Norway (Olweus, 1991). This program was based on Olweus's research indicating that bullying could be deterred among schoolchildren under certain conditions: a school, home, and community culture characterized by warmth, positive interest, and involvement from adults; setting clear limits on unacceptable, antisocial behavior; clear and consistently applied nonhostile sanctions for rule violations; and establishing mechanisms for surveillance of students' activities. Consequently, the bullying-prevention program was designed to change the peer culture in schools nationwide by increasing awareness of bullying, achieving active involvement from teachers and parents, developing clear rules and norms against bullying, and providing support and protection for victims.

Implementing Solutions

"Fools rush in where angels fear to tread" is especially true in violence intervention. Solutions begun without careful diagnosis and planning may not only fail to help but risk causing additional harm. Because there are many kinds of violence, many contexts in which violence occurs, and many kinds of aggressors, no one intervention is suitable for every contingency. Three principles suggested by Morton Deutsch (1993) can guide development of context-specific conflict resolution training:

1. Control your own violence.
2. Do not provoke others.
3. Manage others' aggressive behavior when it occurs.

Like the three aspects of denial in moral exclusion, these principles consider oneself, the other, and the social context and then offer concrete approaches that counteract the tendency for this kind of denial in aggression and violence.

Controlling Your Own Violence. Effective conflict resolution intervention helps individuals reflect on their own conflict resolution style, distinguish between healthy and unhealthy ways of expressing anger, and become aware of the long-term consequences of their violent behavior. Individuals who understand their own conflict resolution style are aware of the situations likely to provoke their emotional arousal; they critically scrutinize their own justifications for anger, aggression, and violence; and they understand the real gains and losses that result from violence. Individuals are more likely to use healthy ways of expressing anger if they can differentiate between assertive and aggressive responses and communicate assertive responses effectively. Individuals need to recognize how pervasive violence is, how small arguments precipitate violence, and how available weapons contribute to violence.

Recognizing What Provokes Others. Effective conflict resolution programs help individuals understand and avoid behaviors that provoke others. This understanding is enhanced by perspective taking. Individuals capable of taking others' perspectives are likely to think flexibly rather than rigidly; acknowledge rather than deny problems; and take a constructive conflict orientation that includes creative problem solving, openness, lack of defensiveness, flexibility, and full use of available resources. Perspective taking facilitates respecting and caring about others, while inability to take the other's perspective can facilitate blame, distrust, and misunderstanding. Perspective taking is difficult amid the arousal of intense conflict. It can be threatening, reveal ugly truths about oneself, and undermine one's worldview.

The Alternative to Violence Project, founded by Quakers and prison inmates in 1975, encourages peaceful individuals, communities, and nations. The program teaches interrelated personal and interpersonal skills that facilitate perspective taking: communication, cooperation, trust, self-esteem building, creative approaches to conflictual situations, handling fear and anger, awareness of stereotyping and prejudice, examination of power structures, and building the capacity for forgiveness.

Managing Aggression When It Occurs. Aggression and violence can escalate rapidly. Effective conflict resolution programs help individuals detect aggression at its early stages and understand the steps that facilitate deescalation. Early detection of incipient aggression or violence can nip it in the bud before conflict gains momentum and escalates out of control. Awareness can be impeded by denying the intensity and persistence of injuries, by failing to see hidden structural violence, and by morally excluding victims. Denial, though counterproductive in the long run, can be less threatening than acknowledging a disappointing or painful truth. As the human history of brutality and atrocity at all levels demonstrates, aggression has no limits. Therefore, the earlier one faces up to dangerous or difficult situations, the better.

A violence prevention program, Fight for Your Rights: Take a Stand Against Violence, cosponsored by the American Psychological Association and MTV, helps youth recognize warning signs for such violence as suicide or murderous intent among peers. Youths exposed to symptoms of incipient violence often lack training to evaluate symptoms for their seriousness. This program fosters youth awareness and encourages actively seeking out skilled assistance to avoid violence and tragedy among their peers.

Ron Fisher and Loraleigh Keashly (1990) propose that each stage of conflict escalation is associated with particular third-party roles and objectives. They suggest that third parties can deescalate conflict stage by stage, rather than attempting to move directly from violence to rational discussion.

At the *destructive stage,* parties try to destroy or subjugate each other. Third parties are peacekeepers who forcefully set norms, define unacceptable violence, and isolate parties when necessary to prevent violence from escalating.

At the *segregated stage,* hostility and threats to basic needs predominate. Third parties discourage further hostility and help parties examine their conflict dynamics and ground rules that can move them toward negotiation.

At the *polarized stage,* conflicts threaten trust and respect. Distorted perceptions and stereotypes prevail. Third parties are consultants who increase mutual tolerance by offering parties an opportunity to scrutinize their assumptions about an adversary's worthiness. They help parties identify mutually acceptable processes toward resolution or reconciliation by encouraging information exchange that can later serve as a basis for negotiation.

At the *discussion stage,* perceptions are accurate, commitment to negotiation is stable, and parties believe in the possibility of joint gains. When needed, third parties facilitate negotiation as mediators to help parties find win-win solutions.

Evaluation

Evaluation is a crucial but underused element of intervention and training. Evaluations help practitioners when a program is under way as well as at its conclusion. Effective evaluation plans are designed as part of an implementation strategy, well before programs are implemented. There are several compelling practical and ethical reasons to use evaluation as a key element of an intervention involving violence, as we now discuss.

Reality Checks. Social contexts inevitably undergo change. Aggression and violence can accelerate this rate of change. Diagnosis and strategies for implementation, no matter how carefully or collaboratively conceived, may miss key elements. Evaluations afford a check that initial diagnosis of the context—not only as it was, but as it continues to evolve—and the selected implementation strategy match. Evaluation builds in the occasion to revisit plans with new insights and knowledge as they emerge.

Unintended Outcomes. The physician's maxim "First, do no harm" has particular urgency in violent relationships. Evaluations can undercut the tendency for denial by offering practitioners concrete data. These data permit evaluation of an intervention's constructiveness and its ability to produce desired outcomes. Evaluative data, therefore, not only serve research purposes but also offer a practical tool for ensuring that an intervention does, in fact, ameliorate violence and that the outcome remains stable over time.

Conflict Residues. Even though intervention transforms conflict into constructive relationship, sticky conflict residues often remain. These residues then serve as a kernel that reproduces destructive conflict, particularly once aggression and violence have become chronic. An observer of intergroup violence in Indonesia reports, "This round of cruelties has roots deep in the past. And it is but one example of what Indonesia fears most: an explosion of religious and ethnic violence that roars out of control, fed by old hatreds and fresh grievances, defying the peacemaking efforts of local leaders and the restraining presence of armed soldiers" (Mydans, 1999, p. 50). Because conflicts transformed from active to quiescent can simmer underground and later erupt, periodic evaluation of key social indicators can monitor conflict residue and detect a shift from benign to malignant symptoms.

Expanding Knowledge. Interventions are especially difficult in violent conflict systems. Evaluations give practitioners and scholars a valuable opportunity to learn from intervention efforts. Learning focuses on effective process and outcomes, and also on pitfalls, dead ends, and quagmires to avoid. This learning is specific to each context; what works well in one context may be ineffective or unsuitable for another. Evaluation, therefore, is a chance for the field to grow by accumulating knowledge about the effects of various kinds of intervention in different contexts.

Ethical Considerations

Interventions in systems characterized by aggression and violence pose special ethical difficulties. An intervenor in a relationship characterized by aggression and violence is also a bystander to past, current, and potential harm. Therefore, intervention has moral as well as practical implications. Naming aggression and violence for what it is invokes particular norms, responsibilities, and obligations. Remaining silent has equally powerful moral implications. Third parties more comfortable with avoidance than with directly addressing aggression and violence may be less effective than those who can motivate parties to view violent processes and outcomes realistically; seek help; make fundamental changes in their own lives and their relationship; and find safe, durable, respectful resolutions.

Practitioners intervening in violent systems must be sufficiently skilled at recognizing violence, coercion, and oppression in relationships. Identifying violence can be surprisingly difficult. Domestic violence is widely underreported by psychologists conducting marital therapy, teachers and counselors in schools, and emergency room doctors. Research in hospital emergency rooms indicates that training, sensitivity, and courage are needed to recognize and document domestic violence (Braziel, 1998). When asked directly, victims and batterers admit to violence. When the answer is "yes," practitioners who ask the difficult questions also need to have sufficient skills to help parties acknowledge real dangers they face, consider use of self-assertion strategies, and make difficult decisions about an appropriate role that they can take in the conflict.

CONCLUSION

We still have a great deal to learn about the precursors of violence. We already know, however, that harsh social contexts throughout a person's life cycle are associated with a violent orientation. We also know that aggression and violence

424 THE HANDBOOK OF CONFLICT RESOLUTION

are embedded in larger social issues: poverty, human rights, land reform, political repression, and economic privation. Effectively addressing aggression and violence considers not just direct violence but social injustice as well. Social resources that can ameliorate structural violence in the lives of children include effective schools, preventive health care, affordable and safe housing, full employment, and environmental safety.

These are investments that can benefit the entire society. Because expression of aggression and violence are susceptible to social context and control, influential public health initiatives include stringent gun control; restricting the amount and intensity of violence in the entertainment media; and training parents, police, school personnel, psychologists, doctors, and politicians as models of cooperative conflict resolution processes.

Peaceful relationships are not simply those without aggression, violence, and war. Cultures of peace address the root causes of many kinds of aggression by emphasizing rights, law, and social justice. Cultures of peace work to implement their values and ideals for human rights, tolerance, democracy, free flow of information, sustainable development, peace education, and gender equality. This chapter offers a moral, systemic perspective as a way of understanding manifestations and causes of aggression and violence in all their complexity. Without simplifying and denying, we can forthrightly and ably address aggression and violence to bring about a culture of inclusion and peace in our personal lives, our communities, and the world.

References

American Psychological Association. *Reducing Violence: A Research Agenda.* Washington, D.C.: American Psychological Association, 1996.

Bandura, A. "Psychological Mechanisms of Aggression." In R. G. Geen and E. I. Donnerstein (eds.), *Aggression: Theoretical and Empirical Reviews.* Vol. 1. Orlando: Academic Press, 1983.

Bandura, A. "Social Cognitive Theory of Moral Thought and Action." In W. M. Kurtines and J. L. Gewirtz (eds.), *Handbook of Moral Behavior and Development,* Vol. 1: *Theory.* Mahwah, N.J.: Erlbaum, 1991.

Baron, R. A. *Human Aggression.* New York: Plenum, 1977.

Baumgarten, M. P. "Violent Networks: The Origins and Management of Domestic Conflict." In R. B. Felson and J. T. Tedeschi (eds.), *Aggression and Violence.* Washington, D.C.: American Psychological Association, 1993.

Berkowitz, L. "Impulse, Aggression, and the Gun." *Psychology Today,* Apr. 1968, pp. 18–22.

Berkowitz, L. *Aggression: Its Causes, Consequences, and Control.* New York: McGraw-Hill, 1993.

Berkowitz, L., and Heimer, K. "On the Construction of the Anger Experience." In M. Zanna (ed.), *Advances in Experimental Social Psychology.* Vol. 22. Orlando: Academic Press, 1989.

Berkowitz, M. W., Guerra, N. G., and Nucci, L. "Sociomoral Development and Drug and Alcohol Abuse." In W. M. Kurtines and J. L. Gewirtz (eds.), *Handbook of Moral Behavior and Development.* Vol. 3. Mahwah, N.J.: Erlbaum, 1991.

Berman, D. "Zap! Pow! Splat!" *Business Week,* Feb. 9, 1998, p. 22.

Bills, R. "Land Mines Maim and Kill Long After Wars Are Over." *The People,* 1996, *106*(4), 5.

Braziel, A. "No Shot in the Dark: Emergency Doctors Develop Picture-Taking Skills to Record—and Prevent—Domestic Violence." *Hospitals and Health Networks,* 1998, *72*(12), 50–51.

Canada, G. *Fist, Stick, Knife, Gun: A Personal History of Violence in America.* Boston: Beacon Press, 1995.

Dellums, R. V. "The Day of the African Child." *Congressional Record,* 1996, *142*(96), E51180.

De Ridder, R., and Tripathi, R. C. (eds.). *Norm Violations and Intergroup Relations.* Oxford: Oxford University Press, 1992.

Deutsch, M. "Interdependence and Psychological Orientation." In V. J. Derlega and F. Grzelak (eds.), *Cooperation and Helping Behavior: Theories and Research.* Orlando: Academic Press, 1982.

Deutsch, M. "Educating for a Peaceful World." *American Psychologist,* 1993, *48,* 510–517.

Dodge, K. A., and Coie, J. D. "Social-Information-Processing Facts in Reactive and Proactive Aggression in Children's Peer Groups." *Journal of Personality and Social Psychology,* 1987, *53,* 1146–1158.

Dollard, J., and others. *Frustration and Aggression.* New Haven: Yale University Press, 1939.

Egan, T. "From Adolescent Angst to Shooting Up Schools." *New York Times,* June 14, 1998, sec. 1, pp. 1, 22.

Fainaru, S. "Alaska School Murders: A Window on Teen Rage." *Boston Globe,* Oct. 18, 1998, pp. A1, A23.

Fingerhut, L. A. *Firearm Mortality Among Children, Youth, and Young Adults 1–34 Years of Age: Trends and Current Status, United States, 1985–1990.* Atlanta: National Center for Health Statistics, Centers for Disease Control and Prevention, 1993.

Fisher, R. J., and Keashly, L. "A Contingency Approach to Third-Party Intervention." In R. J. Fisher (ed.), *The Social Psychology of Intergroup and International Conflict Resolution.* New York: Springer-Verlag, 1990.

Frist, B. "Domestic Violence." *Congressional Record,* 1998, *144*(140), S12024.

Galtung, J. "Violence, Peace, and Peace Research." *Journal of Peace Research,* 1969, *3,* 167–191.

Greene, M. "Youth Violence in the City: The Role of Educational Interventions." *Health Education and Behavior,* 1998, *25,* 173–191.

Grillo, T. "The Mediation Alternative: Process Dangers for Women." *Yale Law Journal,* 1991, *100,* 1545–1610.

Gurr, T. R. *Why Men Rebel.* Princeton, N.J.: Princeton University Press, 1970.

Hien, D., and Hien, N. M. "Women, Violence with Intimates, and Substance Abuse: Relevant Theory, Empirical Findings, and Recommendations for Future Research." *American Journal of Drug and Alcohol Abuse,* 1998, *24,* 419–438.

hooks, b. *Bone Black: Memories of Girlhood.* New York: Henry Holt, 1996.

Maslow, A. *Motivation and Personality.* (Rev. ed.) New York: HarperCollins, 1970.

Maxwell, J. P. "The Effects of Interpersonal Oppressive Violence on Women and Children: Implications for Conflict Management and Violence Prevention Training." *Peace and Conflict: Journal of Peace Psychology,* 1998, *4,* 155–166.

Mydans, S. "Ancient Hatreds, New Battles." *New York Times Magazine,* Mar. 14, 1999, pp. 50–53.

Novicki, M. A. "Protecting Children from War's Impact." *Africa Recovery,* 1996, *10*(3), 10–11.

Olweus, D. "Bully/Victim Problems Among Schoolchildren: Basic Facts and Effects of a School Based Intervention Program." In D. J. Pepler and K. H. Rubin (eds.), *The Development and Treatment of Childhood Aggression.* Mahwah, N.J.: Erlbaum, 1991.

Opotow, S. "Moral Exclusion and Injustice: An Introduction." *Journal of Social Issues,* 1990, *46,* 1–20.

Opotow, S. "Animals and the Scope of Justice." *Journal of Social Issues,* 1993, *49,* 71–85.

Opotow, S., Weiss, L., Lemler, J., and Brown, T. *Air, Sea, and Land: Environmental Conflicts and the Scope of Justice.* Paper presented at the annual meeting of the American Psychological Association, Chicago, 1997.

Peled, E., Jaffe, P. G., and Edleson, J. L. (eds.). *Ending the Cycle of Violence: Community Responses to Children of Battered Women.* Thousand Oaks, Calif.: Sage, 1995.

Phillips, D. P., and Hensley, J. E. "When Violence Is Rewarded or Punished: The Impact of Mass Media Stories on Homicide." *Journal of Communication,* 1984, *34,* 101–116.

Quindlen, A. "Remember Nicole Simpson." *New York Times,* June 22, 1994, p. A21.

Renner, M. "Small Arms, Big Impact: The Next Challenge of Disarmament." *Worldwatch Paper,* Oct. 1997, pp. 5–77.

Renner, M. "An Epidemic of Guns." *World Watch,* 1998, *11*(4), 22–29.

Rule, B. G., and Nesdale, A. R. "Moral Judgment of Aggressive Behavior." In R. G. Geen and E. C. O'Neal (eds)., *Perspectives on Aggression.* Orlando: Academic Press, 1976.

Russell, E. W. "Factors of Human Aggression: A Cross-Cultural Factor Analysis of Characteristics Related to Warfare and Crime." *Behavioral Science Notes,* 1972, *7,* 275–312.

Sheppard, D. "Strategies to Reduce Gun Violence." *OJJDP Fact Sheet,* no. 93. U.S. Department of Justice, Feb. 1999, p. 1.

Sherman, L. W., and Berk, R. A. "The Specific Deterrent Effects of Arrest for Domestic Assault." *American Sociological Review,* 1984, *49,* 261–272.

Smetana, J. *Concepts of Self and Morality: Women's Reasoning About Abortion.* New York: Praeger, 1982.

UNICEF. "UNICEF Report: Modern Wars Imperil Children." *Newsnotes,* 1996, *21*(1), 20–21.

University of Michigan. "Damage to Children of Abused Mothers Starts Early, Is Often Severe, U-M Studies Finds." News release, Nov. 18, 1997.

U.S. Department of Justice. "Homicide Trends in the United States: Nation's Largest Cities Lead the Way as Homicides Fall to Lowest in Decades." News release, Jan. 2, 1999.

Venne, P. "Government Orders: Criminal Code." *Canada Parliament House of Commons Debates,* June 15, 1995, pp. 13928–13939.

Worldwatch Institute. "Small Arms Proliferation: The Next Disarmament Challenge." News release, Oct. 25, 1997.

CHAPTER TWENTY-ONE

Intractable Conflict

Peter T. Coleman

When conflicts that are deeply important to people remain unresolved for long periods of time, they tend to escalate, transform, and resurface repeatedly, eventually becoming stuck at a high level of intensity and destructiveness. These are intractable conflicts. They can occur between individuals (as in prolonged marital disputes) and within or between groups (as evidenced in the antiabortion–pro-choice conflict) or nations (as seen in the tragic events in Northern Ireland, Rwanda, and the former Yugoslavia). They often involve many parties for an extended period of time; they concern an intricate set of historical, religious, cultural, political, and economic issues. They give rise to a threat to basic human needs or values and result in destructive outcomes ranging from mutual alienation and contempt to mutual atrocities such as murder, rape, and genocide among the conflicting parties.

Unfortunately, intractable conflicts are common. Globally, 25 percent of the wars being waged at the time of this writing, both intranationally and internationally (conflicts with more than one thousand deaths per year), have persisted for more than two decades (Lederach, 1997). Some conflicts (such as the current disputes in Kosovo and Cyprus) have been maintained for centuries. Domestically in the United States, we face intractable intergroup conflicts over racial, class, and gender inequality, as well as such issues as abortion rights, the death penalty, and euthanasia. Similarly, the list of intractable interpersonal disputes, grudges, and feuds among family members, with former friends, and personal enemies is substantial.

This chapter has three sections. It begins with a discussion of the characteristics, causes, and consequences of intractable conflict, emphasizing the difference between intractable and manageable conflict. The second section addresses strategies for intervention in intractable conflict. It begins with offering some general guidelines for intervening in such conflicts and then outlines several constructive approaches, emphasizing intervention that is multimodal and multidisciplinary. The chapter concludes with a discussion of implications for training intervenors and disputants.

INTRACTABLE CONFLICTS: CHARACTERISTICS, CAUSES, AND CONSEQUENCES

Although intractable conflict often begins in much the same manner as manageable conflict, it commonly involves a distinct set of issues, circumstances, and dynamics that contribute to its transformation into an entrenched and dangerous process. Although there exists a great difference between one type of intractable conflict (a family dispute) and another (the civil war in Sri Lanka), they do share some common features. My emphasis in this section is on the common social psychological factors contributing to the particular set of problems associated with such conflicts.

Characteristics: Tractable Versus Intractable

An intractable conflict can be broadly characterized as one that is recalcitrant, intense, deadlocked, and extremely difficult to resolve. A more specific definition of intractable conflict can be generated by identifying those characteristics that distinguish an intractable conflict from a manageable one.

Time and Intensity. Intractable conflicts tend to persist and cycle over time, with sporadic increases in intensity and occasional outbreaks of violence. These protracted social conflicts typically last at least a generation, often many generations. At times, they may go underground and appear to be resolved, but if their root causes are not addressed they tend to resurface and intensify when external circumstances permit or encourage their expression. This pattern of suppression and resurgence is exemplified by the conflict over racial inequality in the United States. Thus, the rioting in the streets of South Central Los Angeles in 1994 can be seen as a resurgence of the violence over the same concerns for opportunity and self-determination that were voiced but insufficiently addressed during the Watts riots in Los Angeles twenty-five years earlier.

Issue Centrality. Intractable conflict tends to involve needs or values that the disputants experience as critical to their own (or their group's) survival. Often, these concerns are unrelated to the issues that initially trigger the conflict, but as the conflict escalates the issues are often transformed and ultimately take on a basic and threatening character. Deutsch (1985) offered the label "malignant social processes" to characterize this stage of intense, conflict-filled relationship that is "increasingly dangerous and costly and from which the participants see no way of extricating themselves without becoming vulnerable to an unacceptable loss in a value central to their self-identities or self-esteem" (p. 263).

Conflict Pervasiveness. The experience of threat associated with such conflict is often so central and basic to the human experience that the effects of the conflict spread and become pervasive, affecting most aspects of a person's or a community's social and political life. Cultural, religious, educational, public, and political institutions become involved with the conflict, as do many of the community's scholars and leaders. Many residents of Tel Aviv, for example, report that the enduring conflict in their community has affected much of their day-to-day existence, including some of the most mundane aspects of their lives.

Hopelessness. Typically, the disputants in an intractable conflict reach a point where they feel hopeless about the potential for constructive resolution. At this stage, the parties become unable to envision any approach to resolving the conflict other than that of continued use of force aimed at annihilating the other. The conflict is usually experienced as a tragic lose-lose situation.

Motivation to Harm. At this stage of intensity, the motivations of the disputants are typically at a point where their primary objective is to harm one another. At this level of escalation there generally exists a great mutual fear. This, coupled with the tendency in these extreme situations to exclude the enemy from one's moral universe (viewing them as undeserving of moral treatment) and the profound desire to seek revenge for one's losses, motivates disputants to want to inflict as much physical and psychological harm on the other as possible.

Resistance to Resolution. Finally, intractable conflicts are resistant to repeated and concerted attempts to resolve them. Traditional approaches such as diplomacy, negotiation, mediation, and unilateral use of threats or force by either side often fail to bring about conflict deescalation or resolution. Intractable conflicts require development of extraordinary alternatives to be resolved.

Causes of Intractable Conflict

Other chapters in this volume discuss the causes of conflict escalation, perpetuation, and destructive or violent outcomes (see Chapters One, Two, Eight, and

Twenty). This section builds on those discussions, emphasizing the causes that distinguish intractable from tractable conflicts.

The Issues. In general, conflicts can involve a variety of interrelated issues such as resources, values, power, or basic human needs (see Ronald Fisher's elaboration on Katz's conflict typology in Chapter Eight of this volume). Most conflicts involve more than one type of issue either directly or indirectly; as an example, a marital conflict over finances might disguise a deeper conflict over power and control in the relationship.

A few important distinctions can be made, however, in considering the issues common to intractable conflict. Burgess and Burgess (1996) identified three types of issue that often lead to intractability. First are *irreconcilable moral differences,* which are conflicts over questions of fundamental moral, religious, or personal values that have no verifiable answers and thus are not easily changed or compromised. The Catholic-Protestant conflict over the "correct" Christian doctrine is one example. A second type are *high-stakes distributional conflicts* over finite or scarce resources. A border dispute over territory between clans, tribes, or nations is an example. Third are *"pecking-order" conflicts,* struggles over relational power, ranking, or political dominance among individuals or groups. Many protracted conflicts between siblings are of this nature. All three types of issue are of high importance to the parties involved in any of them and are commonly experienced as zero-sum or win-lose.

John Burton (1987), Jay Rothman (1997), and John Paul Lederach (1997)—eminent conflict scholars—have distinguished between issues that primarily concern divisible *resources* (such as time, money, or land) and those that concern the less tangible, basic issues of personal and group *identity* (such as respectful and fair treatment, security, safety, and a sense of control over one's life). Identity-based concerns are thought to be tied to the most fundamental human needs; therefore conflicts over them are often experienced by people as threatening their very existence. The resource-or-identity distinction has implications for how we understand and approach these conflicts. Although most intractable conflicts involve both types of issue, identity-based issues tend to be more salient in intractable situations. Thus, Lederach (1997) indicates that almost two-thirds of the world's current armed conflicts can be defined as identity conflict.

Because identity conflicts are experienced by disputants as more basic and threatening than resource conflicts, practitioners suggest that they need to be approached and resolved through different channels (such as through the use of extended dialogue sessions, truth commissions, or town meetings). The various methods developed to address predominantly resource-based conflict (such as negotiation, mediation, community problem solving) appear to be inadequate for resolving problems that are primarily related to the sense of self and group identity. The conflict in Kosovo, for example, is a conflict over not only the territory in that region but the symbolic meanings of this territory for the Serbian people (who were brutally defeated there more than six hundred years ago) and for the Kosovo Albanians (who make up the great majority of its residents). Attempts to resolve this conflict would benefit from providing a venue for national dialogue over these differences, thereby supporting the sustainability of any peace agreement.

A third important dimension of the issues in intractable conflict is time. Such conflicts typically have an extensive past, a turbulent present, and a murky future. Western society is mainly present- to future-oriented, which often fosters an understanding of problems and their solutions that shares this same time perspective. Although a forward-looking perspective may have many benefits, it can neglect the need of individuals and groups to heal wounds festering from their past and to fulfill their obligations to their ancestors. Ancestors who were murdered or who have not been buried properly may produce strong obligations with important psychological and social consequences for their descendants today. For example, in some East African religious traditions, death (even murder) is often attributed to the ill will of wrathful ancestors who, feeling betrayed by their ancestors, are believed to poison or bewitch their victims by occult means. Comprehensive analysis of the issues must be mindful of differences in temporal orientation.

Finally, it is common in these situations of highly escalated, protracted conflict for a complex web of latent and manifest issues to develop that are difficult to understand, analyze, and respond to. In addition, the destructive processes involved in conflict escalation often generate issues regarding the "immoral" conduct of both parties during the conflict. This leads to further complexity. The centuries-old conflict in Northern Ireland is a classic example (see the introductory chapter of this volume). The Irish "troubles," long understood as a religious conflict between Catholics and Protestants, is at base a conflict between those who wish to see Northern Ireland remain part of the United Kingdom and those who wish to see the island unified. Religion, of course, plays a role in this conflict, as do international affairs, a history of international dominance, economic and other types of inequality (access to education, health care, housing, and so on), issues of social identity, the existence of multiple factions within each community, and serious concerns over human rights and the use of terrorist tactics. This kind of complexity and interrelatedness of issues is common in intractable conflicts, from the interpersonal to the international.

The Context. Intractable conflicts, particularly at the intergroup or international level, are typically rooted in a history of colonialism, ethnocentrism, racism, sexism, or human rights abuses in relations between the disputants. They regularly occur in situations where there exists a severe imbalance of power between the parties, in which the more powerful exploit, control, or abuse the less powerful. Often, the power holders in these settings use the existence of salient intergroup distinctions (such as ethnicity) as a means of maintaining or strengthening their power base. Such was the case in Rwanda (Smith, 1998). Frequently, intractable conflict occurs in a place where the opportunity structures favor one person or group over the other. These factors contribute to a setting where difficult material circumstances and political conflict lead to social disorganization, making it harder for people to meet their basic physical and psychological needs.

Often, at the heart of the identity-based issues is what Edward Azar (1990) has called "structural victimization" and Deutsch (see Chapter Two) discussed under "social injustice." Participants are seen to be victimized to the extent that they suffer from (1) denial of their identity (typically through lack of recognition from the majority), (2) lack of security for their culture or for other important group memberships, and (3) absence of effective political participation (also known as "voice") through which victimization can be remedied. I add to this list other forms of structural violence and injustice that jeopardize the physical safety and security of people through the effects of poverty, environmental degradation, poor access to health care, and the like. The essence of structural victimization is that someone's most basic human needs for dignity, safety, and control over life are jeopardized or denied. Attempts at conflict resolution that do not address the structural roots of such victimization are not likely to be successful or, even if momentarily successful, enduring.

Cultural or societal norms that legitimate using force create an environment particularly conducive to the use of violence in conflicts. For example, in an analysis of ninety preindustrial societies, Ross (1993) found that exceptionally intense violence is significantly likely in cultures where children are typically reared in cold or harsh families, particularly when it is routine for them to be physically or emotionally abused. Availability of lethal weapons is another factor that increases the probability of violence. Also, periods of rapid social and political change leading to shifts or ambiguity in the power structure, or to lack of communication between the conflicting parties, can increase the chances of a violent, destructive response during conflict.

Escalatory Dynamics. Fisher and Keashly (1991) offered a simple model of conflict escalation that characterizes the various shifts occurring in social processes as a conflict intensifies. They conceptualized conflict as "a mixture of objective and subjective elements that escalates and de-escalates over time" and proposed that "the subjective elements increase and take on greater importance as conflict escalates" (p. 234). For example, they described how, as conflict escalates, the issues tend to shift from "substantive interests and positions to concerns regarding the relationship, to basic needs or values, and ultimately to the very survival of the parties" (p. 236). Fisher and Keashly labeled the four stages of conflict escalation as discussion, polarization, segregation, and destruction. They proposed that destructive changes occur in several processes, including the disputants' communications, interactions, perceptions, and relations with the other; issue identification; and their perception and management of the outcomes. The last stage of this model, destruction, depicts highly escalated conflicts where communication is nonexistent and there are direct attacks; the other is viewed as nonhuman; relations are seen as hopeless; the issues shift to survival needs; and the outcomes are seen as lose-lose, with a desire to inflict as much harm on the other as possible.

The extensive literature on conflict escalation has identified a variety of social psychological processes that can fuel a conflict's intensity, particularly at a high level of escalation. They include elements such as misperception (negative and simplified stereotypes), selective perception (selective evaluation of behavior, discovery of confirming evidence, and attributional distortions), self-fulfilling prophecies (when negative attitudes and perceptions have an impact on the other's behavior), overcommitment (escalation of commitment), and entrapment (a special form of escalation where the parties expend more resources in the conflict than seems appropriate by external standards).

Other factors include a win-lose or competitive orientation (of the parties to the conflict), the tendency toward cognitive rigidity (constriction of thought and inability to envision alternatives) for the parties in an escalated conflict, a gamesmanship orientation (which turns the conflict away from issues of what in real life is being won or lost and toward an abstract conflict over images of power), miscommunication (a breakdown in open and direct communication), and autistic hostility (the tendency to stop interacting and communicating with those whom we are in conflict). Finally, ego-defensive processes such as deindividuation and dehumanization of the enemy can act to exempt one's behavior toward the other from the norms that exist within one's moral community and free the way for committing violent atrocities.

In summary, the particular combination of contextual factors such as structural victimization, the resulting identity-based survival concerns that arise from such settings, and the escalatory dynamics that play out as parties struggle to survive often act in concert to escalate a conflict to a level of high intensity and intractability. The consequences of such a mixture are often dire.

Consequences of Intractable Conflict

There is a litany of negative consequences due to highly escalated destructive conflicts. Below, I highlight those consequences that are specific to intractable conflicts.

Economic Costs. Typically, the costs of intractable conflict in terms of time and money spent are exceedingly high. They span from expensive legal fees, medical bills, and time off from one's employment to the costs incurred from maintaining a large security presence, rebuilding communities destroyed by war, lost investment in communities and revenues from tourism, and humanitarian aid to refugees.

Violence. The most obvious consequence of these conflicts is physical and psychological violence. This can range from psychological violence such as humiliation and abuse progressively upward to destruction of property, terrorist attacks, limited military engagement, ethnic cleansing, genocide, or full-scale war. What is unique to intractable conflict is the pervasiveness and persistence of the psychological and physical violence, how it typically leads to counterviolence and some degree of normalization of violent acts, and the extreme level of destruction it typically inflicts.

Intergenerational Perpetuation. Often the atrocities associated with these conflicts generate considerable long-term animosity between the disputants, which becomes integrated into the socialization processes of the respective families, groups, or societies involved. Through such socialization processes, new generations of potential disputants are propagated and fed on the images of the evil enemy, as well as rage due to past wrongs.

Divisions. In these situations, it is often necessary to separate the disputants in order to contain the violence and protect them from annihilation. Separation can reduce the violence, but the lack of human contact between the parties can also reinforce the negative, stereotypical images that each party holds of the other, which, in turn, can perpetuate their hatred and desire for revenge. The separation of the Greek-Cypriot and Turkish-Cypriot communities on their small island has shown the effects of communal separation.

Mental Health. The experience of prolonged trauma associated with many intractable conflicts produces what is perhaps its deepest wound. Long-term exposure to horrible atrocities and human suffering, the loss of loved ones, rape, bodily disfigurement, and chronic health problems can destroy people's spirit and impair their capacity to lead a healthy life. After the genocide in Rwanda, one study found that 90 percent of all survivors showed signs of psychological trauma (Carney, 1994). Children who are exposed or subjected to abuse and violence, orphaned by war, or inducted into service as child soldiers or as soldiers' "wives" are often the most deeply traumatized.

IMPLICATIONS FOR INTERVENTION
IN INTRACTABLE CONFLICT

Increasingly, important work is being conducted in preventing and intervening in intractable conflicts. This section offers some general propositions or guidelines for intervention. It then outlines several constructive approaches to intractable conflict, emphasizing intervention that is multimodal, multidisciplinary, well coordinated, and oriented to aspects of the conflict that are rooted in the past, the present, and the future.

The set of guidelines given here has been informed by the work of Dean Pruitt, Paul Olczak, Heidi Burgess, Guy Burgess, John Paul Lederach, Herbert Kelman, and Michael Wessells. The guidelines are useful for resolving many types of conflict, but they have particular relevance for addressing intractable conflict. All should be considered important; however, they are presented here in a crude chronological sequence to suggest that the initial guidelines be emphasized in the earlier stages of intervention.

Guideline 1: Conduct a thorough analysis of the conflict system (history, context, issues, and dynamics) prior to intervention.

Generally speaking, there are three phases in approaching such complex conflicts effectively: the problem-analysis phase, the problem-engagement phase, and the problem-resolution phase (Fisher, 1994). They are rarely sequential and are often cyclical in practice, but problem analysis should be carefully thought through so that the resulting initiatives directly address the issues of concern to the conflicting parties. Given the complexity, character, and interrelatedness of the many causal factors of intractable conflict previously outlined in this chapter, it is paramount that the intervenor take the time to begin with a comprehensive analysis of the situation. Our tendency to act before fully comprehending the system of a conflict often exacerbates it. This type of error was depicted in the John Sayles film *Men with Guns,* in which a physician who desires to alleviate the suffering of mountain peasants victimized by civil war introduces a team of young medical doctors into their villages. This well-meaning act backfires by inciting the suspicion of the government's army that the doctors are aiding the peasant revolutionaries; the army retaliates, and the result is more harm inflicted on the peasants. Ideally, assessment of an intractable conflict situation should be systemic in scope (considering important elements of the history and context), informed and verified by those directly involved with the conflict, and reassessed over time as important changes occur.

There are many types of analytical framework that are useful for analyzing conflict systems (see Dugan, 1996, and Lederach, 1997). Pruitt and Olczak (1995) offered a simple yet comprehensive framework for use in analyzing and approaching intractable conflict. Their MACBE model is an eclectic, multimodal systems approach to addressing social conflict that traces the source and potential resolution of a conflict to changes in five distinct yet interdependent "subsystems" of the individuals involved: as the acronym alludes, their motivation, affect, cognition, behavior, and surrounding environment. Highly escalated conflicts entail hostile elements in all five components. Motives are to harm or destroy the other; the affect is hostile and rage-filled; cognitions include negative stereotypes, perceptions, and a large measure of distrust; behaviors are violent and destructive; and the environment is usually polarized.

The model views these five modes of experience as interactive and working with "circular causality," affecting and being affected by changes in the other modes. This feeds the escalation of the system through internal conflict spirals. The authors of the model argue that to address "seemingly intractable" conflicts most effectively, one must understand the interrelationship of these experiences and look to produce changes in several, if not all, of these modes.

Take, for example, a seemingly intractable family dispute between a stepfather and a stepson. The conflict sprang from myriad identity and resource-based issues, persisted for several years, affected the entire family system, and eventually reached a stage where interactions between the disputants alternated between autistic hostility and violence. The family was referred to mediation by the police, and the mediator eventually involved a family therapist. This team of intervenors found it useful to separate those aspects of the conflict that were cognitively based (distrust and stereotypical misperceptions), feeling-based (rage and fear), behaviorally based (lack of effective conflict-resolving skills), motivationally based (unwillingness to engage), and environmentally based (schisms among the broader family system). The intervenors found these distinctions, in light of the interrelatedness of these issues, useful in proposing a comprehensive strategy for intervention.

Guideline 2: Initial concern for the intervenors should be to establish or foster an authentic experience of "ripeness" among disputants or among key representatives of each of the groups involved in an intractable conflict.

The MACBE model recommends a sequential method for intervening in intractable conflict that begins by addressing ripeness. Ripeness has the primary emphasis in their model because "the initial step [toward conflict resolution] must be the development of motivation to escape the conflict" (Pruitt and Olczak, 1995, p. 83). Elsewhere, I have defined *ripeness* as "a commitment by the parties to change the direction of the normative social processes of the relations towards de-escalation" (Coleman, 1997, pp. 3–4). Here, I emphasize the notion of an *authentic* commitment to deescalation to distinguish between ripeness that is short-term and false (typically feigned as a tactical move) from that which is genuine and motivated by a true desire for peace.

In systems experiencing highly escalated conflict, destructive conflict processes can gradually come to be experienced as normative by the parties involved. This is experienced individually (through each person's subjective experiences and expectations of the other in the conflict) as well as through each party's actions and the destructive group norms that come to be established in the system. When this occurs, ripeness can be defined as a commitment by the parties to change the direction of the normative escalatory and destructive social processes toward deescalation. Such commitment can produce a change in the nature of the relations of the parties from a competitive, hopeless, destructive orientation toward a cooperative, constructive coexistence with the potential for mutual gain. Ripeness can either develop unplanned as a result of time and circumstances associated with the conflict or be intentionally facilitated by the conflicting parties and third parties. Differences in how it is introduced, however, have important implications for the conflict system.

Lewin (1947) developed a model for conceptualizing change in systems that offers important insight into these processes (see also Chapter Eighteen). He wrote that "the study of the conditions for change begins appropriately with an analysis of the conditions for 'no change', that is, for the state of equilibrium" (p. 208). Lewin indicated that a state of "no social change" refers to a state of "quasi-stationary social-equilibrium," that is, a relatively constant state. Therefore, to better locate and comprehend the various paths to ripeness in a conflict it is valuable to attempt to understand the dynamic forces that keep a conflict in a state of "unripeness." During the Cold War, for example, the combination of fear, misunderstanding, mutual distrust, and investment in military hardware and industry between the United States and the USSR acted to contain the conflict at a costly level for a prolonged period of time. Lewin compared this state to "that of a river which flows with a given velocity in a given direction during a certain time interval," and added, "a social change is comparable to a change in velocity or direction of that river" (p. 208).

Lewin offered two basic methods for bringing about change in the direction of the flow of a system: by adding forces in the desired direction of the change or by diminishing the opposing forces that resist the change. Typically, the change forces that can induce ripeness include

- Threats and the use of physical force
- The perception of a hurting stalemate (suffering losses in a conflict that cannot be won)
- The experience of a recent or near catastrophe
- The awareness of an impending catastrophe or deteriorating position (Zartman and Aurik, 1991)

Adding change forces to the conflict system induces a state of increased tension that is accompanied by "greater fatigue, higher aggressiveness, higher emotionality, and lower constructiveness" (Lewin, 1947, p. 26). Obviously, this is risky in the already high-tension state of an escalated conflict process. Therefore, it may be beneficial to initially consider the alternative method of *removing the resistance forces opposing ripeness,* thereby facilitating it while lowering relative tension.

Returning to the family conflict previously described, several key factors contributed to unfreezing both the adolescent's and the stepfather's resistance to ripeness and moving them toward resolution of their conflict and a change in their relations. The mediation process (to a small degree) and the individual counseling sessions (to a larger degree) allowed both parties the *cathartic experience* they needed to ventilate their feelings and feel heard and respected by understanding third parties. This helped them both get over their intense blaming of the other and to begin taking some responsibility for their respective situations. These experiences also helped to establish some *trust* between the parties. The counselors and mediator also modeled and discussed the use of appropriate *social skills* for dealing with anger and when engaged in conflict. This helped the parties begin to see alternative methods of responding to each other. Finally, the adolescent's counselor involved other key members in family therapy as a means of educating them to their role in the conflict and making them part of the solution. These interventions worked in combination to move the parties toward ripeness and resolution.

Through identifying and removing the obstacles (such as distrust, rage, and lack of skills) that act to resist ripeness, it becomes possible to create or enhance a disputant's commitment to peace without increasing the overall level of tension in the system. Resistance obstacles differ in their amenability to change and in the level of impact they have on the system. Intervenors would benefit from targeting the obstacles that are of high importance and most amenable to change. Often, the forces that act to resist ripeness can be a valuable source of information regarding where energy is locked up in a system, as well as what the members of the system value and find satisfying. This information can be critical in locating and developing potential interventions.

Guideline 3: Initially, orient disputants toward the primary objective of defining a fair, constructive process of conflict engagement, and away from the objective of achieving outcomes that resolve the conflict.

The work of Burgess and Burgess (1996) on intractable conflict has identified a subtle but important reframing of the approach to these problems (see also Chapter Thirteen). They contend that, because of the zero-sum nature of most intractable conflicts, confrontation over the core issues at stake is inevitable and comprehensive resolution is unrealistic. However, they argue, the processes need not be destructive. Consequently, they advocate that conflict resolvers working in such a situation emphasize creating a process of confrontation that the disputants find to be both effective (in terms of minimizing the negative costs of the conflict and maximizing the benefits) and fair or just (in terms of broad moral concerns). They suggest that conflict resolvers see this as a shift to an incremental approach to resolving conflict, which has the potential of reducing the damage of the conflict process despite the lack of any ultimate resolution.

To a large extent, this is what has emerged with the current peace agreement in Northern Ireland, where a political process has been established (home rule and a power-sharing arrangement between the communities) whose agenda it will be to tackle some of the substantive problems associated with the conflict (such as disarming the IRA). My own sense is that this emphasis on establishing a constructive process might be a particularly useful strategy in the early phases of a conflict resolution process, but that eventually, if the stakes are high, the disputants will demand a focus on the substance of their concerns.

Guideline 4: Given the complexity of intractable conflict, analysis and intervention must be embedded in a multidisciplinary framework.

Because of the complexity and multidimensionality of intractable conflicts, it is imperative that intervenors understand the system of the conflict from various perspectives and approach it comprehensively. Social psychology is but one lens through which to see. In fact, every disciplinary perspective (political science, international affairs, public health, economics, history, law, and so on) is limited in that it focuses our attention on certain aspects of a phenomenon and away from others. This is particularly problematic when it comes to understanding and resolving complex conflicts. Well-intentioned psychosocial interventions (as well as political or economic interventions) that are ignorant of political, economic, and cultural realities can be ineffective or have disastrous consequences. However, the narrow specialist training in disciplines, the complexity of using diverse methods, and the lack of incentive to work across disciplinary boundaries makes a multidisciplinary approach to these conflicts particularly difficult to realize.

Guideline 5: Elicitive approaches to conflict intervention, particularly when working across cultures, tend to be more respectful of disputants, more empowering and sustainable, and generally more effective than prescriptive approaches.

There is a current concern among scholars and practitioners about whether the models in use in many conflict resolution interventions are implicitly oriented toward Western males and are therefore not sufficiently sensitive and respectful of "differences" (of gender, race, culture, class, and so on) in how conflict is understood, approached, and ideally resolved. (For additional discussion of the relation between culture and conflict, see the two chapters in the next part of this volume.)

Responding to these concerns, some scholars have recommended an "elicitive" approach to conflict resolution across cultures (Lederach, 1995; Mays, Bullock, Rosenzweig, and Wessells, 1998). They contend that "prescriptive" approaches to intervention, which view the intervenor as the expert and the participants as passive recipients of predetermined knowledge, models, and skills, are often inappropriate. They endorse another type of approach, where the local, cultural expertise of the participants is elicited and emphasized and where the intervenor and the participants together design interventions that are specifically suited to the problems, resources, and constraints of the specific cultural context. An elicitive approach not only corrects for the bias of a prescriptive approach but also is experienced as empowering by the participants in that it respects, embraces, and accommodates the voices of local people. It can also foster great commitment to the peace process by those involved and therefore lead to plans and initiatives with prolonged sustainability.

Guideline 6: Short-term (crisis-management) interventions need to be coordinated and mindful of long-term objectives and interventions.

Intractable conflict sometimes brings on an extended period of crisis and intense human suffering. It is often these events that capture the attention of outside parties (such as the police, the media, and the international community). When this occurs, intervenors typically focus their efforts on containing the immediate crisis and stopping the violence. This form of crisis management is, of course, essential. However, it is often carried out with little thought for the implications for the larger conflict system and longer-term peace objectives.

Lederach (1997) describes the various time frames inherent in the aspects of peace work. Short-term crisis intervention work (such as emergency relief and humanitarian aid) orients intervenors to immediate, life-saving tasks that typically occur in a framework of two to six months. Short-range planning (such as preparation and training to reduce the likelihood of recurring violence) requires forward thinking, looking ahead one or two years. The longer-term perspective, which Lederach defines as "generational thinking" or thinking twenty-plus years out, is uncommon in peace work but used by some to visualize peace and social harmony between disputants and to identify the steps necessary to reach such an idealized state. Nested between short-range planning and generational thinking is what Lederach refers to as "decade thinking" (five to ten years), where fundamental social change can be designed and implemented.

Lederach encourages practitioners to see each time frame as nested in the longer-term schemas, and to be mindful of the impact of crisis management and short-term planning on long-term objectives. He suggests that thinking in terms of decades can help coordinate peace work in a manner that links the immediate experience of crisis intervention with initiatives toward a better future where such problems can be prevented. This broad time frame is more realistic when addressing protracted conflicts that have been in existence for several generations and may take that long to resolve effectively.

Guideline 7: When working with conflicts between large groups (such as ethnic groups and communities), it is useful to concentrate interventions on the "midlevel" leadership representing each group.

The work of John Burton, Herbert Kelman, John Paul Lederach, and others has emphasized targeting for intervention certain types of leader within groups and communities engaged in protracted social conflicts. These leaders, labeled "track II diplomats" or "middle-range leaders," are typically influential, unofficial representatives (members of the media; former or potential government officials; leaders of business, educational, religious, union, and other local institutions) from the opposing sides of a conflict who represent the mainstream of each community and reflect the attitudes and interests of their respective communities. These leaders are distinguished from both the top-tier leaders (government officials and diplomats) and the grassroots leaders (local leaders and community developers).

There are several advantages to working with such midlevel community representatives. First and most simply, it is efficient. The top-level leaders are usually inaccessible, while the grassroots leaders are often too unconnected with the top level as well as too numerous. Midlevel leaders tend to have both top-down influence with their constituencies as well as bottom-up influence in that they often have the attention of official leaders. Midlevel leaders are often realistic in their assessment of the conflict situations thanks to their direct connection with their constituents (where most of the suffering occurs) and their understanding of the complexities of leadership and diplomacy. Also, midlevel leaders are usually not as constrained by their roles and by the expectations of their constituents (and by media attention) as are top-level leaders. Finally, in the future these leaders may move into formal leadership roles in the government, where they can have direct impact on official diplomacy.

Guideline 8: The general intervention strategy must integrate appropriate approaches for issues rooted in the past, the present, and the future.

As previously mentioned, intractable conflicts tend to revolve around concerns from the past, the present, and the future. In fact, anthropologists have found that members of distinct cultures often differ in the relative importance that they assign to events of the past, present, and future. For intractable conflict to be resolved effectively, the intervention approach must be fashioned to be respectful of these time orientations and comprehensive in addressing the salient issues from each temporal dimension. Furthermore, these interventions must be introduced in a manner inclusive and respectful of past and current approaches to the conflict that have made gains in addressing the problems. In Table 21.1, I outline some of the current methods in the field of conflict resolution that have been designed to address these areas of concern constructively. The primary objectives of these methods are to offer security to the disputants and their communities and to foster better relations among the disputants.

Addressing the Present Situation

Of course, all new interventions begin in the present. However, interventions differ in the degree to which they are mainly directed at stabilizing the current situation and identifying possible inroads to the conflict. Here are some of the many initiatives involved in addressing the present situation.

Crisis Management. Crisis management aims at stopping the violence and reducing human suffering brought on by the conflict. This includes separating the disputants, peacekeeping, humanitarian relief (food, housing, sanitation, medical attention, counseling), introducing international observers, and containing criminal activities.

Conflict Analysis. Systematic identification of the manifest and latent issues (resource and identity), parties, history, escalatory dynamics, and other factors helps define the parameters of the conflict and thereby make it manageable by providing a prognosis and recommendations for intervention. Frameworks such as the MACBE model or the Coleman-Raider "chip-chop" planning analysis (see Chapter Twenty-Four) are useful in organizing these analyses.

Fostering Ripeness. As previously outlined, establishing an authentic commitment to peace among the disputants is a prerequisite to most other interventions.

Table 21.1. Constructive Approaches to Addressing Intractable Conflict.

Past	Present	Future
• Reflexivity • Dialogue • Forgiveness and reconciliation • Traditional approaches	• Crisis management • Conflict systems analysis • Creating ripeness • Constructive confrontation • Problem-solving workshops	• Sustainable reconciliation • Focused social imaging

Constructive Confrontation. The goal of this approach is constructive trans-formation of a conflictful relationship. This is achieved by focusing the inter-vention on fostering a constructive conflict process, not by identifying or achieving a resolution to the conflict (Burgess and Burgess, 1996). The method aims to improve disputants' understanding of both sides of the conflict, sepa-rate the core issues of the conflict from the "conflict overlay," and develop a conflict strategy with the potential to meet the needs of the disputants *and* be fair and just.

Problem-Solving Workshops. The work by Kelman and others (see Rouhana and Kelman, 1994) on using interactive problem-solving workshops in ad-dressing intractable conflict offers a useful prototype of track II diplomacy at work in ongoing disputes. These workshops intentionally involve influential, unofficial representatives (such as members of the media, community activists, and former or potential government officials) from the opposing sides of a con-flict, with emphasis on individuals from the mainstream of each community who reflect the attitudes and interests of their respective communities. During the workshop, the participants engage in formal, collaborative problem-solving work on the needs-based issues that have been identified as central to the con-flict; they also have informal social contact with members of the opposing party or parties.

These interventions are founded on the twin theoretical propositions that equal-status contact in pursuit of superordinate goals can transform the issues and relations between conflicting parties, and that the experiences and inter-actions of the *individuals* involved in these workshops can affect the larger out-comes of the conflict *system.* Workshops of this type often affect the ripeness of individual participants by addressing their areas of resistance, altering their perception of the enemy from evil to human, initiating a sense of requiting and trust in the process of interactive problem solving, allowing the participants an opportunity to begin feeling listened to and respected by the other party, and proposing workable solutions to specific areas of contention. This occurs in an environment relatively free from the external pressures of media scrutiny and formal constituent accountability, pressures that tend to lock formal negotiators into rigid positions.

This experience can foster a shift in one's ripeness and engender commit-ment to the peace process and to a basic change in relations with the other party. If this occurs, the individuals return to their communities and begin to affect the larger system of their conflict through their respective areas of influ-ence. This type of work has been and continues to be done with intractable con-flicts around the world, as in Cyprus (through AMIDEAST), and with ethnic relations in America (through Federal Community Relations Services).

Addressing the Past

Working with concerns in conflicts rooted in the past is a complex but essential process. It is complicated by such factors as bias in memory recall, blocks in memory retrieval because of trauma, and the fundamentally different experiences of the past that exist across cultures in terms of the role and importance of ancestors and the effects of the past on one's present life. Regardless of how the past is understood, in intractable conflict it is necessary to attempt to address the past in order for healing to occur in the present. Here are some of the approaches that have been designed to work with events in the past.

Reflexivity. Building on the work of many others, Rothman (1997) has developed this process. It is essentially a method for individuals to reflect on their own role and responsibility in the escalation of a conflict. It is an active attempt to move disputants out of the antagonistic frame of blaming the other, splitting good and evil (us versus them), making hostile attributions regarding the other, and projecting negative aspects of oneself onto the other. This is done by encouraging disputants to slow down the reactive process to conflict, and to carefully examine what the conflict means to them, why it is important, and why they have become so deeply invested in a destructive approach. The objectives are to help clarify and deepen the disputants' understanding of their own contributions to the escalation of events, and ultimately to support their expression of this understanding in the presence of the other party.

Dialogue. This is a facilitated, interactive process between disputants or former adversaries that is aimed at establishing contact, allowing pain and suffering to be expressed, and fostering deep understanding of the human experience in conflict. Its primary objective is not to solve problems but to reconnect individuals and groups estranged by conflict. Du Bois and Hutson (1997) describe it as "an inclusive, facilitated forum for the face-to-face exchange of information, sharing of personal stories, honest expression of emotion, affirmation of values, clarification of viewpoints and deliberations of solutions to serious concerns" (p. 11). The dialogue process calls for inquiry, not advocacy; temporary suspension of judgment and positions for purposes of exploration; and public acknowledgment of the value of the other's needs. President Clinton's national dialogues on race are one example of this process in action.

Forgiveness and Reconciliation. Forgiveness is one aspect of reconciliation, but reconciliation as a process moves beyond it (see Deutsch's discussion of forgiveness in Chapter Two). Reconciliation is a relational encounter (focused on the relationships between essential elements in the conflict system) that emphasizes acknowledging past wrongs. Lederach (1997) wrote that "reconciliation-as-encounter suggests that space for acknowledging of the past and envisioning of the future (which) is the necessary ingredient for reframing the present" (p. 27). It includes such processes as reflexivity, dialogue, and forgiveness, but it also incorporates the search for *justice* (equality and restitution), *truth* (transparency, revelation, and clarity), *mercy* (acceptance, compassion, and healing) and *peace* (harmony, security, and respect). Lederach suggests that reconciliation is both a process and an objective or ideal. The truth and reconciliation commissions of South Africa, Guatemala, and Haiti are formal examples of these processes.

Traditional Approaches. There exists within both modern and traditional societies an elaborate series of pageants, rituals, ceremonies, and other individual and group experiences and activities that have evolved and been passed on as methods for respecting and managing the past. These experiences incorporate music, dance, costumes, poetry, and prose into a variety of processes aimed at grieving over loss and respecting the dead. More work should be done to understand the relationship of these activities with past events and to clarify the role they could play in helping disputants heal past wounds.

There is great need for innovation in developing new (or perhaps embracing old) methods for addressing problems rooted in the past. Developing expressive and symbolic processes such as the truth and reconciliation commissions, town meetings and dialogue sessions in this country, and family and couples counseling to support mediation processes are all attempts along these lines. These processes are often very time consuming, with the focus of such initiatives less on action and more on healing, forgiving, and reconciling. Ultimately, conflict practitioners need to develop enhanced capacity for understanding the power of the past, as well as the patience and tolerance that some of these time-consuming approaches to addressing the past demand.

Working with the Future

A chief of the Mohawk nation, native peoples of Quebec, once noted that Mohawk tradition makes it the responsibility of the chiefs to think in terms of seven generations. This is based on the belief that the decisions made seven generations ago affect people today, and that the decisions made today will affect the next seven generations (Lederach, 1997). Unfortunately, this type of long-term thinking about malignant conflicts, although essential, is uncommon in the work of scholars and practitioners of conflict resolution. What follows are two important exceptions.

Sustainable Reconciliation. In his book *Building Peace: Sustainable Reconciliation in Divided Societies* (1997), John Paul Lederach describes a strategy and process of peace building in protracted social conflicts that is oriented toward reconstructing relationships and addressing the original structural inequities that contributed to the intensity of the conflict. Lederach's comprehensive approach to peace work emphasizes interventions where short-term and long-term initiatives are coordinated, and where the primary locus of the interventions is in the subsystems of the conflict. These subsystems are the organizations and institutions in the societies (which are often directed by midlevel leaders) that have the capacity for addressing both individual and group-level needs, as well as the ability to influence the constructive changes necessary at the systems or societal level. Again, Lederach's approach emphasizes "decades thinking" as a means of connecting present interventions to future peace.

Focused Social Imaging. Elise Boulding (1986) has designed and conducted a series of workshops that offer a creative and hopeful process for working with disputants who are stuck in the web of malignant social conflict. The approach is quite simple. The workshop actively involves participants who are parties to a dispute (such as Arab and Israeli youths). They begin by identifying some of the shared social concerns regarding the conflict (such as reducing community violence or improving community health services). The participants are then asked to temporarily disregard the current realities of the situation and to step into the future. They are asked to put themselves into a future approximately twenty to thirty years from the present, in which their concerns have been effectively dealt with.

As the participants begin to develop some sense of the social arrangements and institutions in this idealized future, discussion ensues. Together, they begin to create a vision for a community that has the institutions and relationships necessary to effectively address their shared concerns. Then the participants are asked to move slowly backward in time, and to begin identifying the steps that would precede establishment of such institutions and relationships. This is both a creative and a critical process of examining the achievement of their ideal future in the context of the circumstances that are likely to exist between the present and such a future. Ultimately, this process results in both a vision and a plan for making the vision reality. It also can serve to open up the participants' awareness of options and approaches to the current conflict that they previously found impossible to imagine.

IMPLICATIONS FOR TRAINING

Space does not allow detailed discussion of the needs for training in this area. However, the guidelines and processes I have described outline many of the objectives to be addressed in a comprehensive training program for practitioners working with intractable conflict. In summary, such training should address:

Systems thinking and analysis. An introduction to general systems theory (von Bertalanffy, 1973) that offers a conceptual framework for understanding the interrelationships of various elements within systems and their interface with the external environment. Participants should also be trained in using a variety of analytical frameworks for conflict intervention such as those developed by Dugan (1996); Lederach (1997); Fisher and Keashly (1991); Pruitt and Olczak (1995); and Raider, Coleman, and Gerson (see Chapter Twenty-Four).

Coordination of complex activities. Training should develop skills in working with multitask, multimethod approaches that can integrate multidisciplinary perspectives and methodologies to address immediate, short-term, and long-term goals in a comprehensive and coordinated fashion. Training should also emphasize the temporal distinctions of past, present, and future orientations in intervention.

Creating ripeness. Intervenors would benefit from training in understanding and developing strategies and tactics for assessing, fostering, and maintaining authentic commitment to a constructive conflict process among disputants or representatives from disputing groups. Such training should emphasize the distinct effects of introducing change forces in contrast to removing resistance obstacles when fostering ripeness.

Working with crisis and trauma. Conflict resolvers working with disputants in an intractable conflict need to be trained in working with individuals in emotional or physical crisis. Awareness of the symptoms of posttraumatic stress syndrome and understanding of how to do crisis intervention when emergencies occur are important in conducting work in this area.

Facilitating constructive conflict processes. Training in conflict-process facilitation should include instruction in collaborative negotiation, mediation, and other forms of third-party intervention (arbitration, med-arb, and so on) as well as in facilitating reflexivity and dialogue sessions. Intervenors should also be trained in the skills of working elicitively, in particular cross-culturally.

Creativity, innovation, and artistry. There is a substantial need for innovation in this area. Training in the process of focused social imaging (Boulding, 1986) is a good beginning. But practitioners would benefit greatly from applying a creative problem-solving process (see Chapter Seventeen) to the methods for working with intractable conflict, particularly for working with deep, intangible identity conflict.

CONCLUSION

There are no simple solutions to intractability. Once conflict reaches this level of destructiveness, we can only hope to contain the violence and bloodshed and begin the considerable work of repairing the damage to people, places, and relationships. This is a daunting task, but there is hope. Hope in prevention. Intractable conflicts usually have a long history of escalation prior to reaching crisis and entrenchment. We must find ways to intervene earlier, when disputants can still see the humanity and the validity of the other's needs. Unfortunately, it is typically the squeaky wheel of crisis that grabs the attention of the media, the international community, and our systems of governance. Therefore, we must be proactive in establishing early-warning systems at the community, regional, national, and international levels. Their charge would be to monitor emerging disputes and focus our attention on situations before they become impossible to address. Our greatest hope in working intractable conflicts is to find the means to avert them.

References

Azar, E. E. *The Management of Protracted Social Conflict.* Hampshire, England: Dartmouth, 1990.

Boulding, E. "Enlivening Our Social Imagination." In D. Carlson and C. Comstock (eds.), *Citizen Summitry: Keeping the Peace When It Matters Too Much to Be Left to Politicians.* Los Angeles: Tarcher, 1986.

Burgess, H., and Burgess, G. "Constructive Confrontation: A Transformative Approach to Intractable Conflicts." *Mediation Quarterly,* 1996, *13,* 305–322.

Burton, J. *Resolving Deep-Rooted Conflict: A Handbook.* Lanham, Md.: University Press of America, 1987.

Carney, A. "Lack of Care in Rwanda." *British Journal of Psychiatry,* 1994, *165,* 556.

Coleman, P. T. "Redefining Ripeness: A Social Psychological Perspective." *Peace and Conflict: Journal of Peace Psychology,* 1997, *3,* 81–103.

Deutsch, M. (1985). *Distributive Justice: A Social Psychological Perspective.* New Haven: Yale University Press, 1985.

Du Bois, P. M., and Hutson, J. J. *Bridging the Racial Divide: A Report on Interracial Dialogue in America.* Battleboro, Verm.: Center for Living Democracy, 1997.

Dugan, M. "A Nested Theory of Conflict." *Women in Leadership,* 1996, *1,* 9–20.

Fisher, R. J. "Third-Party Confrontation: A Method for the Resolution and Study of Conflict." *Journal of Conflict Resolution,* 1994, *16,* 67–94.

Fisher, R. J., and Keashly, L. "A Contingency Approach to Third Party Intervention." In R. J. Fisher (ed.), *The Social Psychology of Intergroup and International Conflict Resolution.* New York: Springer-Verlag, 1991.

Lederach, J. P. *Preparing for Peace: Conflict Transformation Across Cultures.* Syracuse, N.Y.: Syracuse University Press, 1995.

Lederach, J. P. *Building Peace: Sustainable Reconciliation in Divided Societies.* Washington, D.C.: U.S. Institute of Peace Press, 1997.

Lewin, K. "Frontiers in Group Dynamics." *Human Relations* 1947, *1,* 5–41.

Mays, V. M., Bullock, M., Rosenzweig, M. R., and Wessells, M. "Ethnic Conflict: Global Challenges and Psychological Perspectives." *American Psychologist*, 1998, *53*, 737–742.

Pruitt, D., and Olczak, P. "Beyond Hope: Approaches to Resolving Seemingly Intractable Conflict." In B. B. Bunker and J. Z. Rubin (eds.), *Cooperation, Conflict, and Justice: Essays Inspired by the Work of Morton Deutsch.* Thousand Oaks, Calif.: Sage, 1995.

Ross, M. H. *The Management of Conflict: Constructive and Destructive Processes.* New Haven: Yale University Press, 1993.

Rothman, J. *Resolving Identity-Based Conflict in Nations, Organizations, and Communities.* San Francisco: Jossey-Bass, 1997.

Rouhana, N. N., and Kelman, H. C. "Promoting Joint Thinking in International Conflicts: An Israeli-Palestinian Continuing Workshop." *Journal of Social Issues,* 1994, *50,* 157–178.

Smith, D. N. "The Psychocultural Roots of Genocide: Legitimacy and Crisis in Rwanda." *American Psychologist,* 1998, *53,* 743–753.

von Bertalanffy, L. *General Systems Theory.* New York: Braziller, 1973.

Zartman, I. W., and Aurik, J. "Power Strategies in De-Escalation." In L. Kriesberg and S. J. Thorson (eds.), *Timing the De-Escalation of International Conflicts.* Syracuse, N.Y.: Syracuse University Press, 1991.

PART SIX

CULTURE AND CONFLICT

CHAPTER TWENTY-TWO

Culture and Conflict

Paul R. Kimmel

As our world becomes a global village, the need for better understanding and communication among people from different cultures increases. Many of today's issues transcend local or national interests and action (Berman and Johnson, 1977). For example, common markets, resource shortages, ethnic conflicts, nuclear proliferation, natural disasters, drugs, and environmental problems cannot be handled by individual nations. Relations among nations require meeting and communicating with people of diverse cultural backgrounds.

Whether the situation is bilateral or multilateral; the issue, technical or ideological; or the standard for success, victory or a problem solution, individuals from many cultures must interact. Ideally, they come to understand their basic cultural differences and create commonality in their interaction, which facilitates communication and problem solving. More likely, they assume that they all share the same reality and consequently experience conflict in their interactions until they find that they do not have one reality in common.

I employ the term *microcultures* to refer to commonalities in meaning, norms of communication, and behavior; shared perception and expectation; roles; and the like, which develop among individuals from varying cultural backgrounds as they interact over time. If no microcultures are in place or created, misunderstanding and breakdown in international meetings may result from the often unconscious expectations that negotiators, mediators, and educators bring to these encounters from their own cultures—expectations that are not shared by their counterparts from other cultures. Since each negotiator thinks that the others could (and should) share his expectations, he assumes that the others are misbehaving or not serious about reaching agreement when they do the unexpected. A dramatic case in point was the meeting between the representatives of the United States and Iraq in Geneva in January 1991.

Prior to this meeting between Secretary of State James Baker and Foreign Minister Tariq Aziz, the United States appointed a woman, April Glaspie, as its ambassador to Iraq. The ambassador's gender and her status as a "Westerner" made her a very weak representative in the estimation of the Iraqis. Her status and the ambiguity of the message she had delivered, warning Saddam Hussein against invading Kuwait, signaled to Hussein that the United States was not concerned with what he called the "retaking of Iraq's territory." To him, what was not said by the United States was more important than what was said.

The January meeting in Geneva was plagued by cultural misunderstanding (Stewart, 1991; Kimmel, 1994). The two groups could not have done a better job of alienating each other had they tried. The Associated Press reported that Baker was "genuinely stunned" when Aziz refused to take to his superior Bush's letter explaining what the United States would do if Iraq invaded Kuwait. Aziz judged the Bush letter too explicit to be presented to Hussein. Although we do not know the contents, it is likely that they were blunt and unequivocal. Such communications are not acceptable in cultures whose officials expect room to maneuver so as not to be embarrassed (lose face). An explicit, written statement from one head of state to another was the wrong kind of message sent in the wrong way to the wrong person. Aziz and the Iraqis decided that the Americans were not serious about negotiating and were deliberately insulting them.

Publicly humiliating officials from a face-saving culture can create enemies for life. Such humiliation stiffens their resolve and reduces the possibility of change. After Aziz had been scolded by the U.S. delegation in Geneva, one Iraqi delegate said in a "quaking voice" as he left the meeting, "I never thought that you Americans could be so arrogant. Such a free and open country you have, and still you refuse to see our viewpoint." Here is a man who felt condescension and accused of something he did not intend.

Lacking microcultures, low levels of cultural awareness can contribute to or cause destructive conflict, as this example illustrates.

THEORY

To clarify what we mean by culture and cultural awareness, I discuss and illustrate some relevant social science concepts and theories used in the field of intercultural communication.

Subjective Culture and Mindsets

Intercultural communication specialists think of culture as "a growing, changing, dynamic thing consisting most significantly of shared perceptions in the minds of its members" (Fontaine, 1989, p. 2). It is to a people as personality is to a person (Tyler, 1987). Our learned shared perceptions, or subjective culture as Triandis (1972) has called it, contains the "categories, plans and rules people employ to interpret their world and act purposefully in it" (Spradley and McCurdy, 1989, p. 2). Your subjective culture serves as a highly selective screen between you and the outside world that "directs the organization of the psyche, which in turn has a profound effect upon the ways people look at things, behave politically, make decisions, order priorities, organize their lives, and . . . how they think" (Hall, 1976, p. 212). It gives meaning and intention to your acts and your understanding of the acts of others. Your subjective culture provides the underlying grammar for sending, receiving, and interpreting communications. Many of the expectations that you share with others in your culture have to do with how to communicate.

Edward Hall (1976) hypothesizes that the majority of our cultural categories, plans, and rules are unconscious. To understand our cultural frame of reference, or mindset (Fisher, 1988), in any given situation—that is, how we typically think and feel—requires understanding our unconscious subjective culture and the context of the situation. In the past, when societies were simpler and more homogeneous than today, such understanding was often based on such familiar ethnographic markers as skin color, religion, nationality, gender, or ethnic background. As societies become complex and fluid, the subjective cultures of their members diversify, and these same ethnographic markers are often unreliable guides for predicting and understanding their mindsets and behaviors (Avruch and Black, 1990, 1991).

Constructing Reality

You acquire a subjective culture through socialization by and with other human beings. In this process, what becomes your reality and common sense is selected from an array of alternatives in your social and physical environment. Your consciousness is built or constructed through your contacts with others who have already learned or incorporated certain alternatives from that environment. You perceive what you expect to perceive through selecting information that fits your learned categories. A classic example of the results of this construction process is Bagby's study of Mexican and American schoolchildren (1957), in which two dissimilar pictures were simultaneously projected (one to each eye) through a tachistoscope, a device that allows pictures to be flashed on a screen for an instant. American children saw only a baseball player, while Mexican children saw only a bullfighter.

We develop and use symbols (such as words and sentences) that give meaning to our social activity. Language, our most complete category system, is the primary mode of communication in our symbolic environment. Its inherent reciprocity makes it ideal for constructing common meaning. As individuals (parents, children, teachers, students) interact within a symbolic environment, the shared meanings they create and use become beliefs and attitudes in their subjective culture, and norms and values in their common culture or society.

Through using language, human beings participate in, shape, and spread their common culture. Communication is relatively easy within a language community not only because of similar conversational styles but also because members have learned most of the verbal and nonverbal categories, plans, assumptions, and rules that are part of that language's common culture. Although we develop individualized, unique subjective culture through localized (for example, familial) interaction, people from the same common culture have more or less equivalent realities and mindsets. Thus, there is a strong relationship among the common culture of a people, their language, and their communication and cognitive style.

Most of us are unaware of many of the important differences between our subjective culture and those of individuals from other well-known cultures because few of us are in direct contact with such individuals. Although we sometimes experience aspects of other cultures in the news or when traveling, these aspects are filtered through our own common culture as stereotypes and have little impact on our predisposition to perceive, reason, and communicate in accordance with our own subjective culture. Only extended contact with "foreigners" plus training in intercultural communication can expand our adult subjective culture and mindset.

Cultural Identity

As we are socialized, we learn to center our judgments around values and procedures fundamental to our own common culture. Children learn that the values and procedures of their culture are natural and normal. They are what we call common sense. Children develop a cultural identity grounded in their immediate community and family connections, including their religion, language, customs, and traditions. These congruities of blood, speech, land, and religion possess a powerful, emotional coerciveness.

The bridge between one's common culture and subjective culture is the identification process that binds us together into cohesive groups. There are other possibilities for individual cultural identity formation than one's primordial roots, of course, but the primordial grouping of family and local community is encompassing because it comes first in our enculturation (Volkan, 1992). Those who share primordial roots are sometimes referred to as an ethnic group or a people.

Almost all peoples believe that their way of thinking about and doing things is the best way. They learn to evaluate other ways of thinking about and doing things as unusual, wrong, or inferior. Unless they have had mediated experiences with everyday life in other common cultures, they seldom become aware of the roots or uniqueness of their own and other peoples' realities. Without such awareness, they are likely to misunderstand those from other cultures in face-to-face meetings because of basic and unconscious differences in nonverbal communication, cognition, perception, and reasoning.

To question the universality of your own reality or mindset, or to acknowledge that the reality or mindset of others may fundamentally differ from your own is disorienting. It is easier to believe that all participants in an international meeting, for instance, use one's own established approaches. Contemplating the existence of a variety of approaches to and assumptions about negotiating is daunting and uncomfortable. If you are negotiating within your own common culture or with those from similar common cultures, your expectations of commonality are often met. If dissimilar cultures are involved, there will be surprises (Cohen, 1991).

Attribution Error and Miscommunication

Since most adults' subjective cultures are relatively stable and internally coherent, it is difficult for them to understand fully others whose meanings are inconsistent with their own mindset. Even in formal negotiations, as at Camp David, where negotiators follow the rules of "diplomatic culture," research on intercultural communications (Glenn, 1962) shows that negotiators usually perceive and think in terms of the familiar patterns of their subjective culture. They assume that their mindset is the one that makes sense. If the communication and behavior of "foreigners" do not square with their own mindset, they usually attribute the communication and behavior to undesirable character traits and motivations of the "misbehaving" or "unreasonable" foreigners, rather than attributing the "inappropriate" acts and messages to cultural differences. (Attribution is a judgment about the cause of behavior.) The tendency to assume that the perceived negative behavior exhibited by an unfamiliar person or group is a result of personal factors is part of a well-known psychological process called attribution error (see Chapter Eight for a detailed discussion). Many communication problems in international negotiation have resulted from such attribution errors (Cohen, 1991).

Even sending a signal interculturally is not simple. Attribution error makes misunderstanding likely among those with differing subjective cultures, especially during political conflict. Thus, when Nikita Khrushchev visited the United States during the Cold War, his "We will bury you" speech (discussed in detail in Chapter Six) also included a gesture of clasped hands held overhead, not unlike a winning U.S. politician. Edmund Glenn, chief interpreter for the U.S.

Department of State at the time, pointed out that in the Russian's common culture, the gesture means friendship. For most Americans, of course, it signaled victory or conquest and in combination with his words seemed malevolent. Coming from the leader of the Soviet Union, the message had a threatening and aggressive attribution for Americans.

The intent of the message, according to Glenn, was not that hostile. Khrushchev's meaning should be set in the context of Soviet Communist doctrine, which postulates that communism will overtake and replace capitalism as a way of (economic) life. Hence, when capitalism "dies," it will be the responsibility of communism to bury it. Thus, Khrushchev meant that the communists would live to see the capitalists buried—"We will bury you" meaning we will survive you. The gesture of friendship suggests that the intention of his message might have been analogous to telling a dying relative that you will take care of the funeral. U.S. analysts instead perceived Khrushchev as a villain threatening murder. The difference between the intended and received meanings had to do with the context of the communication and the mindset of the communicators. Without awareness of cultural differences, attribution error reinforces existing images and feelings and creates or exacerbates misunderstanding, misperception, and conflict.

Stereotypes

The content of an error in attribution is not random. The character traits and motivations we attribute to those who behave differently are those associated with such behaviors in our own common culture. They fit our stereotypes. A foreigner "jumping the queue" in England or cutting in line in the United States is seen by compatriots as rude (a character trait) and aggressive (motivation), since those are typically the characteristics of people in England and the United States who engage in such behavior. An international negotiator, mediator, or educator who works at a slower and less persistent pace than an American is seen as stalling (motivation) or lazy (character trait), as an American behaving in this manner might be. A non-Westerner who prefers saving face to giving a direct no is seen as evasive (motivation) or devious (character trait) by a Westerner who is not familiar with the other culture. In each case, the foreigner may be exhibiting behavior that is normal in that culture. The less intercultural experience we have, therefore, the more likely we are to make an attribution that fits our own cultural experience. The attribution perpetuates a stereotype.

If you communicate a negative attribution to those who "violate" your cultural expectation, they are likely to become less receptive to your perspective and ideas. Being accused of laziness or deviousness hurts, especially when the other party was intending just the opposite (that is, careful thinking and preserving harmony). The other party may become defensive, accusing you of misbehaving, being unreasonable and impolite, or condescending—as indeed you are, from their perspective. Negative attribution leads to negative emotions and behavior.

Reasoning and Cognition

Cultural differences also play an important role in how we gather information, arrive at a conclusion, and make a decision; how we think and reason. There are always general principles involved in any style of reasoning. If we do not articulate these general principles (as is usually the case), our mindset may not be apparent, and it may be hard to understand our thinking.

Glenn (1981) has developed a theory of reasoning based on the opposition between relying on authority, principle, and precedent (intuitive reasoning) and relying on observation, experience, and pragmatism (conceptual reasoning). The intuitive method of reasoning is prevalent in homogeneous, smaller, traditional, less specialized societies in which people's experiences are shared and there is reliance on precedent and historical experience as the bases for knowledge. In somewhat more specialized and economically developed societies, authorities are looked to in any new and unfamiliar situation. Their ideas are initially limited, but as their conceptualization becomes broadly accepted, they become what Glenn calls collective representations for that society. In their meeting with U.S. counterparts, the Iraqis were intuitive in their reasoning, relying on both historical experience and authority to make their points.

In still more diverse, urbanized, industrialized, and specialized societies, individuals rely more on pragmatic rather than consensual criteria in their reasoning. Glenn suggests that in these societies the conceptual method of reasoning is prevalent. Collective representations come to be seen as hypotheses to be tested rather than absolute truths. Principles are ideas to be applied empirically and to be changed or discarded if they do not work. The U.S. negotiators' appeals to international law, UN resolutions, and diplomatic precedents in their discussion with the Iraqis were examples of looking to such principles. Scientists also make use of the conceptual method of reasoning.

What you consider the most valid information and how you handle uncertainty are closely related to your usual method of reasoning and thinking. Those who use the intuitive method of reasoning usually rely on fixed ideas and beliefs as the most valid kind of information. They rank high on uncertainty avoidance, being unwilling to tolerate ambiguity (Hofstede, 1980). The Iraqis' comments in Geneva, as reported in the press, were often based on absolute ideological belief. Those who apply concepts in their reasoning are quite likely to look at actions and data as the most valid information. They rank low on what Hofstede has called uncertainty avoidance, tending to have a high tolerance for risk and ambiguity.

High-Context and Low-Context Communications

Instead of criticizing "foreigners" for how we feel about their communications, we can understand them (and ourselves) better by looking for differences in conversational style. An important conceptual dimension of all communication is that of high versus low context (Hall, 1976) or restricted versus elaborated codes (Bernstein, 1975). As Hall puts it, "a high context communication is one in which most of the information is either in the physical context or internalized in the person, while very little is in the coded, explicit, transmitted part of the message. A low context communication is just the opposite. . . . The mass of the information is vested in the explicit code" (1976, p. 91).

According to Hall, languages tend to favor one or the other end of this dimension of context in communication. He characterizes Japanese, Chinese, Arabic, and Mediterranean languages as often high-context; German, English, and Northern European languages are more often low-context. Bernstein's linguistic codes are also useful guides to the level of context being used in a given conversation. The restricted code categories (which often appear in high-context communications) take the listener's meanings for granted. The elaborated codes (indicative of low-context communications) are used to make meaning explicit and fit the conversation to the listener.

Ascertaining your own and others' level of context by listening and looking for these codes can help you understand and monitor conversational styles in intercultural situations. High-context communication is often used in a situation in which social relations are important. This is most likely to be directed to one's own people. In the Iraqi and U.S. meetings in Geneva, much of the Iraqi communication was high-context, especially to their own group. The low-context approach is likely to be used in situations where social relationships are not so important; much of the U.S. communication to the Iraqis was low-context.

Using English as the major language in such international meetings also plays a role in slighting cultural factors. With its grammatical construction of subject-predicate, English creates a world of objects that act or are acted on, with fixed relationships between things and their attributes. English speakers think of a causal world of actors-actions-results (Stewart, 1987). English also engenders a thought process based on a dichotomy between perception and thinking, and on dichotomies within thinking. Use of linguistic dichotomy supports divisive analysis, exclusive categories, and adversarial relationships (Trudgill, 1974), both within the negotiations where English is the major language and in negotiation research done by English-speaking researchers. It is no coincidence that practically all of the English-language research on communications in international negotiation is devoted to bilateral negotiation.

EDUCATION

We can learn to become aware of our own and others' subjective cultures and to avoid misperception and errors of attribution. Although experience in international encounters is critical to such learning, experience alone is not sufficient. Feedback from the other negotiators, mediators, and educators (and from trainers) is also necessary to make us aware and capable of dealing with the impact of our behavior and perception during such encounters. We can be trained to understand and explicate our own position, including values and assumptions, so as to be understood by those who may not share the same style of perceiving, cognizing, reasoning, or communicating (Kimmel, 1992; Emminghaus, Kimmel, and Stewart, 1997).

Training Programs

To achieve such understanding and develop appropriate communication skills, professional training in what I call the process of intercultural exploration is necessary. I have found that realistic role play with, and feedback from, intercultural communication specialists and "cultural representatives" can teach intentional empathic collaboration in communicating and problem-solving interculturally (Kimmel, 1992, 1995). Intercultural exploration training does not try to persuade practitioners to develop or accommodate a particular set of values, assumptions, or styles of perceiving, cognizing, reasoning, and communicating. Trainers in the intercultural exploration process work with negotiators, mediators, and educators on their cultural awareness and communication skills so that they can continue to learn on their own in real meetings. Trainees are confronted with their own cultural assumptions and mindset during the role play.

To make intercultural exploration training relevant and transferable to today's permanent negotiations, emotional involvement and practical skills are needed. A program presented through seminar, discussion, and lecture is unlikely to get at the emotional aspects of cultural difference. Mere information about your own and others' cultures does not affect your mindset nor provide a solid basis for intercultural exploration; training that stimulates real emotion and communication among the trainees does. Effective intercultural training is specific, with scenarios that take place within and in relation to real cultural situations. Current cultural topics set the context for role play and generate the emotions that make it meaningful. As Edward C. Stewart notes, "Trainees gain subjective insight into how their own culture is perceived by others and how its assumptions and strategies contribute to or detract from cross-cultural interaction" (1995, p. 56).

Cultural Awareness

Any training program should be tailored to the participants' background, experience, and skill level. In the intercultural exploration training program the participant's level of cultural awareness is determined early in the program to establish the pace and duration of the individual's training (Bennett, 1986; Kimmel, 1994, 1995).

For purposes of our discussion, there are five levels of cultural awareness:

1. Cultural chauvinism: best exemplified by the narcissistic and egocentric world of early childhood. Individuals at this level of awareness have little knowledge of or interest in people with other subjective cultures.

2. Ethnocentrism: differences among peoples are linked to obvious ethnic, religious, racial, or national characteristics of the individuals involved. Individuals at this level of cultural awareness are convinced of the superiority of their ways of doing and thinking about things.

3. Tolerance: foreign behavior and communication are attributed to living in another society or country, rather than being inherent. The difference is not necessarily seen as undesirable, but the practice of one's own society is regarded as more realistic and effective than that of the other.

4. Minimization: inherent cultural differences are acknowledged but trivialized. Individuals at this level of awareness emphasize what they believe are basic universal patterns of behavior: religious, economic, political, historical, or psychological "laws" that suggest all adult humans are in some ways basically alike. Learning to minimize cultural difference may be culturally based; "Americans typically believe that everyone is basically alike, and other people have the same needs that they have. Since the important differences among people are believed to be individual, not cultural or social, Americans are sensitive to similarities in others rather than to differences" (Stewart and Bennett, 1991, p. 151).

5. Understanding: individuals at this level of cultural awareness believe that their reality and common sense and the reality and common sense of those from other cultures are fundamentally different and can be explained. They recognize that values are created and passed on through the same processes by which other meanings are created and passed on.

Trainees may be at any level of awareness and may change levels over time and situation. Trainers can determine the cultural-awareness level of each participant with regard to a given training situation by observing how the trainee reacts to and judges the values, assumptions, and behavior of others. The ethnocentric sees few, if any, values and beliefs as negotiable, while the understanding person sees many as worth discussing.

For trainees at the ethnocentric level of awareness, the main goal of the initial training is to understand cultural difference while emphasizing the relativity of some of their own values. For trainees with cultural experience and knowledge of cultural difference, it is possible to illuminate some of their basic assumptions and improve their skills in intercultural communication. They can learn how to learn.

Learning to Learn

Training in learning how to learn begins with developing cultural self-awareness and results in acquiring skills to participate effectively in intercultural dialogue or intercultural exploration (Kimmel, 1989). The culturally aware person is conscious of many of the cultural assumptions he or she has internalized unconsciously over a lifetime. To achieve cultural understanding is to be aware of your enculturation, from the concrete level of perception to the abstract level of values.

Many of the skills for successfully interacting with people from varied cultural backgrounds are similar to social skills developed while growing up. It may be possible to help children avoid developing strong cultural identities by providing them with mediated experiences in learning these skills with other children who have differing cultural identity. There are examples of such experiences in the educational programs discussed in Chapter Twenty-Four. However, the problem-solving, decision-making, and negotiating skills most of us learn in our own culture are usually not cross-culturally mediated and thus often interfere with successful communication in an intercultural situation.

To learn how to learn, we must be taught less-culture-specific skills by someone who understands our culture and the other culture(s) in question, both personally and as an outsider. Since all perceptions involve stereotypes that enable us to organize and categorize the characteristics of unfamiliar experience, an intercultural exploration trainer must be familiar with the relevant stereotypes in each trainee's culture. Trainers must also know which social actualities (race, ethnicity, religion, language, tradition, and region) are relevant. Role play that makes such contextual information explicit enables trainees to understand and grow beyond their current cultural identity. The trainer must take an active, personal role in such training.

A technique that I have found useful for expanding cultural self-awareness and understanding is the culture-contrast training exercise (Kimmel, 1992, 1995; De Mello, 1995; Stewart, 1995), in which a trainee tries to persuade a role player whose mindset about a meaningful situation is in opposition to that of the trainee. The role player is a "cultural representative" whose subjective culture is constructed to contrast dramatically with the trainee's. Realistic scenarios are used to involve the trainees. Through focused discussion before and interview after the role play, the trainer helps the trainee understand his or her behavior and reactions in an intercultural meeting. By directly experiencing their own misperceptions and miscommunications—sometimes on video—and then discussing them with the trainers and cultural representatives, trainees become aware of their subjective culture and its impact on others. Through repeated participation in such simulations, a trainee also improves skills in intercultural communication and conflict management.

Cultural Relativism

A criticism often made of a training program like ours is that it condones or even encourages behavior and values that may be inefficient or abhorrent in the name of cultural understanding. This criticism rests on the mistaken assumption that to understand another's subjective culture is to accept or endorse that subjective culture (a position sometimes known as cultural relativism). The intercultural exploration process does not require us to condone the values of another or to demean our own. In the process of creating a new set of meanings (microculture) in an international meeting, we are arguing for some of our own values while remaining open to others' arguments for theirs. It is the openness to different ideas and values and to counterpersuasion that is crucial to cultural understanding and intercultural exploration (Brummett, 1981).

Once we develop such understanding, we can effectively communicate with others as equals and learn about their subjective cultures. We can urge aspects of our own cultural reality through conviction and persuasion rather than through dogma and coercion. As negotiators, mediators, and educators, we become involved in examining and critiquing our own and others' values, assumptions, and beliefs. Especially important is consideration of how functional these are in light of the context or ecology of our current situation.

However, even those with much cultural understanding find that some of their values, assumptions, and beliefs are not negotiable. Both the negotiable and nonnegotiable values, assumptions, and beliefs of the culturally understanding can be explicated through the intercultural exploration process. What is currently nonnegotiable (universals) may slowly change as we engage in creating microcultures and as the ecology on which our common culture is based changes.

Creating a Microculture: An Illustration

In the 1960s, the Fulbright program selected several American nuclear physics professors to take part in a two-summer public diplomacy program for advanced Indian graduate students. The professors were chosen on the basis of their teaching reputation. They were well liked by U.S. students, who appreciated their warmth, humor, and informality in the classroom, as well as their knowledge of the subject matter. They communicated well with these students through discussion and question-and-answer periods. Of course, they took these American teaching techniques and communication styles with them to India.

Since it is quite warm in India in the summer, the professors dressed in short-sleeved, open-neck shirts and light trousers or Bermuda shorts. They often sat on the edge of their desks or leaned back in chairs when lecturing; they frequently asked the Indian graduate students for their questions, ideas, or criticism. They used jokes and anecdotes in their presentation, and they expected the students to "think for themselves," to challenge established ideas in the textbook.

This American style of communication and approach to teaching was quite unfamiliar to the Indian students. Their system of education (heavily influenced by the British colonial system) considers the professor to be an expert in the subject matter, whose job it is to pass on specific information to the students. The students copy what the teacher says, memorize it, and repeat it on an examination. The professor is expected to be formal and reserved and somewhat aloof from the students, who are not expected to know anything before they are taught.

Needless to say, the students and the American professors did not communicate well. The professors were disturbed to find that the students would not take part in discussion or respond to a direct question unless it was on subject matter that had been covered explicitly. None would challenge the professor's remarks (however outrageous) or the information in the textbook. Even worse, they began to talk among themselves during lectures and drop out of the class. The professors' best jokes and anecdotes did not hold their attention.

From the students' point of view, the professors were incompetent. They did not know how to dress, present their material, or relate to students. They appeared not to know the material, since they often asked the students for information that the professor should have known. The students became confused when they were asked to challenge the authority of the professor or the textbook. Worst of all, they did not know what to learn, since the professor did not make clear what information they would be tested on. As a result, they consulted each other for information or dropped out of the class to avoid the embarrassment of not doing well on the examination.

In the middle of the summer, the frustrated professors contacted the Fulbright officials and asked to come home. The officials contacted Bryant Wedge, a psychiatrist and intercultural communications specialist, and asked him to go to India to straighten things out. Wedge asked the professors for a meeting. He explained that the Indian students had very different expectations about education than American students and asked the professors to modify their teaching accordingly. When some of them objected, he suggested that they treat the new approach as an experiment (hoping that as scientists they would find this an interesting idea).

For the remainder of the summer, the professors dressed formally, presented their material in a traditional lecture format, and tested the students only on the information in the textbook and the lecture. There were no discussions or jokes. The students responded well to this approach and did graduate-level work in the course. The professors were quite uncomfortable with this teaching style, however, and all agreed that they would not return to India for the second summer of the program.

Once again, the Fulbright officials called on Wedge. It had not been too difficult to show the professors how to accommodate to expectations about teaching that were similar to some they had experienced before in the United States. It was a challenging assignment to persuade them to continue to use a different approach when they found it intolerable. What was needed was an accommodation that would allow all parties to be comfortable. Intercultural communication is seldom effective if only one party continually adjusts to the other's values, attitude, or style of perceiving, cognizing, reasoning, and communicating. What was needed was empathic collaboration so that the professors and students could learn how to better communicate and do problem solving together—how to create a microculture.

Wedge looked at the problem from the point of view of the professors. What was it about the accommodation that was making them feel uncomfortable? Having been a teacher in the United States and abroad, he knew that they thought the Indian approach to education was rigid, authoritarian, and ineffective. But was there something beyond these perceptions that made them intolerant of this approach; something in their own mindsets?

After several months, he had the Fulbright officials call the professors together on the promise that if they did not like his new plan, they would not have to complete the program in India. When they met, he told them that they should go back to India for one week and continue to behave as the Indians expected professors to behave. However, at an appropriate time during this week they were to tell their students they had neglected to discuss their philosophy of education; a philosophy that they knew to be the best approach to education. It stated that in their classrooms the professor is in charge; whatever he wants to do or wants the students to do is for the best and must be done. They expected all of their students to comply with this philosophy and accept how they dressed and their pedagogy.

The professors were stunned. They considered themselves very pragmatic and not to have any universal educational principles. But they could clearly see that Wedge had discovered such a principle in their behavior, one that was at the root of their discomfort in using a style of teaching other than the one they preferred. Doing as Wedge suggested, they found that the Indian students quickly grasped their teaching philosophy. One professor reported that a student asked, "Why did you not tell us earlier about your philosophy, so that we could have understood what you were doing?"

The second summer of education was more collaborative as both the students and the professors did some accommodating and learning. As they became aware of their universals and effectively shared them with one another, they developed a microculture around their discussion and began intercultural exploration.

IMPLICATIONS FOR CONFLICT MANAGEMENT

The mutual problems faced by parties in international conflict and permanent negotiations are more amenable to solutions when seen from a wide perspective with many alternatives. Problem solving is facilitated if participants have the ability to intentionally shift the cultural frame of reference (mindset). This result of training in intercultural exploration enables them to understand each other and the issues more fully. Intercultural exploration can avert and clarify cultural misunderstanding and misperception and ameliorate destructive conflict by creating new meanings and relationships.

For negotiators, mediators, and educators to create a microculture, both high-context and low-context communication and intuitive and conceptual styles of reasoning are important. The primary process for creating and expressing new ideas is the intuitive style of reasoning, which is rich in meaning (Bordon, 1991). The primary process for organizing and elaborating those ideas is the conceptual approach, which is precise. When mindsets are quite different, the participants who are explicit, direct, and concise (low-context and conceptual) in their communications may be able to share information effectively; such sharing is especially important early in meetings when the negotiators, mediators, and educators are trying to define their situation. When building and maintaining a relationship is of greater concern, high-context communication with its affiliative connotations (restricted codes) may be more important.

Intercultural exploration can help to combine the ideas and approaches of individuals with dissimilar subjective cultures into something new that none of them could conceive alone. Collaboration produces success in problem solving, which in turn strengthens the relationship of the collaborators. Saunders (1989) writes: "Defining a problem publicly can itself become part of the political process for dealing with it. The act of defining a problem together can become part of building a relationship among actors for dealing with it. Publicly redefining a problem can become a symbolically important act in shifting political support for dealing with it" (p. 111).

A Diplomatic Example: Camp David

There is a great deal of evidence of major differences in the style of reasoning used by the Egyptian and Israeli negotiators in their meetings at Camp David in the late 1970s. As Weizman (1981) notes, much of the hostility between the Egyptians and Israelis during these negotiations was fueled by remarks and actions that the negotiators felt were insulting and offensive and reflected badly on their honor. U.S. diplomacy added a third style of reasoning to the negotiations. There were also differing cognitive and communication styles among the negotiators.

The Americans' style of communication was usually frank and to the point, with most of the meaning explicitly contained in the words. It was low-context and conceptual. The Egyptians' style was usually rhetorical; many of their communications were intended to preserve and promote social interests. It was high-context and intuitive. It is not surprising that the Egyptians sometimes found the Americans blunt and tactless, while the Americans felt the Egyptians were at times unclear, evasive, and elliptical (Cohen, 1991). The Israelis' style of communication varied more than that of the Americans or the Egyptians during these negotiations. When dealing with the substantive aspects of the negotiations, they were often more blunt, legalistic, and to the point than the Americans. But in their relationships with the other parties, they were often very sensitive to the social context and the implicit meanings of communications.

Even though many of the American negotiators acknowledged the importance of honor and face, they became impatient with these "distractions" from the substance of the negotiations and seldom saw these cultural factors as a potential resource for reaching agreement (Ting-Toomey, 1988). They usually preferred "reasoned persuasion." The pragmatic Americans were frustrated when Egyptian or Israeli negotiators overlooked the facts and gave credence instead to ideology.

The Americans at Camp David felt that developing a mutually acceptable framework would facilitate working out later agreement on details. When focused on detail early on, the Israelis and the Egyptians brought up their familiar bargaining positions, increasing the adversarial atmosphere in the negotiations. In an effort to implement a conceptual, low-context approach, the Americans kept Menachem Begin and Anwar Sadat physically separated at Camp David and worked from a single text, using jurists from each delegation to try to find wording acceptable to both sides. The hope was that the text would evolve into a peace agreement.

However, the Israelis came to see the Americans as favoring the Egyptians, whom they felt were impulsive and eager to foil the conference. The Egyptians saw the Israelis as intransigent and offensive, and the Americans as ineffective in producing Israeli compliance with important principles. The Americans were upset with both the Egyptians and the Israelis for their unwillingness to be "realistic," and their lack of appreciation for all that the United States was doing for them. It took pressure on Begin from factions within the Israeli delegation, a concession wrested from Sadat by Carter on one of his principles, and agreement to leave open many important issues to get a last-minute signing at Camp David of two framework agreements (not the single text that was hoped for) that were to be completed within three months (Weizman, 1981).

Although these agreements broke down some of the barriers between the Israeli people and the Arab world, they neither improved relationships among the Egyptians, Israelis, and Americans nor created a microculture within which their negotiation efforts could continue. There was little growth in cultural understanding and much miscommunication in these Egyptian-Israeli-American negotiations.

As this example illustrates, developing an international microculture is a difficult process. Negotiators, mediators, and educators with their own cognitive and communication styles are unlikely to achieve creative solution and lasting agreement if they lack the skills to shift to another mindset. With more intercultural training than these negotiators had, it is possible that Camp David outcomes would have been more like those in the Fulbright situation described above. Saunders (1987) recommends that nations focus on their relationships before and while engaging in such international policy making. In our terms, he is suggesting personal interaction that contributes to developing or enriching microcultures. Saunders hopes to change the perception of policy makers in a conflict situation from *us-and-them* to *we.* If the policy makers in question have differing subjective cultures, training in intercultural exploration is crucial to making this change.

Constructive Controversy, Intercultural Exploration, and Peace Building

Discussions among those who can intentionally shift their mindset have the quality of what David and Roger Johnson call constructive controversy (see Chapter Three). The international microculture that comes out of such constructive controversy benefits all parties in their efforts to end destructive conflict, solve problems, and build relationships. When we engage in such constructive controversies we are challenged to clearly represent our values and the cultural assumptions underlying them. Instead of polemicizing on the truth or virtue of a fixed position, as we might when speaking exclusively from our own mindset, we must examine our positions in the context of the larger ecologies in which they are embedded. In this way, constructive controversy becomes intercultural exploration and promotes peace building.

Peace-building skills include empathy, imagination, innovation, commitment, flexibility, and persistence. To be effective peace builders, we must be devoted to developing relationships and creating consensual meaning and outcomes (Kimmel, 1992). Instead of relying on the Golden Rule, which emphasizes one's own subjective culture, peace builders follow the "Platinum Rule": "Do unto others as they would do for themselves if they could." The Platinum Rule requires genuine cultural understanding.

As Stanley Hoffman (1984) and Lloyd Etheridge (1987) point out, modesty and graciousness are key personal ingredients in intercultural explorations. Negotiators, mediators, and educators with cultural understanding and the ability to engage in intercultural exploration with others have a sense of modesty and graciousness that serves them well in peace building. Those with ethnocentric views and adversarial approaches often project a sense of arrogance and righteousness that does not promote constructive controversy. If you are culturally understanding, you are modest because you are aware of the context, cultural assumptions, and limitations of your own position. You are gracious because you more accurately perceive how your actions and words affect others.

There is little possibility that ethnocentrism, calculation, and misrepresentation can succeed in intercultural exploration. Attempts to misuse the intercultural exploration process to deceive other negotiators, mediators, and educators may have limited success with ethnocentric negotiators, mediators, and educators, but only until later actions undermine the deceiver. At this point the latter alienates the others, hurts his own reputation (and perhaps the people he represents), and misses potential solutions to existing problems and conflicts. Such deceptions are eventually uncovered by those with cultural understanding, especially in permanent negotiation situations; "word about you will get around a conference very quickly. If you are viewed as dishonest or malevolent, your effectiveness declines accordingly" (McDonald, 1984, p. 3).

It is important to remember that in times of stress and frustration, even the most culturally understanding among us will make attribution errors. As I have discussed, such errors can be detrimental to communicating and developing an international microculture, which, Fontaine reminds us, "does not usually have documentation, institutional support, or historical precedent. As such it can be a very fragile thing. Its development and maintenance relies on sustained good intentions, constant monitoring, and mutual trust" (Fontaine, 1989, p. 100). But these microcultures and the relationships within them can get us through the stress and frustration that are inevitable in international conflict.

Maslow's Needs Hierarchy

A basic assumption of Western diplomats and social scientists is that there are generic principles of human behavior. This assumption underlies the American use of a single text at Camp David. It can also be seen in John Burton's work (1987) on deep-rooted conflicts. He attributes a basic ontological set of needs to all humans and assumes that deep-rooted conflict among people results from denying or frustrating those needs. His perspective is grounded in Maslow's needs hierarchy (1954), which stressed that our needs for survival, security, identity, recognition, and control are innately given to an appreciable degree (see Chapter Fourteen for a fuller discussion of Maslow).

This ahistorical, biological perspective pays little attention to the cultural meaning of the individual's needs. It ignores how these meanings vary over time or from one group of people to another. Burton acknowledges that deep-rooted conflict may involve the "culturally determined ways in which needs are expressed" (Burton and Sandole, 1986, p. 343), but he agrees with Maslow that the behaviors involved in this expression follow patterns orchestrated by the biology of the individual rather than the social or cultural context provided by the group. As Burton (personal communication, 1989) wrote, "culture is a set of customs and beliefs followed by the members of a given society, and accommodated to by members of other societies, that are not as important as their more fundamental, ontological, universal, biologically based needs." Thus, for Burton, the most basic conflict is about needs, not about cultural meaning or assumption.

Although this theoretical perspective may be useful in understanding some conflicts within or between similar common cultures—especially English-speaking Western cultures—it can be misleading in conflict between people from dissimilar cultures or ethnic groups (such as the Egyptians and the Americans). The intercultural perspective described in this chapter assumes that the most basic intercultural conflicts are grounded in cultural difference and are about the nature of social reality (Black and Avruch, 1989; Avruch and Black, 1991; Emminghaus, Kimmel, and Stewart, 1997). Such conflict is usually found in international situations but may also occur between peoples within heterogeneous nations, as illustrated by current conflicts among ethnic and religious groups in newly independent states—the former Yugoslavia, Ireland, Sudan, and Sri Lanka, for example.

The great danger in being oblivious to the impact of one's own culture when building a theory to explain human behavior lies in promoting one's own cultural beliefs to the status of formalized "scientific knowledge" (Black and Avruch, 1989; Avruch and Black, 1991). The premature search of Western science for such universal schemes often blinds us to other cultural perspectives and information that would increase our ability to understand and improve negotiation and conflict management processes among different peoples (Kimmel, 1984; Emminghaus, Kimmel, and Stewart, 1997). We are functioning at the minimalist level of cultural awareness, when we should be striving for cultural understanding.

CONCLUSION

In this chapter, I have argued that international meetings and negotiations ultimately depend on human perception and behavior, and that such perception and behavior are critically affected by the mindset of every negotiator, mediator, and educator. Differences in perception, cognition, reasoning, and communication styles can lead to misperception and miscommunication that hamper these meetings and create conflict. What you feel in an intercultural conflict and what others intend for you to feel are not always the same thing. Avoiding or ameliorating intercultural communication problems and the dysfunctional conflicts that they create or exacerbate requires training in cultural awareness and intercultural communication that promotes intercultural exploration and learning how to learn.

Intercultural exploration uses differences in mindset to develop new options and approaches, build relationships, and create unique solutions.

Intercultural exploration is becoming ever more needed as we move from the traditional world of bilateral diplomacy to the complex world of multilateral, permanent negotiations (Winham, 1979). Those who use adversarial procedures and hold to official positions—behaviors that have (or had) some merit in traditional diplomacy—are counterproductive in the new situation. Similarly, the traditional techniques of Western peacekeeping and peacemaking may temporarily reduce the level of violence in destructive conflict, but they are unlikely to produce long-term problem solving and peace building (Kimmel, 1992, 1998). Peace builders trained in the intercultural exploration process can locate the larger issues, manage complexity, inspire confidence, get beyond immediate differences, and build relationships.

As the examples in this chapter have illustrated, egalitarian relationships are crucial in today's world of multilateral negotiations and consensual agreement. Without good faith and trust, multilateral agreement and resolution does not hold and negotiations break down. The recognition and respect that emerge when negotiators, mediators, and educators genuinely feel that they are equals are a foundation on which these people can engage in constructive controversy and collaborate regardless of major differences in mindset. Modesty and graciousness are prerequisites to constructive controversy and peace building. (See Chapters One, Two, and Three for full discussion of cooperation, equality, and constructive controversy.)

We are facing impasses in our political, economic, and diplomatic negotiations on more and more occasions. Ethnocentric and tolerant (or, more often, intolerant) diplomatic approaches have harmed our international relationships. A great deal of effort has gone into getting nations and ethnic groups that are in destructive conflict to meet. Persuading them to recognize and talk to each other has not been easy (Saunders, 1987). A similar level of effort is required to develop and implement programs to make their negotiations successful through developing microcultures. Hopefully, future policy makers will invest in the training programs needed to produce culturally aware negotiators, mediators, and educators who can learn how to learn. I believe we can build international microcultures to create a global village in which we can all live, a village in which groups of equals who desire each other's welfare all participate and learn from each other.

References

Avruch, K., and Black, P. W. "Ideas of Human Nature in Contemporary Conflict Resolution Theory." *Negotiation Journal*, 1990, *6*, 221–228.

Avruch, K., and Black, P. W. "The Culture Question and Conflict Resolution." *Peace and Change*, 1991, *16*, 22–45.

Bagby, J. W. "Dominance in Binocular Rivalry in Mexico and the United States." *Journal of Abnormal and Social Psychology,* 1957, *54,* 331–334.

Bennett, M. "A Developmental Approach to Training for Intercultural Sensitivity." *International Journal of Intercultural Relations,* 1986, *10,* 179–196.

Berman, M., and Johnson, J. E. (eds.). *Unofficial Diplomats.* New York: Columbia University Press, 1977.

Bernstein, B. *Classes, Codes and Control.* London: Routledge and Kegan Paul, 1975.

Black, P. W., and Avruch, K. "Some Issues in Thinking About Culture and the Resolution of Conflict." *Humanity and Society,* 1989, *13,* 187–194.

Bordon, G. A. *Cultural Orientation: An Approach to Understanding Intercultural Communication.* Upper Saddle River, N.J.: Prentice Hall, 1991.

Brummett, B. "A Defense of Ethical Relativism as Rhetorically Grounded." *Western Journal of Speech Communication,* 1981, *45,* 286–298.

Burton, J. W. *Resolving Deep-Rooted Conflict: A Handbook.* Lanham, Md.: University Press of America, 1987.

Burton, J. W., and Sandole, D. "Generic Theory: The Basis of Conflict Resolution." *Negotiation Journal,* 1986, *2,* 333–345.

Cohen, R. *Negotiating Across Cultures: Common Obstacles in International Diplomacy.* Washington, D.C.: U.S. Institute of Peace Press, 1991.

De Mello, C. "Acting the Culture Contrast." In S. M. Fowler and M. Mumford (eds.), *Intercultural Sourcebook: Cross-Cultural Training Methodologies.* Vol. 1. Yarmouth, Me.: Intercultural Press, 1995.

Emminghaus, W. B., Kimmel, P. R., and Stewart, E. C. "Primal Violence: Illustrating Culture's Dark Side." *Peace and Conflict: Journal of Peace Psychology,* 1997, *3,* 167–191.

Etheridge, L. *Can Governments Learn?* New York: Pergamon Press, 1987.

Fisher, G. *Mindsets.* Yarmouth, Me.: Intercultural Press, 1988.

Fontaine, G. "Managing International Assignments: The Strategy for Success." Upper Saddle River, N.J.: Prentice Hall, 1989.

Glenn, E. "Semantic Difficulties in International Communication." In S. I. Hayakawa (ed.), *The Use and Misuse of Language.* New York: HarperCollins, 1962.

Glenn, E. *Man and Mankind: Conflict and Communication Between Cultures.* Norwood, N.J.: Ablex, 1981.

Hall, E. T. *Beyond Culture.* New York: Anchor/Doubleday, 1976.

Hoffman, S. "Détente." In J. Nye (ed.), *The Making of America's Soviet Policy.* New Haven: Yale University Press, 1984.

Hofstede, G. *Culture's Consequences: International Differences in Work-Related Values.* Thousand Oaks, Calif.: Sage, 1980.

Kimmel, P. R. "Peace and Culture Shock: Can Intercultural Communication Specialists Help Save the World?" *Abstracts, Tenth Annual SIETAR Conference,* 1984, pp. 1–4.

Kimmel, P. R. *International Negotiation and Intercultural Exploration: Toward Culture Understanding.* Washington, D.C.: U.S. Institute of Peace Press, 1989.

Kimmel, P. R. "Assessing the Impact of Peace Building Processes." *Modern Science and the Vedic Science,* 1992, *5,* 125–133.

Kimmel, P. R. "Cultural Perspectives on International Negotiation." *Journal of Social Issues,* 1994, *50,* 179–196.

Kimmel, P. R. "Facilitating the Contrast-Culture Method." In S. M. Fowler and M. Mumford (eds.), *Intercultural Sourcebook: Cross-Cultural Training Methodologies.* Vol. 1. Yarmouth, Me.: Intercultural Press, 1995.

Kimmel, P. R. "Cultural and Ethnic Issues of Conflict and Peacekeeping." In H. J. Langholtz (ed.), *The Psychology of Peacekeeping.* New York: Praeger, 1998.

Maslow, A. H. *Motivation and Personality.* New York: HarperCollins, 1954.

McDonald, J. *How to Be a Delegate.* Washington, D.C.: Center for the Study of Foreign Affairs, Foreign Service Institute, U.S. Department of State, 1984.

Saunders, H. H. "Beyond 'US and THEM': Building More Mature International Relationships." Washington, D.C.: Brookings Institution, 1987.

Saunders, H. H. "The Arab-Israeli Conflict in a Global Perspective." In J. D. Spradley and D. McCurdy (eds.), *Conformity and Conflict: Readings in Cultural Anthropology.* New York: Little, Brown, 1989.

Spradley, J. D., and McCurdy, D. (eds.). *Conformity and Conflict: Readings in Cultural Anthropology.* New York: Little, Brown, 1989.

Stewart, E. C. "The Primordial Roots of Being." *Zygon,* 1987, *22,* 87–107.

Stewart, E. C. "An Intercultural Interpretation of the Persian Gulf Crisis." *International Communication Studies,* 1991, *4,* 1–47.

Stewart, E. C. "Contrast-Culture Training." In S. M. Fowler and M. Mumford (eds.), *Intercultural Sourcebook: Cross-Cultural Training Methodologies.* Vol. 1. Yarmouth, Me.: Intercultural Press, 1995.

Stewart, E. C., and Bennett, M. "American Cultural Patterns: A Cross-Cultural Perspective." (Rev. ed.) Yarmouth, Me.: Intercultural Press, 1991.

Ting-Toomey, S. "Intercultural Conflict Styles: A Face-Negotiation Theory." In Y. Y. Kim and W. B. Gudykunst (eds.), *Theories in Intercultural Communication.* Thousand Oaks, Calif.: Sage, 1988.

Triandis, H. *The Analysis of Subjective Culture.* New York: Wiley, 1972.

Trudgill, P. *Sociolinguistics: An Introduction.* New York: Penguin, 1974.

Tyler, V. L. *Intercultural Interacting.* Provo, Utah: D. M. Kennedy Center for International Studies, Brigham Young University, 1987.

Volkan, V. "Ethnonationalistic Rituals: An Introduction." *Mind and Human Interaction,* 1992, *4*(1), 3–19.

Weizman, E. *The Battle for Peace.* New York: Bantam Books, 1981.

Winham, G. "The Mediation of Multilateral Negotiations." *Journal of World Trade Law,* 1979, *13,* 193–208.

CHAPTER TWENTY-THREE

Cooperative and Competitive Conflict in China

Dean Tjosvold
Kwok Leung
David W. Johnson

C hina is a powerful test of the universalistic aspirations of Deutsch's theory of cooperation and competition (1949, 1973, 1980, 1990), in particular its utility in understanding the conditions and dynamics through which conflict becomes constructive. Because theirs is a collectivist culture, Chinese people are expected to be particularly wary of conflict and its open discussion (Leung, 1997). Many social scientists consider application of Western-developed theories to Asia unwarranted, even "imperialistic." Since 1994, we have conducted cooperation and competition research in China and East Asia using experimental, survey, and interview methods to understand interdependence and conflict and their manifestations in such areas as organizational teamwork, quality service, and leadership.

Deutsch's original theory (1949) aims to explain the development of relationships and values; actors are assumed to have motives and goals but without assuming particular values and preconditions. Although this supports the universality of the theory, it does not of course reflect most situations. China presents an opportunity to understand how values and other preconditions affect cooperative and competitive management of conflict. Chinese people are,

The work described in this chapter was fully supported by a grant from the Research Grants Council of the Hong Kong Special Administrative Region, China, to the first author (project nos. LC 890/96H and LC 3004/98H).

for example, expected to be particularly oriented toward projecting and protecting social face and to rely on high-context, nonverbal communication. Studies have focused on how Chinese values influence cooperative conflict.

Findings support the theory's major propositions and suggest that it may well be useful for diagnosis and intervention in Chinese conflict, and even between Westerners and Chinese in such venues as international joint ventures. Believing themselves to be open and responsive, Westerners conclude that Chinese people avoid conflict and are closed to dealing with differences. They see themselves as democratic and Chinese as autocratic. Our studies explore—and explode—these generalizations about China.

This chapter first outlines the North American research base for our research and summarizes arguments against generalizing Deutsch's theory to China and East Asia. It then describes our experimental and survey research approaches. Our studies show that Chinese have been found to use open discussion productively, especially within a cooperative context, and to value relationship-oriented, democratic leadership. Research in China is just beginning to challenge and extend the theory. The last sections of the chapter outline major research and practical implications, including how to manage conflict in Sino-American joint ventures.

CONSTRUCTIVE CONTROVERSY

Deutsch's theory of cooperation and competition proposes that goal interdependence very much affects expectations, interactions, and effectiveness (see Chapters One and Three in this volume for detailed discussion). Deutsch argued that cooperative (compared to competitive) goals contribute to productive conflict management. Our experimental research on constructive controversy documents that discussion of opposing positions can contribute to cooperative problem solving and specifies the dynamics by which controversial discussion becomes constructive (Tjosvold, 1985). It also helps detail the nature of the promotive interaction that cooperative goals induce. But social scientists have challenged the validity and usefulness of applying these ideas, developed in North America, to China.

North American Research

Controversy occurs when persons discuss their opposing views about how a problem should be solved. (See Chapter Three for a detailed research review.) Research has documented that controversy promotes curiosity, exploration, understanding, and integration. It has been found that when confronted with an opposing view, people feel uncertain about the most adequate solution, are curious, and seek to understand opposing views. Expressing various views, defending and articulating their rationales, and following internal uncertainty to search for new and more complete information and understanding all develop new, useful solutions to the problem that the protagonists accept and implement. Controversy has been found to be highly constructive if protagonists have cooperative goals because they are willing to integrate opposing views and reach a high-quality agreement. Field research has shown that the dynamics of cooperative controversy can be highly useful for solving an array of complex problems for organizations (Tjosvold and Tjosvold, 1991, 1995).

Should the Theory Be Applied in China?

Many social scientists are skeptical that Western theory can be applied in such collectivist cultures as China, arguing that such theory has inherent weakness in understanding other cultures. An imposed theoretical framework captures the cultural experience of the West, not China. Social scientists should use indigenous values and perspectives to understand and appreciate how Chinese people actually experience interdependence and conflict.

Specific objections have been raised to applying the Deutsch theory. The theory assumes that individuals are self-interested. Their actions and feelings are hypothesized to depend on whether they believe their self-interests are cooperatively or competitively related. As collectivist rather than individualist, Chinese are thought to pursue the interests of their group rather than their individual interests. Is the Deutsch assumption that self-interest motivates group behavior justified in China?

A related objection is that because of their collectivist inclination, Chinese people are highly oriented toward cooperation, where competition and independence are not preferred. Are the Chinese able to interact competitively and independently, or are these experiences infrequent and countercultural?

Deutsch argued that conflict is an inevitable aspect of social interdependence and that, even with highly cooperative goals, group members conflict. Our research emphasizes the value of constructive controversy for cooperative problem solving. However, the Chinese culture highly values harmony, making conflict anathema. Is conflict an important aspect of Chinese organizations?

A related, though somewhat inconsistent, objection is that conflict, when surfaced, is inevitably competitive, although Deutsch argued that conflict has a cooperative face. The Chinese word for conflict connotes warfare, suggesting that conflict is invariably win-lose. Is a cooperative conflict approach viable in China?

Several central Chinese values are theorized to underline their embrace of harmony. Chinese people are thought to avoid conflict because they are particularly sensitive to social face and highly averse to interpersonal hostility and assertive ways of handling frustration and problems. These values make it difficult to initiate conflict; just disagreeing easily and nonverbally communicates an aggressive affront to face. With social face values, can conflict be dealt with directly and open-mindedly?

Chinese society is thought to be a traditional, hierarchical one where employees readily defer to their superiors. Autocratic organizations and leadership are the cultural norm. Open conflict is consistent with participative management. Is constructive controversy consistent with organizational values in China?

Generally, the open-minded teamwork proposed by Deutsch's theory supports organizations pressured to maximize value for customers. Deming and other popular theorists have argued that teamwork and conflict are necessary because of market demands to serve customers with quality products and services, or face diminished resources. China is still a centrally controlled economy dominated by state-owned enterprises (SOEs) that appease ministers, not serve customers. Are Chinese organizations using cooperative conflict to serve customers?

Deutsch's theory, like any other, cannot be assumed to apply automatically in another culture, but applying it in China may be particularly questionable. Before examining our findings, we review our experimental and field methods.

RESEARCH METHODS IN CHINA

Like the theory itself, North American research methods to test it cannot be assumed to apply in China. East Asian researchers have modified our North American methods. Trained both in the East and West and based in Hong Kong, mainland China, Korea, Japan, Taiwan, and other East Asian countries, researchers have debated the theory and developed the methods. The network itself has demonstrated the value of cooperative teamwork and constructive controversy! We are most grateful for our colleagues' openness and contributions to the research.

The first step was to assess whether the theory had potential for understanding interdependence. Network members as well as managers in the region argued that cooperation and competition were both important phenomena in Chinese organizations. Concretely, they translated the major concepts and research questions into Cantonese (the local Hong Kong dialect), Mandarin (the national language of China), Japanese, and Korean. This process also simplified and improved the English operations. Interview, questionnaire, and experimental methods have all been used to test the theory.

Interviews

The interview studies employed the critical-incident methodology (Flanagan, 1954). Rather than having our respondents try to summarize a great number of ratings of how they generally interact with each other, as demanded by most questionnaires, respondents describe concrete experiences. Interviewers can establish a relationship with the respondents, create an informal and personal climate, clarify and answer questions, and encourage the respondent. Chinese people, with their relationship-oriented culture, were thought likely to respond positively to this climate.

The interview has a highly defined structure. For example, in a study on developing commitment to Japanese organizations in Hong Kong, Japanese and Chinese managers were asked to identify a specific interaction that affected their commitment and to describe the setting, what occurred, and the consequences (Tjosvold, Sasaki, and Moy, 1998). Then they answered specific questions that allow statistical tests of the framework and hypotheses. Interviewees specified their goals and the other's goals. Then, using seven-point Likert-scale items, they first indicated how much they perceived that their goals were positively, negatively, or independently related, and second, described their reasoning for goal interdependence. They rated the extent they expressed their own views fully, considered the other's views open-mindedly, tried to understand the other's concerns, worked together for mutual agreement on the issue, and tried to put together the best of the various ideas expressed. After they rated themselves on these dimensions, the interviewers rated their colleague on the same items. The Cronbach alphas of these constructive controversy scales, as usual, were above .80. The employees also described the consequences of the incident for themselves and the organization and rated the effects of the incident on their work relationship, task productivity, and commitment.

The interviews afforded rich descriptive information about effective and ineffective interaction between Japanese and Chinese that affected commitment. Data were coded and sorted to identify the reasons for cooperative, competitive, and independent goals; the interaction behaviors that occurred in them; and the consequences of the interaction. Careful training and supervision of interviewers, explicit guidelines for conducting the interview, and the specific Likert-type questions were all designed to improve the validity of the data collected (Fowler, 1993).

These interview methods have been used to study cooperation and competition and constructive controversy in a variety of organizational contexts. For example, studies test the relevance of the theory to understanding customer service in a restaurant, empowerment of employees, motives and methods for avoiding conflict, customer complaint dynamics, the impact of social face in conflict, and Hong Kong senior accountants' leadership of employees in China.

Questionnaires

Questionnaire surveys complement the interview studies. They allow for sampling of more people and use of independent sources for outcome measures. For example, 191 pairs of supervisors and employees were recruited from ten SOEs in Nanjing and Shanghai to participate in a leadership study on goal inter-dependence, justice, and citizenship behavior (Hui, Tjosvold, and Ding, 1998).

Employees completed questionnaires on measures of cooperation, competition, independence, and constructive controversy with their supervisor, and their level of procedural, distributive, and interactional justice. Their supervisors completed questionnaires on the extent of employee in-role performance (productivity) and extra-role performance (organizational citizenship).

The overall model tested was that a strong sense of justice promotes cooperative goals, which lead to open-minded, constructive controversy. Controversy in turn was expected to lead to strong levels of job performance and citizenship behavior. Structural equation analysis was used to examine the underlying causal structure among justice, goal interdependence, constructive controversy, and in-role and extra-role performance.

Experiments

Experiments directly test hypothesized causal relationships with high internal validity. They provide an alternative to the heavy reliance on questionnaire surveys in management research in China.

We theorized, for example, that open discussion of conflict need not affront social face in China and could contribute to effective problem solving if face was confirmed (Tjosvold, Hui, and Sun, 1998). Eighty participants from a university in Guangzhou were randomly assigned to four conditions: (1) open discussion with affront to face, (2) open discussion with confirmation of face, (3) avoiding discussion with affront, and (4) avoiding discussion with confirmation.

To begin, the participants read that as supervisors they had to meet with employees about job rotation. The employees had developed a practice of trading their positions every hour. The supervisor, as a representative of management, would oppose this job rotation as inefficient.

The "open" participants read that their organization valued frank discussion of differences and could earn up to five chances in a lottery if they discussed their differences openly and directly. The "avoiding" participants would earn chances to the extent that they minimized their disagreement. During the discussion, the confederate taking the role of an employee reinforced these conditions.

After eight minutes of discussion, the participant and confederate completed questionnaires that included the social-face induction. Then the confederate unexpectedly swapped the questionnaires "to increase communication." The "affront" participants thus saw the confederate's ratings, indicating that they were seen as ineffective, and the "confirm" participants learned that they were seen as effective. After another ten minutes, participants made the job rotation decision, were fully debriefed, and were given a small gift and one chance in the lottery.

To measure curiosity, the confederate counted the number of questions the participants asked them about their position. Participants also indicated on seven-point scales their interest in hearing more of the other's arguments and the extent they had explored the position of the other discussant. Participants indicated the extent to which they saw their relationship with the other discussant as cooperative, engaged in mutual give-and-take, and felt confidence in the relationship. To measure learning, participants listed the arguments of the other discussant, and these were scored for accuracy. They also rated the degree to which they had learned from the discussion and found the opposing views useful. Their decisions were coded as to how well they integrated the opposing view into their decision.

Interviews, surveys, and experiments have their strengths and limitations. Our results are not method-specific and deserve confidence because they have been developed through diverse methods.

Results of East Asian Tests of the Theory

Studies offer internal and external validity for the theory and respond to the objections raised about the application of Western (and in particular Deutsch's) theory to China. Chinese people have been found to distinguish cooperation and competition and respond much as do North Americans. Experiments indicate that conflicting opinions, if discussed in a cooperative context, promote open-mindedness and integrated views. Studies are showing how Chinese values can contribute to positive conflict. Field studies document that cooperative conflict dynamics contribute to effective teamwork, leadership, and quality customer service in today's Chinese organizations.

Open-Minded Discussion

Similar to research in North America, cooperative (vis-à-vis competitive) contexts were found to yield openness toward the opposing position and discussant (Tjosvold and Sun, 1998a). Chinese participants in cooperative (rather than competitive) situations were committed to mutual benefit, were interested in learning more about the opposing views, considered these views useful, came to agree with them, and tended to integrate them into their own decisions. They were more attracted to the other protagonist and had greater confidence in working together in the future than participants in the competitive condition.

Surprisingly, openness itself has been found highly valued and useful in conflicts among Chinese. Open controversy (compared to avoiding conflict) strengthened relationships and induced epistemic curiosity, with Chinese people asking questions, exploring opposing views, demonstrating knowledge, and working to integrate views (Tjosvold, Hui, and Sun, 1998). They characterized protagonists who disagreed directly and openly as strong persons and competent negotiators, whereas "avoiding" protagonists were considered weak and ineffectual. In another experiment, open discussion (relative to avoiding) developed a cooperative relationship and open-minded understanding of the opposing view (Tjosvold and Sun, 1998b).

Field studies also support the value of open-minded discussion in a cooperative context. In a study of thirty-nine groups and their supervisors in Hanzhou, China, work teams that used open-minded, constructive discussion of opposing teams promoted product quality and cost reduction; these discussions were more likely with cooperative rather than competitive goals (Tjosvold and Wang, 1998). The measures of product quality and cost reduction were taken independently of the measures of goal interdependence and interaction. Earlier studies found that cooperative conflict was useful for Singaporean managers and employees to resolve issues and work productively together (Tjosvold and Chia, 1989; Tjosvold and Tsao, 1989).

Another study, on conflict values and teams in China, involved 106 pairs of employees and their leaders from SOEs in Shanghai and Nanjing (Tjosvold, Hui, Ding, and Hu, 1998). Employees described their conflict attitudes and relationships; immediate supervisors rated team effectiveness and citizenship. Teams that believed conflict was positive were able to work together effectively and developed strong relationships. These relationships in turn laid the foundation for team effectiveness and employee citizenship.

Teamwork, Quality Service, and Effective Resource Use

Surveys and interview studies have documented generalization of the theory of cooperation and competition, and in particular that cooperative conflict promotes productive teamwork, quality service, and effective leadership. Cooperative, open-minded discussions of service problems helped restaurant employees work together to serve their customers (Tjosvold, Moy, and Sasaki, 1996). Waiters and cooks who had a shared purpose to serve customers well and a common task to increase tips for their team trusted each other, wanted to share the workload, avoided customer complaints, and supported one another. However, showing off one's superior position, evincing a mistrustful attitude based on failure to keep one's word, and background and age differences led to competitive, closed-minded discussions that frustrated quality customer service.

Cooperative conflict, but not competitive or avoiding conflict, helped Hong Kong, Korean, Taiwanese, and Japanese building contractors work successfully with their subcontractors (Tjosvold and others, 1998). Manufacturing managers in Hong Kong who handled conflict cooperatively used their frustration with suppliers in mainland China to improve product quality (Wong, Tjosvold, Wong, and Liu, forthcoming). Dealing with customer complaints in Hong Kong was effectively handled through cooperative conflict (Tjosvold, 1998a).

Conflicts over scarce resources have been thought particularly divisive. However, an open-minded discussion helped Hong Kong accountants and managers dig into and resolve budget issues, strengthen their relationships, and improve budget quality so that limited financial resources were used wisely (Poon, Tjosvold, and Pike, 1998). These discussions were much more likely with cooperative goals than with competitive ones.

Cooperative goals also promoted the open-minded discussion that helped teams of mass-transportation employees obtain organizational support they needed to reduce costs and improve quality (Tjosvold, 1998b). Cooperative, constructive controversy interactions were also found critical for Chinese staff to work productively and develop relationships with Japanese managers, outcomes that in turn built commitment to their Japanese companies (Tjosvold, Sasaki, and Moy, 1998).

Chinese Values for Cooperative Conflict

Experimental and field studies confirm Deutsch's proposition that with cooperative goals, Chinese people make constructive use of controversy. But how do Chinese develop cooperative goals? It is commonly asserted that underlying Chinese values make open, constructive conflict management difficult. Chinese people are thought to avoid conflict in part because they are particularly sensitive to social face, and averse to strong influence and interpersonal hostility. Our studies suggest that Chinese values of social face, implicit communication, and social hierarchy provide boundary conditions for the theory in China because they can frustrate developing cooperative goals. However, experiments show that these values, if constructively expressed, can contribute to conflict management.

Social Face. Social face assumes that people attempt to project a desirable image and want assurance that their image is accepted (Tjosvold, 1983). Goffman (1967), a pioneer in social-face research, proposed that face is "an image of the self delineated in terms of approved social attributes" (p. 2). Showing respect to people confirms face in that it communicates acceptance of this positive image, whereas disrespect affronts face.

Chinese people have been found to be particularly alert to protecting social face to promote relationships. Given their sensitivity to the collective and relationships, they seek harmony and communicate that they respect their partners as capable and worthy (Ting-Toomey, 1988). Their collectivism and their understanding of social face lead them to be hesitant about engaging in aggressive interaction that may challenge the face of others. They want to avoid conflict and, once engaged, use compromise and accommodation to deal with it (Kirkbride, Tang, and Westwood, 1991; Leung, 1988; Tse, Francis, and Walls, 1994). Western managers are advised that they should be careful to protect the face of their East Asians colleagues, or risk severe disruptions in joint ventures and other international arrangements (Tung, 1991).

However, Chinese values related to face may not inevitably make managing conflict indirect and difficult. Indeed, their sensitivity to protecting face can make discussing differences constructive.

Chinese negotiators who confirmed social face were able to manage their conflict cooperatively (Tjosvold and Sun, 1998a). Participants in an experiment in which face was confirmed (in that they received direct feedback that they were seen as effective) emphasized their cooperative goals with the other discussant. They demonstrated epistemic curiosity in that they explored opposing views and were interested in hearing more of the other's arguments. Confirmed participants were prepared to pressure the other and dealt with their disagreement collaboratively. They also indicated that they learned in the discussion, considered the opposing views useful, and had come to agree with some of them. Confirmed participants indicated that they made more effort to integrate than did participants who lost face. A field study also indicated that confirmation of face helped Chinese people discuss their frustrations cooperatively and productively (Tjosvold, 1998b).

Persuasion and Implicit Communication. Chinese people have been expected to avoid conflict because they assume that conflict requires coercion, and they prefer persuasion. However, conflict can give rise to either persuasion or coercion. Persuasive influence was found to result in feelings of respect, cooperative relationships, and openness to the other person and position (Tjosvold and Sun, 1998a). Protagonists who were targets of persuasion compared to coercion sought mutual benefit in the discussion, were open to listening to the other, were interested in learning about the opposing view, and integrated their reasoning. Protagonists in persuasion (as opposed to coercion) were also more attracted and confident in their relationship with the opposing negotiator.

Conflict is also thought to be avoided because in the high-context Chinese culture, where implicit communication is influential, Chinese people assume that conflict communicates interpersonal hostility (Gudykunst, Ting-Toomey, and Chua, 1988; Hall, 1976). However, implicit and nonverbal communication can help develop a cooperative context for conflict discussion. Expressing interpersonal warmth was found to have wide-ranging effects on conflict management (Tjosvold and Sun, 1998b). Participants who discussed with a "warm" rather than a "cold" protagonist developed a cooperative, mutually beneficial relationship. They explored the other's position, incorporated the opposing view and reasoning into their decision and thinking, and were more in agreement with the other's position than participants in the cold condition. Participants in the warm (versus the cold) condition had greater confidence they could work with the other in the future.

A field study suggests that even anger can contribute to conflict management in East Asia; Chinese team members who emphasized their cooperative goals were able to discuss their frustrations directly and effectively to reduce their anger and solve problems (Tjosvold, 1997b). However, with competitive and independent goals, they refused to consider the other's views, protected their self-interest, and remained frustrated.

Chinese people are thought to be more indirect and discreet in their approaches to conflict (Leung, 1997). Their proclivity to save face, use persuasive influence attempts, and communicate indirectly and nonverbally have been assumed to result in conflict avoidance. However, our studies show that these values, when appropriately expressed, can facilitate controlled, but direct, cooperative and open-minded discussion of opposing views. These values may also promote cooperative conflict in the West (Tjosvold, 1983, 1993).

Leadership in a Hierarchical Society

A persistent Western stereotype is that Chinese leadership is autocratic, where followers quickly and automatically follow the wishes and decisions of leaders. Consistent with this image, power distance (where employees accept hierarchy and power differences) has been widely used to understand leadership in China and East Asia (Hofstede, 1980). Chinese employees are thought to accept unilateral decision making and prefer that their leaders be benevolent autocrats.

Studies support the idea of greater acceptance of authority in East Asia than in low-power-distance Western countries (Leung, 1997; Smith, Dugan, and Trompenaars, 1996). However, this generalization has limitations. Superior power in the West is often associated with domination and authoritarianism, but leaders in China are expected to be supportive and nurturing (Pye, 1985; Spencer-Oatey, 1997).

Our research challenges Western stereotypes and indicates that leaders in China must develop an open, mutual relationship with employees. Authority cannot be assumed; leaders must earn it by demonstrating commitment to employees and openness with them. In an examination of the leader relationship in mainland China, 170 supervisor-subordinate dyads in a watch case factory in southern China completed questionnaires (Law, Hui, and Tjosvold, 1998). Strong cooperative goals were found to be critical for a high-quality leader relationship, and this relationship in turn led to employees being effective organizational citizens.

To study power and democracy, eighty-nine Hong Kong leaders and employees were interviewed on specific incidents (Tjosvold, Hui, and Law, 1997). Open-minded discussion of opposing views between leaders and employees was found to be crucial, resulting in productive work, strong work relationships, experience of the leader as being democratic, and belief that both the leader and employee are powerful.

In today's global economy, leaders must at times supervise employees working in another country. Hong Kong senior accounting managers were found to be able to lead employees working in the mainland when they had cooperative goals, but not when their goals were competitive or independent (Tjosvold and Moy, 1998). Then they were able to discuss their views open-mindedly, which led to stronger relationships and productivity—consequences that in turn induced future internal motivation.

Democratic, open-minded leadership is valued in China; Chinese employees want a relationship with their leaders and, although hesitant to initiate conflictful discussions, expect them to consider their needs and views. Cooperative conflict is a concrete way for managers in China to develop the leader relationship and demonstrate their openness. Despite power-distance values, leaders and employees in China can benefit a great deal by managing their conflicts cooperatively. Cooperative conflict is an ideal to which both managers and employees, in China and in the West, can aspire.

THE VALUE OF APPLYING THE THEORY IN CHINA

The theory of cooperation and competition has performed well in China, with the amount of variance explained comparing favorably with studies in North America. This was true despite technical issues such as translation and the inexperience of employees in completing questionnaires—conditions that should increase measurement error.

However, our results do not indicate that the theory of cooperation and competition is highly useful for fully capturing how Chinese people experience and manage conflict. Documenting Chinese conflict management will take many years of research. Our research, though, does demonstrate major alternatives that Chinese people have in managing their conflicts, and it explodes stereotypes and assumptions that interfere with our understanding.

Chinese people in the studies clearly distinguished and understood cooperation and competition. They recognize that they can promote their own goals as well as those of team members. It is not necessary to project that Chinese are collectivists who emphasize their group interests without concern for their own. They can pursue joint outcomes if they believe their goals are cooperative.

Recently, researchers have argued that, although the framework has been highly productive, collectivism and individualism have unresolved conceptual confusion and measurement shortcomings (Earley and Gibson, 1998). Our research in China questions the unidimensionality of collectivism-individualism. Individuals can be highly committed to the collective with strong cooperative goals, but this does not presume lack of individuality. Indeed, cooperative, collective commitment has been found to promote open expression of individual opinions and needs. A strong cooperative team fosters outspoken, assertive, and confident individuals; an effective cooperative team depends on members' willingness to express their individuality (Tjosvold, 1997a). Individuals can be both self-assertive and team-oriented; cooperative goals encourage both.

Although a theory developed in the West has guided our research, the resulting studies have exposed Western stereotypes of China. In contrast to the ideas that Chinese consider conflict anathema and that they inevitably deal with open conflict competitively, Chinese people were found to welcome and value open discussion of opposing views and used conflict to explore opposing views and integrate them. However, these constructive effects depend on the Chinese people's understanding that their goals are cooperative—a condition that cannot be assumed.

Chinese values on social face, persuasion, and nonverbal communication need not imply conflict avoidance. These values, if appropriately expressed, contribute to open-minded, cooperative conflict management. Organizational values in China support developing effective, two-way relationships among leaders and employees. Chinese leaders are more effective and appreciated if they seek the views of employees and develop cooperative relationships with them.

Cooperative conflict was also found to develop the teamwork required to deliver high-quality, high-value service to customers, a competitive advantage needed to survive and flourish in China's growing market economy. Ironically, although the theory of cooperation and competition has been developed in the West, it may be particularly applicable to relationship-oriented China.

Expanding the Theory Through Cross-Cultural Research

In addition to the practical importance of understanding management of conflict in the global marketplace, studying conflict in varied cultural contexts can challenge and refine the present understanding of conflict management. Incorporating ideas and practices of other cultures can develop more enduring, elegant, and universal theories (Gergen, Gulerce, Lock, and Misra, 1996; van de Vijver and Leung, 1997).

Our research in China so far has yet to capitalize on this possibility. For instance, we are not certain about the conditions under which competitive or independent goals are productive, nor the conditions in which cooperative approaches to conflict are costly and risky. However, research in China has the potential to widen our understanding of conflict and the theory of cooperation and competition.

Responsiveness to Goal Interdependence

One potential cultural difference is that Chinese people, as highly relationship-oriented, may be particularly responsive to the effects of goal interdependence differences. That Chinese can be categorized as collectivist does not mean they are necessarily more cooperative and trusting than members of individualistic societies. They are highly flexible and responsive to the situation, and hence they may be very conscious of the goal relationship they have with others.

Many scholars have argued that Chinese and other collectivists very much distinguish between in-group and out-group members. In-group members are allies worthy of trust; out-group members are suspect. Leung (1988) found that Chinese were more likely to criticize a stranger, and less likely to criticize a friend, than were Americans. An English literature professor of Chinese nationality now based in the United States concluded, "Americans are nice to strangers; Chinese are nice to their friends."

In North America, independent goals have an impact on dynamics and outcomes similar to, but not as powerful as, competition. However, in some field studies in China, interactions with independent goals have been more powerful and destructive than ones with competitive goals (Tjosvold, 1998b). It can be speculated that Chinese people are particularly suspicious and closed-minded toward persons with whom they are not involved. They find the lack of relationship implied by independent goals more highly disruptive of effective collaborative work than competition.

Antecedents of Cooperative Goals

Research in North America has concentrated on the consequences of the type of goal interdependence; studies in China may stimulate progress in understanding its antecedents. Chinese society has a unique relation system, *guanxi*, wherein personal connections are central to work. Maintaining good relations is a key job motivator and ingredient in success (Chow and Luk, 1996). Particular ties—coming from the same village, attendance at the same school, and prior connections between fathers—all can build *guanxi* (Farh, Tsui, Xin, and Cheng, 1998).

Research on *guanxi* may illuminate how cooperative goals evolve. *Guanxi* bases may be prima facie evidence that the partners are on the same side, with cooperative goals, and these beliefs of cooperative interdependence in turn lead to mutual trust and assistance. *Guanxi* bases, however, do not inevitably result in mutual relationship. Perhaps the development of competitive goals between partners can explain the failure to capitalize on *guanxi* bases. At present, it is unclear how *guanxi* may facilitate or hinder development of cooperative goals. Studies could also explore the extent that Westerners have similar relational ties that help them develop strongly cooperative relationships.

Research in China has begun to suggest conditions conducive to forming cooperative goals. Confirmation of face, implicit communication to convey warmth, benevolent and participative leadership, and in-group relationships and *guanxi* may convince Chinese people that their goals are cooperative. These conditions may also promote cooperative goals among Westerners.

Harmony Motives and Cooperative Goals

Leung (1996, 1997) has argued that harmony in Chinese societies has two underlying motives. The first is instrumental in nature and regards maintaining harmony as means to other ends. *Disintegration avoidance* refers to the tendency to avoid actions that strain a relationship and lead to its disintegration. Under this motive, people use harmony-seeking behavior as a way to further their self-interest and avoid potential problems with others. *Harmony enhancement* refers to the desire to engage in behavior that strengthens relationships. It represents genuine concern for harmony as a value in and of itself.

Harmony enhancement is "solid" and involves feelings of intimacy, closeness, trust, and compatible and mutually beneficial behavior, whereas disintegration avoidance involves difference in values and interpersonal style as well as avoidance of contact and conflict (Hwang, 1996). Research can explore the hypothesis that harmony enhancement induces cooperative goals and disintegration motives lead to competitive ones.

Practical Implications

Cultures express themselves to a great extent in how they manage conflict. Conflict is a window to understanding national cultures (Leung and Tjosvold, 1998). Although research supports the theory of cooperation and competition in China, results do not imply that goal interdependence is operationalized in the East in a way highly similar to that in the West.

Although the genotype (the underlying conceptual structure of the theory) appears to be similar, the phenotypes (how the theory is manifested in particular situations) often are not. In particular, the actions that develop cooperative goals or communicate an attempt to discuss conflicts open-mindedly may be quite different in China than in North America, as may be the general level of goal interdependence and cooperative conflict.

Even if they have common goals and objectives, people from different cultures may have various views of right and wrong, how best to accomplish goals, the value of a long-term versus short-term perspective, appropriate etiquette, and the value of the contributions people make to a joint venture (Rahim and Blum, 1994). They are also likely to have dissimilar views of how they should manage their conflicts (Kirkbride, Tang, and Westwood, 1991). Although some studies suggest the utility of a cooperative conflict approach between East and West (Tjosvold, 1996; Tjosvold, Lee, and Wong, 1992), more research is needed to document its potential for managing cross-cultural conflicts.

Cooperation theory has the advantage of already developed procedures for applying it in the West, which suggests the broad outlines of how Chinese managers and employees may proceed (Deutsch, 1994, 1994a; Tjosvold, 1991, 1993). Several general steps, which we present in sequential outline, can guide application of cooperative conflict research for Chinese organizations and between China and the West in international joint ventures and other venues. The procedures must be modified to take into account the culture, situation, and people involved in China. Common sense and sensitivity are needed to modify and apply these steps in the West as well.

First, the organization and its teams adopt cooperative conflict as a common vision. Executives, managers, and employees indicate their commitment to develop their cooperative conflict management capabilities. They study, review the research, and debate the theory to decide whether they are committed to using cooperative conflict. Once they are committed, they have developed a strong cooperative goal of learning to manage conflict cooperatively.

Second, all teams develop their cooperative conflict abilities. People come to understand that they need open-minded discussion within their group to create effective solutions to problems, work collaboratively with other teams, and serve customers with quality. They practice expressing their positions and feelings directly; exploring opposing views; demonstrating that they understand the other; using the best ideas from each; and agreeing to a mutually beneficial, high-quality solution. They confirm face, use persuasion influence, and express interpersonal warmth as they disagree with each other. They reflect on their experiences, give feedback, and strive continuously to improve their conflict skills. Positive conflict experiences within their groups leave them confident and prepared to manage conflict with colleagues and customers.

Third, frustration and irritations are vented and used, rather than suppressed. Intense emotions engendered in conflict, when properly expressed, aid conflict management (Tjosvold, 1997b); they reaffirm interdependence, focus energy on solving underlying problems, and discharge frustration. Suppressing feelings can leave people anxious and self-righteous. A rational, effective approach to managing conflict requires skilled expression of feelings, especially for tough, persistent conflict.

Fourth, the goal is gradual, systematic change. Especially in organizations with a history of competition, escalated conflicts have developed reinforcing investments in coercive and combative procedures, suspicious attitudes, and patterns of hostile interaction. Cooperative conflict requires people to create forums for direct discussion, trusting values, and promotive interaction patterns that are relevant, effective, and appropriate for all. To find the endurance needed to move away from competition and conflict avoidance, people need confidence that their colleagues want to manage conflict cooperatively.

The theory of cooperative and competitive conflict does not offer simple techniques that dissolve division. Rather it outlines the relationships and skills needed to deal directly and constructively with them (Tjosvold, 1993). We need more experimentation to understand how to use this knowledge to deal with our many, often complex cross-cultural conflicts.

CONCLUSION

Our research has used Deutsch's theory to understand teamwork, leadership, and conflict in China. In today's diverse and global marketplace, theories—especially about conflict—that can only be applied in one culture are increasingly irrelevant. We need theories that have been validated in various cultures to understand and facilitate cross-cultural teamwork and conflict.

If the framework of cooperative, constructive controversy continues to be successfully demonstrated in Europe as well as East Asia (Kluwer and others, 1993; Tjosvold and De Dreu, 1997), it has the potential to act as a common guide for how people from various cultures can develop their own ways of managing conflict. Diverse people together decide that they want to use a cooperative approach to conflict as the major way of handling their disputes and then put in place the incentives and procedures that support cooperative goals and constructive controversy.

Contrary to the argument that applying Western theories is culturally insensitive, developing a theory of cooperation and competition so that it can be applied in various cultural texts contributes to building organizations that promote and value diversity. With a common framework, people from several cultures can agree on how they are going to disagree. They develop ways of managing conflict that are appropriate and effective for them. They are then able to express their diversity and use conflict to solve problems. Cooperative open-mindedness strengthens their relationships and their appreciation of diversity.

Without a common framework, organizations are apt to impose the procedures of one culture on another—for example, insisting that everyone conform to the ways of the head office. Or they may use trial-and-error in the hope of developing new procedures. However, these approaches are apt to result in an organization characterized by destructive conflict and conflict avoidance.

Harmony has traditionally been highly valued in China, but considering conflict as negative and avoiding conflict appear generally ineffective for promoting successful organizations in China. Chinese people want harmony, but they appear to recognize the necessity of managing conflict to develop authentic harmony, where frustrations are resolved and relationships maintained (Leung, 1997).

Our studies in China suggest that conflict management is critical for modern development. Chinese employees who use their conflicts cooperatively have been found to improve the quality of products and services and reduce costs. Democracy requires that leaders be responsive and open; cooperative conflict contributes to open-minded, productive relationships between leaders and employees.

Our research is only a beginning. More work is needed on how Chinese values and settings have an impact on the underlying dynamics of cooperation and competitive interdependence. We have not proceeded far in using studies in China to modify the theory. We also need to further our knowledge with regard to the critical ways the theory is operationalized, the important antecedents to cooperative goals, the frequency of cooperative and competitive conflict, and how such knowledge can be used to characterize Chinese conflict management. However, our research does suggest possibilities, and it documents that cooperative conflict is a viable, highly constructive approach with great potential in China.

References

Chow, W. S., and Luk, V.W.M. "Management in the 1990s: A Comparative Study of Women Managers in China and Hong Kong," *Journal of Managerial Psychology,* 1996, *11,* 24–36.

Deutsch, M. "A Theory of Cooperation and Competition." *Human Relations,* 1949, *2,* 129–152.

Deutsch, M. *The Resolution of Conflict: Constructive and Destructive Processes.* New Haven: Yale University Press, 1973.

Deutsch, M. "Fifty Years of Conflict." In L. Festinger (ed.), *Retrospections on Social Psychology.* New York: Oxford University Press, 1980.

Deutsch, M. "Sixty Years of Conflict." *International Journal of Conflict Management,* 1990, *1,* 237–263.

Deutsch, M. "Constructive Conflict Management for the World Today." *The International Journal of Conflict Management,* 1994, *5,* 111–129.

Deutsch, M. "Constructive Conflict Resolution: Principles, Training, and Research." *Journal of Social Issues,* 1994a, *50,* 13–32.

Earley, P. C., and Gibson, C. B. "Taking Stock in Our Progress on Individualism-Collectivism: 100 Years of Solidarity and Community." *Journal of Management,* 1998, *24,* 265–304.

Farh, J. L., Tsui, A. S., Xin, K., and Cheng, B. S. "The Influence of Relational Demography and *Guanxi*: The Chinese Case." *Organization Science,* 1998, *9,* 471–488.

Flanagan, J. C. "The Critical Incident Technique." *Psychological Bulletin,* 1954, *54,* 327–358.

Fowler, F. J., Jr. *Survey Research Methods.* (2nd ed.) Thousand Oaks, Calif.: Sage, 1993.

Gergen, K. J., Gulerce, A., Lock, A., and Misra, G. "Psychological Science in Cultural Context." *American Psychologist,* 1996, *51,* 496–503.

Goffman, E. *Interaction Ritual: Essays in Face-to-Face Behavior.* Hawthorne, N.Y.: Aldine de Gruyter, 1967.

Gudykunst, W. B., Ting-Toomey, S., and Chua, E. *Culture and Interpersonal Communication.* Thousands Oaks, Calif.: Sage, 1988.

Hall, E. T. *Beyond Culture.* New York: Doubleday, 1976.

Hofstede, G. *Culture's Consequences: International Differences in Work-Related Values.* Thousand Oaks, Calif.: Sage, 1980.

Hui, C., Law, K. S., and Tjosvold, D. "The Effects of Cooperation and Competition on Leader-Member-Exchange and Extra-Role Performance in China." Unpublished manuscript, Hong Kong University of Science and Technology, 1997.

Hui, C., Tjosvold, D., and Ding, D. "Mediating the Relationship of Justice and Organizational Citizenship Behavior: Global Interdependence." Paper submitted for publication, Chinese University of Hong Kong, 1998.

Hwang, L. L. "Conflict and Interpersonal Harmony Among Chinese People: Theoretical Constructs and Empirical Studies" (in Chinese). Unpublished doctoral dissertation, National Taiwan University, Republic of China, 1996.

Kirkbride, P. S., Tang, S.F.Y., and Westwood, R. I. "Chinese Conflict Preferences and Negotiating Behaviour: Cultural and Psychological Influences." *Organization Studies,* 1991, *12,* 365–386.

Kluwer, E., and others. "Doelinterdependentie en Conflicthantering in Profit- en Non-Profit-Organisaties [Goal Interdependence and Conflict Management in Profit and Nonprofit Organizations]. *Toegepaste Social Psychologie [Applied Social Psychology].* Eburon, Netherlands: Delft, 1993.

Law, S. A, Hui, C., and Tjosvold, D. "Relational Approach to Understanding Conflict Management: Integrating the Theory of Cooperation and Competition, Leader-Member Relationship, and In-Role and Extra-Role Performance." Paper submitted for publication, Hong Kong University of Science and Technology, 1998.

Leung, K. "Some Determinants of Conflict Avoidance: A Cross-National Study." *Journal of Cross-Cultural Psychology,* 1988, *19,* 125–136.

Leung, K. "The Role of Harmony in Conflict Avoidance." Paper presented at 50th anniversary conference of the Korean Psychological Association, Seoul, June 1996.

Leung, K. "Negotiation and Reward Allocations Across Cultures." In P. C. Earley and M. Erez (eds.), *New Perspectives on International Industrial-Organizational Psychology.* San Francisco: Jossey-Bass, 1997.

Leung, K., and Tjosvold, D. "Conflict for Doing Business in the Pacific Rim." In K. Leung and D. Tjosvold (eds.), *Conflict Management in the Asia Pacific Rim.* Singapore: Wiley, 1998.

Poon, M., Tjosvold, D., and Pike, R. "Budget Participation in Hong Kong: Goal Interdependence and Controversy as Contributors to Budget Quality." Unpublished manuscript, City University of Hong Kong, 1998.

Pye, L. W. *Asian Power and Politics: The Cultural Dimensions of Authority.* Cambridge, Mass.: Harvard University Press, 1985.

Rahim A., and Blum, A. A. *Global Perspectives on Organizational Conflict.* New York: Praeger, 1994.

Smith, P. B., Dugan, S., and Trompenaars, F. "National Culture and the Values of Organizational Employees: A 43 Nation Study." *Journal of Cross-Cultural Psychology,* 1996, *27,* 231–264.

Spencer-Oatey, H. "Unequal Relationships in High and Low Power Distance Societies: A Comparative Study of Tutor-Student Role Relations in Britain and China." *Journal of Cross-Cultural Psychology*, 1997, *28*, 284–302.

Ting-Toomey, S. "A Face Negotiation Theory." In Y. Y. Kim and W. B. Gudykunst (eds.), *Theory and Intercultural Communication*. Thousand Oaks, Calif.: Sage, 1988.

Tjosvold, D. "Social Face in Conflict: A Critique." *International Journal of Group Tensions*, 1983, *13*, 49–64.

Tjosvold, D. "Implications of Controversy Research for Management." *Journal of Management*, 1985, *11*, 21–37.

Tjosvold, D. *Conflict-Positive Organization: Stimulate Diversity and Create Unity.* Reading, Mass.: Addison-Wesley, 1991.

Tjosvold, D. *Learning to Manage Conflict: Getting People to Work Together Productively.* San Francisco: New Lexington Press, 1993.

Tjosvold, D. "Bridging East and West to Develop New Products and Trust: Interdependence and Interaction Between a Hong Kong Parent and North American Subsidiary." Unpublished manuscript, Lingnan College, Hong Kong, 1996.

Tjosvold, D. "Conflict Within Interdependence: Its Value for Productivity and Individuality." In C. De Dreu and E. van de Vliert (eds.), *Using Conflict in Organizations*. Thousand Oaks, Calif.: Sage, 1997a.

Tjosvold, D. "Managing Anger for Teamwork in Hong Kong: Goal Interdependence and Open-Mindedness." Paper submitted for publication, Lingnan College, Hong Kong, 1997b.

Tjosvold, D. "Dealing with Retail Customer Complaints: Managing Conflict for Relational Marketing in Hong Kong." Paper submitted for publication, Lingnan College, Hong Kong, 1998a.

Tjosvold, D. "Social Face in Conflict Management Among Chinese: A Study of Respect and Goal Interdependence." Paper submitted for publication, Lingnan College, Hong Kong, 1998b.

Tjosvold, D., and Chia, L. C. "Conflict Between Managers and Employees: The Role of Cooperation and Competition." *Journal of Social Psychology*, 1989, *129*, 235–247.

Tjosvold, D., and De Dreu, C. "Managing Conflict in Dutch Organizations: A Test of the Relevance of Deutsch's Cooperation Theory." *Journal of Applied Social Psychology*, 1997, *27*, 2213–2227.

Tjosvold, D., Hui, C., Ding, D., and Hu, J. "The Positive Role of Conflict on Teams and Citizenship Behavior in China." Paper submitted for publication, Lingnan University, Hong Kong, 1998.

Tjosvold, D., Hui, C., and Law, K. S. "Empowerment in the Leader Relationship in Hong Kong: Interdependence and Controversy." *Journal of Social Psychology*, 1997, *138*, 624–637.

Tjosvold, D., Hui, C., and Sun, H. *Social Face Affronts, Harmony, and Open Disagreement in the Leader Relationship in China.* Paper submitted for publication, Lingnan College, Hong Kong, 1998.

Tjosvold, D., Lee, F., and Wong, C. L. "Managing Conflict in a Diverse Workforce: A Chinese Perspective in North America." *Small Group Research,* 1992, *23,* 302–332.

Tjosvold, D., and Moy, J. "Managing Employees in China from Hong Kong: Interaction, Relationships, and Productivity as Antecedents to Motivation." *Leadership and Organization Development Journal,* 1998, *19,* 147–156.

Tjosvold, D., Moy, J., and Sasaki, S. "Managing for Customers and Employees in Hong Kong: The Quality and Teamwork Challenges." *Journal of Market-Focused Management,* 1996, *1,* 339–357.

Tjosvold, D., Sasaki, S., and Moy, J. "Developing Commitment in Japanese Organizations in Hong Kong: Interdependence, Interaction, Relationship, and Productivity." *Small Group Research,* 1998, *29,* 560–582.

Tjosvold, D., and Sun, H. "Openness Among Chinese in Conflict: Effects of Direct Discussion and Warmth on Integrated Decision Making." Paper submitted for publication, Lingnan College, Hong Kong, 1998a.

Tjosvold, D., and Sun, H. "Persuasive and Coercive Influence: Respect and Cooperative Context for Conflict Management in China." Paper submitted for publication, Lingnan College, Hong Kong, 1998b.

Tjosvold, D., and Tjosvold, M. M. *Leading the Team Organization: How to Create an Enduring Competitive Advantage.* San Francisco: New Lexington Press, 1991.

Tjosvold, D., and Tjosvold, M. M. "Cooperation Theory, Constructive Controversy, and Effectiveness: Learning from Crises." In R. A. Guzzo, E. Salas, and Associates, *Team Effectiveness and Decision Making in Organizations.* San Francisco: Jossey-Bass, 1995.

Tjosvold, D., and Tsao, Y. "Productive Organizational Collaboration: The Role of Values and Cooperative Goals." *Journal of Organizational Behavior,* 1989, *10,* 189–195.

Tjosvold, D., and Wang, Z. M. *Cooperative Goals and Constructive Controversy in Work Teams in China: Antecedents for Performance.* Paper presented at the annual meeting of the Academy of Management, San Diego, Aug. 1998.

Tjosvold, D., and others. "Interdependence and Managing Conflict with Subcontractors in the Construction Industry in East Asia." Paper submitted for publication, Lingnan College, Hong Kong, 1998.

Tse, D. K., Francis, J., and Walls, J. "Cultural Differences in Conducting Intra- and Inter-Cultural Negotiations: A Sino-Canadian Comparison." *Journal of International Business Studies,* 1994, *24,* 537–555.

Tung, R. "Handshakes Across the Sea: Cross-Cultural Negotiating for Business Success." *Organizational Dynamics,* 1991, *14,* 30–40.

van de Vijver, F., and Leung, K. *Methods and Data Analysis for Cross-Cultural Research.* Thousand Oaks, Calif.: Sage, 1997.

Wong, A., Tjosvold, D., Wong, W., and Liu, C. K. "Relationships for Quality Improvement in the Hong Kong–China Supply Chain: A Study in the Theory of Cooperation and Competition." *Journal of Quality and Reliability Management,* forthcoming.

PART SEVEN

MODELS OF PRACTICE

Teaching Conflict Resolution Skills in a Workshop

Ellen Raider
Susan Coleman
Janet Gerson

T his chapter describes the Coleman Raider model, used to teach negotiation and mediation skills to adult learners. By making explicit our teaching philosophy, course objectives, and methods, we hope to stimulate discussion and research about how conflict resolution is taught. Although there is an extensive theoretical and empirical literature on the nature of conflict and the processes of negotiation and mediation as applied in diplomacy, business, and labor relations, there is very little systematic research on the pedagogy of conflict resolution or on the models and methods used to teach these skills to adult or student learners (Raider, 1995; also see Chapter Twenty-Seven).

We first share six pedagogical insights derived from our practice that have come to underpin our training design. Then we discuss the objectives of the course as a whole and the learning activities in each of our seven training modules. We conclude with some recommendations for social science researchers and theorists.

INSIGHTS FROM PRACTICE

The first pedagogical insight is that *each learner has a unique and implicit "theory of practice" for resolving conflicts.* Each individual's theory of practice has been developed over a lifetime, influenced by many factors, such as various individual

---

We wish to express special thanks to Marc Roennau for preparing the graphics for this chapter.

differences, skills, and competencies (see Chapters Fourteen and Fifteen), as well as salient cultural and identity groups norms and values (see Chapter Twenty-Two), and situational roles and hierarchies.

Second, *learners need both support and challenge to examine their own theory of practice.* Intellectual and experiential comparison of competitive and collaborative processes can create challenging internal conflict for most learners. From our experience, learners experience two types of internal conflicts. The first is felt by those who embrace collaboration as an ideal and yet experience dissonance as they discover through course exercises how much of their own behavior is viewed by others and themselves as competitive, accommodating, or compromising (see discussion of the dual-concern model in Chapter Fourteen). The second is felt by those who resist or reject collaboration and then experience dissonance between their own theory of practice and the alternative paradigm presented in the workshop. Although the first group is typically larger, as most participants in our training are volunteers, the trainers must create a learning community where *all* feel safe enough to try on new skills and attitudes.

The third insight is that *experiential exercises shift the responsibility for learning from the trainer to the participant.* For many adult learners, role playing and subsequent public debriefing are powerful learning tools as well as unfreezing devices for behavioral and attitudinal change. The excitement, fun, and support of mutual self-discovery counteract the potential embarrassment of being less-than-perfect in front of the other students.

Fourth, *self-reflection based on video or audio feedback gives many learners motivation to modify problematic behavior.* Videotaping or audiotaping the role-play exercise, for later review, enables each learner to observe and reflect on his or her own behavior in terms of general knowledge about the collaborative conflict resolution process presented by the trainers.

Fifth, *user-friendly models and a common vocabulary enable a group of learners to talk about their shared in-program experience.* Conceptual frames, like the ones taught in modules two through seven (discussed in the next section), are broad enough to illuminate the underlying structure of a collaborative process across many contexts because they leave room for cultural variation. The trainer needs to be contextually sensitive to explain and illustrate the heuristic frames in ways that are culturally and situationally relevant.

The final insight is that *learners need follow-up and support after workshop training to internalize new concepts and skills.* As in other areas of skills training, most participants need additional coaching in a supportive environment for behavioral change to occur (Raider, 1995). A three- to six-day workshop in conflict resolution can make the learner aware of what she does *not* know, thereby beginning the learning process; but more work is needed if a collaborative process is to become the preferred response to mixed-motive conflicts. This humbling but valid observation needs serious consideration by the conflict resolution field—by trainers as well as organizations that sponsor trainings.

OVERVIEW OF THE COLEMAN RAIDER WORKSHOP DESIGN

Developed by Ellen Raider and Susan Coleman, Conflict Resolution: Strategies for Collaborative Problem Solving is a highly interactive workshop typically conducted in a three-day or six-day format. (It is based on Raider's 1987 training manual, *A Guide to International Negotiation*.) The three-day format is for groups requesting training in collaborative negotiation. The longer format includes an extensive three-day module on mediation. All participants receive a training manual, which is divided into sections corresponding to the seven course modules.

Module one presents an overview of conflict resolution, with emphasis on distinguishing between competitive and collaborative resolution strategies.

Module two introduces a structural model, the Elements of Negotiation. In this module, we focus on the difference between positions and needs or interests, as well as the skill of *reframing* and the use of a prenegotiation planning tool.

Module three describes five communications *behaviors* or tactics that are typically used during negotiations, and it emphasizes the difference between the *intent* and the *impact* of any communication.

Combining the learning from the previous modules, module four gives the learner a sense of the flow of a collaborative negotiation by introducing a stage model.

Module five describes how cultural differences affect the conflict resolution process.

Module six helps participants understand and deal with emotions, which typically arise during interpersonal and cross-cultural conflict.

In its short form, module seven introduces mediation as an alternative if negotiation breaks down. The longer form teaches participants the skill and practice of mediation.

Although the information contained in these seven modules is the foundation for every workshop, the material presented is customized to meet the needs of each client. This is accomplished through selecting or creating case simulations, including previously recorded video examples of negotiations or mediations from our library, and prior assessments of the trainee group.

This precourse assessment and customization is an important part of our work. During the assessment, the training team builds rapport with the client and discovers many of the conflicting issues currently in the client's system. This information enables the team to anticipate, recognize, and then incorporate relevant "teachable moments" during the training, that is, to link the training material to real concerns of the learner as they emerge. In this way, we have been able to teach this course to such diverse groups as school teachers in New York, Dallas, and Skopje; corporate executives in Buenos Aires, Paris, and Tokyo; grassroots community groups dealing with tenant organizing and environmental justice; diplomats from the Association of South-East Asian Nations and the European Union; and United Nations staff throughout the world. The course has been taught over the past twelve years to about ten thousand people. The materials have been translated into French, Spanish, and Macedonian, and a book based on our manual has been published in Japanese.

So far, we have trained thirty individuals from diverse backgrounds to teach our workshop. To be certified as a trainer, an individual must acquire important content, presentation, and group-dynamics skills and successfully apprentice with us for three or four workshop trainings. Some trainers are certified to teach in certain cultural or organizational settings but not in others; we feel there are important contextual differences between educational, diplomatic, and business settings as well as between people with differing cultural norms and values.

WORKSHOP OBJECTIVES AND PEDAGOGY

Like other educators, we find it useful to identify for ourselves specific knowledge, skills, and attitude objectives for the training.

Knowledge Objectives

A glance at the table of contents of this volume indicates that there are many areas of academic inquiry that affect the study of conflict and its resolution. How much of this body of knowledge can be included in an introductory experiential workshop?

We have decided to emphasize the distinction between competitive and collaborative approaches to conflict resolution (see Chapter One). Thus, we want participants to understand conceptually and experientially why and under what conditions cooperative conflict resolution processes such as collaborative negotiation and mediation are a better choice for individuals and society than are the commonly used strategies of competition and avoidance. Although we make it clear that we value cooperation, we also believe that we must not impose it on others. Our pedagogy encourages participants to "try on" this new paradigm to see if it is useful. Ultimately, each participant must be self-motivated to make meaningful changes in his or her conflict-resolving behavior. We hope to provide information and experiences during our training that foster this exploration.

Through short essays in the training manual and minilectures, the trainers highlight and summarize in nontechnical language key insights from the field.

In the graduate program at Columbia University, we supplement these essays and minilectures with additional assigned readings. Although specific knowledge objectives are associated with each module, there are some "global" knowledge objectives for the course:

- To develop understanding that conflict is a natural and necessary part of life, and that how one responds to conflict determines if the outcomes are constructive or destructive

- To develop awareness that competition and collaboration are the two main strategies for resolving conflict and for negotiation

- To develop awareness of one's own tendencies in thinking about and responding to conflict

- To become a better conflict manager—in other words, to know which conflict resolution method is best suited for a particular conflict problem (for example, avoidance, negotiation, mediation, arbitration, litigation, or force)

- To become aware of how critical it is to the process of constructive conflict resolution to share information about one's own perspective without attacking the other, and to listen and work to understand the perspective of the other side

Skills Objectives

The most fundamental skills objectives of our training are the following:

- To effectively distinguish positions from needs or interests

- To reframe a conflict so that it can be seen as a mutual problem to be resolved collaboratively

- To distinguish threats, justifications, positions, needs, and feelings and to be able to communicate one's perspective using these distinctions

- To ask open-ended questions in a manner that elicits the needs, rather than the defenses, of the other and, by so doing, communicate a desire to engage in a process of mutual need satisfaction

- When under attack, to be able to listen to the other and reflect back the other's needs or interests behind the attack

- To create a collaborative climate through the use of informing, opening, and uniting behaviors

Attitude Objectives

What attitudes might the participant acquire or confirm after attending an introductory conflict resolution training? Does the learner believe that collaborative conflict resolution skills are useful in their own lives? Do they commit to the larger goal of increasing the use of cooperative conflict resolution skills at all levels to create a more just and caring society? We know from empirical observation that the answers to these questions can be, and often are, affirmative.

Our process permits exploring this continuum through whole-group and small-group discussions and reflection through personal journaling. This investigation varies in depth and breadth depending on the specific audience and the time available for the training.

SEVEN WORKSHOP MODULES

Focus on each of the seven modules in the training sequence is adjusted according to the learning objectives of the audience.

Module One: Overview of Conflict

The first module presents an overview of conflict. The focus is on exploring the participants' existing attitudes. The exercises chosen are intended to create internal conflict within each participant, so that he examines his own attitudes toward conflict, competition, and collaboration. The main activities include a diagnostic case, a physical game, and an interactive video-based minilecture illustrating various methods of conflict resolution.

Collaborative negotiation and mediation are introduced by locating them along the spectrum of conflict resolution approaches that range from avoidance to war. Both negotiation and mediation are explained as consensual alternatives that focus on the parties' underlying needs and interests and require their buy-in to try to reach an agreement. This is contrasted with quasi-judicial and power-based methods such as arbitration, litigation, or combat (see Figure 24.1). In the minilecture we connect these strategies to important theories, such as Deutsch's Crude Law (see Chapter One) and the dual-concern model (see Chapter Fourteen).

A diagnostic case is the first experiential learning exercise. Small groups of four to six people are divided in half to represent each side of the dispute. The groups negotiate for twenty-five minutes—competitively for ten minutes, then collaboratively for fifteen. A frequently used diagnostic situation, the "Ossipila Case," is a conflict between international developers who, with local government backing, want to strip-mine on the ancient farmland used by villagers (who have support from environmental groups).

The exercise is recorded on audio (or video) and played back to the small groups; it is also used in module three for an in-depth analysis. There is a short debriefing immediately after the exercise.

Figure 24.1. Coleman Raider Conflict Resolution Continuum.

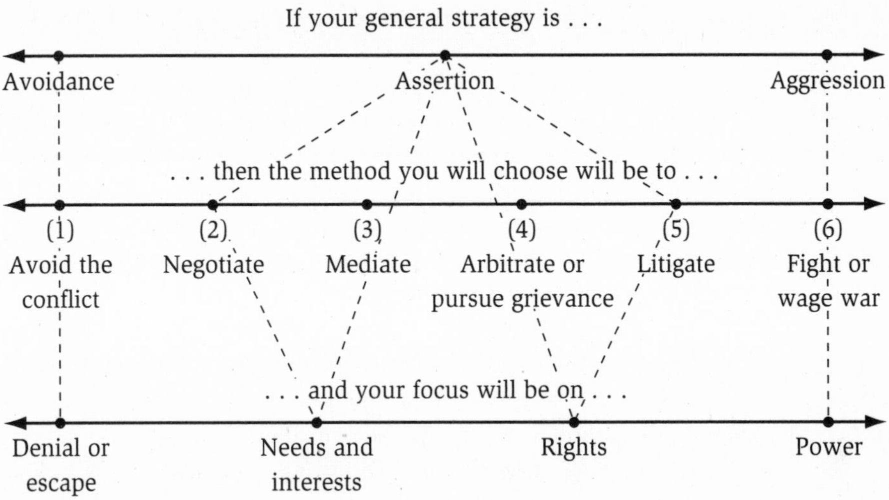

If your general strategy is . . .

Avoidance   Assertion   Aggression

. . . then the method you will choose will be to . . .

(1)   (2)   (3)   (4)   (5)   (6)
Avoid the   Negotiate   Mediate   Arbitrate or Litigate   Fight or
conflict   pursue grievance   wage war

. . . and your focus will be on . . .

Denial or   Needs and   Rights   Power
escape   interests

Source: Copyright © 1992, 1997 Ellen Raider International, Inc., and the Coleman Group International, Inc. Permission has been given for use in *The Handbook of Conflict Resolution.* Other use is prohibited without written permission of the copyright holder.

The diagnostic case serves six functions:

1. It immediately involves both skeptics and believers in our process.

2. It generates a baseline assessment for participants to discern those specific skill areas they need to work on during the rest of the training.

3. It brings out the inherent discrepancy between what we propose and what participants are actually doing.

4. It demonstrates that the learning exercises in the workshop are highly participatory.

5. It allows learners to experience the difficulty of switching from one negotiation strategy to the other, as well as the possible consequences of each approach.

6. It initiates a positive atmosphere of shared learning.

The power of this experience comes from the direct challenge to the participants' views of competition and collaboration. As they listen to themselves and hear the group's feedback, the participants contrast their behavior with their own implicit theories and self-perceptions. This creates a discomfort that is the pivotal stimulus for change during the training. We have found that even if people cognitively grasp the principles of collaboration and want to use them, they still act out a competitive or avoidant orientation.

Module Two: The Elements of Negotiation

In module two, the goal is to introduce a framework we call the elements of negotiation. The elements serve as the underlying grammatical structure of a negotiation. Just as parsing a sentence for verbs, nouns, and adjectives fosters understanding in any language, so too understanding the elements of negotiation fosters analysis of a conflict prior to and during a negotiation. We identify six structural elements: worldview, climate, positions, needs and interests, reframing, and bargaining "chips" and "chops."

Worldview comprises one's deeply held beliefs, attitudes, and values. They are derived from one's culture, family, and other important groups with which one identifies. Worldview is a central component of one's identity. It is almost always nonnegotiable, although it can change over time.

Climate is the mood of the negotiation. It reflects the competitive or collaborative orientation of the parties in the negotiation.

Positions are the specific demands or requests made by each party as negotiation commences—the party's preferred solution to the conflict. If someone is competitive in her orientation, she may inflate her position or state it as nonnegotiable. A collaborative approach requires positions that are specific, clear, and honest with respect to negotiability.

Needs and interests are what each negotiating party is looking to satisfy. If the position is "what you want," the need is "why you want it." Collaboration sometimes requires sorting through layers of positions and needs to arrive at a place where both sides' salient needs can be adequately addressed and met.

Reframing is a way to refocus the conflict issue on needs—not positions. It is essentially the question, "How can we satisfy the priority needs of the parties to the conflict?"

"Chips" and *"chops"* are bargaining offers or threats that each side can use to influence the negotiation. Chips are positive "need satisfiers" that one side proposes so as to meet the needs of the other. They are effective only if perceived as valuable by the other party, while also not undermining one's own interests. Chops are negative "need thwarters," such as threats or insults. They may be useful to counter threats or to level a power imbalance between the disputants. However, they can encourage competition and undermine the trust needed for collaboration, so we discourage their use.

This shared frame of reference, with its common language, becomes a tool to make clear what the students often know intuitively. They learn to analyze the elements of each conflict presented and to use this analysis to prepare for negotiation. A key learning goal is to be able to distinguish needs from positions and to reframe conflict from a competitive clash of positions to collaboration based on understanding and acknowledgment of underlying needs and worldviews. The theoretical discussion underlying reframing in Chapter One of this book constitutes the intellectual context of our emphasis here.

The main learning activities include analysis of simple or complex cases to practice recognition of needs, positions, and reframing (see Figure 24.2) and use of the elements as a prenegotiation planning tool. We describe an example shortly.

After a minilecture explaining the elements, the trainers lead the group through analysis (using a form similar to Figure 24.3, the "negotiation planning form") of a conflict presented in two parts on video. Part one shows a heated conflict, and part two shows one possible resolution. Using a video to display the conflict grounds the discussion in a specific real-world context. The choice of which case to use is an important design decision and is made with understanding of its suitability for a particular client group. One case, "A Community Dispute," has proved useful in many contexts, so we briefly describe it here to illustrate the definitions given earlier.

The mayor of Centerville has called a meeting to address citizen complaints that a factory in the town is emitting powerful toxins that are causing respiratory illness. The owner of the chemical plant, the town's main employer, is present, as are three members of Concerned Citizens of Centerville (made up of plant workers and community members). The mayor cautions that the cause of the illness is as yet undetermined but announces that the results of a preliminary environmental report require the factory to close for one week to see if it is the source of the problem.

As the video begins, it is not immediately clear whether this conflict is a clash of worldviews or an apparent conflict of interests. Assumptions abound,

Figure 24.2. Coleman Raider Reframing Formula.

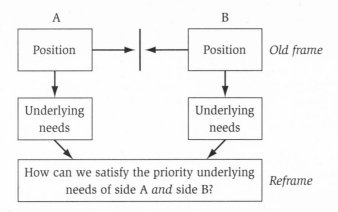

Figure 24.3. Coleman Raider Negotiation Planning Form: "A Community Dispute."

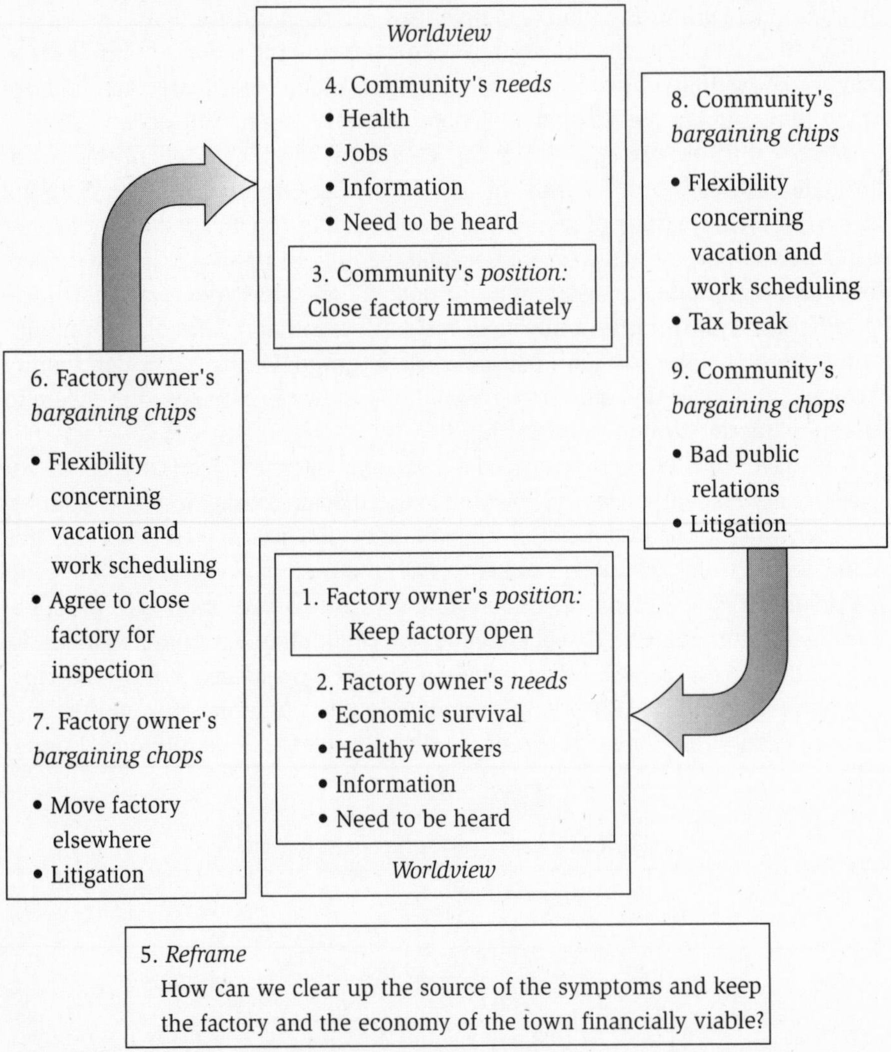

Worldview

4. Community's *needs*
- Health
- Jobs
- Information
- Need to be heard

3. Community's *position*: Close factory immediately

8. Community's *bargaining chips*
- Flexibility concerning vacation and work scheduling
- Tax break

9. Community's *bargaining chops*
- Bad public relations
- Litigation

6. Factory owner's *bargaining chips*
- Flexibility concerning vacation and work scheduling
- Agree to close factory for inspection

7. Factory owner's *bargaining chops*
- Move factory elsewhere
- Litigation

1. Factory owner's *position*: Keep factory open

2. Factory owner's *needs*
- Economic survival
- Healthy workers
- Information
- Need to be heard

Worldview

5. *Reframe*
How can we clear up the source of the symptoms and keep the factory and the economy of the town financially viable?

Source: Copyright © 1992, 1997 Ellen Raider International, Inc. Permission has been given for use in *The Handbook of Conflict Resolution.* Other use is prohibited without written permission of the copyright holder.

however, during class discussion. Is the factory owner a "greedy capitalist" unconcerned with the well-being of the town? Are the concerned citizens merely "environmental crazies" out to destroy the factory, as the owner implies? The workshop discussion generated by the ambiguity helps participants distinguish among position, interest, and identity conflict, and to better understand the concept of worldview.

In part one of the video, the climate is very hostile and competitive. The disputants interrupt, yell, contradict, and accuse one another as well as make it clear that each side sees the other as unreasonable. The position of the community group is to close the factory immediately. The owner's counterposition is to keep the factory open, and he asserts that his plant is not causing the infections.

Through analysis, the class members come to understand that the community needs health *and* jobs. The owner needs profits *and* healthy workers. In addition, all have the need for accurate information about the source of the infections, as well as having their perspective acknowledged and understood. Much common ground is uncovered in what initially appears to some as a worldview clash. The rhetoric of the competitive climate simply makes it difficult to see what calm analysis reveals.

After part one, the trainers lead the class in forming a reframing question. When they view part two of the video, they are able to compare their own reframe with the one used by the mayor: "How can we clear up the source of the symptoms and keep the factory and the economy of this town financially viable?"

In part one, community members' chops include the threat to take the environmental report to the local newspapers, thereby undermining the factory owner's reputation and bottom line. Among the owner's chops is the implied threat to move the factory to another town, taking jobs with him.

In part two, after hearing the mayor's reframing question, the group exchanges chips. At the psychological level, both sides listen to one another as they meet their mutual needs for respect and understanding. On the tangible level, the chips from the worker-and-community side are the workers' willingness to take paid vacation time all together during the same week in July, and an agreement by the community to consider a tax break if the inspection finds that the factory is not the source of the problem. The factory owner's chips include his willingness to close the factory for the inspection and to be flexible concerning the workers' vacation and work scheduling.

After analyzing the video, the participants divide into dyads to continue practicing the skills of identifying positions and needs and forming reframes, using a series of small cases. Through repetition, these drills pose the opportunity to try, err, and retry applying cognitive learning until learners thoroughly understand the skill. Mastery may or may not occur during the workshop. We hope that sufficient value and understanding are experienced so that the learning can continue to be practiced and applied in the participants' lives.

The participants then use a similar format (see Figure 24.3) as a planning tool for further conflict simulation. The planning process helps each party not only clarify its own side of the conflict but also begin to understand the other side better. We caution participants that identifying the other's positions, needs, etc. can only reveal party A's assumptions about Party B and vice versa, and that these assumptions must be tested during the upcoming negotiation. We also ask parties to think of all their chops, and the other's, in this planning process so they can prepare *not* to use or react to them negatively, which would nullify the attempt to be collaborative.

Module Three: Communication Behaviors

In an ideal collaborative negotiation, each side thoroughly communicates its perspective and arrives at understanding of the other side. In reality, the unique and particular worldviews of individuals and groups often make our interactions very complicated. Even though two people speak the same language and know each other well, they may feel that they don't really understand one another. Furthermore, conflict can exacerbate misunderstanding. When our buttons are pushed, our ability to communicate can become quite imprecise and problematic.

To develop collaborative skills and enhance understanding of the communication process, we introduce a second frame, which is grounded in a research tool known as behavioral analysis (Rackham, 1993; Situation Management Systems, 1991). We identify five communication behaviors that occur during negotiation:

1. Attacking
2. Evading
3. Informing
4. Opening
5. Uniting

The mnemonic for these behaviors is the familiar English-language vowel series *AEIOU*. These categories encompass nonverbal as well as verbal communications. We employ only these five types of communication behavior because they amount to an easily learned framework for understanding core communication behavior in conflict.

At the beginning of the module, the trainers present and role-play a two-line interchange. An example of a context-relevant miniskit frequently used with groups of managers is an employee reminding his boss about his upcoming vacation. Each time the interchange is repeated, the boss responds by demonstrating another behavior. The trainers elicit from the group a description of the kind of behavior they are observing. Then the trainers label the behavior:

- Attacking (*A*) includes any type of behavior perceived by the other side as hostile or unfriendly: threatening, insulting, blaming, criticizing without being helpful, patronizing, stereotyping, interrupting, and discounting others' ideas. It also includes nonverbal actions such as using a hostile tone of voice, facial expression, or gesture.

- Evading (*E*) occurs when one or both parties avoid facing any aspect of the problem. Hostile evasions include ignoring a question, changing the subject, not responding, leaving the scene, or failing to meet. Friendly or positive evasions include postponing difficult topics to deal with simple ones first, conferring with colleagues, and taking time out to think or obtain relevant information.

- Informing (*I*) includes behavior that, directly or indirectly, explains one side's perspective to the other in a nonattacking way. Information sharing can occur on many relevant levels: needs, feelings, values, positions, or justifications.

- Opening (*O*) invites the other party to share information. It includes asking questions about the other's position, needs, feelings, and values (nonjudgmentally); listening carefully to what the other is saying; and testing one's understanding by summarizing neutrally what is being said.

- Uniting (*U*) emphasizes the relationship between the disputants. This behavior sets and maintains the tone necessary for cooperation during the negotiation process. The four types of uniting behavior are (1) building rapport, (2) highlighting common ground, (3) reframing the conflict issues, and (4) linking bargaining chips to expressed needs.

After a presentation of *AEIOU,* the class returns to the small groups that were formed for the diagnostic case in module one. The participants listen to the audio (or video) of the case. Together they fill in an *AEIOU* coding form (see Table 24.1) by identifying each comment as an attacking, evading, informing, opening, or uniting behavior. Within their groups, each member receives very specific feedback on how his or her statements are perceived. The type of behavior is identified by its impact on the receiver rather than by the intent of the speaker.

Each group has its own insights and, as a result, is often motivated to try on new skills after people hear how they themselves sound. They also learn to give safe feedback by focusing on the impact the behavior has on them, rather than assuming the intent of the sender. Self-awareness is also heightened when a speaker finds that her actions have an unintended effect. This disparity gives her the opportunity to clarify or rectify her message. It also gives her a chance to think of how she generally comes across to others. It is clear from the debriefing of this exercise that the participants learn about the complexity of the communication process and its importance in maintaining a collaborative process.

We believe that for most trainees this experiential learning is necessary, beyond cognitive understanding, for behavioral changes to take place. Multiple

Table 24.1. Coleman Raider *AEIOU* Coding Sheet (abridged).

Negotiating Styles

Attack: threats, hostile tones or gestures, insults, criticizing, patronizing, stereo-typing, blaming, challenging, discounting, interrupting, defending

Evade: ignore, change subject, withdraw, postpone, table issue, caucus

Inform: reasons, justifications, positions, requests, needs, underlying positions, feelings

Open: listen quietly, probe, ask questions nonjudgmentally, listen actively, paraphrase, summarize understanding

Unite: ritual sharing, rapport building, establish common ground, reframe, propose solutions, dialogue or brainstorming

Source: Copyright © 1992, 1997 Ellen Raider International, Inc. Permission has been given for use in *The Handbook of Conflict Resolution.* Other use is prohibited without written permission of the copyright holder.

skills exercises combined with personal feedback motivate learners to produce the effort needed to change conflict-behavior habits (Raider, 1995). Learners often describe this part of the course as a life-changing event. But because we know how difficult it is to integrate these skills and change one's behavior, we surmise that continued learning may require a supportive postworkshop environment or heightened self-motivation. Empirical research into the long-term effect these workshops have on participants, in the context of supportive or resistive environments, would be very helpful.

Module Four: Stages of the Negotiation

Even though there is usually a back-and-forth flow to the negotiation process, it is useful to break it down into stages for training purposes. In module four we posit four stages:

1. Ritual sharing
2. Identifying the issues (positions and needs)
3. Prioritizing issues and reframing
4. Problem solving and reaching agreement

Although we present the stages linearly, we acknowledge that unless both parties want to be collaborative and are equally competent in collaborative skills, most real-life negotiations do not follow this simple pattern. However, this is not to say that they cannot.

The minilecture by the trainers starts this segment, using a video of a rehearsed "bare-bones" negotiation (see Figure 24.4): one in skeletal form that places each element and behavior in its ideal spot within the framework of the four stages.

Ritual sharing involves preliminary and often casual conversation to build rapport, establish common ground, and pick up critical background information (such as the other's values), which may affect the negotiation. Uniting behavior predominates during this stage.

Identifying the issues has two phases: identifying the positions that frame the conflict, and clarifying the needs that drive them. Informing and opening behaviors

Figure 24.4. Coleman Raider "Bare-Bones" Model.

Stage 1	Ritual sharing 1. Both A and B engage in *uniting* behavior.

Stage 2

Position 2. A states his position 　 flexibly. (*informing*)	Position 4. B states his position 　 flexibly. (*informing*)
Underlying needs 3. B probes for and 　 paraphrases A's 　 underlying needs. 　 (*opening*)	Underlying needs 5. A probes for and 　 paraphrases B's 　 underlying needs. 　 (*opening*)

Stage 3	Reframe 6. Either A or B asks, "How can we satisfy the priority 　 needs of sides A and B?" (*uniting*)
Stage 4	Problem solving 7. A and B brainstorm a number of possible alternative ways 　 (*chips*) to satisfy their needs. (*uniting*)
	Reaching agreement 8. A and B evaluate the alternatives, pick the best combination 　 for both sides, and summarize their agreement.

predominate during this phase, the first being used to tell where you are coming from, and the second to understand the other.

Prioritizing issues and reframing has two parts. Prioritization is needed if there is more than one key issue, and an order must be established (through a mininegotiation) for manageable problem solving. Reframing invites the parties to engage in creative problem solving around needs. It is characterized by a neutral and inclusive question, such as, "How can we satisfy the needs of A while also satisfying the needs of B?"

Problem solving and reaching agreement, the final stage, is characterized by brainstorming (using the informing, opening, and uniting behaviors) that facilitates fresh, novel solutions to the now-shared problem. Humorous and even apparently absurd ideas are encouraged because they increase open-mindedness and often inspire clever solutions. Uniting and opening behaviors are used to diffuse any perceived attacks, highlight common ground, and reiterate the objective: to find mutually satisfying solutions. The negotiators then choose from the brainstormed list those solutions that are feasible and timely and that optimize the satisfaction of each party's needs and concerns. Success depends, in part, on maintaining a continued collaborative, positive climate that encourages creativity.

The trainers present the stages as a linear progression, but real-life negotiations rarely flow so predictably. A good negotiator develops the ability to identify the essence of each stage to diagnose whether the essential tasks embedded within it have been accomplished, and to feel comfortable with the surface disorder. As certain needs are addressed, others may surface. Recognition and processing of all of these needs is necessary for a good and sustainable agreement.

After the stages have been covered, participants practice their own bare-bones negotiation. Trainers explain that this is more like a map of the territory than the territory itself. As with maps, we must make a mental leap from a symbolic portrayal to what is seen when navigating the real landscape. The more clearly the underlying structure and process of bare bones is embedded in our thinking, the more effectively we as negotiators can deal with the variations that occur in actuality.

The bare-bones framework is the most prescriptive in our training. Therefore, great caution has to be used by the training team to make sure that examples used to illustrate this module are context-relevant in form and substance, so that the model is seen as doable in various cultural contexts. The participants analyze conflict cases taken from their own lives and then present a skeletal and ritualized performance in front of the whole group (see Table 24.1). Each step is abbreviated, thus revealing whether the role players really understand the essence or bare bones of the conflict. The trainer coaches the role players and gives feedback at each point of the process. It is in this way that the role players and other participants begin to internalize all the previously learned material.

Module Five: Culture and Conflict

From its inception, our training model has woven the topic of culture throughout the process of teaching and learning negotiation skills. Our original audiences were made up of managers from multinational organizations eager to learn how to negotiate across borders. Building on the work of Weiss and Stripp (1985), Hofstede (1980), Ting-Toomey (1993), and others, we enabled trainees through readings, video clips such as "Going International, Part Two" (Griggs Productions, 1983), and role plays to understand and internalize cultural variables such as high or low power distance, high or low communication context, individualism or collectivism, uncertainty avoidance, and polychronic or monochronic time.

One role-play exercise has been particularly instructive and enjoyable for the participants. The group is divided into small groups of four. One pair from the foursome is instructed to create a fictitious cultural ritual based on the Hofstede dimensions. The other pair comes to the role play unaware that they are entering a "new culture" and, as a result, experiences a simulated form of culture shock as they interact with the classmates who have taken on different persona. The experience is videotaped and then reviewed by each foursome, with much laughter. The educational point is made that it is ideal to know the rules and norms of another culture and, at a minimum, to avoid negative judgments in order to have a successful negotiation.

Video clips and exercises like this are debriefed by using our "filter check model" (see Figure 24.5). For example, one of the video clips from "Going International, Part Two" shows a businessman from the United States (Mr. Thompson) waiting for his Mexican counterpart (Sr. Herrera) in an outdoor cafe in Mexico City. Mr. Thompson reacts negatively to the late arrival of Sr. Herrera (to whom he is trying to make a sale), apparently assuming the lateness is some form of disrespect or power play.

The video captures elegantly and with humor how monochronic and polychronic individuals can misunderstand each other. Sr. Herrera, the polychronic of the two, is late because he is greeting important people along the way. He also does not want to get down to business until he has gotten to know something about the man with whom he is doing business. Mr. Thompson, though, is driven by the task, always looking at his watch and pushing to get the contract signed—so *then* he can go out and have a good time!

By working through the filter-check chart, participants come to see that the misunderstanding displayed is based on cultural assumptions (filters) of the meaning of time, task, and relationships. Neither way is the right way; they are just different. Of course, it is noted that "when in Rome, do as the Romans do"; certainly so if you are in a lower power position, as a seller typically is relative to a buyer.

Figure 24.5. Coleman Raider Filter Check Model.

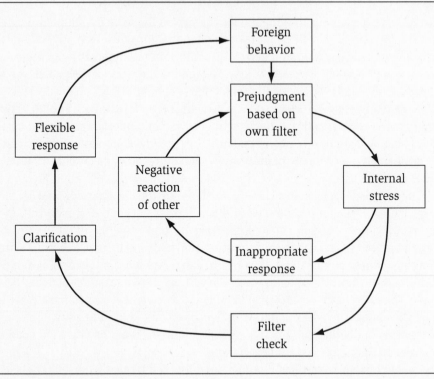

For audiences of educators, we use role-play simulations such as Melting Pot or Salad Bowl to surface issues of class, race, and gender. The disputants in this case are two groups: the Black Teachers Caucus (BTC) and the predominantly white school governance committee at an urban high school in New York City. (This case is based on a real conflict mediated by Raider; it is also discussed in the Introduction and Chapter One of this volume.) The BTC demands a black seat on the governance committee, claiming that the student population is predominantly "of color." The governance committee rejects this demand for a "race-based" seat, countering that representation should be by academic department, not by racial or ethnic identity group.

One way to use this case is to divide a group of four into sides A and B. In round one of the negotiation, each side presents its point of view while the other side tries hard to listen and paraphrase the underlying needs it is hearing. In round two, sides A and B switch and repeat the negotiation, following the model of academic controversy (Johnson and Johnson, 1987). This technique helps not only to move the conflict toward resolution but to get participants to realize how difficult it is to step into the shoes of the other side.

Module Six: Dealing with Anger and Other Emotions

To effectively work with emotions that arise during conflict, a negotiator must have good listening, communication, and problem-solving skills. This section outlines how these skills can be employed to direct emotions into a positive and productive component of the negotiation process. Anger is our main focus because it presents one of the biggest challenges to resolving conflict.

A Philosophy for Dealing with Anger. The philosophy we present to participants is that if someone blames you, states his position inflexibly, confronts you, or attacks you:

1. Avoid the defend-attack spiral and ethnocentric and egocentric responses. Assume that the other has a perspective different from yours and that you need to find out where he is coming from.

2. Listen actively. Your needs are more likely to be heard by the other if he knows through your active-listening behavior that you have understood his needs.

3. Continue to change the climate from competition to cooperation by acknowledging that there are differing perspectives at play, each with part of the truth.

4. Work with the other as a partner to solve the problem.

To build awareness on this topic, participants read an essay in the training manual covering such topics as the relationship of anger to unmet needs, anger as a secondary response that masks more vulnerable emotions, the attack-defend spiral, and additional destructive and constructive responses. Sometimes in the workshop participants form groups of four to discuss the essay. Members offer examples from their own lives, sharing situations in which they themselves were angry or were dealing with another person's anger.

Skills Practice. A key exercise we use in building skills in this area is a round-robin, with one side of each negotiation team working competitively and the other collaboratively. In the first round, the traveling partners are competitive. This means they can use attacking and evading behaviors to act angry, patronizing, and unfair. They are encouraged to make their attacks personal if possible. The stationary partners take on the role of skilled collaborative negotiators. They work to change the climate by using predominantly opening, and some uniting, behaviors to draw out the needs, feelings, and concerns of the others. This round lasts for ten minutes. The goal of the exercise is not to reach an agreement but simply to build readiness for negotiation by changing the climate. In the second round, all the traveling pairs rotate to the next table. The group reverses roles so that the stationary pair is now competitive and the traveling partners are collaborative. In the final round, the traveling pairs move to a third table, where a new foursome attempts to solve the conflict by having both sides use collaboration.

The whole group debriefs after each section so that the participants learn as they proceed. The rounds are often tape-recorded for review. The trainers guide the discussion with questions: "How did the emotions affect the process?" "Were the negotiators able to draw out emotions, unexpressed perspectives, and underlying needs?" "Were they able to create distance between the other's position and needs in their paraphrases?" and "What could they have done better?"

In this exercise, participants experience how difficult it can be to manage another's attacks, emotions, and blaming behavior. Many acquire the insight that people have little control over someone else's responses apart from developing their own collaborative skills. This is when they become "consciously incompetent"—beginning to know what they don't know. We consider this an important learning milestone because handling another's anger is a common motivating concern for participants coming to the workshop. This exercise further motivates them to develop their own skills of listening and "going to the balcony," or rising above the conflict to see it objectively from all perspectives (Ury, 1993).

Module Seven: Introduction to Mediation

In the Coleman Raider model, we often introduce a brief, one-hour overview of mediation in our three-day workshop. The longer version teaches mediation skills. Here we briefly discuss the longer program (see Figure 24.6).

The negotiation model already learned forms the framework for understanding mediation. We might move into the mediation segment of the program by asking participants to create a model for mediation based on what they already know about collaborative negotiation. This task is surprisingly simple as students realize how closely mediation is related to negotiation.

Participants are introduced to four stages of the mediation process (which almost parallel negotiation): (1) setting up the mediation, (2) identifying the issues, (3) facilitating informing, opening, and uniting behaviors and problem solving, and (4) brainstorming and reaching agreement. The vehicles used to practice these stages are skill practice and role playing, the latter constituting the bulk of the activity.

The role plays offer the participants the opportunity to practice everything learned in both the negotiation and mediation segments of the course. Each mediation stage is practiced in trios, rotating the role of mediator. In debriefing, the mediator receives feedback from the trainers and the disputants themselves—how they felt the mediator moved or blocked the process, and how

Figure 24.6. Coleman Raider Mediation Model.

Stage 1:
Set up the mediation
    1. Set up the room.
    2. Deliver an opening statement.

Stage 2:
Identify the issues
    1. Listen to each side, one at a time; probe
       for their priority underlying needs. (*opening*)
    2. Reframe. (*uniting*)
    3. Prioritize the issues.

Stage 3:
Facilitate IOU and problem solving
    1. Help them negotiate directly. (*informing, opening,*
       and *uniting*)
    2. Keep reframing. (*uniting*)
    3. Clear up assumptions. (*cultural issues*)
    4. Brainstorm alternative solutions. (*uniting*)

Stage 4:
Reach Agreement
    1. Have disputants confirm their understanding
       of their future commitments to each other.
    2. Write the agreement, if appropriate.
    3. Close the mediation.

specifically the mediator could have helped their role-play character. (For further discussion of mediation, see Chapter Twenty-Five.) Cases are either furnished by the trainers or elicited from the audience. In addition to small-group mediations, trainers may facilitate the role plays in the center of the room, fishbowl-style, with the class watching. Audio or videotape is often used in various ways and in any segment of the program.

    Throughout the program, trainers present numerous videos of experienced mediators, each with a distinctive style. These show differences in pacing, amount of questioning or silence, and a variety of techniques. The message we intend to impart is that there is no one right way to mediate. We present our model like training wheels on a bicycle: as soon as the learner-mediator grasps the process, he can begin to discover how to make it his own.

Relevant topics (such as caucusing, shuttle diplomacy, getting the parties to the table, organizational context, and culture) are discussed at intervals throughout the program. Prepared videos are used wherever available and relevant to elaborate on these topics and enrich the participants' learning.

CONCLUSION

In this chapter, we have tried to give the reader a sense of the theoretical underpinnings and pedagogical techniques used in our delivery of a conflict resolution training program. We have enumerated a number of insights, drawn from our years of practice, that inform our training designs. We have summarized the knowledge, skill, and attitude objectives we strive for in conducting the program. Finally, we have described in some detail the typical learning activities used in each module of the program.

It is our view that practitioners are a largely untapped resource for researchers in the field of conflict resolution. Practitioners intuitively know a great deal from years of experience. Researchers would do well to cull from trainers what they believe is true, and develop systematic methods to verify it. We at the International Center for Cooperation and Conflict Resolution, Teachers College, Columbia University, researchers and practitioners alike, are excited by the cross-pollination we have nurtured among us, but more is needed. Researchers and practitioners need to seek out opportunities where both can be useful to each other and to the clients they serve. Such a marriage may very well make the difference between a field that loses steam and one that forever changes the ways humans deal with their differences.

References

Griggs Productions. "Going International, Part Two." [Video]. 1983. (Available from Griggs Productions, Inc., 2046 Clement Street, San Francisco, CA 94121; 415/668–4200.)

Hofstede, G. *Culture's Consequences: International Differences in Work-Related Values.* Thousand Oaks, Calif.: Sage, 1980.

Johnson, D. W., and Johnson, R. T. *Creative Conflict.* Edina, Minn.: Interaction, 1987.

Rackham, N. "The Behavior of Successful Negotiators: Huthwaite Research Group, 1980." In R. J. Lewicki, J. A. Litterer, D. M. Saunders, and J. W. Minton (eds.), *Negotiation Readings, Exercises, and Cases.* Burr Ridge, Ill.: Irwin, 1993.

Raider, E. *A Guide to International Negotiation.* Brooklyn, N.Y.: Ellen Raider International, 1987.

Raider, E. "Conflict Resolution Training in Schools: Translating Theory into Applied Skills." In B. B. Bunker and J. Z. Rubin (eds.), *Conflict, Cooperation, and Justice: Essays Inspired by the Work of Morton Deutsch.* San Francisco: Jossey-Bass, 1995.

Raider, E., and Coleman, S. *Conflict Resolution: Strategies for Collaborative Problem Solving.* Brooklyn: Ellen Raider International and Coleman Group International, 1992.

Situation Management Systems. *Positive Negotiation Program.* (4th ed.) Hanover, Mass.: Situation Management Systems, 1991.

Ting-Toomey, S. "Managing Intercultural Conflict Effectively." In L. A. Samovar and R. E. Porter (eds.), *Intercultural Communication: A Reader.* (7th ed.) Belmont, Calif.: Wadsworth, 1993.

Ury, W. *Getting Past No.* New York: Bantam Books, 1993.

Weiss, S. E., and Stripp, W. "Negotiating with Foreign Businesspersons: An Introduction for Americans with Propositions on Six Cultures." Unpublished manuscript, International Business Department, Graduate School of Business Management, New York University, 1985.

CHAPTER TWENTY-FIVE

Mediation

Kenneth Kressel

Mediation may be defined as a process in which disputants attempt to resolve their differences with the assistance of an acceptable third party. The mediator's objectives are typically to help the parties search for a mutually acceptable solution to their conflict and to counter tendencies toward competitive win-lose strategies and objectives. Mediators are most commonly single individuals, but they also can be twosomes, threesomes, or even larger groups.

Although mediation is a pervasive and fundamental human activity—try to imagine family life devoid of parents' interceding in their children's squabbles—in the last two decades formal mediation has begun to play a role at all levels of society and in virtually every significant area of social conflict. Some of the most prominent examples are divorce mediation, peer mediation in the schools, community mediation, mediation of public-resource disputes, judicial mediation, mediation of disputes within organizations, and increasing visibility for mediation in international conflicts between and within nations.

THEORY AND RESEARCH

Use of mediation in its myriad forms far outstrips systematic research on the process. Nonetheless, with increased use has come widening understanding.

The research findings and evidence about mediation mentioned in this chapter are presented in greater detail in Carnevale and Pruitt (1992) and Kressel and Pruitt (1985, 1989).

Our knowledge of mediation as a social psychological process has three major sources: extrapolation from theories of conflict (for example, Deutsch, 1973; Fisher, Ury, and Patton, 1981), empirical research (for example, Kressel and Pruitt, 1989), and the in-depth "case wisdom" of practitioners (Kolb and Associates, 1994; Moore, 1996).

In this chapter, my primary goal is to give a concise account of what this collective literature has to tell us about the factors influencing use of mediation and what happens during the mediation process, particularly in terms of mediator behavior. I begin with what is known about the efficacy of mediation and the types of conflict for which it appears most (and least) effective.

The Efficacy of Mediation

The rise in mediation services over the last two decades has generally occurred in the context of offering disputing parties an alternative to traditional use of lawyers and the courts, particularly in disputes between divorcing parents, neighbors, and disputants who file in small-claims court. The proponents of mediation have argued that it should provide superior outcomes in settings such as these because it is based on a model of cooperative conflict, rather than the win-lose orientation of the adversarial legal system, and because it involves the parties directly and actively in searching for solutions to their differences rather than imposing a solution on them. This intensive participation, it is argued, should lead to psychological commitment to whatever agreements are reached, as well as to agreements that are enduring because they well reflect the needs and circumstances of the disputants. Much of the research on mediation has sought to evaluate whether these and other presumed advantages of mediation reliably occur. The results are generally favorable to mediation, but not unequivocally.

The most positive results are in terms of client satisfaction, settlement rates, and compliance with the agreements reached. On the order of 70–90 percent of disputing parties who have tried mediation say they were pleased with the process, would recommend it to a friend, think it should be available to others in similar circumstances, and things of this kind. Even for those who fail to reach agreement in mediation, the satisfaction rate is typically above 75 percent. These results compare favorably with public satisfaction with kindred services, such as use of attorneys (66 percent) and the role of the courts (40–50 percent).

Mediation also fares reasonably well in terms of its ability to produce a formal settlement agreement, with settlements occurring in the 40–70 percent range across a variety of settings, the median being about 60 percent. These may appear modest figures in contrast with the 90 percent settlement rate achieved by attorneys without recourse to judicial intervention, but it is important to remember that the settlement figures for mediation include many intractable cases in which attorneys have already tried and failed to produce settlement.

Evidence on the rate of compliance with mediated agreement is also generally favorable. For example, in small-claims disputes, compliance with mediated agreements has been reported at 81 percent of the cases, compared to 48 percent for those using traditional adjudication. Similar findings have been reported in management of disputes between divorcing parents.

Although there are occasional nonconfirmatory, contradictory findings, there is also evidence that compared to adjudication mediation produces more compromise and more equal sharing of resources; produces settlements more quickly; and is less costly, both to the parties and the courts that provide the service.

The most consistent negative evidence about mediation is that it typically has little power to alter long-standing, deeply entrenched negative patterns of relating. Results of this kind come from studies of neighborhood justice centers, divorce mediation, and international conflict. The evidence on mediation's effects also suffers from a number of methodological problems common to most new areas of inquiry, and it ignores almost entirely the types of informal mediation that occur outside of traditional legal settings, such as within families or friendship circles or among coworkers. On balance, however, it is clear from a large number of empirical studies that mediation is a helpful and satisfying procedure for many people in a variety of disputes.

Conditions for Effective Mediation

Mediation is not a magic bullet for resolving any and all conflicts. The accumulating evidence suggests that mediation is most apt to be successful in conflicts occupying a general middle range of difficulty. I have selected six factors from among those associated with decreased probability that mediation will produce agreement.

High Levels of Conflict. In empirical studies of mediation, a high level of conflict is the most consistent factor associated with mediator difficulty in helping the parties reach agreement. The measures of conflict intensity that correlate negatively with settlement include the severity of the prior conflict between the parties; a perception that the other is untrustworthy, unreasonable, angry, or impossible to communicate with; and the existence of strong ideological or cultural differences.

Low Motivation to Reach Agreement. In industrial mediation, mediator perceptions that the parties have low motivation to resolve the conflict have been found negatively associated with the probability of settlement; mediation of disputes between nation-states has been closely linked to what is referred to as a "hurting stalemate" (Touval and Zartman, 1989). There is evidence that divorce mediation tends to fail if one spouse has a high level of continuing psychological attachment to the partner or refuses to accept the decision to divorce.

Low Commitment to Mediation. It is a widespread conviction among experienced labor mediators that the chances for agreement are reduced if only one of the parties requests mediation services; empirical studies confirm this. The settlement rate is also lower if the chief negotiators are unenthusiastic about mediation or do not trust the mediator.

Shortage of Resources. Mediation is especially unlikely to succeed under conditions of resource scarcity, as studies of labor and divorce mediation have documented. Resource scarcity presumably limits the range of mutually acceptable solutions that can be found and may reduce the motivation of both the parties and the mediator to search for them.

Disputes Involving "Fundamental Principles." Several lines of evidence support the long-cherished notion of experienced mediators that disputes involving matters of "principle" are especially difficult to resolve. This has been documented for international disputes (when ideology is at stake), for labor mediation (when the dispute is about union recognition as opposed to wages), and in mediation of environmental conflict (where disputes about general policies are half as likely to be resolved compared to site-specific conflict).

Parties of Unequal Power. It is widely felt by practitioners that disputes in which one side is much more powerful than the other (more articulate, more self-confident, better able to withstand the economic and political consequences of a stalemate) are among the most difficult to mediate. The belief is given a measure of support from studies of the mediation of conflicts as disparate as those between warring states and between warring spouses.

It is important to note that mediation often succeeds in disputes with one or more of these characteristics. This is because the skillful mediator may be able to modify some of them in a favorable direction. It is also true that parties in such disputes may attain notable benefit from mediation even if they do not succeed in reaching an agreement: issues may be clarified, the opponent may be humanized, or partial agreement may be reached. Nonetheless, even in isolation, these factors are bound to present the mediator with serious challenges. Collectively, they suggest why the practice of mediation is so stressful and why mediator burnout is a well-recognized phenomenon.

Factors Determining Use of Mediation

Conceptually, mediation should be helpful in any conflict in which the basic framework for negotiation is present (Moore, 1996). The framework includes these elements:

- The parties can be identified.
- They are interdependent.

- They have the basic cognitive, interpersonal, and emotional capabilities to represent themselves.
- They have interests that are not entirely incompatible.
- They face alternatives to consensual agreement that are undesirable (for example, a costly trial).

Mediation is especially likely to prove useful whenever there are additional obstacles that would make unassisted negotiations likely to fail:

- Interpersonal barriers (intense negative feelings, a dysfunctional pattern of communicating)
- Substantive barriers (strong disagreement over the issues, perceived incompatibility of interests, serious differences about the "facts" or circumstances)
- Procedural barriers (existence of impasse, absence of a forum for negotiating)

Although many disputes meet these formal criteria, getting mediation started turns out to be something of a challenge. In interpersonal disputes of all kinds, one-third to two-thirds of those given the opportunity to use formal mediation decline it. It is also apparent that in work settings where informal mediation could be used (as by a manager), the would-be mediator declines to intervene, looks the other way, or chooses to employ power and authority rather than the skills of facilitation. Characteristics of the social environment, the disputing parties, and the potential mediator are among the variables that determine whether or not mediation occurs.

Characteristics of the Social Environment. Anthropologists have shown that in many nonindustrial societies the community is frequently unwilling to tolerate the disruption in social life that would be triggered by intense conflicts between clans having many cross-cutting kinship ties. In such cases, much social pressure may be brought to bear for the parties to mediate, and powerful community leaders are likely to be involved in making sure that mediation occurs and that the parties take it seriously.

There are, of course, notable instances in our own society in which mediation is socially mandated, as in labor laws that require mediation once bargaining has reached an impasse. Less formal but equally powerful mandates occur, as when a judge to a small-claims or divorce dispute "suggests" to the parties that they try mediation before proceeding to a judicial hearing. One of the important research findings is that such pressure does not appear to decrease the effectiveness of divorce, small claims, or neighborhood mediation.

In work settings, the environment may work for and against the use of mediation. Support for the process comes from, say, an organization's need to get work done by means of a task force comprising individuals or groups with equal standing and no common superior. Conflict frequently erupts in such a group and poses an opportunity for informal mediation for a manager with conflict resolution skills. On the other hand, although the modern organization is comfortable with the notion of conflict with its competitors, it is often much less disposed to acknowledge that conflict exists within the organization. Managers often behave accordingly, preferring conflict-avoidant strategies to mediation. They are inclined to bolster these approaches by defining conflicts as being rooted in the parties' personalities and thus not amenable to resolution.

Perceptions of the Disputants. A decision to mediate often depends on the parties' attitudes toward alternative means of attaining their objectives. Thus, a nation may choose to mediate when the human and financial costs of continuing conflict become too high; divorcing parents may mediate as a preferred alternative to the expense and unpredictability of relying entirely on lawyers and the court. In divorce mediation, a modicum of goodwill also appears helpful in making the commitment to mediate. Compared to nonmediating divorcing couples, those who choose mediation have a more positive view of their spouse, more optimism about the prospects for cooperating as parents, and greater willingness to accept responsibility for the marital breakup.

The choice of mediation may also hinge on whether a party perceives that the mediator has leverage with the adversary. Thus, industrial mediators report that management sometimes prefers a mediator with whom the union is very comfortable if they perceive that the union is being inflexible. In the sphere of international mediation, the classic illustration is Egypt's eagerness to have its 1974 dispute with Israel mediated by the United States because of its known affinities with and strong economic influence over Israel. Receptivity to mediation may also be a function of the justice orientation of the party; a disputant with a strong desire for revenge is likely to find mediation unappealing because of the wish to retaliate.

Characteristics of the Potential Mediator. The crucial distinction here is between *contractual* and *emergent* mediation. In contractual mediation, the mediator is an outsider with whom the parties contract for the specific purpose of helping them resolve their dispute. The contractual mediator's relationship with the parties usually ends when the mediation ends. Moore (1996) points out that this form of mediation is common in cultures with an independent judiciary that provides a model of fair procedures and use of third parties as impartial decision makers.

In emergent mediation, the parties and the mediator are part of a continuing relational set with enduring ties to one another. Emergent mediation is found in families, friendship groups, organizations of all kinds, and international relations. Emergent mediators often have a strong vested interest in the outcome of the dispute (for example, family stability), are usually willing and able to mobilize considerable social and other pressure toward resolving the conflict, and maintain ongoing ties to the parties after the mediation effort ends.

In the contractual case, getting mediation started is comparatively straightforward. All that is required is that the disputants (or a party such as the court that controls their interests) decide on mediation. In emergent mediation, by contrast, potential mediators may decline to serve even if the parties wish assistance, or the parties themselves may need to be persuaded to mediate. For these reasons, mediator characteristics are especially important in determining whether emergent mediation occurs.

Third parties may choose to mediate if important interests of their own are at stake. Thus, in organizational settings managers are willing to take on the mediational role if an important agreement between organizational task forces is being negotiated; in an international conflict, nation-states are willing to mediate to protect or extend their own spheres of influence. Whether in international politics or in communal affairs, powerful mediators with self-interested motives for mediating a conflict are more likely than less powerful ones to be able to convince (or oblige) the disputants to make use of their services.

There is also some evidence about variables that deter third parties from mediating. In organizational settings, mediation does not appear to be a popular choice among managers, despite some lip service to the contrary. Speculation about why this is so includes lack of training in mediational skills for managers and the perception that the informal mediational role is not generally valued in organizations or may not be highly visible to the would-be mediator's superiors. There is also evidence that third parties decline to mediate if they feel there is little likelihood of a win-win solution (little common ground) or if they are not concerned about whether the parties attain their aspirations.

Mediator Behavior

It is impossible to give a universally accurate account of what transpires in mediation since the process occurs across so many domains of conflict and since mediators often strive for quite contrasting goals, ranging from settling the substantive issues narrowly defined to accomplishing broad relational, psychological, or social objectives.

Despite these differences, researchers and reflective practitioners have captured certain regularities in mediator behavior. Most of the knowledge on this subject is derived from studying the contractual mediator operating in what may be loosely described as a problem-solving model, oriented to ending a dispute with legal or quasi-legal overtones, as in a labor conflict or divorce.

In describing mediator behavior, I use a typology that I first developed while studying experienced labor mediators. With modifications, the typology has also been used to describe other forms of mediation (Kressel, 1972, 1985; Kressel and Deutsch, 1977; Kressel and Pruitt, 1985; Carnevale, Lim, and McLaughlin, 1989). It divides mediator behavior into *reflexive, contextual, and substantive* strategies. Mediator behavior also varies in the degree of *assertiveness,* a dimension that cuts across these three categories. Here I am not attempting a comprehensive catalogue in each area but rather trying to convey the overall flavor. The reader wishing detailed accounts may consult the works cited in this paragraph.

Before proceeding, I want to make two preliminary observations that may be helpful. First, any categorizing schema of mediator behavior is an obvious over-simplification. Mediation is a fluid, multifaceted activity in which the same act may serve several purposes. Second, it is commonplace among practitioners that successful mediation is a structured activity proceeding in distinctive stages, with various mediator behaviors predominating in each stage. Empirical evidence supports this general proposition, although the precise number and characteristics of such stages may vary considerably, depending on the nature of the parties involved, the complexity of the conflict, and the skills of the mediator. Thus, Figure 25.1 presents Moore's twelve-stage model (1996) for professional mediators dealing with complex conflicts, while Exhibit 25.1 (Deutsch and Brickman, 1994) presents a simpler stage model for students, parents, or other nonprofessionals to use in mediating simple conflicts.

Reflexive Interventions. By reflexive intervention, I refer to mediators' efforts to orient themselves to the dispute and to establish the groundwork on which later activities will be built. Of necessity, they are of primary importance early in mediation, although they occur throughout. Establishing rapport and diagnosis are the most important of the reflexive strategies.

Absent rapport with the parties, mediators can hope to accomplish little. Among the many things mediators can do to establish rapport, we may include giving a convincing and credible introduction to the mediation process and the role of the mediator, conveying sincere concern about the dispute, showing empathic understanding of each side, and behaving evenhandedly. Although rapport building is a central tenet of the practitioner community, it does not receive wide attention from researchers. Such strategies are associated with favorable outcomes in studies of labor mediation and mediation of interpersonal disputes in a community justice center.

Maintaining neutrality toward the parties and impartiality about the issues is often invoked as the sine qua non of rapport building and effective mediation generally, but as we have seen, many mediators (especially those of the emergent variety) hold decided preferences and biases and are often selected by the parties for precisely this reason. Perhaps more crucial than neutrality and impartiality is

Figure 25.1. Twelve Stages of Mediator Moves.

Stage 1: Establishing relationship with the disputing parties
• Make initial contacts with the parties
• Build credibility
• Promote rapport
• Educate the parties about the process
• Increase commitment to the procedure

Stage 2: Selecting a strategy to guide mediation
• Assist the parties to assess various approaches
  to conflict management and resolution
• Assist the parties in selecting an approach
• Coordinate the approaches of the parties

Stage 3: Collecting and analyzing background information
• Collect and analyze relevant data about the people,
  dynamics, and substance of a conflict
• Verify accuracy of data
• Minimize the impact of inaccurate or unavailable data

Stage 4: Designing a detailed plan for mediation
• Identify strategies and consequent noncontingent moves that
  enable the parties to move toward agreement
• Identify contingent moves to respond to situations peculiar
  to the specific conflict

Stage 5: Building trust and cooperation
• Prepare disputants psychologically to participate in
  negotiations on substantive issues
• Handle strong emotions
• Check perceptions and minimize effects of stereotypes
• Build recognition of the legitimacy of the parties and issues
• Build trust
• Clarify communications

Stage 6: Beginning the mediation session
• Open negotiation between the parties
• Establish an open and positive tone
• Establish ground rules and behavioral guidelines
• Assist the parties in venting emotions
• Delimit topic areas and issues for discussion
• Assist the parties in exploring commitments, salience,
  and influence

Source: C. W. Moore, *The Mediation Process,* 2nd ed. San Francisco: Jossey-Bass, 1996, pp. 66–67.
Reprinted by permission.

Stage 7: Defining issues and setting an agenda
- Identify broad topic areas of concern to the parties
- Obtain agreement on the issues to be discussed
- Determine the sequence for handling the issues

Stage 8: Uncovering hidden interests of the disputing parties
- Identify the substantive, procedural, and psychological interests of the parties
- Educate the parties about each other's interests

Stage 9: Generating options for settlement
- Develop an awareness among the parties of the need for multiple options
- Lower commitment to positions or sole alternatives
- Generate options using either positional or interest-based bargaining

Stage 10: Assessing options for settlement
- Review the interests of the parties
- Assess how interests can be met by available options
- Assess the costs and benefits of selecting options

Stage 11: Final bargaining
- Reach agreement through incremental convergence of positions, final leaps to package settlements, development of a consensual approach, or establishment of procedural means to reach substantive agreement

Stage 12: Achieving formal settlement
- Identify procedural steps to operationalize the agreement
- Establish an evaluation-and-monitoring procedure
- Formalize the settlement and create an enforcement-and-commitment mechanism

Exhibit 25.1. A Mediation Outline for Parents.

I. Introduction
   1. Get the quarreling children's or adolescents' attention.
   2. Ask them if they want help in solving their problem.
   3. If they do, move to a "quiet area" to talk.
   4. Explain and get their agreement to four rules:
      • Agree to solve the problem.
      • Do not use name calling.
      • Do not interrupt.
      • Be as honest as possible.

II. Listening
   5. Decide which child will speak first.
   6. Ask Child #1 what happened, how he or she feels, and his or her reasons.
   7. Repeat what Child #1 said so that Child #2 can understand.
   8. Ask Child #2 what happened, how he or she feels, and his or her reasons.
   9. Repeat what Child #2 said so that Child #1 can understand.

III. Solution
   10. Ask Child #1 what he or she can do here and now.
   11. Ask Child #2 what he or she can do here and now.
   12. Ask Child #1 what he or she can do differently in the future if the same problem arises.
   13. Ask Child #2 what he or she can do differently in the future if the same problem arises.
   14. Help the children agree on a solution they both think is fair.

IV. Wrap up
   15. Put the agreement in writing, read agreement out loud if necessary, and have both sign it.
   16. Congratulate them both.

Source: Deutsch, M. and Brickman, E. "Conflict Resolution." *Pediatrics in Review*, 1994, p. 21. Reprinted by permission.

mediator *acceptability,* the route to which appears to be through rapport-building activities.

Before they can intervene effectively, mediators must also educate themselves about the dispute and the disputing parties. Among the diagnostic tasks we may count deciding—with the parties' input—whether or not mediation is an appropriate and mutually acceptable forum (in a case of extreme power imbalance or where there is a history of violence and intimidation, it may not be), separating the manifest from the latent (and more genuine) issues, identifying the real leaders and power brokers (in complex, multiparty disputes), and understanding the relationship dynamics between the parties. Among the mediator's common diagnostic tactics are use of sustained interrogatories (often in conjunction with separate caucuses with each side, where "sensitive" questions can be asked easily) and keen observation of the parties' behavior in joint sessions.

Contextual Interventions. Contextual interventions refer to the mediator's attempts to produce a climate conducive to constructive dialogue and problem solving. This class of strategy embodies the traditional view that a mediator ought to be a catalyst and facilitator, not an arm-twister or proponent of a specific solution. Among the contextual strategies, we may include improving communications, establishing norms for respectful listening and language, managing anger constructively, maintaining the privacy of negotiations, educating the parties about the negotiating process, and establishing mutually acceptable procedures for fact finding. There is evidence that many of these behaviors, especially those associated with improving communication flow, are associated with favorable mediation outcome.

Structural intervention, such as deciding who should be present at negotiation sessions and conducting separate meetings with the parties (caucusing), may also be used as a method of "climate control." Using the caucus is both common and somewhat controversial. The majority of practitioners see caucusing as an essential mediation tool for managing intense emotions, getting at sensitive information, and overcoming impasse. But some mediators avoid the caucus on the grounds that it fosters distrust between the parties, places an undue burden on the mediator for maintaining confidentiality, and engenders secrecy and scheming. Research on mediation of interpersonal disputes in a community justice center (Pruitt, McGillicuddy, Welton, and Fry, 1989) documents that mediators spent approximately one-third of their time in caucus and tended to do so when hostility was high and positions rigid. Although the caucus was used by many disputants as an occasion to bad-mouth the other side to the mediator, the results were a strong decline in direct hostility between the parties and an increase in problem-solving activity. More equivocal results for the caucus have been reported in labor mediation under particularly unfavorable conditions (unmotivated parties, large positional differences, and high hostility), where mediators sometimes fared better by eschewing the caucus altogether.

Substantive Interventions. Substantive interventions refer to tactics by which the mediator deals directly with the issues in dispute. All mediators are obliged to deal with the issues in some way, although some philosophies of the mediator's role deemphasize a substantive, problem-solving focus in favor of relational objectives, such as increased understanding of self and other (Bush and Folger, 1994). Competence at formulating an overarching *strategic direction* for the negotiations—a flexible plan for reaching agreement informed by a sound understanding of each party's interests, constraints, and limitations—is considered a central cognitive ability for the mediator in models that emphasize a problem-solving focus (Honoroff, Matz, and O'Connor, 1990). Certain contexts appear to promote a substantive focus for the mediator. This appears to be the case for mediators who work directly in the shadow of the law, such as divorce mediators or judges who elect to play a mediational role as part of pretrial conferencing.

Research on mediator behavior suggests three distinct but overlapping substantive domains for mediator activity: issue identification and agenda setting, proposal shaping, and proposal making. Mediator interventions in all of these domains have been associated with favorable mediation outcomes, although the pattern is not always uniform.

There is also increasing awareness of the importance of substantive activities aimed at increasing the probability that agreements reached in mediation are implemented and complied with. The risk of noncompliance may rise with increasing number and complexity of the issues, the number of parties involved, the level of tension and distrust between the disputants, the strength and number of internal factions within each party whose cooperation is needed to implement the agreement, and the length of time during which the obligations set forth in the agreement must be performed (Moore, 1996). Among the important substantive activities of the mediator in this final stage of agreement implementation, we may include assistance in selling the agreement to various constituencies, help in developing criteria and procedures for monitoring and evaluating compliance, procedures for dealing with intentional or unwitting noncompliance, encouraging a return to mediation if disagreements arise during the implementation stage, and preparing the parties to maintain their agreements in the face of opposition and resistance from extremist factions (Coleman and Deutsch, 1995).

Assertiveness. Assertiveness refers to how forcefully the mediator behaves in the reflexive, contextual, or substantive domain. It describes a continuum ranging from mild and nondirective at one end to forceful and highly directive at the other. Assertive behavior is most common in the substantive domain. Mediators frequently engage in arm-twisting to persuade reluctant parties to accept particular agreements, particularly during the later phases of mediation. Reflexive and contextual activities are not generally insistent, but even here mediators can act forcefully to overcome obstacles. Thus, judicious diagnostic questioning can yield to demanding and pointed interrogatories if the mediator suspects dishonesty or concealment; interventions aimed at improving the flow of communications and fostering mutual understanding can become stern and confrontational if one or both parties persist abrasively or provocatively.

Although the practitioner literature conveys a decidedly ambivalent attitude about behaviors at the assertive end of the spectrum, it is clear that pressure tactics are commonly used, especially if the dispute involves very high levels of tension and hostility, if a mediator's own interests or values are at stake, if the mediator is under strong institutional pressure to avoid the costs of adjudication, or if the mediator wields power over the disputants (a far-from-rare occurrence in some settings, as with judicial mediators). It is also clear from the research literature and more than a few case studies that assertive and even downright heavy-handed and coercive mediator tactics are often effective in producing settlements, particularly if conflict is intense and positions badly polarized. What is not yet clear are the long-term effects of exercising such pressure, particularly on compliance and future willingness to use mediation.

Mediator Style

Although most empirical studies of mediator behavior have focused on discrete intervention of the kinds just summarized, it is clear that mediators also have distinctive stylistic leanings. Mediator style refers to a cohesive set of strategies that characterize the conduct of a case. There is evidence that mediators are often unaware of their stylistic inclinations, even though they tend to enact the same style from case to case, despite variety in issues and dynamics.

Most stylistic accounts portray the mediator acting in either a *task-oriented* or a *socioemotional* style. The task-oriented style gives priority to active grappling with the issues in the form of shaping and making proposals and liberal use of pressure tactics. The style is often combined with skepticism about the parties' ability to deal with each other and a corresponding sense that the mediator needs to do the lion's share of the work, often through caucusing. The task-oriented approach frequently characterizes mediation of highly polarized disputes in which the costs of unabated conflict are onerous or where the time available for mediation is limited.

Within the broad task-oriented category there appear to be stylistic subtypes. (This may be true for the socioemotional style as well.) My colleagues and I have identified two contrasting approaches to court-annexed divorce mediation, both of which are of the task-oriented variety, but they work on quite different implicit assumptions about the goal of mediation and the role of the mediator (Kressel and others, 1994).

The first subtype, the so-called settlement-oriented mediator, is primarily interested in reaching agreement on any terms acceptable to the parties, attaches great salience to maintaining neutrality, and acts in a manner that suggests that the primary responsibility for problem solving rests with the parties. By contrast, a mediator enacting what is called the problem-solving subtype attaches greater importance to sound problem solving than to settlement per se, subordinates neutrality to the task of correctly identifying the relevant sources of the conflict, and acts in a manner suggesting that leadership of the problem-solving effort rests with the mediator rather than the parties. Both settlement-oriented and problem-solving substyles are able to resolve disputes in a relatively low-level conflict, but the problem-solving style tends to produce structured and thorough problem solving, frequent and durable settlements (especially with high-conflict cases), and favorable attitudes toward the mediation experience.

In contrast to task-oriented styles, socioemotional styles focus less on the issues and more on opening lines of communication and clarifying underlying feelings and perceptions. Mediators with this orientation tend to be optimistic about the parties' ability to manage their own affairs and emphasize the need of the parties to work through to their own solution. The orientation is ordinarily combined with interest in improving the parties' long-term relationship.

Transformational mediation, as proposed by Bush and Folger (1994), is perhaps the best articulated, and certainly the most popular, of the socioemotional approaches to the mediation role. The transformational mediator's allegiance is to the twin objectives of empowerment and recognition. Empowerment refers to strengthening each party's ability to analyze its respective needs in the conflict and to make effective decisions; recognition refers to improving the capacity of the disputants to become responsive to the needs and perspectives of the other (Folger and Bush, 1996). The approach is avowedly critical of mediator activities to produce settlement, direct problem solving, or substitute mediator judgment or analysis for that of the parties. All of these activities are felt to narrow the parties' opportunity for self-reflection, mutual recognition, and enhancement of autonomy.

The unique virtues claimed for the transformative approach may be more apparent than real, however. For example, the ten "hallmarks" of transformative mediation outlined by Folger and Bush (1996) are, in many ways, remarkably consistent with the mediator attitudes and behavior characteristic of the problem-solving style of divorce mediation and other well-grounded variants of the task orientation. The hallmarks include leaving responsibility for the outcome with the parties, remaining nonjudgmental about the parties' views and decisions, taking an optimistic view of the parties' competence and motives, and allowing for and exploring the parties' uncertainty. Polemical claims notwithstanding, there is no empirical evidence for preferring one mediation style over another. Comparative studies, pitting well-defined stylistic models against each other in disputes with well-delineated characteristics, have yet to be conducted.

IMPLICATIONS FOR UNDERSTANDING
AND MANAGING CONFLICT

I divide my thoughts on the practical meaning of our knowledge about mediation into two segments: the relevance of this knowledge for the user (or would-be user) of mediation, and its relevance for the mediation practitioner.

Implications for the Mediation User

Although mediation has become more familiar in recent years, this chapter reviews evidence that its use is often hindered by ignorance, resistance, and a lack of social support. Embroiled parties and the individuals with formal or informal authority over them can do a number of things to offset these tendencies.

Encourage Use of Mediation. Whereas research indicates that mediation is effective in many conflicts, parties are often reluctant to try it because they are unfamiliar with the process and distrustful of their adversary. For this reason, exercising tactful but firm pressure on antagonists to try mediation is often extremely helpful. Those in a position to exercise such pressure can take comfort from the evidence that it has not been found damaging to the mediation process, so long as the parties retain the right to withdraw from mediation at any time.

A more pervasive issue is the unavailability of mediation in many settings, particularly in the workplace. There are at least two things that people with organizational authority can do in this regard. The first is to promote establishment of formal mediation services. Typical settings for such services are as part of a human resource department or ombuds office, but other creative locations can be found (in one university, a faculty development center became the locus for informal mediation of faculty disputes). Such services need to be careful to respect confidentiality and privacy, and the employee mediators need assurances that their work is valued.

A second way to foster use of mediation in the workplace is to give managers mediation training. Such education can be useful in helping them make informed and appropriate referrals to mediation. Mediation training can also empower managers and other emergent mediators to intervene directly in conflict between subordinates in new and productive ways. Although managers often fear to mediate the conflicts of their subordinates on the grounds that they are not "neutral," it is clear that neutrality is not a sine qua non for effective mediation. More important is acceptability built on rapport and the mediator's evenhandedness. These qualities depend on skills and attitudes basic to all good human interaction: active listening, patient inquiry, respect for differences, skepticism about win-lose solutions, and avoidance of premature closure whenever complex issues and feelings are involved. People taught such skills and attitudes as part of a mediation training program often report general improvement in their interactions with others, quite apart from their usefulness in mediation proper.

Be Prepared to Participate. Voluntarily seeking or accepting referral to mediation is almost always a sensible thing to do in any conflict. Disputants should enter mediation willing to suspend distrust and competitive stratagems at least long enough to give the process a chance. It is also important to keep in mind that active participation in the mediation process is likely to produce benefits even if a comprehensive settlement is not reached. Benefits include such things as gaining a clearer perspective on your interests and objectives as well as those of the other, making progress toward agreement on some issues, and the satisfaction of knowing that a thorough and sincere effort to work collaboratively has been made. In addition, parties who have made a good-faith initial effort at mediation often return to the process later in the trajectory of their dispute, with positive results.

For managers or others with authority over the disputants, active participation in the mediation process can mean a number of things. Making appropriate referrals is one. Disputants who are given an enthusiastic, informed referral are likely to derive greater benefit than those referred to mediation in a less knowledgeable or lukewarm way or by mangers using mediation as a dumping ground for conflicts they do not wish to deal with. Authoritative third parties should also be receptive to participating directly in the mediation process if invited to do so, since many conflicts are a reflection of broad dynamics that the parties alone may have limited ability to influence. Managers and similar authorities often have knowledge or resources that can greatly expand the opportunities for creative problem solving in such circumstances. The failure of mediation in organizational settings is often an indicator that the focal conflict was only a symptom of wider group or organizational problems. In some "failed" mediations of this type, the parties and the mediator may have important information on these matters, and disputants sometimes authorize a "mediator report" on the subject. Encourage this where possible—and take such reports seriously.

Accept a Broad Definition of the Mediation Role. Mediation comes in a great range of strategies and styles, and all appear useful under some circumstances. This fact contrasts with the mythic belief—strangely persistent, even among many mediators—that a proper mediator must be neutral, nondirective, and impartial. From the evidence at hand, strong departures from this mythic ideal are not only common but particularly needed in highly polarized conflicts. The consumer of mediation services needs to be aware of this pluralistic world of practice and be prepared to evaluate proffered mediation services accordingly. The important thing in judging the suitability of a given mediator—and we are always talking about that, not some abstract process—is to be able to give positive answers to some basic questions: Does the mediator communicate a reasonable definition of his or her role? appear evenhanded? make you feel safe? understood? free to make your own decisions?

Implications for the Practitioner

Mediation is an inordinately stressful social role. Mediators work under conditions that are often emotionally unpleasant, and they typically work in isolation. The role also contains contradictory and ill-defined elements and is often poorly understood by disputants and referral sources alike. (Detailed discussion of the nature and consequences of role stress for the mediator may be found in Kressel, 1985; and Kolb and Associates, 1994). Mediator stress is further compounded by the lack of proven theory on many central issues of professional behavior. Three practical implications for avoiding mediator burnout can be drawn: maintain realistic expectations, develop awareness of your own role and stylistic preferences, and become a reflective practitioner.

Maintain Realistic Expectations. Like the participants in mediation, the mediator too should have realistic expectations for success. Since so much depends on the motivation and circumstances of the parties, do not expect every case to settle; as many as one-third or more do not, regardless of your best efforts. Settlement mania is an unfortunate occupational hazard among mediators, who need to bear in mind that disputants often derive benefits from mediation independent of their ability to reach agreement, and that parties leaving mediation without an agreement but with a good feeling about the process and the mediator often return at a later point when their motivation and circumstances are more suitable to using the process effectively.

Know Your Own Style and Role Preferences. Mediator activity is driven by strong, if sometimes unarticulated, ideas about how the mediation role should be enacted. There is evidence that some of these role interpretations may be superior to others for certain types of conflict, but our knowledge about these matters is sketchy. It is important that mediators become aware of their own role predilections. A mediator without this kind of self-awareness may be particularly vulnerable to unrealistic expectations for success and to social pressure from referral sources and others to produce settlements. Being clear about your own vision of the role also helps you give the parties appropriate expectations of what mediation requires of them—a crucial matter since disputants often enter the process with notions that are either vague or unacceptable (to you) of what will happen. For example, my colleagues and I tried to be clear with the divorcing couples referred to us by the family court that we saw our primary role as helping orchestrate a good problem-solving process, more or less independent of the goal of settlement (the problem-solving style discussed earlier). We did our best to socialize the parties to this version of the mediation role, but if they had other motives from which they could not be dissuaded (to reach a speedy agreement, or to give cover to a behind-the-scenes deal, or to extract revenge or expiate guilt), we learned to tactfully refer the case back to the attorneys and the court.

Become a Reflective Practitioner. Although not every case can reach resolution, every case can be an occasion for reflective learning. A reflective practitioner can also make an important contribution to conflict theory since practitioners often have much intuitive wisdom about the dynamics of conflict that inform their strategic choices. Cultivating habits of systematic reflection can make these intuitions explicit and available for systematic verification.

Reflective learning can be done in many ways, but a number of suggestions may be helpful (a detailed account of these ideas is found in Kressel, 1997). First, *be systematic.* Try to think reflectively after every session where possible, or certainly at the conclusion of mediation. Reflection can be made systematic with the help of even very simple debriefing protocols. Among the items that such a protocol might include are questions about the characteristics of the parties or their circumstances that appeared to facilitate or inhibit the mediation process, and interventions or strategies that were particularly helpful or unhelpful. Much of what occurs in mediation is relatively familiar and uneventful. Periodically, however, puzzling, unanticipated, vexatious, or transforming episodes occur for which training and prior experience provide no ready answers. These "indeterminate zones of practice" (Schön, 1983) represent the greatest challenge to professional competence. Reflective case study protocols can be tailored to help identify and understand them.

Second, *reflect with others.* Interaction with others can enrich reflective learning; indeed, it may be a precondition for it. A reflective partner or team can also serve as at least a provisional check on wishful or incomplete thinking and extend emotional as well as intellectual support. There are many ways to structure the interaction with teammates. Ideally, team meetings should be regular and give each member of the team an equal opportunity to debrief using the same reflective protocol to organize dialogue. A useful approach is to build the dialogue around persistent questioning of each other's tactical choices. The best interrogatory moments are those in which the team is able to simultaneously convey a supportive stance toward the mediator whose case is being discussed, while pushing for articulation of hidden hunches about the conflict or the mediation role that produced the intervention being scrutinized. A typical series of queries might ask: "Why did you do (or not do) X?" "What were you thinking when you did X?" "Can you say more about the cues in the situation that led you to do that?" "Why didn't you do Y or Z?"

Interestingly, team discourse of this kind relies on the same sort of skill that mediation requires: empathy, persistent questioning, attentive listening, curiosity about underlying ideas, and willingness to tactfully challenge positions. In this sense, a reflective team can help develop an explicit understanding of mediation theories-in-action, while simultaneously presenting an opportunity to practice the interpersonal skills needed in mediation.

The third suggestion is to *formulate and test reflective hypotheses.* No reflective method is immune to subjective bias or distortion, but the insights of reflection can be subject to a crude but useful verification procedure. The approach is essentially this: first, establish a reflective hypothesis based on observed similarities over a number of sessions or cases; second, at the next appropriate occasion, use the hypothesis to fashion a relevant mediation strategy; third, evaluate the consequences of the intervention strategy. Did it make sense to the parties? reduce tensions? lead to creative problem solving?

My colleagues and I used this procedure to identify the central role of mediator question asking in divorce mediation. We noticed that even though we experienced a strong press to control conflict by using exhortations and advice, they appeared far less useful than persistent and focused queries on topics directly related to the focal conflict. A mediation strategy was formulated reflecting this possibility ("In the next session, try to avoid exhortations and suggestions. Instead, ask as many open-ended, relevant questions as you can think of") and its effects observed. Several things became apparent. Asking good questions was easier said than done, there were distinctive types of question that were useful for different purposes, and question asking was indeed a powerful vehicle for reducing tensions and moving the parties toward problem solving. Here again, the team discourse reinforced skills needed in mediation itself. In both contexts, it is important to develop hypotheses about underlying phenomena by persistent questioning, and to devise strategies to test them.

IMPLICATIONS FOR TRAINING

The ability to effectively manage conflict may well be considered one of the basic characteristics of the truly educated person. Training in mediation is an important subset of this ability. There is evidence that such training may profitably begin as early as the elementary school years. Ironically, although there is an extensive cottage industry in mediation skills training, much of it is geared to preparing contractual mediators to handle formalized conflict of the kind that typically ends up in court. Relatively speaking, training in generic mediation skills for the nonspecialist has been left to languish. This is doubly unfortunate, since conflict in the workplace, school, home, and community is ubiquitous and would often respond well to mediation—if only there were a mediator prepared to handle it! Several implications for training the nonspecialist in mediation may be derived from the material presented in this chapter.

Train Leadership

The most effective way to multiply the benefits of mediation training is to offer the training first and foremost to the leaders of a group or organization. Leaders who understand the mediation process can make effective and meaningful referrals to mediation within the organization, can stimulate others within the organization to acquire and use such training, and are likely to turn to mediation in the event that serious conflict arises. In addition, leaders often need the skills of mediation as much as others in an organization or group, if not more, because the power and authority that leaders possess often leads them away from collaborative modes of influence for resolving their differences with others. Mediation training can, in theory, reduce this tendency. In sum, organizations wishing to convey to the rank and file their serious commitment to collaborative conflict management can send no clearer message than to train their leaders.

Teach a Hierarchy of Mediation Concepts and Skills

We are still far from a complete understanding of which mediator activities and styles are most appropriate under which conditions of conflict, but for training purposes it is obviously useful to distinguish between two broad classes of intervention: foundational and higher-order activities. Foundational activities are the reflexive and contextual interventions by which mediators establish rapport and provide a meaningful negotiating structure within a collaborative (rather than adversarial) set of norms. Skill in active listening and the ability to gather information about the dispute and the parties' perspectives on it are the most salient foundational activities. Foundational activities also rest on mastery of certain basic concepts, such as the importance of distinguishing interests from positions and the primacy of situational forces rather than personality attributes in fostering destructive conflict. The higher-order activities are substantive and assertive behaviors by which mediators interject themselves forcefully into a conflict and play an active role in the problem-solving process, including imparting strategic direction to negotiations and shaping the substantive proposals.

Although the more vigorous higher-order activities are often necessary in an intensely polarized dispute, the foundational skills and concepts are often sufficient to produce a collaborative orientation in the low-to-moderate-intensity conflict that permeates organizational and group life. They also have broad general utility for trainees, quite apart from their usefulness in mediation. For these reasons, the foundational skills should be emphasized in mediation training programs where training time is limited, as is especially likely if the trainees are organizational or community leaders.

Create a Supportive Environment for Reflective Learning

Learning the skills of mediation, including the foundational skills, requires direct practice and active learning through role play and simulation. These are often done to greatest collective profit in a fishbowl setting, where the entire group can share the same experience and compare ideas and reactions. Practicing skills in front of others also duplicates some of the tension associated with actual practice; for this reason it is often highly valued by trainees for its verisimilitude. However, such a context also stirs anxiety and evaluation apprehension, which can be inimical to skill development and inhibit a reflective stance toward the learning experience. There are many ways to conduct experiential learning to produce a supportive and reflective learning environment. A four-stage schema for debriefing mediation role play has proved useful in this regard, and I describe it here for illustrative purposes.

Reflective debriefing of a role play begins with a *"ventilation" stage*, during which the person who has been the mediator is encouraged to describe immediate feelings and impressions associated with the role play. The trainee is instructed to emphasize spontaneity ("here and now" feelings) and to deemphasize cerebral analysis. It is meant partly to be cathartic and partly to begin the reflective process. The other trainees are encouraged to respond to the target person by exercising empathic listening skills; they are also instructed to avoid critical evaluation or advice giving.

There then follows a stage of *supportive feedback,* during which members of the training group are asked to praise the mediator for things that were done well during the role play, with the injunction to be as specific and concrete in their remarks as possible (not "You were calm" but "When one of the parties challenged your lack of experience as a mediator, you answered nondefensively and reasonably").

Once all supportive feedback has been given, a third, *reflective, stage* begins. The target person is instructed to describe any source of puzzlement, frustration, or surprise that occurred during the role play. Once again, the other trainees are required to respond in an empathic, nonevaluative manner. They are also encouraged to ask questions that may help clarify the underlying issues raised, and to offer suggestions to the mediator role player on strategies for handling them.

A final, *implementation, stage* follows, with a return to the role play and an attempt to make use of any lessons learned from the reflective debriefing. Throughout the process, the trainer (1) ensures that trainees adhere to the debriefing procedures and (2) models appropriate behavior and attitude.

CONCLUSION

The empirical and practitioner literatures of more than two decades make clear that mediation is an important and useful instrument for managing many forms of social and interpersonal conflict. Mediation is of documented value for conflicts occupying a broad middle range of difficulty, but for highly polarized disputes as well it can bring distinctive benefits even if settlement is not reached. They include reducing tension, clarifying issues, and humanizing the adversary. Research and practice have also identified the structured, if never precisely predictable, stages that constitute the mediation process and the skills, attitudes, and behaviors characterizing the mediator's art. Certain of these skills and attributes (such as the ability to establish rapport with angry parties, gather information through sustained questioning, listen actively and empathetically to contending points of view, suspend judgment, and foster norms of collaboration) would seem of such demonstrable value that training in mediation can well be justified as part of the learning experience of the well-educated person.

My review also suggests some intriguing ironies. Thus, even though mediation is an empirically validated process, getting disputants to use it often amounts to a hard sell, requiring the persuasive powers of a court or application of other powerful social and cultural pressures. A second irony: most of our knowledge about mediation comes from the formal arena of legally definable conflicts; about use of mediation in the informal and ubiquitous conflicts of everyday life we know a good deal less. Here too, there is evidence that the process is underused. It also appears to be the case that for all its established value, those who assume the mediation role enter a world of significant ambiguity and stress, where the potential for burnout seems high. A final irony, or perhaps merely the inevitable result of a field still in its relative infancy, is that the successful mediation process is still something of a mystery, as is illustrated by argument over such things as the meaning and importance of mediator neutrality, the appropriateness of highly assertive mediator tactics, and the relative merits of problem-solving versus transformative approaches to the mediation role.

This blend of positive findings, intriguing ironies, and demonstrable role stresses and ambiguities amounts to a rich opportunity for researchers and practitioners, especially those of the reflective variety, who can approach the conundrums and debates of the field in the same tolerant, focused, and inquisitive manner that characterizes the constructive mediation process itself. My broad overview also suggests a seminal role for the friends and supporters of mediation. By familiarizing themselves with mediation and encouraging its use, managers, parents, and leaders (of a community, an institution, a group) can transform mediation from a frequently untapped resource to a familiar and common instrument for resolving the disputes of everyday life.

References

Bush, R.A.B., and Folger, J. P. *The Promise of Mediation: Responding to Conflict Through Empowerment and Recognition.* San Francisco: Jossey-Bass, 1994.

Carnevale, P. J., Lim, J. D., and McLaughlin, M. E. "Contingent Mediator Behavior and Its Effectiveness." In K. Kressel and D. G. Pruitt (eds.), *Mediation Research: The Process and Effectiveness of Third-Party Intervention.* San Francisco: Jossey-Bass, 1989.

Carnevale, P. J., and Pruitt, D. G. "Negotiation and Mediation." *Annual Review of Psychology,* 1992, *43,* 531–582.

Coleman, P. T., and Deutsch, M. "Interethnic Conflict in Schools." In W. D. Hawley and A. W. Jackson (eds.), *Toward a Common Destiny: Improving Race and Ethnic Relations in America.* San Francisco: Jossey-Bass, 1995.

Deutsch, M. *The Resolution of Conflict: Constructive and Destructive Processes.* New Haven: Yale University Press, 1973.

Deutsch, M., and Brickman, E. "Conflict Resolution." *Pediatrics in Review,* 1994, *15,* 16–22.

Fisher, R., Ury, W., and Patton, B. *Getting to Yes: Negotiating Agreements Without Giving In.* Boston: Houghton Mifflin, 1981.

Folger, J. B., and Bush, R.A.B. "Transformative Mediation and Third-Party Intervention: Ten Hallmarks of a Transformative Approach to Practice." *Mediation Quarterly,* 1996, *13,* 263–278.

Honoroff, B., Matz, D., and O'Connor, D. "Putting Mediation Skills to the Test." *Negotiation Journal,* 1990, *6,* 37–46.

Kolb, D., and Associates. *When Talk Works: Profiles of Mediators.* San Francisco: Jossey-Bass, 1994.

Kressel, K. *Labor Mediation: An Exploratory Survey.* New York: American Association of Labor Mediation Agencies, 1972.

Kressel, K. *The Process of Divorce: How Professionals and Couples Negotiate Settlement.* New York: Basic Books, 1985.

Kressel, K. "Practice-Relevant Research in Mediation: Toward a Reflective Research Paradigm." *Negotiation Journal,* 1997, *13,* 143–160.

Kressel, K., and Deutsch, M. "Divorce Therapy: An In-Depth Survey of Therapists' Views." *Family Process,* 1977, *16,* 413–443.

Kressel, K., and Pruitt, D. G. "Themes in the Mediation of Social Conflict." *Journal of Social Issues,* 1985, *41,* 179–198.

Kressel, K., and Pruitt, D. G. (eds.). *Mediation Research: The Process and Effectiveness of Third-Party Intervention.* San Francisco: Jossey-Bass, 1989.

Kressel, K., and others. "The Settlement Orientation vs. the Problem-Solving Style in Custody Mediation." *Journal of Social Issues,* 1994, *50,* 67–84.

Moore, C. W. *The Mediation Process: Practical Strategies for Resolving Conflict.* (2nd ed.) San Francisco: Jossey-Bass, 1996.

Pruitt, D. G., McGillicuddy, G. L., Welton, G. L., and Fry, W. R. "Process of Mediation in Dispute Settlement Centers." In K. Kressel and D. G. Pruitt (eds.), *Mediation Research: The Process and Effectiveness of Third-Party Intervention.* San Francisco: Jossey-Bass, 1989.

Schön, D. A. *The Reflective Practitioner.* New York: Basic Books, 1983.

Touval, S., and Zartman, I. W. "Mediation in International Conflicts." In K. Kressel and D. G. Pruitt (eds.), *Mediation Research: The Process and Effectiveness of Third-Party Intervention.* San Francisco: Jossey-Bass, 1989.

CHAPTER TWENTY-SIX

Managing Conflict Through Large-Group Methods

Barbara Benedict Bunker

This chapter begins in practice and works backward toward a theoretical question: Are there situations where managing conflict is enough—situations in which our socialized desire for conflict *resolution* may be more than is really needed for joint action?

We live in a world in which our environment is continuously changing. Organizations and communities are constantly dealing with new developments and pressures. A predictable and stable world surrounding our organizations and communities is a luxury we used to take for granted but that no longer exists. In the United States, we are also living in communities in which our diversity and our awareness of our differences in values, ethnicity, and religion are increasing. Thus, managing these differences is ever more important to us. This new situation requires organizations that are far more flexible and responsive than those in our past. It requires that communities develop ways of gathering people for input and planning immediately, not six months hence. It requires methods that can acknowledge and deal with difference, not suppress it in the service of homogeneity.

The author is grateful for wonderful conversations about conflict in large groups with the following practitioners, whose ideas contributed greatly to this chapter: Billie Alban, Dick and Emily Axelrod, Bridgett Bolton, Al Fitz, Robert Jacobs, Harrison Owen, Larry Peterson, Kris Quade, Nancy Cebula, and Roland Sullivan.

In the last ten years, practitioners who consult with organizations and communities have developed new methods of working with "the whole system" in large groups. These remarkable new methods allow groups from fifty to several thousand to gather and work together. Billie Alban, an internationally known organization development (OD) practitioner, and I have been studying these methods since the early 1990s (Bunker and Alban, 1992). Our book, *Large Group Interventions: Engaging the Whole System for Rapid Change* (1997), is a conceptual overview of twelve major methods, what underlies their effectiveness, and why they work.

This chapter is organized in three sections, each about one type of method now in use: Methods for Creating the Future, Methods for Work Design, and Methods for Discussion and Decision Making. After an explanation of each type of large-group method and case examples, I describe and speculate about the processes that allow conflict to be managed, and sometimes resolved, in these events. In the final section, underlying principles that make these methods effective in dealing with differences are proposed.

WHAT ARE LARGE-GROUP INTERVENTION METHODS?

These large-group intervention methods create large-scale changes, such as a new strategic direction for a business or agency, the redesign of work for higher productivity, or the resolution of some community or systemwide problem. In contrast to older methods, where decisions were made by an executive group at the top of the business, or in the mayor's office, these methods gather those who are affected by the decision or action, to participate in the discussion and decision making. In business organizations, this might include employees, customers, suppliers, and even competitors. In school districts, teachers, administrators, and board members might be joined by students, parents, and community representatives. In a community, we might see agencies, schools, churches, the police, housing areas, and local and state government all present.

Depending on the nature of the issue, the questions are, Who is affected by this decision or action? Who has a stake in the outcome? The idea is to get the whole system into the room (all of the stakeholders) for a new kind of dialogue about the situation they face. The size of the group assembled is determined by the critical mass of people needed to bring about real change; it is constrained only by limitations of budget and available meeting space.

Why bring together so many people? Why not let the decision makers do their job and make the decision? This question leads us to the second major defining assumption of large-group intervention: if people have an opportunity to participate in shaping their future, they are apt to make change work. People support what they help to create. These are very participative events. By participative, I mean that people express their views, they listen to others, they have "voice," and they are heard. They do not necessarily make every decision, but they have the opportunity to influence other people as well as the decisions.

Stakeholders in communities and organizations bring knowledge, values, and experience to these events. The kinds of decision that face us today are often enormously complex and need the best thinking and experience of all those involved, not just a few. Executives who participate in large-group events for the first time are often moved by the amazing variety of talent and capacity in their organization. They make remarks such as, "I had no idea how great and how talented the people in this organization are! It's been a revelation to me!"

Underlying these methods is an assumption that a democratic process rather than a hierarchical or bureaucratic one is most effective for moving forward in one direction. This assumption closely matches Deutsch's ideas about the values underlying collaboration and cooperation (see Chapter One).

THREE TYPES OF LARGE-GROUP METHOD

A convenient way to organize these methods is by the outcomes they produce. Here is a brief description of each type, with an illustrating anecdote.

Methods That Create the Future

The Search Conference (Emery and Purser, 1996), Future Search (Weisbord and Janoff, 1995), Real-Time Strategic Change (Jacobs, 1994), and the Institute of Cultural Affairs (ICA) Change Model for strategic change (Spencer, 1989) are four methods that gather systems to define and set goals for the future (see Figure 26.1 for a brief summary). "What kind of school system," people might ask, "do we want to be by 2005?" "What new market niche can we create in the next three years?" "How can we become a community free from fear?" "How can we be a community with housing for all by 2010?" "What are the unique contributions of our hospital to this metropolitan community?" All these are appropriate theme questions for these future-oriented conferences.

Planning a Future Search. Each future-oriented event is carefully planned by a group representing the sponsoring system, working with a consultant who is expert in the method. For example, when I ran a Future Search for the business school of a small Jesuit college on what they needed to do about their curriculum to create a successful future for the M.B.A. program, the planning committee included representatives from the dean's office, faculty, staff, students, and business community. Having the stakeholders present for the planning helps to understand what the system is like and also helps anticipate conflict that may emerge in the large-group meeting. If there are unions, it is essential that they be part of the planning committee. Sometimes, these conflicts

Figure 26.1. Large-Group Methods for Creating the Future.

The Search Conference
Purpose: To Create a Future Vision
Emery and Emery

- Set format: environmental scan, history, present, future
- Criteria for participants: within system boundary
- Theory: participative democracy
- Search for common ground
- Rationalize conflict
- No experts
- Total-community discussions
- 2.5 days minimum
- 35 to 40 + participants
- Large groups—multisearch
- $\frac{1}{3}$ total time is action planning

Future Search
Purpose: To Create a Future Vision
Weisbord and Janoff

- Set format: past, present, future, action planning
- Stakeholder participation, no experts
- Minimizes differences
- Search for common ground
- Self-managed small groups
- 18 hours over 3 days
- 40 to 80 + participants
- Larger groups—multisearch conference

Real-Time Strategic Change
Purpose: To Create a Preferred Future with Systemwide Action Planning
Dannemiller and Jacobs

- Format custom designed to issue
- Highly structured and organized
- Theory: Beckhard change model
- Common database
- 2 to 3 days + follow-up events
- Use of outside experts as appropriate
- Use of small groups and total community
- Self-managed small groups
- 100 to 2,400 participants
- Logistics competence critical
- Daily participant feedback
- Planning committee and consultants design events

ICA Change Model
Purpose: Strategic Planning

- Stakeholder participation
- 2 to 7 days
- 50–200 participants
- Planning committee and consultants design events

Source: B. B. Bunker and B. T. Alban, *Large Group Interventions.* San Francisco: Jossey-Bass, 1997. Reprinted by permission.

can even be resolved in the committee, so they do not emerge on the floor of the large group.

What are the meetings like? Here I wish I could show a video, but let me try to create the image in words. I am going to describe a Future Search that occurred in Danbury, Connecticut. The initiating concern that brought the community together was a rapid increase in violence in schools as well as in the community as a whole. Realizing that reducing violence was too limited an emphasis for the future they wanted, they finally chose "creating a community free from fear" as the theme.

Imagine 180 people arriving at a big hall. They pick up name badges that assign them to one of twenty-three round tables five feet in diameter that each seats eight. They are purposely assigned as heterogeneously (or "max-mix") as possible. This means that they meet and work with representatives of all the other stakeholder groups at their assigned tables. Each table is designed to be a microcosm of the system in the room.

A Future Search begins with a statement of purpose from the sponsors. Then everyone is asked to participate at their tables in an activity that reviews the history of the community, the world, and each person himself or herself over the last thirty years. Using a worksheet, people think about the important events in these histories first. After a while, everyone gets up and writes these important events on long sheets of butcher paper that have been posted on the walls and labeled by decade. After the thoughts have been put up, the facilitators assign each table to do an analysis of the patterns they see in a specific decade and report their analysis to the whole assembly. This activity gets people involved and working together at the tables. In the course of the analysis, the history of the system is shared with everyone, the impact of the environment on the system is better understood, and people get to know each other personally.

The Future Search method has developed a "design" or series of activities that is standard and can be used with very little modification. It involves discussion, self-disclosure, imagining, analyzing, and planning. These activities have both an educational and an emotional impact on participants. They represent the major steps in any open systems planning process. Thus, there are activities that scan the external environment and notice the forces affecting the organization or community. Next, there are activities that look at the capacity of the organization to rise to the challenge it faces. Then there are activities that ask people to dream about their preferred future in the face of the reality they now confront. Finally, there is work to agree on the best ideas for future direction, and action planning to begin to make it happen. Although the overall plan is rational, the activities themselves are interesting, fun, and challenging. The interactions that occur among people create energy and motivation for change.

In two days, the conference attendees in Danbury discover in their history that a sense of community has been disrupted by the loss of industry moving out, the building of a new superhighway that bisects the town, and the demise of the well-known community fairgrounds that once brought the community together. In addition, new groups are moving into the area. The attendees learn that forty-two languages are now spoken in the high school, creating new educational issues. When they assess the resources of the community, they find that many groups do not know what other groups are doing, and that there are untapped opportunities for synergy, coordination, and cooperation.

The skits that the groups create develop themes about housing, racism, hospital services in underserved areas of the city, and summer recreation transportation for children. Action planning groups are formed (some of which are still working actively two years after the conference). In two days, 180 people create more than a dozen major initiatives to improve life in the community. (Two years later, we are pleased to report, a number of these task forces are still at work and several major initiatives have been completed.)

The other three methods—Search Conference, the ICA Change Model, and Real-Time Strategic Change—all have elements in common with Future Search. They vary in design activities, in the structure of decision making, and in how many people they can accommodate. Real-Time Strategic Change, for example, has been used for a group of twenty-two hundred employees of the Ford Mustang plant in Dearborn. They gathered in three ballrooms at a convention center in Detroit to plan the future of the plant when it reopened in 1993. So, when we say large groups, we really mean large!

Dealing with Differences About the Future. One would think that bringing together people of so many interests and perspectives is bound to generate conflict, or at least major differences about perception and future direction. What keeps these methods from blowing up? So many aspects of organizational and community life disintegrate into bedlam; why don't these unwieldy events do so?

First, of course, there are differences—real, and many of them. But all of these events operate under an assumption unlike those of, say, a New England town meeting or a hearing in front of the city council. The key here is *the search for common ground.* People are asked to focus their minds and energy on what is shared. Early activities in all of these events create a shared database of information as well as knowledge about the views of those present; sometimes, invited experts and relevant outsiders bring information that contributes to the shared database as well. People are encouraged to notice and take differences seriously, but not to focus on them or give a lot of energy to conflict resolution. Rather, they try to discover what they agree on, and this becomes the base for moving forward. People are generally surprised by how much agreement there actually is when they look for it. This is because the usual process of noticing and focusing on differences is disrupted.

When we gather in a group or meet as individuals, there is a tendency (at least in Western cultures) to feel comfortable with others who share our views, values, and attitudes. We notice if people are different or if groups do not seem to share our assumptions. When that happens, the tendency is either to withdraw and ignore the difference, or to become competitive and attempt to change the others over to our view. In the latter case, the more competitive the situation becomes, the more win-lose the atmosphere. People focusing on making their points stick, on winning, tend to lose sight of what they have in common with others and only see the difficult differences.

Some years ago, National Public Radio had a story that illustrates this unconventional approach. The report came from St. Louis, where the pro-life and pro-choice forces were certainly not in agreement, except that some leadership in both groups wanted to avoid violence. They asked, "Is there anything that we agree on that could become a source of common ground?" Although there is much that they will never agree on, the two sides discovered that there was common ground: in their mutual concern for pregnant teenagers. As a result of this discovery, they created a successful, jointly sponsored project to help pregnant adolescents that did a great deal to manage the incipient violence in that city.

Merrelyn Emery's thinking about the relationship between conflict and common ground in her writing on the Search Conference makes these issues very clear (Emery and Purser, 1996). She sees the conference setting as a "protected site" where people can come together and search for commonalities despite their fear and natural anxiety about conflict. She believes that "groups tend to overestimate the area of conflict and underestimate the amount of common ground that exists" (p. 142). "Rationalizing conflict" is the important process that takes conflict seriously when it arises, so that substantive differences are clarified and everyone understands and respects what they are. If the conflict is rationalized and everyone is clear about exactly what the agreements and disagreements are, it is possible to wait for a short time to see if it can be resolved. If not, the name of the conflict is posted visibly on a "disagree list," meaning that although the issue does not receive further attention, the differences are acknowledged.

The Seventh American Forestry Conference, held in 1996 using the Real-Time Strategic Change method, further illustrates the importance for conflict management of the principles and processes we have just discussed. Beginning in 1882, Forestry Conferences were convened by the president of the United States to set forest policy for the upcoming decades. They included nurserymen, forest scientists, representatives of lumbering interests, and citizen advocates. Early congresses created momentum for a system of forest reserves set aside for public use and for creation of the U.S. Forest Service.

The American Forestry Association eventually had enough credence to be able to call for congresses, which were held in 1953, 1965, and 1975. After 1975, however, the various interests grew so conflicting that no one group was strong enough to call a seventh congress. Finally, in 1995, the Yale Forest Forum brought together a round table of fifty stakeholders from environmental groups, industry, public agencies, small owners, community-based groups, research, and academia. Despite their diversity, by using participative methods they were able to agree on visions and principles to guide the congress, set for the next year. They grew strong in their commitment to making the congress happen and formed the nucleus group that called the Seventh American Forestry Conference.

Before the conference was convened, more than fifty local round tables and collaborative meetings were held all over the United States to develop draft visions for the next ten years and principles to support them. These meetings were structured and sponsored by a citizens' involvement committee. In addition, there was a Website for the conference and some visits to other countries to benchmark best practices. In this prework, it became clear to the conference planning committee that they could not use the traditional "talking heads" conference format. They chose Kristine Quade and Roland Sullivan of Minneapolis (experts in Real-Time Strategic Change) as their consultants.

When the fifteen hundred people invited to the three-and-a-half-day conference convened in Washington, D.C., in 1996, the draft visions and principles already created by the local meetings formed the basis of discussion at the tables. The table task was to incorporate the various visions and principles into one set that most people concerned with forestry issues could endorse as the desirable policy for the next decade and to avoid the win-lose confrontations so typical of public issues with diverse stakeholders.

Several tactics were important factors in their being able to do this. First, the leadership did not take positions on controversial issues even though there were interest groups present that wanted them to do so. The process was a collaborative search for agreement at tables of ten diverse participants each.

Second, voting or showing where you stood was done with colored cards. Green signaled agreement, yellow indicated uncertainty or ambivalence, and red meant disagreement. Agreement was declared if more than 50 percent of the congress showed green cards. This method created space to explore people's views—especially the meaning of a yellow vote.

Third, some potentially explosive issues (such as divisive pending legislation) were avoided in the agenda for the congress. In other words, the level of conflict was managed. Practitioners of large-group methodology have rules of thumb for dealing with conflict, such as "Don't open up anything you don't have time to work with and resolve" and "Don't open up conflicts late in the event, when there's no time to adequately deal with it."

Much of the first day was devoted to table groups working together and getting to know each other. At the end of the first day and the beginning of the second, many information sessions and topic conversations were offered by knowledgeable experts. Attendees at the tables decided where they wanted members to go, and they came back to report what they had learned to their table team after each session. During the second and third days, table deliberations were integrated, creating visions and principles that more than 50 percent of those assembled agreed on. Finally, time was devoted to planning next-step initiatives to carry forward the vision and principles.

The processes that create this kind of agreement across diverse interests occur within individuals as well as at the group and system levels. Individually, people arrive seeing the world and the future from the perspective of their own interest. At this point individuals are egocentric, meaning they do not fully understand other views or interests. In the course of discussions, acquiring new information, and trying to move toward agreement, they begin to understand (if not agree with) others at the table. Their boundaries become less rigid and they become flexible in looking for solutions that might offer gains both for themselves and for others in their table team. As they engage in this cooperative process, the atmosphere at the group level becomes supportive and affirming. The group begins to feel successful. One symptom of this shift in perspective is that rather than saying *I* there is a noticeable increase in the use of *we*.

Interestingly, at this congress, there was a group of about two hundred people who did not like the way the congress was organized. They met in rump sessions to plan disruption of the congress at which they were participants. They wanted the leadership to take specific positions, and they were prepared to picket and heckle in order to influence others to join them. As the table groups pursued their worked together, fewer and fewer of the original dissident members were still willing to go to a rump meeting or participate in a disruptive demonstration. They realized that they could get some of what they cared about through this collaborative process. Toward the end, only a single person, the leader of the movement, was still walking around the floor picketing and trying to arouse others! The process had clearly captured and involved all of the others.

Methods for Work Design

The second set of large-group methods can involve stakeholders in redesigning work (see Figure 26.2 for a summary). Since the 1970s, with global economic pressures affecting American business, we have experienced a series of popular and even faddish processes—notably "total quality" and "reengineering"—that were adopted to improve quality, decrease the cost of manufacturing or service delivery, and respond to consumer requirements.

The idea that work could be organized so that it is productive and also satisfying to the human beings who do it was articulated in the 1950s by a British theorist, Eric Trist, and an Australian collaborator, Fred Emery (Emery and Trist, 1960). They called it "socio-technical systems" (STS). The idea developed as they

Figure 26.2. Large-Group Methods for Work Design.

The Conference Model
Axelrod and Axelrod

- Uses five conferences:
  - Vision
  - Customers
  - Technical
  - Design
  - Implementation
- Data-assist teams work between meetings to involve larger organization
- 80 participants
- 2 + days for each conference
- Small groups self-managed

Fast-Cycle Full-Participation Work Systems Design
Passmore, Fitz, and Frank

- System preparation work
- Minimum critical specs
- Five meetings:
  - Future search (1.5 days)
  - Meeting external expectations (1 day)
  - Work systems analysis (2 days)
  - Work life analysis (1 day)
  - New design and implementation (4 days)
- 30 to 80 attend meetings
- Parallel design of support process changes
- Between-meetings STS work

Real-Time Work Design
Dannemiller and Tolchinsky

- Whole system present at launch or implementation (50 to 2,400)
- Process, design, deep-dive conferences representative
- One-day conferences on key design support issues
- Design team manages process and does STS work
- Implementation team oversees miniconferences

Participative Design
Emery and Emery

- Bottom-up process
- Companywide education is first step
- Management sets minimum specifications
- Basic principle: each level coordinates and controls own work
- Each unit designs its own work
- Six design principles used to redesign work
- Multiskilling the norm

Source: B. B. Bunker and B. T. Alban, *Large Group Interventions.* San Francisco: Jossey-Bass, 1997. Reprinted by permission.

were studying the introduction of new technology into coal mines. Observing that the social organization of the workers could impede or facilitate the new technology, they created a process for redesigning work that paid attention to efficiency and quality as well as to a social structure that would organize workers in compatible groups.

The method that emerged, STS Redesign, was widely used in Scandinavia in the 1960s but did not become popular elsewhere in the West until the late 1970s and early 1980s. The usual practice in the United States was that a design team that represented all of the stakeholders closeted itself for months at a time to do the technical analysis of the workflow and propose ways to organize that would improve the work, reduce waste, and create good social relationships. When they finally emerged with a new design, the other folks at work who had been waiting anxiously for many months were more than slightly skeptical. They had to be sold, and so the whole process developed another iteration. It took years to accomplish the reorganization.

Dick Axelrod, an STS practitioner based in Chicago, created a process called the Conference Model, which uses four large-group events, two-day conferences to involve many more people in the process of redesign. This process can create a new work design in four to six months, one in which most of the people feel they have had some input.

In the Mercy Healthcare system in Sacramento, California, for example, five hospitals needed to redesign their patient care delivery processes, a core process in a hospital. They needed to save a lot of money and at the same time improve patient care. The first two sessions, the vision conference and the customer conference, create a vision of the goal of patient care and consultations with customers (in this case, former patients and the community) about their desires. (In recent years, the two conferences have often been combined.) Then there is an analysis of the current patient care process and where it needs to be improved—the technical conference—and a design conference to make changes and create an improved process and the organizational structure to support it. Finally, the decisions are refined and acted on in an implementation conference.

The technical conference was held in five adjacent ballrooms, one for each hospital, so that if necessary there could be coordination among the hospitals. For example, at certain moments in the process, selected members of each hospital went on a treasure hunt to the other four ballrooms to look for good ideas that they could incorporate from what others had created.

These conferences are usually held about a month apart, which gives time for a specially designated team to go back into the system and present to those not attending what has happened at the conference and get their input. When Mercy Healthcare surveyed three thousand people in the hospital system, 85 percent said that they felt involved and able to give input to the process. This is remarkable, since only about 150 people from any one hospital attended any conference.

The underlying principle here, again, is that the people who do the work and deliver the service possess a great deal of wisdom and experience. They, better than others, usually know where the problems are and what goes wrong at work. Therefore, they need to be involved in the analysis and redesign process. Even if jobs are at stake—and they were, at Mercy Healthcare—people would ordinarily rather have a voice in what is changing than simply have it done to them. In situations like these, anxiety runs high. It is very helpful to people during anxious times if there is openness about the process of change as well as lots of communication about how decisions will be made.

When we wrote our book about these methods (Bunker and Alban, 1997), we identified four approaches to work design (see Figure 26.2). Increasingly, however, the Conference Model, Real-Time Work Design, and Fast-Cycle Full-Participation Work Design have moved toward each other, influenced by coming from the same STS tradition and an annual collaborative professional meeting (the STS Roundtable) where practitioners discuss matters of theory and practice with each other. What seems to occur now is that large conferences or meetings are interspersed with smaller task forces, or work by the steering group, in a pattern that makes sense for each client. This always includes addressing future goals for the organization as both a business and a social system, assessing the impact of the environment on the organization, doing a technical analysis of the core work process, and redesigning that process and the structure that supports it.

Participative Design: A Distinctive Approach. The fourth method is still distinctive. Participative Design, created by Fred Emery and Merrelyn Emery (1989), is a method that redesigns work and the work organization from the bottom up (Emery, 1995). It is based on the idea that the people who do the work need to be responsible for, control, and coordinate their own work. This is in sharp contrast to the bureaucratic principle, where each level controls the work of those below.

Work is redesigned to conform to the six critical human requirements that create meaningful and productive work:

1. Autonomy
2. Opportunity to learn and keep learning on the job
3. Variety in work
4. Mutual support and respect in a cooperative work environment
5. Meaningful work product and community contribution
6. A desirable future at work

Management decides in advance what constraints or minimum critical specifications the unit must work within—for example, that they cannot add jobs or exceed certain budgetary levels. Then, within these limits, the whole work unit analyzes what skills are needed to do the work of the unit, and who has the skills. Next, they redesign the unit to meet both the objective criteria for satisfying work and their own requirements. After the bottom of the organization is redesigned, the people at the next higher level then ask, "Given this new work design, what's our work?" They proceed to redesign their work. Theoretically, this continues to the very top of the organization. To be successful, Participative Design requires that top management understand and endorse this very democratic approach to working with employees.

Interpersonal conflict occurs most often in the Participative Design workshop when people in the work unit are analyzing their work and creating a new organization that they will manage and be responsible for. According to Nancy Cebula, a practitioner having much experience with this method, about halfway through the redesign process the group wakes up to the fact that in the new world they are creating, they will have to deal with and manage their own conflict. This is usually a new experience, because in hierarchically controlled organizations people can run to the boss, complain, and expect him or her to do something. A self-managing unit must develop processes for dealing with conflicts in its own team and with other teams.

It has been observed that interpersonal conflict that festers on and on in teams is often a cause of dissolution. For this reason, consultants suggest that teams work out a script for the steps to take if conflict appears. They may start by having the affected parties try to talk it out, so that it becomes team business. Some teams have rotating roles for mediators. Or the steps can include calling in people from human resources to mediate as a last resort. If the process is defined in advance, it helps people openly deal with issues.

In one team on the verge of becoming self-managing, the process faltered when the group seemed unable to select people for the two new teams that were proposed. Someone finally blurted out to the inquiring facilitator, "Our problem is that we have two slackers in the group and no one wants them on their team." The facilitator asked, "What's the best way to deal with this?" The group decided to go off into a room and handle it without their manager or the facilitator. The facilitator said they could take one hour. They retired to the room, from which angry sounds emerged from time to time. But thirty minutes later, they emerged with two teams—each including one of the slackers, who had been told they would have to shape up or depart. Everyone survived this first experience at managing their own conflict. (Interestingly, one of the slackers quit within a few days. The other turned herself around. She could no longer be mad at the system; there were now peers in her world to whom she was accountable.)

Training in conflict management, particularly in systems where there is a strong history of conflict, is often part of the prework that gets a system ready to do Participative Design.

Conflict and the Redesign Process. Unlike methods for future planning that can be used in groups such as communities, associations of like interest, and organizations, Methods for Work Design are always used by organizations to improve their own processes. This means that the people who come to these events belong to the same organization and have a stake in its future. Even in a case where labor relations have been troubled and there is an intraorganizational battlefield, it is not in anyone's self-interest to let the organization die. Thus, there is always a certain level of energy for change and improvement available in these settings.

One of the first issues to understand in doing this kind of work is the organization's conflict history and the climate in which redesign occurs. Participative methods give people a chance to engage and have input into how their job life is structured. For some organizations with a long history of mistrust between labor and management, such an invitation is not easily believed (and management needs to seriously consider its own willingness to accept participation before it embarks on this course).

This history is likely to be in evidence in the large-group meeting. It appears in a number of forms, often evinced by outspoken individuals who make themselves known on the floor. Although the rules of large-group events say that people and their views are listened to and treated with respect, what does a facilitator do when someone grabs a microphone and produces a tirade against management? On the one hand, the speaker deserves to be treated with respect. On the other, he or she is not authorized to speak, and the speech violates acceptable behavior. The person might instigate others who also have an axe to grind. In all likelihood, they represent only a small percentage of those present, but their aggressiveness can intimidate those whose views are moderate and who are hesitant to express themselves in front of five hundred people.

One perspective on this kind of emotional display is catharsis theory. The idea is to let these people have their say, even if it disrupts the time schedule that you planned, but you do not let them have the day. They are not allowed to filibuster or totally disrupt proceedings. After a reasonable time, if they do not seem to have finished, you may call a short break (everyone else departs for the coffee and restrooms) and then go on to the next activity.

I had this experience in one plant in the Midwest that had a troubled labor history. A vocal group of disbelievers in management's good intentions was holding forth on the floor, and it was affectively very negative and very strong. I had had my fill after about fifteen minutes and wandered out into the hall, where to my surprise I found a group of employees grousing, saying things like, "It's always the same people, and they always say the same things. Why don't they shut up and see what happens? I'm tired of listening to them." After the break, when we went back to work on the next activity, the energy level in the room was high and very positive. People were deeply engaged and made suggestions for changes that would improve work at the plant.

A second strategy that is sometimes useful is to respectfully engage the whole group in reacting to what is being said by the vocal minority. A facilitator might ask for an indication of who agrees with what is being said, and then ask for those with different views to make themselves known. The facilitator can ask questions that bring out other points of view. Moderates need encouragement to express their views, but as they do so a clear picture of the views of the whole system begins to emerge. As others get into the discussion, the community begins to manage it. Some might say to the person hogging the floor, "Joe, you know, you're taking advantage of this, and you know we don't support you. Why don't you sit down and be quiet?" Working in this context, the facilitator senses when the group has had enough and is ready to move on and guides the process to the next step.

There are times, however, when the frustration and aggravation with the organizational situation and with management is very strong (and for good reason). People who have not been treated well really have a right to be angry; they need to say so publicly to management and hear its response. This level of conflict, though, has the potential to escalate and take a destructive turn. If voices from the floor become personally accusative and cross the invisible line of acceptable public behavior toward superiors, a bad situation can result. This is everyone's black fantasy about large groups—that an irreparable explosion might do permanent damage.

Although this possibility always exists, it is interesting to consider the other forces working in this setting to keep conflict within responsible limits. An organization is not an association of persons with no particular bonds. There is a history, a present, and hopefully a future. It is in everyone's self-interest that things come out better rather than worse. These are forces encouraging collaboration and helping to keep the conflict responsible. In a large-scale event, conflict is a public process that occurs with the whole system present. Its public nature is also a force for responsible management of the conflict. The facilitator's skill to martial the positive forces while at the same time allowing expression of the conflict is critical to successful management of the event.

Methods for Discussion and Decision Making

The third category of large-group methods seek diagnosis and finding solutions to problems. They are predominantly oriented toward fixing specific problems that have developed in the past.

The large-group methods used for this purpose differ substantially among themselves (Figure 26.3). Work-Out is a method developed at General Electric that is being used in numerous companies to solve serious organizational problems by bringing together all of the stakeholders in a time-limited problem-solving format. Simu-Real (Klein, 1992) creates a simulated organization with the people who actually hold the roles acting out their own jobs so as to understand problems, or even test a new design for organizational structure.

Figure 26.3. Large-Group Methods for Discussion and Decision Making.

Simu-Real

Purpose: Real-Time Work on Current Issues, Test Future Designs, Learn About System
Klein and Klein

- Organization selects issue for work
- Room arrangement reflects organization structure
- People act their organization role
- Periods of stop action and reflection
- Decision process agreed to in advance
- 1 day
- 50 to 150 people
- Facilitator needs expertise in process consultation

Work-Out (GE)

Purpose: Problem Identification and Process Improvement

- Improvement target selected
- Employee cross-functional meeting
- Process—discuss and recommend
- Senior management responds immediately
- Champions and sponsors follow through to implementation
- Follow up as needed
- 1 to 2 days

Large-Scale Interactive Events

Purpose: Problem Solving
Dannemiller and Jacobs

(Same methodology as Real-Time Strategic Change.)

- Many uses

Open Space Technology

Purpose: Discussion and Exploration of System Issues
Harrison Owen

- Least structured of large-group technologies
- Divergent process
- Large group creates agenda topics
- Interest groups form around topics
- Periodic town meetings for sharing information across interest groups
- One facilitator—lays out format, ground rules, "holds the space"
- Requires understanding of large-group dynamics
- 1 to 3 days

Source: B. B. Bunker and B. T. Alban, *Large Group Interventions.* San Francisco: Jossey-Bass, 1997. Reprinted by permission.

Large-Scale Interactive Events (Jacobs, 1994) uses the Real-Time Strategic Change framework (recall Figure 26.1) to solve many types of problem, from diversity issues to intergroup coordination problems, one example being encouraging police, emergency rooms, agencies, and homeless shelters to better deal with the rise of tuberculosis among homeless people in New York City.

In terms of conflict resolution, these three methods use many of the principles described earlier of creating common ground, acknowledging but not dwelling on conflicts, rationalizing conflict, and creating new conditions for resolution.

Open Space Technology (Owen, 1992, 1995) is unique among these methods. Instead of using designed activities in preplanned groupings, it places the responsibility for creating and managing the agenda on the participants. Its founder, Harrison Owen, describes it as effective in highly conflicted situations. For this reason, I focus the discussion in this section on Open Space alone of the four methods for decision making.

Briefly, this "agendaless" method creates a simple process in which people coming to an Open Space meeting create their own agenda for one, two, or three days of discussion of a chosen topic or issue. For example, the Presbyterian Church USA invited five hundred people to an Open Space to discuss some difficult and contentious issues, just prior to their annual national meeting. In another instance, a series of Open Space meetings were held in Canada to consider the Quebecois issue. And a hospital system in California, faced with the need to cut costs, held an Open Space in each hospital community to get input from citizens about their concerns and priorities. This method has been used in hundreds of venues to create good conversation about a wide range of issues.

What is Open Space technology? What is an Open Space meeting? The simplest way to put it is that Open Space is a self-managing meeting in which the people attending create their own agenda in the first hour of the event. Everyone sits in a large circle, with open space in the middle. The facilitator introduces the theme of the meeting and describes the norms for participation. Then people are invited to come forward and declare to the whole assembly a topic on which they have strong feelings, so an issue group can be convened to talk about it. A person writes a topic and her name on newsprint and tacks it on a wall called the "community bulletin board." She selects a time and place from the choices that are organized for this purpose and written on Post-it notes. She sticks the time-and-place Post-it on her topic sheet and hangs it on the wall.

The posted topics create the visual agenda for a meeting that will go on for several days. People can add new topics whenever they want by tacking a notice on the bulletin board. Each person who proposes a topic agrees to show up, start the discussion, and after it is over go to the "newsroom" and type a summary of what was said, using a simple computer template. These meeting reports are printed out and immediately posted on another long wall so that everyone can keep up with what is being said in other groups.

After the initial agenda-setting meeting, the only gatherings of the total group are brief ones in the morning and evening for comments and new topic announcements. The group discussion periods are usually about ninety minutes long. This means there can be four or five sessions (with multiple groups convening at each session) during a day, and more if the evening is also used.

A unique feature of Open Space is its set of rules and norms. Far from being an uptight event where everyone is supposed to attend everything but people play hooky and feel mildly guilty, Open Space encourages self-management and freedom to do what is needed to maintain individual focus and energy. The "Law of Two Feet" suggests that if you do not feel engaged in the group you are attending, you get your two feet under you and go somewhere else, to another session that you do find productive. There is a lot of floating around and in and out, which is quite freeing and energizing. Other norms suggest that things begin to happen when people have the energy to make them happen. "Whenever it starts is the right time," they say. "Whoever comes are the right people." "Whatever happens is the only thing that could have." "When it's over, it's over."

Open Space meetings remove the oughts, shoulds, and musts; they suggest that you "follow your bliss," to quote Joseph Campbell. What happens is usually quite interesting, even remarkable. An example may be helpful in getting a better feel for this unusual methodology and how conflict is dealt with. In this example, an intact organization, the business school in a public college, uses Open Space three times over a period of a year to deal with long-term conflict in the system.

The dean, now in her third year, believed that the business school had fallen behind in its ability to produce "job ready" B.A. graduates because faculty were using old methods, texts, and technology. Shrinking government funding intensified the competition for resources and exacerbated ever-present interdepartmental rivalries. The faculty was unionized, as was the staff. This was a faculty that was angry at each other, at the dean, and at the administration.

Owen has said that Open Space should be used (1) for issues that affect the whole organization or system, (2) in situations of high conflict, and (3) when you can't think of anything else to do. It is possible that all three reasons were part of the dean's decision to try an Open Space meeting. The theme to be explored was "issues and opportunities for the future of the faculty of business." The event was held during working hours at the college, over two and a half days. Fifty of eighty faculty attended, plus staff and administration. The first two days were Open Space, as described earlier. The final half day was a convergence process, which is often added to the Open Space experience to plan for action.

In the initial agenda-setting circle, the facilitator was struck by the fact that no one looked at anyone else (a common symptom of deep conflict in a system). Although there were about the expected number of topics posted, given

564 THE HANDBOOK OF CONFLICT RESOLUTION

the main theme they were superficial: "the cleanliness of the college," "academic excellence," and so on. There was a general air of anger toward the administration. Comments at the end of the day were bland.

The overnight soak time clearly had an effect. The next morning, new issues were posted that were quite unlike those of the first day; two examples were "conflict and conflict resolution" and "the strategic direction to get out of this mess." The dean posted a topic, "the human face of management," and its issue-group session was attended by everyone present. In that discussion, she talked personally about her role and views and became a real human being to those present. As the day progressed, a number of individuals approached the facilitators, saying things like, "You wouldn't believe what's happening in our group!" There was excitement and energy on the second day, in contrast to the flat affect and withdrawal of the first day.

The Open Space exploration was closed at the end of day two with a "talking stick" circle (a version of a Native American custom). The stick is passed around the circle; when you have it, you may speak if you choose to and others are expected to listen respectfully. These are not group reports, but just what people are thinking and feeling at the end of the day. From the comments, it was clear that the faculty had begun to move from being frozen by conflict to another posture. A representative quote in the circle was, "I haven't spoken to [another faculty member] for fifteen years because of a disagreement we had, but that is going to change." A number of participants reported the first meaningful conversations in years. Others talked about the need to sort out relationships and move on.

Open Space technology is a divergent process for allowing ideas to emerge and develop. It creates really good conversation. Many people, particularly we Westerners with our need for visible results and action, add on a half-day convergent structure to plan and take action. In the case of the business college, everyone voted on the issues as they emerged in the group reports; they named the top vote-getting issues and formed voluntary task forces to tackle them. The group decided to hold another open space four months later to hear reports from the task forces and to continue the conversation.

At that next Open Space, forty-five members reassembled for a two-and-a-half–day event. This time it opened with a ninety-minute session to hear reports from the task forces. Then the facilitator opened the space for new agenda, and the meeting continued in the manner we have described. This time, there was much more willingness to address the complex and difficult issues they faced as a faculty trying to create a better future. Many more academic issues were addressed, as were the difficulties of dealing with departments where everyone is tenured and out-of-date. Again, the last half day was used to prioritize and organize new task forces having another four-month reporting date.

The third and final Open Space meeting was run completely by the faculty. They had learned to use the methodology and made it a way of working together. Many changes have occurred, and the faculty is continuing to work with the dean to create a secure future. One marker event that happened between the second and third open space meetings has diagnostic value. A dismissed faculty member tried to rally support for ousting the dean. When he went to antiadministration fellows who had been his supporters, he was rebuffed and told, "This dean is the best one we've ever had."

What principles explain this shift in energy, from being dug into conflict, blaming, and attacking to being able to solve problems and work together? One major dynamic is removing the hierarchical authority structure by way of open space technology. There is no *they*. It's all *we*. Facilitators *wait* for people to create their own agenda. They believe that what is on the wall is what the group needs to talk about. Nothing is imposed. Although there is a theme, participants decide what issues they will address. The dean was there, but only as a member of the group.

If hierarchy is absent, the well-worn patterns of manipulation and control are disrupted. There is no decision structure or way of getting power. The normal way of doing business is suspended, and people are asked simply to follow their own energy and commitments so they both get and give. In Open Space, the Law of Two Feet, the Four Principles (see endnote for a statement of Four Principles), and constructive conflict processes replace hierarchy with guidance for individuals. It creates huge freedom to act, which is delightful even though it makes people a bit anxious. But everyone else is in the same situation, and people enjoy exploring their freedom; they work it out. It leaves the participants with one very important question in mind: "What is it that *we* have energy and the will to do?"

What impact do participatory meetings have on the whole system after the event is over? What happens back at work? There is anecdotal evidence that one meeting of this type can create new plans and get action going that strongly affects the system. Another effect of all of these methods is to create new networks and relationships that have ongoing value. In the case of the business school, the attendees began using open space as "their" way of working together.

When something like this happens, hierarchy and the bureaucratic process in the organization are modified. It should be pointed out strongly that senior management's understanding of the collaborative nature of these meetings is crucial. Leaders need to understand and agree to this method of working, and their very important role in it, well in advance.

CONCLUSION

Practitioners of large-group methods have created processes that work at the organizational and community levels either to manage or to resolve conflict.

Here are some principles about large-group processes that account for their effectiveness.

- Focus on *common ground,* an area of agreement rather than difference or competitive interest.

- *Rationalize conflict.* This means acknowledge and then clarify conflict rather than ignore or deny it. Agree to disagree and move on to areas of agreement.

- *Manage conflict* by avoiding incendiary issues or those that cannot be dealt with in the time available.

- *Expand individuals' egocentric view of the situation* by exposing them to many points of view in heterogeneous groups that do real tasks collaboratively and develop group spirit. This broadens views and educates.

- Allow time to acknowledge the group's *history of conflict* and feelings before expecting people to work together cooperatively.

- *Manage public airing of differences and conflict.* Treat all views with respect. Allow minority views to be heard but not to dominate discussion. Preserve time for expression of views held by people "in the middle" as well as those who are at the extreme.

- *Reduce hierarchy* as much as possible. Push responsibility for working together and for managing conflict down in the organization so that people are responsible for their own activity.

Large-group interventions tackle conflict in various ways at a number of points in its development—sometimes dealing with past history, sometimes putting differences aside and simply managing them, and sometimes directly addressing and resolving issues that divide people and groups. The principles I have described are primarily at the systems level. These processes, however, simultaneously affect the group and the individual, as reflected in the principle of creating new conditions for resolution of conflict. These methods also document many of the principles developed in the research on conflict and conflict resolution. We hope that they also stimulate new theoretical thinking about how conflict is managed and resolved.

Note

1. The Four Principles are (1) Whenever it starts is the right time; (2) Whatever happens is the only thing that could have; (3) Whomever come are the right people; and (4) When it's over, it's over.

References

Bunker, B. B., and Alban, B. T. (eds.). "Large Group Interventions." *Journal of Applied Behavioral Science,* 1992, *28* (entire issue 4).

Bunker, B. B., and Alban, B. T. *Large Group Interventions: Engaging the Whole System for Rapid Change.* San Francisco: Jossey-Bass, 1997.

Emery, F. E. "Participative Design: Effective, Flexible and Successful, Now!" *Journal for Quality and Participation,* 1995, *18,* 6–9.

Emery, F. E., and Emery, M. "Participative Design: Work and Community Life." In M. Emery (ed.), *Participative Design for Participative Democracy.* Canberra: Centre for Continuing Education, Australian National University, 1989.

Emery, F. E., and Trist, E. L. "Socio-Technical Systems." In C. W. Churchman and others (eds.), *Management Sciences, Models, and Techniques.* New York: Pergamon Press, 1960.

Emery, M., and Purser, R. E. *The Search Conference: A Powerful Method for Planning Organizational Change and Community Action.* San Francisco: Jossey-Bass, 1996.

Jacobs, R. W. *Real-Time Strategic Change.* San Francisco: Berrett-Koehler, 1994.

Klein, D. "Simu-Real: A Simulation Approach to Organizational Change." *Journal of Applied Behavioral Science,* 1992, *28,* 566–578.

Owen, H. *Open Space Technology: A User's Guide.* Potomac, Md.: Abbott, 1992.

Owen, H. *Tales from Open Space.* Potomac, Md.: Abbott, 1995.

Spencer, L. J. *Winning Through Participation.* Dubuque, Iowa: Kendall/Hunt, 1989.

Weisbord, M. R., and Janoff, S. *Future Search.* San Francisco: Jossey-Bass, 1995.

PART EIGHT

LOOKING
TO THE FUTURE

CHAPTER TWENTY-SEVEN

A Framework for Thinking About Research on Conflict Resolution Training

Morton Deutsch

I n this chapter, I sketch out a framework for thinking about research on conflict resolution training (CRT). First, I consider types of research and for what kind of issue each is most suited. Second, I discuss briefly types of audience, or users of research, and what they want. Here, I describe some substantive issues or questions for research that practitioners consider to be important. Next, I consider some of the difficulties in doing research in this area as well as what kind of research strategies may be helpful in overcoming these difficulties. Finally, I offer a brief overview of existing research in this area.

TYPES OF RESEARCH

There are many kinds of research, all of which have merit. They have differing purposes and often require varying types of skill. There is a tendency among both researchers and practitioners to derogate research that does not satisfy their specific needs or that does not require their particular kind of expertise. Thus, "action research" is frequently considered to be second-class research by basic researchers and "basic research" is often thought of as impractical and wasteful by practitioners. Elsewhere (Deutsch, 1973), I have termed such conflict, which is based on misunderstanding (rather than on a valid conflict of value, fact, or interest), a "false" conflict.

I now turn to a discussion of several types of research that are relevant to conflict resolution: basic research, developmental research, field research, consumer research, and action research. Some researchers work primarily in one type; others move back and forth among them. I start my list with a discussion of basic research, but I do not assume the natural flow is unidirectional from basic to developmental research, and so forth. The flow is (and should usually be) bidirectional: basic does not mean initial.

Basic Research

There are many unanswered questions basic to knowledge and practice in the field of conflict resolution. To illustrate just a few:

- What is the nature of the skills involved in constructive conflict resolution? How are they the same or different from the skills involved in such physical activities as playing tennis? What is it that limits or enables their use according to circumstances?

- What determines when a conflict is ripe for intervention or mediation? What gives rise to intractable conflict, and how can it be changed constructively?

- What are the basic dimensions along which kinds of culture vary in their response to and management of conflict?

- How can people learn to control transference and countertransference (to use psychoanalytic terms) so that their emotional vulnerability does not lead to counterproductive behavior during conflict?

- What are the important similarities and differences in conflict processes at the interpersonal, intergroup, and international levels?

- What are reliable, valid, and reasonably precise ways of measuring the knowledge, attitudes, and skills involved in constructive conflict resolution?

- What are the intervening psychological processes that lead to enduring and generalized change in managing conflict, and what are the psychological and social consequences of such change?

- What are the most effective ways of dealing with difficult conflict and difficult people?

- What type of value system is implicit in the current practice of conflict resolution?

These are only a few of the important questions that must be addressed if we are to have the kind of knowledge that is useful for those interested in making conflict constructive—whether it be in school, the family, industry, or community. Many other questions are implicit in the various chapters of this book.

Developmental Research

Much developmental research is concerned with helping to shape effective educational and training programs in this area. Such research is concerned with identifying the best ways of aiding people to acquire the knowledge, attitudes, and skills necessary for constructive conflict resolution by answering such questions as, How should something be taught (for example, using what type of teaching methods or pedagogy)? What should be taught (using what curriculum)? For how long? Who should do the teaching? In what circumstances? With what teaching aids? These best ways are apt to vary as a function of the age, educational level, cultural group, and personality of the children and adults involved.

There is a bidirectional link between developmental and basic research. To assess and compare the changes resulting from various educational and training programs, it is necessary to know what changes these programs were seeking to induce and also to develop valid and reliable measuring instruments and procedures for measuring these changes.

I note that there has been very little of the kind of research suggested here. Some evaluation research has indicated that CRT is viewed as worthwhile by its consumers; some has demonstrated that such training has worthwhile effects on self-esteem and on reducing destructive forms of conflict. We are now at the point where we need to go beyond demonstrating that CRT can be worthwhile; we have to start studying what types of training are most effective and most efficient.

Field Research

Much developmental research can be done in experimental classrooms or workshops. However, field research is needed to identify the features of political systems, cultures, and organizations that facilitate or hinder effective CRT. Can CRT have desirable effects with inner-city high school students living and studying under adverse circumstances? What kind of culture is most favorable to such training, and what kind makes it unfeasible or ineffective? Which levels in an organizational hierarchy must be knowledgeable and supportive of CRT for it to be effective? In schools, what type of CRT model should be employed: extracurricular activity, a specific course in CR, an infusion model in all school courses, use of constructive controversy, or all of the above? Is cooperative learning a necessary precondition or a complement to CRT? Who should teach CR: a specialist in CRT, a teacher, a student, or a parent? What criteria should be employed in selecting CR trainers? And so forth.

Most of these questions have to be asked and answered in terms of the specific characteristics of the individual school, taking into account the resources, organization, personnel, student body, and social setting. Little if any research has been done on questions of this type because it is difficult and expensive to do direct research on them. In a subsequent section, we discuss *experience surveys* as an alternative, feasible approach to such issues.

Consumer Research

It would be valuable to have periodic surveys of where CRT is taking place, who is being trained, what kind of qualification the trainers have, and so on. Also, it would be good to know how their CRT training is evaluated by its recipients, immediately after training and one year later. In addition to studying those who have had CRT, it would be useful to assess what the market is for CRT among those who have not had it.

Most of the research on CRT in schools and other organizations has been essentially study of "consumer satisfaction." The research has usually involved studying the effects of CRT in a particular classroom, workshop, or school. Results are quite consistent in indicating a considerable degree of approval among those exposed to CRT, whether in the role of teacher, student, or parent of a student. This is indeed encouraging, but awareness of the Hawthorne effect suggests both caution in our conclusions and the need to go considerably beyond consumer-satisfaction research. (The Hawthorne effect, of course, refers to research suggesting that almost every program that is introduced has beneficial effects on the people involved simply because of the increased attention they receive.)

Action Research

Action research is a term originally employed by Kurt Lewin to refer to research linked to social action. To be successful, it requires active collaboration between the action personnel—the trainers, school personnel, and practitioners—and the research personnel. What the action personnel do can be guided by feedback from the research concerning the effectiveness of their actions. To study the processes involved in successfully producing a change (or failing to do so) in a well-controlled, systematic manner, the researchers depend on the action personnel being cooperative. Most research on CRT in the schools—no matter how it is otherwise labeled—is a form of action research.

There are two main ways in which successful collaboration with practitioners increases the likelihood that research findings are used. First, participation usually raises the practitioners' interest in the research and its possible usefulness. Second, collaboration with practitioners helps to ensure that the research is relevant to problems as they appear in the actual work of the practitioners and the functioning of the organization in which their practice is embedded.

However, there are many potential sources of difficulty in this collaboration. It is time consuming and hence often burdensome and expensive to both the practitioners and researchers. Also, friction may occur because of the disparate goals and standards of the two partners: one is concerned with improving existing services, the other with advancing knowledge of a given phenomenon. The practitioner may well become impatient with the researcher's attempt to have well-controlled independent variables and the intrusiveness involved in extensive measuring of dependent variables. The researcher may become exasperated with the practitioner's improvisation and reluctance to sacrifice time from other activities to achieve the research objectives. In addition, there is often much evaluation apprehension on both sides: the practitioners are concerned that, wittingly or unwittingly, they will be evaluated by the research findings; the researchers fear that their peers will view their research as not being sufficiently well controlled to have any merit.

AUDIENCES FOR RESEARCH

There are several audiences for research: foundations and government agencies, executives and administrators who decide whether CRT takes place in their organization, CRT practitioners and teachers who do CRT, and researchers who do one or more of the types of research described earlier. The audiences rarely have identical interests.

Funding Agencies

In my limited experience with foundations, I have gained the impression that most are less interested in supporting research than they are in supporting pilot training programs, particularly if such programs focus on preventing violence. Their interest in research is mainly oriented to evaluation, to answering the question, "Does it work?" Many government agencies have interests that are similar to those of private foundations, but some, such as the National Science Foundation and the National Institute of Mental Health, are willing to support basic and developmental research if the research is clearly relevant to their mission.

It is my view that research on the question of "Does it work?" is a waste of scarce resources. Unfortunately, this view is not widely shared by funding agencies. There is enough credible evidence to indicate that CRT *can* have positive effects. The appropriate question now is under what conditions such effects are most likely to occur—for example, *who* benefits, *how,* as a result of receiving *what type of training* and by *what kind of trainer,* in *what kind of circumstance*? That is, the field of conflict resolution has advanced beyond the need to answer the oversimplified question of "Does it work?"; it must address the more complicated questions discussed in the section on types of research—particularly the questions related to developmental research.

Executives and Administrators

The executive and administrative audience is also concerned with the question of "Does it work?" But depending on their organizational setting, they may have different criteria in mind in assessing the value of CRT. A school administrator may be interested in such criteria as the incidence of violence, disciplinary problems, academic achievement, social and psychological functioning of students, teacher burnout, and cooperative relations between teachers and administrators. A corporate executive may be concerned with manager effectiveness, ease and effectiveness of introducing technological change, employee turnover and absenteeism, organizational climate, productivity, and the like.

It is fair to say that, with rare exceptions, CRT researchers and practitioners have not developed the detailed causal models that would enable them to specify and measure the mediating organizational and psychological processes linking CRT to specific organizational or individual changes. Most executives and administrators are not much interested in causal models. However, it is important for practitioners and researchers to be aware that the criteria of CRT effectiveness often used by administrators—incidence of violence, academic achievement, employee productivity—are affected by many factors other than CRT. It may, for example, be successful in increasing the social skills of students, but a sharp increase in unemployment, significant decrease in the standard of living, or greater use of drugs in the students' neighborhood may lead to deterioration of the students' social environment rather than the improvement one can expect from increased social skills. The negative impact of such deterioration may counteract the positive impact of CRT training.

One would expect executives and administrators to be interested in knowing not only whether CRT produces the outcomes they seek but also whether it is more cost-effective in doing so than alternative interventions. Some research has evaluated the effectiveness of alternative dispute resolution procedures, such as mediation (see Chapter Twenty-Five) compared to adjudication, but otherwise there is little research examining the cost-effectiveness of CRT.

Practitioners

Recently, I was at a conference of practitioners, educators, and researchers who were concerned with developing suggestions for a research agenda on conflict resolution in the schools. Practitioners suggested a large number of varied issues for possible research. Many are similar to the research questions listed earlier under types of research.

The suggestions had two interrelated foci: issues relating to individual change and those relating to institutional change. With regard to each focus, the practitioners articulated a need to have measuring instruments that they could use to assess the effectiveness of their training. Some felt that such instruments would be of particular value to them in relation to funding agencies and policy makers. A number of practitioners sensibly felt that the methods they used during their training and consulting, to check on the effects they were having, were more detailed and sensitive than the typical questionnaires used in evaluation. Their own methods were more useful to them even if less persuasive to funding agencies. As a researcher, it seemed to me that a lot could be learned of general value from a study of the implicit theoretical models underlying the work of practitioners, as well as a study of how practitioners go about assessing the impact of what they are doing.

The focus on individual change was concerned with such issues as these:

- How much transfer of training is there from the school to the student's other social contexts? How long do the effects of training endure? What factors affect transfer and long-term outcomes?

- How can training be responsive to individual differences among students in personality, intelligence, age level, social class, ethnic group, gender, and religion?

- How important is similarity in social cultural background between trainer and student in promoting effective CRT? Are well-trained student trainers particularly effective in training other students?

- What models of training are being employed among trainers?

- Can levels of expertise be characterized? How long and pervasive does training have to be for these levels?

- What selection and training procedures should be employed with regard to CRT trainees? with regard to trainers of trainers?

- How early should CRT begin?

The focus on institutional change was concerned with other questions:

- Must the adults in the system—the administrators, teachers, parents, staff, and guards—receive CRT training if students' training is to be effective? Must other community institutions be involved, such as the church, the police, health providers, and other community agencies?

- What are the most effective models for institutionalizing CRT in the schools?

- What changes in the curricula, pedagogy, and school culture are typically associated with a significant institutional change?

- What critical mass of students, teachers, administrators, and parental involvement is necessary for systemic change?

It is evident that the issues raised by the practitioners are important but complex and not readily answerable by a traditional research approach. In addition, the complexity suggests that each question contains a nest of others that have to be specified in greater detail before they are accessible to research.

Researchers

Psychologically, other researchers are usually the most important audience for one's research. If your research does not meet the standards established for your field of research, you can expect it to be rejected as unfit for publication in a respected research journal. This may harm your reputation as a researcher—and may make tenure less likely if you are a young professor seeking it. This may be true even if funding agencies, administrators, and practitioners find the research to be very useful to them.

The research standard for psychology and many other social sciences is derived from the model of the experiment. If one designs and conducts an experiment ideally, one has created the best conditions for obtaining valid and reliable results. In research as in life, the ideal is rarely attainable. Researchers have developed various procedures to compensate for deviation from the ideal in their attempt to approximate it. However, there is a bias in the field toward assuming that research that looks like an experiment (for example, it has control groups, and before-and-after measures) but is not because it lacks randomization and has too few cases (more on this later) is inherently superior to other modes of approximation. I disagree. In my view, each mode has its merits and limitations and may be useful in investigating a certain type of research question but less so in another.

I suggest three key standards for research: (1) the mode of research should be appropriate to the problem being investigated, (2) it should be conducted as well as humanly possible given the available resources and circumstances, and (3) it should be knowledgeable and explicit about its limitations.

RESEARCH STRATEGIES

Many factors make it very difficult to do research on the questions outlined in the previous sections, particularly the kind of idealized research that most researchers would prefer to do. For example, it is rarely possible to assign students (or teachers, or administrators) randomly to be trained (or not trained) by randomly assigned expert trainers employing randomly assigned training procedures. Even if this were possible in a particular school district, one would face the possibility that the uniqueness of the district has a significant impact on the effectiveness of training; no single district can be considered an adequate sample of all or other school districts. To employ an adequate sample (which is necessary for appropriate statistical analysis) is very costly and probably neither financially nor administratively feasible.

Given this reality, what kind of research can be done that is worth doing? Here I outline several mutually supportive research strategies of potential value.

Experimental and Quasi-Experimental Research

Experimental research involves small-scale studies that can be conducted in research laboratories, experimental classrooms, or experimental workshops. It is most suitable for questions related to basic or developmental research, questions specific as to what is to be investigated. Thus, such approaches would be appropriate if one sought to test the hypothesis that role reversal does not facilitate constructive conflict resolution when the conflict is about values (such as euthanasia) but does when it centers on interests. Similarly, it would be appropriate if one wished to examine the relative effectiveness of two different methods of training in improving such conflict resolution skills as perspective taking and reframing.

This kind of research is most productive if the hypothesis or question being investigated is well-grounded in theory or in a systematic set of ideas rather than when it is ad hoc. If well-grounded, such research has implications for the set of ideas within which it is grounded and thus has more general implications than testing an ad hoc hypothesis does. One must, however, be aware that in this type (as well as in all other types) of hypothesis-driven research, a hypothesis may not be supported—even if it is valid—because implementation of the causal variables (such as the training methods), measurement of their effects, or the research design may be faulty. Generally, it is easier to obtain nonsignificant results than to find support for a hypothesis. Thus, practitioners have good reason to be concerned about the possibility that such research may make their efforts appear insignificant even though their work is having important positive effects.

In good conscience, one other point must be made. It is very difficult and perhaps impossible to create a true or pure experiment involving human beings. The logic involved in true experiments assumes that complete randomization has occurred for all other variables except the causal variables being studied. But human beings have life histories, personalities, values, and attitudes prior to their participation in a conflict workshop or experiment. What they bring to the experiment from their prior experience may not only influence the effectiveness of the causal variables being studied but also be reflected directly in the measurement of the effects of these variables.

Thus, an authoritarian, antidemocratic, alienated member of the Aryan Nation Militia Group may not only be unresponsive to CRT but also, independently of this, score poorly on such measures of the effectiveness of CRT as ethnocentrism, alienation, authoritarianism, and control of violence because of his or her initial attitudes. Such people are also less likely to participate in CRT than democratic, nonviolent, and nonalienated people. The latter are apt to be responsive to CRT and, independently of this, to have good scores on egalitarianism, nonviolence, lack of ethnocentrism, and the like, which also reflect their initial attitudes.

With appropriate "before" measures and correlational statistics, it is possible to control for much (but far from all) of the influence of initial differences in attitudes on the "after" measures. In other words, a quasi-experiment that has some resemblance to a true experiment can be created despite the prior histories of the people who are being studied.

Causal Modeling

Correlations, by themselves, do not readily permit causal inference. If you find a negative correlation between amount of exposure to CRT and authoritarianism, as I have suggested, it may be that those who are authoritarian are less apt to expose themselves to CRT, or those who have been exposed to CRT become less authoritarian, or the causal arrow may point in both directions. It is impossible to tell from a simple correlation. However, methods of statistical analysis developed during the past several decades (and still being refined) enable one to appraise with considerable precision how well a *pattern* of correlations within a set of data fits an a priori causal model. Although causal modeling and experimental research are a mutually supportive combination, causal modeling can be employed even if an approximation to an experimental design cannot be achieved. This is likely to be the case in most field studies.

Consider, for example, a study we completed several years ago on the effects of training in cooperative learning and conflict resolution on students in an alternative high school (Deutsch, 1993; Zhang, 1994). Prior theoretical analysis (Deutsch, 1949, 1973; Johnson and Johnson, 1989) as well as much experimental and quasi-experimental research (see Johnson and Johnson, 1989, for a comprehensive review) suggested what effects such training could have and also suggested the causal process that might lead to these effects. Limitation of resources made it impossible to do the sort of extensive study of many schools required for an experimental or quasi-experimental study, or to employ the statistical analysis appropriate to an experiment. So we constructed a causal model that, in essence, assumed training in cooperative learning and/or conflict resolution would improve the social skills of a student. This, in turn, would produce an improved social environment for the student (as reflected in greater social support as well as less victimization from others), which would lead to higher self-esteem and more sense of personal control over one's fate. The increased sense of control would enhance academic achievement. It was also assumed that improvement in the student's social environment and self-esteem would lead to increased positive sense of well-being as well as decreased anxiety and depression. The causal model indicated what we had to measure. Prudence suggested that we also measure many other things that potentially might affect the variables on which the causal model focused.

The results of the study were consistent with our causal model. Even though the study was quite limited in scope—having been conducted in only one alternative high school—the results have some general significance. They are consistent with prior theory and also with prior research conducted in very different and much more favorable social contexts. The set of ideas underlying the research appears to be applicable to students in the difficult, harsh environment of an inner-city school as well as to students in well-supported, upper-middle-class elementary and high schools.

Nonexperimental field research is either exploratory or testing of a causal model, or some combination of both. Exploratory research is directed at describing the relations and developing the set of ideas that underlie a causal model. Typically, it is inappropriate to test a causal model with the data collected to stimulate its development. Researchers are notoriously ingenious in developing ex post facto explanations of data they have obtained, no matter how their studies have turned out. A priori explanations are much more credible. This is why nonexploratory research has to be well grounded in prior theory and research, if it is to be designed to clearly bear on the general ideas embedded in the causal model. However, even if a study is mainly nonexploratory, exploratory data may be collected so as to refine one's model for future studies.

Survey Research

This form of research is widely used in market research, preelection polling; opinion research; research on the occurrence of crime; and collection of economic data on unemployment, inflation, sales of houses, and so on. A well-developed methodology exists concerning sampling, questionnaire construction, interviewing, and statistical analysis. Unfortunately, little survey research has taken place in the field of CRT. Some of the questions that could be answered by survey research have been discussed earlier, under the heading of consumer research. It is, of course, important to know about the potential (as well as existing) consumers of CRT. Similarly, it is important to know about current CRT practitioners: their demographics, their qualifications to practice, the models of training they employ, how long they have practiced, the nature of their clientele, the goals of their training, and their estimation of the degree of success.

Experience Surveys

Experience surveys are a special kind involving intensive in-depth interviews with a sample of people, individually or in small focus groups, who are considered to be experts in their field. The purpose of such surveys may be to obtain insight into the important questions needing research through the experts' identification of important gaps in knowledge or through the opposing views among the experts on a particular topic. In addition, interviewing experts, prior to embarking on a research study, generally improves the researcher's practical knowledge of the context within which her research is conducted and applied and thus helps her avoid the minefields and blunders into which naïveté may lead her.

More important, experts have a fund of knowledge, based on their deep immersion in the field, that may suggest useful, practical answers to questions that would be difficult or unfeasible to answer through other forms of research. Many of the questions mentioned earlier under the heading of field research are of this nature. Of course, one's confidence in the answers of the experts is eventually affected by how much they agree or disagree.

There are several steps involved in an experience survey. The first is to identify the type of expert you want to survey. For example, with respect to CRT in schools, one might want to survey practitioners (the trainers of trainees), teachers who have been trained, students, or administrators of schools in which CRT has occurred. The second step is to contact several experts of the type you wish to interview and have them nominate other experts, who in turn nominate other experts. After several rounds of such nominations, a group of nominees usually emerges as being widely viewed as experts. The third step is to develop an interview schedule. This typically entails formulating a preliminary one that is tried out and modified as a result of interviews with a half dozen or so of the experts individually and also as a group. The revised schedule is formulated so as to ask all of the questions one wants to have answered by the experts, while leaving the expert the opportunity to raise issues and answer the questions in a way that was not anticipated by the researcher.

Many years ago, Mary Collins and I (Deutsch and Collins, 1951) conducted an experience survey of public housing officials prior to conducting a study of interracial housing. Our objective was to identify the important issues that could be the focus of our future study. It led us to study the effects of the occupancy patterns: whether the white and black tenants were housed in racially integrated or racially segregated buildings in a given housing project. Additionally, the survey created a valuable handbook of the various other factors that, in the officials' experience, affected race relations in public housing. It was a useful guide to anyone seeking to improve race relations in public housing projects.

Although it is possible for the experts to be wrong—to have commonly held, mistaken, implicit assumptions—their articulated views are an important starting point either as constructive criticism or as a guide to informed practice.

Learning by Analogy

Not only can the field of CRT learn from its experienced practitioners, it can also learn from the work done in other closely related areas. Many of the issues involved in CRT have been addressed in other areas: transfer of training is of considerable concern to learning theorists and to the field of education generally; communication skills have been the focus of much research in the fields of language and communication as well as social psychology; anger, aggression, and violence have been studied extensively by various specialities in psychology and psychiatry; and there is an extensive literature related to cooperation and competition. Similarly, creative problem solving and decision making have been the focus of much theoretical and applied activity. Terms such as attitude change, social change, culture change, psychodynamics, group dynamics, ethnocentrism, resistance, perspective taking, and the like are common to CRT and older areas. Although CRT is relatively young, it has roots in many well-established areas and can learn much from the prior work in these areas. The purpose of this handbook is, of course, to provide knowledge of many of these relevant areas to those interested in conflict resolution.

As an educational innovation, CRT is also relatively young. There is, however, a vast literature on innovation in education and the factors affecting the success or lack of success in institutionalizing an innovation in schools. In particular, by analogy cooperative learning could offer much useful experience for CRT in this regard. Cooperative learning, which is conceptually closely related to CRT, has accumulated a considerable body of experience that might help CRT practitioners understand what leads to success or failure in institutionalizing a school program of CRT.

RESEARCH EVALUATING
CONFLICT RESOLUTION PROGRAMS

A few years ago, I wrote that "there is an appalling lack of research on the various aspects of training in the field of conflict resolution" (Deutsch, 1995, p. 128). The situation has been improving since then. There is now much evidence from school systems of the positive effects of conflict resolution training on the students who were trained. Most of the evidence is based on evaluations by the students, teachers, parents, and administrators. In Lim and Deutsch's international study (1997), almost all institutions surveyed reported positive evaluations by each of the populations filling out questionnaires. Similar results are reported in evaluations made for school programs in Ohio, Nevada, Chicago, New York City, New Mexico, Florida, and Texas (see Bodine and Crawford, 1998; Lam, 1989). Most of the evaluations were based on questionnaires or interviews. Some of the studies also focused on mediation training. Generally, highly positive effects were found for the student mediators on their self-esteem as well as their conflict behavior in and out of school, as reported by their teachers and parents. Also, most of the disputants who participated in the mediation had positive reactions to it.

Very few of these evaluation studies have control groups or before-after measures, which would allow the kind of statistical analyses that determine whether the changes are due to the CRT. Kmitta (1998) has recently reported a meta-analysis of eight such studies. His findings reveal only a few statistically significant effects of CRT. However, he points out that the studies all had major methodological problems and that the number of studies, eight, is too small for a meta-analysis.

Supplementing the questionnaire studies, some of the schools have reported on the effects of training on school violence, discipline problems, and other student behavior. Here are some typical examples cited in Bodine and Crawford (1998):

- In evaluation of the New York City Resolving Conflict Creatively Program, 71 percent of teachers involved reported moderate or great decreases in physical violence in the classroom, and 66 percent observed less name-calling and fewer verbal put-downs.

- A mediation program in a number of New York City high schools reported suspensions for fighting decreased by 46, 45, 70, 60, and 65 percent in five of the high schools during the first year of program operation.

- The Peace Education Foundation's Conflict Resolution and Peer Mediation Program in Dade County and Palm Beach County in Florida also indicates a significant decrease in referrals for disruptive behavior. In one elementary school, referrals dropped from 124 between September and December in 1992 to 5 during the same period in 1994.

In addition, there is a very small body of systematic research (see Deutsch and others, 1992; Johnson and Johnson, 1989, 1995, 1996) indicating that the students who participate in such programs develop social skills, more self-esteem, a greater sense of personal control over their lives, higher academic achievement, and so on. However, it should be noted that the amount of high-quality, systematic research of long enough duration is small. There have been few systematic studies of the effects of such programs on youth violence.

A series of fourteen studies by Johnson and Johnson (1995, 1996) as well as two recent, as yet unpublished, studies of which I have seen preliminary reports (Jones, 1997; Aber and others, forthcoming), have been well designed and have significant findings.

Johnson and Johnson Studies

Johnson and Johnson (1995) and Stevahn, Johnson, and Johnson (1996) offer systematic small-scale studies of the effects of implementing their Peacemaker Program in classrooms, involving students from kindergarten through the tenth grade. Their program includes teaching students problem-solving negotiations and peer-mediation procedures, as well as involving them in constructive controversy. The results can be summarized here:

- Students and faculty tended to develop shared understanding of how conflicts should be managed and a common vocabulary to discuss conflicts.

- Students also tended to learn the negotiation and mediation procedures, retain their knowledge throughout the school year and into the following year, apply the procedures to their own and other people's conflicts, transfer the procedures to nonclassroom settings such as the playground and lunchroom, transfer the procedures to nonschool settings such as the home, and use the procedures similarly in family and school settings.

- Further, students learned to view conflict as potentially positive, and faculty and parents viewed the conflict training as constructive and helpful.

- The number of discipline problems teachers had to deal with decreased by about 60 percent; referrals to administrators dropped about 90 percent. Faculty and administrators no longer had to arbitrate conflict among students; instead they spent their time maintaining and supporting the peer-mediation process.

- The conflict resolution procedures tended to enhance the basic value of respect in the classroom and school, making those locations calmer.

Comprehensive Peer Mediation Evaluation Project

The Comprehensive Peer Mediation Evaluation Project (CPMEP), conducted by Jones and her colleagues, involved twenty-seven schools with a student population of about twenty-six thousand, a teacher population of approximately fifteen hundred, and a staff population of about seventeen hundred (Jones, 1997). They employed a three-by-three design: three levels of schools (elementary, middle, and high school); each level of school was exposed to either peer mediation only (a "cadre program"), peer mediation plus (a "whole school program"), or no training at all ("control groups"). The training and research occurred over a two-year period.

I do not have the space to report all of their interesting findings. Instead, I draw on their summary of general conclusions.

- *Peer-mediation programs yield significant benefit in developing constructive social and conflict behavior in children at all educational levels.* It is clear that exposure to peer-mediation programs, whether cadre or whole school, has a significant and lasting impact on students' conflict attitude and behavior. Students who are direct recipients of program training benefit the most; however, students without direct training also benefit. The data clearly demonstrate that exposure to peer mediation reduces personal conflict and increases the tendency to help others with conflict, increases prosocial values, decreases aggressiveness, and increases perspective taking and conflict competence. These effects are significant, cumulative, and sustained for long periods, especially for peer mediators. Students trained in mediation, at all educational levels, are able to enact and use the behavioral skills taught in training.

- *Peer-mediation programs significantly improve school climate.* The programs had a significant and sustained favorable impact on teacher and staff perceptions of school climate for both cadre and whole-school programs at all educational levels. The programs had a limited-to-moderate favorable effect on student perceptions of climate. There is no evidence that peer-mediation programs affected overall violence or suspension rates.

- *Peer mediation effectively handles peer disputes.* When used, peer mediation is very effective at handling disputes. There is a very high rate of agreement at all educational levels on high mediator and disputant satisfaction. However, the number of cases documented suggests that mediation may be underused given its effectiveness.

- *Both cadre and whole-school programs yield significant benefits. Cadre programs yield better individual outcomes, while whole-school programs yield better climate outcomes.* The results do not support the assumption that whole-school programs are clearly superior to cadre programs. The latter have a strong effect on students' conflict attitudes and behaviors, and whole-school programs have a strong impact in terms of school climate. Based on this evidence, schools that cannot afford a whole-school approach may secure similar, or even superior, benefits with a cadre program that is well implemented.

- *Peer-mediation programs are effective at all educational levels.* The programs have more influence on climate at the elementary school level, largely because of the ability to diffuse the impact in the smaller population. Otherwise, the difference between middle and high school levels is relatively unimportant. Peer-mediation programs have significant positive effect at all levels.

It is important to recognize that not only was this study well designed from a research point of view but also the conflict resolution training was well-designed and systematic. The training for the peer-mediation-only and peer-mediation-plus (whole-school program) conditions are outlined here.

For peer mediation only:

- Grades trained included fourth and fifth (elementary); sixth, seventh, and eighth (middle); and ninth, tenth, eleventh, and twelfth (high school).

- Eighteen to twenty-four students were trained per school in year one, and a second group was trained in year two.

- A minimum of fifteen hours of training was given in elementary schools and twenty to thirty hours in middle and high schools. Training was completed in four weeks or less and took place at the beginning of the fall semester in each year.

- Each school had a site leadership team (SLT) of four or five adults, with at least one teacher, one nonteaching staff member, and (where possible) one administrator. The SLT was responsible for day-to-day implementation and oversight of the peer-mediation program.

- Each training organization gave SLTs one day of front-end program implementation training and contacted SLTs biweekly to monitor program implementation, offer program activities, and debrief cases.

For peer-mediation-plus or whole-school programs, in addition to the peer-mediation training and activities, each whole-school program received (1) curriculum infusion training and (2) conflict skills training for staff.
Regarding curriculum infusion:

- Six to eight hours of training were given, using a standardized curriculum.

- A select group of teachers were trained (voluntarily, although any teacher could attend the training), who committed to using at least one period (forty-five minutes) per week of class time to teach from the conflict curriculum.

- One or two teachers per grade in elementary schools and two teachers per grade in middle and high schools delivered the conflict training in curriculum-infusion classes for at least one full semester following training.

- Participating teachers received ongoing contact and support from the training organization.

As for conflict skills training:

- It totaled six to eight hours of conflict skills training.

- It was offered to all adult staff of the school (teachers, nonteaching staff, and administrators).

- Curriculum infusion teachers and SLT members were required to attend.

The Resolving Conflict Creatively Program (RCCP)

The data for the study, conducted by Aber and others (forthcoming), come from evaluation of the Resolving Conflict Creatively Program (RCCP), a comprehensive intervention in violence prevention and intergroup understanding that involves seventeen hundred teachers and forty-five thousand children in 112 elementary, middle, and high schools throughout New York City. The evaluation focuses on more than eight thousand children and nearly four hundred teachers in fifteen elementary schools across four districts in New York City. The elementary schools are divided into four groups in varying stages of intervention: nonintervention, beginning stage, integration of some program components, and integration of all program components. This quasi-experimental evaluation design allows the relative effects of no-program implementation to be compared to varying levels of implementation, and it examines whether RCCP meets its own self-defined goals and objectives in fifteen schools.

At this writing, only data for the first year of the two-year study are available. Three interesting findings have emerged so far. First, the initial measurements (prior to training) indicate that as grade level increases (comparing grade one with grades two and three with grades four, five, and six), children have more aggressive fantasies, employ aggressive strategies more frequently, attribute hostility to others more frequently, and have fewer prosocial fantasies as well as employ prosocial strategies less frequently in a conflict scenario. The implication is that children become more aggressive over time unless CRT counteracts these tendencies. The second finding is that from the first to the second measurement, during the first year of training, the children overall become more aggressive and less prosocial.

The third finding is that this negative trend is significantly affected by how much the teachers implemented CRT in the classroom. The children with teachers who received a moderate amount of training and gave most lessons showed the least negative trend, and the children with teachers having a high amount of training but giving few lessons showed the most pronounced negative trend, more so than the teachers with no training who gave no lessons.

These findings are quite evocative. One wants to know whether the negative trend associated with age is general or confined to the sort of inhospitable environment to which many schoolchildren in New York City are exposed. (The data from the Jones study should shed some light here.) Does the negative trend plateau at a certain age? And so forth.

Perhaps an even more important question has to do with understanding the conditions that lead to implementing CRT. Why did many of the teachers with a high level of training implement only a few or no lessons in the classroom? Tom Roderick, director of the RCCP in New York, points out "of the 20–25 teachers who get involved in the RCCP in a school over a period of several years, four or five typically embrace the program and teach the curriculum regularly, while the rest drop away" (1998, p. 20). Are there systematic differences between the teachers who embrace the program and those who don't? Is it more a question of school readiness and support for CRT than teacher readiness? Are teachers and schools apt to implement one type of CRT program more than another?

CONCLUSION

This chapter was stimulated by the paucity of research on the various aspects of training in the field of conflict resolution. The paucity is due to a number of factors, including lack of adequate funding to support the kind of research that would be valuable to do. Another important factor is lack of appreciation of the large range of worthwhile questions in CRT that can be addressed by research, and the research strategies that are available to address them. In response to this latter factor, I have sketched out a framework for thinking about the research possibilities related to CRT.

References

Aber, J. L., and others. "Resolving Conflict Creatively: Evaluating the Developmental Effects of a School-Based Violence Prevention Program in Neighborhood and Classroom Context." *Developmental Psychopathology,* forthcoming.

Bodine, R. J., and Crawford, D. K. *The Handbook of Conflict Resolution Education: A Guide to Building Quality Programs in Schools.* San Francisco: Jossey-Bass, 1998.

Deutsch, M. "A Theory of Cooperation and Competition." *Human Relations,* 1949, *2,* 129–151.

Deutsch, M. *The Resolution of Conflict: Constructive and Destructive Processes.* New Haven: Yale University Press, 1973.

Deutsch, M. "The Effects of Training in Cooperative Learning and Conflict Resolution in an Alternative High School." *Cooperative Learning,* 1993, *13,* 2–5.

Deutsch, M. "The Constructive Management of Conflict: Developing the Knowledge and Crafting the Practice." In B. B. Bunker and J. Z. Rubin (eds.), *Conflict, Cooperation, and Justice: Essays Inspired by the Work of Morton Deutsch.* San Francisco: Jossey-Bass, 1995.

Deutsch, M., and Collins, M. E. *Interracial Housing: A Study of a Social Experiment.* Minneapolis: University of Minnesota Press, 1951.

Deutsch, M., and others. "The Effects of Training in Cooperative Learning and Conflict Resolution in an Alternative High School." Unpublished manuscript, Teachers College, Columbia University, 1992.

Johnson, D. W., and Johnson, R. T. *Cooperation and Competition: Theory and Research.* Edina, Minn.: Interaction, 1989.

Johnson, D. W., and Johnson, R. T. "Teaching Students to Be Peacemakers: Results of Five Years of Research." *Peace and Conflict: Journal of Peace Psychology,* 1995, *1,* 417–438.

Johnson, D. W., and Johnson, R. T. "Conflict Resolution and Peer Mediation Programs in Schools: A Review of the Research." *Review of Educational Research,* 1996, *66,* 459–506.

Jones, T. S. "Comprehensive Peer Mediation Evaluation Project: Preliminary Final Report." Report submitted to the William and Flora Hewlett Foundation and the Surdna Foundation, 1997.

Kmitta, D. "A Preliminary Meta-Analysis of School-Based Conflict Resolution Programs." *Fourth R,* 1998, *82*(5–6), 22–24.

Lam, J. *The Impact of Conflict Resolution on Schools: A Review and Synthesis of the Evidence.* (2nd ed.) Amherst, Mass.: National Association for Mediation Education, 1989.

Lim, Y., and Deutsch, M. *International Examples of School-Based Programs Involving Peaceful Conflict Resolution and Mediation Oriented to Overcoming Community Violence: A Report to UNESCO.* New York: International Center for Cooperation and Conflict Resolution, Teachers College, Columbia University, 1997.

Roderick, T. "Evaluating the Resolving Conflict Creatively Program." *Fourth R,* 1998, *82*(3–4), 19–21.

Stevahn, L., Johnson, D. W., and Johnson, R. T. "Integrating Conflict Resolution Training into Academic Curriculum Units: Results of Recent Studies." Paper presented at the annual meeting of the American Educational Research Association, New York, 1996.

Zhang, Q. "An Intervention Model of Constructive Conflict Resolution and Cooperative Learning." *Journal of Social Issues,* 1994, *50*, 99–116.

CONCLUDING OVERVIEW

Peter T. Coleman

I would like to begin the conclusion of this volume with a story of hope. For the past two years, our center, the International Center for Cooperation and Conflict Resolution, has cosponsored a course with our colleagues at Columbia University's School of International and Public Affairs on the theory and practice of preventive diplomacy and conflict resolution at the United Nations. This has been an innovative course, bringing eminent theorists and researchers from academia together with highly skilled international practitioners and encouraging lively dialogue among them. The students for the course have been a mix of graduate students from Columbia and UN personnel.

I began the course this year with a conceptual overview of Deutsch's theory of cooperation and competition (see Chapter One) and discussion of its relevance for resolving international conflict. After my remarks, we asked the students to work in small groups to apply the ideas from the theory to the emerging conflict in Kosovo (this was in January 1999, prior to the NATO bombing campaign), with the objective of generating recommendations for the UN and for the international community.

At the conclusion of this exercise, one particularly articulate student, a military attaché to a UN ambassador, summarized his group's discussion. He said they felt there were few feasible options to the crisis other than recommending that NATO threaten to bomb or use other force against the Serbians to stop the ethnic cleansing in the area. There was general consensus on this conclusion among the students in the class.

Three months later, at the final meeting of the course, Richard Holbrook (whose position as U.S. ambassador to the UN was at that time pending approval in Congress) spoke to the class about what was then current US and NATO policy in Kosovo and Serbia. Holbrook spoke passionately for the need to continue the bombing campaign against the Serbs. His argument was detailed, articulate, and very convincing. After Holbrook concluded his statement, he left the room—but discussion of the situation in the former Yugoslavia continued.

It was at this point that the same young attaché who had advocated bombing earlier in the term spoke again. He began by saying that he had been struck by something during Holbrook's remarks: the fact that the military initiatives that were typically employed in these situations, such as use of bombing missions or sending in ground troops, were rarely successful in achieving their political objectives. The objectives, he claimed, in many such situations were to inflict enough harm on the general population that either the leadership feels its pain and acquiesces, or the people organize and remove the leaders. The use of military force, he said, as we had seen in Vietnam, Iraq, and now in Kosovo, rarely achieved these objectives. I paraphrase him: "The notion of bombing a village in order to save it, as in Vietnam, is insane. The Serbs are bombing Kosovo in order to save it, and we are bombing Serbia in order to save it. It simply makes no sense. There has to be a better way!"

He continued, as best I recall: "Every day I look at a map of Africa hanging in my office, and I think that if these are the types of solutions we have to offer the many conflicts on that continent, there will never be peace." Here was an accomplished U.S. Marine, someone who had risen in the ranks of the military to a position of substantial importance, stating emphatically, "There has to be a better way!" In subsequent discussion with this student, he thanked me for my role in the course and said that learning about a constructive approach to conflict had challenged his thinking about conflict resolution and peacemaking in important ways.

For more than seventy years, scholars and practitioners in the field of conflict resolution have been searching for a better way. As is evident in the many chapters of this handbook, a great deal of progress has been made toward understanding conflict and resolving it constructively. However, a great deal of work remains to be done.

I find this opening story hopeful because it illustrates how education in conflict resolution, particularly when presented in practical terms to individuals who are in influential positions, can begin to have an important impact on our world. The story also points out, however, that there are no simple answers to complex conflicts, and that we all must keep striving to find a better way.

THE CHALLENGES THAT LIE AHEAD

In the last section of the Introduction to this handbook, Morton Deutsch outlined eight questions that the field of conflict resolution has been, or is currently

addressing. In this, the final chapter, I outline some of the questions and challenges that theorists, researchers, and practitioners of conflict resolution will
face in their work in the years ahead. Many of the issues outlined here are
themes that run throughout the book, but I summarize them here for purposes
of clarity and to begin to set out a new agenda for scholar-practitioner collaboration in the field.

Readiness

The first question is, how can readiness to resolve conflict constructively be fostered in individuals, groups, and nations?

This raises many issues, several of which were touched on in the chapters
on personality, intractable conflict, training, and large-group intervention in this
volume. However, many questions remain. People and institutions are seldom
ready to undertake significant change. Yet competitive and avoidant approaches
to resolving conflict are ingrained in many people and institutions; collaborative, integrative approaches represent a new way of thinking and acting for
them. The collaborative approach generally goes against the prevalent competitive style of resolving conflict modeled in families; by the media; and by many
of our leaders in sports, business, and government.

The first task is, quite often, simply to make people aware that there are options available to them when in conflict other than to fight or flee. This is largely
what most preliminary training or coursework in conflict resolution attempts to
achieve: to make people aware of their own competitive or avoidant tendencies
in conflict, and of the fact that they have a broad menu of available options. For
these educational experiences to be successful, it is important that they effectively engage and inspire students sufficiently to motivate them to try something new and to develop the skills necessary to begin resolving conflict
constructively.

A separate but related concern with regard to readiness has to do with our
ability to assess and engender a degree of *authentic readiness* for disputants involved in a conflict. Collaborative negotiation and mediation are voluntary
processes that require the disputants to engage in them willingly if they are to
make real progress toward understanding each other's needs and reaching
agreement. At times, disputants may "act cooperative" during a negotiation
process, while having no intention of following through once an agreement has
been reached. This was thought to have occurred at the Cambodian Peace Ac-
cords in the mid-1990s, an exemplary collaborative peace process that fell apart
upon implementation because the parties reneged on the agreement. Work
needs to be done on developing better methods of assessing and fostering disputants' genuine willingness to collaborate and make peace.

Systems must also be readied. Research has shown that unless schools and
districts are sufficiently motivated to embrace a change initiative such as insti-
tuting a program of conflict resolution training, it is likely to fail. This readiness

must exist for a majority of the system, including regents, board members, superintendents, principals, teachers, other professional staff, students, and parents. One method for assessing organizational readiness in schools is being used in the Learning Communities Project, initiated by the New York City Resolving Conflict Creatively Program, or RCCP (Roderick, 1998; see also the last part of Chapter Twenty-Seven). For a school to be included in the project, 70 percent or more of the faculty must vote in favor of its implementation. This approach could be taken for entire school districts, or even for statewide school initiatives. Administrators and conflict practitioners need to work to develop innovative methods of assessing and fostering readiness throughout these and other systems.

Finally, awareness of constructive responses to conflict needs to be widespread among the general population. One way of attaining this is for the field to attempt educating prestigious individuals in high-profile positions within a given society. In 1995, a campaign was initiated in Australia through the leadership of the nationwide Conflict Resolution Network (CRN), which sought to influence the campaign process of local, state, and federal elections in that country. Their basic objective was to ensure high-level political dialogue by encouraging the candidates to adopt an orientation to *issues, not insults; dialogue, not debate; and collaboration, not confrontation.* Immediate response to the campaign was very positive, with 32 percent of candidates for their House of Representatives committing to the CRN conflict-resolving principles. In the United States, the League of Women Voters has been doing important work in promoting its Code of Fair Campaign Practices, which requires candidates for public office to commit to uphold basic principles of decency, honesty, and fair play.

These efforts hope to foster a new type of political process, and a government that models respect, care, and common sense in addressing the issues, conflicts, and visions of the people it represents. A general shift in attitude and response to conflict could come about if those in influential positions of high visibility (political leaders; sports, entertainment, and media celebrities; and business leaders) were to model constructive strategies and skills.

Change Agents

Second, How can we help people in the field of conflict resolution understand and develop skills in their roles as change agents?

The field is increasingly aware of the fact that very often conflict professionals have to act as change agents within the systems in which they work. Whether intervening in a professional relationship, a family, an organization, a community, or a nation, it is useful to think about conflict resolution systemically. This has two implications, one practical and one political. The practical concerns the need to broaden understanding of what we do. Much of the emphasis of past work in the field has been on training conflict specialists in the skills of getting disputants to the table, facilitating a constructive process, and reaching an agreement. However, there is increasing recognition of the problems that occur in implementation, both in helping to ensure that disputants can effectively implement their agreements and in implementing effective mediation and training programs within larger systems.

In the case of disputes between individuals, it is not uncommon for good agreements to fall apart because of problems with implementation or changes that occur after the agreement is made. Conflict specialists need to be better trained to help disputants anticipate future problems and to build in feedback mechanisms so that if problems occur with implementation the disputants will attempt to resolve them collaboratively or return to the table to work them out.

Considerable challenges can also occur in implementing mediation or training programs within systems. There is increasing recognition of the difficulties of implementing any lasting change in systems with regard to dispute resolution mechanisms and the need to identify the processes and conditions that give rise to successful implementation. Introducing cooperation and conflict resolution concepts and practices into systems often involves, in a sense, a paradigm shift in how people see and approach problems. Fostering this type of fundamental change in the norms and practices of a system requires that conflict specialists have the necessary skills to motivate and persuade, organize, mobilize, and institutionalize the change. These skills need to be adequately integrated into the training of conflict specialists who work in systems, particularly complex ones.

The second implication of defining our work in terms of change concerns the conflict resolver's level of awareness of the political repercussions of his work. Intervening in part of any system in some way affects the whole system. If one department in an organization undergoes a substantial change in how it functions, this is likely to have an impact on the entire organization. It is therefore important for the intervenor to be informed about the political context in which he works and to be aware that the intervention has a potential impact on the balance of power existing within the system.

This is both a moral and a practical obligation. In *The Promise of Mediation* (1994), Bush and Folger discussed this issue under the heading "The Oppression Story" of mediation. They argued that in some settings, mediation can serve to oppress those in low power by masking patterns of injustice within systems or by allowing those in high power to set the agenda and intimidate. Conflict specialists must be trained to think in terms of the social and political processes within organizations, and to reflect critically on their own role in the power dynamics within institutions so that they can work fairly and effectively.

The Importance of Cultural Differences

The third challenging issue is, How can our growing recognition of the importance of cultural differences be used to improve the practice of constructive conflict resolution and to help develop universally valid theories in this area?

Most scientific theories and models of practice have the laudable aim of being universally true. Theorists commonly assume that the basic ideas in the theories related to cooperation and competition, equity theory, social judgement, communication, self-control, persuasion, and so on, are applicable to, say, the aborigines in Kakadu as much as to Park Avenue sophisticates, to people living in caves as well as to astronauts. However, most theories are developed in particular societies with their particular cultures, gender roles, and other characteristics.

Theorists often do not articulate their assumptions about the relations between the theory and the social context in which it is to be applied. Does a theory developed in the United States implicitly assume that the social context is one in which there is a market economy and individualistic values are strongly held? If so, it may only be applicable in social contexts similar to the ones in which it was developed. There is a strong need for the field of conflict resolution, and the social sciences generally, to develop explicit knowledge about the social context that is assumed in its relevant theories.

Even if the basic ideas of a theory are applicable in a variety of social contexts, specific implementation of its ideas is always dependent on the characteristics of the social context in which they are applied. Thus effective implementation of any of the theoretical ideas in this book depends on whether a practitioner is working in a social context (such as the American one) that is individualistic, has low power distances, is strongly task-oriented, has low uncertainty avoidance, and is masculine and modern, or in a social context that differs significantly on any of these dimensions.

In general, scholars and practitioners can respond to these concerns in several ways. First, it is important that both scholars and practitioners be aware of their own gendered, cultural, and societal mindsets with regard to their work (see Fisher, 1988). Kimmel (Chapter Twenty-Two) offers a useful stage model for self-examination in this area along a dimension from ethnocentricism to understanding. Some degree of mindfulness of our own biases and assumptions can help us examine our theories, models, and practices for similar biases and make them explicit.

Second, a significant amount of work has been conducted in the last two decades on identifying the psychological dimensions on which people differ due to variations in culture, ethnicity, religion, and gender (see Hofstede, 1980; Kolb and Coolidge, 1991; Markus and Kitayama, 1991; Segall, Lonner, and Berry, 1998). Conflict specialists working cross-culturally need to be informed about these dimensions and be mindful of how they affect the way people make meaning in conflict situations.

Third, scholars and practitioners need to better distinguish those elements of conflict resolution that are universal and therefore applicable across cultures from those that are not. For example, Deutsch (in Chapter One) has suggested that specific values such as reciprocity and nonviolence universally occur in enduring, voluntary, and significant relations of cooperation and constructive conflict resolution. The cross-cultural universality of the linkage between such values and constructive conflict resolution is different from the culturally specific usefulness of certain prescribed processes (such as recommendations to "separate the people from the problem," to openly express one's needs, or to take an analytical approach to understanding the issues); these are likely to vary considerably across cultures, gender, class, and so on.

Lederach (1995) has suggested practicing an "elicitive" approach when offering conflict resolution training across cultures. He argues that "prescriptive" approaches to training, which view the trainer as the expert and participants as passive recipients of predetermined knowledge, models, and skills, are often inappropriate in many cultures. Lederach advocates an approach where the context expertise of the participants is emphasized and combined with the process and content expertise of the trainer, so that the trainer and the participants together create a new model of constructive conflict resolution that is specifically suited to the resources and constraints of the particular social context in which the participants are embedded.

Conflict Within the Field of Conflict Resolution

Fourth, given the existence of much conflict in the field of conflict resolution (as among the scholarly disciplines, between theorists, researchers, and practitioners; and among training programs and graduate studies for scarce resources—students, clients, grants, and so on), how can the field learn to walk its talk and model how conflicts can be resolved constructively?

The field of conflict resolution has become, ironically, a fairly competitive arena. This competition and the resulting conflict between individuals, disciplines, programs, and institutions pose serious challenges to progress in our field.

For example, the various scholarly disciplines often approach conflict from contrasting perspectives. Take a dispute over water rights between two neighboring tribal groups. A social psychologist is first concerned with the characteristics of the parties, their prior relationship, the strategies and tactics they use in the dispute, their respective needs in the situation, escalatory dynamics, and so on. A legal scholar working in this area, however, is concerned with prior treaties or contracts, land rights, the existence of legal precedents, and so on. A scholar of international affairs may be oriented to contextual or structural factors such as the balance of power in the dispute or the national or regional sources and implications of the conflict. Scholars from anthropology, business, history, and economics may emphasize still other aspects of the situation.

At one level, these orientations are due simply to the varieties of educational training and task orientation. At a deeper level, however, beneath many of the disciplinary contrasts are ideological and value differences. If conflict is believed to exist within a unitary ideological frame (where society is seen as an integrated whole in which the interests of the individual and society are one) as opposed to a radical frame (where society is seen as comprising antagonistic class interests), it requires one kind of response and not another. Similarly, whether one's primary orientation to conflict is competitive or cooperative dictates strategy.

These and other variations in how conflict is understood and approached typically come into conflict themselves when scholars or practitioners attempt to work together. These days, because many of the significant conflicts that societies face are rooted in political, economic, and social histories and are fueled by social psychological dynamics, we are finding that analysis and resolution cannot be adequately conducted from any one disciplinary perspective; a multidisciplinary framework is required. But the traditional reward systems and orientations of the disciplines lessen the chances for such an approach. Combining traditional disciplinary paradigms and methodologies with multidisciplinary ones is a daunting task, though an essential one if the field of conflict resolution is to offer effective solutions to some of the worlds most perplexing problems.

Second, there is growing concern in the field of conflict resolution over the substantial gap between theory and practice. As described by Deutsch in the Introduction, many practitioners of conflict resolution dismiss the contributions of theorists and researchers, particularly if the research challenges their own opinions or methods. At the same time, scholars often fail to use the expertise of highly skilled practitioners in their development of theory, and research designs often fail to take into account what practitioners and policy makers want or need to know. In fact, a recent evaluation of the eighteen, mostly university-based, Hewlett Theory Centers found that the work of most practitioners surveyed was largely unaffected by the important contributions generated by the various centers (theory, publications, and so forth). At the same time, much of the research conducted at these centers was found to be "removed from practice realities and constraints." This lack of effective collaboration between scholars and practitioners hinders the development of the field and is a significant loss for both scholars and practitioners.

We must practice what we preach, and learn to work together across orientations, organizations, and disciplines, and between theory and practice. There is much strength in the diversity of our field, but we must come together to realize it. One such attempt has been initiated at Columbia University. Our vision is to establish Columbia University's Conflict Resolution Network (CU-CRN) as an arena for multidisciplinary work in conflict resolution emphasizing the theory-practice link. The network will offer important opportunities for scholars and practitioners from various disciplines to collaborate on research, theory development, practical models, and conflict-intervention services. To this end, the network is developing a series of coordinated activities such as multidisciplinary courses, seminars, international conferences, publications, a senior fellows program, and conflict resolution training and intervention services to the Columbia

University community and beyond. Our intention is to begin this work by engaging in a series of discussions exploring the various ideological, value, disciplinary, and theory-practice conflicts that exist in the field and affect our ability to work together. Initiatives such as this one can begin to build the bridges needed for collaborative, multidisciplinary scholarship and practice.

Learning to Learn

The fifth challenge is, How can we learn to learn about our methods and practice?

The field of conflict resolution has been criticized for being broad, but not deep. The issue is whether work in this area is both based on sound theoretical thinking and systematically studied and evaluated in a manner that allows the field to grow. I believe this volume attests to the rich theoretical foundations of the field. However, I do agree that much of the practice of conflict resolution is not evaluated, or poorly evaluated. This is a lost opportunity to learn from our work, to understand the conditions under which certain tactics and strategies are more or less effective, and to build on what is effective and discard what is not. This type of research is still uncommon, despite its increase in the past ten years (see Chapter Twenty-Seven). Systematic evaluation of conflict resolution practices needs to be conceptualized and implemented at the onset of intervention, not as an afterthought. Additionally, there would be much benefit from longitudinal studies examining the long-term effects of training and mediation programs.

Encouraging Innovation

Finally, How can we foster creative innovation in our thinking and our practice of resolving conflict constructively?

Betty Reardon, a renowned peace educator, has stated that "the failure to achieve peace is in essence a failure of the imagination." In addition to studying what we already do, it is essential that we develop new methods and ways of thinking about conflict that move beyond our current approaches. As the nature of the conflicts that we face changes, so must our thinking and our strategies for resolution. This often requires adopting a novel point of view (Chapters Sixteen and Seventeen). We must continuously view our current understanding of conflict and conflict resolution as merely a beginning—the first few steps toward the much needed means for finding "a better way" of improving and enhancing human conflict interaction.

References

Bush, R.A.B., and Folger, J. P. *The Promise of Mediation: Responding to Conflict Through Empowerment and Recognition.* San Francisco: Jossey-Bass, 1994.

Fisher, G. *Mindsets.* Yarmouth, Me.: Intercultural Press, 1988.

Hofstede, G. *Cultures Consequences: International Differences in Work-Related Values.* Thousand Oaks, Calif.: Sage, 1980.

Kolb, D., and Coolidge, G. G. "Her Place at the Table: A Consideration of Gender Issues in Negotiation." In J. Z. Rubin and J. W. Breslin (eds.), *Negotiation Theory and Practice.* Cambridge, Mass.: Harvard Program on Negotiation, 1991.

Lederach, J. P. *Preparing for Peace: Conflict Transformation Across Cultures.* Syracuse, N.Y.: Syracuse University Press, 1995.

Markus, H. R., and Kitayama, S. "Culture and Self: Implications for Cognition, Emotion, and Motivation." *Psychological Review,* 1991, *98,* 224–253.

Roderick, T. "Evaluating the Resolving Conflict Creatively Program." *Fourth R,* 1998, *82*(3–4), 19–21.

Segall, M. H., Lonner, W. J., and Berry, J. W. "Cross-Cultural Psychology as a Scholarly Discipline." *American Psychologist,* 1998, *53,* 1101–1110.

RECOMMENDED READING

Chapter One

Deutsch, M. *The Resolution of Conflict: Constructive and Destructive Processes.* New Haven: Yale University Press, 1973.

Johnson, D. W., and Johnson, R. T. *Cooperation and Competition: Theory and Research.* Edina, Minn.: Interaction, 1989.

Rawls, J. *Political Liberalism.* New York: Columbia University Press, 1996.

Rubin, J. Z., Pruitt, D. G., and Kim, S. H. (1994). *Social Conflict: Escalation, Stalemate, and Settlement.* (2nd ed.) New York: McGraw-Hill.

Chapter Two

Crosby, F. *Relative Deprivation and Working Women.* New York: Oxford University Press, 1982.

Deutsch, M. *Distributive Justice: A Social Psychological Perspective.* New Haven: Yale University Press, 1985.

Gurr, T. R. *Why Men Rebel.* Princeton: Princeton University Press, 1970.

Lind, E. A., and Tyler, T. R. *The Social Psychology of Procedural Justice.* New York: Plenum, 1988.

Opotow, S. (ed.). "Moral Exclusion and Injustice." *Journal of Social Issues,* 1990, *46* (special issue).

Schulman, M., and Meckler, E. *Bringing Up a Moral Child: A New Approach for Teaching Your Child to Be Kind, Just, and Responsible.* Reading, Mass.: Addison-Wesley, 1985.

Tyler, T. R., Boeckmann, R. J., Smith, H. J., and Huo, Y. J. *Social Justice in a Diverse Society.* Boulder, Colo.: Westview Press, 1997.

Chapter Three

Deutsch, M. "Conflicts: Productive and Destructive." *Journal of Social Issues*, 1969, *25*, 7–41.

Graham, P. (ed.). *Mary Parker Follett—Prophet of Management.* Boston: Harvard Business School Press, 1995.

Johnson, D. W., and Johnson, R. T. *Teaching Students to Be Peacemakers.* (3rd ed.) Edina, Minn.: Interaction, 1995.

Johnson, D. W., and Johnson, R. T. *Human Relations: Valuing Diversity.* Edina, Minn.: Interaction, 1999.

Maier, N. *Problem Solving and Creativity in Individuals and Groups.* Pacific Grove, Calif.: Brooks/Cole, 1970.

Moscovici, S. "Social Influence and Conformity." In G. Lindzey and E. Aronson (eds.), *The Handbook of Social Psychology.* Vol. 2. (3rd ed.) New York: Random House, 1985.

Piaget, J. *The Moral Judgment of the Child.* New York: Free Press, 1948.

Piaget, J. *The Psychology of Intelligence.* New York: HarperCollins, 1950.

Tjosvold, D. *The Conflict Positive Organization.* Reading, Mass.: Addison-Wesley, 1991.

Chapter Four

Gambetta, D. *Trust: Making and Breaking Cooperative Relations.* Cambridge, Mass.: Blackwell, 1988.

Kramer, R., and Tyler, T. R. (eds.). *Trust in Organizations: Frontiers of Theory and Research.* Thousand Oaks, Calif.: Sage, 1996.

Sitkin, S. B., Rousseau, D. M., Burt, R. S., and Camerer, C. (eds.). "Special Topic Forum on Trust in and Between Organizations." *Academy of Management Review*, 1998, *23* (entire issue 3).

Worchel, P. "Trust and Distrust." In W. G. Austin and S. Worchel (eds.), *The Social Psychology of Intergroup Relations.* Belmont, Calif.: Wadsworth, 1979.

Chapter Five

Alinsky, S. D. *Rules for Radicals: A Practical Primer for Realistic Radicals.* New York: Random House, 1971.

Follett, M. P. "Power." In E. M. Fox and L. Urwick (eds.), *Dynamic Administration: The Collected Papers of Mary Parker Follett.* London: Pitman, 1973.

McClelland, D. C. *Power: The Inner Experience.* New York: Irvington, 1975.

McIntosh, P. "White Privilege and Male Privilege: A Personal Account of Coming to See Correspondences Through Work in Women's Studies." Working paper, Center for Research on Women, Wellesley College, 1988.

Mindell, A. *Sitting in the Fire: Large Group Transformation Using Conflict and Diversity.* Portland, Ore.: Lao Tse Press, 1995.

Chapter Six

Clark, H. H. *Using Language.* Cambridge: Cambridge University Press, 1996.

Krauss, R. M., and Chiu, C. Y. "Language and Social Behavior." In D. T. Gilbert, S. T. Fiske, and G. Lindzey (eds.), *The Handbook of Social Psychology.* Vol. 1. (4th ed.) New York: McGraw-Hill, 1998.

Krauss, R. M., and Fussell, S. R. "Social Psychological Models of Interpersonal Communication." In E. T. Higgins and A. W. Kruglanski (eds.), *Social Psychology: A Handbook of Basic Principles.* New York: Guilford Press, 1996.

Chapter Seven

Chaiken, S. L., Wood, W., and Eagly, A. H. "Principles of Persuasion." In E. T. Higgins and A. W. Kruglanski (eds.), *Social Psychology: A Handbook of Basic Principles.* New York: Guilford Press, 1996.

Eagly, A. H., and Chaiken, S. L. *The Psychology of Attitudes.* Orlando: Harcourt Brace, 1993.

Petty, R. E., and Wegener, D. "Attitude Change: Multiple Roles for Persuasion Variables." In D. T. Gilbert, S. T. Fiske, and G. Lindzey (eds.), *The Handbook of Social Psychology.* Vol. 1. (4th ed.) New York: McGraw-Hill, 1998.

Chapter Eight

Blake, R. R., and Mouton, J. S. *Solving Costly Organizational Conflicts.* San Francisco: Jossey-Bass, 1984.

Blake, R. R., Shepard, H. A., and Mouton, J. S. *Managing Intergroup Conflict in Industry.* Houston: Gulf, 1964.

Brown, L. D. *Managing Conflict at Organizational Interfaces.* Reading, Mass.: Addison-Wesley, 1983.

Deutsch, M. "Subjective Features of Conflict Resolution: Psychological, Social, and Cultural Influences." In R. Vayrynen (ed.), *New Directions in Conflict Theory.* London: Sage, 1991.

Fisher, R. J. *The Social Psychology of Intergroup and International Conflict Resolution.* New York: Springer-Verlag, 1990.

Fisher, R. J. *Interactive Conflict Resolution.* Syracuse, N.Y.: Syracuse University Press, 1997.

Janis, I. L. *Groupthink.* (2nd ed.) Boston: Houghton Mifflin, 1982.

Rubin, J. Z., Pruitt, D. G., and Kim, S. H. *Social Conflict: Escalation, Stalemate, and Settlement.* (2nd ed.) New York: McGraw-Hill, 1994.

Taylor, D. M., and Moghaddam, F. M. *Theories of Intergroup Relations.* (2nd ed.) New York: Praeger, 1994.

White, R. K. *Fearful Warriors: A Psychological Profile of U.S.-Soviet Relations.* New York: Free Press, 1984.

Chapter Nine

Bazerman, M. H., and Neale, M. A. *Negotiating Rationally.* New York: Free Press, 1992.

Brett, J. M. "Negotiating Group Decisions." *Negotiation Journal,* 1991, *7,* 291–310.

Janis, I. L., and Mann, L. *Decision Making: A Psychological Analysis of Conflict, Choice, and Commitment.* New York: Free Press, 1977.

Rubin, J. Z., Pruitt, D. G., and Kim, S. H. *Social Conflict: Escalation, Stalemate, and Settlement.* (2nd ed.) New York: McGraw-Hill, 1994.

Chapter Ten

Thompson, L. *The Mind and Heart of the Negotiator.* Upper Saddle River, N.J.: Prentice-Hall, 1998.

Thompson, L., and Gonzalez, R. "Environmental Disputes: Competition for Scarce Resources and Clashing of Values." In M. Bazerman, D. Messick, A. Tenbrunsel, and K. Wade-Benzoni (eds.), *Environment, Ethics, and Behavior: The Psychology of Environmental Education and Degradation.* San Francisco: New Lexington Books, 1997.

Thompson, L., Nadler, J., and Kim, P. H. "Some Like It Hot: The Case for the Emotional Negotiator." In L. Thompson, J. M. Levine, and D.M. Messick (eds.), *Shared Cognition in Organizations: The Management of Knowledge.* Hillsdale, N.J.: Erlbaum, in press.

Thompson, L., Medvec, V. H., Seiden, V., and Kopelman, S. "Poker Face, Smiley Face, and Rant and Rave: Myths and Realities About Emotion in Negotiation." In M. Hogg and S. Tindale (eds.), *Blackwell Handbook in Social Psychology: Group Processes,* Vol. 3, forthcoming.

Chapter Eleven

Ross, L., and Nisbett, R. E. *The Person and the Situation.* New York: McGraw-Hill, 1991.

Tavris, C. *Anger: The Misunderstood Emotion.* New York: Simon & Schuster, 1989.

Weiner, B. *Judgments of Responsibility: A Foundation for a Theory of Social Conduct.* New York: Guilford Press, 1995.

Chapter Twelve

Metcalfe, J., and Mischel, W. "A Hot/Cool System Analysis of Delay of Gratification: Dynamics of Willpower." *Psychological Review,* 1999, *106,* 3–19.

Mischel, W. "From Good Intentions to Willpower." In P. M. Gollwitzer and J. A. Bargh (eds.), *The Psychology of Action: Linking Cognition and Motivation to Behavior.* New York: Guilford Press, 1996.

Mischel, W., Cantor, N., and Feldman, S. "Principles of Self-Regulation: The Nature of Willpower and Self-Control." In E. T. Higgins and A. W. Kruglanski (eds.), *Social Psychology: A Handbook of Basic Principles.* New York: Guilford Press, 1996.

Chapter Thirteen

Dweck, C. S. *Self-Theories: Their Role in Motivation, Personality, and Development.* Philadelphia: Psychology Press, 1999.

Chapter Fourteen

Bandura, A. *Social Foundations of Thought and Action: A Social Cognitive Approach.* Upper Saddle River, N.J.: Prentice Hall, 1986.

Hall, C. S., and Lindzey, G. *Theories of Personality.* (3rd ed.) New York: Wiley, 1978.

Heitler, S. M. *From Conflict to Resolution: Strategies for Diagnosis and Treatment of Distressed Individuals, Couples, and Families.* New York: Norton, 1990.

Saklofske, D. H., and Zeidner, M. (eds.). *International Handbook of Personality and Intelligence.* New York: Plenum, 1995.

Chapter Fifteen

Cartledge, G., and Milburn, J. F. *Teaching Social Skills to Children and Youth: Innovative Approaches.* (3rd ed.) Needham Heights, Mass.: Allyn & Bacon, 1995.

De Vries, R., and Zan, B. *Moral Classrooms, Moral Children: Creating a Constructivist Atmosphere in Early Education.* New York: Teachers College Press, 1994.

Jensen, E. *Teaching with the Brain in Mind.* Alexandria, Va.: Association for Supervision and Curriculum Development, 1998.

Shantz, C. U., and Hartup, W. W. (eds.). *Conflict in Child and Adolescent Development.* New York: Cambridge University Press, 1992.

Chapter Sixteen

Gruber, H. E. *Darwin on Man: A Psychological Study of Scientific Creativity.* (2nd ed.) Chicago: University of Chicago Press, 1981.

Chapter Seventeen

Blake, R. R., and Mouton, J. S. *Restoring Trust Between Groups in Conflict*. San Francisco: Jossey-Bass, 1984.

Boulding, E. "Enlivening Our Social Imagination." In D. Carlson and C. Comstock (eds.), *Citizen Summitry: Keeping the Peace When It Matters Too Much to Be Left to Politicians*. Los Angeles: Tarcher, 1986.

Cleese, J. "And Now for Something Completely Different." *Personnel*, Apr. 1991, pp. 13–15.

Treffinger, D. J., Isaksen, S. G., and Dorval, K. B. *Creative Problem Solving: An Introduction*. (Rev. ed.) Sarasota, Fla.: Center for Creative Learning, 1994.

Chapter Eighteen

Beckhard, R., and Harris, R. *Managing Organizational Transitions*. (2nd ed.) Reading, Mass.: Addison-Wesley, 1987.

Klein, G. "Some Notes on the Dynamics of Resistance to Change: The Defender Role." In G. Watson (ed.), *Concepts for Social Change*. Washington, D.C.: National Training Laboratories, 1966.

Lewin, K. "Group Decision and Social Change." In E. E. Maccoby, T. Newcomb, and E. Hartley (eds.), *Readings in Social Psychology*. Austin, Tex.: Holt, Rinehart and Winston, 1947.

Salancik, G. "Commitment Is Too Easy." *Organizational Dynamics*, 1977, *6*, 62–80.

Chapter Nineteen

Argyris, C., Putnam, R., and Smith, D. M. *Action Science: Concepts, Methods, and Skills for Research and Intervention*. San Francisco: Jossey-Bass, 1985.

Cranton, P. *Understanding and Promoting Transformative Learning: A Guide for Educators of Adults*. San Francisco: Jossey-Bass, 1994.

Marsick, V. J., and Watkins, K. E. *Facilitating the Learning Organization: Making Learning Count*. London: Gower, 1999.

Mezirow, J. D., and Associates *Fostering Critical Reflection in Adulthood: A Guide to Transformative and Emancipatory Learning*. San Francisco: Jossey-Bass, 1990.

Chapter Twenty

Baron, R. A., and Richardson, D. R. *Human Aggression*. (2nd ed.) New York: Plenum Press, 1994.

Eron, L. D., Gentry, J., and Schlegel, P. *Reason to Hope: A Psychological Perspective on Violence and Youth*. Washington, D.C.: American Psychological Association, 1994.

Green, R. G. "Aggression and Antisocial Behavior." In D. T. Gilbert, S. T. Fiske, and G. Lindzey (eds.), *The Handbook of Social Psychology.* Vol. 2. (4th ed.) New York: McGraw-Hill, 1998.

Kurtz, L. R. (ed.). *Encyclopedia of Violence, Peace, and Conflict.* Vols. 1–3. Orlando: Academic Press, 1999.

Chapter Twenty-One

Boulding, E. "Enlivening Our Social Imagination." In D. Carlson and C. Comstock (eds.), *Citizen Summitry: Keeping the Peace When It Matters Too Much to Be Left to Politicians.* Los Angeles: Tarcher, 1986.

Harris, P., and Reilly, B. *Democracy and Deep-Rooted Conflict: Options for Negotiators.* Stockholm: International IDEA, 1998.

Lederach, J. P. *Preparing for Peace: Conflict Transformation Across Cultures.* Syracuse, N.Y.: Syracuse University Press, 1995.

Lederach, J. P. *Building Peace: Sustainable Reconciliation in Divided Societies.* Washington, D.C.: U.S. Institute of Peace Press, 1997. (esp. ch. 6)

Rothman, J. *Resolving Identity-Based Conflict in Nations, Organizations, and Communities.* San Francisco: Jossey-Bass, 1997. (esp. ch. 1)

Chapter Twenty-Two

Avruch, K., and Black, P. "The Culture Question and Conflict Resolution." *Peace and Change*, 1991, *16*, 22–45.

Fisher, G. *Mindsets.* Yarmouth, Me.: Intercultural Press, 1988.

Lumsden, M., and Wolfe, R. "Evolution of the Problem-Solving Workshop: An Introduction to Social Psychological Approaches to Conflict Resolution." *Peace and Conflict: Journal of Peace Psychology*, 1996, *2*, 37–67.

Stewart, E. C., and Bennett, M. "American Cultural Patterns: A Cross-Cultural Perspective." (Rev. ed.) Yarmouth, Me.: Intercultural Press, 1991.

Chapter Twenty-Three

Leung, K., and Tjosvold, D. *Conflict Management in the Asia Pacific Rim: Assumptions and Approaches in Diverse Cultures.* New York: Wiley, 1998.

Tjosvold, D. *Conflict-Positive Organization: Stimulate Diversity and Create Unity.* Reading, Mass.: Addison-Wesley, 1991.

Tjosvold, D. "The Cooperative and Competitive Goal Approach to Conflict: Accomplishments and Challenges." *Applied Psychology: An International Review*, 1998, *47*, 285–313.

Chapter Twenty-Four

Broad, M. L., and Newstrom, J. W. *Transfer of Training.* Reading, Mass.: Addison-Wesley, 1992.

Bush, R.A.B., and Folger, J. P. *The Promise of Mediation: Responding to Conflict Through Empowerment and Recognition.* San Francisco: Jossey-Bass, 1994.

Deutsch, M. *The Resolution of Conflict: Constructive and Destructive Processes.* New Haven: Yale University Press, 1973.

Fisher, R. J., Ury, W., and Patton, B. *Getting to Yes: Negotiating Agreement Without Giving In.* (2nd ed.) New York: Penguin, 1991.

Gudykunst, W., and Kim, Y. Y. *Communicating with Strangers: An Approach to Intercultural Communication.* New York: McGraw-Hill, 1992.

Lewicki, R. J., Litterer, J. A., Minton, J. W., and Saunders, D. M. *Negotiation.* (2nd ed.) Burr Ridge, Ill.: Irwin, 1994.

Rubin, J. Z., Pruitt, D. G., and Kim, S. H. *Social Conflict: Escalation, Stalemate and Settlement.* (2nd ed.) New York: McGraw-Hill, 1994.

Chapter Twenty-Five

Bush, R.A.B., and Folger, J. P. *The Promise of Mediation: Responding to Conflict Through Empowerment and Recognition.* San Francisco: Jossey-Bass, 1994.

Honeyman, C. "Five Elements of Mediation." *Negotiation Journal,* 1988, *4,* 149–158.

Irving, H. H., and Benjamin, M. *Family Mediation: Contemporary Issues.* Thousand Oaks, Calif.: Sage, 1995.

Kolb, D., and Associates. *When Talk Works: Profiles of Mediators.* San Francisco: Jossey-Bass, 1994.

Kressel, K., and Pruitt, D. G. *Mediation Research: The Process and Effectiveness of Third-Party Intervention.* San Francisco: Jossey-Bass, 1989.

Moore, C. W. *The Mediation Process: Practical Strategies for Resolving Conflict.* (2nd ed.). San Francisco: Jossey-Bass, 1996.

National Institute for Dispute Resolution. *Performance-Based Assessment: A Methodology for Use in Selecting, Training, and Evaluating Mediators.* Washington, D.C.: National Institute for Dispute Resolution, 1995.

Riskin, L. L. "Understanding Mediators' Orientations, Strategies, and Techniques: A Grid for the Perplexed." *Harvard Negotiation Law Review,* 1996, *1,* 7–51.

Rubin, J. Z. (ed.). *Dynamics of Third-Party Intervention: Kissinger in the Middle East.* New York: Praeger, 1981.

Schrumpf, F., Crawford, D. K., and Bodine, R. J. *Peer Mediation: Conflict Resolution in Schools. Student Manual.* (Rev. ed.) Champaign, Ill.: Research Press, 1997.

Yarbrough, E., and Wilmot, W. *Artful Mediation: Constructive Conflict at Work.* Boulder, Colo.: Cairns, 1995.

Chapter Twenty-Six

Bunker, B. B., and Alban, B. T. *Large Group Interventions: Engaging the Whole System for Rapid Change.* San Francisco: Jossey-Bass, 1997.

Emery, M., and Purser, R. E. *The Search Conference: A Powerful Method for Planning Organizational Change and Community Action.* San Francisco: Jossey-Bass, 1996.

Jacobs, R. W. *Real-Time Strategic Change.* San Francisco: Berrett-Koehler, 1994.

Owen, H. *Open Space Technology: A User's Guide.* Potomac, Md.: Abbott, 1995.

Chapter Twenty-Seven

Bodine, R. J., and Crawford, D. K. *The Handbook of Conflict Resolution Education: A Guide to Building Quality Programs in Schools.* San Francisco: Jossey-Bass, 1998. (esp. ch. 6)

Johnson, D. W., and Johnson, R. T. "Conflict Resolution and Peer Mediation Programs in Schools: A Review of the Research." *Review of Educational Research,* 1996, 66, 459–506.

CONTRIBUTORS

Morton Deutsch is E. L. Thorndike professor and director emeritus of the International Center for Cooperation and Conflict Resolution (ICCCR) at Teachers College, Columbia University. He studied with Kurt Lewin at MIT's Research Center for Group Dynamics, where he obtained his Ph.D. in 1948. He is well known for his pioneering studies in intergroup relations, cooperation-competition, conflict resolution, social conformity, and the social psychology of justice. His books include *Interracial Housing; Research Methods in Social Relations; Preventing World War III: Some Proposals; Theories in Social Psychology; The Resolution of Conflict; Applying Social Psychology;* and *Distributive Justice.* His work has been widely honored by the Kurt Lewin Memorial Award, the G. W. Allport Prize, the Carl Hovland Memorial Award, the AAAS Socio-Psychological Prize, APA's Distinguished Scientific Contribution Award, SESP's Distinguished Research Scientist Award, and the Nevitt Sanford Award; he is a William James Fellow of APS. He has also received lifetime achievement awards for his work on conflict management, cooperative learning, peace psychology, and applications of psychology to social issues. In addition, he has received the Teachers College Medal for his contributions to education, the Helsinki University medal for his contributions to psychology, and the doctorate of humane letters from the City University of New York. He has been president of the Society for the Psychological Study of Social Issues, the International Society of Political Psychology, the Eastern Psychological Association, the New York State Psychological Association, and several divisions of the American Psychological Association. It is not widely known, but after postdoctoral training Deutsch received a certificate in psychoanalysis in 1958 and conducted a limited practice of psychoanalytic psychotherapy for more than twenty-five years.

Peter T. Coleman holds a Ph.D. in social and organizational psychology from Teachers College, Columbia University, and was a professional actor prior to his graduate studies. He was trained as a mediator by the New York state criminal court system and worked as a mediator from 1991 to 1993. He currently is an assistant professor at Teachers College and teaches both theory and practicum courses in conflict resolution. He is also director of the International Center for Cooperation and Conflict Resolution (ICCCR) at Teachers College and coordinator of the Columbia University Conflict Resolution Network. He works frequently as a consultant and trainer in conflict resolution and systems change. He has conducted research on in-group and out-group formation, gender discrimination, mediation of interethnic conflict, ripeness of conflict, and resistance to power sharing.

Keith G. Allred, assistant professor of public policy at Harvard University's Kennedy School of Government, teaches and conducts research on negotiation. At the applied level, he investigates organizational, legal, and international negotiations and conflicts. At the theoretical level, his research investigates anger-driven, retaliatory conflict; the conditions under which disputants prefer types of third-party involvement (mediation, arbitration, litigation); and how personalities react to various negotiation and conflict situations. His research has recently appeared in the annual volume of *Research on Negotiation in Organizations* and in journals such as *Organizational Behavior* and *Human Decision Processes.* Before Harvard, he was assistant professor in social and organizational psychology at Columbia University. Allred earned his Ph.D. in organizational behavior, with an emphasis on social psychology, from UCLA.

Caryn J. Block is associate professor of psychology and education in the Program in Social-Organizational Psychology, Teachers College, Columbia University. She obtained her Ph.D. in 1991 from New York University. Her publications include work on the influence of racial identity in organizational contexts, perception of affirmative-action programs, and the influence of sex-role stereotypes on perception of men and women as managers. Her research also focuses on organizational learning and the type of climate likely to foster a learning organization.

Susan K. Boardman is associate professor of psychology and director of the Center for Dispute Resolution at the University of New Haven. She is also codirector of research at the International Center for Cooperation and Conflict Resolution (ICCCR) at Teachers College, Columbia University. After receiving her Ph.D. from Columbia University in 1986, she was awarded a National Institute of Mental Health postdoctoral fellowship, during which she played a key role in the ICCCR's first research project. Her research and writing have focused on the effects of personality and communication on conflict resolution, and the dynamics of latent conflict in the workplace. She has been teaching and conducting training in negotiation and mediation for more than ten years.

Barbara Benedict Bunker is professor of psychology at the State University of New York at Buffalo. Her research and writing interests focus on organizational change and organizational effectiveness. She is a frequent lecturer in university executive development, human resources, and organizational development programs sponsored by Columbia (from which she received her Ph.D.), Michigan, Harvard, and Pepperdine universities. Her recent research and writing includes studies of Japanese senior executive women and commuting couples in the United States; she edited a special edition of the *Journal of Applied Behavioral Science* on large-group interventions that accelerate system change, *Conflict, Cooperation, and Justice* (with Jeffrey Rubin), *and Large Group Interventions: Engaging the Whole System for Rapid Change* (Jossey-Bass, 1997) with Billie Alban.

Shelly L. Chaiken received her Ph.D. in social psychology in 1978 from the University of Massachusetts-Amherst. She is a professor in the Department of Psychology at New York University and has held previous professorial appointments at the University of Toronto and Vanderbilt University. Her research has been on social cognition, persuasion, and attitude.

Kathleen M. Cochran received an M.S. in early childhood education from Bank Street College and an Ed.M. in curriculum design, with a concentration in conflict resolution, from Teachers College, Columbia University. Her teaching and training experience ranges from preschool to adult. She developed a nationally distributed series of K–12 conflict resolution materials and produced award-winning staff development videos on school-based conflict resolution. Her interests include the relationship of social skills learning to the development of language and literacy.

Susan Coleman is a principal of Coleman International, Inc., a firm specializing in conflict management and resolution through training, mediation, and consulting. She has graduate degrees from Hofstra and Harvard universities and teaches negotiation and mediation at Columbia University. She has conducted training in conflict resolution and intercultural communication for thousands of business executives, diplomats, health care professionals, and educators. She has also mediated a variety of business and community disputes. Her clients have included the United Nations Secretariat, American Express, AT&T, the New York City Board of Education, Schering International, the Ministry of Foreign Relations of the Colombian Government, and other organizations. Susan Coleman and Ellen Raider's training materials have been used around the world.

Aaron L. DeSmet is a doctoral student in the department of organization and leadership at Teachers College, Columbia University, and is finishing his Ph.D. in social and organizational psychology. His research focuses on self-awareness and self-regulation and their effects on leadership and group performance. He is also an organization and change strategy consultant. His independent consulting work includes strategic planning, team building, process reengineering, employee surveys, and 360-degree feedback design.

Ronald J. Fisher is professor of psychology and founding coordinator of the Applied Social Psychology Graduate Program at the University of Saskatchewan in Saskatoon, Canada. He has a Ph.D. in social psychology with a minor in international relations from the University of Michigan. He is currently a member of the U.S. National Research Council's Committee on International Conflict Resolution as well as the steering committee for the Joint Presidential Initiative on Ethnopolitical Warfare of the American and Canadian Psychological Associations. His writings include *The Social Psychology of Intergroup and International Conflict Resolution* and *Interactive Conflict Resolution,* as well as numerous articles and chapters. His primary scholarly interests are in third-party intervention directed toward protracted social conflict at the intergroup and international levels. He also has more than twenty years' experience as a trainer and consultant in the areas of conflict management and resolution, small-group leadership, team building, and strategic planning.

Janet Gerson teaches conflict resolution at the International Center for Cooperation and Conflict Resolution (ICCCR) at Teachers College, Columbia University, has directed its Mediation Center, and was a co-creator of the course "Issues in Power, Rank, and Privilege: Race, Class, and Gender in the United States." A peace educator, she is the alternative representative of the World Council on Curriculum and Instruction to the United Nations. She is also a member of the Gender and Human Security Network, an international women's group of human rights and peace activists who are developing a paradigm and strategies as alternatives to the prevailing militarized security system. She continues to combine her previous work as a choreographer with conflict analysis and peace education as an associate member of the Theater of the Oppressed Laboratory in New York City. She is an Ed.M. candidate in cultural studies and philosophy of education at Teachers College.

Howard E. Gruber is professor emeritus of the University of Geneva (Switzerland) and currently adjunct professor at Teachers College, Columbia University. He obtained his Ph.D. from Cornell University in 1950. He was professor of genetic psychology in Geneva, a chair previously held by Jean Piaget. At Rutgers University, he was codirector with Solomon Asch of the Institute for Cognitive Studies. His major field of work is studying the creative process, with special emphasis on intensive case studies of highly creative people. He has authored some two hundred articles and such books as the much-honored *Darwin on Man.* His work in progress is entitled *Piaget: A Man Thinking.* He has been a member of the Institute for Advanced Study at Princeton and has been awarded Guggenheim, Ford, and National Institute for Mental Health fellowships. He has also received the Rudolph Anheim Award for his contribution to psychology and the arts.

Deborah H. Gruenfeld received her Ph.D. in social psychology in 1993 from the University of Illinois, Urbana-Champaign. She is an associate professor at Northwestern University's Kellogg Graduate School of Management. Her work has involved the study of group decision making, negotiation, and information sharing.

David W. Johnson is a professor of educational psychology at the University of Minnesota. He is codirector of the Cooperative Learning Center. He held the Emma M. Birkmaier Professorship in Educational Leadership at the University of Minnesota from 1994 to 1997. He received his master's and doctoral degrees from Columbia University in social psychology. He has published more than four hundred research articles and book chapters and authored more than forty books. A past editor of the *American Educational Research Journal,* he has received numerous awards for outstanding research and teaching from many national and international professional associations. For the past thirty years, Johnson has served as an organizational consultant to schools and businesses in North America, Central America, Europe, Africa, Asia, the Middle East, and the Pacific Region. He is a practicing psychotherapist.

Roger T. Johnson is a professor of curriculum and instruction at the University of Minnesota. He holds his doctoral degree from the University of California, Berkeley, in science education. He is the codirector of the Cooperative Learning Center. His public school teaching experience includes kindergarten through eighth grade instruction in self-contained classrooms, open schools, nongraded situations, cottage schools, and departmentalized (science) schools. At the college level, he has taught teacher-preparation courses for undergraduate through Ph.D. programs. He has consulted with schools throughout the United States and Canada, Panama, England, Germany, Norway, Sweden, Finland, and New Zealand. He has received many local, national, and international awards for his teaching and research. He is the author of numerous research articles, book chapters, and books and is a leading authority nationally on inquiry teaching and science education.

Charles M. Judd received his Ph.D. in social psychology in 1976 from Columbia University. He is a professor in the department of psychology at the University of Colorado-Boulder and has held previous professorial appointments at Harvard University and the University of California, Berkeley. His research has focused on social cognition, stereotyping, political attitudes, and research methods.

Tal Y. Katz is a faculty member in the Program in Social-Organizational Psychology, Teachers College, Columbia University, and in the School of Business Administration at the Interdisciplinary Center, Herzliya, Israel. She earned her Ph.D. (1999) in social-organizational psychology at Teachers College. Her research interests are individual work in teams and team performance as a function of the interaction of situational and dispositional factors.

Paul R. Kimmel received his Ph.D. in social psychology from the University of Michigan in 1963. He has taught at the Saybrook Graduate School and Research Center, Iowa State University, American University, UCLA, and Pepperdine University. He was the first public fellow of the American Psychological Association and a peace fellow of the U.S. Institute of Peace. In addition to his publications in cross-cultural communication, he has done major evaluation studies in this area for the Department of State and the U.S. Agency for International Development. For more than thirty years, he has been designing and conducting programs in intercultural communication for diplomats, UN personnel, the police, Americans going abroad, and other groups. He has found his training and work as a professional actor valuable in conducting workshops on intercultural communication.

Robert M. Krauss is professor of psychology at Columbia University. His research examines the role of language and coverbal behaviors in communication. He is coauthor (with Morton Deutsch) of *Theories in Social Psychology* and has written numerous widely renowned articles on interpersonal communication.

Kenneth Kressel is professor of psychology at Rutgers University, Newark, New Jersey, and director of the campus Teaching Excellence Center and the Program in Conflict Management. He received his Ph.D. from Columbia University in social psychology. He is the author *of The Process of Divorce: How Professionals and Couples Negotiate Settlement* and coeditor of an issue of the *Journal of Social Issues* on mediation of social conflict (with Dean Pruitt) and the book *Mediation Research: The Process and Effectiveness of Third-Party Intervention* (also with Pruitt). He served as an associate editor of *the International Journal of Conflict Management* and is on the editorial boards of *Negotiation Journal* and *Mediation Quarterly.*

Kwok Leung is professor and chairman of the Department of Psychology at the Chinese University of Hong Kong. He was an associate editor of the *Journal of Cross-Cultural Psychology* and is currently an associate editor of the *Asian Journal of Social Psychology.* He coedited *Innovations in Cross-Cultural Psychology, Progress in Asian Social Psychology* (volume one), and *Conflict Management in the Asia Pacific Rim;* he also coauthored *Methods and Data Analysis for Cross-Cultural Research.* He is the current president of the Asian Association of Social Psychology. His research interests include justice and conflict resolution, joint ventures in China, cross-cultural psychology, and cross-cultural research methodology. He received his Ph.D. from the University of Illinois.

Roy J. Lewicki is the Dean's Distinguished Teaching Professor at the Max M. Fisher College of Business, Ohio State University. He received his Ph.D. in social psychology from Teachers College, Columbia University, in 1969. Before joining the faculty at Ohio State, he held faculty positions at Yale University, Dartmouth College, and Duke University. He is the author or editor of many research articles as well as twenty-one books, including *The Fast Forward MBA in Negotiation and Dealmaking; Negotiation; Negotiation: Readings, Exercises, and Cases; Essentials of Negotiation;* and *Research on Negotiation in Organizations.* In 1988, he received the first David Bradford Outstanding Educator Award from the Organizational Behavior Teaching Society for his contributions to the field of teaching in negotiation and dispute resolution. He was elected the first chairperson of the Conflict Management Division of the Academy of Management, and he will serve as president of the International Association of Conflict Management in 1999–2000; he is also a trustee of the Columbus Council for Ethics in Economics.

Eric C. Marcus obtained his Ph.D. in 1985 from Columbia University in social psychology. He has been a consultant to organizations since 1984. He is a principal of the Marcus Group, a consulting firm that specializes in issues of organizational change and individual and group development. In this capacity, he has worked with various public and private sector client systems. He currently serves as president of the Organization Development Network of Greater New York. He is an adjunct faculty member in the Department of Management at Baruch College and in the Department of Organization and Leadership at Teachers College.

Victoria J. Marsick is a professor of adult and organizational learning in the Department of Organization and Leadership, Teachers College, Columbia University. She directs graduate programs in adult education. Prior to joining Teachers College, she was a training director at the UN Children's Fund. She holds a Ph.D. in adult education from the University of California, Berkeley. She consults on learning organizations and on action learning with such clients as AT&T, Coca Cola, Exxon, Travelers, Arthur Andersen, the Canadian Imperial Bank of Commerce, and the U.S. Department of Defense. She has written many books and articles on informal learning, action learning, team learning, and the learning organization.

Walter Mischel received his Ph.D. in psychology from the Ohio State University in 1956 and was awarded an honorary doctor of science degree from the same institution forty-one years later. He currently is the Robert Johnston Niven Professor for Humane Letters in Psychology at Columbia University, to which he came after serving as professor, and twice chair, of the psychology department of Stanford University. He is a fellow of the American Academy of Arts and Sciences; his honors include the Distinguished Scientific Contribution Award from the American Psychological Association and the Distinguished Scientist Award from its Division of Clinical Psychology. His research and theoretical work has addressed the nature of personality and of the self-regulatory processes that enable individuals to exert greater control and willpower over the course of their lives.

Ezequiel Morsella is a third-year graduate student in the Department of Psychology at Columbia University. His current research concerns the process by which gesturing facilitates lexical retrieval.

Janice Nadler is a doctoral student in the Department of Psychology at the University of Illinois, Urbana-Champaign, and a doctoral dissertation fellow at the American Bar Foundation. Her research interests include negotiation and conflict, psychology and law, and group decision making.

Susan Opotow is associate professor in the Graduate Program of Dispute Resolution at the University of Massachusetts, Boston. Her research focuses on conflict and injustice, as well as examining psychosocial conditions that permit harmful behavior toward those seen outside the scope of justice. Her publications focus on justice in public schooling, environmental conflict, and public-policy debates such as affirmative action and accommodating disability. She earned her Ph.D. at Columbia University.

Ellen Raider is a mediator, trainer, and program developer whose training materials are used by educational, business, and governmental organizations throughout the world. In partnership with Morton Deutsch, she launched the International Center for Cooperation and Conflict Resolution (ICCCR) and graduate studies in conflict resolution at Teachers College, Columbia University. She has also done training and mediation in many school systems, including New York City, where her training of the staff from 150 high schools launched a major citywide effort to reduce youth violence by increasing their conflict resolution and mediation skills. She is a member of the Advisory Council of CREnet, a professional organization of conflict resolution educators. In her own consulting practice, she has designed cross-cultural conflict resolution training programs for the worldwide staff at UNICEF; the Committee for National Security, a Washington-based arms control group; the American Friends Service Committee; and the U.S./USSR Trade Negotiation Project, sponsored by the U.S. National Science Foundation and the Soviet Academy of Foreign Trade. She holds a B.S. degree in communications and an M.Ed. degree in educational psychology from Temple University and has done additional graduate work in cultural anthropology at the New School of Social Research.

Sandra V. Sandy is the International Center for Cooperation and Conflict Resolution (ICCCR)'s director of research, Teachers College, Columbia University. She is also executive director of the Peaceful Kids ECSEL Program, which offers conflict resolution education to preschoolers, parents, and day care staff. She earned her Ph.D. in social psychology from Columbia University. Before joining the ICCCR in 1994, she was assistant professor and research associate at Cornell University Medical College. Her primary research focus has been on conflict resolution with children. She has published articles on conflict resolution in early childhood, conflict resolution from preschool to adolescence, the effects of personality on conflict, constructive conflict management and social problems, the role of mediation and conflict resolution in creating safe learning environments, conflict management among homeless children, and the policy and research implications of managing conflict. She also teaches conflict resolution from a developmental perspective and has served as a consultant to a number of private and public organizations involved with educating young children.

Alfonso Sauquet holds an M.B.A. from ESADE in Spain and an M.A. in organizational psychology from Columbia University, where he is currently a doctoral candidate. He is professor of organizational psychology at ESADE and is currently researching the relationship between conflict and group learning and directing a multinational research project in four European countries.

Leigh Thompson is the John L. and Helen Kellogg Distinguished Professor of Organization Behavior at Northwestern University's Kellogg Graduate School of Management. Her research interests include negotiation, group decision making, problem solving, and team performance. She is the author of *The Mind and Heart of the Negotiator.*

Dean Tjosvold is chair, professor, and head of management, Lingnan College, Hong Kong. He received his Ph.D. in social psychology from the University of Minnesota. In 1992, Simon Fraser University awarded him a university professorship for his research contributions. He has received numerous awards, including one from the American Educational Research Association for outstanding research on cooperation and competition. He is past president of the International Association of Conflict Management. He has published more than 150 articles and fifteen books on managing conflict, cooperation and competition, decision making, power, and other management issues. He is on several editorial boards, among them the *Academy of Management Review* and the *Journal of Organizational Behavior.* He is a partner in his family health care business, based in Minnesota.

Carolyn Wiethoff is an advanced doctoral student in the Department of Management and Human Resources at the Max M. Fisher College of Business, Ohio State University. She earned her A.B. in philosophy from Kean University, and her M.A. in speech communication from Indiana University, Bloomington. Before returning to graduate school, she spent twelve years in various management positions in public accounting firms.

Eben A. Weitzman received his Ph.D. in social and organizational psychology from Columbia University. He is currently assistant professor, Graduate Programs in Dispute Resolution, University of Massachusetts, Boston. His interests are in organizational development, cross-cultural conflict, conflict resolution, and intergroup relations. His current research focuses on intragroup conflict in mediation, cultural differences in attitudes toward conflict, organizational conflict, and the effects of cooperation and competition on small-group processes.

Patricia Flynn Weitzman is an instructor in the Department of Social Medicine, Harvard Medical School, and the coordinator of the Harvard Geriatric Education Center. She received her Ph.D. in developmental psychology from New York University in 1996. Her research interests center on social cognitive development and the influence of contextual variables on individual responses to interpersonal conflict. She has done research on decision making and conflict resolution during adolescence, young adulthood, and old age.

NAME INDEX

A

Abelson, R. P., 196, 207
Aber, J. L., 584, 587, 589
Acton, Lord, 117
Adler, A., 271, 290
Adorno, T. W., 116, 128
Ahern, 6
Alban, B. T., 547, 557, 566
Alinsky, S. D., 123, 126, 128, 366, 380
Allport, G., 178
Allred, K. G., 236, 243, 244, 245, 246, 250, 252
American Psychological Association, 407, 421, 424
Ames, C., 279, 287
Archer, J., 279, 287
Arcuri, L., 138, 143
Argyris, C., 370, 380, 385, 386–387, 398
Aristotle, 66
Armor, D., 149, 165
Asch, S. E., 135, 143, 345, 349, 354
Atkinson, J. W., 298, 314
Aurik, J., 438, 450
Austin, J. L., 141, 143
Averill, J., 242, 249, 252

A (continued, col. 2)

Avruch, K., 455, 471, 472, 473
Axelrod, D., 555, 556–557
Azar, E. E., 170, 433, 449
Aziz, T., 454

B

Babcock, L., 225, 233
Bagarozzi, D., 99, 105
Bagby, J. W., 455, 473
Baker, G., 454
Balke, W. M., 222, 233
Bandura, A., 282, 288, 299–300, 313, 412, 416, 424
Banks, C., 120, 129, 167, 184
Banton, M., 12, 17
Barnard, C. I., 120, 128
Baron, R. A., 404, 424
Barry, B., 243, 252
Bartunek, J. M., 243, 252, 371, 381
Basoglu, M., 59, 63
Baucom, D. H., 248, 252
Baumeister, R. F., 249, 253, 268, 274
Baumgarten, M. P., 414, 424
Bavetta, A. G., 304, 315
Bazerman, M. H., 156, 158, 160, 165, 195, 198, 199–201,

202, 204, 207, 208, 209, 217, 218, 219, 234, 304, 315
Beckhard, R., 364, 365, 367, 370–371, 381
Begin, M., 468
Bell, E. C., 304, 314
Bem, S. L., 305, 314
Bennett, M., 462, 473, 474
Bennett, P., 196, 208
Benton, A. A., 223, 234
Berk, R. A., 411, 427
Berkowitz, L., 249, 252, 410, 411, 416, 424, 425
Berman, D., 414, 425
Berman, M., 453, 473
Bernoulli, 196
Bernstein, B., 460, 473
Berry, J. M., 149, 165
Berry, J. W., 596, 600
Bettman, J. R., 149, 164
Bierce, A., 131
Bies, R. J., 87, 90, 101, 106, 249, 251, 253
Bigley, G. A., 87, 104
Bills, R., 403, 425
Black, P. W., 455, 471, 472, 473
Blair, T., 6

Blake, R. R., 167, 168, 178, 183, 184, 305, 314, 364, 365
Blakeney, R. N., 304, 314
Block, C. J., 279, 280, 281, 287, 288, 307
Block, J., 314
Blum, A. A., 489, 493
Boardman, S. K., 289, 308, 309, 314, 315
Bobo, L., 116, 130
Bodine, R. J., 583, 584, 589
Boon, S. D., 87, 104
Bordon, G. A., 467, 473
Borris, E. R., 59, 61, 63
Bottom, W. P., 100, 104
Boud, D., 382, 388, 399
Boulding, E., 364, 365, 447, 448, 449
Bowen, C. D., 354
Bradbury, T. ., 248, 249, 253
Bram, S. J., 63
Branstetter, W. H., 325, 341
Braque, 347
Brauer, M., 163, 164
Braziel, A., 423, 425
Brehm, J. W., 98, 105
Brennan, S. E., 139, 143
Brett, J. M., 196, 206–207, 208
Brezhnev, L., 135–136
Brickman, E., 529, 545
Bridges, W., 367, 376, 381
Bronfenbrenner, 318
Brown, L. D., 168, 184
Brown, R., 137, 138
Brown, T., 417, 426
Brummett, B., 464, 473
Bucher, A. M., 249, 254
Bullock, D. H., 318, 341
Bullock, M., 441, 449
Bunker, B. B., 86, 87, 88, 89, 98, 99, 104n.1, 104n.3, 105, 546, 547, 557, 566
Burdette, M. P., 95, 105
Burgess, G., 285, 287, 431, 436, 439–440, 444, 449
Burgess, H., 285, 287, 431, 436, 439–440, 444, 449
Burke, W. W., 376, 381
Burnham, D. H., 117, 129
Burrell, G., 115, 128
Burt, R. S., 87, 106, 107
Burton, J. W., 61, 64, 170, 299, 314, 431, 442, 449, 470, 471, 473

Bush, G., 454
Bush, R.A.B., 194, 208, 285–286, 287, 533, 536, 544, 545, 595, 599
Bushman, B. J., 249, 253
Butler, D., 248, 254, 281
Butler, J. K., 96, 98, 104, 105
Butler, R., 287

C
Cairns, E., 4–5, 17
Camerer, C., 87, 106, 107, 225, 233
Campa, R., 68
Campbell, D. T., 168, 184
Campbell, J., 563
Canada, G., 412, 425
Cantor, N., 260, 270, 275
Cantril, H., 12, 17
Carnevale, P. J., 191, 192, 206, 208, 306, 315, 356, 359, 363, 365, 529, 544
Carney, A., 435, 449
Carter, J., 468
Cebula, N., 558
Ceci, S. J., 318, 341
Chaiken, S. L., 98, 105, 144, 146, 147, 149, 150, 151, 152, 153, 159, 164
Chapman, D. I., 243, 253
Chee, Y. K., 193, 209
Chen, M., 250, 253
Chen, S., 147, 151, 152, 153, 164
Cheng, B. S., 488, 492
Cheraskin, L., 88, 89, 106
Chervaney, N. L., 91, 106
Chia, L. C., 482, 494
Chiongbian, V., 244, 252
Chirico, D. M., 347, 354
Choi, I., 241, 253
Chow, W. S., 488, 492
Chua, E., 484, 492
Chui, C. Y., 143
Clark, H. H., 139, 143
Clark, R. A., 298, 314
Cleese, J., 359, 360, 361, 365
Clinton, B., 6, 150
Coch, L., 374, 381
Cochran, K. M., 316, 328, 342
Cohen, R., 382, 388, 399, 457, 468, 473
Coie, J. D., 413, 425

Coleman, P. T., 111, 115, 118, 128, 355, 428, 437, 449, 534, 545, 591
Coleman, S., 443, 448, 499, 501, 521
Collins, M. E., 582, 589
Collins, W. A., 339, 341
Connor, D. R., 373, 381
Cook, B. W., 316, 341
Coolidge, G. G., 596, 600
Copley, B., 398, 399
Costa, P. T., Jr., 306, 308, 314
Courtright, J. A., 99, 105
Crawford, D. K., 583, 584, 589
Creyer, E. H., 149, 164
Cseh, M., 382, 385, 399
Csikszentmihalyi, M., 337, 341
Cummings, L. L., 91, 106

D
Dahl, R. A., 110, 128
Damon, W., 320–321, 323, 334, 341
Daniels, S., 100, 104
Dannemiller, 549, 555, 561
Dant, R. P., 191, 208
Darby, J., 4–5, 17
Darling, N. E., 337, 342
Darwin, C., 11, 345–346, 348, 357
Davis, J., 98, 106
Davis, K. E., 238–239, 240, 254
Davis, W., 338, 342
De Dreu, C., 491, 494
De Harpport, T., 229, 235
De Mello, C., 463, 473
De Ridder, R., 415, 425
De Rivera, J., 242, 253
DeSmet, A. L., 256
De Vries, R., 318, 319, 322, 341
Deci, E., 375, 381
Dellums, R. V., 403, 425
Deming, W. E., 495
Deutsch, M., 1, 2, 13, 14, 15, 17, 21, 22, 39, 40, 41, 43, 47, 48, 64, 66, 70, 84, 88, 89, 91, 99, 100, 105, 111–112, 114, 118, 120–121, 122, 125, 126, 128, 142, 143, 168, 174, 180, 184, 248, 253, 279, 284, 287, 289, 300–303, 305, 314, 315,

317, 341, 355, 374–375, 381, 414, 420, 425, 430, 433, 445, 449, 475– 478, 481, 483, 489, 491, 492, 504, 523, 529, 534, 545, 548, 571, 580, 582, 583, 584, 589, 590, 591–593, 596–597, 598
Dewey, J., 382–383, 399
Ding, D., 480, 482, 493, 494
Dodge, K. A., 192, 208, 413, 425
Dollard, J., 409, 425
Dorval, K. B., 204, 209, 359, 365
Downing, J. M., 163, 164
Du Bois, P. M., 445, 449
Duckitt, J. H., 125, 128
Dugan, M., 436, 448, 449
Dugan, S., 485, 493
Dweck, C. S., 279, 280, 281, 284, 287, 326, 334, 341
Dyce, J. A., 307, 314
Dye, D. A., 308, 314
Dyson, F., 348–349

E

Eagly, A. N., 146, 149, 150, 151, 159, 164
Earley, P. C., 486, 492
Eastwood, C., 136
Eberle, B., 364, 365
Edleson, J. L., 412, 426
Egan, T., 408, 425
Eichmann, A., 60, 118
Einstein, A., 348, 357
Elias, J., 318, 341
Elliott, E. S., 281, 287
Emery, F. E., 549, 554, 555, 556, 557, 566, 567
Emery, M., 548, 549, 552, 555, 557, 567
Emminghaus, W. B., 461, 471, 473
Engels, F., 11
Erikson, E. H., 290, 310, 314, 318, 332, 336–337, 341
Etheridge, L., 469, 473
Euwema, M. C., 191, 209

F

Fainaru, S., 408, 425
Fairbairn, W.R.D., 290
Fan, E. T., 149, 165
Farh, J. L., 488, 492

Farver, J. M., 325, 341
Feldman, S., 260, 270, 275
Fenichel, O., 295, 314
Feynman, R., 349
Fincham, F. D., 248, 249, 253
Fingerhut, L. A., 403, 425
Fischer, K. W., 318, 341
Fischoff, B., 338, 342
Fisher, G., 455, 473, 596, 599
Fisher, R. J., 104n.2, 105, 123, 128, 166, 167, 168, 184, 249, 283, 287, 364, 365, 375, 381, 421, 425, 431, 433–434, 436, 448, 449, 523, 545
Fiske, S. T., 125, 129
Fitz, A., 555
Flanagan, J. C., 478, 492
Flavell, J. H., 318, 341
Fletcher, G.J.O., 240, 254
Flippen, A. R., 241, 253
Foeman, A. K., 97, 105
Folger, J. P., 194, 208, 285–286, 287, 533, 536, 544, 545, 595, 599
Follett, M. P., 111, 129
Fontaine, G., 455, 470, 473
Fountain, S., 127–128
Fowler, F. J., Jr., 479, 492
Francis, J., 483, 495
Frank, M. G., 216–217, 234
Frank, 555
Franklin, 13
French, J.R.P., 374, 381
Frenkl-Brunswik, E., 116, 128
Freud, A., 47, 64, 290, 302, 314
Freud, S., 11, 65, 290, 294, 295, 296–297
Frist, B., 403, 425
Froehle, T., 250, 253
Fromm, E., 290, 347, 354
Fry, W. R., 533, 545
Fussell, S. R., 143

G

Gabarro, J. J., 96, 97, 102, 105
Galtung, J., 405, 426
Gambetta, D., 86, 105
Gardner, H., 317, 341
Garmezy, N., 76
Gentner, D., 230, 231, 234
Gephardt, R., 150
Gergen, K. J., 487, 492

Gerson, J., 448, 499
Gibson, C. B., 486, 492
Gibson, K., 100, 104
Gick, M. L., 230, 231, 234
Gilbert, D. T., 240, 253
Gilovich, T., 216–217, 234
Giner-Sorolla, R., 147, 151, 152, 164
Girrotto, V., 223, 234
Gist, M. E., 304, 315
Glaspie, A., 454
Glenn, E., 457–458, 459, 473
Goffman, E., 483, 492
Goleman, D., 257, 275, 317, 341
Gollwitzer, P. M., 270, 275
Gordon, W.J.J., 364, 365
Gorsuch, R. L., 307, 315
Gottman, J. M., 99, 105, 317, 341
Graham, S., 251, 255
Grant, P. R., 167, 184
Greene, M., 419, 426
Greenhalgh, L., 243, 253
Griffin, D. W., 102, 107
Griffith, M., 220
Griggs Productions, 515, 520
Grillo, T., 419, 426
Gruber, H. E., 345, 354, 355–359, 361
Gruenfeld, D. H., 144, 149, 165
Gudykunst, W. B., 484, 492
Guerra, N. G., 416, 425
Gulerce, A., 487, 492
Gurr, T. R., 50, 64, 410, 426

H

Hall, A., 316
Hall, D. G., 167, 184
Hall, E. T., 455, 460, 473, 484, 492
Hammond, K. R., 222, 233, 346, 354
Haney, C., 120, 129, 167, 184
Harper, M. V., 396–397, 399
Harris, R., 370, 381
Hartmann, H., 290
Harvey, J. B., 108, 129, 248
Harvey, J. H., 253
Hastie, R., 217, 235
Heatherton, T. F., 268, 274
Hedlund, J., 198, 208
Heider, F., 238, 240, 241, 253
Heimer, K., 411, 425

Heitler, S. M., 309, 314
Henriquez, M., 339, 342
Hensley, J. E., 412, 426
Henslin, J. M., 223, 234
Heron, J., 388, 399
Hewstone, M., 241, 254
Hien, D., 410, 426
Hien, N. M., 410, 426
Hitler, A., 408
Hoffman, S., 469, 473
Hofstede, G., 121, 129, 459, 473, 485, 493, 515, 520, 596, 600
Holbrook, R., 592
Hollenbeck, J. R., 198, 208
Hollingshead, A. B., 149, 165
Holmberg, M., 339, 342
Holmes, J. G., 87, 104
Holubec, E., 68, 85
Holyoak, K. J., 230, 231, 234
Honoroff, B., 534, 545
hooks, b., 410–411, 426
Horn, W. F., 317, 341
Horney, K., 290
Hornstein, H. A., 241, 253
Howard, D., 138–139
Hrebec, D., 217, 222, 235
Hu, J., 482, 494
Hui, C., 480, 481, 482, 485, 493, 494
Huismans, S. E., 191, 209
Hull, C. L., 13, 17
Hume, J., 6
Hussein, S., 454
Huston, T. L., 98, 105
Hutson, J. J., 445, 449
Hwang, L. L., 489, 493
Hyman, S. E., 11, 17

I
Ickes, W., 305, 315
Ilgen, D. R., 198, 208
Isaksen, S. G., 204, 209, 359, 365
Issacharoff, S., 225, 233

J
Jacobs, R. W., 548, 549, 561, 562, 567
Jaffe, P. G., 412, 426
Janis, I. L., 68, 84, 173, 184, 197–198, 204, 205, 207, 208
Janoff, S., 548, 549, 567
Jarvis, P., 382, 399
Jefferson, T., 65, 79, 83, 84, 135

Jennings, E. E., 96, 105
Jensen, E., 317, 318, 323, 328, 330, 341
Johnson, D. W., 22, 27, 65, 68, 70–72, 75, 76, 79, 84–85, 341, 469, 475, 516, 520, 580, 584–585, 589, 590
Johnson, J. E., 453, 473
Johnson, J. T., 159, 165
Johnson, M., 364, 365
Johnson, R. T., 22, 27, 40, 65, 68, 70–72, 75, 76, 79, 84–85, 341, 469, 516, 520, 580, 584–585, 589, 590
Jones, E. E., 238–239, 240, 241, 254
Jones, R. A., 98, 105
Jones, T. S., 99, 106, 584, 585, 590
Jones, W. H., 95, 105
Jose, P. E., 242, 254
Judd, C. M., 144, 159, 163, 164, 165
Jung, C., 290, 297

K
Kahn, R. L., 217, 234
Kahneman, D., 195, 196–197, 198, 206, 208
Kanter, R. M., 111, 126, 128, 129
Kaplan, S. J., 301, 315
Katz, D., 169, 431
Katz, T. Y., 279, 281, 288
Keashly, L., 176, 421, 425, 433–434, 448, 449
Kelley, H. H., 104n.2, 107, 223, 234, 237, 238, 240–241, 248, 250, 254, 284, 288
Kelman, H. C., 61, 64, 314, 436, 442, 444, 450
Keltner, D., 220, 221, 234
Khrushchev, N., 134, 135, 137, 457–458
Kilmann, R. H., 305, 308, 314
Kim, P. H., 149, 165
Kim, S. H., 168, 184, 188, 189, 190, 195, 206, 208, 222, 235, 249, 255, 279, 288, 305, 315, 364, 365
Kimmel, P. R., 453, 454, 461, 462, 463, 469, 471, 472, 473, 474, 596
King, M. L., Jr., 79

King, R., 266
Kipnis, D., 122, 124–125, 129
Kirkbride, P. S., 483, 489, 493
Kitayama, S., 596, 600
Klein, D., 560, 561, 567
Klein, G., 373, 381
Klein, M., 290
Klein, 561
Klineberg, O., 12, 17
Kluwer, E., 491, 493
Kmitta, D., 584, 590
Kohlberg, L., 117–118, 129, 318, 319, 320–321, 323, 334, 342
Kohut, H., 290
Kolb, D., 243, 252, 254, 382, 388, 399, 523, 539, 545, 596, 600
Kramer, R., 87, 105, 217, 227, 234, 235, 249, 253
Krasnor, L. R., 192, 208
Krauss, R. M., 131, 140, 142, 143
Kray, L. J., 226, 235
Kressel, K., 190, 191, 194, 208, 522, 523, 529, 535, 539, 540, 545
Kurtzberg, T. R., 228, 234

L
Lacan, J., 290
Lakoff, R., 364, 365
Lam, J., 583, 590
Langer, E. J., 223, 234, 398, 399
Larson, J. M., 100, 105
Larson, R., 337, 341
Laursen, B., 339, 341
Law, K. S., 485, 493, 494
Law, S. A., 485, 493
Lawler, E. J., 156, 158, 165
Lazarus, R. S., 242, 255
Leachman, R., 398, 399
Lederach, J. P., 428, 431, 436, 441–442, 446–447, 448, 449, 597, 600
Ledoux, J., 261, 275
Lee, F., 252, 254, 489, 495
Leggett, E. L., 279, 287
Lemler, J., 417, 426
Lenin, V. I., 135
Lenney, E., 305, 314
Leung, K., 475, 483, 485, 487, 488, 489, 491, 493, 495
Levi, A., 196, 207

Levine, J., 144, 165
Levine, R. A., 168, 184
Levinger, G., 98, 105
Levinson, D. J., 116, 128
Levkoff, S. E., 193, 209
Lewicki, R. J., 86, 87, 88, 89,
  90, 96, 98, 99, 100, 101,
  102, 104*n*.1, 104*n*.2, 104*n*.3,
  105, 106, 112–113, 119, 129,
  243, 252, 304, 314, 371
Lewin, K., 12–13, 17,
  367–370, 381, 438–439,
  449, 574
Lewis, 13
Lewis, S. A., 149, 165
Lewis, W. A., 249, 254
Liebling, R. M., 223, 234
Lim, J. D., 529, 544
Lim, Y., 583, 590
Lincoln, A., 79
Lind, E. A., 226, 235
Lindaman, E., 370, 381
Lippitt, R., 367, 370, 381
Litterer, J. A., 112–113, 119,
  129, 304, 314
Liu, C. K., 482, 495
Lock, A., 487, 492
Loewenstein, G. F., 199, 200,
  201, 205, 208, 209, 219,
  225, 230, 231, 233, 234
Lonner, W. J., 596, 600
Lowell, E. L., 298, 314
Luckman, T., 132
Luk, V.W.M., 488, 492
Lumpkin, J. R., 191, 205, 209
Lyman, S. M., 251, 255

M
Maass, A., 138, 143
Maccoby, E. E., 327, 342
Macdonagh, K., 196, 208
Mahler, 13
Malle, B. F., 116, 129
Mallozzi, J. S., 244, 252
Malone, P. S., 240, 253
Mann, L., 196, 197–198, 204,
  205, 207, 208
Mannix, E. A., 199, 200, 205,
  208
Marcus, E. C., 366, 370, 381
Markus, H. R., 596, 600
Marsick, V. J., 382, 383–385,
  393–394, 395, 399
Martin, R. P., 290, 304, 314
Martz, J. M., 100, 106

Marx, K., 11, 12, 66, 115, 134,
  135, 137
Maslow, A., 170, 297,
  298–299, 409, 426, 470, 474
Mastern, A., 76
Matrocchio, J., 282, 288
Matsui, F., 244, 252
Matz, D., 534, 545
Maxwell, J. P., 419, 426
Mayer, R., 98, 106
Mays, V. M., 441, 449
McAllister, D. J., 87, 90, 96,
  98, 101, 102, 106
McArthur, L. A., 240, 254
McClelland, D. C., 113–114,
  117, 129, 298, 314
McCrae, R. R., 306, 308, 314
McCurdy, D., 455, 474
McDonald, J., 470, 474
McGaugh, J. L., 342
McGillicuddy, G. D., 533, 545
McKersie, R. B., 222, 235
McKnight, D. H., 91, 106
McLaughlin, M. E., 529, 544
Mershon, B., 307, 315
Merton, R. K., 174, 184, 354
Messick, D. M., 219,
  224–225, 234
Metcalfe, J., 261, 275
Meyer, G. D., 222, 233
Mezirow, J. D., 385–386, 392,
  393, 397, 399
Michela, J. L., 237, 240–241,
  254
Michels, R., 110, 129
Mill, J. S., 65
Millar, F. E., 99, 105
Miller, A. G., 240, 253
Miller, N. E., 13, 17
Milton, J., 74
Mindell, A., 125, 129
Mink, O., 395–396
Minow, M., 59, 64
Minton, J., 104*n*.2, 106,
  112–113, 119, 129, 304, 314
Mischel, W., 256, 257–258,
  260, 261, 270, 275, 305,
  307, 315
Misra, G., 487, 492
Mitchell, G., 6
Mize, J., 318, 342
Moghaddam, F. M., 168, 184
Moore, C. W., 523, 525, 527,
  529, 534, 545
Moore, D. A., 228, 234

Morgan, G., 110, 115, 128, 129
Morgenstern, O., 13–14, 17
Morran, K., 250, 253
Morris, M. W., 223, 228, 234
Morsella, E., 131
Mouton, J. S., 167, 168, 178,
  183, 184, 305, 314, 364, 365
Moy, J., 479, 482, 483, 486,
  495
Murnighan, J. K., 100, 104
Murray, H. A., 297, 315
Mydans, S., 423, 426

N
Nadler, J., 213, 231, 234
Neale, M. A., 156, 158, 160,
  165, 195, 198, 199–201,
  202, 204, 205, 207, 208,
  209, 217, 218, 234, 304, 315
Nesdale, A. R., 416, 426
Newton, I., 354
Niebuhr, 347
Nisbett, R. E., 240, 241, 253,
  254
Novicki, M. A., 403, 426
Nucci, L., 416, 425

O
Ochberg, F., 59, 64
O'Connor, D., 534, 545
Olczak, P., 436–437, 448, 450
Oliver, R. L., 243, 252
Olweus, D., 419–420, 426
Olzack, P., 176
Opotow, S., 118, 129, 403,
  417, 426
Orivis, B. R., 248, 254
Osborn, A. F., 364, 365
Osgood, C., 97, 106
Oskamp, S., 228, 234
Ovsiankina, 13
Owen, H., 561, 562, 567

P
Packard, T., 317, 341
Paine, J. W., 149, 164
Parlamis, J., 244, 252
Passmore, 555
Patton, B., 104*n*.2, 105, 123,
  128, 249, 253, 283, 287,
  364, 365, 523, 545
Pavlov, 267
Pearce, J. L., 87, 104
Pearsall, S., 281, 288
Peled, E., 412, 426

Pelton, L. E., 191, 205, 209
Peter, O., 251, 255
Peterson, R. S., 149, 165
Petty, R. E., 146, 149, 151, 155, 165
Pfeffer, J., 112, 129
Phillips, D. P., 412, 426
Phillips, J. M., 198, 208
Piaget, J., 318, 319, 325, 331–332
Picasso, P., 347
Pike, R., 483, 493
Plato, 349, 353
Poon, M., 483, 493
Postle, D., 388, 399
Poze, T., 364, 365
Pratto, F., 116, 129, 130
Probst, T. M., 356, 363, 365
Pruitt, D. G., 144, 149, 157, 165, 168, 174, 176, 184, 188, 189, 190, 191–192, 195, 206, 208, 222, 235, 249, 255, 279, 288, 305, 306, 315, 364, 365, 436–437, 448, 450, 523, 529, 533, 544, 545
Purser, R. E., 548, 552, 567
Putnam, L. L., 99, 106, 243, 254
Pye L. W., 485, 493

Q
Quade, K., 553
Quadrel, M. J., 338, 342
Quindlen, A., 416, 426

R
Rackham, N., 510, 520
Rahim, A., 489, 493
Rahim, M. A., 178, 305, 306, 315
Raia, C. P., 244, 252
Raider, E., 4, 443, 448, 499, 500, 501, 512, 516, 520, 521
Rawls, J., 40
Raya, P., 318, 341
Reagan, R., 135–136
Reardon, B., 365, 599
Regan, D. T., 250, 254
Renner, M., 403, 426
Reuben, H. T., 364, 365
Robinson, R. J., 220, 221, 234, 252, 254
Robinson, S. L., 100, 106

Roderick, T., 588, 590, 594, 600
Rodriguez, M. L., 257, 275
Rogers, L. E., 99, 105
Rokeach, M., 356, 365
Roosevelt, E., 316
Roseman, I. J., 242, 254
Rosenzweig, M. R., 441, 449
Ross, L., 220, 221, 228, 234, 240, 253, 254
Ross, M., 219, 235, 240, 254
Ross, M. H., 433, 450
Rotenberg, E. J., 318, 341
Rothman, J., 97–98, 106, 310, 315, 431, 445, 450
Rotter, J. B., 91, 106, 304, 315
Rouhana, N. N., 444, 450
Rousseau, D., 87, 106, 107
Rubin, J. Z., 168, 174, 184, 188, 189, 190, 191–192, 195, 206, 208, 222, 235, 249, 255, 279, 288, 305, 315, 364, 365
Rule, B. G., 416, 426
Rusbult, C. E., 100, 106
Russell, B., 109, 129
Russell, E. W., 414, 427

S
Sadalla, G., 339, 342
Sadat, A., 468
Salacuse, J. W., 122–123, 124, 125, 129
Salancik, G. R., 112, 129, 369, 381
Salvi, D., 138, 143
Sandole, D., 470, 473
Sandy, S. V., 289, 308, 309, 314, 315, 316, 328, 342
Sanford, R. N., 116, 128
Sapolsky, R. M., 256, 275
Sasaki, S., 479, 482, 483, 495
Sashkin, M., 111, 129
Saunders, D. M., 104n.2, 106, 112–113, 119, 129, 304, 314, 467, 469, 472
Saunders, H. H., 474
Sauquet, A., 382
Sayles,J., 436
Schachtel, E. G., 11, 17
Schelling, T. C., 14, 17
Schön, D. A., 382, 383–384, 385, 386–387, 398, 399, 540, 545

Schoorman, F. D., 98, 106
Schul, P. L., 191, 208
Schultz, L. H., 193–194, 209
Schweber, S. S., 349, 354
Schweitzer, A., 49
Scott, M. B., 251, 255
Segall, M. H., 596, 600
Selman, R. L., 193–194, 209, 318, 320–321, 323, 332, 337, 338, 342
Semin, G. R., 138, 143
Sentis, K. P., 224–225, 234
Shakespeare, W., 407
Shapiro, D., 88, 89, 106, 251, 253, 255
Shepard, H. A., 168, 184
Sheppard, B. H., 88, 89, 106
Sheppard, D., 403, 427
Sherif, M., 167, 184, 349, 354
Sherman, D. M., 88, 106
Sherman, L. W., 411, 427
Shoda, Y., 257, 275
Shore, R., 317, 318, 323, 342
Shriver, D. W., Jr., 59, 64
Shure, M. B., 192, 209, 335, 342
Sicoly, F., 219, 235
Sidanius, J., 116, 129, 130
Siegal, W. E., 241, 253
Siegler, R. S., 318, 342
Sillars, A. L., 248, 249, 255
Sim, D. S., 223, 234
Sitkin, S. B., 87, 106, 107
Situation Management Systems, 510, 521
Smetana, J. G., 339, 342, 416, 427
Smith, C. A., 242, 255
Smith, D. N., 433, 450
Smith, P. B., 485, 493
Snyder, M., 305, 315
Sole, K., 358, 359, 373
Spencer, L. J., 548, 567
Spencer-Oatey, H., 485, 494
Spindel, M. S., 242, 254
Spivack, G., 192, 209, 335, 342
Spradley, J. D., 455, 474
Stack, A. D., 249, 253
Stahelski, A. J., 284, 288
Stallworth, L. M., 116, 129
Staub, E., 50, 64
Steil, J. M., 47, 64
Stein, M., 356, 365
Steinberg, L., 337, 342

Stephens, J. B., 115, 130
Stevahn, L., 584, 590
Stevens, C. K., 304, 315
Stevenson, M. A., 89, 96, 98, 100, 106
Stewart, E. C., 454, 460, 461, 462, 463, 471, 473, 474
Stillinger, C., 228, 234
Stripp, W., 515, 521
Strutton, D., 191, 205, 209
Suedfeld, P., 149, 165
Sullivan, G. R., 396–397, 399
Sullivan, H. S., 290
Sullivan, R., 553
Sun, H., 480, 481–482, 484, 494, 495

T
Tait, A., 196, 208
Tajfel, H., 168, 184
Tang, S.F.Y., 483, 489, 493
Tavris, C., 249, 250, 255
Taylor, A. D., 63
Taylor, D. M., 168, 184
Tetlock, P. E., 149, 165
Thibaut, J., 104n.2, 107
Thomas, K. W., 178, 243, 255, 305, 308, 314
Thompson, L., 144, 165, 199, 200, 201, 205, 208, 209, 213, 217–218, 219, 221–222, 226, 227, 228, 229, 230, 231, 234, 235, 365
Thompson, M. M., 102, 107
Tice, D. M., 268, 274
Ting-Toomey, S., 468, 474, 483, 484, 492, 494, 515, 521
Tjosvold, D., 65, 70, 71, 85, 111, 120, 121, 130, 475, 476, 477, 479, 480, 481–482, 483, 484, 485, 486, 487, 488, 489, 490, 491, 493, 494, 495
Tjosvold, M. M., 477, 495
Tolchinsky, 555
Totten, J., 250, 254
Touval, S., 524, 545
Treffinger, D. J., 204, 209, 359, 365
Triandis, H., 474
Trimble, D., 6
Tripathi, R. C., 415, 425
Tripp, T. M., 249, 253
Trist, E. L., 554, 556, 567
Trompenaars, F., 485, 493

Trope, Y., 147, 164
Trudgill, P., 460, 474
Tsao, Y., 482, 495
Tse, D. K., 483, 495
Tsui, A. S., 488, 492
Tung, R., 483, 495
Tunstall, B., 368, 381
Turner, J., 168, 184
Tversky, A., 198, 208
Tyler, T. R., 87, 105, 455
Tyler, V. L., 474

U
UNICEF, 427
U.S. Dept. of Justice, 404, 427
University of Michigan, 403, 427
Ury, W., 104n.2, 105, 123, 128, 249, 253, 283, 287, 364, 365, 518, 521, 523, 545

V
Valley, K. L., 199, 209, 227, 235
Van Boven, L., 231, 234
Van de Vijver, F., 487, 495
Van de Vliert, E., 191, 209
Van Gogh, T., 347
Van Gogh, V., 347
Venne, P., 403, 427
Volkan, V., 456, 474
Von Bertalanffy, L., 448, 450
Von Neumann, J., 13–14, 17
Vuchinich, S., 339, 342
Vygotsky, 318

W
Walker, D., 382, 388, 399
Walls, J., 483, 495
Walton, R. E., 222, 235
Wang, Z. M., 495
Ward, A., 220, 221, 234
Watkins, K. E., 382, 383–385, 393–394, 395, 399
Watson, D., 241, 255
Watson, J., 367, 381
Wedge, B., 465–466
Wegener, D. T., 146, 149, 151, 155, 165
Weiner, B., 241–242, 245, 251–252, 255
Weisbord, M. R., 371, 381, 548, 549, 567
Weiss, L., 417, 426

Weiss, S. E., 515, 521
Weitzman, E. A., 185, 193, 205, 206, 209, 241, 253
Weitzman, P. F., 185, 193, 205, 206, 209
Weizman, E., 467, 468, 474
Welton, G. L., 533, 545
Wentzel, K. R., 337, 342
Wessells, M., 436, 441, 449
Westerley, B., 367, 381
Westwood, R. I., 483, 489, 493
White, R., 174
White, S. B., 199, 209
Wiethoff, C., 87
Williams, A., 138
Winham, G., 472, 474
Winnicott, D., 290
Wish, M., 301, 315
Witkin, 345
Wong, A., 482, 495
Wong, C. L., 489, 495
Wong, W., 482, 495
Wood, R. E., 282, 288
Wood, W., 151, 164
Woolf, V., 345
Worchel, P., 86, 87, 107
Worldwatch Institute, 403, 427

X
Xin, K., 488, 492

Y
Yeates, K. O., 193–194, 209

Z
Zajonc, R. B., 160, 165
Zan, B., 318, 319, 322, 341
Zander, A., 369, 374–375, 381
Zanna, M. P., 102, 107
Zartman, I. W., 438, 450, 524, 545
Zeigarnik, 13
Zey, M., 209
Zhang, Q., 580, 590
Zillman, D., 267, 275
Zimbardo, P., 120, 129, 167, 184
Zmuidinas, M., 251, 255
Zojonc, R. B., 165
Zubek, J. M., 190–191, 194, 209
Zuckerman, 153

SUBJECT INDEX

A

Ability: childhood development and, 326–328; as fixed *versus* malleable, 281–287, 326–328

Abortion conflict, 34, 51, 137, 416, 428

Academic learning, constructive controversy in, 79–83

Accountability, 77, 81

Accuracy motivation, 150–151, 153–154, 158–163

Accuser bias and bias of the accused, 244–248, 250–251

Achievement: constructive controversy and, 72–74; goal orientation and framing of, 279, 280–282; need, 298; social-emotional skills and, 316–317

Action: bungling type of, 22, 24, 29; effective type of, 22, 24, 29; reflection in, 384–385, 390–394

Action planning, 551

Action research, 571, 574–575

Action science, 386–387, 390–394, 395–396, 397–398

Active listening, 140, 542

Activity inhibition, 117

Actor-observer bias, 240–241, 244

Addictive personality, 311

Adlerian counseling, 271–272

Adolescence: collaborative creativity in, 349–353; developmental stages in, 321, 332, 336–338; naïve conflict resolution strategies in, 339; role of conflict in, 339–340

Adolescent-parent conflict: adolescence development and, 339; implications of power in, 121–126

Advocacy teams, 77–79, 81–82

Affective domain of learning, 387–388, 397

Affiliation needs, 298

Affirmative action conflict, 54

After-action review (AAR), 395–396

Agenda-setting circle, 563–564

Aggression, 403–424; forms of, 404–405; intervention in, 418–423; levels of analysis of, 405, 406; management of, 421–422; moral theories of, 414–417; nested model of, 405, 406; reactive *versus* proactive, 413; theories of, 404–414. *See also* Anger; Violence

Aggressor, identification with, 47, 302

Agreeableness, 307, 309, 311–312, 313

Agreements: lose-lose, 221–222; nature of, 15; renegotiation of, 233; types of win-win, 189–190, 364. *See also* Outcomes; Solutions

Alcohol use, 266, 407

Alienation, 122, 125

Alternative dispute resolution, 576

Alternative to Violence Project, 421

Ambiguity, tolerance for, 181, 368, 372, 459

Ambivalence: self-regulatory failure and, 264; of trust in relationships, 95, 102–103

American Forestry Conference, 552–554

American Psychological Association, 421

AT&T breakup, 368

Anal stage, 291, 293

Analogical reasoning, 230–231

Analogy: learning by, 230–231, 582–583; use of, 364

Analysis, conflict: in Coleman Raider model, 506–509; of intergroup conflict, 176, 177–178; of intractable conflict, 436–437, 443, 448; in problem-solving and decision-making approach, 198, 207

Analytical skills, 180–181

Analytical *versus* synthetic approach, 9–10

Ancestors, 432

Anchors and anchoring, 196–197, 198, 200, 204

Anger and angry conflict: attribution and, 237, 242–252; behavioral responses to, 242–243, 257, 260–261; as cause of violence, 411; in China, 484–485; destructiveness of, 243–244; expression of, 249–250; management of, 249–252, 268–274; moral component of, 415; self-perpetuating cycle of, 246–249; self-regulation and, 257–274; strategies for cooling, 268–272; training in dealing with, 517–518. *See also* Aggression

Annihilation, goal of, 430

Antisocial personality disorder, 407–408

Anxiety, 264–265, 312; cognitive rigidity and, 363; intrapsychic conflict and, 294–296

Apology, 251

Application, social context of, 38

Approach-approach and approach-avoidance conflict, 13

Arms race debate, 221

Arousal, 409–410

Arrogance, 470

As-if technique, 271–272

Aspiration level, power imbalance and, 200

Assertiveness: in intergroup conflict resolution, 178–179; mediator, 534–535; strategy of, 123, 126

Asymmetry: in goal interdependence, 23; in scope of justice, 51, 57; in sensitivity to injustice, 45–46

Attachment needs, 298, 409

AEIOU (attack, evade, inform, open, unite) behaviors, 510–512

Attitude change: constructive controversy and, 74; facilitating, 161–163; persuasion and, 144, 160–163

Attitudes, 29–30, 503–504; defined, in cooperation-competition model, 23–24; information processing and, 150, 152–153; negative, 24; positive, 24

Attribution(s), 7, 236–252, 434; emotional and behavioral implications of, 241–243; implications of, for conflict, 243–249; implications of, for conflict resolution and training, 249–252; in intercultural communication, 241, 457–459, 470; in intergroup conflict, 171; research and theory on, 236–241

Auction procedure, 62, 63

Audience: impression motives and, 159; problem of multiple, 139; for research, 575–578

Australia, Conflict Resolution Network (CRN), 594

Authoritarianism, 116–117, 304

Autistic hostility, 26, 434

Autonomous information processors, 139

Autonomous strategy, 123

Autonomy needs, 298

"Autonomy *versus* shame and doubt" stage, 332, 336, 339

Avoidance, 13; concurrence seeking as, 69; as conflict style, 306, 308, 309, 311–312; as conflict style in China, 476, 481–482, 484, 487, 489, 491; as defense mechanism, 294–295; uncertainty, 459

Avoidance-avoidance conflict, 13

Awareness development: for children, 325; of individual differences, 289–291; of power differences, 126; of social identity, 57. *See also* Cultural awareness; Self-awareness

B

Backcasting, 271–272

Back-channel communication, 140

Balkan conflicts, 357

Bargaining experiment, 142

Bargaining strategies. *See* Negotiation strategies and tactics

Basic research, 571, 572

Behavioral analysis, 510–512

Behavioral decision making (BDM), 199–200, 204–205

Behavioral perspective on aggression, 411–412

Behavioral synchrony cues, 228–229

Belongingness and love needs, 298, 409

BATNA (best alternative to a negotiated agreement), 123

Bias: accuser, and of the accused, 244–248, 250–251; attributional, 236–252, 457–459, 470; cognitive or judgmental, 8, 171, 174, 213–233; defined, 215; in group decision making and problem solving, 198–201, 204–205; in intergroup conflict, 171; linguistic intergroup, 138; reduction of, 229–233, 249–252; in systematic and heuristic processing, 149–150, 151–154, 158–163, 214–215. *See also* Attribution; Cognitive or judgmental biases

Biased punctuation of conflict, 217

Binding third-party judgment, 177–178

Biosocial-behavioral shift, 318

Blaming: justice and injustice and, 52; of low-power groups, 125–126; social norms and, 415; the victim, 51

Bone Black (hooks), 410–411

Bosnia conflict, 49

Brainstorming, 204, 364

Bridging, 189–190

Buddhists, 49

Building Peace: Sustainable Reconciliation in Divided Societies (Lederach), 446–447

Bullying-prevention program, 419–420

Bungling actions, 22, 24, 29

Burundi conflict, 49

C

Calculus-based distrust (CBD): calculus-based trust (CBT) *versus,* 92; strategies to manage, 96–97; usefulness of, 101

Calculus-based trust (CBT), 88–89, 90–91, 92; actions that build, 96, 101–102; calculus-based distrust (CBD) *versus,* 92; relationships characterized by, 93–95

Camp David, 457, 467–469, 470

Capitalism, 134, 458

Cases: in action science, 397–398; diagnostic, 504–506

Catastrophizing, 265

Catharsis, 439, 559

Causal modeling, 580–581

Ceremonies, 446

Change agents, 378–380, 594–595

Change and change processes: conflict and, 366–380; for conflict with aggression or violence, 418–423; defined, 366–367; for intractable conflict, 438–439; management of, 371–378; management of large-group conflict and, 546–566; planned, management of, 370–371; practitioners' questions about, 577; reflection and, 382–398; theoretical conceptions of, 367–378. *See also* Social change work

Character traits, 304. *See also* Personality; Traits

Childhood development of conflict resolution skills: in adolescence, 336–340; in early childhood, 317, 318–331; educational programs for, 328–331, 335–336, 339–340, 583–588; implicit theories and, 326–328; individual differences and, 324–326; in middle childhood, 331–336; neurological development and, 323–324; self-control and, 327; social-emotional learning and, 316–318. *See also* Individual development

China and Chinese culture: collectivism in, 476, 477–478, 483, 486–488; cooperative and competitive conflict in, 475–492; face saving in, 454, 476, 477–478, 480, 483–484; goal interdependence in, 487–488, 489; hierarchy and leadership in, 478, 485–486; international joint ventures and, 489–490; open-minded discussion in, 481–482; persuasion and implicit communication in, 484–485; research methods in, 478–486; value of harmony in, 477–478, 489, 491; values for cooperative conflict in, 483–485

Chips and chops, 443, 506

"Chutes and Ladders," 89

Circular causality, 437

Civil disobedience, constructive controversy example about, 79–83

Class conflict, 66

Climate, 506, 533

Closed mode, 362–363

Coercion and coercive tactics, 26, 35, 122; persuasion *versus,* 157–158

Cognition and reasoning: constructive controversy and, 65–66, 73; cultural differences in, 459; impact of stress on, 197–198, 204; intuitive *versus* conceptual, 459, 468

Cognitive bias. *See* Attribution; Bias; Cognitive or judgmental biases

Cognitive change: facilitating, 162–163; in persuasion and negotiation, 160–161, 162–163

Cognitive complexity, 149

Cognitive factors: in aggression, 412–413; in intergroup conflict, 170–171; in problem solving, 192–194

Cognitive needs, 409

Cognitive or judgmental biases, 8, 213–233, 413; defined, 215; heuristic processing and, 149–150, 151–154, 158–163, 214–215; implications of, for conflict resolution, 220–229; implications of, for training, 229–233; in intergroup conflict, 171, 174; reduction of,

229–233; types, sources, and effects of, 215–220. *See also* Attribution

Cognitive orientations: defined, 301–302; fixed *versus* malleable, 283–287; to power, 114–116; in single-trait approach, 304

Cognitive processing modes, 148–163, 459. *See also* Heuristic processing; Heuristic-systematic model; Systematic processing

Cognitive psychology, 192

Cognitive rigidity, 283–287, 362–363, 434

Cognitive schemas, 371–372

Coherence *versus* correspondence theories, 346

Cold War, 134, 135, 137, 457–458

Coleman Raider workshop model, 443, 499–520; bare-bones negotiation framework in, 512–514; modules in, 504–520; objectives and pedagogy of, 502–504; overview of, 501–502; reframing formula in, 507

Collaboration: for aggression and violence intervention, 418–420; creativity and, 347–365; individual work *versus*, 352–353, 357–359; skills of, 70–71

Collective identity, 89, 310

Collectivist culture, 476, 477–478, 483, 486–488

Colocation, 89

Columbia University, 318, 328–331, 520, 591–592, 598–599

Comforting behavior, 325

Commitment: to change, 369–370, 377–378, 379–380; group decision making and, 198–201, 205; to mediation, 525; over-, 175, 434; ripeness and, 437–439; to solution, 205

Commitment testing, 370

Common ground: cultural differences in, 136–137; intentionalist communication and, 136–137; misperceptions of, 137–139; search for, 551–554, 566

Communication, 7, 131–143; behavioral analysis of, 510–512; childhood training in, 325; concepts of, 132; in cooperative *versus* competitive relations, 25; creative collaboration and, 348–349; cultural differences in, 453–472, 484–485; dialogic paradigm of, 139–141; electronic *versus* face-to-face, 228–229; encoding-decoding paradigm of, 132–134; form of, 141–142; high-*versus* low-context, 460, 468; implicit, 484–485; intentionalist paradigm of, 134–137; intercultural, 453–472; microcultures for, 453–454, 464–471; perspective-taking paradigm of, 137–139; principles of, 133, 135, 138, 140, 141, 142; role of, in conflict resolution, 131, 141–143; substance of, 141–142; for trust restoration,

99–100; in writing, 269. *See also* Information transfer; Persuasion

Communication skills: for intervenors in intergroup conflict, 181; for problem solving, 192–193. *See also* Intercultural communication; Skills

Communism, 134, 135, 458

Community, shared, 35. *See also* Moral community

Community conflict management, 546–566. *See also* Large-group intervention methods

"Community Dispute" exercise, 507–508

Community-based antiviolence programs, 419

Community-level aggression, 405, 406

Comparative imbalance, 43–44, 226–228, 410

Competence, mutual confirmation of, 71

Competition: anxiety in, 363; characteristics and effects of, 25–26; constructive and destructive, 27–28; debate and, 69; destructive conflict and, 27; initiators of, 28–30; usefulness of, 28. *See also* Cooperation-competition dynamics

Competitive orientation (win-lose), 7, 21–22; destructive controversy and, 70; goal orientation and, 283–284; harmful effects of, 31, 122; intractable conflict and, 434; negative attitude and, 24; power and, 120–122

Competitive struggle, view of conflict as, 11–12, 363

Compliance, 370, 375, 377–378, 380

Comprehensive Peer Mediation Project (CPMEP), 585–587

Compromise, 189, 306, 339

Conceptual frames for learning, 500, 506–507

Concession making, 224

Concrete operational stage, 319

Concurrence seeking: constructive controversy *versus*, 66, 67, 68, 69; outcomes of constructive controversy *versus*, 72–76

Conference Model, The, 555, 556–557

Conflict: attributions and, 236–252; basic questions about, 6–9; change processes and, 366–380; cognitive bias and, 213–233; commitment testing and, 370; communication and, 131–143; within conflict resolution field, 597–599; constructive controversy and, 65–85; cooperation-competition model of, 12–13, 21–39, 475–492; creativity and, 345–365; culture and, 453–495, 515–517; deep-rooted, 470–471; diagnosis of, 202–204; examples of, 1–6; goal orientations and, 279, 282–287; involving fundamental principles, 525; justice and injustice and, 41–63; level of, 524; overview of, 1–16, 504–506; personality and, 289–313; persuasion theory and, 144–165; power and, 108–128; research questions about, 15–16; residues of, 422–423; resistance and, 373; role of, in childhood development, 322–323, 335–336, 339–340; self-regulation and, 256–274; social psychological processes of, 7–9, 27; social psychological theorizing about, 11–16; trust and, 86–104; typology for intergroup, 169–170; value of, 65–66. *See also* Destructive conflict; Escalation; Intergroup conflict; Intractable conflict; Intrapsychic conflict

Conflict pervasiveness, 430

Conflict resolution: for aggression and violence, 418–423; attribution theory and, 249–252; challenges of future, 593–599; change management and, 366, 371–380; childhood development and, 316–340; cognitive biases and, 213–233; Coleman Raider model of, 499–520; communication in, role of, 131, 141–143; conflict management *versus*, 546–547; continuum of, 505; cooperation-competition model of, 30–37; creativity in, 345–365; decision-making approach to, 201–207; destructive, unfair procedures and, 53–54; fair rules for, 61; intercultural exploration approach and, 467–472; intergroup, 174–183; for intractable conflict, 436–447; issues in contemporary, 14–16; large-group methods of, 546–566; personality types and, 309–313; persuasion in settings of, 144–145, 155–163; power and, 121–126; problem solving and decision making (PSDM) model of, 186–207; problem-solving approach to, 201–207; process *versus* outcomes focus in, 439–440; reflective practice in, 389–399; self-regulation and, 256–274; situational determinants of goal orientation in, 285–286; trust management in, 96–103; universal elements of, 595–597; values underlying, 34–35, 548. *See also* Constructive controversy; Mediation; Negotiation; Negotiation strategies and tactics; Skills; Training

Conflict Resolution: Strategies for Collaborative Problem Solving. *See* Coleman Raider workshop model

Conflict Resolution Network (CU-CRN), 598–599

Conflict resolution skills. *See* Skills; Training

Conflict resolution training (CRT) research, 571–589; audiences for, 575–578; examples of, 583–588; strategies for, 578–583; types of, 571–575. *See also* Conflict study; Social psychological research; Training

Conflict study: conflict in, 597–599; cooperation-competition theory and, 31–34, 475–492; cross-cultural, 475–492, 595–597; on effectiveness of conflict resolution training programs, 583–588; of intergroup conflict, 167–168; on mediation, 522–536; research strategies in, 578–583; research types in, 571–575; social psychological theories and, 11–16; themes for future, 593–599; themes in contemporary, 14–16, 572. *See also Research headings;* Social psychological research; Social psychological theory

Conflict styles and strategies, 310–313; in adolescence, 339; multidimensional measures of, 306–309; naïve, 339; single measures of, 305–306

Conflict system analysis, 436–437, 443, 448. *See also* Analysis, conflict

Conformity, 354

Confrontation: constructive, 285–286, 444; of intergroup conflict, 178, 181, 182

Conscientiousness, 306–307, 309, 311–312, 313

Constructive competition, 27–28

Constructive conflict: conditions giving rise to, 15, 28–30; cooperative orientation and, 27, 31–34. *See also* Change; Conflict resolution; Creativity

Constructive conflict resolution. *See* Conflict resolution

Constructive confrontation, 285–286, 444

Constructive controversy, 9, 28, 65–85, 476–477; academic learning and, 79–83; benefits of, 72–76; Chinese research on, 477–492; compared to concurrence seeking, debate, and individualistic learning, 66–68; conditions determining, 70–72; decision making and, 76–79; definition and characteristics of, 66–68; democracy and, 83; example of academic use of, 79–83; example of structured use of, 76–79; intercultural exploration and, 469–470; North American research on, 476–477; outcomes of, 72–76; peace building and, 469–470; resources for, 76; skills for, 70–72, 81; structuring, 76; theory of, 68–70; value of, 65–66

Consultation skills, 182–183

Consumer research, 574

Contending strategies, 192, 308, 309, 311

Context: learning and, 385; power and, 124; risk taking and, 198. *See also* Social contexts

Contextual interventions, 533

Contingency modeling, 176

Control: attribution and perceptions of, 242; invalid perceptions of, 222–224; locus of,

304; mechanisms of, 291; of personal violence, 420; self-regulation and, 260. *See also* Self-regulation

Controversy, constructive *versus* destructive, 70–72. *See also* Constructive controversy

Conventional stage, 321

Convergence, 362–363

Cool cognitive factors, 149, 150

Cool system and response, 261–263

Cooling strategies, 268–272

Cooperation: anxiety reduction in, 363; characteristics and effects of, 25–26; constructive controversy and, 68–70; development of, in adolescence, 338; development of, in middle childhood, 334; in dialogic communication, 139–141; initiators of, 28–30; norms of, 32–34, 61–62, 70–71; reconciliation and, 62; reframing and, 31–32. *See also* Conflict resolution

Cooperation-competition dynamics and theory, 7, 12–13, 21–39, 248; applied to China, 475–492; attitudes in, 23–24; Coleman Raider model of training in, 501–520; creativity and conflict under conditions of, 358–363; development of theory of, 12–13, 22; as dimension of relationships, 301; dual-concern models and, 305–306; example of, 21; false dichotomy view of, 216, 218–219; game theory and, 13–14; generalizability of, across cultures, 475–492; goal orientation and, 282–284; implications of, for conflict resolution, 35–37; implications of, for training, 37–39; implications of, for understanding conflict, 31–34; initiators of cooperation and competition in, 28–30, 202–203; in intergroup conflict, 166–167, 174; Lewin's field theory and, 12–13; orientations in, 7, 21–22, 24, 31, 37; overview of, 22–24; predictions of, 24–27; substitutability in, 23; summary of, 30–31

Cooperative conflict resolution skills, 36. *See also* Conflict resolution; Skills; Training

Cooperative learning, 38, 327–333

Cooperative orientation (win-win), 7, 21–22; Chinese values for, 483–485; constructive controversy and, 70; creative collaboration and, 352–353; importance of, 31; positive attitude and, 24; power and, 120–122, 123; social support for, 31, 38; strategic creativity and, 218–219. *See also* Conflict resolution

Cost cutting, 364

Counterphobia, 295

Countertransference, 296

Creative Response to Conflict (CRC), 335–336

Creativity, 8, 345–365; conditions for, in conflict, 355–356; in conflict resolution field, 599; constructive controversy and, 66, 73–74, 84; egg drop exercise in, 358–363; evolving systems approach to, 346–349; guidelines for conflict and, 359–363; in intractable conflict resolution, 448; moral domain of, 346–347, 349; myths about, 359–360; resistance as, 373; shadow box experiments on, 349–354; strategic, 218–219; techniques for stimulating, 363–365; time frame of, 348–349, 357

Criminal-justice systems, 411–412

Crisis management, 441–442, 443, 448

Critical-incident methodology, 478–479

Cuban missile crisis, 222

Cultural anthropologists, 12

Cultural awareness, 453–472; education for, 461–466, 515–517; levels of, 462–463, 596; need for, 453–454; theoretical concepts for, 454–460

Cultural chauvinism, 462

Cultural differences, 453–472; in acceptable aggression, 414; in attribution, 241, 457–459, 470; challenge of, 595–597; in common ground, 136–137; in communication, 460; in cooperative and competitive conflict, 475–492; elicitive *versus* prescriptive approaches and, 440–441, 597; intergroup conflict theory and, 267; in needs, 470–471; in power experience, 121; in reasoning and cognition, 459; sensitivity to, 181; in time orientation, 432, 442–443; trust development in situations of, 97

Cultural identity, 456–457, 463

Cultural relativism, 464

Culture, 8, 9, 16, 453–495; conflict and, 453–472, 515–517; dispositions to violence *versus* peace in, 408–409, 424, 433; influence of, on aggression, 414; subjective, 455–466; theories of, 454–460. *See also* Intercultural communication

Culture-contrast training exercise, 463–464

Customer service, in China and North America, 482–483

Cypress conflict, 299, 428, 435, 444

D

Danbury, Connecticut, Future Search conference, 550–551

Death penalty debate, 221

Debate: constructive controversy *versus*, 66, 67, 69; outcomes of constructive controversy *versus*, 72–76

Decision making, 185, 186, 187, 195–207; behavioral model (BDM) of, 199–200, 204–205;

changing, as part of intergroup conflict resolution, 176, 179; in conflict resolution, 185, 186, 187, 195–201; conflict resolution and, 201–207; conflict theory of, 197–198; constructive controversy and, 76–79; large-group methods for, 560–565; participative, 386–387; problem solving *versus,* 185; rational choice model of, 196–198; stress and, 197–198, 204; training for, 205–207. *See also* Group decision making; Group problem solving; Problem solving

Deep structure, 108–109, 113

Deescalation of conflict, 15; cooling strategies for, 268–272; resistance to, in intergroup conflict, 174–175, 430; third-party role in, 270, 421–422; training for, 272–274, 421–422

Defense mechanisms, 291, 292–293, 294–296

Defense motivation, 151–152, 153–154, 158–163; in intergroup conflict, 174

Definition of the problem, 363

Dehumanization: conditions for moral exclusion and, 49–52, 58, 60; empathy *versus,* 58; humanization *versus,* 61; in intractable conflict, 434

Deliberate discourse, 66

Democracy: participation and, 548; role of civil disobedience in, constructive controversy about, 79–83; role of constructive controversy in, 83

Demonstrations, 272

Denial, 295, 417

Dependence: personality of, 312; power strategies and, 125–126; powerlessness and, 111

Dependent strategy, 122

Deprivation, relative, 43–44, 50, 410

Desensitization, 51

Destructive competition, 27–28

Destructive conflict, 7; aggression and violence in, 403–424, 449–450; anger and attribution in, 243–249; competitive orientation and, 27; conditions giving rise to, 15, 28–30; cultural misunderstanding as cause of, 453–454, 471–472; defined, 168; distrust and, 86; intergroup, 166–183; intractable, 428–449; processes of perpetuation of, 26–27. *See also* Aggression; Escalation; Intractable conflict; Violence

Detachment, intervenor, 181

Deutsch's cooperation-competition theory. *See* Cooperation-competition dynamics and theory

Deutsch's Crude Law of Social Relations, 29–30, 174, 248, 504

Developmental psychology, 65–66. *See also* Childhood development; Personality; Individual development

Developmental research, 573

Deviance, 407–408

Devil's Dictionary, The (Bierce), 131

Diagnosis: in conflicts with aggression or violence, 418; in mediation, 532–533; in problem solving, 202–204, 383

Diagnostic skills, 183

Dialogic paradigm, 139–141

Dialogue: in action science, 397–398; for intractable conflict resolution, 445; for reflective mediators, 540

Difficult conflicts. *See* Aggression; Destructive conflict; Escalation; Intractable conflict; Violence

Disagreement, skills for constructive, 70–72. *See also* Constructive controversy

Discourse, 66, 397–398, 540

Discrimination, 170–171

Displacement, 295

Dispositions: for aggression, 408–409; attribution based on, 238–241; single-trait approach to, 304–305. *See also* Attribution; Personality

Dissatisfaction, 355–356, 361–362

Distraction, 263, 265

Distributive justice and injustice, 42–44; defined, 41; example of, 52–53; principles of, 42–44; systemic social, 56

Distrust, 7; calculus-based, 92; conflict management and, 96–103; identification-based, 93; in intergroup conflict, 174; management of, 103; relationships characterized by elements of, 93–95; trust *versus,* 90; usefulness of, 101. *See also* Calculus-based distrust; Identification-based distrust; Trust

Divergence *versus* convergence, 362–363

Diversity management, 546–547

Divide-and-choose procedure, 62–63

Divisions, 435

Doctrine and Discipline (Milton), 74

Dogmatism, 304

Domain theories, 416

Domestic violence and abuse, 265, 403, 405, 406, 410, 414; deterrence of, 418–419, 423; moral dimension of, 416. *See also* Aggression; Violence

Double-loop learning, 386–387, 390, 397

Dow Chemical, 222

Driving forces, 367–368

Dual-concern models, 178, 192, 305–306

Dual-process models, 145, 147; heuristic-systematic model as, 147–163

E

Early childhood, 316, 318–331; role of conflict in, 322–323; stage theories of, 319–323

Economic costs of intractable conflict, 435

Economic structures, changing, 179

Economics perspective on trust, 87

Education: academic, constructive controversy in, 79–83; in attributional bias, 250–252; for childhood conflict resolution skill development, 316–340; in conflict management, 15–16; in conflict resolution, Coleman Raider model of, 499–520; for constructive conflict resolution, framework for, 37–39; for cultural awareness, 461–466, 515–517; importance of, 591–592; in win-win-attitude, 31. *See also* Childhood development of conflict resolution skills; Conflict resolution training research; Training

Educational programs: for childhood development of conflict resolution skills, 328–331, 335–336, 339–340; for cultural awareness, 461–466; effectiveness of, 583–588; for school-based conflict resolution, 583–588. *See also* Conflict resolution training research; Training

Effective actions, 22, 24, 29

Effective power: conditions for, 112; in conflict resolution, 124

Effort, attributed lack of, 241–242

Egalitarianism: in multilateral negotiations, 472; power orientations and, 118

Egg drop exercise, 358–363

Egocentric impulsive stage, 320, 323

Egocentric judgment, 216, 219, 229; and interpretations of fairness, 200, 205, 216, 219; and invalid perceptions of control, 222–224

Egoistical deprivation, 44

Ego-reality conflict, 294

Egyptian-Israeli negotiations, 467–471, 470, 527

Electronic communication, 228–229

Elicitive *versus* prescriptive approaches, 440–441, 597

Emotional intelligence (EQ), 257

Emotional milestones, 323–324

Emotional-management education, 324–326

Emotions: attributions and, 237–238, 241–252; brain structure and, 261; in decision making, 197–198; expression of, 249–250, 490, 559, 566; in identification-based trust, 98, 99; in learning, 387–388; reflection on, 387–388, 397; self-regulation and, 259, 260–274; snowballing and, 266–267; training in dealing with, 517–518. *See also* Anger; Social-emotional competence; Social-emotional learning

Empathy: development of, 55, 57–58, 250; development of, in childhood, 320–323, 325–326; resilience and, 76. *See also* Perspective taking

Empowerment, 111, 286, 441, 536

Encoding and self-regulation, 257–259

Encoding-decoding paradigm of communication, 132–134

Enduring *versus* useful truths, 10

English language, 460

Enterprise, 348–349

Entitlements: rising expectations regarding, 44

Entrapment, 175, 434

Environmental power, 112

Epistemic code, 385

Epistemic curiosity, 65, 69

Equality: in distributive justice, 42, 43; human, 34–35; power distribution and, 301, 302. *See also* Power

Equity, 42, 43; belief in, in middle childhood, 334; in intergroup conflict resolution, 179

Escalation: anger and attribution in, 243–252; anger and self-regulation in, 267–272; intergroup, dynamics of, 173–175; motives and, 159–160; narcissistic, 295–296; processes and dynamics of, 26–27, 421–422, 433–434; violence prevention and, 421–422. *See also* Aggression; Anger; Intergroup conflict; Intractable conflict; Violence

Espoused theories, 386–387, 395

Esteem needs, 299, 409. *See also* Self-esteem

Ethics: of intervention, 423; of research, 579

Ethnic aggression, 405, 406

Ethnic identity, 456–457

Ethnocentrism, 170–171, 172, 462–463, 469–470, 472, 596

Evaluation: of conflict resolution practice, 599; of conflict resolution programs, 583–588; of intervention, 422–423; skills, 183

Evolution, 406–407

Exaggeration of conflict, 220–221

Execution and homicide, 411–412

Executives and administrators, 575

Expectancy: and self-regulation, 259, 260; and social norms, 415

Expectations: cultural, 453–454; mediator, 539; rising, 44; structures of, 115; trust and, 87, 92–93, 104n.3, 104n.4

Expected-utility principle, 196

Experience over time, trust and, 92

Experience surveys, 574, 581–582

Experiential learning, 387–388, 500, 504–506, 511–512, 542–543. *See also* Learning; Reflection; Role play

Experimental paradigm for persuasion, 145–146

Experimental research, 579–580

Experiments, in China study, 480–481

Expertise exchange, constructive controversy and, 74

Explanations, 251–252

Exploratory research, 581

Expressive and symbolic processes, 446

Extremists, curbing, 61–62

Extroversion-introversion, 306, 309, 311–312

F

Face-saving cultures, 454, 476, 477–478, 480, 483–484

Face-saving strategies, 269

Fair campaign practices, 594

Fair outcome, 41, 43–44, 52–53. *See also* Distributive justice

Fair procedure, 21, 44–45, 53–54; development of, 61; inventing, 62–63; as problem-solving outcome, 189. *See also* Procedural justice

Fair treatment, 41, 53

Fairness: development of rules of, in middle childhood, 334; egocentric interpretations of, 200, 205, 216, 219; reciprocity and, 34; scope of justice and, 49–52. *See also* Injustice; Justice

Fallibility, 35

False dichotomy between cooperation and competition, 216, 218–219

Family-level aggression, 405, 406. *See also* Domestic violence

Fast-Cycle Full-Participation Work Systems Design, 555, 557

Feedback: for developing self-regulation, 273–274; for generating motivation to change, 372; goal orientations and, 281, 286; for overcoming bias, 229–230

Feminist perspectives: on power differences, 119

Field research, 573–574, 581

Field theory, 12–13

Fight for Your Rights: Take a Stand Against Violence, 421

Fight-or-flight response, 193, 261, 264, 267, 311–312, 413; in childhood development, 320, 323

Filter check model, 515–516

Final-offer arbitration, 53

First impressions, 216–217

Five-factor trait model (FFM), 306–308; conflict resolution strategies and, 308–309, 310–313

Fixed orientation, 281–287, 326–327, 362–363

Fixed view of ability, 281–284

Fixed-pie view: defined, 217; feedback and, 229–230; mythical, 199

Flipping a coin, 62

Focused social imaging, 447, 448

Force field analysis, 367–368

Forgiveness: in addressing conflicts rooting in the past, 445–446; defined, 58–59; development of, 60–61; for grievous harm, 55, 58–62

Formal operational stage, 319, 338

Formal *versus* informal relationships, 301

Foundations, 575

Fractionating of conflict, 375

Frames and framing: cultural mindsets and, 455; goal orientations and, 279–287; of goals, for deescalating conflict, 270–272; ladders of inference and, 392–393; in problem solving, 196–197, 198, 199, 204; of reference, 345. *See also* Reframing

Fraternal deprivation, 44

Free choice, 380

Friendship and friends: conflict styles and, 309; constructive controversy and, 75; dimensions of, 302–303; influence of, in adolescent development, 337–338; influence of, in early childhood development, 322; influence of, in middle childhood development, 333–334. *See also* Relationships

Frustration, 407, 409–410, 490, 560

Fulbright professor public diplomacy program, 464–466, 469

Fundamental attribution error, 240, 250. *See also* Attribution

Funding agencies, 575

Future orientation, 432; conflict resolution approaches in, 443, 446–447; large-group methods addressing, 548–554

Future Search, 371, 548–552

Future state, imagining or envisioning, 364, 370–371, 379

G

Game theory and games, 13–14

Gamesmanship orientation, 434

Gender: adolescent development and, 337–338; aggression and, 410–411; middle childhood conflict and, 335; power orientation and, 119; sensitivity to differences of, 181

Gender role expectancies, 410–411

General Electric Work-Out, 560, 561

Generational conflict, 435

Geneva meeting, Iraq and United States, 454, 459, 460

Global village or economy, 453, 485–486, 546, 554

Goal interdependence, 29–30, 476–477; asymmetrical, 23; in constructive controversy, 70, 77, 80–81; cultural differences in, 487–488;

defined, 22; emotional reactivity and, 264; independence *versus*, 23; negative, 22, 23, 77; persuasion and, 156–157; positive, 22–23, 77, 80–81; power and, 120–121

Goal orientation: in conflict situations, 282–287; framing and reframing, 270–272, 279–287; process and outcome, 280–287; theory of, 280–282

Goal pursuit: flexible or malleable, 270–272, 281–287; persistence in, 259, 260

Golden rule, 71, 469

Good-child morality, 321

Government agencies, 575

Graciousness, 469–470, 472

Group cohesiveness, 172–173, 175

Group decision, in constructive controversy: consensus, 78; defined, 77

Group decision making, 68, 173, 198–201; bias in, 198–201, 225–226; commitment and, 198–201; procedure for, 201–205; skills for, 36–37, 180–183. *See also* Decision making; Problem solving

Group norms, 172–173, 175

Group pressures, 345, 349, 354

Group problem solving, 8; concurrence seeking and, 68; constructive controversy for, 66, 76–79; intergroup, 181–182; skills for, 36–37, 180–183. *See also* Constructive controversy; Decision making; Problem solving

Group *versus* self-interest, 225–226

Groupthink, 68, 173

Guanxi, 488

Guatemala, 446

Guide to International Negotiation, A (Raider), 501

Guided imagination, 58

H

Habitual responses, 267–268

Haiti, 446

Harm, motivation to, 430

Hate crimes, 416

Hatred, moral exclusion and, 49–52

Helping, attributions and, 237

Heuristic processing, 147–163, 164*n*.2; cognitive biases and, 149–150, 151–154, 158–163, 214–215; cognitive consequences of, 148; defined, 147–148; motivation and, 150–154, 158–163; sources of bias in, 149–150

Heuristic-systematic model of persuasion, 147–164; applied to negotiation, 155–163; information processing modes in, 147–150; motivation in, 150–154; overview of, 147–150

Hewlett Theory Centers, 598

Hierarchy: in China, 478, 485–486; power and, 120; reduction of, in large-group methods, 565, 566

High-power groups (HPGs) or parties: power strategies of, 122–123, 124–125; tendencies of, 124–125

High-stakes distributional conflicts, 431

Historical context of structural power, 119, 433

Histrionics, 295–296, 306, 311

Homicide, 411–412. *See also* Violence

Hopelessness, 430

Hot buttons, 34

Hot motivational factors, 149. *See also* Motivation

Hot system and reactions, 257, 260–268

Howard Beach incident, 220

Human Judgment and Social Policy (Hammond), 346

Humanistic psychology, 298–299

Humanization, 61

Humor, 269, 361

I

Idea checklists, 204

Idea stimulation techniques, 204, 363–365, 564

Identification with the aggressor, 47, 302

Identification-based distrust (IBD): identification-based trust *versus*, 93; strategies to manage, 98–99

Identification-based trust (IBT), 89–91; actions that build, 97–98; identification-based distrust (IBD) *versus*, 93; relationships characterized by, 93–95; restoration of, 99–101; value of, 102

Identity conflict, 310–313, 431–433, 448

Identity formation, in adolescence, 336–338

Identity groups, 456–457

"Identity *versus* role confusion" stage, 332

Ideology: in conflict resolution field, 597–598; intergroup conflict about, 169; lexical choice and, 133–134; power orientation and, 115. *See also* Cognitive or judgmental biases

Idiographic models of personality, 290–303

Id-superego conflict, 294

Immediacy, 181

Implementation of decision or solution: change agents and, 594–595; for conflict with aggression or violence, 420–422; in constructive controversy process, 79

Implementation strategies, 269–270, 418–420

Implicit communication, 484–485

Implicit theories: about personality, 326–328; about power, 115–116, 118

SUBJECT INDEX **639**

Importance of relationship, 301
Impression motivation, 151, 152–153, 158–163
Impulse control. *See* Self-regulation
Inaction strategy, 192
Independence, 23, 111
India, Fulbright professor public diplomacy program in, 464–466, 469
Individual as decision maker, 196–198
Individual development, 8; of conflict resolution skills in childhood, 316–340; constructive controversy and, 65–66, 75–76; hot-cool system balance and, 262; neurological, 323–324; power orientations and, 113–119; problem-solving competencies and, 192–193; psychoanalytic theories of, 291–293; role of conflict in, 322–323, 335–336, 339–340; stage theories of, 318, 319–323, 331–335, 336–338. *See also* Childhood development of conflict resolution skills; Social-emotional learning
Individual differences, 277–242; in goal orientation, 279–287; in personality, 289–313; that affect socioemotional competence, 324–326
Individualist cultures, 477, 486–487
Individualistic learning or orientation: constructive controversy *versus*, 66, 67, 68, 70; creative collaboration and, 352–353, 357–359; outcomes of constructive controversy *versus*, 72–76
Individual-level aggression, 405, 406
Individuation, 162
Inducibility, 29–30; defined, 24; negative, 24
Induction, 325–326
"Industry *versus* inferiority" stage, 332, 337
Influence strategies, 112–113, 224. *See also* Negotiation strategies and tactics
Informal dispute resolution, 419
Information processing modes: cultural differences in, 459; in persuasion theory, 147–164; problem solving and, 192. *See also* Heuristic processing; Heuristic-systematic model; Systematic processing
Information transfer: communication as, 132; for trust building, 232. *See also* Communication
Ingratiation, 269
"Initiative *versus* guilt" stage, 332, 336
Injustice, 7, 41–63; in the course of conflict, 53–54; implications of, for training, 55–63; implications of, for understanding conflict, 52–55; scope of, 42, 49–52, 57; sense of, 45–48, 410; social, systematic forms of, 55–57; as source of conflict, 52–53; types of, 41–52. *See also* Justice

Instinctivist theories, 11–12, 406–407
Institute of Cultural Affairs (ICA) Change Model, 548, 549, 551
Instrumental morality stage, 320, 334
Integration: creativity and, 346–348; of personality, 312
Integrity, intervenor, 181
Intellectual conflict, value of, 65–66. *See also* Constructive controversy
Intellectualization, 296
Intensity of relationship, 301
Intentionalist paradigm, 134–137
Interactionist approach to personality, 299–300
Intercultural communication, 453–472; creating a microculture for, 464–466; cultural theories and, 454–460; diplomatic example of, 467–471; intercultural exploration training for, 460–466, 467
Intercultural exploration training, 461–472
Interdependence, goal. *See* Goal interdependence
Interests, 506; conflict of, *versus* identity conflict, 310; focus on, *versus* positions, 162; identifying and analyzing, 190, 513–514; level of concern with, 191–192
Intergroup attributional bias, 241
Intergroup conflict, 8, 16, 166–183; analysis of, 176, 177–178; deescalation of, 175–183; defined, 168; escalation dynamics in, 173–175; group-level factors in, 172–173; implications of, for conflict confrontation, 178; implications of, for conflict resolution, 178–179; implications of, for training, 180–183; implications of, for understanding and practice, 175–179; individual level factors in, 169–171; intervention skills for, 180–183; intractable, 428; objective-subjective mix in, 176; perceptual and cognitive factors in, 170–171; principles for resolution of, 176–179; resistance to resolution in, 174–175; resolution of, 175–183; settings and levels of, 166, 180–181; social psychological approach to, 167–168; sources and dynamics of, 169–175; tension in, 361–363; theoretical approaches to, 168–169; typology of, 169–170. *See also* Intractable conflict
Intergroup simulations, 57
Internal conflict, 291. *See also* Intrapsychic conflict; Personality
International Center for Cooperation and Conflict Resolution, 591–592
International negotiation, 457–458, 467–471, 471–472, 591–592. *See also* Culture; Intercultural communication; Intergroup conflict

Interpersonal attraction, 75–76

Interpersonal negotiation strategies (INS), 193–194

Interpersonal orientation to power, 119

Interpersonal-level aggression, 405, 406, 428. *See also* Aggression

Interpretation. *See* Attribution

Intervenors or facilitators for intergroup conflict, 180–183. *See also* Mediators

Interviews: in China study, 478–479; as research strategy, 581–582

Intractable conflict, 8, 16, 428–449; causes of, 430–434; characteristics of, 429–430; consequences of, 434–435; constructive confrontation approach to, 285–286, 444; defined, 428; intervention in, 436–447; levels of, 428. *See also* Aggression; Destructive conflict; Escalation; Intergroup conflict; Violence

Intrapsychic conflict, 256–274; as cause of development, 65–66; as cause of moral exclusion of others, 51–52; personality and, 289–313; sources of, 294–296; of trust and distrust, 102–103

Iraq, 454, 459, 460

Irreality, 348

Israeli-Egyptian negotiations, 467–471, 470, 527

Issues: centrality of, 430; in intractable conflict, 430, 431–432; prioritizing, 514

J

Johnson and Johnson studies, 584–585

Joint products or goals, 89

Judgmental bias. *See* Bias; Cognitive or judgmental biases

Justice, 7, 15, 41–63; developmental stages of, 320–321; implications of, for training, 55–63; implications of, for understanding conflict, 52–55; principles of, conflict about, 54; principles of, conflict-resolving combinations of, 55, 62–63; types of, 41–52. *See also* Injustice; Scope of justice; Sense of justice

K

Knowledge, 35–37

Knowledge-based trust, 104*n*.1

Kosovo conflict, 428, 432, 591–592

L

Labeling of children, 324

Ladders of inference, 392–393

Language, 456, 460; for conflict resolution training, 500, 506–507; microcultures for, 453–454, 464–471

Large Group Interventions: Engaging the Whole System for Rapid Change (Bunker and Alban), 547

Large-group conflict, 9, 442; about the future, 548–554; about work design, 554–560; management of differences and, 546–547

Large-group intervention methods, 546–566; for creating the future, 548–554; defined, 547–548; need for, 546–547; principles of, 566; for problem solving, 560–565; for work design, 554–560

Large-Scale Interactive Events, 561, 562

Laser tag, 414

Law of Two Feet, 563, 565

Layered personality, 294, 295

Leadership: in China *versus* North America, 482–483, 485–486; in intergroup conflict, 173, 442; mediation training for, 541–542

League of Women Voters, 594

Learning: by analogy, 230–231, 582–583; informal and incidental, model of, 383–385; insights about, 499–501; to learn, 463–464, 599; multimodal, 388, 398; social, theory of, 299–300; social context of, 38; through experience, models of, 382–385; through reflection, 382–398, 539–541, 542–543. *See also* Reflection; Social-emotional learning

Learning Communities Project, 594

Lexical choice, 133–134

Liking, 225–226

Linguistic codes, 460

Linguistic intergroup bias, 138

Linkage, positive and negative, 30

Listening: active, 140, 542; in decoding paradigm, 132–134; in dialogic paradigm, 140–141; in intentionalist paradigm, 134–137; in perspective-taking paradigm, 137–139; in persuasion theory, 150; training in, 517–518

Logrolling, 189, 364

Long-term thinking, 441–442, 446–447

Los Angeles riots, 429

Lose-lose situations, 217–218, 430. *See also* Intractable conflict

Loss and mourning, 376

Loss-averse, 197

Low-power groups (LPGs) or parties: integrative solutions and, 205; power strategies of, 122–123, 125–126; tendencies of, 125–126

M

MACBE model, 437, 443

Machiavellianism, 119, 304

Malleable orientation, 281–287, 326–327

Managerial grid, 305

Manipulation, as conflict style, 308–309

Mapping: of assumptions to actions, 393–394; of solutions to solutions, 230–231

Marital conflict: attributional dynamics in, 248–249; emotional reactivity and escalation of, 265, 267; example of, 1–2; intractable, 428; trust restoration in case of, 99–100. *See also* Domestic violence

Marshmallow test, 257–258, 263, 265

Marxism, 11, 12, 66, 134, 135

Maslow's hierarchy of needs, 298–299, 409, 470–471

MIT Research Center for Group Dynamics, 13

Mastery orientation, 280–287

Meaning: cultural construction of, 455–456, 470–471; joint construction of, 140–141; location of, in communication paradigms, 140; personal, self-regulation and, 259, 264; perspectives or schemas of, 385–386, 392–393

Media violence, 412

Mediation, 9, 15, 522–544; childhood development in, 336, 339; Coleman Raider model stages of, 518–520; conditions for effective, 524–525; contractual *versus* emergent, 527–528; for decision making, 196; disputants' participation in, 537–538; disputants' perceptions of, 527; efficacy of, 523–524; for facilitating reflection, 396–399; factors determining use of, 525–528; for fostering creative conflict, 364–365; implications for practitioners of, 538–541; implications for users of, 537–538; interventions in, 528–535; ironies of, 544; problem-solving *versus* settlement-oriented styles of, 190–191, 194, 535–536; stages of, for complex conflicts, 529, 530–531; stages of, for simple conflicts, 529, 532; student or peer, 585–587; theory and research on, 522–536; training in, 541–543; transformational, 536. *See also* Intervenor or facilitator; Third-party intervention

Mediators: behaviors and guidelines for, 528–535, 538–541; characteristics of, 527–528; goal orientation and, 285–286; problem-solving and decision-making training for, 205–207; reflective practice by, 529–541, 532–533; role definition for, 538, 539; role of, in overcoming bias, 221, 250–251; stage outlines of moves by, 529, 530–532; styles of, 530.*535–536;* types of, 522; videotapes of, 519–520. *See also* Intervenors; Practitioners

Men with Guns, 436

Mental illness, 407–408

Mercy Healthcare, 556–557

Message form, 141–142

Metaphors, 364

Microcultures, 453–454, 464–471

Middle childhood, 331–336; role of conflict in, 335–336; stage theories of, 331–335

Middle East conflicts, 147–148, 357, 467–469

Midlevel leadership, 442

Militant leaders, 173, 175

Mindfulness, 398, 596

Mindsets, cultural, 455–460

Minimization, 51, 296; stage of cultural awareness, 462

Mirror images, 171

Mr. Clown Box, 274

Misunderstanding: angry conflict and, 244–249, 434; cognitive bias and, 214; cultural, 453–454, 457–458, 463–464; as false conflict, 571. *See also* Attribution; Cognitive or judgmental biases; Communication

Mob behavior, 265–266

Model I and Model II values, 387, 388, 397

Modeling, 272, 325–326, 412

Modesty, 469–470, 472

Mohawk tradition, 446

Moods, 153–154, 197–198

Moral community: enlarging, 55, 57, 58–59; exclusion and inclusion in, 49–52, 56–57, 57, 60, 118, 302, 417; retributive and reparative justice and, 48–49; systemic exclusion from, 56–57, 417

Moral conduct, in intractable conflict, 432

Moral development, 117–118, 416; friendship and, 322, 333; stages of, 320–323, 333

Moral differences, intractable, 431

Moral disengagement, 416–417

Moral domain: of aggression and violence, 414–417; of creativity, 346–347, 349

Moral orientations, 301, 303; defined, 302; to power, 114–115, 117–119

Moral reasoning and judgments, 415–416

Moral relativity stage, 321

Moral rule breaking, 48–49

Moral superiority, 48, 50, 51, 54–55, 57, 302

Morals, 414–415

Motivation and motives, 7; for aggression, 409; for change, 270, 367, 368, 371–372, 376, 378–379; childhood development and, 326–328; constructive controversy and, 65–66, 73; goal orientations and, 279–287; to harm, 430; implicit theories about, 326–328; information processing and, 150–154; for mediation, 524; multiple or mixed, 153–154, 218; personality and, 297–299, 304, 326–328; persuasion and, 150–154, 158–162; theories of, 297–299

Motivational orientations, 301; defined, 302; to power, 116–117
Motivational psychology, 297–299
Movement for change, 369, 372–377
MTV, 421
Multidisciplinary approach: to conflict resolution field, 12, 597–599; to intractable conflict, 440, 448
Multiple audience problem, 139
Mutual respect, 61
Mutual security, 61
Mutual third-person stage, 321

N

Naïve conflict resolution strategies, 339
Narcissistic personality, 295–296, 311
National Institute of Mental Health, 575
National Public Radio, 552
National Science Foundation, 575
Nationalism, 172
National-level aggression, 405, 406; intractable conflict and, 428
Need for power (nPower), 117
Need principle, 42
Need theories, 297–299, 311–312; of aggression, 409; cultural differences and, 470–471
Needs, 506, 513–514; conflict of, 169–170, 179, 310–313; substantive *versus* personality, 310–313
Negotiation: elements of, 506–510; interpersonal strategies for, 193–194; as joint decision making, 196–197, 198; motive processing in, 158–163; of the nonnegotiable, 2; persuasion in settings of, 144–145, 155–164; settings of, 146; stages of, 512–514; between victim and victimizer, 60–61. *See also* Conflict resolution
Negotiation planning form, 507–508
Negotiation strategies and tactics, 15; interpersonal, 193–194; justifying as, 54–55. *See also* Conflict resolution; Influence strategies
Neo-Piagetian theories, 318, 319, 322
NEO-PI-R five-factor model questionnaire, 308–309, 311–312
Networks of enterprise, 348–349
Neurological deficits, 407
Neurological development, 318, 323–324
Neuroticism, 306, 309, 311–312
Neutrality, 529, 532, 538
New York City school-based conflict resolution programs, 584, 587–588, 594
Noise, 133
Nomothetic models of personality, 290, 303–309
Nonliteral language, 135–136
Nonspecific compensation, 189, 364

Nonviolence, defined, 35. *See also* Violence
Norms, group, 172–173
Norms, social: aggression and, 415–417; formation of, 349, 354
Norms of cooperative behavior, 32–34; for constructive controversy, 70–71; listed, 32–33; for reconciliation, 61–62; violation of, 33–34, 415
Norms of moral community: breaking of, retributive and reparative justice for, 48–49
Norms of redress, 415
Northern Ireland conflict, 4–6, 428, 432, 440, 471

O

Observational learning, 299–300, 412
Obsessive-compulsive personality, 306, 312, 313
Offers, simultaneous multiple, 232
Open Space Technology, 561, 562–565
Open-minded discussion, in China *versus* North America, 481–482, 483, 485–486
Openness to experience, 306, 309, 311–312, 362–363
Opposing-forces bias, 216, 217–218, 229–230
Oral stage, 291, 292
Organizational conflict management, 546–566. *See also* Large-group intervention methods
Organizational readiness, 593–594
Ossipila Case, 504–506
Outcome or performance goals, 280–287
Outcomes: comparative satisfaction and, 225–228; focus on process *versus*, 439–440; of intergroup conflict resolution, 178–179; of problem-solving approaches, 189–191. *See also* Agreements; Solutions
Overcommitment, 175, 434
Overconfidence, 200

P

Paired stimulus-response, 267–268
Paranoia, 311
Parent involvement, 330–331
Participation: in change planning and management, 376–377, 379–380; in large-group interventions, 547–548, 555, 557–558, 562–565
Participative Design, 555, 557–558
Past orientation, 432; conflict resolution approaches in, 443, 445–446
Peace: constructive controversy and, 469–470; cultures of, 424; intercultural exploration and, 469–470; skills for building, 469–470, 472
Peace Education Foundation, Conflict Resolution and Peer Mediation Program, 584

Peaceful Kids Early Childhood Social-Emotional Learning (ECSEL) Program, International Center for Cooperation and Conflict Resolution, Columbia University, 318, 328–331
Peacemaker Program, 584–585
Pecking-order conflicts, 431
Peer mediation, 585–587. *See also* Educational programs
Perceptual bias. *See* Bias; Cognitive or judgmental biases
Personal power, 112
Personal relationships. *See* Relationships
Personal responsibility, denial of, 51
Personality, 8, 289–313; aggression and, 408–409; attribution and, 238–241; conflict resolution and, 309–313; implicit theories about, 326–328; models of, 290–309; multitrait measures of, 305–309; needs, 310–313; single-trait measures of, 304–305; socioemotional competence and, 324–326; trust and, 87, 91. *See also* Dispositions; Individual development
Personalized power orientation, 117
Perspective taking: as communication paradigm, 137–139; in constructive controversy process, 78, 82; development of, in adolescence, 338; development of, in early childhood, 320–323, 325–326; development of, in middle childhood, 334, 336; friendship and, 322; in problem solving, 192–194, 198, 200, 204, 206; for reducing aggression and violence, 420–421; for reducing attributional bias, 250; as skill for constructive controversy, 71–72
Persuasion, 7, 144–165; in Chinese *versus* North American culture, 484–485; defined, 144; facilitating, 161–163; heuristic-systematic model of, 147–164; in negotiation and conflict settings, 155–164; research paradigm for, 145–146; settings of, *versus* negotiation settings, 146, 155–163; theory and research on, 144–154
Phallic stage, 291, 293
Physiological needs, 298, 409
Physiology, 406–407
Piagetian theory, 318, 319, 322, 331–332, 338
Pie, expanding the, 189, 364. *See also* Fixed-pie view
Platinum rule, 469
Plato's parable of the cave, 349, 353
Play, 348–349, 357, 361
Pluralist frame of power, 115
Points of view: creativity and, 345–354; critical reflection and, 385–386, 398; importance of, 353–354; novel, 346–365, 599; of the other (POVO), 353–354; synthesis of (POVOSYN), 354
Political structures, 179
Positions, 506; in academic constructive controversy, 81–83; focus on interests *versus*, 162; identifying, differentiating, and integrating, 72, 513–514; view of as fixed *versus* malleable, 283–284, 286
Postmodern nihilism, 353
Postsettlement settlements, 233
Posttraumatic stress disorders (PTSD), 59–60, 403, 435, 448
Power, 8, 108–128; and compliance *versus* commitment, 377–378; concepts of, 109–113; conflict and, 108–128, 431; corruption by, 117, 124–125; decision making and, 200; dimensions of, 111–113, 301, 302; exercise for training in, 127–128; goal interdependence and, 120–121; implications of, for conflict resolution, 121–126; implications of, for training, 126–128; intergroup conflict resolution and, 179; intervention strategies and, 419; intractable conflicts and, 432–433; mediation and unequal, 525, 595; needs, 298; perception of, 123–124; perspectives on, 110–111; prevailing, competitive orientation to, 120–122; psychological orientations to, 113–119; situational factors in, 113, 119–121; social structures and, 119–121; strategies for conflict resolution and, 122–123, 124–126; working definition of, 111–113
Power bases, 112
Power conflict, 169
Power distance, 121, 485–486
Power over, 111, 123
Power use, 112
Power with, 111, 123
Powerful, the, as victimizers, 45–47, 51. *See also* High-power groups; Victimizers
Powerless, the, as victims, 45, 51. *See also* Low-power groups; Victims
Powerlessness and dependence, 111, 125–126
Practice *versus* theory orientation, 9–10, 598–599
Practitioners: as change agents, 378–380, 594–595; orientation of, *versus* scientist, 9–10; reflective, 39, 382, 539–541; as research audience, 576–578. *See also* Intervenors; Mediators
Pragmatic *versus* skeptical approach, 10
Preconventional stage, 320, 323
Predispositions: for aggression, 407–408; single-trait approach and, 304–305. *See also* Dispositions; Personality

Preoperational stage, 319

Presbyterian Church USA, 562

Present situation, addressing, 443–444

Principled stage, 321

Prioritization, 514

Problem: defined, 188; identification of, 203–204

Problem solving, 186–195, 201–207, 514; analogical reasoning in, 230–231; approaches to, critiques of, 194–195; approaches to, evidence for, 190–191; approaches to, overview of, 188–192; childhood education in, 335, 336; conditions that encourage, 205–206; conflict resolution and, 201–207; constructive controversy and quality of, 73; decision making *versus*, 185; defined, 188; individual and social interaction perspectives on, 192–194; intergroup, 181–183; large-group methods for, 560–565; learning through experience in, 383–385; as personal conflict strategy, 308, 309, 312; predictors of use of, 191–192; training for, 205–207. *See also* Decision making; Group problem solving

Problem solving and decision making (PSDM) model, 186–207; applied to conflict resolution, 201–205

Problem-solving dialoguing, 335

Problem-solving workshops, 299, 444

Procedural justice and injustice, 44–45; defined, 41; development of, 62–63; examples of, 52–54; questions of, 45; systemic or social, 56; values and, 45

Process or learning goals, 280–287, 326

Productivity, constructive controversy and, 72–74

Projection, 51–52, 295, 296, 311

Promise of Mediation, The (Bush and Folger), 595

Psychodynamic theories: of aggression, 409–410; critique of, 296–297; of personality and conflict, 290–297; of power orientation, 116–117

Psychological approach: to conflict studies, 12, 256–274; to power, 113–119; to trust, 87. *See also* Intrapsychic conflict; Personality; Social psychological theory

Psychological health, constructive controversy and, 75–76

Psychological mechanisms: in change process, 366, 367; in escalation, 434; for moral exclusion and inhumane treatment, 51. *See also* Defense mechanisms; Personality

Psychological orientations: aggression and, 414–415; to power, 113–119; social situations and, 300–303; trust and, 91–92

Psychosexual development, 11. *See also* Personality; Individual development

Psychotherapy, 313

Punishment, 48–49, 411–412

Q

Quasi-experimental research, 579–580

Quebecois debate, 562

Questioning, 163, 232, 335, 364

Questionnaires, in China study, 479–480

Questions: in simple *versus* critical reflection, 388–389; stimulation of, 345–346, 356–357

R

Radical frame of power, 115

Rape, 405

Rapport-building skills, 36, 37, 181

Rational argumentation, 72

Rational choice model, 196–198

Rationality, attributional, 240–241

Rationalization, 294–295

Rationalizing conflict, 552, 565, 566

Reaction formation, 295

Reactive devaluation, 227–228

Readiness, 593–594

Realistic group conflict theory, 168–169, 171

Reality checks, 422

Real-Time Strategic Change, 548, 549, 551, 552–554, 562

Real-Time Work Design, 555, 557

Reasoning. *See* Cognition and reasoning

Rebuttal, in constructive controversy, 78

Reciprocal reflective stage, 321, 322, 332

Reciprocity, 34, 596–597

Recognition, 536

Reconciliation, 55, 58–62; in addressing problems rooted in the past, 445–446; cooperative principles for, 61–62; defined, 61; sustainable, 446–447

Redesigns, 395

Reference points in problem solving, 196–197, 204. *See also* Points of view

Reflection: before action or conflict, 384, 395–396, 397–398; in action or during conflict, 384–385, 389–390, 396–397; after action or conflict, 384, 390–394, 397–398; for conflict resolution, 389–399; for conflict resolution training, 500; critical, 385–389; experiential learning and, 387–388; for intractable conflict resolution, 445; learning through, 382–398, 539–541, 542–543; mediator, 539–541, 542–543; roles of, in problem-solving stages, 383–385; simple *versus* critical, 388–389; support for, 542–543; using, to learn from experience, 388–389

Reflective hypothesis, 540–541

Reflective practitioner, 39, 382, 539–541

Reflexive intervention, 529, 532–533

Reflexivity, 445

Reframing, 31–32; in Coleman Raider model, 506, 507, 514; for creative conflict, 356–357, 363; for deescalation, 270–272; of intractable conflict, 439–440; persuasion and, 161; resonance and, 97–98

Refreezing, 369–370, 377–378

Refutation, in constructive controversy, 78

Rehearsal, 272

Relabeling, 51

Relationship power, 112

Relationships, personal: ambivalence of trust in, 95, 102–103; attributional dynamics in, 248–249; characterization of, based on trust elements, 93–95; decision making and types of, 201, 205; as developmental and multifaceted, 90–92; dimensions and psychological orientations of, 301–303; professional relationships *versus,* 88, 90–91, 201; self-interested behavior and, 225–226; trust in, 88–104; type of, and conflict style, 309. *See also* Friendship

Relative deprivation, 43–44, 50, 410

Relativism, 353, 464

Relaxation, 263

Relearning, 300

Religious conflict, 431

Repression, 295

Reputation, trust and, 92

Research questions: for basic research, 572; for consumer research, 574; contemporary themes and, 14–16; for developmental research, 573; of executives and administrators, 576; for field research, 573–574; of funding agencies, 575; for the future, 593–599; of practitioners, 576–577. *See also* Conflict resolution training research; Conflict study; Social psychological research

Research strategies, 578–583

Research types, 571–575

Researchers, 578

Resilience, 76

Resistance: to change, 369, 372–377, 379, 439; competitive orientation and, 122, 125; conditions for strengthening, 374–375; conditions for weakening, 375–377; and conflict, 373, 374–375; to eliminating injustice, 47; to high-power groups, 125; to intergroup conflict deescalation and resolution, 174–175, 430; to mediation, 534

Resolution of Conflict, The: Constructive and Destructive Processes (Deutsch), 15

Resolving Conflict Creatively Program (RCCP), 584, 587–588, 594

Resonance, 97–98

Resource availability and scarcity: change and, 376; mediation and, 525

Resource conflict, 409; Chinese management of, 482–483; in intergroup conflict, 169; in intractable conflict, 431

Resources, power, 112, 123–124. *See also* Power

Responsibility, judgments of harm and, 245–248, 251–252

Restraining forces, 367–368

Retaliation, 237, 242–252

Retention, constructive controversy and, 73

Retributive and reparative justice and injustice, 42, 48–49, 56

Ripeness, 437–439, 443, 448

Risk taking: contexts and, 198; individual factors in, 196–198; self-confidence and, 362; trust building and, 203

Ritual sharing, 513

Rituals, 446

Role assignment, and judgment of fairness, 225

Role modeling, 272

Role play, 58, 272, 273; in conflict resolution skill training, 500, 510–512, 515–516, 518–519; in intercultural exploration training, 461, 463; in mediation training, 542–543

Role reversal, 58, 272

Role theory, 119–120

Romeo and Juliet, 407

Round-robin, 517–518

Rule-based games, 331–332, 334

Rumination, 264–265

Rwanda conflict, 49, 428, 433, 435

S

Safety needs, 298, 311, 409

San Francisco Community Board Program (CBP), 339–340

Scaffolding, 329, 335

Scenario backcasting, 271–272

Schizophrenia, 407–408

Schmooze effect, 228–229

School conflict and conflict resolution programs: BTC-SBM case example of, 3–4, 32, 54, 516–517; causal modeling research on, 580–581; evaluative research on, 583–588

School-related violence, 408

Scientist orientation, 9–10

Scope of justice, 42, 49–52; enlarging, 57; power orientation and, 118

Search Conference, 548, 549, 551, 552

Self-actualization needs, 299, 409

Self-awareness: cultural, 462–464, 596; of goal orientation, 285, 286; for intervenors in intergroup conflict, 181; mediator, 539–541; of social identity, 181; training in, 511. *See also* Awareness development

Self-confidence: fostering, 362; intervenor, 181

Self-control, 7, 327, 335, 420. *See also* Self-regulation

Self-development: as goal orientation, 280–287; stage theories of, 319, 322, 332–333. *See also* Individual development

Self-efficacy, 299–300, 411

Self-esteem: constructive controversy and, 75–76; development of, in adolescence, 337–338; development of, in middle childhood, 333–334; process orientation and, 280; sense of injustice and, 46–47; in single-trait approach, 304

Self-fulfilling prophecies, 26, 174

Self-instruction messages, 274

Self-interest: bias *versus,* 213; collective interest and, 225–226

Self-perpetuating cycle of anger-driven conflict, 246–249

Self-regulation, 256–274; affects and, 260–261; childhood development of, 327, 334–335; cooling strategies for, 268–272; failure of, in interpersonal conflict, 264–268; hot and cool systems and, 260–268; implications of, for training, 272–274; process and conditions of, 258–260; stress and, 262–263, 264–266

Sense of justice and injustice, 45–48; activation of, 47–48; appeal to, by low-power groups, 126; defined, 41–42; differential sensitivity to, 45–46, 410; self-esteem and, 46–47; victims and victimizers in, 45–47

Sensorimotor stage, 319

Shadow box experiments, 349–354

Sharing information, 232

Simplification and bias, 215–217

Simulation, 273–274. *See also* Role play

Simu-Real, 560, 561

Single-loop learning, 386–387, 390

Situational factors and cues: in aggression, 410; dispositions and, 304–305; in goal orientation, 281–284, 285–286; mapping, 393–394; in power orientation, 113, 119–121; in psychological orientation, 300–303. *See also* Social contexts

Skeptical *versus* pragmatic approach, 9–10

Skeptic's critique of problem solving, 195

Skills: behavioral, for overcoming bias, 231–233; of change agent, 38; childhood development of, 316–340; for constructive conflict resolution, 35–37, 38, 503; for constructive controversy, 70–72, 81; for intergroup conflict resolution, 180–183; mediation, 542,

543–544; peace-building, 469–470, 472; for problem solving, 192–193; self-control, 259; of self-regulation, 272–274; for stress management, 266, 270, 330; types of, 36–37. *See also* Childhood development of conflict resolution skills; Education; Perspective taking; Training

Slavery, 404, 417

Snowballing, 266–267

Social change. *See* Change

Social change work, 48, 53–54. *See also* Change

Social cognitive approaches: to aggression, 412–413; to development, 318, 319–322

Social competence: aggression and, 413; constructive controversy and development of, 75–76; problem solving and, 192–194. *See also* Social-emotional competence

Social Conflict (Rubin et al.), 188

Social contexts: for aggression, 406, 408–409, 414, 422, 423–424; of application, 38; cooperation-competition in, 29–30; development and, 318; distributive justice principles in, 43–44; implicit power theories and, 115–116; for intractable conflicts, 432–433; of learning, 38; of meaning and communication, 140; for mediation, 526–527; for moral exclusion, 50, 417; psychological orientations and, 300–303; for trust in relationships, 90–91, 92. *See also* Situational factors and cues

Social Darwinism and determinism, 11–12

Social dominance orientation (SDO), 116

Social identities: conflict of, 310, 431–432; moral dimension of, 415; self-awareness of, 57

Social identity theory, 168–169, 170–171, 182

Social injustice, 7; moral exclusion and, 417; systematic forms of, 55–57, 417, 433. *See also* Injustice

Social interaction perspectives on problem solving, 192–194

Social justice, 7, 15. *See also* Justice

Social learning theory, 299–300, 412. *See also* Social-emotional learning

Social media, 29–30

Social norms. *See* Norms, social

Social perspective coordination, 192–193, 206

Social psychological processes affecting conflict, listed, 7–9

Social psychological research: on conflict resolution training, 571–589; on mediation, 522–536; themes of, listed, 14–16. *See also* Conflict resolution training research; Conflict study; *Research headings*

Social psychological theory: of attribution, 236–252; of communication, 141–143; of constructive controversy, 65–85; cooperation-competition model of, 12–13; cultural differences and, 16, 595–597; of culture and cultural awareness, 454–460; empirical orientation in, 12; field theory and, 12–13; game theory and, 13–14; of goal orientation, 279–287; historical overview of, 11–16; of intergroup conflict, 167–168; of justice and injustice, 41–63; on mediation, 522–536; of persuasion, 144–165; of power orientation, 109–113; of problem solving and decision making, 185–207; of trust, 87

Social structures: changing, for intergroup conflict resolution, 179; power differences in, 119–121, 124

Social systems: change process in, 367–380; levels of, and change, 367; levels of, and intractable conflict, 428; levels of, and violence, 404–405, 406

Social-cognitive theory of power orientation, 115–116

Social-emotional competence: domains of, 318; individual differences that affect, 324–326

Social-emotional dimension of relationships, 301, 303

Social-emotional learning: in adolescence, 336–340; of aggression, 412; conflict management skills and, 316–318; in early childhood, 318, 319–331; in middle childhood, 331–336; role of conflict in, 322–323, 335–336, 339–340

Social-emotional mediator style, 535, 536

Socialization and subjective culture, 455–460

Socialized power orientation, 117

Social-relational morality, 321, 333

Sociobiological approaches, 406–407

Sociological perspective on trust, 87

Sociomoral judgments of aggression, 415–416

Socio-technical systems (STS), 554, 556–557

Solution quality: constructive controversy and, 73; decision-making approach and, 206–207

Solutions: evaluating and choosing, 204–205; identifying alternative, 204; integrative, 189–190, 204–205; mapping, 230–231. *See also* Agreements; Outcomes

South Africa, 446

Speech acts, 141–142

Spiraling effect, 328–329

Sri Lanka, 471

Standoff, 339

Stanford University role play study, 120

Stereotypes and stereotyping: cognitive bias and, 214, 216–217; cultural, 458–459, 463; in intergroup conflict, 171, 434; trust and, 92. *See also* Bias; Cognitive or judgmental biases

STAR (stop, tell, ask, resolve) model, 329–330

Strategic competencies, 259

Strategic creativity, 218–219

Strategic direction, 533–534

Strategy focus, 283

Stress: attribution errors and, 470; decision making and, 197–198, 204; education in management of, 266, 270; education in management of, for children, 330; hot-cool system balance and, 262–266, 270; of mediators, 538–539

Structural intervention, 533

Submission, 312, 339

Substance use, 266, 407

Substantive interventions, 533–534

Substantive need, 310–313

Substitutability, 29–30; defined, 23; negative, 23

Sudan, 471

Superiority claims, 50, 302. *See also* Moral superiority

Support: for cooperative orientation, 31, 38; for eliminating injustice, 47; for generating motivation to change, 372; post-training, 38, 500–501; for reflective learning, 542–543

Suppression, 295

Surprisingly positive behavior, 269

Survey research, 581–582

Sustainable reconciliation, 446–447

Symbols, 456

Sympathy, 237

Synectics, 364

Synthesis: in academic constructive controversy, 82–83; in creative conflict, 346–354

Synthetic *versus* analytical approach, 9–10

Systematic processing, 147–163; cognitive consequences of, 148–149; defined, 147; motivation and, 150–155, 158–163; sources of bias in, 149–150

Systems approach: to conflict analysis, 436–437, 448; to conflict resolution, 438–439, 448; to creativity, 346–349; to large-group conflict management, 547, 561, 562–565; to readiness, 593–594

T

Talking stick circle, 564

Task involvement, constructive controversy and, 74

Task leadership, 181

Task orientation, 301, 303, 535–536

Task structure, in academic constructive controversy, 80–83

Teamwork: in China, 478, 482–483, 487; constructive controversy and, 478; in international joint ventures, 490

Temperament, 324. *See also* Dispositions; Personality

Tension: as condition for change, 368, 371–372, 376, 439; as condition for creativity, 356, 361–362; escalation and, 439; fostering optimal, 361–362

Testosterone, 407

Theories of action, 386–387, 390

Theories of practice, 499–500

Theory, social psychological. *See* Social psychological theory

Theory of Games and Economic Behavior, The (von Neumann and Morgenstern), 13–14

Theory of Interdependence and Psychological Orientation (Deutsch), 414

Theory *versus* practice orientation, 9–10, 598–599

Theory-in-use propositions, 395–396

Third Reich, 408

Third-party intervention, 9, 15, 339; for deescalating conflict, 270, 421–422; for fostering creative conflict, 364–365; in intergroup conflict resolution, 176, 177–178, 180–183. *See also* Intervenors or facilitators; Mediation; Mediators

Time frame: for creative work, 348–349, 357, 360; in intractable conflict, 429–430, 432, 441–442; in peace work, 441–442

Time orientation: cultural differences in, 442; intervention according to, 442–447

Time-outs, 268–269

Time-space oasis, 359

Tolerance, 462, 472

Track II diplomats, 442

Traditional approaches, 446

Training: attribution theory and, 249–252; for change agents, 378–380; in cognitive bias effects and reduction, 229–233; Coleman Raider model of, 499–520; for conflict with aggression or violence, 418–423; cooperation-competition theory and, 37–39; effectiveness of, 583–588; follow-up support after, 38, 500–501; in goal orientation, 285; intercultural exploration, 461–466; intergroup conflict theories and, 180–183; for intractable conflict intervention, 447–448; justice and injustice and, 55–63; in mediation, 541–543; personality theory and, 313; power theories and, 126–128; problem solving and decision making (PSDM) model and, 205–207; research on, 571–589; self-regulation theory and, 272–274; substantive content of, 39. *See*

also Childhood development of conflict resolution skills; Conflict resolution training research; Education

Traits and trait models, 303–309; defined, 303–304; multidimensional, 305–309; single, 304–305; use of, in conflict resolution, 309–313

Transcendence, 266, 409

Transference, 296

Trauma. *See* Posttraumatic stress disorders

Trust, 7, 86–104; criticality of, to relationships, 88–95; defined, 87; dimensions of, 87; distrust *versus*, 90; expectations and, 87, 92–93; factors in, 91; fair procedure and, 53; forms of, 88–90; implications of, for conflict management, 101–103; information sharing and, 232; management of, in conflict situations, 96–103; model of, 92–93; perspectives on, 86–87; power orientation and, 119; in problem solving, 203; reconciliation and, 62; relationship dimension of, 87–104; relationships characterized by elements of, 93–95; restoration of, 99–101, 103; theories of, 87; violations of, 99–101, 103, 104n.3. *See also* Calculus-based trust; Identification-based trust

"Trust *versus* mistrust" stage, 332, 336

Truth and reconciliation commissions, 446

Truths, enduring *versus* useful, 10

Twelve-step model, 372

U

Uncertainty avoidance, 459

Unconscious, 291; belief systems, 385–386, 390; personality needs and, 310; subject culture, 455

Understanding stage of cultural awareness, 462, 596

Unfreezing, 367, 368, 370, 371–372, 378–379

Unilateral one-way stage, 320

Unilateral power assertion, 339

Unintended consequences or outcomes, 384, 385, 422

Unitary frame of power, 115

United Nations, 591–592

U.S. Army, 395–396

Unwitting commitments, 26–27

Useful *versus* enduring truths, 10

V

Values: in conflict resolution field, 597–598; of constructive conflict resolution, 34–35, 548; cultural relativism and, 464; different, distrust and, 98–99; intergroup conflict in, 169; with regard to procedural justice, 45; self-regulation and, 259; shared, as basis of trust, 89

Venting, 249–250, 397, 490

Victimizers: forgiveness and reconciliation and, 58–62; moral exclusion by, 49–52, 60; sense of justice in, 45–47; sense of justice in, activation of, 47–48; systemic exclusion by, 56–57

Victims: focus on, 60; forgiveness and reconciliation and, 58–62; moral exclusion of, 49–52, 60; sense of injustice in, 45–47; sense of injustice in, activation of, 47–48; systemic exclusion of, 56–57

Videotape and audiotape training, 500, 515–516, 519–520

Violence, 8, 403–424; causes of, 404–417; direct, 404–405; failure of self-regulation and, 265–266, 267; forgiveness and reconciliation and, 58–62; forms of, 404–405; intervention in, 418–423; of intractable conflict, 435; levels of analysis of, 405, 406; by low-power groups, 126; management of, 421–422; moral dimension of, 414–417; moral exclusion and conditions for, 49–52, 60, 417; myths about, 418; nested model of, 405, 406; prevalence of, 403–404; structural, 404–405, 416–417; unfair procedure as source of, 53–54. *See also* Aggression; Anger

Volition, 369–370

W

War, 403–404; moral disengagement in, 416; societies characterized by, 414. *See also* Aggression; Anger; Intractable conflict; Violence

Weapons, 403–404, 408, 433

Whole system, 547

Willpower. *See* Self-regulation

Win-lose orientation. *See* Competitive orientation

Win-win orientation. *See* Cooperative orientation

Win-win outcomes: problem solving and, 191; types of, 189–190, 364

Withdrawal, 311–312, 339

Work design: conflict and process of, 559–560; large-group methods for, 554–560

Work-Out (General Electric), 560, 561

Workplace diversity efforts, 97

Worldview, 506

Y

Yielding strategy, 192

Yugoslavia, former, 428, 471

Z

Zero-sum approach, 280, 283–284, 439–440. *See also* Competitive orientation